# Los Angeles & Southern California

Andrea Schulte-Peevers, John A Vlahides

# Contents

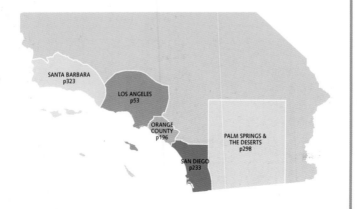

SANTA BARBARA
p323

LOS ANGELES
p53

ORANGE COUNTY
p196

PALM SPRINGS & THE DESERTS
p298

SAN DIEGO
p233

# Destination Los Angeles & Southern California

It's been a tingling presence in your mind ever since you were a child. And how could it not be? The images, the mythology, the sheer sexiness and velocity generated by Southern California have swamped the airwaves ever since the beginnings of broadcast and film. The sun, the fun, the wildly creative experiments in every field of human endeavor: this is where great ideas – and dreams – are born and launched into the world's psyche. And where else can you surf at dawn, four-wheel drive along jagged desert roads beneath the sweltering noon sun, schuss down alpine slopes in the evening and then party 'til closing time in a swank club?

There is great boldness and youthful exuberance in Southern California. Its collection of 'thrill rides' is unparalleled, whether your thrills come from roller coasters, horseback riding or simply enjoying mouthwatering wines and seafood as the sun plunges into the Pacific. You can start your trip in the dynamo that is LA and hunt for the California Dream along the Walk of Fame in Hollywood, the bizarre Venice Boardwalk or on achingly beautiful beaches. Then head to the legendary Disneyland, or to San Diego with its lush parks, SeaWorld and celebration of Mexican and American culture. North of LA, a breathtaking coast delivers you to the sparkling mission city of Santa Barbara, where strolling is an education in the arts and California history. Go inland for the rugged desert beauty of Joshua Tree National Park or Palm Springs, the famous spa and playground city.

SoCal is the ultimate frontier for questing spirits, and when you arrive, you'll feel little need to search any further

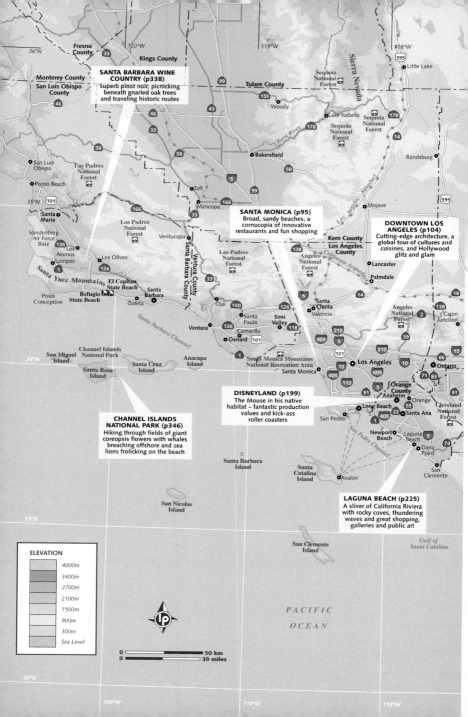

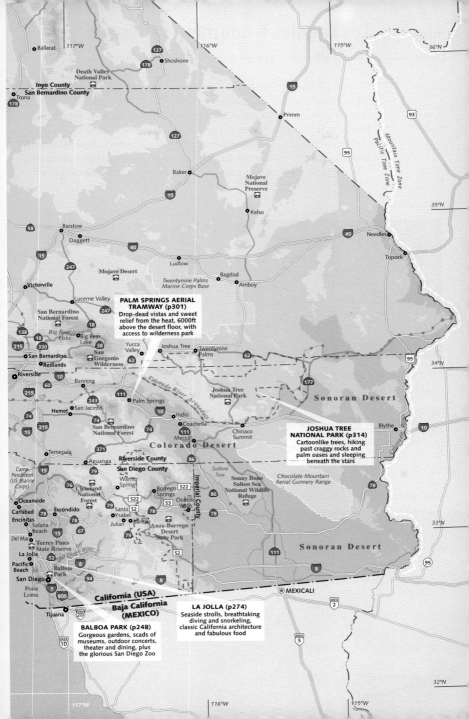

**PALM SPRINGS AERIAL TRAMWAY (p301)**
Drop-dead vistas and sweet relief from the heat, 6000ft above the desert floor, with access to wilderness park

**JOSHUA TREE NATIONAL PARK (p314)**
Cartoonlike trees, hiking past craggy rocks and palm oases and sleeping beneath the stars

**LA JOLLA (p274)**
Seaside strolls, breathtaking diving and snorkeling, classic California architecture and fabulous food

**BALBOA PARK (p248)**
Gorgeous gardens, scads of museums, outdoor concerts, theater and dining, plus the glorious San Diego Zoo

Visiting Los Angeles and Southern California is like rummaging through Aladdin's cave of treasures. Besides the gems depicted in these photos, be sure to catch these highlights: take a virtual trip around the world in **Downtown Los Angeles** (p149), work on your tan on the fine beaches of **Santa Monica** (p95), visit Mousetown, aka **Disneyland** (p199), and its new neighbor, **Disney's California Adventure** (p204), explore the rugged beauty of **Channel Islands National Park** (p346) or soar from sand to snow on the **Palm Springs Aerial Tramway** (p301).

ADINA TOVY AMSEL

Pretend you're a movie star at Universal Studios Hollywood (p121)

Throw yourself into the scene at Venice (p97), LA's most outlandish beach

DALLAS STRIBLEY

Catch some waves at Malibu (p93), one of LA's legendary surf beaches

RAY LASKOWITZ

BRENT WINEBRENNER

Savor superb wines in the Santa Barbara Wine Country (p338)

Delight in the variety of animals at the world-famous San Diego Zoo (p253)

JOHN BORTHWICK

LEE FOSTER

Beach-hop along the coast of Laguna Beach (p225) in Orange County

RICHARD CUMMINS

Dine alfresco in Palm Springs (p300)

RICHARD CUMMINS

Soak up the rays and snorkel the waters of La Jolla Cove in San Diego's La Jolla (p274)

Marvel at the distinctive trees and dramatic landscape of Joshua Tree National Park (p314)

RICHARD CUMMINS

# Getting Started

Southern California (SoCal) has excellent tourism infrastructure, making traveling around the region a great pleasure. From backpackers to jetsetters, all will find their needs and expectations met. Room and travel reservations are a good idea in summer and around holidays, but otherwise you can keep your advance planning to a minimum.

## WHEN TO GO

SoCal's a great destination year-round, but most people visit in July and August when sunny skies and warm temperatures are pretty much guaranteed. This is the best time for frolicking on the beach, engaging in water sports, enjoying alfresco dinners and attending outdoor events. The mountains are beautiful too during this season, especially if you're into hiking, biking or other outdoor activities. Summer is not ideal for exploring the desert where the mercury can soar as high as 120°F. In all areas but the desert lodging is at a premium during these months and lines at such major attractions as Disneyland can be frustratingly long. Note that a pair of weather phenomena called 'June Gloom' and 'California Eddy' often blanket the coastal towns in thick fog in late spring – not so great if you're here for the sunshine.

See Climate Charts (p352) for more information.

The shoulder seasons (March to May and September to November) bring smaller crowds and lower prices. In spring, wildflowers often brighten meadows, mountains and parts of the desert, while in fall it can still be warm enough to swim in the Pacific. Unless you're planning a beach vacation, winter (December to February) is a great time to visit, despite the greater chance of rain. It's ideal for exploring the desert, when temperatures are mild and pleasant. Meanwhile, the higher mountain elevations, for instance around Big Bear Lake, have turned into a winter wonderland, drawing ski hounds to the slopes. In coastal cities, the cultural calendars are in full swing, skies are clear, temperatures still agreeable and, yes, lines at Disneyland and other theme parks are as short as they'll ever be (except around holidays).

Check the weather before you pack for your trip at the National Weather Service's home page for Los Angeles: www.wrh.noaa.gov/lox.

For information on holidays see p356, and for details of festivals and special events see p354.

## COSTS & MONEY

SoCal is a rather expensive region to visit, thanks, at least in part, to relatively comfortable income levels and a high overall standard of living. What you spend depends largely on what kind of traveler you are, what experiences you wish to have and the season in which you're visiting. In summer

---

**DON'T LEAVE HOME WITHOUT...**

- Checking the latest passport and visa requirements (p356)
- Hotel or camping reservations, especially in summer (p348)
- Driver's license and car documents, if driving, along with liability insurance and car-hire reservations (p366)
- A sweater and jacket for evenings, mountain travel and those days when the SoCal sun is a no-show
- A Beach Boys CD for driving down the coastal highway
- This book and an open mind

## TOP TENS

### Celluloid Faves

What better way to build your excitement about traveling to the world's biggest dream factory than by watching some movies set right in SoCal? Check out these flicks – all set in LA except for the two most recent, which are set in Orange County and the Santa Barbara Wine Country respectively. For reviews see p34.

- *A Star is Born* (1937)
  Director: David O Selznick
- *Chinatown* (1974)
  Director: Roman Polanski
- *Stand and Deliver* (1988)
  Director: Ramón Menéndez
- *Boyz N the Hood* (1991)
  Director: John Singleton
- *Short Cuts* (1993)
  Director: Robert Altman
- *Pulp Fiction* (1994)
  Director: Quentin Tarantino
- *LA Confidential* (1997)
  Director: Curtis Hanson
- *Mulholland Drive* (2001)
  Director: David Lynch
- *Orange County* (2002)
  Director: Jake Kasdan
- *Sideways* (2004)
  Director: Alexander Payne

### Top Reads

Great storytelling opens up a window on a destination's culture and people. Get ready for your trip by curling up with these works penned by some of SoCal's finest writers. For reviews see p32.

- *Ramona* (1884) Helen Hunt Jackson
- *The Big Sleep* (1939) Raymond Chandler
- *Day of the Locust* (1939) Nathanael West
- *The Last Tycoon* (1940) F Scott Fitzgerald
- *The Loved One* (1948) Evelyn Waugh
- *Less than Zero* (1985) Bret Easton Ellis
- *Palm Latitudes* (1988) Kate Braverman
- *Devil in a Blue Dress* (1990) Walter Moseley
- *The Handyman* (1999) Carolyn See
- *Where I Was From* (2003) Joan Didion

### Party In the Streets

Southern Californians are always up for a good time, and there's almost always something going on, especially in LA. Here's a list of favorites, but also have a look at p354.

- Rose Parade (Pasadena, Los Angeles, p137) January 1
- Los Angeles Times Festival of Books (Westwood, Los Angeles, p137) Third weekend in April
- Coachella Valley Music & Arts Festival (Indio, Palm Springs, p308) Late April or early May
- Cinco de Mayo (Downtown Los Angeles, p137) Early May
- LA Pride (West Hollywood, Los Angeles, p84) Mid-June
- Pageant of the Masters (Laguna Beach, Orange County, p228) July to August
- Sunset Junction Street Fair (Silver Lake, Los Angeles, p137) Mid-August
- Fleet Week (Downtown San Diego, p259) Mid- to late September
- West Hollywood Halloween Carnival (West Hollywood, Los Angeles, p138) October 31
- Doo Dah Parade (Pasadena, Los Angeles, p138) Sunday before Thanksgiving, November

and around holidays, renting a car, staying in mid-range hotels, enjoying two sit-down meals a day, spending some money on sightseeing, activities and going to bars or clubs will cost between $150 and $250 per day (per person, traveling as an adult couple). Families can save by booking into hotels that don't charge extra for children staying in the same room as their parents and by taking advantage of the numerous discounts available at museums, theme parks and other sights. (For information on traveling with children, see p351.) Even for mere survival, you probably won't be able to spend less than $50 to $70 per day, and this will have you sleeping in hostels, riding buses, preparing your own meals or eating snack- and fast-food, and limiting your entertainment. For ways to keep costs down, see p354.

Comfortable mid-range accommodation starts at around $100 for a double room. A two-course meal in an average restaurant without alcoholic drinks costs between $20 and $30, plus tax and tip. Museums charge anything up to $15, while attractions such as Disneyland will set you back $50 per person. Car rentals start at $20 per day, excluding tax and insurance.

## TRAVEL LITERATURE

To get you in the mood for your trip, read some of these titles. They'll paint vivid pictures of the land and society you're about to visit.

*My California: Journeys by Great Writers* (2004) is an insightful collection of stories about the Golden State by 27 of its finest chroniclers, including Pico Iyer, Rubén Martinez, Patt Morrison and Carolyn See. Proceeds benefit the California Arts Council. Literary bigwigs like Walter Mosley and new voices like Sandra Tsing Loh contributed to *LA Shorts* (2000), a superb anthology of essays portraying the City of Angels in all its diversity.

*Hollywood Babylon* (1958), Kenneth Anger's 'tell-all' book about the tawdry, sad and scandalous life and times of Hollywood's Golden Era stars, is a classic, even if reportedly rooted more in rumor than reality.

One of the first travelers to record his impressions of California, Richard Henry Dana visited the state in 1835 during the Mexican Rancho period. He recounts his thoughts in *Two Years Before the Mast,* a good read that's still available.

Charles Phoenix' *Southern California in the '50s* (2001) and *Southern Californialand* (2004) are colorful, high-spirited pictorial romps taking you back to the era that gave birth to car culture, suburbia and Disneyland.

For a little light-hearted reading, try Dianna Gessler's *Very California: Travels Through the Golden State* (2001) in which she captures her adventures and the state's character in whimsical watercolors and short vignettes.

Peter Theroux' *Translating LA: A Tour of the Rainbow City* (1994) is a solid and interesting – if now slightly dated – piece of storytelling that takes you into various neighborhoods and explores what makes them tick.

## INTERNET RESOURCES

For more cool websites see p56.

**@LA** (www.at-la.com) Well-organized portal puts SoCal at your fingertips.

**California State Government** (www.ca.gov) Links to general information, history, culture, doing business and environmental protection.

**California State Parks** (www.parks.ca.gov) Indispensable site for history, information and reservations at all state parks.

**California Tourism** (www.visitcalifornia.com) Links to all visitors bureaus throughout the state.

**Lonely Planet** (www.lonelyplanet.com) Travel news and summaries, the Thorn Tree bulletin board and links to more web resources.

**Theme Park Insider** (www.themeparkinsider.com) Visitors rate and evaluate rides and attractions at major theme parks in SoCal and elsewhere.

### HOW MUCH?

Cappuccino $2.50

Roll of 36-exposure film $4

Pack of cigarettes $4.40

Movie ticket $9-11

Map of the stars' homes $6

### LONELY PLANET INDEX

Gallon (3.78L) of gasoline $2.30

Liter of bottled water $1

Bottle of Budweiser in a bar $2.50-3

Souvenir T-shirt $10-15

Street snack (chicken taco) $1.50

# Itineraries

## CLASSIC ROUTES

### THE GRAND CIRCLE

Two to Three Weeks

**Prepare for a roller coaster of urban and rural delights on this 850- to 950-mile loop that will have you going from the beach to the desert, up into the mountains and back down to the coast.**

Kick things off in **Los Angeles** (p53), where you'll be spoiled for choice with top-notch sights, beautiful beaches and SoCal's best cuisine scene. Then head to Anaheim for a date with Mickey at **Disneyland** (p199) and a day of R and R in **Laguna Beach** (p225). Dip into the famous mission in **San Juan Capistrano** (p231) before arriving in **San Diego** (p233), where the sights will have you burning up the pixels in your digicam. Leaving civilization behind, head to **Anza-Borrego Desert State Park** (p319), a remote expanse of subtle beauty. Continue north, skirting the **Salton Sea** (p313) to **Joshua Tree National Park** (p314) with its whimsical trees. Squeeze in a day of margarita-sipping and golfing in nearby **Palm Springs** (p300) before climbing from the desert floor to the alpine village of **Big Bear Lake** (p126) for biking, hiking and skiing. Head west via the scenic Rim of the World Dr to **Ventura** (p343), the gateway to the **Channel Islands National Park** (p346). From here drive to **Santa Barbara** (p323) where you can tour downtown's historical sights or vineyard-hop around the **Santa Barbara Wine Country** (p338) before heading back to LA.

## COASTAL DELIGHTS

**One Week**

Book-ended by two of SoCal's great cities, San Diego and Santa Barbara, this route hugs the Pacific for most of the 240 miles it covers. Start out in **San Diego** (p233), where you can hang with modern-day hippies in **Ocean Beach** (p279), eat a fish taco or ride a roller coaster in **Mission Beach** (p277) and promenade around posh downtown **La Jolla** (p274). In northern San Diego County, stop in pretty, slow-paced **Carlsbad** (p294), where Legoland California scores big with kids, or plow on to the beautifully restored mission in **San Juan Capistrano** (p231). Secluded beaches and eucalyptus-shrouded hillsides imbue artsy **Laguna Beach** (p225) with a Riviera-like feel. Next up, sophisticated **Newport Beach** (p219) has great shopping, a huge pleasure-craft harbor and an amusement center. **Huntington Beach** (p215), aka 'Surf City, USA,' epitomizes the SoCal surfing lifestyle, while in laid-back **Long Beach** (p102) the historic *Queen Mary* ocean liner is a major draw.

You're in densely populated LA now, where you'll be barreling through a string of bustling beach towns, most notably **Venice** (p97), with its boardwalk and cast of quirky characters, and **Santa Monica** (p95) – its lively pier has a solar-powered Ferris wheel and the nearby promenade makes for great people-watching. From here it's off to **Malibu** (p93) via the ultrascenic Pacific Coast Hwy, beautifully hemmed in by the ocean and mountains. The road travels inland around Oxnard but goes coastal again in **Ventura** (p343), whose charming downtown has a pretty mission and cool thrift shops. Your final stop is **Santa Barbara** (p323), a symphony of red-tile roofs, great architecture and restaurants.

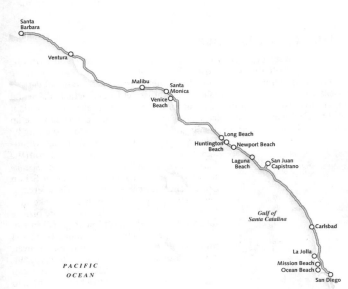

Southern California's coast is a ribbon of myth and legend, immortalized in film, song, word – and the imagination. This 240-mile route will have you traveling along its entire length, passing through some of the best in nature, culture and character the region has to offer.

# TAILORED TRIPS

## JUST FOR KIDS

It's no secret: kids love Southern California with its glorious beaches, near-perfect weather and cluster of blockbuster attractions. Topping most of their must-do lists is, of course, **Disneyland** (p199), the original 'mouse house,' although its new neighbor, **Disney's California Adventure** (p204), also has some fun rides. Nearby, **Knott's Berry Farm** (p211) gets high marks for its neat Old West theme, several fun-but-scary thrill rides and the spookiest Halloween party around. Pre-teens adore the rainbow-colored fantasy world at **Legoland California** (p294), a quick drive south in Carlsbad, while San Diego is all about animal magnetism. The famous

**San Diego Zoo** (p253) has an entire Noah's Ark worth of critters, from cuddly koalas to playful pandas. **SeaWorld** (p278) is a watery zoo where you'll be entertained by the antics of Shamu, the killer whale, and his finned friends. Another highlight is the safari-style **Wild Animal Park** (p254), where large mammals such as giraffes and zebras roam 'freely' in large enclosures. Los Angeles, meanwhile, lets you take a peek at movie magic at **Universal Studios Hollywood** (p121), although its thrill rides are tame compared to what awaits at **Six Flags Magic Mountain** (p122) whose hair-raising roller coasters should satisfy even the most speed-crazed teen.

## OFFBEAT FUN & ADVENTURE

If you're not into Disney or maybe the beaches don't excite you anymore, you can get off the beaten path and explore some, shall we say, more *unusual* attractions. Deep in the desert, near Joshua Tree National Park, is **Pioneertown** (p315), a 1940s Wild West movie set turned actual village and home to the quirkiest honky-tonk around. Getting there takes you past giant fields of **windmills** (p306), blades whirling wildly in the desert sun like an army of demented dervishes. Windmill worshippers should also swing by

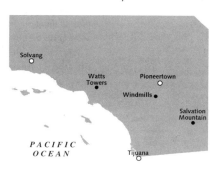

**Solvang** (p342), north of Santa Barbara, a whim-sical Danish village seemingly plucked from the fairy tales of Hans Christian Andersen. Speaking of worshippers, down south near the Salton Sea is **Salvation Mountain** (p313), whose creator has been saving souls one brush stroke at a time for nearly two decades. For more bizarre folk art, head to the **Watts Towers** (p117) in LA, a city that practically defines weird (see p134 for more offbeat suggestions). It does, however, have serious competition from **Tijuana** (p269), across the border in Mexico, where you can have your picture taken with a burro painted to look like a zebra and wearing a sombrero.

## THE GREAT OUTDOORS

On land, in the water and in the sky – opportunities to get your heart pumping abound no matter where you are in Southern California. Water babies especially have plenty of action to look forward to. Don a mask or strap on a tank for close-up encounters with glowing garibaldi, sea anemones and other marine life at the **San Diego-La Jolla Underwater Park** (p275) or the **Casino Point Marine Park** (p102) on Catalina Island, both protected ecological reserves. Catalina, with its craggy, coved coastline, is also perfect kayaking terrain, although to truly get off the beaten path, you'll want to do battle with the waves at **Channel Islands National Park** (p346). There's great mountain biking in several places, but nowhere more so than in **Big Bear Lake** (p126), whose ski mountains morph into championship-level bike parks in the summer. Rock climbers will be spoiled for challenge on the desert-baked boulders of **Joshua Tree National Park** (p314), while golfers will enjoy smacking a Titleist down the fairway at one of more than 100 golf courses in nearby **Palm Springs** (p300). Hiking trails beckon all over SoCal, even in ultra-urban LA, where the **Santa Monica Mountains** (p130) are laced with wonderful trails, including one to the former *M\*A\*S\*H* film set.

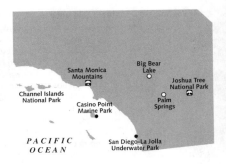

## ROAD RAVES

In Southern California the road always beckons, and numerous routes do a lot more than get you from point A to point B. If you have time for only one drive, head north from Santa Monica on the **Pacific Coast Hwy** (Hwy 1; p94), an epic stretch of road that reveals ocean vistas of surreal beauty as it meanders past Malibu before skirting inland at Point Mugu. North of here, **San Marcos Pass Rd** (Hwy 154; p343) rises from Santa Barbara into the Santa Ynez Mountains, taking you past Chumash rock art, thick forests and placid Lake Cachuma to the Santa Barbara Wine Country. Away from the coast, several gorgeous mountain roads await, of which the **Angeles Crest Hwy** (Hwy 2; p124), above Pasadena in LA, offers the easiest access. The most spectacular, though, is the **Rim of the World Dr** (Hwy 18; p127), which puts you above the congestion and pollution on its climb into the San Bernardino Mountains all the way to Big Bear Lake. You'll be treated to equally terrific views on the aptly named **Palms to Pines Hwy** (Hwys 243 and 74; p314), carved into the San Jacinto Mountains above Palm Springs. This drive is ideal for escaping the summer heat.

# The Authors

## ANDREA SCHULTE-PEEVERS     Coordinating Author, Los Angeles

By the time she was 20, Andrea had lived in Germany and the UK and racked up thousands of miles traveling on all continents except Antarctica. When it came time to settle down, she found Southern California's sunny disposition – and skies – simply irresistible. Armed with a degree from the University of California, Los Angeles (UCLA), she managed to feed her wanderlust by becoming a travel writer and, since 1996, has authored or updated about two dozen books for Lonely Planet. Andrea makes her home in Los Angeles with her husband, David, and their cat, Mep the Fierce.

**My Los Angeles & Southern California**

The first time I set foot in LA was in Downtown (p104), a rich tapestry of human experience that instantly intrigued me. Years later, it's still a favorite spot, a place for enjoying concerts at the Walt Disney Concert Hall (p107), foraging for hip clothes in the Fashion District (p185) or wolfing down ceviche at the Grand Central Market (p111). I'm equally fond of the beaches – especially those in chic Santa Monica (p95), outlandish Venice (p97) and fun-loving Hermosa (p100) – and the Santa Monica Mountains (p130), whose meandering trails are perfect for beating the blues and the belly-fat. To truly escape the urban velocity, though, there's no better place than Joshua Tree National Park (p314), followed closely by Big Bear Lake (p126) in the San Bernardino Mountains and the artsy oceanside enclave of Laguna Beach (p225).

## JOHN A VLAHIDES     Orange County, Palm Springs & the Deserts, San Diego, Santa Barbara

A native New Yorker, John studied cooking in Paris, then worked as a luxury-hotel concierge and earned membership in Les Clefs d'Or, the international union of the world's elite concierges. John now works as a freelance travel writer and lives in San Francisco, where he spends his free time touring California by motorcycle, sunning beneath the Golden Gate Bridge, skiing the Sierra Nevada and singing tenor with the San Francisco Symphony Chorus. He also cowrote Lonely Planet's *Coastal California*.

## CONTRIBUTING AUTHORS

**Rose Dosti** wrote the boxed text 'The LA Food Scene.' A veteran food writer for the *Los Angeles Times*, she wrote the 'Culinary SOS' column for 25 years. Author of eight cookbooks, including *Dear SOS: Favorite Restaurant Recipes* (2001), Rose is a 2004–05 Fulbright scholar and teaches cookbook and food-memoir writing at Emeritus College at Santa Monica College.

**David Goldberg MD** wrote the Health chapter. He completed his training in internal medicine and infectious diseases at Columbia-Presbyterian Medical Center in New York City, where he has also served as voluntary faculty. David is an infectious diseases specialist in Scarsdale, New York, and the editor-in-chief of the website www.mdtravelhealth.com.

**Alisha Snider** wrote the 'Living the Hollywood Cliché' boxed text. After graduating from Ithaca College with a BA in drama and clinical sociology, Alisha lived in New York for seven years performing in musical theater before moving to LA in 2003. She is currently performing in a children's theater show at Garry Marshall's Falcon Theatre and trying to break into film and television.

**John Payne** wrote the Music section of the Culture chapter. He is an LA-based film and theater composer, as well as the music editor of *LA Weekly* and contributor to various music, art and news publications. John is the author of the forthcoming *Pathfinders*, a collection of his articles on influential new-genre artists of the 1970s and '80s.

# Snapshot

Every year millions of people worldwide watch a TV show or film – or maybe the New Year's Day Rose Parade – and have their dreams of Southern California confirmed. The sunshine. The mythology. The stars. The creativity, drive and sheer fun of living here. Thousands come for a visit. Many of them stay. And therein lies the problem…

The single biggest issue affecting Southern California in the 21st century is its ballistic population growth. In 2004, nearly 21 million people made their homes in the seven-county area between Santa Barbara and San Diego and out to the Arizona state border, an increase of almost 20% since 1990. By 2020 that number is expected to swell by another six million. Such growth is the result of both migration from other countries and US states and an increase in the birth rate, especially among Latinos, who, at about 40%, make up the largest ethnic group in the region (see p30). How to fit in all of these folks while retaining SoCal's much-envied lifestyle is becoming an increasingly huge dilemma for politicians, urban planners and residents.

The writing has been on the wall for quite some time. Anyone trying to make it along the freeways during rush hour knows that traffic congestion is a huge problem. Car emissions are the biggest culprit behind the region's air quality, which ranks among the worst in the country. Meanwhile, housing shortages have driven up prices, making it virtually impossible for average wage earners to buy houses in urban neighborhoods. This, of course, is spawning suburban sprawl as giant cookie-cutter developments invade outlying areas.

Water continues to be another hot-button issue. Built in what is essentially a desert, Southern California has to import most of its water from central and northern California as well as the Colorado River. But thanks to a prolonged drought (since 2000), the Colorado River has seen its water levels plunge while being called upon to slake the thirst not only of Southern California but of other fast-growing cities such as Phoenix and Las Vegas. To help alleviate the problem, Congress passed the California Water Bill in October 2004, which will restore the Sacramento-San Joaquin delta river system in northern California and increase the water flow to the south by about 5%.

Despite such 'clouds' hanging over Southern California, people are not all down in the mouth. The region certainly hasn't lost its cutting edge, as was again confirmed in June 2004 when the first private space flight was launched from the Mojave desert, about 80 miles north of LA. SoCal also continues to be the main driving force behind the state's economic recovery. In 2004, it created about 100,000 new jobs, especially in the tech sector, aerospace, international trade and tourism. At about $800 billion, Southern California's gross product is only slightly lower than that of Spain and higher than Mexico's. Still, many people believe California can and should do better, foremost among them Governor Arnold Schwarzenegger who has made improving the state's business climate a major focus of his administration. Only time will tell if the governor's star power and policies will succeed in making California the 'Golden State' once again.

# History

Most people think of Southern California as being only recently settled by the Brady Bunch, but a lot happened before the suburban dream became the dominant cultural paradigm.

## PREHISTORIC TIMES

Settlement of North America began at least 12,000 years ago with one of the most significant human migrations ever. The ancestors of Native Americans, taking advantage of lowered sea levels during the Pleistocene epoch, walked from Siberia to Alaska via a land bridge across the Bering Strait. They weren't exactly speedy about moving south, and, according to radiocarbon dating of artifacts such as shell middens (ancient refuse heaps), stone tools and arrowheads, it took descendants of these migrants about 2000 years to reach Southern California. Curiously, though, San Diego's coastal areas hold middens dating back 20,000 years, making it some of the oldest known human-inhabited land in the US. But the most spectacular artifact left behind by California's early inhabitants is rock art, dating from 500 to 3000 years ago. In the age of computer graphics, the ancient art may not look like much at a glance, but historically speaking, it's stunning. Many sites are closed to the public in the interest of preservation, but you can visit Chumash Painted Cave State Historic Park (p343), near Santa Barbara.

## NATIVE CALIFORNIANS

Archaeological evidence paints a clear picture of the day-to-day lives of Native Americans at the time of European contact. Though their culture left behind nothing so spectacular as the Mayan and Aztec pyramids further south, California's earliest inhabitants lived in highly adapted societies that made the most of the land. They belonged to more than 20 language groups with around 100 dialects, and lived in small communities and villages, often migrating with the seasons from the coast to the mountains.

Their dietary staple was meal, made from ground acorns, which came from 20 native oak species (though most of the trees have since been cut down to make way for subdivisions). They supplemented their diets with small game, such as rabbit and deer, and fish and shellfish along the coast, and made clothing out of plants. California Indians used earthenware pots, fish nets, bows, arrows and spears with chipped stone points, but their most developed craft was basket making. Not only were the baskets functional – some of them were so tightly woven that they could even hold water – they were also beautiful. You'll have several great opportunities to see these and other artifacts while on the road at the Southwest Museum of the American Indian (p122) in LA, the excellent Museum of Man (p250) in San Diego, and the Palm Springs Desert Museum (p304), which has a comparatively small, but fine collection of baskets by local tribes.

Coastal and inland peoples traded, but generally they didn't interact much, partly because they spoke different languages. Conflict was almost nonexistent. California Indians had neither a warrior class nor a tradition of warfare – at least not until the Europeans arrived.

If you're wondering what happened to California's Native-American population, find definitive answers in *Handbook of North American Indians*, edited by Robert Heizer; California is covered in Volume 8.

| 10,000 BC | AD 1542 |
|---|---|
| Shoshonean Indians occupy the area now known as Los Angeles | Explorer Juan Rodríguez Cabrillo sails to LA and claims land for the king of Spain |

## BOATS & BUCCANEERS

After the conquest of Mexico in the early 16th century, there was much fanciful speculation about a golden island beyond Mexico's western coast. It was California, named even before it was explored after a mythical island queen in a Spanish novel. The precise etymology and meaning of the name 'California' have never been convincingly established, but there is wide consensus that it is a derivation of 'Calafia,' the book's heroine queen, who ruled a race of gold-rich black Amazons.

In 1542 the Spanish crown called on Juan Rodríguez Cabrillo, a Portuguese explorer and retired conquistador, to lead an expedition up the west coast to find the fabled land. He was also charged with finding the equally mythical Strait of Anian, an imagined sea route between the Pacific and the Atlantic.

He had no such luck. But when Cabrillo sailed into San Diego and named it San Miguel, he and his crew became the first Europeans to see mainland California. The ships sat out a storm in the harbor, then sailed northward. On arriving at Santa Monica Bay, a brown smoky haze hung in the air, no doubt from campfires in the Gabrieleño Indian village of Yangna, the site of present-day Downtown LA. In what might be considered a stroke of clairvoyance, Cabrillo named the bay Bahía de los Fumos, or 'Bay of Smokes.' Continuing north, they made a stop on the Channel Islands where, in 1543, Cabrillo fell ill, died and was buried. (If you're visiting San Diego, pay a visit to Point Loma and the Cabrillo National Monument, p279, where you can learn more about the cantankerous explorer's journey.)

The expedition continued as far as Oregon, but returned with no evidence of a sea route to the Atlantic, a city of gold or islands of spice. The unimpressed Spanish authorities forgot about California for the next 50 years. No European returned to Southern California until 1602, when Sebastian Vizcaino arrived in what is now San Diego Bay on the feast day of San Diego de Alcalá and couldn't resist renaming the place San Diego. He and his crew recorded their findings and moved on.

The website of the Historical Society of Southern California (www.socalhistory.org) has biographies, information on the region's historical places and excellent links to other websites on SoCal history.

## MISSION IMPROBABLE

Everyone wanted a toehold on the west coast of the New World in the 18th century. Around the 1760s, as Russian ships sailed to California's coast in search of sea otter pelts, and British trappers and explorers were spreading throughout the West, the Spanish king worried about the encroaching threats to his claims. Conveniently for him, the Catholic Church was anxious to start missionary work among the native peoples, so the two got together and created an army – of God, that is – setting up Catholic missions inside military forts (presidios). Native-American converts would live in the missions, learn trade and agricultural skills and ultimately establish pueblos (small Spanish towns) and the military would supposedly protect them. It didn't work out very well.

The first Spanish colonizing expedition, called the 'Sacred Expedition,' proved nearly disastrous. On July 1, 1769, a sorry lot of about 100 missionaries and soldiers, led by the Franciscan priest Junípero Serra and the military commander Gaspar de Portolá, hobbled ashore at San Diego Bay. They had spent several weeks at sea on their journey from Baja California,

To learn more about Southern California's missions, their cultural influence and their historical significance, log on to the California Missions website: www.californiamissions.com.

where Serra had already founded one mission, and about half of their cohorts had died en route. Many of the survivors were sick or near death. It was an inauspicious beginning for the Mission San Diego de Alcalá (p255), the 'mother' of the chain of 21 California missions.

Ostensibly, the purpose of the presidios was to protect the missions and deter foreign intruders. In fact, the garrisons created more threats than they deterred. Drunken troublemaking soldiers raped and pillaged, infuriating the Native Americans. Not only were the presidios militarily weak, but their weakness was well known to Russia and Britain, which did nothing to strengthen Spain's claims to California.

**DID YOU KNOW?**

The distance between California's missions equals a day's journey by horseback.

The mission period was an abject failure. The Spanish population remained small, the missions achieved little more than mere survival, foreign intruders were not greatly deterred, and more Native Americans died than were converted.

They're little more than shells of what they once were, but some of the presidios remain. The San Diego Presidio was largely destroyed by fire in 1872, but the 1782 El Presidio de Santa Barbara (p329) still stands with several of its original buildings intact. If you're heading south of LA, take a detour to see the Mission San Juan Capistrano (p231), whose chapel is one of the prettiest of its kind.

## THE PATH TO STATEHOOD

Mexico gained independence from Spain in 1821, and the new nation's people looked to California to satisfy their thirst for private land. By the mid-1830s the missions had been secularized, with a series of governors doling out hundreds of free land grants, giving birth to the rancho system. The new landowners, called rancheros or Californios, prospered quickly and became the social, cultural and political fulcrums of California. The average rancho was a whopping 16,000 acres and largely given over to livestock to supply the trade in hide and tallow.

American explorers, trappers, traders, whalers, settlers and opportunists showed up in droves in California, seizing on prospects that the Californios foolishly ignored. Some of the Americans who started businesses converted to Catholicism, married locals and assimilated into Californio society. One American, Richard Henry Dana, author of *Two Years Before the Mast* (1840), worked on a ship in the hide trade in the 1830s and wrote disparagingly of Californians as 'an idle and thriftless people who can make nothing for themselves.' But of Los Angeles, which at the time had a population of only 1200 souls, he wrote, 'In the hands of an enterprising people, what a country this might be.'

He wasn't the only one to see great possibilities. Impressed by California's potential wealth and hoping to fulfill the promise of Manifest Destiny (the imperialist doctrine to extend US borders from coast to coast), US president Andrew Jackson sent an emissary to offer the financially strapped Mexican government $500,000 for California, an offer that was tersely rejected.

Mexico's troubles were just beginning. In 1836 Texas had seceded from Mexico and declared itself an independent republic. When the US annexed Texas in 1845, Mexico was downright apoplectic and broke off diplomatic relations, ordering all foreigners without proper papers to

| 1850 | 1892 |
|---|---|
| California becomes a state | Oil is discovered in Downtown LA, sparking a major oil boom |

be deported from California. Outraged Northern Californians revolted, captured the nearest Mexican official and, supported by a company of US soldiers led by Captain John C Frémont, declared California's independence from Mexico in June 1846 by raising their 'Bear Flag' over the town of Sonoma. The Bear Flag Republic existed for all of one short month. (The banner lives on, however, as the California state flag.)

Meanwhile, the US had declared war on Mexico following the dispute over Texas, which provided the US all the justification it needed to invade Mexico. By July, US naval units occupied every port on the California coast, including the then capital Monterey.

On Christmas day 1846, Frémont took the city of Santa Barbara without bloodshed. Though an ambush waited for him to descend on the city from the north over Gaviota Pass, Benjamin Foxen warned him and guided him along what is now Foxen Canyon Rd and over San Marcos Pass. (Look for the historical marker on Foxen Canyon Rd, 14 miles north of Los Olivos in the Santa Barbara Wine Country, p338).

When US troops captured Mexico City in September 1847, putting an end to the war, the Mexican government had little choice but to cede much of its northern territory to the US. The Treaty of Guadalupe Hidalgo, signed on February 2, 1848, turned over California, Arizona and New Mexico to the US. Only two years later, California was admitted as the 31st state of the United States. (An interesting detail of this treaty guarantees the rights of Mexican citizens living in areas taken over by the US. Many Mexicans feel that this provision still entitles them to live and work in those states, regardless of their country of birth.)

By an amazing coincidence, gold was discovered several days before the signing of the treaty and quickly transformed the newest American outpost. The population surged from 15,000 to 90,000 over the course of a year between 1848 and 1849.

## RAILROAD, AGRICULTURE & INDUSTRY

**DID YOU KNOW?**

The *Los Angeles Times* published its first issue in 1881.

The transcontinental railroad shortened the trip from New York to San Francisco from two months to five days, opening up markets on both coasts. Tracks were laid simultaneously from the east and the west, converging in Utah in 1869. By the 1870s, speculation had raised land prices to levels no farmer or immigrant could afford, the railroad brought in products that undersold the goods made in California, and some 15,000 Chinese laborers – no longer needed for rail construction – flooded the labor market; many of them moved south to LA.

**DID YOU KNOW?**

The first Los Angeles telephone book, issued in 1882, was only three pages long.

For all its power today, LA was largely ignored in the 19th century until 1876, when the Southern Pacific Railroad (SP) laid tracks from San Francisco to the fledgling city. The SP monopoly was broken in 1887, when the Atchinson, Topeka & Santa Fe Railroad Company (AT&SF) laid tracks linking LA across the Arizona desert to the East Coast. The competition was so fierce between the rival railroads that at one point you could cross the entire continent for only $2, causing the so-called 'boom of the '80s,' a major real estate explosion lasting from 1886 to 1888. More than 120,000 migrants, mostly from the Midwest, came to Southern California, settling in the 25 new towns laid out by AT&SF in the eastern part of Los Angeles County.

| 1913 | 1924 |
|---|---|
| Owens Valley Aqueduct brings water to LA (allowing the population to continue exploding) | LA city planners approve the building of 40 new subdivisions per week |

Coinciding with the arrival of the railroad was the establishment of an orange-growing industry in Southern California. Around 1874 the US Department of Agriculture shipped three Brazilian navel (seedless) orange trees to Eliza and Luther Tibbetts, botanists in Riverside, a town east of LA. So successful were these trees, which produce their fruit in winter, that a second crop of summer-producing Valencia oranges was established in what is now Orange County. By 1889 orange trees covered more than 13,000 acres, sending the previously woebegone local economy through the roof.

Unlike many fruits, oranges easily survive long-distance rail shipping. As California oranges found their way onto New York grocery shelves, coupled with a hard-sell advertising campaign, Easterners heeded the self-interested advice of crusading magazine and newspaper editor Horace Greeley to 'Go West, young man.' LA's population jumped from 2300 in 1860 to 11,000 in 1880, to more than 50,000 in 1890, and a stunning 100,000 in 1900.

Much of the land granted to the railroads was sold in big lots to speculators who also acquired, with the help of corrupt politicians and administrators, a lot of the farmland that was released for new settlement. A major share of the state's agricultural land became consolidated into large holdings in the hands of a few city-based landlords, establishing the pattern (which continues to this day) of industrial-scale 'agribusiness' rather than small family farms.

In the absence of coal, iron ore or abundant water, heavy industry developed slowly, although the 1892 discovery of oil in the LA area stimulated the development of petroleum processing and chemical industries.

San Diego, meanwhile, had become a civilian pueblo after the missions broke up, around 1833, and remained a ramshackle village at the base of Presidio Hill (p257), with only a few hundred residents, until the 1850s when William Heath Davis, a former sea captain and San Francisco property speculator, bought 160 acres of bay-front land and erected prefabricated houses, a wharf and warehouses. Everyone thought the plan preposterous. Dubbed Davis' Folly, the development was ahead of its time. But in 1867 Alonzo E Horton, another San Francisco speculator, acquired 960 acres of waterfront land and promoted it as 'New Town.' This time the new subdivision prospered, particularly after an 1872 fire devastated much of the settlement near Presidio Hill.

The 1869 discovery of gold in the hills east of San Diego sparked a frenetic mining boom, which in 1884 brought the railroad to the city. After the gold ran out, half the population left, and San Diego went back to being a sleepy little town of only 2000 souls. Despite the never-ending rah-rah efforts of city boosters, San Diego remained without an industry until the 20th century.

## THE 20TH CENTURY

The population, wealth and importance of Southern California increased dramatically throughout the 20th century. The revolutionary years in Mexico, from 1910 to 1921, caused a huge influx of immigrants from south of the border, re-establishing Latino communities that had been

**DID YOU KNOW?**

At the 1884 World's Fair in New Orleans, the world tasted San Bernardino Valencia oranges for the first time, effectively putting Southern California on the map.

**DID YOU KNOW?**

Without the 1913 construction of the Owens Valley Aqueduct, LA would never have grown beyond 100,000 inhabitants.

| 1927 | 1931 |
| --- | --- |
| Academy of Motion Picture Arts & Sciences is founded at the Biltmore Hotel | Los Angeles International Airport (LAX) opens |

smothered by American dominance. The Panama Canal, completed in 1914, made shipping feasible between the eastern and western US, and the new port of San Pedro, 21 miles south of LA's City Hall, sprang up as the busiest port on the West Coast. The Lockheed brothers and Donald Douglas – taking note of LA's ideal test-flight weather and its capacity to house large work forces – established aircraft manufacturing plants in the area during WWI. Around the same time, aviation pioneer Glenn H Curtiss founded a flight camp in San Diego and helped develop ship-based aircraft on San Diego Bay. Ryan Airlines built the *Spirit of St Louis* for Lindbergh's transatlantic flight in 1927, and Consolidated Aircraft opened its San Diego factory in 1931. At long last, San Diego had a raison d'être.

Roman Polanski's *Chinatown* (1974) stars Jack Nicholson and Faye Dunaway in the story of Los Angeles' early-20th-century water wars. Robert Towne's brilliant screenplay deftly navigates the shrewd deceptions that made Los Angeles what it is today.

The Great Depression saw another wave of emigrants, this time from the impoverished prairie states of the Dust Bowl. The immigrants were broke, and competition for work was fierce. Mexicans took it on the chin, bearing the blame for an oversaturated workforce, never mind that they had arrived first. Outbreaks of social and labor unrest led to a rapid growth of the Democratic Party in California, which remains the dominant party in California. Some of the party's Depression-era public works projects had lasting benefits, great and small, especially dams and reclamation projects, which imported vast amounts of water for large-scale irrigation of Southern California's crops.

Southern California has always had a love-hate relationship with its changing population. Immigrants are typically welcomed in periods of rapid growth, only to be rejected when times get tough. Chinese railroad workers, for instance, were in great demand in the 1860s but ended up victimized in the 1870s. The Webb Alien Land Law of 1913 prevented some Asian minorities from owning land. During WWII, 93,000 people of Japanese heritage – many of them American citizens – were forcibly placed in internment camps. African Americans came in large numbers to take jobs in the postwar boom, but found themselves unemployed when the economy slowed down. Ironically, California owes much of its success to its cultural diversity. For more on multiculturalism, see p31.

## GUNNING AHEAD

Although California has never been the scene of a major conflict, it's one of the most militarized places on earth. During and after WWI, aircraft industries were established by Douglas and the Lockheed brothers in LA, and Curtis in San Diego. Two decades later, with another world war brewing, the aviation industry helped lift California out of the Great Depression. By the end of WWII, billions of federal dollars had been poured into Southern California military contracts.

WWII had a huge impact on Southern California. After the devastating 1941 bombing of the US Naval Fleet in Pearl Harbor, San Diego became (and remains to this day) headquarters for the Pacific Fleet, forever transforming the city: the harbor was dredged and man-made islands built; vast tracts of housing appeared; public spaces were turned into training camps, storage depots and hospitals; and the city's population doubled in a couple of years. Further north, Camp Pendleton, the huge Marine base, was established in southern Orange County. The Colorado Desert,

| 1955 | 1960 |
|---|---|
| Disneyland opens in Anaheim | University of California, San Diego (UCSD) opens |

near Palm Springs, temporarily became one of the biggest military training grounds in history. Los Angeles had established itself as the center of the aviation industry, and aircraft plants in the area turned out planes by the thousands. Hollywood even got on the bandwagon and produced propaganda films.

Many of the service people who had passed through the state during WWII liked the place so much that they returned to settle here. The military-industrial complex continued to chug along in Southern California, providing jobs in high-tech, Cold War industries, from avionics and missile manufacturing to helicopter and nuclear submarine maintenance. The marine corps continues to train recruits here, and the navy holds advanced training for fighter pilots. There are submarine bases, aircraft testing facilities, air force bases and sprawling gunnery ranges. Military spending peaked in the 1980s under President Ronald Reagan (a former California governor), but by 1990 it had become clear that the honeymoon was over. Budget cutbacks resulted in the closure of numerous bases and forced hundreds of defense-related companies to downsize and restructure. Workers who had grown accustomed to regular paychecks from McDonnell Douglas and other aerospace companies suddenly got laid off. However, America's recent and ongoing 'war on terror' has lately sparked renewed interest in the armed forces and its related industries in the region.

Southern California swells with pride over its military history, most obviously in San Diego, where you can not only visit the decommissioned aircraft carrier USS *Midway* (p248), but you can even board visiting naval ships that are currently in service (see p259). And if you're a military history buff and plan to visit the inland deserts, be sure to check out the Palm Springs Air Museum (p306).

## CELLULOID & STARS

Few industries have symbolized Southern California, especially LA, more than moviemaking. Independent producers came as early as 1908, primarily for the sunny climate, which allowed indoor scenes to be shot outdoors – a necessity, given the unsophisticated photo technology of the day. And in this land of little rain and varied terrain, any location, from ocean to desert to alpine forest, could be realized nearby on almost any day of the year. What's more, the proximity of the Mexican border enabled filmmakers to rush their equipment to safety when challenged by the collection agents of patent holders such as Thomas Edison. A little known fact, though, is that Santa Barbara, not LA, was the original center for film production. The American Film Company, founded in Santa Barbara at the corner of Mission and State Sts in 1910, was the largest in the world for about three of its 10 years in existence. (The set for the *Ten Commandments* lies buried in Guadalupe Dunes, north of the city near Santa Maria.)

The film industry – or simply 'The Industry,' as it's known in LA – has done much to promote California's image throughout the country and the world. As film, and later TV, became the predominant entertainment medium of the 20th century, California took center stage in the world of popular culture.

**DID YOU KNOW?**

In 1915 DW Griffiths produced *Birth of a Nation* and paved the way for the LA film industry.

| 1968 | 1988 |
|---|---|
| Robert Kennedy assassinated at the Ambassador Hotel in LA | Smog report issued; EPA imposes strict standards on LA County |

## SHIFTING PARADIGMS

Unconstrained by the burden of traditions, bankrolled by affluence and promoted by film and TV, California leads the world in new attitudes and social movements. As early as the 1930s, Hollywood was promoting fashions and fads for mass consumption, even as the nation struggled to move beyond the Depression.

Though you'd never know it today, LA and San Diego once had extensive, efficient public rail systems, specifically electric trains and streetcars. In the 1940s General Motors secretly bought them up by establishing dummy corporations, then dismantled them so that citizens would be forced to ride diesel buses or drive cars. Suddenly the car was king.

With 1950s affluence, the emerging middle class moved to the suburbs, and no place in America better defined suburban life than Orange County. The Irvine Company, owner of more than 100,000 acres of agricultural land (the legacy of 19th-century Spanish land grants), built the first 'master-planned' communities. Strict rules governed their design – hence the county's uniform beige-box architecture. Everybody lived on a quiet street, where children could safely play; shopping centers and strip malls were kept separate, concentrated along wide, multilane boulevards. Everyone had a new freezer, a family sedan and a garage.

The 'Beat' movement was a reaction against the banality and conformism of suburban life, turning to coffeehouses for jazz, philosophy, poetry and pot. When the postwar baby boomers hit their late teens, many took up where the Beat generation left off, rejecting their parents' values, heeding Tim Leary's counsel to 'turn on, tune in, drop out.' Though the hippie counterculture was an international phenomenon, Southern California was at the leading edge of its music, its psychedelic art and its new libertarianism. Sex, drugs and rock and roll ruled the day.

In the late 1960s and early '70s, New Left politics, the anti–Vietnam War movement and Black Liberation forced their way into the political limelight, and flower power and give-peace-a-chance politics seemed instantly naive. The 1968 assassination of Robert Kennedy in LA, the sometimes violent repression of demonstrations, and the death of a spectator at a Rolling Stones concert at the hands of their security guards (Hell's Angels they had hired for the occasion) stripped the era of its innocence.

What a difference a decade makes. In the 1980s and '90s, Southern California's new obsession became the healthy lifestyle, with more aerobic classes and self-actualization workshops than you could shake your totem at. Leisure activities such as in-line skating, snowboarding and mountain biking all originated in California. But be careful what you laugh at. From pet rocks to soy burgers, Southern California's flavor of the month will probably be next year's world trend.

## THE FUTURE IS NOW

The world looks to California for drama of all kinds, from TV and movies to celebrity gossip, so it should come as no surprise that, in 2003, the state made worldwide headlines when Arnold Schwarzenegger, a Republican, won the governor's seat in a highly contentious recall election that ousted former Democratic governor Gray Davis from power. Davis had ridden

*Ask the Dust* (1939), by John Fante, follows the fame-and-fortune fantasies of a struggling writer in Depression-era Los Angeles, where 'the smell of gasoline makes the sight of palm trees seem sad.'

**DID YOU KNOW?**

John F Kennedy was nominated president at the Democratic Convention in LA in 1960.

In *Coast of Dreams* (2004) Kevin Starr, the former state librarian, scoops together in journalistic style California's recent history, from 1990 to 2003, during which unprecedented social upheaval forever changed the state's cultural direction.

| 1992 | 1994 |
|---|---|
| LA riots (after acquittal of police officers who beat Rodney King) | Northridge earthquake (6.7 on Richter scale) causes 57 deaths |

high on the wave of good times in the late 1990s, but when the state's economy fell apart, so did his popularity.

No place in America was more affected by the year-2000 demise of the dot-coms and subsequent plunge of world markets than California, the nation's wealthiest state and the world's fifth-largest economy. To add insult to injury, the same year brought rolling blackouts to California's recently deregulated electricity market, forcing the state to buy its energy on the spot market, day by day, at ridiculously inflated prices. Consumers' bills doubled overnight. Governor Davis, forced into a corner, negotiated expensive long-term contracts that locked in very high rates for electricity, but he successfully stabilized the market. Then, after the contracts had been signed, allegations emerged that power generators, among them failed energy giant Enron, had created an artificial energy crisis by pulling electricity off the state's grid in a conspiracy to drive up prices. Then the companies went bust. The money vanished.

In November 2002 Democratic Governor Davis won a second four-year term, but Republican malcontents forced an October 2003 recall election on the grounds of 'malfeasance,' blaming the governor for the $40 billion budget deficit. Citizens were angry at Davis' bad habit of favoring big-money 'special interests,' and Republicans played on it. Arnold Schwarzenegger entered the race and won on an anti–'special interest' platform, despite receiving hefty campaign donations. But this is a state that loves its celebrities. Californians will always forgive an action hero more easily than a state bureaucrat.

*Cadillac Desert: The American West and Its Disappearing Water* (1986), by Mark Reisner, chronicles in compelling prose the history of water in Southern California and the ruthless politics that surround it.

# The Culture

## REGIONAL IDENTITY

Believe everything you've ever heard about Southern Californians – as long as you realize that the stereotypes are almost always exaggerated. Sure, Valley girls snap chewing gum in the shopping malls north of LA, surfer boys shout 'Dude!' across San Diego beaches and harried soccer moms occasionally flip out in Orange County's rush-hour traffic, but all in all, it's still hard to peg the population. Bear in mind that this chapter addresses general trends, not hard-and-fast rules.

Los Angeles is by far the most cosmopolitan city in SoCal, and it sometimes seems that everyone works in 'The Industry' (film and TV). Indeed, the first question you'll often hear from a resident is 'What do you do for a living?' Based upon your answer, much will be assumed about you. People define themselves – and their social status – by their jobs. Then, of course, there's the car you drive. It's a common joke, but there's an underlying truth to it: in LA, you simply *must* have the right car. Class consciousness expresses itself in one's choice of internal-combustion engine. Remember, this is the land of valet parking. People notice these things. Even the poor.

Politically speaking, LA leans to the left and strongly supports the Democratic Party, unlike almost every other Southern California city (except Santa Barbara). Angelenos tend to have a sophisticated, expansive worldview, likely the result of the city's culturally diverse society (see p31). But LA's residents don't always get along well, mostly because of the great disparity between the haves and have-nots.

Between LA and San Diego in Orange County (beyond the so-called 'orange curtain'), George W Bush is welcomed with open arms at $2000-a-plate Republican fundraising dinners. Many people live in gated communities and have limited tolerance for (or exposure to) outsiders. The conservative politics extend to San Diego, largely because of the high numbers of military personnel who live there, but extreme right-wing fundamentalists are few and far between. This is California, after all, not the Bible Belt.

## LIFESTYLE

When it comes to how people live, LA is a city of extremes, from the palm-tree-lined streets and palatial mansions of Beverly Hills to the embattled neighborhoods of East LA and South Central. California has the world's fifth-largest economy, and much of the money is concentrated in SoCal, in the hands of a few. But there's also a significant middle class – SoCal is the birthplace of the planned suburb – and many people live out the American dream on quiet, residential streets with grassy backyards. Just as it's impossible to generalize what type of people live in SoCal, it's equally difficult to qualify *how* people live.

Woody Allen called Los Angeles a 'suburb in search of a city.' If you've never been there before, then as you travel around the vast LA Basin, you may come to the same conclusion. No matter where you're going in LA, you'll have to drive to reach your destination (just like in the suburbs), and it will usually take you at least 20 or 30 minutes to get there. Everyone in LA has a car.

Meanwhile, people in SoCal – particularly Orange County and San Diego – exhibit odd social behavior in pedestrian areas such as Hunting-

Los Angeles is the birthplace of countless rumors and urban legends. Find out what's true and what's not at the Urban Legends Reference Pages at www .snopes.com.

ton Beach (p215) and La Jolla (p274). When you pass someone on the street, expect to be looked up and down, head to toe, then completely disregarded. Again, blame it on car culture. People spend so much time in their vehicles and ignoring others around them that, on the rare occasion they walk somewhere, they inadvertently treat passersby with the same indifference they would a motorist in another vehicle on the freeway. It takes some getting used to. Don't personalize it: everyone gets the same treatment – unless you're a celebrity, of course.

Frank Lloyd Wright built only a few houses in the LA area, but his designs heavily influenced the work of later architects, such as Rudolph Schindler and Richard Neutra, who sought to bring the outdoors inside, with vast panes of glass opening up onto patios that connect to other parts of the house. This open style of floor plan is a recurring theme today around SoCal, where many people have swimming pools and barbecues and even outdoor refrigerators and ice makers, permitting outdoor entertaining with the main house serving as little more than a backdrop for the patio and pool. Remember, it rarely rains in SoCal, and people take full advantage of the balmy weather. For more on SoCal's architecture see p36.

By contrast, southern Orange County's architectural design styles are strictly controlled by the Irvine Company, the privately held real estate company that built America's first master-planned suburban communities on subdivided land, which was once part of the original 93,000-acre Irvine Ranch. The chairman of the board so liked Tuscany that he decided that all the homes in the new communities should have stucco facades. (If you dislike the region's beige, boxy architecture and rows and rows of strip malls, blame him.) Residential areas are kept separate from shopping districts so everyone has a safe place in which to raise a family. Though residents own their homes, the Irvine Company owns most of the retail space, including Fashion Island shopping center in Newport Beach, as well the adjacent Four Seasons Hotel. To the company's credit, it has set aside 50,000 acres as open space – even if it did recently bulldoze the hilltops above Crystal Cove State Park to build more multimillion-dollar boxes overlooking the sea, something a lot of locals justifiably resent.

Despite any regional or political differences, in everyday life most people are pleasant – sometimes to a fault. Sure, there are exceptions, such as between developers and conservationists, but in society, everyone is so determined to get along that it can be hard to find out what somebody really thinks. Political correctness thrives in SoCal. Sometimes it's annoying. If you stick around for a while, you'll inevitably exchange telephone numbers with a person who expresses interest in seeing you again. In most parts of the world that means, 'Call me.' Not in SoCal. It's just a nicety. Often the other person never calls, and if you make an attempt to do so, you may never hear back.

Then again, some might say that you're 'codependent' for holding expectations of your new friend. The jargon of self-help groups has completely infiltrated the daily language of Southern Californians. For example, the word 'issue' gets bandied about so frequently that, unless you've mastered the lexicon, you can't be sure what precisely the speaker is trying to convey. (Generally speaking, it's a polite way to refer to someone else's problems without implying that the person has…well, problems.) It's all about getting along and being nice.

However, this all flies out the window on the state's always-busy freeways when a driver's extended middle finger often pops up. Road rage has

Nobody could break down into simpler terms the psychology of SoCal's culture of fads better than Dr Seuss (Theodor Geisel) in his story *The Sneeches* (1961). Visit his library at the University of California, San Diego (UCSD; p276).

become a serious problem, especially in LA. If you plan to do any driving whatsoever, before you put the key in the ignition, take a deep breath and meditate on remaining calm throughout your journey. Expect to encounter people who won't hesitate to cut you off, and then flip you off. Factor it in, let it go and – most importantly – don't engage the other driver in a game of one-upmanship. Rumors of freeway shootings are *not* urban legends. Take heart: they're not the norm. If driving stresses you out, then point your car toward the coast, don flip-flops and a pair of shorts and join laid-back locals who know where to find the real SoCal experience: at the beach.

## POPULATION

California is the most populous state in the US. It's also one of the fastest growing, posting increases of more than 5 million residents between 1990 and 2000. In 2003, 35.5 million people called the Golden State home.

California is a diverse society, and most native-born Americans who live in SoCal came here from somewhere else. As of 2003, nearly one in four California residents was foreign-born – even the state's Austrian-born celebrity governor, Arnold Schwarzenegger. Today approximately 30% of America's total immigrant population lives in California; Mexicans compose the largest group, followed by those from the Philippines, China, India, El Salvador, Guatemala, Iran, Korea and Taiwan (in that order). California also has large communities of Armenians and Indians. Most immigrants live in urban areas and bring their cultures and languages with them, creating richly textured neighborhoods and districts, particularly in LA, where most of California's 'just-off-the-boat' immigrants live.

The state's racial makeup continues to shift. Hispanic, Latino and Asian populations steadily increase, while the number of whites declines. In 2000 the US census found Caucasians still had the highest numbers, making up about 47% of the population. Hispanics and Latinos weren't far behind, with just over 32%. By contrast, African Americans comprised just over 7% of the population, Asians and Pacific Islanders about 11%, and Native Americans only 1%.

Most Southern Californians live within about 30 miles of the coast. The reason is simple: much of SoCal is semidesert, and the further inland you go, the hotter it gets. Besides, the beach is what draws most people to SoCal in the first place.

## SPORTS

If you're into sports, you'll love SoCal. As in most of the rest of America, competitive sports play a vital role in local cultural life. From Little League baseball and soccer games for kids, to adult-league softball and even bowling, sports are everywhere in SoCal life – even in the language (you can barely get a job unless you identify as a 'team player'). Sports stadiums are to SoCal what the Coliseum was to Rome, and there's no shortage of opportunities to book a seat and cheer the big leagues.

Professional games are played by one National Football League (NFL) team, the San Diego Chargers; three Major League Baseball (MLB) teams, the LA Dodgers, Disney-owned Anaheim Angels and San Diego Padres; two National Basketball Association (NBA) teams, the LA Lakers and LA Clippers; one Women's National Basketball Association (WNBA) team, the LA Sparks; two National Hockey League (NHL) teams, the LA Kings and the Mighty Ducks in Anaheim; and one Major League Soccer (MLS) team, LA Galaxy. Games can be sold out – especially Lakers and Kings games – so buy tickets early. Football season runs from August to mid-January, baseball from March to October, basketball from November to April, women's basketball from June to August, ice hockey from October to April and soccer from March to November. For details on where teams play and how to book seats, see the relevant Entertainment sections in destination chapters.

For a more homegrown sporting event, consider taking in a Minor League Baseball game. The games are a great slice of Americana. To find out more about the league, check out www.minorleaguebaseball.com.

Beach volleyball grows more popular every year, especially on the beaches of Orange County, such as Huntington Beach (p215). Seaside towns in LA host several professional tournaments each summer, the most important of which are the Hermosa Beach Open (p100) and Manhattan Beach Open (p99).

Motor sports are also a huge obsession. Long Beach hosts the Toyota Grand Prix of Long Beach (p102), a Formula 1 race, every April. In September San Diego hosts the Thunderboat Regatta (p259), in which superfast speed boats race on Mission Bay.

## MULTICULTURALISM

Since California gained statehood in 1850, most of its growth has come from immigration. This has resulted in a richly multicultural society, but one in which race relations have often been strained.

During the mid-19th century, pioneers essentially walked across the continent on a crapshoot they'd find gold in California. By the end of the century Easterners were arriving by rail to stake agricultural claims and grow oranges, the new cash crop. During the Great Depression and Dust Bowl years, Okies came in droves with the modest goal of living in a land where the top soil didn't blow away. And after WWII, soldiers migrated with their young wives to start families in the new suburbs. The unifying theme? Fortune and success. From the earliest days of California history, immigrants have all come seeking a better way of life. (For more, see p19.)

After the fall of Saigon in 1975, many Vietnamese, Cambodian and Hmong refugees (from the mountains of Laos) fled to America, aided by the US government, which tried to disperse the new immigrants across the nation. Nonetheless many relocated to California, with the highest concentration of Vietnamese immigrants settling in Westminster, Orange County, because of the city's inexpensive retail space and housing.

Black, not blonde, is now the dominant hair color in LA, due largely to the enormous Mexican population. Forty percent of LA County's residents are Mexican by birth or ancestry, and by 2020 they will surpass whites as the majority. Other groups from South and Central America continue to arrive in droves, mostly because opportunities in the their home countries are narrowing. Their collective influence is huge. From radio and TV stations to Spanish-language billboards, you'll see and hear Latino culture everywhere as you drive through LA.

Latino LA is constantly evolving, coming out of the shadows 200 years after the city's founding, and Hispanics have taken a leadership role in local political, community and cultural life. Nearly every kitchen in SoCal is run in Spanish, and there are a host of Latino products on grocery-store shelves: Cacique cheese, Juanita's Menudo and MexiCola, to name a few. The salsa-dancing scene is red hot, seven nights a week. Home-grown musicians such as Los Lobos and Ozomatli have crossed over to the international mainstream. And of all the groups that play major venues such as the Universal Amphitheatre and Greek Theater, Latino artists top the list as the most popular.

Each successive generation has acculturated differently. Twenty years ago, Latino-Americans had little say in politics. Today the LA County sheriff

San Diego's carefree outward appearance belies a dark underbelly. Get the dirt in *Under the Perfect Sun: The San Diego Tourists Never See* by Mike Davis et al (2003).

is Latino, as is one of the most powerful members of the county's board of supervisors, and Latinos are increasingly well represented in the California State Assembly and US Congress. Gone are the days of corralling Latinos into a few isolated communities. Sure, the barrio still exists, most notably in the 'gateway' community of Pico/Union, where recent Mexican and Central American immigrants first get a toehold in the USA, but the formerly white-only suburban dream of the 1950s has been adopted by Latinos, particularly in Huntington Park, Bell and Cudahy. The more-moneyed middle class resides in the suburbs of Alhambra, San Gabriel and points east. As inevitably happens with first- and second-generation Americans, a few adventuresome kids ditch the perceived oppression of their parents' suburban tract homes in search of the freedom of urban subculture; in the case of young Latino hipsters, most head to West LA, Santa Monica and Venice.

For all this upward mobility, Mexican and Latino workers still do most of the farm labor and domestic work, and many of them are without proper papers. It's estimated that as many as 2.3 million illegal aliens (always a politically hot topic) currently live in California, which amounts to 40% of the total number of illegals in the entire country. In 1994, in the face of increasing unemployment and state government deficits, Californians voted in favor of Proposition 187, which denied illegal immigrants access to state government services, including schools and hospitals. Legal challenges blocked it from becoming law, but the knee-jerk anti-immigration sentiment remains, especially in pockets of Orange County, which has an alarming concentration of white supremacists and neo-Nazis.

But California has a way of integrating its people, although it sometimes takes a generation or two. Today, SoCal's astonishingly diverse population is both its weakness and its strength. Race-related incidents receive high-profile exposure, as with the 1992 Los Angeles riots following the acquittal of four white police officers charged with beating Rodney King. Following the attacks of September 11, 2001, security got tough, and discrimination against minorities, especially Muslims and Arabs, worsened. Yet you never hear about the day-to-day civility between races. The arrival of people from every corner of the globe makes everyday SoCal one of the most tolerant, cosmopolitan and open-minded societies anywhere. On an errand run, you might drop off shirts with your Japanese dry cleaner, pick up groceries from the Korean shopkeeper and get a parking ticket from a Greek police officer. The mythical promise of hope and new beginnings looms large for all.

To find galleries, museums, fine-art exhibition spaces and calendars of upcoming shows throughout SoCal, check out ArtScene at www.artscenecal.com.

## ARTS

Los Angeles is SoCal's cultural hub. Indeed, few cities in the US can boast such artistic diversity, and thanks to the movie industry, no other city can claim the cultural influence – both high and low – that LA exerts worldwide. Despite lacking the dynamism of the LA scene, Orange County's Laguna Beach and San Diego still have lively arts communities. For the lowdown on what's happening now, check the Entertainment sections of the destination chapters later in this book.

**DID YOU KNOW?**

Author Raymond Chandler is famous for writing pulp fiction set in LA, but he lived in San Diego, where he died in 1959.

### Literature

Los Angeles has sheltered many illustrious 20th-century writers, among them William Faulkner, F Scott Fitzgerald and Aldous Huxley. During WWII, German writers Bertolt Brecht and Thomas Mann resided in LA, exiled from their war-torn homeland.

While much of the local writing talent always seems to be harnessed to the film industry – even Faulkner and Fitzgerald were in LA primarily to make a living by writing screenplays – LA provides an immense wealth of irresistible material to writers. Bookworms will find that novels about the city make for fascinating reading.

Los Angeles has been a favorite subject of novelists since the 1920s. Many have regarded LA in political terms, often viewing it unfavorably as the ultimate metaphor for capitalism. Classics in this vein include Upton Sinclair's *Oil!* (1927), a muckraking work of historical fiction with socialist overtones. Aldous Huxley's novel *After Many a Summer Dies the Swan* (1939) is a fine ironic work based on the life of publisher William Randolph Hearst (also the subject of Orson Welles' film *Citizen Kane*). F Scott Fitzgerald's final work, *The Last Tycoon* (1940) makes scathing observations about the early years of Hollywood by following the life of a 1930s movie producer who is slowly working himself to death.

Despite the city's literary tradition, it is pulp fiction that best captures the gritty side of LA, and Raymond Chandler is the genre's undisputed king. Start with *The Big Sleep* (1939), and after following Philip Marlowe, private eye, for one book, you may wind up reading all the others, too.

LA fiction's banner year was in 1970. Terry Southern's *Blue Movie* concerned the decadent side of Hollywood. Joan Didion's *Play It as It Lays* looked at Angelenos with a dry, not-too-kind wit. *Post Office,* by poet-novelist Charles Bukowski, captured the down-and-out side of downtown (Bukowski himself worked at downtown's Terminal Annex, p106). *Chicano,* by Richard Vasquez, took a dramatic look at the Latino barrio of East LA.

The mid-1980s brought the startling revelations of Bret Easton Ellis' *Less Than Zero,* about the cocaine-addled lives of wealthy Beverly Hills teenagers. For more comedic insights into LA during the go-go '80s, pick up Richard Rayner's *Los Angeles Without a Map* (1988), which follows a British man who gets lost in his Hollywood fantasies while chasing a Playboy bunny. Kate Braverman's *Palm Latitudes* (1988) traces the intersecting lives of a flamboyant whore, a murderous housewife and a worn-out matriarch who manage to maintain their strength and dignity against the backdrop of the violence and machismo of LA's Mexican barrio.

In more recent years, literary pulp fiction has once again made a big bang. Walter Mosley's famed *Devil in a Blue Dress* (1990), set in Watts, places its hero in impossible situations that test his desire to remain an honest man. Elmore Leonard's *Get Shorty* follows a Florida loan shark who moves to SoCal and gets mixed up in the film industry. Both stories – like many of the genre – translate brilliantly into film.

More recently, the novels of Carolyn See, who teaches at UCLA, are well crafted and inspiring, for example *The Handyman* (1999), in which a frustrated artist becomes a not-so-good handyman who winds up repairing the lives of his clients. *In the Heart of the Valley of Love,* by Cynthia Kadohata (1997), tells the story of survival of a young girl in a near-apocalyptic LA in 2052 and explores struggle in the face of adversity. San Diego novelist Joseph Wambaugh draws on his own experience as a detective to craft his crime-fiction novels; *Floaters* (1996) centers on the 1995 America's Cup race. Abigail Padgett, also from San Diego, writes engaging mysteries that weave together themes of Native American culture, mental illness and the SoCal desert. Sue Grafton, author of the Kinsey Millhone mystery series and the alphabet mystery series (*A is for Alibi,* et al) sets her novels in Santa Barbara – though in the books it's called Santa Theresa.

One of the best – and most cynical – novels about Hollywood ever written, *Day of the Locust* (1939), by Nathanael West, paints a noir picture of the savagery of Tinseltown; its biting insights still hold true more than a half-century later.

Few writers nail SoCal's culture as well as Joan Didion. In *Where I Was From* (2003), the author contrasts the mythology of California with the actuality of life in the Golden State, with special emphasis on suburban LA.

Helen Hunt Jackson's *Ramona* (1884) is a socially critical story about the star-crossed love between an adopted orphan girl who grows up on a California rancho and a Native-American boy. Their tale becomes a metaphor for the bigotry and injustices perpetrated against indigenous people throughout time.

## Cinema & TV

Angeleno culture is unique in that the city's primary art forms – film and TV – are also a major export. LA media has a powerful presence in the lives of not only Americans, but of people around the world. Images of LA are distributed far beyond the city's limits, ultimately reflecting back upon the city itself. Few people come to LA without some cinematic reference to the place – nearly every street corner has been or will be a movie set – and many of the newbies who have settled here make every effort to live up to the city's sexy image.

The movie and TV industry is hardly unaware of the relationship between celluloid and the city. With increasing regularity, Hollywood films feature the city not only as a setting but as a topic, and in some cases, almost as a character. Lately the high cost of filming in LA has sent location scouts beyond the San Fernando Valley (where most of the movie and TV studios are found today) north of the border to Canada, where they're welcomed with open arms (and pocketbooks) in 'Hollywood North,' particularly in Vancouver, Toronto and Montréal.

Los Angeles loves to turn the camera on itself. Perhaps the greatest film about the city is Roman Polanski's *Chinatown* (1974), a story about LA's

For a wonderful overview of the Santa Barbara Wine Country, watch Alexander Payne's *Sideways* (2004), which follows two middle-aged buddies on a week-long romp through the wine country region.

---

### MUSIC   *John Payne*

The LA music 'scene' has steadfastly resisted easy characterization, and has waxed and waned on the fortunes of the film and TV sectors and the vagaries of American pop culture in general.

Originally, the music biz and its attendant club scene arose out of the city's film industry and the massive post-WWII influx of classically trained European refugees and American jazz, R&B and country-music hopefuls to Southern California. The city has been regarded as the ostensible center of the nation's music industry at least since the late 1950s.

Los Angeles, especially following the WWII boom days, was a churning, exploding mecca for live jazz, R&B, soul, gospel and rock-and-roll groups. Beat music clubs dotted the infamous Sunset Strip in Hollywood, along La Brea Ave toward the Leimert Park/Crenshaw district and all the way down into 'the community' of Watts, Inglewood, Compton and all over South Central LA.

But by the mid-1970s, live music in LA had pretty much dried up, at least for bands who presented their own material and an original vision. Rock and pop bands had few places to play, and even less say in the kind of material they could perform in the clubs. A limited number of venues presented either Top 40 cover combos or, worse, were pay-to-play showcases. At these latter venues, bands routinely paid club owners for the privilege of being seen and heard on a stage, where, with any 'luck,' a major-label rep would spot their commercial potential, after which they'd sign away their lives and get layered hairdos.

The scene got rudely shaken up by the disgruntled rumblings of the Sex Pistols/Clash–inspired kids of 1977. The start of a few clubs, such as Masque, and punk magazine *Slash* that year showed that something was up. Local news and arts papers seized the day with vigorous profiles of the music and its scenesters. In fact, many *LA Weekly* reporters were musicians themselves, and were on the streets and in the clubs, playing a major part in the creation of a legitimate music scene.

An updated definition of latter-day punk rock has to include rappers and DJs, nu-folk strummers and nu-metal thrashers, art-rock and experimental noise. In this respect, LA punk refuses to curl up and die. The late 1980s rise of hip-hop greats such as NWA, Freestyle Fellowship and Cypress Hill showed that punk rock's do-it-yourself ethos translated very well in non-rock (ie black and brown) circles. Seemingly legitimized by the enormous spate of rap-metal hybrid acts such as Korn, Limp Bizkit and Linkin Park, the local hip-hop scene rolls on to large and appreciative mixed crowds, although more hard-core rap acts are mostly confined to tightly controlled venues such as the Sunset Strip's House of Blues and the Key Club.

Today, the LA underground/backpack hip-hop and DJ scene is immense and incredibly fertile. Future stars can be seen to best advantage underground at Santa Monica's BossaNova club and

early-20th-century water wars. Vincent Minelli's *The Bad and the Beautiful* (1952) takes a hard look at the filmmaking business, with Lana Turner recalling the exploits of an aggressive, egotistic film producer, played by Kirk Douglas. In David O Selznick's *A Star Is Born* (1937), Janet Gaynor plays a woman rising to stardom as her movie-star husband (Fredric March) declines in popularity. A 1954 remake starred Judy Garland; a 1976 remake starred Barbra Streisand. The most memorable of James Dean's famous scenes in *Rebel Without a Cause* (1955) takes place above LA in Griffith Park. A violent world of deals, sexual betrayal and double-crossing drive both good and bad cops to hubristic destinies – and deaths – in the LA of the crime-ridden '50s in *LA Confidential* (Curtis Hanson, 1997); starring Kevin Spacey, Kim Basinger and Danny DeVito.

For more contemporary commentary on Hollywood, see Robert Altman's *The Player* (1992), starring Tim Robbins and Fred Ward. It's a classic satire on the moviemaking machinery, featuring dozens of cameos by the very actors and actresses being spoofed. Also by Altman, *Short Cuts* (1993) weaves several stories by Raymond Carver, showing a sadly depraved Los Angeles, leaving no aspect of LA culture unexamined. Starring Lily Tomlin, Andie MacDowell, Tim Robbins and Robert Downey Jr.

Billy Wilder's classic *Sunset Boulevard* (1950), starring Gloria Swanson and William Holden, is a thrilling study of how Hollywood discards its aging stars. There are great shots of post-WWII LA, including the now-gone Schwab's Drugstore.

---

nearby Temple Bar, as well as at Temple Bar's sister club, Little Temple, Gabah on Melrose Ave and El Cid restaurant in Silver Lake. Plug into the scene at Santa Monica's KCRW (89.9 FM), which airs eclectic music, artist interviews and upcoming club events, especially on its after-dark music shows such as Jason Bentley's hypnotic 'Metropolis' and Garth Trinidad's delish 'Chocolate City.'

This being LA, almost nothing but nostalgia lasts, and historically the cohesive music scenes here have gotten trampled by a predictable inventory of commercial, bureaucratic and encroaching middle-aged concerns. But someone in the upper echelons here finally made the connection: live music is *big* money, and it attracts investment – that, for better or worse, is what LA is all about.

Today, nightlife in LA is booming. On most any night of the week, there's more music of almost any variety (a few that have yet to be named) than even the most insatiable music fan could consume and digest. True, all over Hollywood and the Westside you'll find your more punishing club experiences as well (eg proper dress code enforced, New York–style velvet ropes, $10 to $20 parking fees and the pleasure of being patted down by muscle-bound goons at the doors). But legendary clubs such as the Troubadour on Santa Monica Blvd and Spaceland in Silver Lake have benefited from booking state-of-the-art progressive rock and electronic bands on national tours, as well as local garage, electronic and hip-hop acts. The Sunset Strip's House of Blues brings a generally excellent assortment of the best in rock, world music, R&B and hip-hop. Recent upgrades to midsize concert halls such as the Henry Fonda Theater on Hollywood Blvd, Vine St's Avalon and the El Rey on Wilshire Blvd have resulted in lines around the block. At the Echo in Echo Park or the all-ages Smell downtown, you'll find abstract DJs, dubstyle dance freakerie and all manner of electronic/experimental rock and nu-music bands in a funkily eerie atmosphere. The Hotel Café in Hollywood hosts the best of the new raft of singer-songwriter types. And fans of 'serious music' should not miss a visit to the new Walt Disney Hall, which presents what may be the world's greatest symphony orchestra, the LA Philharmonic, led by the dazzling Esa-Pekka Salonen.

LA's music scene has long seemed nothing more than a vast assemblage of sequestered monocultures that have neither the ability nor the desire to talk to each other, but ever so slowly one feels the walls coming down and a new kind of creative friction is being generated around town, especially with the recent major renovations and subsequent crowds on Hollywood Blvd and the Sunset Strip. In the meantime, though, a lot of musicians and writers enjoy the opportunity for isolation that LA provides, as a peerless opportunity to carve out a truly alternative music scene right in the eye of the bullshit hurricane known as the recording industry.

Ridley Scott's sci-fi thriller *Blade Runner* (1982) projects modern LA way into the 21st century, with buildings reaching far into the sky – icy fortresses contrasting starkly with chaotic, neglected streets; starring Harrison Ford and Rutger Hauer.

The films by Quentin Tarantino are self-consciously influenced by noir classics, westerns and even Hong Kong thrillers, and they prominently feature modern-day LA. Violent *True Romance* (1993), written by Tarantino, stars Christian Slater as a naive and unbelievably lucky fugitive who deflects his trouble toward greedy film tycoons. In Chandleresque fashion, Quentin Tarantino creates a surreal Los Angeles, from the bottom up, in *Pulp Fiction* (1994). For all its action, the film is quite realistically stuck much of the time in cars cruising LA's streets.

*Stand and Deliver* (Ramón Menéndez, 1988), based on a true story, stars Edward James Olmos as a take-no-prisoners LA high-school teacher who whips a bunch of Latino gang members into shape by successfully teaching them college-level calculus. John Singleton's *Boyz N the Hood* (1991), starring Cuba Gooding Jr, offers a major reality check on coming-of-age as a black teenager in the inner city, circa 1990.

Surrealist David Lynch's *Mulholland Drive* (2001) is the story of a woman (played by Laura Harring) who tries to put her life back together after suffering from amnesia. Her journey takes her through encounters with weird and terrifying people living out their lives on various edges of dark LA mindscapes. *Laurel Canyon* (2002) shows another strange view of life in LA. A young med-school intern and his fiancée return to live with his pot-smoking mother (Frances McDormand), who's producing her latest boy toy's rock-and-roll record in the house.

On the lighter side, the most outrageously sardonic commentary on LA has to be Tony Richardson's *The Loved One* (1965), based on an Evelyn Waugh novel about the funeral industry, featuring Sir John Gielgud and Liberace (as a huckstering mortician). In *Scenes from a Mall* (1991), Woody Allen and Bette Midler dramatize their relationship while trying to shop in an LA mall. And Steve Martin's *LA Story* (1991) hilariously parodies nearly every aspect of LA life, from enemas to earthquakes. In Jake Kasdan's *Orange County* (2002) a surfer desperately tries to get into Stanford University and escape his oddball family; in the meantime you get a humorous snapshot of OC culture.

Among the most famous TV shows set in LA, *Beverly Hills 90210* made the local zip code famous and glamorized teen life in one of SoCal's ritziest neighborhoods. Now it's *The OC*, set in Newport Beach, Orange County, that delves into teenage angst and showcases the latest in adolescent fashion. *Six Feet Under* gives you a glimpse of modern LA through the eyes of a family running a funeral home. Of course, TV producers often fabricate 'facts' about SoCal. Take, for example, the CBS soap opera *The Bold and the Beautiful*, which depicts LA as America's center of haute couture fashion, when arguably nothing could be further from the truth.

**DID YOU KNOW?**

The 1970s TV show *The Bionic Woman*, starring Lindsay Wagner, was set in Ojai.

## Architecture

Southern California's architecture is a jumble of styles, uses a hodgepodge of materials and reflects various degrees of quality. It's as diverse as the region's population.

In the Spanish-Mexican Period, missions were built around a courtyard, with a garden and a kitchen, with buildings for livestock and horses nearby. Materials reflected what the indigenous peoples and the padres found on hand: adobe, limestone and grass. Even after the church's influence waned, the mission building style remained practical for California's climate. Later, Californians adapted the original Spanish Mission style to create the California rancho, or rancho adobe, style. Outstanding examples of adobes are found in El Pueblo de Los Angeles (p104), Old Town in San Diego (p255) and the Presidio in Santa Barbara (p329).

Also known as Queen Anne or Eastlake style, Victorian architecture became popular in the late 19th century. The upper class built grand mansions to keep up with East Coast fashion that reflected the style popular during the reign of Queen Victoria. Soon smaller, less detailed versions were being produced in great quantities. The Victorian style is most prevalent in Northern California, but you can see one of the finest examples of Victorian whimsy in San Diego at the Hotel del Coronado (p280); a few examples remain around downtown LA, too, particularly the Grier Musser Museum (p114).

With its more simple, classical lines, Spanish Colonial architecture – or Mission Revival, as it's also called – was a rejection of the frilly Queen Anne style and a nostalgic hearkening back to the early days of California missions. Arched doors and windows, long covered porches, fountains, courtyards, solid walls and red-tile roofs typify the design elements. The style's heyday lasted from 1890 to 1915. The arrival of William Templeton Johnson and the young Irving Gill on the architectural scene fortified this trend, especially in San Diego. The train depots in LA, San Juan Capistrano and San Diego were built in this style. San Diego's Balboa Park (p248) also showcases some outstanding examples, all a legacy of the 1915–16 Panama-California Exposition.

For contemporary social criticism, pick up Mike Davis' *City of Quartz* (1990), an excoriating history of LA and a glimpse into its possible future; in *Ecology of Fear*, he examines the decay of the natural environment in the LA Basin.

Bernard Maybeck, Charles and Henry Greene and Julia Morgan ushered in the Craftsman – or Arts and Crafts – movement. Simplicity and harmony were key design principles, which blended Asian, European and American influences to create single-family homes that were both functional and comfortable. The typical house is a bungalow: a one-story wood structure with low-pitched gabled roofs, often with exposed rafters. Overhanging eaves, terraces and sleeping porches function as transitions between, and extensions of, the house and its natural environment. Some of SoCal's most beautiful buildings were built in the Arts and Crafts style, including the Gamble House (p123) in Pasadena and the Marston House (p252) in San Diego.

In the early 1920s, it became fashionable to copy earlier styles, blended into an architectural mishmash that achieved a remarkably appealing aesthetic. No style was off limits: neoclassical, baroque, Tudor, pueblo, French Norman, Mayan, Aztec or Egyptian – it was all fair game. Various revival styles often show up in public buildings such as courthouses, civic auditoriums, museums and exposition spaces. Look out for downtown LA's Richard Riordan Central Library (p109) and the California Quadrangle (p250) in San Diego's Balboa Park.

Art deco took off in the 1920s and 1930s, especially for public and office buildings. Art deco's vertical lines and symmetry create a soaring effect, often mitigated by a stepped pattern toward the top. Heavy ornamentation, especially above doors and windows, might consist of floral motifs, sunbursts or zigzags. Check out the former Bullocks Wilshire Building department store (p114) and Wiltern Theater (p114) in LA. Art deco's close cousin, Streamline Moderne, sought to incorporate the machine aesthetic, in particular the aerodynamic look of airplanes and ocean liners. Distinctive style elements include horizontal bands of smallish, circular windows (like portholes); smooth, curved facades; simulated railings; and heavy use of aluminum and stainless steel. In LA, Streamline Moderne beauties include the Coca-Cola Bottling Plant (p114) downtown and the Crossroads of the World building (p81) on Sunset Blvd in Hollywood.

Also called the 'International style,' modernism was initiated in Europe (mostly Germany) by Bauhaus architects Walter Gropius, Ludwig Mies van der Rohe and Le Corbusier. Characteristics include a boxlike shape, open floor plans, flat roofs, plain and unadorned facades and interior walls and the abundant use of glass. Rudolph Schindler and Richard Neutra, both of whom had come to Southern California from their native Austria, brought early modernism to LA. Both were also influenced by Frank Lloyd Wright, one of America's preeminent architects. In fact, Schindler collaborated with Wright on the Hollyhock House (p82), which was built in a style Wright fancifully called 'California Romanza.' Wright also created 'textile block' houses, made from blocks of prefab concrete, a relatively new medium at the time. The Ennis-Brown House (p82) is one example.

In part a response to the starkness of the International Style, later postmodernism sought to reemphasize the structural form of the building and the spaces between its different parts, as in the heavy-duty concrete blocks of Louis Kahn's Salk Institute (p276) in La Jolla. Today, Richard Meier has perfected and transcended the postmodernist vision. Take a trip to the Getty Center (p91) in West LA, and judge for yourself.

Canadian-born Frank Gehry is arguably the most interesting architect working in the USA today. At the forefront of 3-D computer-aided design, Gehry has been able to create shapes and forms previously unseen in building designs, highlighted by his use of contemporary and expensive materials such as titanium. His Guggenheim Museum in Bilbao, Spain, propelled him to new heights in the architecture world, and recently he improved upon his techniques and design for the impressive, high-profile Walt Disney Concert Hall (p107).

# Environment

## THE LAND

People disagree about the exact boundary between Northern and Southern California, but when you look at a topographic map, it becomes obvious. The northernmost edge of Southern California is marked by a series of east–west-trending mountains called the Transverse Ranges. These mountains, mostly around 5000ft high, divide the state in two. The most visible are the Santa Ynez Mountains, which lord over Santa Barbara (when you drive to the Santa Barbara Wine Country, p338, you'll be heading uphill into Northern California).

To the south, the Los Angeles Basin directly fronts the ocean, bordered by a series of mountains that extend into Mexico. San Diego, on the edge of this plateau 120 miles south of LA, lies right on the border with Mexico.

The Mojave Desert spreads east and north of Los Angeles, all the way into the state of Nevada. To the south and east, the Sonoran Desert includes the Imperial and Coachella Valleys (now heavily irrigated farmland east of Palm Springs) and the Salton Sea. There is no definite line between the two deserts, depending on whom you ask, but there is agreement that the Sonoran Desert extends well into Mexico.

Southern California sits on one of the world's major earthquake fault zones, on the edge of two plates: the Pacific Plate, which consists of the Pacific ocean floor and much of the coastline, and the North American Plate, which covers all of North America and part of the Atlantic ocean floor. The primary boundary between the two is the infamous San Andreas Fault, which runs for 650 miles and has spawned numerous smaller faults. If you want an up-close look at the fault, book a jeep tour from Palm Springs (p307).

Earthquakes are common, although most are too small or too remote to be detected without sensors. In fact, small earthquakes are a good sign. The plates should move at a rate of about 1in per year. When they don't, the energy stores up, eventually resulting in large-scale quakes.

## WILDLIFE

Much of Southern California is desert, but it has been so heavily irrigated and built up that you'll have to get outside metropolitan areas to see native species. Along the coast, because of water carried on shore in the form of fog, there's a narrow greenbelt with a greater variety of visible wildlife than you'll find further inland.

### Animals

Between December and March, people come from far and wide to see gray whales breach offshore on their annual southward migration. Get a good view at Cabrillo National Monument at Point Loma (p279) in San Diego and from Point Vicente on the Palos Verdes Peninsula (p100) in Los Angeles. Most coastal towns have whale-watching boat tours (see the destination chapters). Pods of bottlenose dolphins and porpoises swim close to the shore year-round from north of Santa Barbara to Mexico and love to show off and dive out of the water alongside boats. If you venture to the Channel Islands National Park (p346), you'll likely spot some sort of pinniped, be it an elephant or harbor seal, California sea lion or sea otter. There's an inherent goofiness to their frolicking and great passion in their loud barking; kids love them.

Acclaimed writers, from Norman Mailer to Charles Bukowski, have written about California's awe-inspiring scenery. Look for their work in two outstanding anthologies, *Unfolding Beauty: Celebrating California's Landscapes* (2000) and *Natural State: A Literary Anthology of California Nature Writing* (1998).

The US Geological Survey (USGS) website on earthquakes shows everything from seismic activity to tips on preparedness: www.earthquake .usgs.gov.

Many bird species migrate along the Pacific Flyway, one of the four principle migration routes in North America, and there's a changing roster of birds overhead depending on the season. There are good places on the coast to hunker down with a pair of binoculars – but urban sprawl is encroaching on Southern California wetlands. Still, the Ballona Wetlands near Marina del Rey (p98) in Los Angeles remains a major stopover. In Orange County, head to Bolsa Chica State Ecological Reserve (p217) or to Newport Bay Ecological Reserve (p222) where you can canoe around and watch the geese. In San Diego, bring your Audubon book to the tidal marsh at Batiquitos Lagoon (p295).

Year-round residents include gulls, grebes, terns, cormorants, sandpipers and little sanderlings that chase receding waves along the shore, looking for critters in the freshly turned sand.

Monarch butterflies, beautiful orange creatures that follow remarkable migration patterns in search of milkweed, their only source of food, spend winter in California by the tens of thousands, largely north of Santa Barbara, but also in the eucalyptus groves around the city.

If you're traveling inland to the desert regions, don't expect to see many animals running around in the middle of the day. To cope with the heat, most desert wildlife is nocturnal and only comes out once the shadows get long. Look for roadrunners, little gray birds with long, straight tails and a poof of feathers on top of their heads, which you can often spot on the side of the road. Desert tortoises are harder to spot; their slow pace has landed them on the endangered species list because they're often run over by cars. They tend to seek shade, so make sure that you look under your car if you've left it for many hours at desert parks such as Anza-Borrego (p319) or Joshua Tree (p314).

Though they're extremely shy, you might see several other desert inhabitants such as the reddish kit fox, bobcat (which has no tail), coyote, jackrabbit, kangaroo rat and a variety of snakes, lizards and spiders. If you play golf at sunset or sunrise, you might spot any number of animals, which come for the easy access to water.

## Plants

Along the coast, where flora gets a blast of water from occasional fog banks, look for live oak, with hollylike evergreen leaves and fuzzy acorns; manzanita, treelike shrubs with intensely red bark and small berries; and aromatic California laurel, with long slender leaves that turn purple.

Everywhere except the deserts, the hills turn green in winter, not summer. Because it almost never freezes, as soon as the autumn and winter rains arrive, the dried-out brown grasses spring to life with new growth. Wildflowers pop up as early as February. The most conspicuous and familiar is the bright orange California poppy, the state flower, which blooms in March and April, sometimes longer, depending on rainfall. But don't pick one, or you could face a fine; they're protected by state law. (Regardless, they wilt almost instantly when picked.) Along the coast look for little purple wild irises until June. And everywhere look for oak trees: California has 20 native species of them.

The Torrey pine, a species adapted to sparse rainfall and sandy, stony soils, is extremely rare. Look for them near San Diego at Torrey Pines State Reserve (p276) in La Jolla and on Santa Rosa Island, which is part of Channel Islands National Park (p346).

Considering they look barren at first glance, the deserts of California are rich with plant life – but you need to know what to look for. Some species are tricky to spot because of their discrete profiles.

Tree-huggers will thrill for *Oaks of California*, by Bruce Pavlik et al (1991), which details the history and ecology of California's 20 indigenous species of oak, with gorgeous photographs and excellent locator maps.

Desert plants have adapted to the climate with thin, spiny leaves that resist moisture loss (and deter grazing animals); seed-and-flowering mechanisms kick into high gear during brief winter rains.

Nothing says desert more than a cactus. Indeed, cacti are perhaps the most intriguing life forms out here. The cholla cactus, for instance, appears so furry that one variety is nicknamed 'teddy-bear cactus.' But resist hugging it: what appears to be 'fur' actually consists of extremely sharp, barbed spines that can bury themselves in your skin at the slightest touch. But oh! it's pretty. If you're lucky enough to visit during blooming season in spring, you'll get to see its bright-yellow flower.

Looking like something from a Dr Seuss book, Joshua trees were named by immigrant Mormons, who saw them as Joshua welcoming them to the promised land. The trees grow in the Mojave Desert and, of course, at Joshua Tree National Park (p314). Almost as widespread are prickly pears, flat cacti that produce showy flowers ranging in color from pink and magenta to yellow and orange. The smoke tree, a small, fine-leafed tree with a smoky blue color, is said to indicate the presence of underground water.

The cactuslike creosote is actually a small bush with hard leaves and a distinctive smell. There's also the spiky ocotillo shrub, with its canelike branches that sprout leaves after rainfall and produce bright red-orange flowers in spring; and catclaw, which has garnered the nickname 'wait-a-minute bush' for its small, sharp, hooked spikes that scratch you or grab your clothing if you brush past.

Known from Western movies, tumbleweed grows quickly to become a ball of tough branches attached to the ground by a single stem, which uproots and tumbles across the desert in the summer wind.

**DID YOU KNOW?**

If you look at a map of the California coast, you can see the outline of a man's profile just north of Santa Barbara. Republicans call it Ronald Reagan, Democrats Franklin Delano Roosevelt.

---

### WATER FOR A THIRSTY GIANT

The growth of semi-arid Los Angeles into a megalopolis is inextricably linked to water. When the city's population surged to 200,000 people in the early 20th century, ground-water levels were insufficient to meet the city's needs, let alone sustain further growth. It was apparent that water had to be imported. Fred Eaton, a former LA mayor, and William Mulholland, the city water bureau superintendent, knew just how and where to get it: by aqueduct from the Owens River Valley, at the foot of the Eastern Sierras, some 250 miles northeast.

The fact that Owens Valley itself was settled by farmers who needed the water for irrigation purposes bothered neither the men nor the federal government, which actively supported the city in acquiring land and securing water rights in the valley – though it was done secretly and underhandedly.

Voters gave Mulholland the $24.5 million he needed to build an aqueduct that would carry melted snow from the mountains to the city. Work on the aqueduct began in 1908. An amazing feat of engineering – crossing barren desert floor as well as rugged mountain terrain for 233 miles – it opened to great fanfare on November 5, 1913. An extension to the Mono Basin in 1940 lengthened the aqueduct by 105 miles. The Owens Valley, though, would never be the same. With most of Owens Lake drained, the once-fertile valley became barren, causing farms to close and businesses to go bust. A bitter feud between valley residents and the city ensued; some foes even used dynamite to sabotage the aqueduct. Formal arbitration in 1929 ended with LA making a few concessions. Roman Polanski set his Academy Award–winning film *Chinatown* against the backdrop of these water wars. If you prefer to read the full story of what happened, pick up a copy of *Cadillac Desert* by Marc Reisner.

To this day, LA's Department of Water & Power owns 307,000 acres in the Inyo and Mono Counties and the system supplies more than 75% of the city's water. But residents at the water's source still resent the thirsty giant to the south.

The only palm tree native to California is the Washingtonia palm, which is found naturally in desert oases and produces stalks of rather tasty small black berries.

California has been overrun by introduced species. Ice plant, the ropy green groundcover with purple-and-white flowers that creeps over beach dunes, came originally from South Africa. During construction of the railroads in the 19th century, fast-growing eucalyptus trees were imported from Australia to make railroad ties, but the wood proved poor and it split when driven through with a stake. The trees now grow like weeds, fueling summertime wildfires with their flammable, explosive seed capsules. Even snails come from far away, brought to California in the 1850s from France to produce escargots. Now they're everywhere.

For a comprehensive list of all California State Parks, from beaches to mountains to historical parks, log on to www .parks.ca.gov.

## NATIONAL PARKS

Southern California has two federally protected parks overseen by the National Park Service (NPS): Channel Islands National Park and Joshua Tree National Park.

The Channel Islands National Park (p346) sits off the shore of Santa Barbara and covers roughly 250,000 acres, mostly undeveloped. The islands are prized for their rich marine life and aquatic environments. Unlike other national parks in California, it receives few visitors because of the islands' remote locations: to reach them requires a boat ride on seas that are often choppy, though you can fly the 30 miles to Santa Rosa Island. No bridge connects them to the mainland. The islands support several species of plant and animal, including the rare Torrey pine, found on Santa Rosa Island. From the shore on a rare day without fog or mist, look at the islands and see if you can spot splashes of yellow from the many coreopsis flowers.

For complete information about national parks, from activities to zoology, visit the National Park Service website at www.nps.gov.

Joshua Tree National Park (p314) lies just north of Palm Springs at the convergence zone of the Colorado Desert and the Mojave Desert; the former is lower, hotter and drier, the latter is higher, cooler and more moist. The park covers just over a million acres. The most famous feature is the Joshua tree, a type of yucca that is related to the lily, but there are also many stunning geological formations, attracting rock climbers from around the world. Naturally occurring oases support stands of fan palms. But stay away in summer, unless you like blistering heat; winter is the time to visit.

## ENVIRONMENTAL ISSUES

Southern California's development has come at the expense of the environment. Tons of particulate matter spew into the air from automobile and diesel emissions, causing the development of asthma in children in urban areas. The ocean is overfished, land is disappearing beneath asphalt and landfills, and tankers leak oil off the coast.

**DID YOU KNOW?**

Each year Southern California has about 10,000 earthquakes, nearly all undetectable.

Along the coast, air pollution isn't that bad, due in large part to the prevailing westerly winds that blow in clean air off the ocean. But travel inland, particularly in the LA Basin, and the air takes on a thick haze, obscuring vistas and creating health hazards. Fortunately California leads the nation in emissions control – even if Los Angeles' air quality remains some of the worst in the country.

Of equal concern, water. There never seems to be enough to satisfy demand by coastal cities and inland farms. Most of it comes from the Sierra Nevada Mountains, in the eastern part of the state, but global warming and droughts affect winter snowpack. If it rains in the Sierra – or doesn't snow at all – there's nothing to melt into the reservoirs that supply inland farms and coastal cities. Fortunately the citizenry has learned how to conserve. And you will too: expect a low-flow showerhead in your hotel room.

# Southern California Outdoors

Step outside from spring through fall in Southern California, and the weather will be warm and clear, perfect for a day at the beach or a hike in the woods. Though it's easy to forget about the natural environment when you're stuck on the freeway surrounded by concrete and steel, the beach is never far away. If you prefer a perspective from on high, mountains and parkland surround the Los Angeles Basin. And when winter winds blow, the coast gets too damp and the mountains too chilly, the soothing emptiness and warm sun of the desert await just over the hills to the east.

In addition to the activities listed in this chapter, check the destination chapters for specific information about everything from ballooning to biking to boating.

## SURFING

Surfing is SoCal's signature sport. Invented by Pacific Islanders, surfing was made popular by Duke Kahanamoku in Hawaii in the 1920s but actually arrived in California in 1907, when Henry Huntington invited George Freeth to put on a surfing demonstration in Southern California to help the railroad magnate promote his Redondo–Los Angeles Railway. It has imbued SoCal culture with a look, language and way of life that is, in theory at least, laid-back, easygoing and totally dedicated to sun and sea. (In actuality, many young surfer dudes can be aggressive and territorial.)

SoCal's 'big three' surfing spots are Rincon Point (near Ventura, p343), Trestles (near San Clemente) and Malibu (Surfrider Beach, p94), all point breaks (where swells peak up into steep waves as they encounter a shelflike point) known for consistently clean, glassy, big waves. If you're a beginner or intermediate surfer your jaw will drop as you watch the action. But you won't be alone: these places get crowded. The best spots to learn to surf are at beach breaks of long, shallow bays where waves are small and rolling. San Onofre (north of Oceanside, p296) and San Diego's Tourmaline (Mission Beach, p277) are good spots for beginners. Huntington Beach (p215) is Orange County's surf mecca, with a surfing museum, surfing walk of fame and a pro/am surf series championship contest each September. There's also a surfing competition and nifty museum on the sport in Oceanside (p296) on San Diego's North Coast, held every June.

Long boards are heavy and unwieldy compared to the short boards most commonly used, but they're easier to balance on and less likely to 'pearl' (when the tip of the board takes a dive). Morey Doyle boards, made of spongy foam, are the ultimate beginner's tool. You'll find surfboard rental stands on just about every beach where surfing is allowed. Rentals cost about $10 an hour, and lessons start at around $50 (inquire at surf shops). See the Activities sections of the destination chapters for more detail.

Crowds are a problem on weekends in summer. Any surf spot with a parking lot facing the ocean is likely to be packed, but breaks that require a long walk or paddle will inevitably have fewer people.

Locals aren't always as laid-back and easygoing as the culture paints them to be. Some surfers are so territorial that they're downright hostile toward outsiders, notably at San Diego's Windansea (p275); other spots not open to newcomers have been specified in the destination chapters).

Orange County–based *Surfer* magazine (www.surfermag.com/travel) has travel reports that cover just about every inch of the US coastline.

Even if you don't surf, you'll get an adrenaline rush from the exhilarating cinematography of the surfing documentary *Riding Giants* (Stacy Peralta, 2004). For a retro take on the sport, check out the classic *The Endless Summer* (Bruce Brown, 1966).

## HIKING

Hiking is the best way to see the land up close. Unaided by machinery, moving in sync with nature, you can see, hear, touch and smell so much more than you otherwise could. In Southern California, you can amble along beaches to the sound of the booming surf, summit 10,000ft mountain peaks that are still snowy in June, and trek through cacti and sandy desert landscapes. And if you tread lightly, you'll catch darting glimpses of wildlife, anything from lizards to black bears. In springtime keep your eyes peeled for wildflowers: some are so small and precious they're nearly invisible; others are so large and flamboyant they look like something out of a comic book.

All national and state parks have easy, well-marked, short trails, many under 2 miles. They're primarily aimed at people with little hiking experience, low fitness levels or limited time. They have interpretive displays and are marked on maps as nature trails or self-guided interpretive trails. These trails are the forest equivalent of freeways – fast, easy to navigate and efficient, but not terribly thrilling and sometimes crowded. You'll have a better chance of finding solitude on a longer walk. Longer trails are almost always well marked, so you won't need a topographic map or compass as long as you stick to the main routes. Ask at a ranger station or visitors center for suggestions about routes to suit your interest and ability.

Parks almost always have some sort of on-site visitors center. At major trailheads in national forests and in state parks, look for bulletin boards that show trail maps and other information relative to the hike. Always carry water, snack food and, if inclement weather is on the horizon, an extra layer and raincoat. Pack out your trash. If you're heading to a national forest, information about regulations and the nearest rangers stations are at www.fs.fed.us/r5, the website of the National Forest Service, Pacific Southwest Region.

### Safety

Choose a hike within your range of ability, and seek local advice on trails, equipment and weather before heading out. Be aware of potential dangers, and pay attention on the trail. A minor injury or accident – a twisted ankle or a fall down a hillside – can be life threatening if you're alone. Always let someone know where you're going and how long you plan to be gone. Use sign-in boards at trailheads or ranger stations. If you carry a cell phone, service may be spotty or nonexistent; climb to the highest peak for the best reception.

Look out for western poison oak in forests throughout California, especially below 5000ft elevation. It's a shrub most easily identified by its shiny triple-lobed reddish-green leaves, which turn crimson in autumn. Remember the following trail adage: 'Leaves of three, let it be.' If you brush against it, scrub the area with soap and water or an over-the-counter remedy such as Tecnu, a soap specially formulated to remove the oils from poison oak.

### Books & Maps

Pick up *Los Angeles Times* columnist John McKinney's excellent hiking guides, published by Olympic Press, among them *Day Hiker's Guide to Southern California* and *Day Hiker's Guide to California State Parks*. To learn what wildflowers are sprouting trailside, pick up a copy of the National Audubon Society's *Field Guide to Wildflowers: Western Region,* which fits easily into a daypack.

The **US Geological Survey** (USGS; ☎ 888-275-8747; www.usgs.gov), an agency of the Department of the Interior, publishes highly detailed topographic maps of the entire country at different scales. The USGS 1:125,000 maps with 200ft contour intervals and 1:100,000 maps with 150ft contour intervals are useful planning and backpacking maps. The USGS website has the full product catalog and a database of retailers. The US Forest Service (USFS) also produces good maps of national forests; you can pick them up at forest visitors centers or at the online **National Forest Store** (www.fs.fed.us/recreation/nationalforeststore).

## Fees

Most state parks charge a fee of $5 to $10 per vehicle per entry. You'll need a National Forest Adventure Pass (NFAP) if you're going to visit one of the four following national forests of Southern California: San Bernardino, Cleveland, Angeles and Los Padres. Passes cost $5 per day or $30 per year (seniors and disabled $15) and must be displayed on the windshield of your vehicle. Adventure passes are good for one year from the month of purchase and can be transferred to another person for no additional charge. USFS ranger stations and various sporting-goods stores in SoCal sell passes, or you can order one by phone ( ☎ 909-382-2622). For a list, by city, of all vendors that carry them, log on to www .fsadventurepass.org.

## Hikes

Believe it or not, you can walk all the way from Mexico to Canada along the Pacific Crest Trail (PCT), a 2638-mile-long footpath along the ridgelines of spectacular mountain ranges. The trail passes through 24 national forests, seven national parks, 33 designated wilderness areas and five state parks, following the crest of the Sierra Nevada in California and Cascade Range in Oregon and Washington, at an average elevation of 5000ft.

To hike the trail in its entirety, moving at a fast clip of 15 miles per day, would take nearly six months, the California portion about four months. But you don't have to commit to such a dramatic interstate trek to get a taste of the PCT. Day or weekend hikers can plan short trips on many accessible segments of the trail. In the very south, the trail passes through portions of Anza-Borrego Desert State Park (p319) on its way toward Yosemite National Park, Lake Tahoe and beyond.

The **Pacific Crest Trail Association** ( ☎ 916-349-2109; www.pcta.org), headquartered in Sacramento (California's capital), can provide detailed information on the trail, as well as addresses for regional forest-service and wilderness-area offices, tips on long and short backpacking trips, weather conditions and details about wilderness permit requirements.

Even if you don't have time to trek a portion of the PCT, you'll still find plenty of fantastic hiking throughout SoCal, some right in metropolitan areas. In Los Angeles you can hike for miles in America's largest urban park, Griffith Park (p118) and in the Santa Monica Mountains (p130), amid oak woodlands and other Mediterranean environments.

Though Orange County has been mostly developed, you can find good day hiking in places such as Crystal Cove State Park (p222), in Newport Beach. If you're heading to Laguna Beach, check out the West Ridge Trail (p228), where you can trek along a ridgeline, high above the picturesque little town, with gorgeous ocean views.

The Santa Ynez Mountains lord over Santa Barbara, rising 4000ft from sea level within 10 miles of the ocean, an awesome sight. A 30-minute drive (about 15 miles) from town takes you to the Los Padres National Forest (p343), where you can climb up the rugged mountains from the trailheads near San Marcos Pass. Just off the Santa Barbara coast, at Channel Islands National Park (p346), you can hike past frolicking sea lions and giant sprays of coreopsis flowers.

In San Diego the best hiking is along the coastal bluffs in Torrey Pines State Reserve (p276), at La Jolla's northern boundary, where you can see some of the last remaining stands of *Pinus torreyana* on the mainland. Further inland, about 90 miles (a two-hour drive) out of the city, Anza-Borrego Desert State Park (p319) provides open-trail desert hiking, allowing you to choose your own path, but come prepared: the July heat can be brutal and inescapable.

But if you're in Palm Springs in summer, you'll find relief by ascending 6000ft on the Palm Springs Aerial tram to the relatively cool pine forests of the Mt San Jacinto Wilderness State Park (p301). If you're here in winter, no self-respecting hiker should visit Palm Springs without spending at least a day trekking past giant rock formations at Joshua Tree National Park (p314), where the shaggy trees look like something out of a Dr Seuss book.

If you *really* want to get in on the locals-only scene, then you've got to be introduced by an insider.

## KAYAKING

The 22-year-old Coastwalk (www.coastwalk.org) is dedicated to completing the California Coastal Trail, a continuous public-access trail along the state's entire length. Contact it about day hikes and the annual state-long coast walk.

Quiet and unobtrusive, kayaking lets you view marine life at close range and explore islands, coves and sea caves that might otherwise be inaccessible. If you've never tried it before, it's not as hard as you might think. Sea kayaks, which hold one or two people, are larger and more stable than white-water boats, making them safer and easier to navigate. They also have storage space so you can take them on an overnight or even week-long journey.

The most popular destinations for sea kayaking are the Channel Islands National Park (p346), off the Santa Barbara coast, and Catalina Island (p102), further south toward Los Angeles. They're ideal spots for an overnight trip for experienced paddlers. Day trips are equally rewarding, especially for beginners who can put in at Mission Bay (p277) in San Diego and enjoy the calm, protected waters. In La Jolla (p282) you can explore cliffs and caves and float above the San Diego-La Jolla Underwater Park's kelp forests and reefs. Some outfits offer full-moon paddles. There's nothing quite like seeing the reflection of the moon and stars glittering on the water and hearing the gentle splash of water on your boat's hull.

You can find out more about kayaking in Southern California by contacting **California Kayak Friends** (www.ckf.org) or **American Canoe Association** (www.acanet.org), which provide extensive information on everything from safety and instruction to destinations and events for paddlesports aficionados.

## DIVING & SNORKELING

The waters off the coast of California are wonderful playgrounds for divers and snorkelers. Rock reefs, shipwrecks and kelp beds attract a variety of fish and beg for exploration. There are sites suited for all skill and experience levels; wet suits are recommended year-round.

For scuba-diving resources in Los Angeles and Southern California, log on to www.ladiver.com.

If you want to try diving for the first time, some outfitters offer a short beginner's course that includes brief instruction, followed by a shallow beach or boat dive. The cost ranges from $100 to $150. Great places, especially for first-time divers, are in La Jolla (p281) and on Catalina Island (p102), where kelp beds house a rich marine environment close to the surface. Local dive shops are the best resources for equipment, guides and instructors. Otherwise, to explore California's deep waters, you must be certified. To dive with an operator, or to have tanks filled, the minimum qualification required is an open-water certificate from Professional Association of Dive Instructors (PADI), National Association for Underwater Instructors (NAUI) or another recognized organization such as the British Sub-Aqua Club (BSAC). An open-water certificate course costs from $300 to $400. For instructors and dive schools, contact **NAUI** ( ☎ 813-628-6284, 800-553-6284; www.naui.org).

If you don't have the time, money or desire to take a deep-water dive, rent a snorkel, mask and fins (around $20 for the lot), which are widely available from concessionaires near the respective snorkeling sites. **Scuba Diving** (www.scubadiving.com) and **Sport Diver** (www.sportdiver.com), published by PADI, are widely available magazines dedicated entirely to underwater pursuits.

## GOLF

Once the province of rich old men, golf has become the most fashionable American sport ever since Tiger Woods burst onto the scene. Now everyone from school kids to their grandmothers have gotten in on the game. As a result, golf courses have proliferated faster than bunnies on Viagra, and even small towns have their own greens.

Most regions of Southern California have public courses with reasonable greens fees, although many of the top-ranked courses are at private golf clubs, where you have to be invited by a member or get a referral from the pro at your home club (which doesn't always guarantee admission, depending on the exclusivity of the club). Semiprivate clubs are open to nonmembers, except at peak times, such as Saturday and Sunday mornings. Palm Springs is the undisputed golfing mecca of SoCal and supports more than 100 courses; San Diego and surrounding areas have over 80 courses.

Greens fees vary hugely, from $25 to over $200 for 18 holes. It depends on the course's location and its degree of difficulty. Some courses charge an additional fee for cart rental. Always reserve in advance, but if you can't nail down a time, ask about walk-up policies. For information on golf courses throughout Southern California check out the following websites:

**Los Angeles** (www.laparks.org/dos/sports/golf.htm)
**Orange County** (www.playocgolf.com)
**Palm Springs** (www.palmspringsteetimes.com)
**San Diego** (www.golfsd.com)
**Santa Barbara** (www.santabarbara.com/activities/golf)

Here's a short list of some favorite golf courses:

## Los Angeles
**Harding & Wilson Golf Courses** (Map p75; ☎ 323-663-2555; 4730 Crystal Springs Dr, Griffith Park; greens fee 18-hole weekday/weekend $22/28.50) Two 18-hole courses, par 72.
**Penmar Golf Course** (Map pp72-3; ☎ 310-396-6228; 1233 Rose Ave, Venice; greens fee weekday/weekend $11.50/15) Nine holes, par 33.
**Rancho Park Golf Course** (off Map pp70-1; ☎ 310-838-7373; 10460 W Pico Blvd; greens fee 18-hole weekday/weekend $22/28.50, 9-hole $11.50/15) Near Culver City; 18 holes (par 71) and nine holes (par 35).

## Orange County
**Aliso Creek Golf Course** (Map p226; ☎ 949-499-1919; www.alisocreekinn.com; 31106 Pacific Coast Hwy, Laguna Beach; greens fee $16-28, optional cart $9) Nine holes, par 32.
**Pelican Hill Golf Club** (Map p220; ☎ 949-760-0707; www.pelicanhill.com; 22651 Pelican Hill Rd S, Newport Coast; greens fee incl cart $175-250) Eighteen holes, par 71. Gorgeous ocean views.

## Palm Springs
**La Quinta Resort/PGA West** (Map p302; ☎ 760-564-5729, 800-742-9378; www.laquinta resort.com/golf; 49-499 Eisenhower Dr; greens fee incl cart $50-235) Five courses, 18 holes, par 72.
**Tahquitz Creek Palm Springs Golf Resort** (Map p302; ☎ 760-328-1005; www.tahquitz creek.com; 1885 Golf Club Dr; greens fee incl cart $75-95) Two 18-hole courses, par 72.

## San Diego
**Aviara Golf Club** (Map p246; ☎ 760-603-6900, 800-905-0272; www.sandiegogolf.com; 7447 Batiquitos Dr, Carlsbad; greens fee incl cart $175-195) Eighteen holes, par 72.
**Balboa Park Municipal Golf Course** (Map pp242-3; reservations ☎ 858-570-1234, pro shop ☎ 619-239-1660; www.sandiegogolf.com; 2600 Golf Course Dr; greens fee $36-41, optional cart $26) Eighteen holes, par 72.
**Torrey Pines Golf Course** (Map p247; ☎ 800-867-7397, 858-456-8366; www.torreypines.com; 11480 North Torrey Pines Rd, La Jolla; greens fee incl cart $140-205) Two courses, 18 holes, par 72.

## Santa Barbara
**Sandpiper** (Map pp326-7; ☎ 805-968-1541; www.sandpipergolf.com; 7925 Hollister Ave; greens fee $110-130) Eighteen holes, par 72.
**Santa Barbara Golf Club** (Map pp326-7; ☎ 805-687-7087; www.sbgolf.com; 3500 McCaw Ave; greens fee $27-36, cart $24) Eighteen holes, par 70.

**DID YOU KNOW?**

Golfers can save money – sometimes by as much as 50% – by booking twilight play.

**DID YOU KNOW?**

Kerri Walsh and Misty May, beach volleyball gold medalists at the 2004 Olympics, both live and play volleyball in Southern California.

# Food & Drink

California's food and drink rate among the world's best, and many great trends began here, from the rise of coffee culture (which, contrary to popular belief, did *not* originate in Seattle) to 'fusion' cooking (think Japanese-Italian and Chino-Latino). Though Northern California is the true nexus of California cuisine, Southern California – especially Los Angeles – does its part to expand the genre.

## STAPLES & SPECIALTIES

The Golden State produces almost all of America's tomatoes and artichokes, most of its lettuce and cabbage, and nearly everything else that comes from the earth. You name it, California grows it. Residents love produce. The single most common way to eat vegetables is in salad. Served with a crusty loaf of freshly baked bread, it's a classic SoCal meal.

Salad was once thought of as 'rabbit food' by many a Yankee. Men of Illinois saw men of California eating salads and called them gay (remember 'real men don't eat quiche'?). Thirty years and 300,000 coronary-bypass surgeries later, the rest of America has followed suit – if only with iceberg lettuce (also grown here, east of Palm Springs in the Imperial Valley). In Southern California, where so many ripe avocados, fresh fruits and crunchy nuts originate, there's always something unusual in the salad bowl.

With hundreds of miles of coastline, it's no wonder Californians love fish. Fishing is not only a huge industry, but a tremendously popular sport. As you travel between Santa Barbara and San Diego, spring through fall, you'll often see halibut and tuna on restaurant menus, some of it locally caught. Salmon is especially popular – though much of it comes from Northern California.

People associate California with vegetarianism, but locals love meat. For years the paradigm for beef was corn-fed cattle from the Midwest. In California, however, a reverse trend is in progress. Better restaurants now serve grass-fed beef, from cattle that range freely, without dietary or hormonal supplements. Not only does it improve the meat's texture and flavor, but it's more environmentally friendly, since cattle aren't forced to consume a crop that requires vast amounts of water, fuel and electricity to grow, then process, into feed. But corn is federally subsidized, which makes it cheap; it also causes the animals to grow faster, reducing costs for farmers and eventually consumers.

Still, 'organic' meats and produce have taken off among savvy food lovers and environmentalists. This is ironic, since California's giant agribusiness companies produce huge amounts of genetically modified foods in the Central Valley. But the cognoscenti won't buy it. Top chefs now insist on organics, claiming that they're not only environmentally safer, but they simply taste better, especially tomatoes and strawberries. And in the case of fish, it's more nutritious and healthful, particularly salmon (farmed, so-called 'Atlantic salmon' has color added to turn it orange, and the fish is often raised in polluted waters). At the best restaurants, chefs will print on the menu the names of the farms that grow their produce and supply their meats and cheeses.

As you drive through small inland towns such as Ojai (p344) and other agricultural regions, stop at the mom-and-pop farm stands and buy whatever is in season; you'll often find organically grown items – see if you can't taste the difference. If you don't have a chance to drive to the country, then swing by a farmers market where rural growers bring their produce to towns and cities. They're great fun, and you can pick up a pot of locally produced honey to take home to grandma. Details about farmers markets are listed throughout the destination chapters. For LA markets, see p184.

Each region has its culinary strengths – and weaknesses. Los Angeles rides the wave of new trends more than anywhere else in SoCal, and the results can be wonderful, even if the city's chefs sometimes blur the line between food as sustenance and food as fashion accessory. For the complete low-down, see p153. San Diego, by contrast, shies away from esoteric fads, but the cooking style evolves more slowly. For example, nearly every restaurant there still serves Caesar salad, seared sesame-crusted ahi tuna, and crème brûlée, a three-course menu that soared to popularity in Los Angeles and San Francisco in the late 1980s, but of which San Diegans never seem to tire. No matter. They do it well.

SoCal's food scene benefits hugely from its diverse immigrant populations. Mexican food is a staple for many Californians, and until you've tasted *carnitas* (braised pork) or fish tacos washed down by a cold beer, you haven't experienced California culture. The same goes for Asian cooking. Places like Little Saigon in Orange County (p214) have huge concentrations of Vietnamese people, and you won't find more authentic *pho* (noodle soup; rhymes with paw) outside of Hanoi.

> If you're hiking in the woods, pick some California laurel to take home and dry. Use it in recipes that call for bay leaves, but only use half the amount called for – it's pungent!

## DRINKS

Californians love wine, and ever since Stag's Leap cabernet sauvignon and Chateau Montelena chardonnay (both from Napa Valley) beat French rivals in 1976 at the Paris Tasting – the 'World Cup of Wine' – California has basked in the glow of international attention for its excellent vintages. Though the region only began growing wine grapes in the 1980s, Santa Barbara's Wine Country (p338) produces some outstanding pinot noirs and Rhône-style wines (these include syrah, morvedre and viognier). If you love wine, don't leave the state before you've tried some. Look for them on restaurant menus and at wine bars throughout Southern California.

Unlike in France, locally made wine is pricey. Many prefer instead to drink beer, a perfectly respectable alternative (so long as you drink it from a glass and not the bottle, at least while at the dinner table) especially when it's made locally. If you like handcrafted ales and lagers, make it a point to seek out any of the microbreweries listed in the destination chapters. They usually serve good pub grub as well.

> **DID YOU KNOW?**
> California produces more than 17 million gallons of wine annually.

Spirits are also exceedingly popular. The last decade has seen a big comeback of 1950s-style martini bars, but gin has now taken a back seat to vodka, allowing such wacky deviations as lemon- and chocolate-flavored martinis your grandparents would never have considered drinking. No place in SoCal embraces cocktail culture as much as Palm Springs, where nearly every house has a built-in bar. In fact many people visit the desert city expressly to laze poolside for the weekend in a boozy haze.

In SoCal's cafés – which are everywhere – people love strong coffee. Don't be ashamed to wrinkle your nose at pale brown water. Most baristas respect mud drinkers. In roadside diners, however, expect weak brews.

On the nonalcoholic front many vintners have started bottling their unfermented wine-grape juice. Look for it on restaurant menus and at better non-chain food stores. You'll no doubt see a plethora of places (eg Jamba Juice) dedicated solely to fruit smoothies: fruit blended with ice and yogurt, sorbet, 'vitamin boosters' and other goodies. These concoctions really hit the spot on a hot day.

## CELEBRATIONS

Holidays are feast days, usually spent at home. For Thanksgiving Day and Christmas Day, roast turkey always appears on the table, but lately many California residents – in classic form – have sought new, nontraditional ways to cook them. Starting in late October, food sections of local newspapers brim with alternative recipes for preparing holiday turkeys. The latest craze is to brine the fowl (soak it in saltwater) before cooking it, resulting in a succulent, flavorful, juicy bird.

On other holidays, such as Independence Day and Labor Day, everybody barbecues, cooking everything from hot dogs and steaks, to salmon and veggie burgers over an open fire. Unlike in most regions of the USA, you can safely plan a barbecue months in advance without worrying that it's going to rain. Barely a drop falls between May and November.

## WHERE TO EAT & DRINK

The average Californian eats one good-sized meal a day, usually at dinner. Lunch is more casual than dinner and many people snack throughout the day. Restaurants in California serve lunch between 11:30am and 2:30pm, and dinner between 5:30pm and 10pm, but some close earlier. If a restaurant accepts reservations, book a table. Most people eat dinner between 6pm and 8pm. Lots of residents regularly eat out, and restaurants in metropolitan areas get crowded, even during the week.

As for choosing one restaurant over another, whenever possible pick one where the chef is also the owner. It makes all the difference in consistency and quality.

### California-Cuisine Restaurant

There is no such thing as a typical California-cuisine restaurant. You can't pigeonhole the style. It may draw its primary influences from Europe, or maybe Asia. There are no rules, except that the food should be extremely fresh, minimally processed and perfectly prepared. For sauces, chefs generally rely on flavor-packed reductions of stocks rather than fat-enriched gravies.

One of the hottest trends in California cooking is 'small plate' dining, a variation on the Spanish tradition of tapas, in which diners order a number of diverse appetizer-sized dishes of food, allowing everyone at the table to share. Culinary styles range from Japanese to Mediterranean and just about everything in between.

### Steak House

Despite their reputation, Californians eat a lot of meat. From north to south steak houses are a constant on the state's food scene. Patrons come for cold gin and rare beef. The dining room is candlelit; in the separate full bar, there's a TV showing the ballgame. Steak houses are usually expensive. More and more are featuring grass-fed, as well as Kobe (pronounced *koh*-bay) beef, both of which are premium grades. Kobe beef comes from a Japanese breed of cattle that has been reared in accordance with strict standards; the cows receive daily massages and before they're slaughtered they're fed sake to get them drunk and relax their muscles. There's a lot of fake Kobe; check the source before you spend $80 on a steak.

### Seafood House

California seafood restaurants serve fish in an egalitarian atmosphere of conviviality. The tradition is as old as the gold rush. Virtually anywhere fishing boats are moored, you'll find a California seafood house nearby.

When deciding what to order, ask the waiter which fish have been locally caught (the waters off LA and San Diego aren't as clean as those further north, so you may not find many local fish in those cities). The best dishes are often the chef's specials, which are prepared expressly for that day's menu, based on what's fresh at the market. At casual seafood houses, fried foods are prominent on the menu; at fancier places the fish is usually sautéed or broiled and served with a delicate sauce, often enriched with butter.

### Bar & Grill

It's just what the name says. At its simplest, it's a sawdust saloon that cooks a limited menu on its small grill. At the other end are fabulous places to eat a steak and drink one-too-many martinis without having to worry about talking too loudly. Like the steak house and the seafood house, the bar and grill is an unpretentious place. They serve lots of meat and have full bars, as well as a good selection of beers.

### Quick Eats

Virtually all grocery stores sell to-go food, usually sandwiches, but sometimes freshly roasted chickens, sushi, salads, deli meats and cheeses. Keep an eye out for farmers markets and independent grocery stores listed throughout the book, both great places to grab food on the fly. If you want to eat in a sit-down restaurant but have to get out quickly, tell your waiter as soon as you sit down.

## VEGETARIANS & VEGANS

California may have more vegetarians and vegans per capita than any other state, but outside metropolitan areas restaurants that are strictly vegetarian are few and far between. Take heart: vegetarians may go to virtually any proper sit-down restaurant in SoCal and order a satisfying meal from the regular menu. Sometimes as much as 60% of the offerings will be vegetarian. This is especially true of Chinese and Indian restaurants, both of which are plentiful. Western-style restaurants have the obligatory vegetarian pasta dishes as well as salads, portobello mushrooms in season, baked squashes and eggplant (aubergine), pilafs and pies. Dishes of steamed mixed vegetables dressed with olive oil or an emulsion sauce are popular, and people do astonishing things with tofu. Even many Mexican restaurants will offer vegetarian dishes, a thing unheard of in Mexico – just make sure they don't use lard in the beans.

## WHINING & DINING

If you're traveling with kids, you'll be pleased to know that most restaurants will be happy to see you. Always ask for a children's menu; it's sometimes printed on a take-home coloring book or placemat. There are also loads of mid-range places where mom and dad can enjoy a good bottle of wine and the kids can have ice-cream sundae.

High-end restaurants don't like kids. Meals in such places last two hours or more, too long to expect little ones to sit without squirming or screaming. Unless they're exceptionally well behaved, properly dressed and old enough to appreciate the meal, don't bring children to better restaurants without first calling to inquire if it's appropriate.

For more information about traveling with children see p351.

## HABITS & CUSTOMS

Men, if you're not sure what to wear, choose a long-sleeved collared shirt and tuck it into a nice pair of pants with a good pair of shoes and belt.

Some, but not all, species of seafood are being overfished, causing environmental degradation. To find out what's safe to eat (and what's not), check out the Monterey Bay Aquarium's Seafood Watch List at www.mbayaq.org.

A stunning exposé about food in America, *Food Politics: How the Food Industry Influences Nutrition and Health*, by Marion Nestle (2003), tracks big business' influence on the American diet.

Add some product to your hair, and voilà! You're a local. If you're still uncertain about dress codes, call the restaurant.

General table manners are fairly intuitive. Table servers are politely addressed as 'waiter' or 'waitress,' or possibly 'sir,' but never by shouting, 'Hey, buddy!' or 'Come here!' At better restaurants, *you* must ask for the bill.

Smoking is illegal in restaurants. If you're in the home of someone who smokes, wait until all have finished eating, then ask permission of your host and the others at the table. If anyone objects, it's common practice to go outside or into another room.

Famed culinary writer MFK Fisher's posthumously published memoir *To Begin Again: Stories and Memoirs 1908–1929* (1994) addresses the 'art of living well gastronomically,' and also describes Southern California before it was all built up.

## COOKING COURSES

The following are all reputable courses in Southern California.

**California Sushi Academy** (Map pp72-3; ☎ 310-581-0213; www.sushi-academy.com; 1611 Pacific Ave, Venice, LA) You can study to be a professional sushi chef here, but most people just come for the three-hour basic seminars offered every Saturday and Sunday for $80. Five-day intensive courses are $1620.

**New School of Cooking** (off Map pp72-3; ☎ 310-842-9702; www.newschoolofcooking.com; 8690 Washington Blvd, Culver City, LA) Seasoned instructors run multiweek courses or single-session three-hour classes ($75) built around a theme, technique, ingredient or dish (eg Japanese noodles, reduction sauces, Asian pub food, tacos).

**Laguna Culinary Arts** (Map p226; ☎ 949-494-0745; www.lagunaculinaryarts.com; 550 S Coast Hwy, Laguna Beach, Orange County) Besides comprehensive home and professional chef courses, this outfit also offers three- and four-hour classes ($85 to $95) in which you learn how to prepare a three-course gourmet meal.

**Chez School of Food & Wine** (Map p74; ☎ 310-316-1566; www.chezmelange.com; 1718 Pacific Coast Hwy, Redondo Beach, LA) Attached to the Chez Mélange restaurant (p162), this is a small, energetic and personable cooking school with themed classes ($55), often with a seasonal focus (say, Thanksgiving turkey or classical French cuisine).

# Los Angeles

CONTENTS

Ah, Los Angeles. Everyone knows what to expect, right? Perpetual sunshine. Beaches full of hard bodies. Surfers shredding the perfect waves. Palatial hilltop mansions. Palm trees swaying in the breeze. And, of course, movie stars…everywhere.

Aside from the movie stars, you'll probably find all that and then some in one of the world's most intriguing and complex cities. Sure, cruising the Sunset Strip in a convertible, finding your favorite celebrity's star on the Walk of Fame and window-shopping on Rodeo Dr are all part of the LA experience. But once you've starred in the movie of your imagination, move on and transcend the clichés. Explore the other LA with its superb art museums, cutting-edge architecture, beautiful parks and gardens, and fun shopping. Pick from an international smorgasbord of culinary experiences – Afghani to Zambian – then take in some world-class jazz or Beethoven.

What makes LA so fascinating is its wealth of human experience, its mosaic of cultures living side by side in relative peace, and its beautiful setting by the sea. Not even earthquakes, traffic gridlock and smog can stop LA from thriving. Reality here is never far from the myth, and vice versa. And that's just what makes LA so unique. And fun.

## HIGHLIGHTS

- Bodysurfing at any of LA's legendary **beaches** (p129)
- Traipsing in the footsteps of Chumash Indians and filmmakers in the **Santa Monica Mountains** (p130)
- Feeling your spirits soar during an afternoon at Brentwood's hilltop **Getty Center** (p91)
- Marveling at the wackiness of human existence along Venice Beach's **Ocean Front Walk** (p97)
- Treating your ears to a concert at the breathtaking **Walt Disney Concert Hall** (p107) in Downtown Los Angeles
- Taking a trip around the world and back in time in **Downtown Los Angeles** (p104)
- Immersing yourself in the sassy SoCal vibe in sophisticated **Santa Monica** (p95)
- Guzzling beer or sipping martinis on a **bar-hop** (p168) around Silver Lake and Los Feliz

- LA COUNTY POP: 10.1 MILLION
- AVERAGE TEMPS: JAN 47/66°F, JUL 62/82°F

# ORIENTATION

Los Angeles may be vast and amorphous, but the areas of interest to visitors are fairly well defined. About 12 miles inland, Downtown LA is home to world-class architecture and cultural venues, and imbued with a global-village feel thanks to such enclaves as Little Tokyo, Chinatown, Olvera St and the Fashion District. Pretty Pasadena, to the northeast, is famous for its Rose Bowl and the enchanting Huntington Library, Art Collections & Botanical Gardens.

Northwest of Downtown, Hollywood also encompasses trendy Los Feliz and Silver Lake, which border the large urban playground of Griffith Park. West Hollywood is LA's epicenter of urban chic and the gay and lesbian community. Most TV and movie studios, though, are actually north of Hollywood in the San Fernando Valley.

South of Hollywood, Mid-City's main draws are the museums of the Miracle Mile District, while, west of here, Beverly Hills gives visitors a taste of the 'lifestyles of the rich and famous' along Rodeo Dr and mansion-lined residential streets. Other Westside communities – all linked by Sunset Blvd – include Westwood, home to the University of California, Los Angeles (UCLA); refined Bel Air; and Brentwood with the hilltop Getty Center.

Of the beach towns, sophisticated-yet-relaxed Santa Monica is the most tourist-friendly with some terrific beaches, shopping and dining. Others include ritzy Malibu, funky Venice, the South Bay trio of Manhattan Beach, Hermosa Beach and Redondo Beach, and finally, bustling Long Beach.

Due to LA's huge size, a car is the most efficient way to get around, although if you limit explorations to specific neighborhoods, public transportation is adequate.

For information on how to get to LA's various neighborhoods from Los Angeles International Airport (LAX), see p193.

## Maps

A good map is as essential as sunscreen when exploring LA. Some of the best are published by the **American Automobile Association** (AAA; ☎ 800-874-7532; www.aaa.com), which has numerous branches around town, including one in **West LA** (off Map pp70-1; ☎ 310-914-8500; 1900 S Sepulveda Blvd; 🕒 9am-5pm Mon-Fri) and another in **Hollywood** (Map pp68-9; ☎ 323-525-0018; 5500 Wilshire Blvd; 🕒 9am-5pm Mon-Fri). AAA's *Central & Western Area* map is the single most useful map. Maps cost about $4 each but are free to members of AAA and its foreign affiliates.

Other street maps are also sold at gas stations, supermarkets, convenience stores

---

**LOS ANGELES IN...**

**Two Days**

Start your day with breakfast at the **Griddle Café** (p154) in West Hollywood, then work off the carbs with a stroll along newly revitalized **Hollywood Blvd** (p59). After lunch it's off to **Beverly Hills** (p87) and Rodeo Dr via mansion-lined **Sunset Blvd** (p87). From here, make a beeline to the **Getty Center** (p89) before concluding the day with dinner in **Santa Monica** (p159) and people-watching on **Third St Promenade** (p96).

On the second day, weather permitting, spend the morning frolicking on the beach in Venice and checking out the mad scene along the famous Ocean Front Walk, better known as **Venice Boardwalk** (p97), then hit the road for Downtown. Check out **Olvera St** (p105), the new **Cathedral of Our Lady of the Angels** (p108) and **Walt Disney Concert Hall** (p107), and get your cultural fix at the **Museum of Contemporary Art** (p108). Head back to Hollywood for predinner drinks and sunset views at **Yamashiro** (p169), then let your appetite tell you where to go for dinner.

**Four Days**

Make **Universal Studios Hollywood** (p121) the focus of your third day, then spot real movie stars over dinner at **Spago Beverly Hills** (p157). For a change of pace on your final day, head to **Pasadena** (p123) and the serene **Huntington Library, Art Collections & Botanical Gardens** (p126). After dinner in Old Pasadena, head to the **Sunset Strip** (p83) for one last night on the town.

and tourist offices. Lonely Planet's laminated *Los Angeles* map is available in bookstores or at www.lonelyplanet.com.

## INFORMATION
### Bookstores
Outlets of chain stores Barnes & Noble and Borders abound throughout LA; check the Yellow Pages for branches. Listed here are our favorite indie bookstores, each with their own specialty and eclectic assortment.

**Acres of Books** (Map pp62-3; ☎ 562-437-6980; 240 Long Beach Blvd, Long Beach) Labyrinthine and maddeningly crammed, this is the 'mother' of all used bookstores.

**Bodhi Tree** (Map pp68-9; ☎ 310-659-1733, 800-825-9798; 8585 Melrose Ave, West Hollywood) Celebrity-heavy dispensary of used and new spiritual tomes, soulful music and aura-enhancing incense. Psychic readings, too.

**Book Soup** (Map pp68-9; ☎ 310-659-3110; 8818 W Sunset Blvd, West Hollywood) Solid selection of entertainment, queer studies and fiction. Also great people-watching (high celeb quotient) and big-name book signings.

**California Map & Travel Center** (Map pp72-3; ☎ 310-396-6277; 3312 Pico Blvd, Santa Monica) Well-respected travel bookstore with frequent readings and slide shows.

**Caravan Bookstore** (Map pp64-5; ☎ 213-626-9944; 550 S Grand Ave, Downtown LA) Old-timey shop teeming with Western American history books, including a $1 bargain table.

**Distant Lands** (Map p76; ☎ 626-449-3220; 56 S Raymond Ave, Pasadena) Treasure chest of travel books, guides and gadgets, including luggage and daypacks.

**Eso Won Books** (off Map pp68-9; ☎ 323-294-0324; 3655 S La Brea Blvd, South Central) The city's best bookstore for African-American and African literature; frequent readings and signings.

**Hennessey & Ingalls** (Map pp72-3; ☎ 310-458-9074; 214 Wilshire Blvd, Santa Monica) Mecca for art and architecture lovers.

**Traveler's Bookcase** (Map pp68-9; ☎ 323-655-0575; 8375 W 3rd St, Mid-City) Just what it says.

**Vroman's** (Map p76; ☎ 626-449-3220; 695 E Colorado Blvd, Pasadena) Southern California's oldest bookstore (since 1894) and a favorite with local literati.

### Emergency
**Emergency number** ( ☎ 911) For police, fire or ambulance service.

**Police** ( ☎ 800-275-5273) For nonemergency service.

**Rape & Battering Hotline** ( ☎ 800-656-4673)

**Suicide Prevention Hotline** ( ☎ 877-727-4747)

### Internet Access
Cybercafés are notoriously short lived, so call ahead to confirm that the following are still in business. Besides the ones listed here, the libraries in LA (opposite) also offer limited free Internet access.

**Cyber Java** (Map pp66-7; ☎ 323-466-5600; 7080 Hollywood Blvd, Hollywood; per hr $6; ⏰ 7am-11:30pm)

**Equator Coffeehouse** (Map p76; ☎ 626-564-8656; 22 Mills Pl, Pasadena; per hr $5; ⏰ 8am-midnight Sun-Thu, 8am-1am Fri & Sat)

**Interactive Café** (Map pp72-3; ☎ 310-395-5009; 215 Broadway, Santa Monica; per hr $6; ⏰ 6am-1am Sun-Thu, 6am-2am Fri & Sat)

**Rooms Café** (Map pp70-1; ☎ 310-445-3320; 1783 Westwood Blvd, Westwood; per hr $6; ⏰ 1pm-1am)

### Internet Resources
**www.at-la.com** The ultimate Web portal to all things LA.

**www.blacknla.com** Comprehensive online directory for LA's African-American community.

**www.blogging.la** One of the best LA blogs featuring musings, gripes, observations and tips from about 20 writers.

**www.la.com** Hip guide to shopping, eating and special events around town.

**www.lablogs.com** Gateway to LA-related blogs.

**www.laobserved.com** Insightful, newsy blog maintained by journalist Kevin Roderick, formerly of the *Los Angeles Times,* with a focus on LA culture, media and politics. Great for finding out about the latest hot-button issues; lots of really useful links.

**www.latinola.com** Plugs you right into the Latino arts and entertainment scene.

**www.losangelesalmanac.com** All the facts and figures at your fingertips.

**www.visitlosangeles.info** Official website of the Los Angeles Convention & Visitors Bureau, which operates the Downtown Los Angeles Visitor Information Center (opposite) and the Hollywood Visitors Center (opposite).

### Left Luggage
Since September 11, lockers and left-luggage storage at airports are a thing of the past. The Greyhound bus terminal in Downtown LA (p192) still has coin-operated lockers, but the maximum storage period is 24 hours ($2 per six hours). Amtrak's Union Station (p193) does not offer baggage storage. Your best bet may be to go with an off-site storage service. Charges vary but expect to pay about $10 for the pickup and $3 to $7 per piece per day, depending on the size of the bag.

**AeroEx** ( ☎ 310-670-2834)
**LAX International Baggage Service**
( ☎ 310-646-0222)
**MBI Enterprises** ( ☎ 310-646-7460, 866-202-6348)
**Superior Airline Services** ( ☎ 310-410-1112)

## Libraries

**Beverly Hills Library** (Map pp70-1; ☎ 310-288-2220;
444 N Rexford Dr, Beverly Hills; ☼ 10am-9pm Mon-Thu,
10am-6pm Fri & Sat, noon-5pm Sun)
**Hollywood Library** (Map pp66-7; ☎ 323-856-8260;
1623 Ivar Ave, Hollywood; ☼ 10am-8pm Mon-Thu, 10am-
6pm Fri & Sat, 1-5pm Sun)
**Richard Riordan Central Library** (Map pp64-5;
☎ 213-228-7000; 630 W 5th St, Downtown; ☼ 10am-
8pm Mon-Thu, 10am-6pm Fri & Sat, 1-5pm Sun) Also
see p109.
**Santa Monica Library** (Map pp72-3; ☎ 310-458-8614;
1324 5th St, Santa Monica; ☼ 10am-9pm Mon-Thu,
10am-5:30pm Sat, 1-5pm Sun) Temporary location until
completion of the new permanent facility at 6th St and
Santa Monica Blvd, scheduled for late 2005/early 2006.

## Media

For listings magazines, see p172.
**Daily News** (www.dailynews.com) Caters mostly to San
Fernando Valley readers.
**KCRW 89.9 fm** (www.kcrw.org) National Public Radio
(NPR); world music, intelligent talk.
**KPFK 90.7 fm** (www.kpfk.org) Part of the Pacific radio
network; news and talk.
**La Opinión** (www.laopinion.com) Spanish-language
daily.
**LA Weekly** (www.laweekly.com) Free alternative news
and listings magazine.
**Los Angeles Magazine** (www.losangelesmagazine
.com) Glossy lifestyle monthly with useful restaurant guide.
**Los Angeles Sentinel** (www.losangelessentinel.com)
African-American weekly.
**Los Angeles Times** (www.latimes.com) Nation's fourth-
largest daily and winner of 35 Pulitzer Prizes, including
five in 2004.

## Medical Services

**Cedars-Sinai Medical Center** (Map pp68-9; ☎ 310-
855-5000; 8700 Beverly Blvd, West Hollywood; ☼ 24hr
emergency room)
**LA County/USC Medical Center** (off Map pp64-5;
☎ 323-226-2622; 1200 N State St, Downtown; ☼ 24hr
emergency room)
**Los Angeles Free Clinic** (appointments at any branch
☎ 323-462-4158); Hollywood (Map pp66-7; 6043 Hollywood Blvd); Hollywood (Map pp66-7; 5205 Melrose Ave);
Mid-City (Map pp68-9; 8405 Beverly Blvd) Medical and
dental care, and counseling.

**Sav-On Drugs** ( ☼ 24hr) Mid-City (Map pp68-9; ☎ 323-
937-3019; 6360 W 3rd St); Santa Monica
(Map pp72-3; ☎ 310-828-6456; 2505 Santa Monica Blvd)
Pharmacy chain with dozens of branches across town;
check the Yellow Pages for additional locations.
**UCLA Medical Center** (Map pp70-1; ☎ 310-825-9111;
10833 LeConte Ave, Westwood; ☼ 24hr emergency room)
**Venice Family Clinic** (Map pp72-3; ☎ 310-392-8630;
604 Rose Ave, Venice) Good for general health concerns, with
payment on a sliding scale according to your means.
**Village Health Foundation** (off Map pp68-9; ☎ 323-
733-0471; 4073 Pico Blvd, near Koreatown; ☼ 10am-6pm
Tue-Fri, 9am-4pm Sat) Low-cost,
alternative-health clinic (acupuncture, Chinese medicine,
massage therapy, herbal therapy).
**Women's Clinic** (Map pp70-1; ☎ 310-203-8899; 9911
W Pico Blvd, Suite 500, Century City) Fees are calculated on
a sliding scale according to your capacity to pay.

## Money

**American Express** West Hollywood (Map pp68-9;
☎ 310-659-1682; 8493 W 3rd St; ☼ 9am-6pm Mon-Fri,
10am-3pm Sat); Pasadena (Map p76; ☎ 626-449-2281;
269 S Lake Ave; ☼ 9am-6pm Mon-Fri, 10am-2pm Sat)
**Associated Foreign Exchange** (Map pp70-1; ☎ 310-
274-7610; 433 N Beverly Dr, Beverly Hills; ☼ 9am-5pm
Mon-Fri, 10am-4pm Sat)
**TravelEx** ( ☎ 800-287-7362) West Hollywood
(Map pp68-9; 806 Hilldale Ave, West Hollywood;
☼ 9am-5pm Mon-Fri); Beverly Hills (Map pp70-1;
421 N Rodeo Dr, Beverly Hills; ☼ 10am-6pm Mon-Fri)
**World Banknotes Exchange** (Map pp64-5; ☎ 213-
627-5404; 520 S Grand Ave, Suite L, Downtown; ☼ 9am-
5pm Mon-Fri, 9am-1pm Sat)

## Post

Post offices abound in LA. Call ☎ 800-275-
8777 for the nearest branch.

## Tourist Information

**Beverly Hills Conference & Visitors Bureau**
(Map pp70-1; ☎ 310-248-1015, 800-345-2210; www
.beverlyhillsbehere.com; 239 S Beverly Dr, Beverly Hills;
☼ 8:30am-5pm Mon-Fri)
**California Welcome Center** (Map pp68-9; ☎ 310-
854-7616; Beverly Center Mall, 8500 Beverly Blvd, West
Hollywood; ☼ 10am-6pm Mon-Sat, 11am-6pm Sun)
**Downtown Los Angeles Visitor Information
Center** (Map pp64-5; ☎ 213-689-8822; www.visit
losangeles.info; 685 S Figueroa St, Downtown; ☼ 9am-
5pm Mon-Fri)
**Hollywood Visitors Center** (Map pp66-7; ☎ 323-467-
6412; Hollywood & Highland complex, 6801 Hollywood Blvd, Hollywood; ☼ 10am-10pm Mon-Sat,
10am-7pm Sun)

**Long Beach Visitors Information** (Map pp62-3; ☎ 562-436-3645, 800-452-7829; www.visitlongbeach.com; 100 Aquarium Way, Long Beach; ☒ 10am-5pm daily Jun-Sep, 10am-4pm Fri-Sun Oct-May)

**Marina del Rey Visitor Center** (Map pp72-3; ☎ 310-305-9545; www.visitthemarina.com; 4701 Admiralty Way, Marina del Rey; ☒ 10am-4pm)

**Pasadena Convention & Visitors Bureau** (Map p76; ☎ 626-795-9311, 800-307-7977; www.pasadenacal.com; 171 S Los Robles Ave, Pasadena; ☒ 8am-5pm Mon-Fri, 10am-4pm Sat)

**Santa Monica Visitors Center** (Map pp72-3; ☎ 310-393-7593; www.santamonica.com; 2nd fl, Santa Monica Place Mall, Santa Monica; ☒ 10am-6pm)

**Santa Monica Visitors Kiosk** (Map pp72-3; 1400 Ocean Ave, Santa Monica; ☒ 10am-4pm Sep-May, 10am-5pm Jun-Aug)

**West Hollywood Convention & Visitors Bureau** (Map pp68-9; ☎ 310-289-2525, 800-368-6020; www.visitwesthollywood.com; Pacific Design Center, M-38, 8687 Melrose Ave, West Hollywood; ☒ 8:30am-5:30pm Mon-Fri)

## DANGERS & ANNOYANCES

Walking around LA in the daytime is generally no problem, although extra caution should be exercised in East LA, Compton and Watts, sections of which are plagued by gangs and drugs. Stay away from these areas after dark. Hollywood also yields dangers, especially in poorly lit side streets; ditto for Venice. Crime rates are lowest in Westside communities such as Westwood and Beverly Hills, as well as in the beach towns (except Venice) and Pasadena. Downtown LA is safe in the daytime and not bad at night, but since its streets are nearly completely deserted after dark, most people don't feel safe walking around then. Downtown is also home to many homeless folks, most of whom gather on Skid Row, an area roughly bounded by 3rd, Alameda, 7th and Main Sts.

## SIGHTS

Each of LA's neighborhoods has its own unique appeal and where you concentrate your sightseeing largely depends on your personal interests. Classic sights such as museums and great architecture are in Downtown, Mid-City, Pasadena and Hollywood. West Hollywood has the legendary Sunset Strip and cool shopping, and the beach towns are great for soaking up the SoCal vibe.

---

### LIVING THE HOLLYWOOD CLICHÉ   *Alisha Snider*

Three of the four agents at the casting call were dressed in Halloween costumes. The one prompting me with lines from the tampon ad wore a plastic lion mask and yellow body suit complete with hairy tail. There were no self-deprecating comments, no gestures of apology, no recognition that a feeling, thinking, striving adult woman stood before one animal, one unidentifiable monster and to my best guess, one pole-dancer, and was about to muster all her stage craft and transform into a perky teen, talking about inserting her first-ever female hygiene product into her uncostumed body.

I'd arrived in LA from New York City two months before, determined to break into TV and film work after spending thousands of dollars on professional training and years performing in musical theater. As expected, it wasn't an easy transition. Some days I'd audition as a sweet, innocent fifteen-year-old in the morning and as a hot, sexy 25-year-old in the afternoon. I'd find a secluded spot in the parking lot and change in my car/trailer, but sometimes I'd forget and confuse the sweet and innocent for the hot and sexy. It didn't seem to matter much to the males in the audience.

In LA everyone wants to be an actor or a writer or a director or a producer. There are no normal people. Or if there are, if there are people that actually have professions, they too secretly harbor dreams of stardom.

There's no way around the cliché. It's emotionally confusing when people sometimes stare at me thinking I'm 'somebody' and then turn away disappointed upon a closer look. But I do it too; I can't help thinking everybody is 'somebody.'

I knew before I came to LA that my success would be at least as much about luck as talent, about when you're babysitting the agent's kids, or teaching the screenwriter's wife how to swim or serving the producer a drink at a party – that it's that mythic big break that can make your future. My big break so far came because I look exactly like a particular 15-year-old girl (especially when seen from behind) starring in a pilot for a new series (think *LA Law* meets *The*

## Hollywood, Los Feliz & Silver Lake
Map pp66–7

Aging movie stars know that a face-lift can do wonders to pump up a drooping career, and it seems the same can be done with LA neighborhoods. Millions of dollars have been invested in rejuvenating the legendary **Hollywood Blvd** in recent years. Even if it's still not all that glamorous, it's at least ready for its close-up. Historic movie palaces bask in restored glory, Metro Rail's Red Line makes access easy, some of LA's hottest bars and nightclubs have sprung up here, and even 'Oscar' has found a permanent home in the Kodak Theatre, part of a vast new shopping and entertainment complex called Hollywood & Highland. Lording it above the bustle from its dignified hillside perch is the city's most recognizable landmark, the Hollywood Sign, while east of Hwy 101 (Hollywood Fwy), the neighborhoods of Los Feliz (loss *fee*-les) and Silver Lake have evolved into bohemian-chic enclaves with fun and funky shopping, sleek nightlife and a hopping cuisine scene.

Most of the sights described in this section line up neatly along a 1-mile stretch of Hollywood Blvd between La Brea Ave and Vine St. To learn more about the area's historic significance, look for the red signs installed in front of major and minor landmarks along this stretch, or join a walking tour operated by Red Line Tours (p136).

The Metro Red Line serves central Hollywood (Hollywood/Highland station) and Los Feliz (Vermont/Sunset station) from Downtown LA and the San Fernando Valley. Pay-parking lots abound in the side streets; the cheapest we've found is the one on Cherokee Ave, just north of Hollywood Blvd, which charges $1 for two hours. The Hollywood & Highland parking garage charges $2 for four hours with validation (no purchase necessary) from any of the merchants or the Hollywood Visitors Center (p57).

### HOLLYWOOD WALK OF FAME
Big Bird, Bob Hope, Marilyn Monroe and Sting are just a few of the celebrities being sought out, admired, photographed – and stepped on – day after day on the famous **Hollywood Walk of Fame**. Since 1960 more

---

*Jetsons*). One of the rules in Hollywood is that extravagantly paid teenagers must not only have a guardian and tutor on set, they can only work a certain number of hours in the day. And when the hours are up and the shooting goes on, a desperate adult who resembles the body type of the kid gets to work those long extra hours, usually into the early morning, pretending she is 15.

I didn't complain since the money was great. I'd make more in a week than I'd make working at the health spa (my usual day job) for an entire month. And there were perks. While most of the shooting took place outside a decommissioned nuclear power plant – the one where Britney Spears shot a video – which in another universe could seem dangerous or bleak, there was something about the daily 2am visits by the coffee-cart guy that made it seem glamorous. I always ordered a double macchiato with whipped cream.

Driving one night through Hollywood after a shift at the health club and a disappointing audition for a toothpaste ad, tired and questioning my resolve, I saw two rays of light blast into the night sky – a movie premiere. And close too. I parked, grabbed my camera, and walked toward the lights and the gathering crowd. I'm small so I was able to thread my way to the front, where private security guards were gently pushing the overzealous away from the street. A mother next to me explained to her son that Brad and Jennifer would arrive last. I of course knew who she meant; no need for 'Pitt' and 'Aniston.'

Finally Brad and Jen alighted from their limo like two gods, sparkling and shiny, illuminated by search lights. The screaming fans closed in on me, elbowing me, almost climbing on top of me just for a glance. The roar was deafening and I struggled to reach into my pocket for my camera. Flashbulbs were firing like a machine gun and pleas for the couple to look this way or to come closer were drowned out by high-pitched screams. I wasn't conscious of it at first but I also began to mouth the words, silently at first, then softly, and finally at the top of my lungs, 'BRAD! JEN! LOOK THIS WAY!' When they walked away, it turned into a whimper and a cry as I realized I had just lived one more Hollywood cliché.

0 — 10 km
0 — 6 mi

**E** **F** **G** **H**

Angeles Crest Hwy

(2)

To Wrightwood

Red Box Rd

San Gabriel Mountains

San Gabriel River

**1**

Cogswell Reservoir

Mt Wilson Observatory

Mt Wilson (5710ft)

Angeles National Forest

San Gabriel Reservoir

Morris Reservoir

Mt San Antonio (Old Baldy: 10,064ft)

6

Brookside Park  Altadena

San Antonio Heights

Pasadena

(134)

Foothill Fwy

8  18

Arcadia

Monrovia

(210)

Rancho Cucamonga

San Marino

Azusa

Glendora

(30)

(30)

Pasadena Fwy

17

Temple City

Santa Fe Dam Recreation Area

(30)

(66)

Alhambra

San Gabriel

N Rosemead Blvd

(605)

Baldwin Park

Covina

Bonelli Regional County Park

Montclair

Upland

**2**

(10)

Monterey Park

El Monte

San Bernardino Fwy West Covina

(10)

Pomona

Ontario

Mission Blvd

Ontario International Airport

(60)

(60)

Whittier Narrows Recreation Area

(60)

Industry  La Puente

(57)

(71)

Diamond Bar

(83)

Chino

East Los Angeles

34

Pomona Fwy

(60)

Pico Rivera

San Gabriel River Fwy

Schabarum Regional Park

Rowland Heights

(57)

Calbon Canyon Rd

Riverside County

Chino Hills State Park

**3**

Santa Ana Fwy

(710)

(5)

Whittier

La Habra Heights

Los Angeles County

Orange County

Carbon Canyon Rd

Prado Flood Control Basin

Norco

Downey

(605)

La Mirada

(39)

Imperial Hwy

Brea

Richard Nixon Library

Yorba Linda Blvd

Yorba Linda

(71)

Corona

Paramount

Norwalk

Santa Ana Fwy

Buena Park

La Habra

CSU Fullerton

Fullerton

Placentia

(90)

Artesia Fwy

San Gabriel River Fwy

Cerritos

Knott's Berry Farm

Riverside Fwy

(91)

(91)

(91)

Lakewood

Lincoln Ave

(5)

Anaheim

Carson St

Long Beach Airport

Cypress

(39)

(57)

(55)

Villa Park

Irvine Regional Park

(231)

**4**

E Willow St

Katella Ave

Stanton

Disneyland & Disney's California Adventure

Orange

Cleveland National Forest

CSU Long Beach

(605)

San Diego Fwy

Garden Grove Fwy

Garden Grove

(22)

(22)

Santa Ana Mountains

Belmont Shore  Naples

Westminster

Santa Ana

Tustin

**5**

Beach Harbor

Seal Beach National Wildlife Refuge

Beach Blvd

Costa Mesa Fwy

Eastern Transportation Corridor

Irvine Center Dr

Long Beach Breakwater  Seal Beach Pier

Seal Beach

(405)

(5)

(231)

Portola Hills

San Pedro Bay

Bolsa Chica State Beach

Pacific Coast Hwy

Santa Ana River

John Wayne Airport (Orange County)

(73)

Irvine

UC Irvine

Lake Forest

Huntington Beach

(55)

Costa Mesa

Huntington Pier

(1)

Newport Beach

Mission Viejo

Huntington City Beach  Huntington State Beach

Newport Bay

Corona del Mar

(73)

**6**

Corona del Mar State Beach

Crystal Cove State Park

San Pedro Channel

(133)

Laguna Beach

Aliso Beach

(74)

Ferry to Santa Catalina Island

Laguna Niguel

San Juan Capistrano

**EATING** (pp162–3)
Alegria................................**32** F1
Belmont Brewing Company...**33** F4
Christine..............................**34** C4
Christy's..............................**35** F4
Egg Heaven.........................**36** F4
Hamburger Mary's...............**37** G1
Papadakis Taverna ..............**38** D5
Sir Winston's.................(see 18)
Taco Surf.............................**39** F4

**DRINKING** (p170)
Alex's Bar...........................**40** F4
Yard House..........................**41** F2

**ENTERTAINMENT** (pp171–82)
Blue Cafe.............................**42** F1
Hollywood Park...................**43** C1
Home Depot Center.............**44** D2

**SHOPPING** (p191)
Long Beach Outdoor Antique &
  Collectible Market.............**45** F3

**TRANSPORT**
Catalina Express Port - Long
  Beach................................**46** F3
Catalina Express Port - San
  Pedro................................**47** D5
Eagle Rider..........................**48** B1
Greyhound...........................**49** E4
Transit Mall....................(see 5)

**OTHER**
Gondola Getaway.................**50** F5

Long Beach

0 ━━━━━ 1 km
0 ━━━━━ 0.5 miles

A · B · C · D

Universal Studios Hollywood

Hollywood Franklin Park

Hollywood/ Highland

Hollywood & Highland

Hollywood Blvd

Hollywood Reservoir Dam

Mulholland Dr

Runyon Canyon Park

**Hollywood Hills**

Metro Red Line

Dearborn Dr

Griffith Park

Brush Canyon

Canyon Dr

Wattles Garden Park

Sycamore Ave

Camrose Dr

Scenic Gardens

Orchid Ave  Franklin Ave

Hollywood Fwy

Hollywood/ Western

N Vista Ave

N Franklin Ave

Hollywood Blvd

**See Hollywood Blvd Enlargement**

N Cahuenga Blvd

N Vine St

Hollywood/ Western

CBS Studios

W Sunset Blvd

**Hollywood**

Delongpre Park

Fountain Ave

Hollywood Recreation Center

Warner Hollywood Studios

Poinsettia Recreation Center

Santa Monica Blvd

Beth Olam Memorial Park

Paramount Studios

Melrose Ave

Willoughby Ave

Clinton St

Rosewood Ave

Beverly Blvd

Pan Pacific Park

Robert Burns Park

0 — 1 mi
0 — 0.5 miles

**INFORMATION**
| | |
|---|---|
| Cyber Java | 1 B4 |
| Hollywood Library | 2 C2 |
| Hollywood Visitors Center | 3 A2 |
| LA Gay & Lesbian Center | 4 B2 |
| Los Angeles Free Clinic - Hollywood Blvd | 5 C4 |
| Los Angeles Free Clinic - Melrose Ave | 6 D5 |

**SIGHTS & ACTIVITIES** (pp58–134)
| | |
|---|---|
| Capitol Records Tower | 7 C1 |
| Crossroads of the World | 8 B4 |
| Erotic Museum | 9 B2 |
| Frederick's of Hollywood Lingerie Museum | 10 B2 |
| Guinness World of Records Museum | 11 B2 |
| Hollyhock House | 12 E4 |
| Hollywood Athletic Club | 13 B4 |
| Hollywood Bowl | 14 B3 |
| Hollywood Bowl Museum | 15 B3 |
| Hollywood Entertainment Museum | 16 A2 |
| Hollywood Forever Cemetery | 17 C5 |
| Hollywood Heritage Museum | 18 B3 |
| Hollywood High School | 19 B4 |
| Hollywood Museum | 20 B2 |
| Hollywood Pro Bicycles | 21 B2 |
| Hollywood Sign | 22 C1 |
| Hollywood Wax Museum | 23 B2 |
| Immaculate Heart High School | 24 D3 |
| Junior Arts Center | (see 12) |
| Marshall High School | 25 G3 |
| Municipal Art Gallery | (see 12) |
| Palace Theatre | (see 75) |
| Panpipes Magickal Marketplace | 26 C2 |
| Ripley's Believe It or Not! | 27 B2 |
| Sunset Ranch Hollywood | 28 D1 |

**SLEEPING** (pp139–40)
| | |
|---|---|
| Best Western Hollywood Hills Hotel | 29 C3 |
| Dunes Inn Sunset | 30 D4 |
| Highland Gardens Hotel | 31 B4 |
| Hollywood Celebrity Hotel | 32 A1 |
| Hollywood Hills Hotel & Apartments | 33 B3 |
| Hollywood Roosevelt Hotel | 34 A2 |
| Hotel Bamboo | 35 C3 |
| Liberty Hotel | 36 A1 |
| Magic Castle Hotel | 37 B4 |
| Orange Drive Manor Hostel | 38 A1 |
| Orchid Suites Hollywood | 39 A1 |
| Renaissance Hollywood Hotel | 40 A1 |
| USA Hostels Hollywood | 41 B2 |

**EATING** (pp151–4)
| | |
|---|---|
| Ammo | 42 B5 |
| Birds | 43 C3 |
| Cafe Stella | 44 F5 |
| Carousel | 45 E4 |
| Casita Del Campo | 46 G4 |
| Cheebo | 47 A4 |
| Cobras & Matadors | 48 F4 |
| El Conquistador | 49 G5 |
| Fred 62 | 50 F4 |
| Madame Matisse | 51 G5 |
| Mel's Drive-in | (see 20) |
| Musso & Frank Grill | 52 B2 |
| Palermo | (see 50) |
| Rambutan Thai | 53 G6 |
| Sanamluang | 54 C2 |
| Scooby's | 55 B2 |
| Vermont | 56 F4 |
| Vert | 57 A1 |
| Yuca's | 58 F3 |
| Zankou Chicken | 59 E4 |

**DRINKING** (pp168–9)
| | |
|---|---|
| 4100 Bar | 60 F5 |
| Akbar | 61 F4 |
| Beauty Bar | 62 C2 |
| Cat & Fiddle Pub | 63 B4 |
| Daddy's | 64 C2 |
| Faultline | 65 F5 |
| Formosa Cafe | 66 A5 |
| Frolic Room | (see 96) |
| Good Luck Bar | 67 F4 |
| Lava Lounge | 68 A4 |
| Red Lion Tavern | 69 H4 |
| Three Clubs | 70 C5 |
| Tiki Ti | 71 F4 |
| Yamashiro | 72 B3 |

**ENTERTAINMENT** (pp171–82)
| | |
|---|---|
| Actors' Gang Theatre | 73 C5 |
| American Cinematheque | (see 80) |
| ArcLight & Cinerama Dome | 74 C4 |
| Avalon | 75 C1 |
| Boardner's | 76 B2 |
| Catalina Bar & Grill | 77 B4 |
| Dragonfly | 78 B5 |
| Echo | 79 H6 |
| Egyptian Theatre | 80 B2 |
| El Capitan Theatre | 81 A2 |
| El Cid | 82 F5 |
| El Floridita | 83 C4 |
| Gabah | 84 E6 |
| Garden of Eden | (see 1) |
| Gig | 85 A5 |
| Grauman's Chinese Theatre | 86 A2 |
| Highlands | 87 A1 |
| Hudson Theatres | 88 B5 |
| Improv Olympic West | (see 89) |
| Ivar | 89 B2 |
| John Anson Ford Theatre | 90 B3 |
| King King | 91 B2 |
| Knitting Factory Hollywood | (see 16) |
| Kodak Theatre | 92 A1 |
| Little Temple | 93 F5 |
| M Bar & Restaurant | (see 83) |
| MET Theatre | 94 D5 |
| Nacional | 95 C2 |
| Pantages Theatre | 96 C2 |
| Spaceland | 97 G5 |
| White Lotus | 98 C1 |

**A** **B** **C** **D**

**1**

**INFORMATION**
A Different Light.....................(see 79)
American Automobile
  Association..........................**1** E6
American Express......................**2** C5
Bodhi Tree............................**3** C4
Book Soup............................**4** B3
California Welcome Center..............**5** C5
Cedars-Sinai Medical Center...........**6** B5
Farmers Market Office.................**7** D5
German Consulate.....................**8** D6
Los Angeles Free Clinic...............**9** C5
Sav-On Drugs........................**10** D5
South African Consulate...............**11** D6
Traveler's Bookcase..................**12** C5
TravelEx............................(see 81)
West Hollywood Convention &
  Visitors Bureau....................**13** B4

**2**

**SIGHTS & ACTIVITIES** (pp58–134)
A+D Museum.........................**14** C3
CBS Television City...................**15** D5
Craft & Folk Art Museum..............**16** D6
Crunch Gym.........................**17** D3
Fairfax High School..................**18** D4
Farmers Market (original - LA).......**19** D5
Golden Bridge.......................**20** E5
Greystone Mansion...................**21** A3
Hyatt House.........................**22** C3
La Brea Tar Pits.....................**23** D6

LACMA West.........................**24** D6
Los Angeles County Museum of Art.....**25** D6
MOCA Pacific Design Center...........**26** B4
Pacific Design Center................(see 13)
Page Museum........................(see 23)
Petersen Automotive Museum..........**27** D6
Porno Walk of Fame..................**28** D3
Schindler House.....................**29** C4
Zimmer Children's Museum.............**30** C6

**SLEEPING** (pp140–2)
Alta Cienega Motel...................**31** C3
Argyle.............................**32** C3
Banana Bungalow Hollywood...........**33** D4
Best Western Sunset Plaza Hotel.......**34** C3
Beverly Laurel Hotel.................**35** C3
Chateau Marmont....................**36** C3
Elan Hotel Modern...................**37** C5
Farmer's Daughter...................**38** C3
Grafton on Sunset...................**39** C3
Le Montrose Suite Hotel..............**40** B4
Mondrian...........................**41** C3
Ramada Plaza Hotel & Suites..........**42** C3
San Vicente Inn.....................**43** B4
Secret Garden B&B..................**44** D2
Sofitel Los Angeles..................**45** C3
Standard Hollywood..................**46** C3
Summerfield Suites by Wyndham.......**47** B4
Sunset Marquis Hotel & Villas.........**48** C3
Valadon Hotel......................**49** B4

**3**

**4**

**SHOPPING** (pp182–92)
Agent Provocateur...................**101** D4
Baby Jane of Hollywood.............(see 58)
Baby Melt..........................(see 122)
Beauty Collection
  Apothecary.......................**102** D5
Bristol Farms.......................**103** D3
Chac-Mool Gallery..................**104** B4
Curve.............................**105** B5
Decades & Decades Two..............**106** C4
Erewhon Natural Foods
  Market...........................**107** D5
Fahey/Klein Gallery.................**108** E5
Farmers Market (West
  Hollywood).......................**109** E3
Fred Segal.........................**110** D4
Gelson's...........................**111** C3
Grove.............................**112** D5
Head Line Records..................**113** B3
Hustler Hollywood..................**114** B3
Iturralde Gallery...................**115** E5
Jet Rag............................**116** E4
Kitson.............................**117** B5
Kristin Londgren...................**118** C5
Lisa Kline..........................**119** B5
Lisa Kline Outlet Store.............(see 123)
Margo Leavin Gallery...............**120** B4
Maya.............................**121** D4
Melrose Trading Post...............(see 18)
Meltdown Comics &
  Collectibles......................**122** E3
Necromance.......................**123** E4
Palmetto..........................**124** C5
Pleasure Chest.....................**125** C3
Remix Vintage Shoes...............(see 57)
Tower Records......................**126** B3
Trader Joe's.......................**127** C3
Trashy Lingerie....................**128** C5
Turtle Beach Swimwear.............**129** C5
Wasteland.........................**130** E4
Whole Foods Market (Fairfax
  District).........................(see 7)
Whole Foods Market (West
  Hollywood).......................**131** D3
Wound & Wound Toy Co..............**132** E4

**5**

**6**

Wattle
Garde
Par

Selma Ave

William S
Hart Park

W Sunset Blvd

N Curson Ave
N Nichols Canyon Rd
Laurel Canyon Blvd
N Crescent Heights Blvd

Queens Rd
N Alta
Loma Rd
Fountain Ave

Norton Ave

Santa Monica Blvd

Sunset Plaza Dr
Horn
Ave
W Sunset Blvd

Holloway Dr

Romaine St

Willoughby St

Waring Ave

WEST HOLLYWOOD

Melrose
Pl

Melrose Ave

Clinton St

Rosewood Ave

Fairfax
District

Oakwood Ave

Beverly Blvd

Alden Dr

Beverly
Center

W 1st St

Burton Way

W 3rd St

Pan
Pacific
Park

Dayton Way
Colgate Ave

Clifton Way

Colgate Ave

Wilshire Blvd

Hancock Park

La Cienega
Park

To Bikram Yoga
Studio (0.75mi)

Greystone
Park

Lomo Vista Dr

Doheny Rd

W Sunset Blvd
N Doheny Dr
S Doheny Dr
Cynthia St
Palm Ave

N La
Peer Dr

Santa Monica Blvd

N Robertson Blvd
S Robertson Blvd
N Hamel Dr
N Carson Dr
S Swall Dr
S Clark Dr
S Shenandoah St

N Sweetzer Ave
N Kings Rd
N Flores St
N Orlando Ave

San Vicente Blvd

N Beverly Blvd

S La Cienega Blvd
S La Peer Dr
S Le Doux Rd
S Sweetzer Ave
S Orlando Ave
S La Jolla Ave
S Alfred St
S Crescent Heights Blvd

S Fairfax Ave
S Ogden Dr
S Genesee Ave
S Spaulding Ave
S Stanley Ave
S Curson Ave
S La Brea Ave

Oakhurst Dr

San Vicente Blvd

0 —————————— 1 km
0 —————————— 0.5 miles

| EATING | 🍴 | (pp154–6) |
|---|---|---|
| Alto Palato | 50 | C4 |
| Angelini Osteria | 51 | E5 |
| A.O.C. | 52 | D5 |
| Buddha's Belly | 53 | E5 |
| Campanile | 54 | E6 |
| Canter's Deli | 55 | D4 |
| Chaya Brasserie | 56 | B5 |
| Cobras & Matadors | 57 | D5 |
| French Quarter Market Place | 58 | D3 |
| Griddle Café | 59 | D3 |
| Gumbo Pot | 60 | D5 |
| Hamburger Mary's | 61 | C3 |
| Hugo's | 62 | C3 |
| Kibitz Room | (see 55) | |
| Koi | 63 | C4 |
| La Brea Bakery | (see 54) | |
| Le Pain Quotidien | 64 | B4 |
| Loteria! Grill | (see 60) | |
| Marix Tex Mex | 65 | C3 |
| Mel's Drive-In | 66 | C3 |

| | | |
|---|---|---|
| Pastis | 67 | D5 |
| Pink's Hot Dogs | 68 | E4 |
| Real Food Daily | 69 | C4 |
| Singapore's Banana Leaf | (see 60) | |
| Surya | 70 | D5 |
| Swingers | (see 35) | |
| Tail O' the Pup | 71 | C4 |
| Xiomara | 72 | F4 |

| DRINKING | 🍷 | (p169) |
|---|---|---|
| Abbey | 73 | B4 |
| Bar Marmont | (see 36) | |
| El Carmen | 74 | D5 |
| El Coyote | 75 | E5 |
| Factory/Ultra Suede | 76 | B4 |
| Here Lounge | 77 | B4 |
| Largo | 78 | D4 |
| Micky's | 79 | B4 |
| Palms | 80 | C4 |
| Rage | 81 | B4 |
| Sky Bar | (see 41) | |
| Urth Caffe | 82 | C4 |

| ENTERTAINMENT | 🎭 | (pp171–82) |
|---|---|---|
| Bang Improv Studio | 83 | D4 |
| Cat Club | 84 | B3 |
| Celebration Theatre | 85 | E3 |
| Comedy Store | 86 | C3 |
| Conga Room | 87 | E6 |
| Coronet Theatre | 88 | C4 |
| Groundlings | 89 | E4 |
| Hollywood Improv | 90 | E4 |
| House of Blues | 91 | C3 |
| Laugh Factory | 92 | D3 |
| Pacific Theatres at the Grove | 93 | D5 |
| Parlour Club | 94 | D3 |
| Roxy | 95 | B3 |
| Silent Movie Theatre | 96 | D4 |
| Storyopolis | 97 | B5 |
| Troubadour | 98 | B4 |
| Viper Room | 99 | B3 |
| Whisky-a-Go-Go | 100 | B3 |

A   B   C   D

**1**

**DOWNTOWN BEVERLY HILLS**

0 _____ 300 m
0 _____ 0.2 miles

● 4

W 3rd St

● 13

Cametta Ave

Park Way

Burton Way

● 20

N Crescent Dr

N Alpine Dr

N Canon Dr

N Beverly Dr

34 🏢

Foothill Rd

● 84

18 🏢

1 🏛

55 🏢

N Rodeo Dr

N Camden Dr

Dayton Way

48 🏢

Beverly
Gardens
Park

🏢 12

71 🏢

75 🏢

N Bedford Dr

N Roxbury Dr

N Rexford Dr

Philbert Dr

Santa Monica Blvd

49 🏢

7 🏢

69 🏢

Bella Dr

Cielo Dr

45 🏢

P 🏢
74

10 78

44 🏢

Clifton Way

S Santa Monica Blvd

Brighton Way

77 🏢

Two
Rodeo

70 🏢
76 🏢

52 🏢

To Vibrato Grill
& Jazz (2.5mi);
Groove Riders (4.5mi)

Green
Acres Dr

Wilshire Blvd

41 🏢

57 🏢

S Spalding Dr

S Linden Dr

S McCarty Dr

S Roxbury Dr

S Bedford Dr

S Peck Dr

S Camden Dr

S Rodeo Dr

El Camino Dr

S Beverly Dr

S Rodeo Dr

29 🏢

31 🏢

S Canon Dr

S Crescent Dr

27 ●

Benedict Canyon Dr

**2**

36 🏢

97 🏢

92 ●

98 ●
99 ●
101 ●
85 ●
84 ●

**Bel Air**

N Beverly Glen Blvd

St Pierre Rd

88 ●

83 ●

87 ●

86 ●
90 ●

**3**

25 ●

Bel Air Rd

Bellagio Rd

Clifton Rd

Stone Canyon Rd

**Holmby
Hills**

Monovale
Dr

Bel Air
Country Club

Charing
Cross Rd

96 ●

W Sunset Blvd

Reservoir

Circle Dr E

Mapleton Dr

To Getty Center (0.1mi);
Skirball Cultural Center (3mi);
San Fernando Valley (5mi)

Club View Dr

**Holmby
Park**

80 ●

**4**

38 🏢

● 14

To Brentwood
Motor Hotel
(0.75mi)

Warner Ave

Comstock Ave

Los Angeles
Country Club

De Neve Dr

23 🏛
22
🏢 67

Circle Dr

Gayley Ave

University of
California,
Los Angeles
(UCLA)

Westholme Ave

66 🏢

Circle Dr S

17 🏢

405

8 🏢

Hilgard Ave

Malcolm Ave

**Westwood**

S Beverly Glen Blvd

**5**

Los
Angeles
National
Cemetery

16 🏢
59 🏢

Le Conte Ave

35 🏢

73 🏢

Weyburn Dr

63 🏢 P

Broxton Ave

Lindbrook Dr

Wellworth Ave

West Los Angeles
Veterans
Administration
Center

San Diego Fwy

Kinross Ave

56 🏢

Gayley Ave

24 🏛

60 🏢

Wilshire Blvd

33 ●

Selby Ave

Glendon Ave

21 ●

Westwood Blvd

Ohio Ave

Malcolm Ave

2

🏢 5

Santa Monica Blvd

Santa Monica Blvd

**6**

58 🏢

S Vicente Blvd

S Sepulveda Blvd

Veteran Ave

Westwood
Park

Westwood Blvd

To American
Automobile Association
(0.3mi); Nuart (0.5mi);
Odyssey Theatre (0.75mi)

To Rhino Records (0.1mi);
Gyu-Kaku (1mi); La Serenata
de Garibaldi (1mi); Westside
Pavilion (1mi)

43 🏢

6 @

To British Consulate (0.1mi);
Dutch Consulate (0.1mi); Italian
Consulate (0.8mi); New Zealand
Consulate (0.8mi)

To Nuart
Theatre (0.5mi)

**INFORMATION**

| | |
|---|---|
| Associated Foreign Exchange.1 | B2 |
| Australian Consulate.............2 | E6 |
| Beverly Hills Conference & | |
| Visitors Bureau...................3 | F5 |
| Beverly Hills Library.............4 | B1 |
| French Consulate.................5 | B6 |
| Rooms Café.......................6 | C6 |
| TravelEx..........................7 | B2 |
| UCLA Medical Center.............8 | C5 |
| Women's Clinic..................9 | F6 |

71

## SIGHTS & ACTIVITIES (pp58–134)
24 Hour Fitness....................................(see 9)
Anderton Court...........................................10 B2
Beverly Hills High School............................11 E5
Church of the Good Shepherd.....................12 A2
City Hall......................................................13 B1
Franklin D Murphy Sculpture Garden...........14 C4
Mann Bruin Theatre.....................................15 B5
Mann Village Theatre...................................16 B5
Mildred E Mathias Botanical Garden............17 C5
Museum of Television & Radio....................18 B2
Museum of Tolerance..................................19 F6
O'Neill House..............................................20 A1
Pierce Bros Westwood Memorial Park...........21 C5
Royce Quad.................................................22 C4
UCLA Fowler Museum of Cultural History.23 C4
UCLA Hammer Museum...............................24 C5
UCLA Hannah Carter Japanese Garden.........25 C3
Virginia Robinson Gardens...........................26 C3
Westlake School for Girls.............................27 C3

## SLEEPING (pp142–4)
Avalon Hotel...............................................28 F5
Best Western Beverly Pavilion......................29 C2
Beverly Hills Hotel.......................................30 E3
Beverly Hills Reeves Hotel............................31 C2
Beverly Terrace Hotel...................................32 G4
Century Wilshire Hotel.................................33 C5
Crescent......................................................34 B1
Hilgard House Hotel.....................................35 C5
Hotel Bel-Air...............................................36 C3
Le Meridien.................................................37 H4
Luxe Hotel Sunset Boulevard.......................38 A4
Maison 140.................................................39 E5
Mosaic Hotel...............................................40 E5
Regent Beverly Wilshire................................41 B2
St Regis Los Angeles...................................42 E6

## EATING (pp156–8)
Ambala Dhaba............................................43 C6
Cheesecake Factory.....................................44 B2
Crustacean.................................................45 A2
Gyu-Kaku...................................................46 H5
Il Cielo.......................................................47 G4
Il Pastaio....................................................48 B1
Le Pain Quotidien.......................................49 A2
Mako..........................................................50 B2
Matsuhisa...................................................51 H5
McCormick & Schmick's..............................52 B2
Mulberry Street Pizzeria..............................53 F5
Natalee Thai Cusine....................................54 H5
Nate 'n Al's................................................55 B2
Native Foods...............................................56 C5
Real Food Daily.......................................(see 53)
Restaurant..............................................(see 32)
Spago Beverly Hills......................................57 C2
Sunnin Lebanese Cafe.............................(see 43)
Taiko..........................................................58 A6
Tanino........................................................59 C5
Tengu.........................................................60 C5
Trattoria Amici........................................(see 32)
Urth Caffe...................................................61 F5
Versailles....................................................62 H6
Zen Grill & Sake Lounge..............................63 B5

## ENTERTAINMENT (pp171–82)
Cecchi Gori Fine Arts Theatre.....................64 H5
Joint...........................................................65 H6
Pauley Pavilion...........................................66 B5
Royce Hall..................................................67 C4

## SHOPPING (pp182–92)
Beverly Center............................................68 H4
Cartier........................................................69 B2
Cartier........................................................70 B2

Cheese Store of Beverly Hills.......71 B2
Farmers Market (Beverly
    Hills).......................................72 G4
Farmers Market (Westwood).......73 C5
Harry Winston.............................74 B2
Le Palais des Thés......................75 B2
Tiffany.......................................76 B2
Under G's...................................77 A2
Van Cleef & Arpels......................78 B2
Westfield Shoppingtown
    Century City............................79 E5

## STARS' HOMES
Aaron Spelling Estate...............80 D4
Barbra Streisand House............81 D3
Bugsy Siegel House..................82 E4
Burt Reynolds House................83 D3
Clara Bow House.....................84 A1
Clark Gable House....................85 D3
Diane Keaton House.................86 D3
Elvis Presley House...................87 D3
Errol Flynn House.....................88 C3
George Harrison House.........(see 83)
Gregory Peck House.................89 D3
Ira & George Gershwin
    House...................................90 D3
Jack Benny House.....................91 E3
Johnny Weissmuller Estate.......92 C3
Lana Turner House....................93 E4
Lucille Ball House.....................94 E3
Peter 'Colombo' Falk House......95 E3
Playboy Mansion......................96 D4
Reagan Compound...................97 C3
Rod Stewart House...................98 D3
Stan Laurel House.....................99 E4
Steve Martin House.................100 E4
Walt Disney Estate..................101 D3

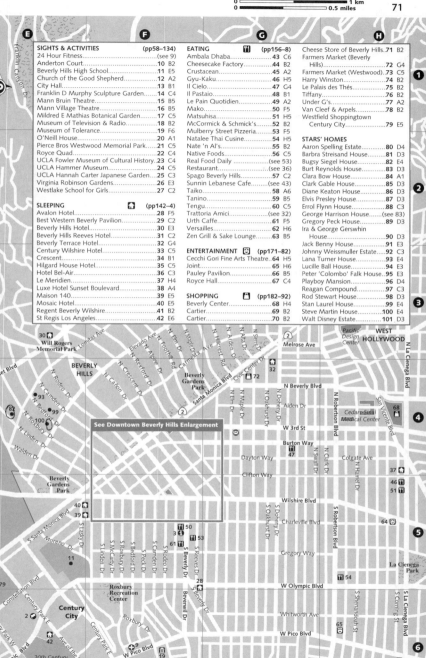

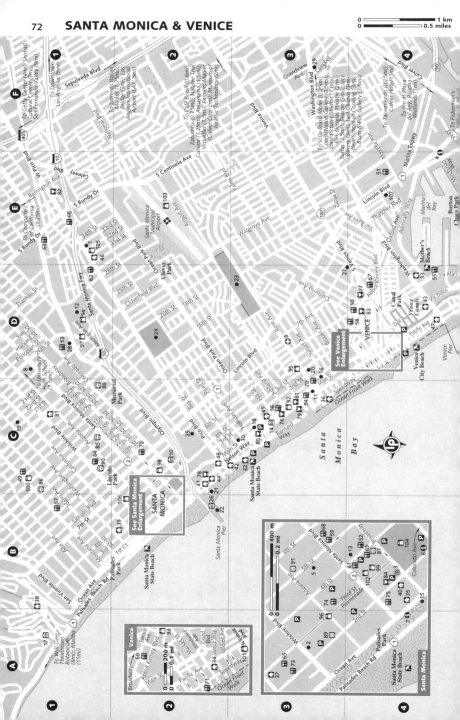

0        1 km
0       0.5 miles

**SIGHTS & ACTIVITIES** (pp99–100)
| | |
|---|---|
| Hermosa Beach Historical Museum............................1 | B3 |
| Roundhouse Marine Studies Lab & Aquarium......................2 | A2 |
| Seaside Lagoon..........................3 | B4 |

**SLEEPING** (pp147–8)
| | |
|---|---|
| Beach House at Hermosa............4 | A4 |
| Best Western Sunrise Hotel........5 | B4 |
| Hawthorn Suites.......................6 | B2 |
| Hotel Hermosa........................7 | B3 |
| Sea Sprite Motel & Apartments...8 | A4 |
| Sea View Inn..........................9 | A1 |
| Surf City Hostel.....................10 | A4 |

**EATING** (p162)
| | |
|---|---|
| Backburner Cafe.....................11 | A4 |
| Beach Hut No 2......................12 | A4 |
| Bluewater Grill.......................13 | B4 |
| Chez Mélange........................14 | C6 |
| El Sombrero...........................15 | A6 |
| Gina Lee's Bistro....................16 | B6 |
| Green Temple........................17 | A6 |
| Mamma D's...........................18 | A6 |
| Spot......................................19 | A5 |
| Uncle Bill's Pancake House.......20 | A5 |
| Versailles..............................21 | B2 |
| Zazou...................................22 | B6 |

**DRINKING** (p170)
| | |
|---|---|
| 705 Bar................................23 | A4 |
| Aloha Sharkeez......................24 | A4 |
| Baja Sharkeez.......................25 | A1 |
| Mangiamo............................26 | A6 |
| Side Door.............................27 | A6 |

**ENTERTAINMENT** (pp171–82)
| | |
|---|---|
| Cafe Boogaloo......................28 | A4 |
| Comedy & Magic Club.............29 | A4 |
| Lighthouse Cafe....................30 | A4 |

**SHOPPING** (pp182–92)
| | |
|---|---|
| Bristol Farms........................31 | B1 |
| Farmers Market (Hermosa Beach)...............................32 | B3 |
| Whole Foods Market..............33 | B4 |

**OTHER**
| | |
|---|---|
| Chez School of Food & Wine....(see 14) | |

Hermosa Beach
0    150    300 m
0    150    300 yards

Manhattan Beach
0    150    300 m
0    150    300 yards

0 ___ 1 km
0 ___ 0.5 miles

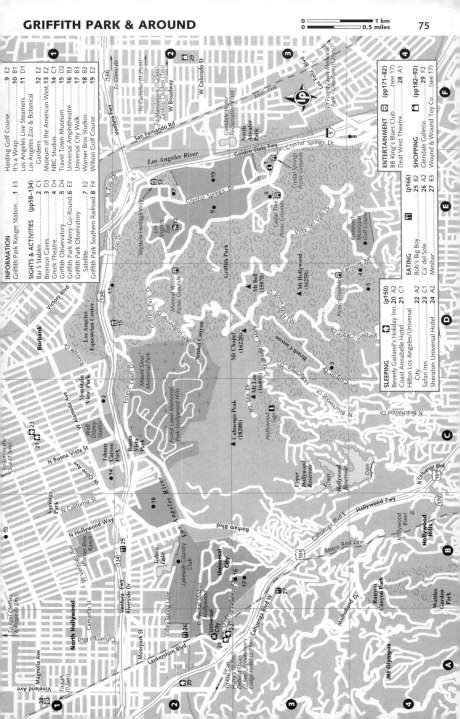

0 | 1 km
0 | 0.5 miles

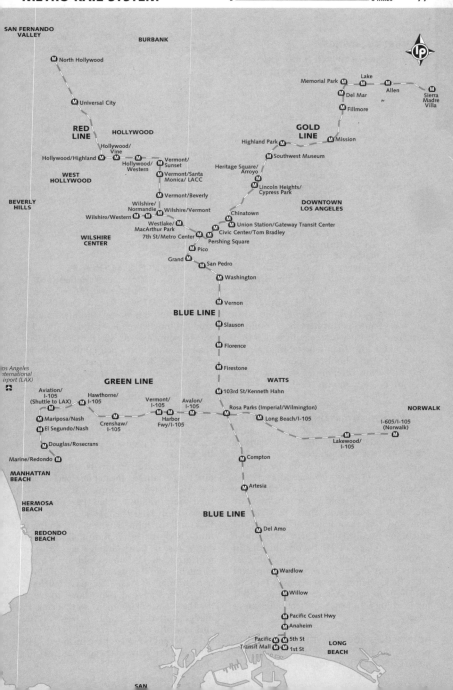

## TICKET TO SAVINGS

The **Hollywood CityPass** (www.citypass.com; adult/child 3-9 $72/49) is a coupon booklet offering one-time admission to Universal Studios, three attractions along Hollywood Blvd (Hollywood Museum, Hollywood Entertainment Museum and Kodak Theatre) and a narrated city bus tour with Starline Tours (p135). The pass is available online or from any of the places mentioned, and will save you about 40% off full admission. The roster of venues participating in this scheme changes periodically, so check the website for updated information.

than 2000 artists of film, recording, TV, radio and live performance have received their own marble-and-bronze star embedded in the Hollywood Blvd sidewalk. Look for them in the stretch between La Brea Ave and Gower St and along Vine St between Yucca St and Sunset Blvd. Actress Joanne Woodward was the first to be honored in this way. Some performers have multiple stars, one for each category in which they made a name for themselves. Singing cowboy Gene Autry holds a record five stars. New induction ceremonies still take place once or twice a month. Call ☎ 323-489-8311 for details.

### HOLLYWOOD ENTERTAINMENT MUSEUM

The history and mystery of movie-making are unmasked at this high-tech **museum** ( ☎ 323-465-7900; www.hollywoodmuseum.com; 7021 Hollywood Blvd; adult/student $10/5; ☼ 10am-6pm daily late May–early Sep, 11am-6pm Thu-Sun mid-Sep–mid-May), tucked away in the basement of the tacky Galaxy mall. The main attractions here are the original sets from *Star Trek, The X-Files* and *Cheers,* which you'll see at the end of the 'Studio Tour.' This is after you've watched a video of Hollywood history in a nutshell and walked by props and costumes from *Forrest Gump, Ben Hur* and other flicks. Before you're released into the gift shop, you get to have some interactive fun learning about special effects and sound effects.

### HOLLYWOOD ROOSEVELT HOTEL

Elegant Spanish Colonial architecture, rich history and delicious gossip rendezvous at this venerable **hotel** ( ☎ 323-466-7000; www.hollywoodroosevelt.com; 7000 Hollywood Blvd; admission free; ☼ 24hr), a Hollywood fixture since 1927. An instant hit with celebrities, it hosted the world's first Academy Awards (then called the Merit Awards) in 1929. F Scott Fitzgerald, Salvador Dalí and other heavy hitters enjoyed jazz and cabaret at its Cinegrill in the '30s. A few years later, Marilyn Monroe shot her first commercial (for toothpaste) by the pool, which was later decorated by British artist David Hockney. Actor Montgomery Clift, who stayed here while filming *From Here to Eternity,* apparently never left: his ghost can still be heard playing the bugle. The Roosevelt has also been featured in many movies, including *Almost Famous* and *Catch Me If You Can.* If you want to stay here, see p140.

### GRAUMAN'S CHINESE THEATRE

The world's most famous **movie theater** ( ☎ 323-463-9576; www.manntheatres.com; 6925 Hollywood Blvd) opened in 1927 with Cecil B DeMille's *King of Kings* and has hosted innumerable star-studded movie premieres and, in the 1940s, the Academy Awards. Movie mogul Sid Grauman personally dreamed up the flamboyant red pagoda design complete with dragons and stone lions to keep the evil spirits away.

You can see the exotic interior by buying a movie ticket (p173) or by joining one of the half-hour tours (adult/child/senior $12/8/8) that take place throughout the day, except during premiere days. Buy tickets at the gift store.

Most Tinseltown tourists, though, gravitate to the famous **theater forecourt** (admission free; ☼24hr), where legions of stars have left their footprints in cement. Few people can resist comparing their shoe size to Mary Pickford's or John Wayne's, or looking for other body parts, including Jimmy Durante's nose or Betty Grable's legs. Also immortalized are Whoopi Goldberg's braids, Groucho Marx' cigar and Harold Lloyd's wire-frame glasses. Douglas Fairbanks Snr, Mary Pickford (who both co-owned the theater with Grauman) and Norma Talmadge started the tradition back in 1927 and box-office superstars still get the nod today. Recent honorees have included Al Pacino, Arnold Schwarzenegger and Michael Douglas.

## HOLLYWOOD & HIGHLAND

Grauman's Chinese Theatre is literally dwarfed by this vast **shopping and entertainment complex** (☎ 323-467-6412; www.hollywoodandhighland.com; 6801 Hollywood Blvd; admission free; 🕑 24hr), a perfect marriage of kitsch and commerce, and the spark plug for the boulevard's rebirth. Its main feature is the circular outdoor **Babylon Court**, whose huge freestanding triumphal arch frames views of the Hollywood Sign. A pair of pompous pachyderms perched on lofty pedestals lord it over the scene, which was inspired by the set of DW Griffith's 1916 movie *Intolerance*. Decorating the pavement is the **Road to Hollywood**, a series of actual quotes from people who have 'made it' in the Industry. The restaurants and shops here are mostly of the chain variety, with the exception of Wolfgang Puck's Vert (p152).

The complex also houses the **Kodak Theatre** (☎ 323-308-6363; www.kodaktheatre.com; tour adult/child/student/senior $15/10/10/10; 🕑 10:30am-2:30pm), which opened in 2001 and has been the permanent home of the Academy Awards show and other glitzy events ever since. The pricey 30-minute tour takes you into the auditorium, the VIP room and past an actual Oscar statuette.

## EL CAPITAN THEATRE

One look at **El Capitan** (☎ 323-467-7674; 6838 Hollywood Blvd), across the street from Hollywood & Highland, and you'll know why they used to call them 'movie palaces.' Beautifully restored by Disney, Hollywood's most glamorous film venue pairs an ornate Spanish Colonial facade with a richly flamboyant East Indian interior. Built for live performances in 1926, it made its movie-house debut in 1941 with the premiere of *Citizen Kane*. The vast auditorium with triple glitter curtains is still a special place to see films, which are often preceded by live show extravaganzas (p172).

## HOLLYWOOD MUSEUM

This is one of the newer **museums** (☎ 323-464-7776; www.thehollywoodmuseum.com; 1660 N Highland Ave; adult/student/senior $15/12/12; 🕑 10am-5pm Thu-Sun) in town, and it's a good one. Time-travel through Hollywood history as you survey a century's worth of props, costumes, photos, posters, scripts and various memorabilia from a galaxy of stars – Marilyn Monroe to Fred Astaire, Russell Crowe to Leonardo DiCaprio. Hannibal Lecter's jail cell from *Silence of the Lambs* is on display, as are sets from *Moulin Rouge* and *Gladiator*. It's all housed in a glorious art deco building where make-up pioneer Max Factor once worked his magic on the stars. His famous 'For Blondes Only' and 'For Brunettes Only' make-up rooms are also part of the museum's collection.

## RIPLEY'S BELIEVE IT OR NOT!

Life's pretty strange and it'll feel stranger after you've visited the *über*-bizarre **Ripley's** (☎ 323-466-6335; www.ripleys.com; 6780 Hollywood Blvd; adult/child $12/8; 🕑 10am-11pm Sun-Thu, 10am-midnight Fri & Sat), where exhibits range from the merely gross to the grotesque. Expect to find shrunken human heads, a sculpture of Marilyn Monroe made from shredded $1 bills, a bikini woven from human hair and a figure of a man with a 4ft crowbar stuck through his head. The place is easy to spot: just look for the plastic T-rex with a clock between its fangs seemingly bursting from building's rooftop. The clock, by the way, runs backwards.

## GUINNESS WORLD OF RECORDS MUSEUM

You know the deal: this **museum** (☎ 323-462-8860; 6764 Hollywood Blvd; adult/child/senior $11/7/8.50; 🕑 10am-midnight Sun-Thu, 10am-2am Fri & Sat) is all about the fastest, tallest, biggest, fattest and other superlatives. Perhaps more interesting is the building itself, which once housed Hollywood's oldest thespian venue, the 1913 Idle Hour Theater. Combination tickets with the wax museum (see following) are $16/9/14 per adult/child/senior.

## HOLLYWOOD WAX MUSEUM

No celebrities around to snare your stare? Don't fret: fantasy can be reality at this **museum** (☎ 323-462-5991; www.hollywoodwax.com; 6767 Hollywood Blvd; adult/child/senior $11/7/8.50; 🕑 10am-midnight Sun-Thu, 10am-1am Fri & Sat). At this campy haven of kitsch you can gawk at life-size waxen likenesses of showbiz greats, athletes, presidents and even Jesus. If you feel you must visit both this and the Guinness World of Records Museum (see previous), you can save with a combination ticket (adult/child/senior $16/9/14).

## EGYPTIAN THEATRE

When the **Egyptian** (☎ 323-466-3456; www.egyptiantheatre.com; 6712 Hollywood Blvd) opened in 1922 as Hollywood's first movie theater, it rang the death knell for Downtown's Broadway Theater District (p110). Its lavish getup, complete with sunburst ceiling, hieroglyphs and sphinx heads, capitalized on the craze for all things Egyptian, which was sparked by the discoveries of archaeologist Howard Carter (coincidentally, it opened just mere days before Carter stumbled upon King Tut's tomb). In its heyday, the theater had live caged monkeys and usherettes clad in Cleopatra-style garb.

The Egyptian got a royal makeover in the late 1990s when it became the permanent home of American Cinematheque, a non-profit film organization. On weekends it usually presents **Forever Hollywood** (adult/student/senior $9/8/8; ☼ 2pm & 3:30pm Sat & Sun), a one-hour documentary about Hollywood history. Behind-the-scenes tours (adult/child under 12/senior $7/5/5) take place sporadically. For film screenings, see p173.

### EROTIC MUSEUM
OK, let's make no bones about it: this **museum** ( ☎ 323-463-7684; 6741 Hollywood Blvd; adult/student/senior $13/10/10; ☼ noon-9pm Sun-Thu, noon-midnight Fri & Sat) is all about sex. Whether its displays are also erotic is entirely up to you. Actual exhibits change periodically but current examples are a crude movie showing porn legend John Holmes in action, images of Marilyn Monroe in the buff and erotic etchings by Pablo Picasso. Upstairs you could reach inside a Plexiglass cube for a little 'hands-on' fun with plastic replicas of male and female sex organs. Elsewhere the raw homoerotic images of Tom of Finland and the more tender works of Julian Murphy were displayed. Check the website for current exhibits.

### MUSSO & FRANK GRILL
Hollywood Blvd may be making a comeback, but for a time warp back to its original golden era, pop into **Musso & Frank Grill** ( ☎ 323-467-7788; 6667 Hollywood Blvd), Tinseltown's longest operating restaurant (since 1919). Charlie Chaplin used to knock back vodka gimlets at the bar, while literati such as William Faulkner and Raymond Chandler used the high-backed booths as a second office. The no-nonsense food (see p153), classic cocktails and noir ambience still lure a catalog of celebs – from the Rolling Stones to Woody Allen – to this day.

### FREDERICK'S OF HOLLYWOOD LINGERIE MUSEUM
If stars' undies get you all hot and bothered, drop into this saucy **exhibit** ( ☎ 323-466-8506; 6608 Hollywood Blvd; admission free; ☼ 10am-6pm Mon-Sat, noon-5pm Sun) in the back of Frederick's of Hollywood, the legendary purveyor of panties, push-up bras and garter belts since 1947 (p186). Actual displays rotate but may include such gems as Madonna's tasseled bustier, Phyllis Diller's training bra, 'Forrest Gump' boxer shorts and bras worn by Tony Curtis and Milton Berle.

### HOLLYWOOD & VINE
The intersection of Hollywood Blvd and Vine St became famous in the 1920s as the hub of the entertainment industry, surrounded by studios, radio stations and the Academy of Motion Picture Arts and Sciences. In 2003 it was named Bob Hope Square in honor of the entertainer's 100th birthday.

Although Hope died a few weeks later, he outlived most of the original structures that once stood here. One exception is the 1956 **Capitol Records Tower** (www.hollywoodandvine .com; 1750 N Vine St), the world's first circular office building. Designed by Welton Becket, it resembles a stack of records topped by a stylus. Across the street, the 1926 art deco **Palace Theatre** (1735 N Vine St) was built for the stage but later hosted such TV shows as Groucho Marx' *You Bet Your Life* and *The Merv Griffin Show*. It's now the Avalon (p178), a glam nightclub.

Back on Hollywood Blvd, a few yards east of Vine, the 1930 **Pantages Theatre** ( ☎ 323-468-1770; www.nederlander.com; 6233 Hollywood Blvd) has been restored to its glamorous art deco glory. Oscars were handed out here from 1949 to 1959, followed by the Emmys in the 1970s. These days, the Pantages is the city's prime venue for musical and Broadway blockbusters (see p179).

### SUNSET BOULEVARD
A short walk south on Vine St takes you to Sunset and Vine, where the glitzy new **Hollywood Marketplace** mall hopes to ride on the coattails of Hollywood & Highland's success. Next door, looking like a giant golf ball sliced in half, is the 1963 **Cinerama Dome** built to screen 'Cinerama' movies, an early wide-screen format that never caught on. It's now part of **ArcLight** (p172), a state-of-the-

art movie-theater complex that's a favorite with Industry types. A bit further west, the epic **Amoeba Records** (p189) lures music fans with its baffling collection of vinyl and CDs and free live concerts.

Continuing west takes you past the 1923 **Hollywood Athletic Club** (6525 W Sunset Blvd), where Rudolph Valentino, John Wayne and other hunks once swam laps and pumped iron, to the 1936 Streamline Moderne **Crossroads of the World** (6671 W Sunset Blvd). Built as one of LA's first malls, it has an eye-catching nautical theme and now houses offices.

Past Highland Ave **Hollywood High School** (1521 N Highland Ave) stretches for an entire block. It has an impressive roster of alumni and nice architecture for a public school.

### HOLLYWOOD SIGN

LA's endless list of publicity seekers included real estate developer Harry Chandler. Back in 1923, Chandler put up 50ft-tall sheet-metal letters spelling out 'Hollywoodland' on the southern slope of Mt Lee to draw attention to his latest venture. The last four letters later disappeared but the remainder became LA's most famous landmark, the **Hollywood Sign**. Once aglow with 4000 light bulbs, the sign even had its own caretaker who lived behind the 'L' until 1939.

In 1932 a young actress named Peggy Entwistle, despondent over her dead-end career, leapt her way from the 'H' into Hollywood lore. In subsequent decades the sign crumbled along with the rest of Hollywood until a celebrity-studded effort restored it to its former glory in 1978.

It's illegal to hike up to the sign, but there are many places where you can catch good views, including Hollywood & Highland (p79), the top of Beachwood Dr and the Griffith Park observatory (p118).

### HOLLYWOOD FOREVER CEMETERY

Some of the best-known and beloved Hollywood stars have found their final rest in this **cemetery** (☎ 323-469-1181; www.hollywoodforever.com; 6000 Santa Monica Blvd; 🕑 8am-6pm), which is filled with magnificent tombstones, monuments and two mausoleums. Come here to pay your respects to silent-era heartthrob Rudolph Valentino; Tyrone Power, who

### FAMOUS ALUMNI

Want to find out where your favorite celeb studied algebra and French? Visit any of the following high schools, community colleges and universities.

**Beverly Hills High School** (Map pp70-1; 241 S Moreno Dr, Beverly Hills) Nicolas Cage, Jamie Lee Curtis, Richard Dreyfuss, Angelina Jolie, Lenny Kravitz, Monica Lewinsky, Rob Reiner, David Schwimmer, Betty White

**Fairfax High** (Map pp68-9; 7850 Melrose Ave, Mid-City) David Arquette, Flea (of Red Hot Chili Peppers), Al Franken, Demi Moore, Slash (of Guns N' Roses)

**Hollywood High School** (Map pp66-7; 1521 N Highland Ave, Hollywood) Carol Burnett, Judy Garland, James Garner, Barbara Hershey, John Ritter, Jason Robards, Mickey Rooney

**Immaculate Heart High** (Map pp66-7; 5515 Franklin Ave, Hollywood) Tyra Banks, Natalie Cole, Mary Tyler Moore

**Marshall High** (Map pp66-7; 3939 Tracy St, Silver Lake) Leonardo DiCaprio

**Palisades High** (Map pp60-1; 15777 Boudoin St, Pacific Palisades) Jeff Bridges, Christie Brinkley, Katey Segal

**Polytechnic High** (Map pp62-3; 1600 Atlantic Ave, Long Beach) Cameron Diaz, Snoop Doggy Dog, Marilyn Horne, Spike Lee

**Santa Monica College** (Map pp72-3; 1900 Pico Blvd, Santa Monica) Buzz Aldrin, James Dean, Dustin Hoffman, Arnold Schwarzenegger, Hillary Swank

**Santa Monica High School** (Map pp72-3; 601 Pico Blvd, Santa Monica) Glenn Ford, Robert Downey Jr, Rob Lowe, Sean Penn, Charlie Sheen

**University High School** (off Map pp72-3; 11800 Texas Ave, near Santa Monica) Jeff Bridges, James Brolin, Bridget Fonda, Marilyn Monroe, Randy Newman, Nancy Sinatra, Elizabeth Taylor, Tone Loc

**University of California, Los Angeles** (UCLA; Map pp70-1; 405 Hilgard Ave, Westwood) Carol Burnett, James Dean, Francis Ford Coppola, Heather Locklear, Jim Morrison, Tim Robbins

**University of Southern California** (USC; off Map pp64-5; 3535 S Figueroa Street, South Central) Neil Armstrong, Frank Gehry, Ron Howard, George Lucas, Tom Selleck, OJ Simpson, John Wayne, Robert Zemeckis

**Westlake School for Girls** (now Harvard-Westlake; Map pp70-1; 700 N Faring Rd, Bel Air) Candice Bergen, Bridget Fonda, Tracy Nelson, Sally Ride, Shirley Temple

died while filming a dueling scene in Madrid; Jayne Mansfield, who literally lost her head in a car accident; John Huston, whose last film was an adaptation of James Joyce's *The Dead*; and many more superstars. The two Douglas Fairbanks (Sr and Jr) lie side-by-side in a grand memorial tomb by a reflecting pool, while gangster Bugsy Siegel is interred in the cemetery's Jewish section. To help you find your favorite stars, pick up a map ($5) at the **flower shop** ( 9am-5pm) near the entrance. Staff also run monthly tours ($10) and the Cinespia outdoor film series (see p173). Call or check the website for upcoming events.

### HOLLYWOOD BOWL & AROUND

A favorite summer performance venue, the **Hollywood Bowl** ( ☎ 323-850-2000; www.hollywood bowl.com; 2301 Highland Ave; late Jun-Sep) was built within a natural amphitheater known as Daisy Dell and has delighted music fans since 1922. Lloyd Wright, Frank's son, added a concert shell a couple of years later but thanks to poor acoustics it was tinkered with repeatedly until a new one was finally built in 2004. The sound is now better than ever, the stage is big enough for a full orchestra, and several large projection screens give the folks in the cheap seats (from $1) a chance to see what's happening onstage. The bowl is the summer home of the Los Angeles Philharmonic (p178) and also hosts big-name rock, jazz and blues acts. Many concertgoers come an hour or two early to enjoy a pre-show picnic on the parklike grounds or in their seats (alcohol is allowed). There are several concessions if you don't want to bring your own food.

For insight into the place's storied history visit the **Hollywood Bowl Museum** ( ☎ 323-850-2058; www.hollywoodbowl.com/event/museum.cfm; 2301 N Highland Ave; admission free; 10am-showtime Mon-Sat & 4pm-showtime Sun late Jun–mid-Sep, 10am-4:30pm Tue-Sat mid-Sep–late Jun).

Just across Hwy 101 from the bowl is the **John Anson Ford Theatre** ( ☎ 323-461-3673; 2580 E Cahuenga Blvd; May-Oct), another beloved, but much smaller, outdoor venue where no seat is more than 96ft from the stage. It presents a far-ranging program of music, dance and theater from around the world.

While here also pop into the **Hollywood Heritage Museum** ( ☎ 323-874-2276; 2100 N Highland Ave; adult/child/senior $3/1/1; 11am-4pm Sat & Sun)

just south of the bowl. It's inside the horse barn used by Cecil B DeMille in 1913 and 1914 to shoot *The Squaw Man,* Hollywood's first feature-length film. Inside are exhibits on early filmmaking, including costumes, projectors and cameras as well as a replica of DeMille's office.

### BARNSDALL ART PARK

This sprawling **park** (4800 Hollywood Blvd) is the legacy of oil heiress Aline Barnsdall (1882–1946), who came to LA from Chicago in 1915 with grand ideas for an experimental theater community. Frank Lloyd Wright drafted the plans but only three of the structures were ever built, including the beautiful **Hollyhock House** ( ☎ 323-644-6269; www.hollyhock house.net), today considered an early Wright masterpiece. It marks his first attempt at creating an indoor-outdoor living space in harmony with LA's sunny climate, a style he later referred to as California Romanza. To please his client, Wright integrated depictions of the hollyhock, Barnsdall's favorite flower, throughout the structure.

In 1927 Barnsdall abandoned her idea and donated the complex to the city of LA with the proviso that it become a public art park, which it did. Today, the **Junior Arts Center** ( ☎ 323-644-6275) offers low-cost art classes for children, while work by grown-up LA artists is on display at the **Municipal Art Gallery** ( ☎ 323-644-6269; admission free; noon-5pm Wed-Sun). The Hollyhock House itself has been under renovation for years, although **tours** (adult/student/senior $5/3/3) of the exterior are currently offered hourly from 12:30pm to 3:30pm on weekends and by appointment Wednesday through Friday. Free maps for self-guided tours are available at the Municipal Art Gallery, which also has daily screenings of a documentary about the history and restoration of Hollyhock House.

The park sits smack dab on the southern edge of Los Feliz in Little Armenia. For a casual Middle Eastern meal, you can try the nearby eateries Zankou Chicken (p166) and Carousel (p152).

### ENNIS-BROWN HOUSE & LOVELL HOUSE

Fans of Frank Lloyd Wright should also make a beeline to the spectacular **Ennis-Brown House** ( ☎ 323-660-0607; www.ennisbrownhouse.org; 2607 Glendower Ave; adult/child 8-12/student/senior $20/10/15/15; tours 11am & 1:30pm Tue, Thu & Sat), about 1 mile north of Barnsdall Art Park. It is one of four 'textile block' houses – inspired by Mayan architecture – Wright built in LA. Tours are by reservation only.

Wright influenced any number of architects, including Austrian immigrant Richard Neutra who achieved international stardom with the nearby **Lovell House** (4616 Dundee Dr). It was prominently featured in the movie *LA Confidential* but is unfortunately closed to the public.

## West Hollywood                    Map pp68–9

West Hollywood (WeHo) is an independent city that, despite its diminutive size of 1.9 sq miles, packs more personality than most larger hoods. It is the heart of gay and lesbian life in LA (see p84), the center of Southern California's design community, and the adopted home of about 6000 immigrants from the former Soviet Union who've turned eastern WeHo into 'little Russia.' LA's fabled nightlife artery, the Sunset Strip, also passes through.

During the day, you'll find two hours of free parking in the structure at 8383 Santa Monica Blvd; additional hours are $1.50 and after 6pm they charge a flat fee of $3. The PDC parking structure in the 800 block of San Vicente Blvd charges $4 per entry. Street parking is heavily restricted. WeHo is also served by the DASH bus (p195).

### SUNSET STRIP

The stretch of Sunset Blvd between Laurel Canyon Blvd and Doheny Dr has been a favorite nighttime playground since the 1920s. The hotel Chateau Marmont (p142) and clubs such as Ciro's (now the Comedy Store; p180), Mocambo and Trocadero (both now defunct) were favorite hangouts of Hollywood high society. The '60s saw the opening of the Whisky-a-GoGo (p174), America's first discotheque, the birthplace of go-go dancing and a launchpad for the Doors, who were the club's house band in 1966. Nearby is the **Hyatt Hotel** (8401 W Sunset Blvd), which earned the moniker 'Riot House' in the '70s when it was a favorite with such rock royalty as Led Zeppelin. At one time, the band rented six floors and raced motorcycles in the hallways.

Today the strip is still nightlife central, although it's lost much of its cutting edge. It's a visual cacophony dominated by billboards and giant advertising banners draped across building facades. The Whisky's still there, as is the Hyatt, but they've been eclipsed by such places as the House of Blues (p174); the Mondrian (p141) hotel, a jet-set haunt and home of the *über*-trendy Sky Bar (p169); and the Viper Room (p175), where actor River Phoenix overdosed in 1993.

### PACIFIC DESIGN CENTER & AROUND

Design is big in WeHo, with around 130 trade-only showrooms at the **Pacific Design Center** (PDC; ☎ 310-657-0800; www.pacificdesigncenter .com; 8687 Melrose Ave; admission free; ☯ 9am-5pm Mon-Fri) alone and dozens more in the surrounding streets, the so-called **Avenues of Art & Design** (Beverly Blvd, Robertson Blvd and Melrose Ave). Thrown into the mix is a healthy smattering of galleries, restaurants and cafés. The PDC showrooms generally sell only to interior design pros, but if you've spotted a must-have, you might be able to get it at a mark-up through their Buying Service.

The PDC itself is an architectural landmark designed by Cesar Pelli in 1975 and nicknamed the 'Blue Whale' for its behemoth dimensions and shiny cobalt-blue glass facade. A green addition (we like to think of it as the 'green turtle') was added in 1988. The West Hollywood Convention & Visitors Bureau (p58) is on the mezzanine level.

Also here is **MOCA Pacific Design Center** ( ☎ 213-626-6222; www.moca.org; admission free; ☯ 11am-5pm Tue, Wed & Fri, 11am-8pm Thu, 11am-6pm Sat & Sun), a small satellite branch of Downtown's Museum of Contemporary Art (p108). Exhibits often focus on architecture and design themes.

### SCHINDLER HOUSE

The former **home and studio** ( ☎ 323-651-1510; www.makcenter.com; 835 N Kings Rd; admission $5, free 4-6pm Fri; ☯ 11am-6pm Wed-Sun) of Vienna-born architect Rudolph Schindler (1887–1953) is one of the most celebrated private modernist residences in LA. It's a prime example of what Schindler called 'space architecture,' inspired by California's sunny yet temperate climate. Its open floor plan, flat roof and glass sliding doors were considered avant-garde back in 1922, but became staples of California architecture after WWII. Tours are available on weekends, but you're free to look around at other times. Today it houses the MAK Center for Art and Architecture, a

## OUT & ABOUT IN LOS ANGELES

LA is one of the country's gayest cities with the rainbow flag flying especially proudly along Santa Monica Blvd in West Hollywood (WeHo). Dozens of high-energy bars, cafés, restaurants, gyms and clubs flank this strip, turning it pretty much into a 24/7 fun zone. Most places cater to gay men, although there's plenty going on for lesbians and mixed audiences as well. Beauty reigns supreme in 'Boystown' and the intimidation factor can be high unless you're buff, bronzed and styled. Elsewhere, the gay scenes are considerably more laid-back and less body-conscious. Silver Lake, another major romping ground, has a large leather and Levi's crowd and a few Latino bars. The beach towns, historically havens of queerness, have the most relaxed, neighborly scenes, especially in Santa Monica, Venice and Long Beach.

Freebie magazines containing up-to-date listings and news about the community are generally strewn about in bars, restaurants and gay-friendly establishments around town. **A Different Light** (Map pp68-9; ☎ 310-854-6601; 8853 Santa Monica Blvd, West Hollywood) is LA's bastion of queer literature, nonfiction and magazines. Staff are chatty and womyn welcome. The **LA Gay & Lesbian Center** (Map pp66-7; ☎ 323-993-7400; www.laglc.org; 1625 Schrader Blvd, Hollywood; 9am-8pm Mon-Fri, 9am-1pm Sat) is a one-stop service and health agency.

The festival season kicks off in late May with the **Long Beach Pride Celebration** (☎ 562-987-9191; www.longbeachpride.com), which basically serves as the warm-up for **LA Pride** (www.lapride.org), a three-day festival in mid-June with nonstop partying and a parade down Santa Monica Blvd. A few months later, on **Halloween** (October 31), the same street morphs into a veritable freak show bringing together tens of thousands of fancifully – and often erotically – costumed revelers of all sexual persuasions. For details about the **Outfest** film festival, see p172.

Fans of homoerotic art pioneer Touko Laaksonen, who is better known as Tom of Finland, should check out the small exhibit at the **Erotic Museum** (p80) in Hollywood or contact the **Tom of Finland Foundation** (☎ 213-250-1685; www.tomoffinland.com) for a tour of Tom's beautiful Craftsman Silver Lake one-time home, which today serves as the foundation headquarters and an art gallery.

If it's gay theater you want, check out what's on at the **Celebration Theatre** (Map pp68-9; ☎ 323-957-1884; www.celebrationtheatre.com; 7051 Santa Monica Blvd, West Hollywood), which ranks among the nation's leading producers of gay and lesbian plays, winning dozens of awards.

You can safely assume any WeHo hotel to be gay-friendly, although you shouldn't encounter problems elsewhere either. The **San Vicente Inn** (Map pp68-9; ☎ 310-854-6915, 800-577-6915; www.gayresort.com; 845 N San Vicente Blvd, West Hollywood; r $70-300; P) is LA's main men-only guesthouse. Rooms and cottages overlook a tropical garden, and frolicking zones include a hot tub, sauna, pool and sundeck.

### Bars & Clubs

**Abbey** (Map pp68-9; ☎ 310-289-8410; www.abbeyfoodandbar.com; 692 N Robertson Blvd, West Hollywood; mains $9-13; 8am-2am, breakfast to 2pm) From its beginnings as a humble coffeehouse, the Abbey has grown into WeHo's funnest, coolest and most varied club, bar and restaurant. There are so many flavored martinis that you'd think they were invented here, plus a full menu of pub grub and desserts (and yes, they still serve coffees). You can take your pick from many spaces which range from outdoor patio to chill room to your own private divan. On weekend nights, they're all busy.

**Factory/Ultra Suede** (Map pp68-9; ☎ 310-659-4551; www.factorynightclubla.com; 652 La Peer Dr, West Hollywood) This giant double club has an edgy New York feel and sports different stripes nightly. On Friday night, the Girl Bar (at the Factory) is the preferred playground of fashion-forward femmes, while male hot bods strut their stuff on Saturdays. Music-wise, anything goes here as long as it's got a good beat.

**Here Lounge** (Map pp68-9; ☎ 310-360-8455; www.herelounge.com; 696 N Robertson Blvd, West Hollywood) This is WeHo's premier venue for S&M (standing and modeling). It's chic and angular, with lots of smooth surfaces – and that goes for both the men *and* the setting. Thursday's Fuse night draws luscious lipstick lesbians.

**Rage** (Map pp68-9; ☎ 310-652-7055; 8911 Santa Monica Blvd, West Hollywood; ⊗ 11:30am-2am) This pulsating double-decker bar and dance club for boy pals has a rotating roster of DJs spinning house, R&B, hip-hop, funk and other sounds. There's no cover for Monday's Alternative Night, while 18+ Tuesdays bring in the younger set.

**Micky's** (Map pp68-9; ☎ 310-657-1176; 8857 Santa Monica Blvd, West Hollywood; ⊗ noon-2am) Not far from Rage, it's 'raining men' at this posing, preening and cruising club where nonstop high-energy dance music translates into an electric party atmosphere. Frequent drinks specials help break down any residual inhibitions.

**Palms** (Map pp68-9; ☎ 310-652-6188; 8572 Santa Monica Blvd, West Hollywood) This scene staple has been keeping lesbians happy for over three decades and even gets the occasional celebrity drop-in, as in Melissa Etheridge or Ellen DeGeneres. Beer is the beverage of choice and the Beer Bust Sundays are legendary.

**Roosterfish** (Map pp72-3; ☎ 310-392-2123; www.roosterfishbar.com; 1302 Abbot Kinney Blvd, Venice; ⊗ 11am-2am) This friendly neighborhood been-there-forever kind of bar still manages to stay current and cool. It's the type of place where you can strike up new friendships while playing pool, shooting electronic darts or nursing your drink. Friday is the busiest night, or go for the Sunday afternoon barbecue.

**Faultline** (Map pp66-7; ☎ 323-660-0889; 4216 Melrose Ave, Silver Lake; ⊗ 6pm-2am Tue-Fri, 2pm-2am Sat & Sun) This indoor-outdoor venue is party central for manly men with nary a twink in sight. Take off your shirt and head to the beer bust on Sunday afternoon (it's an institution), but get there early or expect a long wait.

**Akbar** (Map pp66-7; ☎ 323-665-6810; 4356 W Sunset Blvd, Silver Lake) Best jukebox in town, Casbah-style atmosphere, and a great mix of people that's been known to change from hour to hour – gay, straight, on the fence or just hip, but not too-hip-for-you.

**Dragstrip 66** ( ☎ 323-969-2596; www.dragstrip66.com; 1822 W Sunset Blvd, near Silver Lake; cover $15; ⊗ 2nd Sat of month) This monthly club has been packing them in since 1993. Themes change (from Halloween to Catholic school girls) but your host – fabulous drag queen Gina Lotrimin – doesn't. Super-DJ Paul V mans the decks. Only about 5% of patrons are in drag (and get discounted admission). This club, currently at the Echo (p178), moves around, so be sure to confirm the current location.

**Oil Can Harry's** (off Map p75; ☎ 818-760-9749; www.oilcanharrysla.com; 11502 Ventura Blvd, Studio City, San Fernando Valley; ⊗ Tue & Thu-Sat) If you've never been country-and-western dancing, you'll be surprised at just how sexy it can be, and Oil Can Harry's is the place to do it, three nights a week. On Tuesdays and Thursdays, it even offers lessons for the uninitiated. Saturday night is retro disco.

### Cafés & Restaurants

**French Quarter Market Place** (Map pp68-9; ☎ 323-654-0898; 7985 Santa Monica Blvd, West Hollywood; mains $5-13) This buzzy place with its endearing indoor-outdoor New Orleans–theme does belly-filling California cuisine – eclectic, healthful and heaps of it. Inside are a bunch of one-of-a-kind shops, including Baby Jane of Hollywood (p190).

**Hamburger Mary's** (mains $6-10) Long Beach (Map pp62-3; ☎ 562-983-7001; 740 E Broadway); West Hollywood (Map pp68-9; ☎ 323-654-3800; 8288 Santa Monica Blvd) This wonderfully over-the-top eatery puts everyone in a happy mood with its drinks specials, special events and casual menu (try the Proud Mary burger). The weekend brunches are great for getting in gear for the rest of the day. You won't even mind the bill: it's served in a stylish stiletto.

**Casita Del Campo** (Map pp66-7; ☎ 323-662-4255; 1920 Hyperion Ave, Silver Lake; mains lunch $7-8, dinner $12-14; ⊗ 11am-11pm; Ⓟ ) What's not to love about this Mexican cantina? It's airy, it's fun, and if you go on the right night there's a tiny theater downstairs where you might catch a drag show.

**Marix Tex Mex** (Map pp68-9; ☎ 323-656-8800; 1108 N Flores St, West Hollywood; mains $8-14) Year-in year-out, the open-air Marix has patios for strong margaritas and lots of meeting and greeting, plus decent-sized portions of some of WeHo's best-loved Mexican specialties.

think tank and study center funded by the Austrian Museum für Angewandte Kunst (MAK; Museum of Applied Arts). MAK sponsors numerous exhibitions, lectures, performances and workshops year-round.

### A+D MUSEUM

A + D = the **Architecture + Design Museum** ( ☎ 310-659-2445; 8560 W Sunset Blvd; admission free; 🕙 10am-6pm Mon-Sat, noon-6pm Sun), which moved to the Sunset Strip from Downtown LA in early 2004. Curators mount several exhibits a year, which spotlight individual architects, focus on design themes (eg automotive or aerospace design), or introduce new work by emerging architects.

## Mid-City                    Map pp68-9

Mid-City describes the area east of West Hollywood, south of Hollywood, west of Koreatown and north of I-10 (Santa Monica Fwy). Visitors gravitate to the **Fairfax District**, LA's principal orthodox Jewish neighborhood with Fairfax Ave as its main artery and the Farmers Market as its main attraction. Further south, along Wilshire Blvd, is the **Miracle Mile District**, which is home to several important museums, including the Los Angeles County Museum of Art (LACMA).

There's plenty of street parking and validated parking at the Farmers Market. The entire area is served by DASH shuttles on the Fairfax route (p195).

### FARMERS MARKET

Apples to zucchinis, you'll find these and then some at the landmark **Farmers Market** ( ☎ 323-933-9211; www.farmersmarketla.com; 6333 W 3rd St; admission free; 🕙 9am-9pm Mon-Fri, 9am-8pm Sat, 10am-7pm Sun), in business since 1934 when a handful of farmers started peddling produce from their truck beds. Casual and kid-friendly, it's a fun place to browse for all kinds of stuff, from candles to clothing, from crafts to foods from around the world. Once you're all loaded up, grab a coffee or sandwich (see p155 for recommendations) and settle down for some primo people-watching.

Since 2002 the market has been connected to the **Grove** ( ☎ 323-900-8080; www.thegrovela.com; 189 The Grove Dr; admission free; 🕙 24hr), an attractive outdoor shopping mall built around a central plaza with a musical fountain, which erupts in sound and light every half hour (nicest after dark). A historic trolley connects the Grove with the Farmers Market, but you might as well walk. For store hours at the Grove see p191.

North of here is **CBS Television City** ( ☎ 323-575-2624; www.cbs.com; 7800 Beverly Blvd), where game shows, talk shows, soap operas and other programs are taped, often before a live audience. If you'd like to be part of one, check with the Farmers Market office (near the clock tower on the market's north side) or the **CBS ticket office** ( 🕙 9am-5pm Mon-Fri) to see if free tickets are available.

### LOS ANGELES COUNTY MUSEUM OF ART (LACMA)

Huge, compelling, global – **LACMA** ( ☎ 323-857-6000; www.lacma.org; 5905 Wilshire Blvd; adult/child under 17/student/senior $9/free/5/5, admission free after 5pm & on 2nd Tue of the month; 🕙 noon-8pm Mon, Tue & Thu, noon-9pm Fri, 11am-8pm Sat & Sun) is justifiably regarded as one of the top art museums in the country. The vast collection spreads over five buildings, but it's all neatly organized by geography or period, so you can easily zero in on what interests you most. If your understanding of art is limited, rent an audio guide (adult $3, children aged five to 17 $1).

For masterpieces by Mary Cassatt, John Singer Sargent and Winslow Homer head to the **American Art** section in the Ahmanson Building. Also here is the **European collection** which offers a comprehensive survey of 800 years of painting and sculpture. Come here to feast your eyes on Rembrandt's *Raising of Lazarus* or Cézanne's *Sous-Bois*. On the same floor you can travel back in time to **ancient Egypt, Greece and Rome** or admire the collection of **Islamic treasures**, which includes glazed pottery, tile and glass from Iran and Turkey. For several millennia's worth of ceramics from **China**, plus paintings, lacquerware and a recreated Ming-period scholar's studio, head to the lower level.

**Japanese art** is housed in the museum's most beautiful building, the Pavilion for Japanese Art. Standout exhibits include precious miniature sculpture (called netsuke), woodblock prints from the Edo period (1615–1868) and lots of ceramics and textiles.

The Anderson Building hosts a revolving coterie of temporary exhibits and traveling shows as well as selections from LACMA's **modern and contemporary art** collection, which includes perennial crowd-pleasers Magritte, David Hockney and Anselm Kiefer. German expressionists are a particular strength with canvases by seminal artists George Grosz, Ernst Kirchner and Emil Nolde perfectly expressing 1920s angst.

**Photography** is based in the Hammer Building, with outstanding works by Ed Weston, Ansel Adams, Diane Arbus and the recently deceased Henri Cartier-Bresson. Paintings by Frida Kahlo, her husband Diego Rivera, Rufino Tamayo and other Mexican modernists have found a home in the **Latin American** galleries of LACMA West, a former department store a short walk west of the main museum complex. LACMA West closes at 5pm.

LACMA also organizes temporary exhibits and hosts high-caliber traveling shows. Besides great art, the museum also has a busy events calendar with regular film screenings, concerts and guided tours. Check the listings magazines (p172) or LACMA's website for what's on during your visit. A café and a formal restaurant provide sustenance.

### LA BREA TAR PITS & PAGE MUSEUM

Once upon a time, saber-toothed tigers, mammoths, dire wolves and other extinct critters prowled the land that is now LA. Many of them met their maker between 40,000 and 10,000 years ago in gooey tar bubbling up from deep below the surface along Wilshire Blvd. Animals wading into the sticky muck became entrapped and were condemned to a slow death by starvation or suffocation. Carnivorous mammals and birds, who hopped on to dying or dead animals hoping for an easy meal, found themselves stuck as well. And so it happened that La Brea Tar Pits, filled with the greatest variety of Ice Age plants and animals on earth, are among the world's most famous fossil sites.

Since excavations started in 1906, paleontologists have unearthed over one million fossilized skeleton parts, the most spectacular of which are displayed at the **Page Museum** ( ☎ 323-934-7243; www.tarpits.org; 5801 Wilshire Blvd; adult/child 5-12/student/senior $7/2/4.50/4.50; ❧ 9:30am-5pm Mon-Fri, 10am-5pm Sat & Sun). Excavations still continue in summer (usually July and August) when you can observe scientists at work in **Pit 91** (admission free; ❧ 10am-4pm Wed-Sun). At other times, they're fussing over bones in the glass-encased laboratory inside the museum itself, cleaning, identifying, cataloging and storing their discoveries. Outside the museum, a diorama of a life-

size mammoth family, whose patriarch has become entrapped in the ooze, dramatizes the animals' cruel fate.

### PETERSEN AUTOMOTIVE MUSEUM

LA's love affair with the automobile is celebrated at this **museum** ( ☎ 323-930-2277; www.petersen.org; 6060 Wilshire Blvd; adult/child 5-12/student/senior $10/3/5/5; ❧ 10am-6pm Tue-Sun), which is a treat even to those who can't tell a piston from a carburetor. The permanent exhibit on the ground floor takes you along a mock LA streetscape and back in time about 100 years. En route you'll learn how the city's growth has in many ways been shaped by the automobile. LA is also revealed as the birthplace of gas stations, billboards, strip malls, drive-in restaurants and drive-in movie theaters. Upstairs galleries feature changing exhibits – hot rods to race cars, classic cars to muscle cars, and vehicles used in movies or driven by celebrities. Children will gravitate to the Discovery Center on the 3rd floor where they can learn science by way of the automobile.

### CRAFT & FOLK ART MUSEUM

Founded in 1965 as the Egg and the Eye, a gallery-cum-omelette-parlor, this **museum** ( ☎ 323-937-4230; www.cafam.org; 5814 Wilshire Blvd; adult/child under 12/student/senior $3.50/free/2.50/2.50, admission free on 1st Wed of the month; ❧ 11am-5pm Wed-Sun) has evolved into a well-respected showcase of traditional folk art and handicrafts. Huge crowds turn out for its biennial International Festival of Masks, held in October (next one in 2005), with a parade, performances and workshops.

## Beverly Hills                    Map pp70–1

The mere mention of Beverly Hills conjures images of fame and wealth, which is reinforced by what is shown on film and TV. Fact is, the reality is not so different from the myth. Stylish and sophisticated, this is indeed where the well-heeled frolic. Opulent mansions flank manicured grounds on tree-shaded avenues, especially north of **Sunset Blvd**.

Beverly Hills' residential streets are great for driving around and getting lost. If you're into stargazing, you can follow the little tour in this book (p90), take a guided bus tour (p135) or buy a map to the stars' homes.

In the downtown area, several city-owned garages offer two hours of free parking, including one at 9510 Brighton Way. For two hours of free valet parking, head to the garage underneath Two Rodeo (enter from Dayton Way).

## RODEO DRIVE

Rodeo Dr is a three-block artery of style that ranks right up there with Tokyo's Ginza District and London's Bond St as one of the world's most glamorous and expensive shopping strips. This is where Prada, Gucci, Armani and Valentino trot out their glamorous fashions in sleek emporiums staffed by hotties as svelte as gazelles. It's pricey, pretentious and yet, somehow, oddly irresistible. Sauntering down one side of the street and up the other is still one of the quintessential LA experiences, even if most of us can only gawk at the goods.

Most people gravitate to **Two Rodeo** (cnr Rodeo Dr & Wilshire Blvd), a cobbled and attractively designed lane (1990) inspired by a Tuscan hillside village. Refuel at an outdoor café with great people-watching potential.

For Frank Lloyd Wright fans, there's the 1953 **Anderton Court** (322 N Rodeo Dr), a zany zigzag construction, although clearly not his best work. Also check out the 1988 **O'Neill House** (507 N Rodeo Dr), a few blocks north. It doesn't have a famous architect, but the free-form art nouveau structure in the tradition of Catalán master Antonio Gaudí is unarguably one of the most imaginative structures in Beverly Hills.

## MUSEUM OF TELEVISION & RADIO

Fancy watching the pilot of *Bonanza* or *Star Trek*? How about the Beatles' US debut on the *Ed Sullivan Show*? Or the moon landing? These and thousands more TV and radio broadcasts are only the click of a mouse away in this sparkling **facility** (MTR; ☎ 310-786-1000; www.mtr.org; 465 N Beverly Dr; suggested donation adult/child/student/senior $10/5/8/8; ☺ noon-5pm Wed-Sun), the younger sibling of a similar outfit in New York City.

The museum's amazing collection spans 75 years and includes everything from sports to sitcoms, documentaries to day soaps, and news reels to cartoons, all available for listening and viewing at private consoles. There's also a radio listening room with prerecorded programs and three galleries. Getty Center architect Richard Meier designed the crisp, gleaming white building.

The museum also runs daily screenings in its auditorium, seminars and the occasional live broadcast. Pick up a schedule at the information desk or call ☎ 310-786-1025.

## BEVERLY HILLS CIVIC CENTER AREA

Public buildings tend to be gray behemoths built with little money and even less imagination. Not so in Beverly Hills, whose **City Hall** (455 N Rexford Dr) looks as splendid and dignified as a royal palace. The 1932 Spanish Renaissance confection with its landmark tiled cupola is part of the modern, Mediterranean-style Civic Center complex, which is also home of the excellent Beverly Hills Library (p57). On the other side of Santa Monica Blvd, you can stroll or jog in the **Beverly Gardens Park**, a long and narrow band of green dotted with sculptures and a cactus garden. Near the latter is the Roman Catholic **Church of the Good Shepherd** ( ☎ 310-285-5425; 505 N Bedford Dr), Beverly Hills' oldest church (1923) and a favorite celebrity 'hitching post.' This was where Elizabeth Taylor wed Conrad 'Nicky' Hilton and Rod Stewart led Rachel Hunter down the aisle. Famous funerals have included those of Rudolph Valentino and Frank Sinatra.

## BEVERLY HILLS HOTEL

Featured on the cover of the Eagles' *Hotel California* album, the **Beverly Hills Hotel** ( ☎ 310-887-2887; 9641 Sunset Blvd) is as revered in LA as the countless Hollywood legends who have cavorted here (and still do). Affectionately known as the 'Pink Palace,' this swank hotel has served as unofficial hobnobbing headquarters of the power elite since 1912.

The Polo Lounge was a notorious post-chukker hangout of the lords of the polo crowd, including Darryl F Zanuck, Spencer Tracy and Will Rogers. Marlene Dietrich had her very own 7ft-by-8ft bed installed in Bungalow 11, and Howard Hughes, the billionaire recluse, went progressively off his nut during 30 years of delusional semi-residence here. Elizabeth Taylor bedded six of her eight husbands here in various bungalows. While filming *Let's Make Love,* Yves Montand and Marilyn Monroe were probably doing just that; Marilyn is also reported to have 'bungalowed' both JFK and RFK here as well.

By the '70s, the Pink Palace had lost its luster and the stars went elsewhere to frolic.

Then, in the early 1990s, the Sultan of Brunei took pity on the place and reportedly pumped almost $300 million into her rejuvenation. When she reopened in 1995, the grand dame had regained her blush, lurid wink and ability to seduce the power players. Scripts are once again read, and deals cut, by the pool where young starlets stretch languidly in the hopes of 'discovery.' If you'd like to stay here, see p143 for details.

### VIRGINIA ROBINSON GARDENS
Virginia Robinson, wife of department store mogul Harry Robinson, had a passion for plants and devoted many years of her long life to creating these lovely **gardens** ( ☎ 310-276-5367; 1008 Elden Way; tour adult/child 5-12/student/senior $10/3/5/5; ☟ 10am & 1pm Tue-Thu, 10am Fri). Tucked into a quiet residential area, they surround the Robinsons' magnificent 1911 beaux arts mansion, one of the oldest estates in Beverly Hills. Guided tours (reservations required) take you through this symphony of trees and flowers, harmoniously tossed together in a profusion of color and fragrance. You'll also get a peek inside the mansion where the Robinsons once entertained the Hollywood elite.

### MUSEUM OF TOLERANCE
Run by the Simon Wiesenthal Center, this interactive and high-tech **museum** ( ☎ 310-553-8403; www.wiesenthal.com/mot; 9786 W Pico Blvd; adult/child/student/senior $10/7/7/8; ☟ 11:30am-6:30pm Mon-Thu, 11:30am-3pm Fri Nov-Mar, 11:30am-5pm Fri Apr-Oct, 11am-7pm Sun) deals primarily with the Holocaust, although it also confronts visitors with other incidents of extreme intolerance, from segregation in America to genocides in Bosnia and Rwanda. The goal is to make visitors reflect upon their own closely held beliefs and to suggest ways to overcome prejudice and bigotry. Note that the only way to experience this museum is by following a prescribed route, which can take up to three hours to complete. The last entry is 2½ hours before closing and reservations are suggested.

In the **Multimedia Learning Center**, on the 2nd floor, you can research a variety of Holocaust-related topics. Also here are letters by Anne Frank, a bunk bed from the Majdanek camp and Göring's dress uniform cap. Lectures by Holocaust survivors take place several times a week.

A new separate exhibit called **Finding Our Families, Finding Ourselves** (adult/child under 12/student/senior $8/6/6/7, combination ticket with main museum $15/11/11/13; ☟ same as main museum) examines the diversity of American society and what it means to be an American. It follows the personal histories of poet Maya Angelou, comedian Billy Crystal, musician Carlos Santana and baseball coach Joe Torre.

### GREYSTONE PARK & MANSION
Wedding parties and film producers are no strangers to the sweeping city views from this 22-acre **hilltop park** (Map pp68-9; ☎ 310-550-4654; www.greystonemansion.org; 905 Loma Vista Dr; admission free; ☟ 10am-6pm May-Oct, 10am-5pm Nov-Apr). The 1928 mansion – named for the drab blend of Indiana limestone used in its construction – was a wedding present from oil tycoon Edward L Doheny to his only son Ned. The married couple didn't remain happy for long, for on the night of February 6, 1929, Ned was shot in a murder-suicide by his male secretary. Scenes from *The Bodyguard, Ghostbusters, Indecent Proposal* and other films were shot here. The mansion is only open during special events, including plays, concerts and afternoon tea ceremonies, but you're free to roam around or picnic in the park.

## Westwood, Bel Air & Brentwood
Map pp70-1

Westwood is practically synonymous with UCLA, one of the finest universities in the country. The huge campus borders Sunset Blvd in the north and blends into pedestrian-friendly Westwood Village on its south side. The village is a nice spot for a meal, a bit of shopping or catching a movie in a historic movie theater. The 1931 **Mann Village Theatre** ( ☎ 310-208-5576; 961 Broxton Ave), often used for premieres, and the smallish 1937 art deco **Mann Bruin Theatre** ( ☎ 310-208-8998; 948 Broxton Ave) are favorites. A farmers market (p184) takes place on Weyburn Ave every Thursday afternoon. Parking is expensive and at a premium in Westwood. The only garage offering one hour of free parking is at 1036 Broxton Ave.

North of Westwood, **Bel Air** is a favorite hideaway of stars whose sybaritic homes are generally well hidden behind security gates and dense foliage. **Brentwood**, west of the I-405 (San Diego Fwy), is only a little less exclusive and home to one of LA's headline attractions, the hilltop Getty Center. It

**LOS ANGELES**

---

### TOUR OF THE STARS' HOMES

Seeing where the stars live – or lived – is a guilty pleasure easily indulged in on a visit to LA. Numerous tour companies specialize in celebrity tours, and maps to the stars' homes are sold all along Hollywood and Sunset Blvds, although they're usually out-of-date. For those traveling with wheels, consider following this do-it-yourself tour of the glamorous, the notorious, the frivolous and the ostentatious. You'll see plenty of mansions protected by robotic cameras, armed guards and fierce dogs – look, but don't trespass. Budget about 90 minutes to two hours for this tour (see Map pp70-1).

Start your engine on Bedford Dr, which has been a favorite with celebrities going back to the 1920s when original 'It' girl, **Clara Bow**, reputedly bedded the entire USC football team, including a linebacker named Marion Morrison (later John Wayne), in her home at 512 N Bedford Dr. **Stan Laurel** lived up the street at No 718 and **Steve Martin** once resided at No 721. **Lana Turner**'s one-time haunt at No 730 was where the film star's daughter stabbed her mother's abusive lover to death in 1958 (she was acquitted).

For more gore, turn left on Lomitas Ave, then right on N Linden Dr to No 810, where gangster **Bugsy Siegel** had a deadly encounter with a bullet back in 1947. Continue north to Sunset Blvd, turn right, then left on N Roxbury Dr for a great lineup of former star homes, including **Lucille Ball** (No 1000), **Jack Benny** (No 1002), **Peter 'Columbo' Falk** (No 1004), **Ira & George Gershwin** (No 1019 and 1021, respectively) and **Diane Keaton** (No 1025).

Backtrack, turn right on Lexington Rd and right again on Ladera Dr, which veers left onto Monovale Dr; No 144 was **Elvis Presley**'s home. Monovale merges with Carolwood Dr, another 'celebrity row.' The modest house at No 245 was occupied in happier times by **Burt Reynolds**

---

is comparatively low-key and accessible but still quite exclusive. Marilyn Monroe died in her home at 12305 5th Helena Dr, but Brentwood didn't really become a household name until the OJ Simpson murder trial in 1994 following the slaying of his wife and another man at her condo at 875 Bundy Dr. Simpson was (in)famously acquitted.

### UNIVERSITY OF CALIFORNIA, LOS ANGELES (UCLA)

It may have started out as the southern branch of UC Berkeley back in 1919, but today **UCLA** ( ☎ 310-825-4321, tour reservations ☎ 310-825-8764; www.ucla.edu; 405 Hilgard Ave) has eclipsed its northern cousin in size and, in some areas, prestige. It ranks among the nation's top universities and boasts an outstanding research library (7.5 million volumes), one of the world's finest hospitals, and the country's second-largest film and TV archive (only the Library of Congress has more). Its faculty includes five Nobel Prize winners and four of its alumni are laureates as well. It was the alma mater of Francis Ford Coppola, James Dean and Jim Morrison. These days some 37,000 students try to uphold the university's reputation. Free student-guided tours are offered at 10:30am and 1:30pm Monday to Friday; reservations required.

The 419-acre campus is beautifully landscaped and contains several buildings of architectural interest, as well as museums and exhibit spaces. The prettiest and oldest structures, modeled after Renaissance churches in northern Italy, flank **Royce Quad** in the campus center.

Nearby is the **UCLA Fowler Museum of Cultural History** ( ☎ 310-825-4361; www.fowler.ucla.edu; admission free; ☻ noon-5pm Wed-Sun, noon-8pm Thu) which collects arts, crafts and artifacts from non-Western cultures. This translates into such highly specialized but often intriguing exhibits as the recent 'Saluting Vodou Spirits,' which showcased the museum's collection of Haitian ritual flags. Since it's free (for now), you might as well check it out.

Garden retreats include the pretty **Franklin D Murphy Sculpture Garden** northeast of Royce Quad, which has dozens of works by Rodin, Moore, Calder and other American and European artists. In the campus' southeastern corner, the **Mildred E Mathias Botanical Garden** ( ☎ 310-825-1260; www.botgard.ucla.edu/bg-home.htm; admission free; ☻ 8am-5pm Mon-Fri, 8am-4pm Sat & Sun) has more than 5000 native and exotic plants and flowers as well as 'The Nest,' a public outdoor classroom. Enter on Tiverton Ave. It closes an hour earlier on winter weekdays.

and **Loni Anderson** and, before that, by the late Beatle **George Harrison**. **Barbra Streisand** lived at No 301 and **Clark Gable** at No 325, not far from **Walt Disney**'s estate at No 355 (note the mouse-ear motif in the wrought-iron gate). **Gregory Peck** could be seen shuffling around No 375, while **Rod Stewart** had to keep fans away from his manse at No 391.

Turn around, follow Carolwood south to Sunset Blvd, turn right and then take the first marked left turn lane onto Charing Cross Rd, and watch out for 'bunnies' as you approach Hugh Hefner's **Playboy Mansion** at No 10236. The mansion is big but not as big as TV producer **Aaron Spelling**'s estate at 594 Mapleton Dr, adjacent to the Los Angeles Country Club (follow Charing Cross, then go left on Mapleton). The vanilla-colored chateau has 123 rooms and at one time was inhabited (not counting live-in staff) only by Spelling, his wife and their kids Tori and Randy. It is the largest private residence in all of LA.

Turn right on Club View Dr, right again on S Beverly Glen Blvd and across Sunset Blvd through the gates of swank Bel Air. Turn right on St Pierre Rd and follow it up and back down the hill. On your right at 486 St Pierre Rd is the abandoned hillside estate of **Johnny Weissmuller** of *Tarzan* fame. The actor used to keep in shape swimming in the moat-shaped pool surrounded by junglelike gardens. The house at 345 St Pierre Rd was where, in 1942, **Errol Flynn** allegedly raped a 17-year-old girl during a wild party; he was later acquitted. The incident gave birth to the expression 'in like Flynn,' referring to someone who's quick about getting the girl.

St Cloud Rd veers off to the right and skirts the vast **Reagan** compound. It was here where US President Ronald Reagan died in 2004. The original address was 666 Bel Air Rd, but a superstitious Nancy had the number changed because of its satanic associations. Turning left and following Bel Air Rd south takes you back to Sunset Blvd.

For another green gem travel off-campus to swank Bel Air, home of the **UCLA Hannah Carter Japanese Garden** ( ☎ 310-825-4574; www .japanesegarden.ucla.edu; 10619 Bellagio Rd; admission free; ☺ 10am-3pm Tue, Wed & Fri), a terraced Kyoto-style garden accented with a lily pond, waterfalls and a lively little brook. Other elements are a traditional teahouse, bonsai trees, bridges, antique stone carvings and symbolic rocks. Sorry, no picnics. Reservations required.

### UCLA HAMMER MUSEUM

In Westwood Village, this museum started as a mere vanity project for its main benefactor, the late oil tycoon Armand Hammer (1898–1990), but has since graduated to a widely respected contemporary and period art **museum** ( ☎ 310-443-7000; www.hammer.ucla.edu; 10899 Wilshire Blvd; adult/child under 17/student/senior $5/free/3/3; ☺ 11am-7pm Tue & Wed, 11am-9pm Thu, 11am-7pm Fri & Sat, 11am-5pm Sun). Hammer's passion for European art resulted in a sizable collection of relatively minor paintings by impressionists, postimpressionists and Old Masters as well as lithographs and sculpture by Honoré Daumier, a top 19th-century French satirist. A selection of these is generally on view, but the Hammer really shines when it comes to its often cutting-edge and courageous special exhibits of contemporary

art. Concerts, films, lectures, readings and discussions play a supporting role.

Parking is available under the museum; make sure to have your ticket validated for the $2.75 per three hour rate.

### PIERCE BROS WESTWOOD MEMORIAL PARK

This small, star-studded **cemetery** ( ☎ 310-474-1570; 1218 Glendon Ave; admission free; ☺ 8am-sunset) is embraced by Westwood's office high-rises and a bit hard to find – from Wilshire Blvd, turn south onto Glendon Ave and look for the driveway immediately to your left. Hollywood babe Marilyn Monroe is buried in an above-ground crypt next to an empty one reserved for Playboy owner Hugh Hefner. She's in good company for in the ground you'll find the graves of Natalie Wood, Burt Lancaster, Walter Matthau, Jack Lemmon, Roy Orbison and other stars. Frank Zappa is here as well, albeit in an unmarked spot.

It's a small cemetery, so you should be able to find most graves without too much looking. Otherwise, ask the friendly staff at the office for help.

### GETTY CENTER

In the Santa Monica Mountains, high above the 405 Fwy, the billion-dollar **Getty Center**

### ART FORTRESS IN THE SKY

To many people, even more impressive than the Getty Center's art is its architecture. One of the world's top architects, New York–based Richard Meier, used his billion-dollar budget to come up with a remarkable hilltop complex built along two natural ridges. The architect cleverly juxtaposed sensuously curving buildings with starkly angled ones, making the place seem open, spacious and embracing. Add California sunshine to the mix and you get a most remarkable alchemy of light and shadow. It's an effect further enhanced by the use of travertine, a cream-colored, textured and fossilized stone imported from Italy, for many of the buildings. Reflecting the sunlight in the early morning, it literally seems to absorb the rays during the day and, by the late afternoon, radiates a golden warmth. Ask at the information desk about free architecture tours.

( ☎ 310-440-7300; www.getty.edu; 1200 Getty Center Dr; admission free; ⏰ 10am-6pm Sun & Tue-Thu, 10am-9pm Fri & Sat) presents triple delights: a stellar art collection (Renaissance to David Hockney), the fabulous architecture of Richard Meier, and the superb – and seasonally changing – gardens designed by Robert Irwin. On clear days, you can add breathtaking views of the city and ocean to the list. Even getting up to the 110-acre 'campus' aboard a driverless tram is fun.

The sprawling complex unites the art collections of oil magnate J Paul Getty (1892–1976) with several Getty-sponsored research, education and conservation institutes. Four two-story pavilions house the permanent collection, while a fifth presents changing exhibitions. The skylit upper floors display paintings, while the lower floors showcase sculptures, manuscripts, photographs, drawings, furniture and a spectacular collection of decorative arts. The paintings collection is strongest when it comes to pre-20th-century Europeans. Must-sees include Van Gogh's *Irises,* Monet's *Wheatstacks,* Rembrandt's *The Abduction of Europa* and Titian's *Venus and Adonis.*

Tours, lectures and interactive technology, including audioguides ($3), make the art accessible to all. Even children won't feel bored when taking a Family Tour or visiting the Family Room with its games, books and computers. There's even a separate kid-oriented audioguide, which builds stories and activities into the self-guided tour.

Also check the Getty's cultural events calendar, which includes fabulous concerts, lectures and films. Most events are free but some require reservations (although you can always try standby). A great time to visit is in the late afternoon after the crowds have thinned and you can watch the sunset while enjoying a picnic or a snack from a kiosk or the self-service café. For formal meals, book a table at **Restaurant** ( ☎ 310-440-6810).

Admission is free but parking is $7; both Metro Bus No 761 and the Big Blue Bus No 14 stop here. The Getty is fully accessible to disabled persons.

### SKIRBALL CULTURAL CENTER

A cluster of galleries, performance spaces and educational facilities, the **Skirball** ( ☎ 310-440-4500; 2701 N Sepulveda Blvd; adult/child under 12/student/senior $8/free/6/6; ⏰ noon-5pm Tue-Sat, 11am-5pm Sun) is a celebration of Jewish heritage and the American Jewish experience. It's a lavish space designed by renowned architect Moshe Safdie and named for its main benefactor, Jack Skirball, a rabbi, real-estate tycoon and producer of Hitchcock films.

The main exhibition, *Visions and Values: Jewish Life from Antiquity to America,* is a pastiche of 4000 years of history, tradition, values and accomplishments of the Jewish people from ancient Israel to today. It's all engagingly presented with ceremonial objects, photographs, video, artifacts, archaeological finds and large-scale replicas, most impressively that of a mosaic floor from a 3rd-century synagogue in Galilee. Poignant too are displays of the original copies of the Nuremberg Laws, signed by Hitler, which stripped Jews of their civil rights in Nazi Germany, and Hitler's racist rant *Mein Kampf.* Both were given to the Huntington Library (p126) by General Patton in 1945 and are displayed indefinitely.

The Skirball also hosts traveling exhibits and has a packed schedule of lectures, concerts and performances. Big crowds turn out for the free world music summer concert series. Zeidler's Café (mains $6 to $10) serves strictly kosher light California fare.

## Culver City

Culver City – huh? East of Venice and south of Westwood, modest-looking Culver City doesn't get a lot of attention, even though it is home to one of the oldest and most famous movie studios in the world. From 1924 until its 1990 takeover by Sony Pictures, **Metro-Goldwyn-Mayer (MGM)** produced countless classics in its sprawling lot on Washington Blvd, including *The Philadelphia Story, 2001: A Space Odyssey* and, most famously, *The Wizard of Oz*. Tours of the historic studio, now known as Sony Pictures Studios, are offered during the week (p120).

But there's more going on in Culver City than movie-making, as the city gradually positions itself as the Westside hub of cutting-edge art and performance. At least a dozen galleries, including the prestigious **Blum & Poe** (p183) and the lowbrow **Copro/Nason Gallery** (p183), have recently moved here; the new **Kirk Douglas Theatre** (p179) brings new voices and an experimental approach to the stage; and cool new architecture, such as the **Hayden Tract** (3500 block of Hayden Ave) by Eric Owen Moss, is cropping up in pockets here and there.

Culver City is also home to the strange but irresistibly intriguing **Museum of Jurassic Technology** (p134) and the classy **Jazz Bakery** (p176), which has been bringing in the faithful for over a decade. For directions to these Culver City attractions, see the off-map arrows on Map pp72–3.

## Malibu                                          Map pp60–1

Malibu is not a destination, it's a state of mind. Long synonymous with surfing, celebrities and a hedonistic lifestyle, it hugs 27 spectacularly beautiful miles of coast where the Santa Monica Mountains meet the ocean. The Chumash Indians who first lived here quite appropriately called the place 'humaliwo' ('where the surf sounds').

Malibu has been a popular celebrity retreat since the 1920s when money troubles forced landowner May Rindge to lease out some of her property west of the Malibu Lagoon. Clara Bow and Barbara Stanwyck were among the original residents of what became known as the **Malibu Colony**. Today, this gated and well-policed enclave is still home to A-list celebs including Tom Hanks, Sting and Leonardo DiCaprio. While it's impossible to get past the gate without a personal invitation from a resident, it is legal to walk along the beach – provided you stay below the high-tide mark. For the best views of the colony, head a little up the coast to **Malibu Bluffs Park**. For the best star-spotting, visit Malibu's two shopping areas, the **Malibu Country Mart** (Map pp60-1; 3835 Cross Creek Rd), a lovely outdoor mall with nice cafés, restaurants and boutiques, or the more utilitarian **Malibu Colony Plaza** (Map pp60-1; 23841 W Malibu Rd), which has a Ralphs supermarket and a gas station.

Despite its wealth and high star quotient, Malibu is surprisingly low-key and laid-back, and is best appreciated through its natural assets. Some of the best **beaches** include Las Tunas, Surfrider, Point Dume and Zuma. Rising behind Malibu is **Malibu Creek State Park**, part of the Santa Monica Mountains National Recreation Area and laced with hiking and biking trails (see p130).

There's free parking along some sections of Hwy 1 (Pacific Coast Hwy) but be sure to read the signs. Otherwise you'll find pay parking lots along here charging $6 to $10, depending on the time of year. On summer weekends, they often fill up by midday.

---

### DETOUR: RONALD W REAGAN LIBRARY & MUSEUM

When Ronald Reagan, the country's 40th president, died on June 5, 2004, at age 93, he was buried in the shadow of his **presidential library** (off Map pp60-1; ☎ 800-998-7641; www.reaganlibrary. net; 40 Presidential Dr; adult/child 11-17/senior $7/2/5; ☉ 10am-5pm) in Simi Valley, just across the Ventura county line. Love him or hate him, the exhibits here are really quite fascinating. Galleries cover all phases of Reagan's life from his childhood in Dixon, Illinois, through his early days in radio and acting to his stint as governor of California, although the focus is obviously on his years as president (1980–8). The museum features re-creations of the Oval Office and the Cabinet Room, Reagan family memorabilia, gifts from heads of state and a nuclear cruise missile. The graffiti-covered chunk of the Berlin Wall never fails to impress either. To get there, take I-405 (San Diego Fwy) north to the 118 (Ronald Reagan Fwy) west; exit at Madera Rd South, turn right on Madera and continue straight for 3 miles to Presidential Dr.

**THE ROAD OF DREAMS**

The Pacific Coast Hwy is an epic ribbon of roads extending all the way from Alaska to Chile, more or less hugging the ocean all the way. Some of its most spectacular stretches pass through Southern California as a pastiche of Hwys 1 and 101, a meandering line of asphalt caught between beaches, cliffs and mountains and connecting numerous coastal villages. The most scenic sections of this mythical road are between Dana Point and Seal Beach, between Santa Monica and Point Mugu (past Malibu) and between Ventura and Santa Barbara.

**MALIBU PIER & AROUND**

Closed for nearly a decade due to storm damage, the century-old **Malibu Pier** is once again open for strolling and fishing (no license required) and also offers a good vantage point of **Surfrider Beach**, known to boarders as the holy grail of surfing. The beach sits near where Malibu Creek meets the ocean, an area officially known as the **Malibu Lagoon State Beach** ( ☎ 818-880-0350; 23200 Pacific Coast Hwy; admission free; ♻ 8am-sunset). Birders will have a field day at this popular stopover for migratory birds. Call about nature and cultural history tours.

Up on a bluff overlooking the beach is the **Adamson House** ( ☎ 310-456-8432; www.adamsonhouse.org; 23200 Pacific Coast Hwy; adult/child $5/3; ♻ 11am-2pm Wed-Sat), a national historic site and must-see for architecture buffs and tile enthusiasts. The beautiful 1930 Spanish Moorish villa sits amid lush grounds and is awash in locally made hand-painted tiles. The adjacent **Malibu Lagoon Museum** ( ☎ 310-456-8432; admission free; ♻ 11am-3pm Wed-Sat) chronicles the history of Malibu, from the Chumash Indian period to the battle over the Malibu highway and the formation of the Malibu Colony.

A little way up PCH (Hwy 1) is the turnoff to Serra Rd which, after snaking uphill for about 1 mile, dead-ends at one of Malibu's most enchanting hideaways, the **Serra Retreat** ( ☎ 310-456-6631; www.sbfranciscans.org/communities/retreats/serra; 3401 Serra Rd; admission free; ♻ 9am-4:30pm). Run by Franciscan friars, this religious center has lovely gardens that are usually open to the public. It's a quiet and meditative spot

with sweeping views of the foothills and the ocean. On weekends the free on-site parking is often at a premium.

**NORTHERN MALIBU**

About 1½ miles north of the Malibu Pier, atop a grassy slope with views of the Pacific and the mountains, **Pepperdine University** ( ☎ 310-456-4000; 24255 Pacific Coast Hwy) surely has one of the world's most beautiful campuses. This well-endowed private institution is affiliated with the Church of Christ and counts President Bill Clinton's nemesis, independent investigator Ken Starr, among its faculty (he's the law school dean). Art fans should check out whatever show's on view at the university's **Frederick R Weisman Museum of Art** ( ☎ 310-506-4851; admission free; ♻ 11am-5pm Tue-Sun).

Pepperdine sits right on Malibu Canyon Rd, which makes for a lovely drive through the Santa Monica Mountains. About 11 miles from the uni you'll come upon one of the mountain's hidden treasures, the **Malibu Hindu Temple** ( ☎ 818-880-5552; 1600 Las Virgenes Canyon Rd; admission free; ♻ 9am-noon & 5-8pm Mon-Fri, 9am-8pm Sat & Sun, closes 1hr earlier Nov-Mar). Built in traditional Indian style, it has numerous outdoor and indoor shrines dedicated to Hindu deities. Visitors are welcome, but dress modestly. On weekends, the temple kitchen serves simple vegetarian meals ($4 donation).

**GETTY VILLA**

Long before the hilltop Getty Center (p91) opened, crowds flocked to the J Paul Getty Museum in Malibu, fashioned after the Roman Villa dei Papiri. Closed for renovation since 1997, it is scheduled to reopen in late 2005 as the **Getty Villa** (17985 Pacific Coast Hwy), once again showcasing the museum's precious Greek and Roman statues.

## Pacific Palisades

Pacific Palisades, founded by Methodists in the 1920s, is an upscale community north of Santa Monica. It's rife with celebrities and common millionaires who live ensconced in gorgeous Mediterranean-style villas clinging to the hillsides of five major canyons carving through the Santa Monica Mountains. There are no major sights here, but you can get a feel for the neighborhood by strolling its business district, which is centered on where Sunset Blvd intersects with Strathmore Ave.

In the 1930s the Palisades, as locals call the area, was a favorite with European exiles, including writers Thomas Mann and Lion Feuchtwanger. High up in the hills above Sunset Blvd, Feuchtwanger's old home, the **Villa Aurora** (Map pp60-1; ☎ 310-456-4231; www .villa-aurora.org; 520 Paseo Miramar), is now a German-American artists center hosting numerous cultural events, including readings, film screenings and concerts (prices vary).

Street parking is usually easy to find.

### WILL ROGERS STATE HISTORIC PARK

Will Rogers (1875–1935) was an Oklahoma-born cowboy turned humorist, radio-show host and movie star after coming to California in 1919. In the late '20s he traded his Beverly Hills mansion for a **ranch house** (Map pp60-1; ☎ 310-454-8212; admission free; ☽ 10am-5pm) in the Santa Monica Mountains, where he lived until dying in a plane crash in 1935. The ranch sits near the polo field where Rogers was often joined by his famous buddies Spencer Tracy, Gary Cooper, Walt Disney and others. Matches still take place on weekends from April to September (www .willrogerspolo.org).

The surrounding chaparral-covered hills Rogers loved so much have been preserved as a **state historic park** (Map pp60-1; ☽ 8am-sunset). An easy-to-moderate 2-mile hike leads up to Inspiration Point from where you can enjoy sweeping views of the mountains and the ocean. If you're feeling more ambitious, continue traipsing along the Backbone Trail.

The park entrance is west off Sunset Blvd and is marked by signs. Parking is $5.

### SELF-REALIZATION FELLOWSHIP LAKE SHRINE

No matter your religious persuasion, you'll likely feel any negative vibes evaporate while strolling the beautiful and serene grounds of the **Self-Realization Fellowship Lake Shrine** (Map pp60-1; ☎ 310-454-4114; www.yogananda-srf .org/temples/lakeshrine; 17190 Sunset Blvd; admission free; ☽ 9am-4:30pm Tue-Sat, 12:30-4:30pm Sun). Paths meander around a spring-fed lake and past lush vegetation to a Dutch windmill–turned-chapel and a shrine containing some of the ashes of Mahatma Ghandi. The fellowship was founded in 1920 by charismatic yogi Paramahansa Yogananda and blends beliefs and traditions of Christian and Eastern religions. Overlooking the garden is the hill-top temple, crowned by a gilded lotus, where lectures and services open to anyone take place several times weekly.

### EAMES HOUSE & STUDIO

The striking **Eames House & Studio** (Map pp72-3; ☎ 310-459-9663; 203 Chautauqua Blvd; admission free; ☽ 10am-4pm Mon-Fri), built in 1949 by Charles and Ray Eames, resembles a Mondrian painting in 3-D. It's still used by the Eames family, but you're usually free to look through the glass front at the fully furnished downstairs interior, including the kitchen and living room. Going inside, though, requires an appointment; a fee may be imposed starting in 2005. There's free parking on nearby Corona del Mar.

While here also have a look at the adjacent 1949 **Entenza House** (Map pp72-3; 205 Chautauqua Blvd), a huge gleaming white jumble by Charles Eames and Eero Saarinen; the best view is across the wall from the Eames House garden. Richard Neutra designed the nearby **Bailey House** (Map pp72-3; 219 Chautauqua Blvd), which was built from 1946 to 1948.

## Santa Monica
Map pp72-3

The seaside city of Santa Monica is one of the most agreeable in LA, with its early-20th-century pier, pedestrian-friendly downtown, wide beaches and excellent shopping and dining. It's a posh place, with a phalanx of new buildings, from ultradeluxe beachfront hotels to mansions in the quiet residential area north of Montana Ave and luxury condominium complexes in the town center. 'New' is the operative word, for Santa Monica wasn't always a 'Beverly-Hills-by-the-sea.' In fact, until about 10 or maybe 12 years ago, this was little more than a laid-back beach town whose ultraliberal politics garnered it the moniker of 'People's Republic of Santa Monica.' Today it seems that the only vestige of those days remains a certain largesse towards homeless people, who are fed and tolerated, at least as long as they're quiet and well-behaved.

For visitors, Santa Monica is a central, safe and fun base for exploring LA. Parking is free for two hours at the four large public parking garages on 2nd and 4th Sts between Broadway and Wilshire Blvd. For Main St, the lot at Ocean and Hollister Ave has inexpensive metered parking. The electric Tide Shuttle (25¢ per ride) makes a loop

**LOS ANGELES**

from downtown to the beach, Main St and back every 15 minutes from noon to 8pm (to 10pm Friday and Saturday).

### SANTA MONICA PIER

You've probably seen it dozens of times in movies and on TV: the neon-lit arch of the **Santa Monica Pier** ( ☎ 310-458-8900; www.santa monicapier.org; admission free; 24hr), the oldest amusement pier in California (since 1908) and still a fun place to while away a few hours in the ocean breeze. There are great views of the beach and the Santa Monica skyline, a few casual restaurants, a gaggle of street vendors and diversions of all sorts. On Thursday nights throughout summer, the pier comes to life with a free concert series, the Twilight Dance Series (p171), and the Santa Monica Drive-In movie screenings (p173).

The main attraction at the pier, at least for kids, is **Pacific Park** ( ☎ 310-260-8744; www.pac park.com; admission free; 11am-11pm Sun-Thu, 11am-12:30am Fri & Sat Jun-Aug, shorter winter hours), a small amusement park with the world's first solar-powered Ferris wheel and a rather tame roller coaster, plus a host of kiddy rides, midway games and food concessions. Rides cost between $1.50 to $4.50 each, or you can have unlimited rides for $11/22 (under/over 42in tall); check the website for discount coupons.

The pier's oldest attraction is the 1922 **carousel** ( ☎ 310-395-4248; rides adult/child $1/0.50; 11am-5pm Mon-Thu, 11am-7pm Fri-Sun, closed Tue & Wed Jan–mid-Mar), a cheerful merry-go-round with hand-painted horses, which was featured in the movie *The Sting*.

Right below the carousel, at beach level, is the **Santa Monica Pier Aquarium** ( ☎ 310-393-6149; admission by donation, suggested/minimum $5/1, children under 12 free; 2-6pm Tue-Fri, 12:30-6pm Sat & Sun). Operated by the nonprofit environmental organization, Heal the Bay, this children-oriented facility introduces you to jellyfish, small sharks and other critters residing in Santa Monica Bay. You'll also learn about marine conservation and get to pet sea urchins, starfish and other tidepool animals.

South of the pier is the **Original Muscle Beach**, where the Southern California exercise craze began in the mid-20th century. Brand-new equipment once again draws fitness fanatics. Nearby, the **International Chess Park** brings together people from all walks of life who share enthusiasm for the game. Following the **South Bay Bicycle Trail** (p128), a paved bike and walking path, south for about 1½ miles takes you straight to Venice Beach. Bike or in-line skate rentals are available on the pier and at beachside kiosks.

### THIRD STREET PROMENADE

Stretching for three long blocks between Broadway and Wilshire Blvd, **Third St Promenade** is a case study on how to morph a dilapidated, dying main street into one of the city's most dynamic and happening spots. With cars banished from the strip, there's lots of carefree strolling, mingling and browsing to be done. Peruvian flutes mingle with bluegrass guitar and classical cellos in a parade of free street entertainment. Watch the world go by while sipping cappuccino in an outdoor café. Pick up a sleek outfit, cool knickknack or the latest bestseller; take in a movie; or scarf down a pizza or ice cream. Hobby cooks to professional chefs stock up at the superb farmers market (p184) on Wednesday and Saturday mornings. And it's all anchored by Santa Monica Place (p191), a popular shopping mall designed by Frank Gehry. Did we mention this was a happening place?

### CAMERA OBSCURA

Just north of Santa Monica Pier, in beautiful bluff-top Palisades Park, the **Camera Obscura** ( ☎ 310-458-8644; 1450 Ocean Ave; admission free; 9am-1pm Mon, 9am-3pm Tue-Fri, noon-3pm Sat, 11am-3pm Sun), a precursor to the single-lens reflex camera, was quite a sensation back in 1899 but is now simply a quaint diversion. Ask for the key inside the senior recreation center.

### BERGAMOT STATION ARTS CENTER

A nexus of the LA arts scene, this industrial-chic **art campus** (2525 Michigan Ave; most galleries 10am-6pm Tue-Sat) in a former Red Trolley terminus harbors nearly three dozen galleries, a café, studios and shops. A highlight here is the small **Santa Monica Museum of Art** ( ☎ 310-586-6488; www.smmoa.org; Bergamot Station, Bldg G1; admission by donation; 11am-6pm Tue-Sat), the saucy and irreverent home of changing contemporary art exhibits. Both local and national artists – fledgling to big-name – get exposure here with preference given to those working with new and experimental media. Curators also host an intrepid schedule of public community events. It's about 3 miles from the beach; enter from Cloverfield Blvd.

## MAIN STREET

Main St, especially the stretch between Ocean Park Blvd and Rose Ave, is flanked by one-of-a-kind boutiques and galleries, and is a joy to shop in. Wedged in between the stores is the **Edgemar Complex** (2415-49 Main St), where Frank Gehry has transformed a former ice factory into a sculptural mall housing stores, the Röckenwagner/Brasserie (p160) and the Edgemar Center for the Arts (p180).

Further along is the **California Heritage Museum** ( ☎ 310-392-8537; www.californiaheritagemuseum .org; 2612 Main St; adult/child under 12/student/senior $5/free/3/3; ☉ 11am-4pm Wed-Sun), housed in a grand 1894 mansion. The museum has great collections of decorative, fine and folk arts, as well as California furniture and pottery. The most fun, though, are its special themed exhibits – from surfboards to Craftsman decor. The Sunday morning farmers market (p184) in the museum's parking lot is a lively and interactive affair that brings out the entire community.

## GEHRY HOUSE

In his creative life before the Guggenheim Bilbao in Spain and the Walt Disney Concert Hall (p107), Frank Gehry was primarily known as the guy who sculpted houses from mundane materials such as chain-link fencing, plywood and corrugated aluminum. A great place to see the 'early Gehry' is his 1979 **private home** (1002 22nd St), a deconstructivist postmodern collage that architecture critic Paul Heyer called a 'collision of parts.' It's bold, sculptural and provocative. Neighbors were none too pleased with this work initially, but that was before Gehry had claimed his spot in the pantheon of contemporary American architects.

## ANGELS ATTIC

Toy trains travel along the ceiling, and vintage dolls inhabit pint-sized crenellated castles and Tudor mansions at this sweet little **museum** ( ☎ 310-394-8331; 506 Colorado Ave; adult/child $6.50/4; ☉ 12:30-4:30pm Thu-Sun) in a gorgeously kept 1895 Victorian home. Other highlights include a dollhouse shaped like a shoe, a miniature Versailles and, quite literally, a Noah's ark worth of animal figurines.

## MUSEUM OF FLYING

Here today, gone tomorrow and, soon, back again. The **Museum of Flying** (www.museumofflying .com) has been through a lot in recent years, but at the time of writing looked poised to return to its old haunt, the Santa Monica Airport, albeit with a new focus. A selection of the museum's famous vintage airplanes will now be complemented by historical exhibits about the airport and the Douglas Aircraft company founded here in the 1920s. The plan is to reopen in 2005. Check the website for updates.

## Venice    Map pp72–3

If aliens landed on Venice's famous **Ocean Front Walk** (Venice Pier to Rose Ave; admission free; ☉ 24hr), they'd probably blend right into the human zoo of chainsaw-juggling entertainers, bikini-clad cyclists, a roller-skating Sikh minstrel and zealous 'meat is murder' activists. Known locally as Venice Boardwalk, this 1½-mile strip along the sand is the place to get your hair braided, your skin tattooed or your aura adjusted. It's a freak show that must be seen to be believed, preferably on a hot summer weekend when the scene is at its most surreal. Avoid the boardwalk after dark.

There are some good places for a snack or meal, including the landmark **Sidewalk Café** (p161), an outdoor gym filled with budding Schwarzeneggers and basketball courts where 'hoop dreams' are kept alive. The Sunday afternoon drum circle draws hundreds of revelers for tribal playing and spontaneous dancing. If the noise doesn't show you the way there, just follow your nose towards whiffs of 'wacky tabaccy.'

It's quite appropriate that Venice – SoCal's quintessential bohemian playground – was the brainchild of eccentric, dreamer extraordinaire and cigarette heir Abbot Kinney (1850–1920). Kinney envisioned a cultural theme park on marshy land just south of Santa Monica, complete with imported gondoliers to pole people around his beachfront paradise. The park, which he dubbed 'Venice of America,' opened on July 4, 1905 and also featured a Ferris wheel, a hydrogen-filled balloon, the Rapids water ride and other such diversions. Soon after Kinney's death, Prohibition spelled doom for the venue and eventually the city paved over most of the canals.

These days, it's still possible to catch a glimmer of Kinney's dream. In the 1990s, 3 miles of the original waterways were restored and are now flanked by handsome villas with flowery front yards. The **Venice Canal Walk** threads through this idyllic neighborhood where ducks preen, swans glide and residents putter around on little boats. It's best accessed from either Venice or Washington Blvds, near Dell Ave.

Kinney may have been a little kooky but he unwittingly set the trend for 20th-century Venice, California. Such counterculture royalty as beatniks Lawrence Lipton and Stuart Perkoff and *über*-hippie Jim Morrison made their homes here at one time. Today, Venice is still a cauldron of creativity, peopled by karmically correct New Agers, eternal hippies, cool-conscious musicians, and artists and architects of all stripes.

Galleries, studios and public art abound, much of it with an unsurprisingly surreal bent. Case in point: Jonathan Borofsky's tutu-clad **Ballerina Clown** (Rose Ave & Main St). Nearby stands Frank Gehry's **Chiat/Day Building** (340 Main St), fronted by a three-story-tall pair of binoculars by Claes Oldenburg and Coosje van Bruggen.

Kinney would probably be delighted to find that one of Venice's most individualistic streets bears his name. Sort of a seaside Melrose with a Venetian flavor, the mile-long stretch of **Abbot Kinney Blvd** between Venice Blvd and Main St is chockablock with unique boutiques, galleries, vintage-clothing stores and interesting restaurants, including Hal's Bar & Grill (p161), Joe's (p161) and Abbot's Pizza (p161). In late September, the Abbot Kinney St Festival (p138) draws thousands of revelers.

There's street parking on Abbot Kinney Blvd but for the Ocean Front Walk you'll probably have to shell out $6 to $10 for the privilege of leaving your car in a parking lot, such as the one at the corner of Venice Blvd and Pacific Ave. Rates are higher in summer and on weekends.

### Marina del Rey                    Map pp72–3
Just down the coast from Venice Beach, some 6000 sailboats and yachts are moored in what locals call simply 'the Marina,' the largest artificial small-craft harbor in the US. Wrested from coastal wetlands in the '60s, this watery world is also LA's 'singles capital' with nearly six in 10 people living alone in countless canal-side condos and apartments.

Devoid of major sights, Marina del Rey is really all about the water. You can rent every conceivable watercraft (kayaks, pedal boats, jet skis etc), join a harbor cruise (p134), go whale-watching (from January to March; p134) or head out to hook a halibut or yellowtail.

Most of the action centers on **Fisherman's Village** ( ☎ 310-823-5411; 13755 Fiji Way), a strip of candy-colored New England–style cottages filled with gift shops and restaurants. Just north of here, at the end of Mindanao Way, the small **Burton Chace Park** is a good spot for a picnic, flying a kite or watching the parade of boats coming through the Main Channel. In July and August, there's a free concert series on Thursday and Saturday evenings (p171).

Just south of the marina are the **Ballona Wetlands**, the last remaining wetlands in LA County and home to hundreds of bird species, including the great blue heron. Their

---

**MURAL MANIA**

Public art is big in Venice and murals are a preferred form of expression. You'll see them everywhere but especially along the Ocean Front Walk. Outstanding works include **Chagall Returns to Venice Beach** (1996; 201 Ocean Front Walk at Ozone Ave) by Christina Schlesinger, and **Venice Reconstituted** (1989; 25 Windward Ave) by Rip Cronk. Cronk's **Homage to a Starry Night** (1990; Ocean Front Walk at Wavecrest Ave) was inspired by the Van Gogh original.

With such a strong mural tradition, it's not surprising that Venice is home to the nonprofit **Social & Public Art Resource Center** (SPARC; Map pp72-3; ☎ 310-822-9560; www.sparcmurals.org; 685 S Venice Blvd; admission free; ☻ 10am-6pm Mon-Fri), housed in a historic former police station. Founded by three women artists in 1976, SPARC promotes, preserves and produces public murals throughout LA. The gallery and bookstore are well worth a look if you're interested in this type of art.

habitat, however, has been seriously compromised since construction began on **Playa Vista**, a custom-planned luxury community on land once owned by Howard Hughes. When completed, the new 'city within a city' will be home to about 11,000 residents.

There's free and metered street parking throughout.

## South Bay Beaches                    Map p74

South of LAX, Santa Monica Bay is home to a trio of all-American beach towns – Manhattan Beach, Hermosa Beach and Redondo Beach – far removed from the grit and velocity of urban LA. Lovely if not lavish homes come down all the way to the gorgeous white beach, which is the prime attraction here and paralleled by the **South Bay Bicycle Trail** (p128).

Tourism has been filling local coffers since land baron and railroad tycoon Henry Huntington connected the beach towns to LA with his Pacific Electric Railway in 1905. The luxurious Hotel Redondo (no longer around), a saltwater plunge pool and several piers were among the early attractions, as was the original 'surfer dude' George Freeth (see below).

### MANHATTAN BEACH

The birthplace of surf music and beach volleyball, Manhattan Beach is a casual, pretty and affluent community whose residents don't seem to mind that they're living downwind from a major power plant. Shops, bars and restaurants cluster at the foot of Manhattan Beach Blvd near the pier, which is a major surfing hot spot. In the 1960s, a gaggle of teens from nearby Hawthorne got so inspired watching the longboarders in action, they wrote some songs about them. Shortly thereafter, the Beach Boys gave birth to a new genre of music with *Surfin' Safari, Surfin' USA* and other chart busters. Ironically, only one of them, Dennis Wilson, even knew how to surf.

Walking the pier's entire 928ft length takes you to the small **Roundhouse Marine Studies Lab & Aquarium** ( ☎ 310-379-8117; www.scc.ca.gov/Wheel/lapage/4_man/round.html; suggested donation $2; ☞ 3pm-sunset Mon-Fri, 10am-sunset Sat & Sun). Youngsters will probably get a kick out of close encounters with moray eels, an octopus, reef sharks and a geriatric lobster (he's over 50 years old).

Every summer, you can watch the pros bump, set and spike at the Manhattan Beach Open, the world's oldest and most prestigious beach volleyball tournament (since 1960). Numerous Olympians are usually among its competitors.

The downtown area has several pay-parking garages, the largest being Lot M on

---

### GEORGE FREETH: KING OF THE SURFER DUDES

The Beach Boys, Frankie and Annette, Jan and Dean: surfing mythology and Southern California have long been synonymous, and we may owe it all to Henry Huntington's genius for promotion. Huntington owned a lot of beachfront real estate which he was eager to sell to visitors arriving on his Pacific Electric Railway which, since 1905, connected Downtown LA with the beaches. So in 1907, in order to help lure prospective buyers, Huntington hired a Hawaiian-Irish surfer named George Freeth to perform his miracle of 'walking on water' for visitors to Redondo Beach. The crowds came, and Huntington sold a lot of land.

It was Freeth who fathered the surfing revolution that would eventually become an enormous industry and an entire lifestyle in California. As a child in Hawaii, after seeing an old painting showing his mother's ancestors riding the waves, he decided to try his luck at this ancient art. When the gargantuan, traditional 16ft hardwood boards proved too hard to handle, he cut one in half, thus creating the first 'long board' – and modern surfing was born. Until 1915 Freeth held the Redondo Beach crowds in thrall with daily performances, and he eventually became the first lifeguard in Southern California. (He even received a Congressional Medal of Honor for bravely rescuing a boatload of stranded fishermen.) A bronze memorial to him on the Redondo Beach Pier is frequently draped with leis from surfers who come from around the world to pay their respects.

Freeth died in the great influenza epidemic of 1919 at age 36, but the mark he left on world culture surpassed even the legacy of Huntington himself. Freeth's short, sweet life was the original 'endless summer.'

LOS ANGELES

Valley Dr between Manhattan Beach Blvd and 13th St.

## HERMOSA BEACH

'Hermosa' is Spanish for 'beautiful,' a name that's quite appropriate considering the bevy of buff and bronzed SoCal singles hanging out and partying here, especially on the rambunctious Pier Ave pedestrian mall. Less grown-up and gentrified than Manhattan Beach, Hermosa claims to be the birthplace of surfing. Since 2003 it's even had a **Surfers Walk of Fame** on its pier to cement the boast, which has raised eyebrows, if not ire, in Redondo Beach (below) and Huntington Beach (p215), which both make the same claim. Beach volleyball is big here as well with dozens of nets strung up along the boardwalk called the Strand. Like neighboring Manhattan Beach, Hermosa hosts several volleyball tournaments, including the prestigious Hermosa Beach Open in late July. Worth a quick stop is the little **Hermosa Beach Historical Museum** ( ☎ 310-318-9421; www.hermosabeachhistorical society.org; 710 Pier Ave; admission free; 2-4pm Sat & Sun), which provides an endearing chronicle of the city's past.

Every Memorial Day and Labor Day weekend, Hermosa's three-day **Fiesta Hermosa** (www.fiestahermosa.com), with music, food, kiddy rides and a huge arts-and-crafts fair, attracts large throngs of revelers.

## REDONDO BEACH

Redondo Beach has 2 miles of beach but most visitors gravitate to the foot of Torrance Blvd where the **Redondo Beach Pier** is chockablock with restaurants, bars, souvenir shops and a fishing dock. North of here, along Harbor Dr, is **King Harbor**, a clump of apartment buildings adjacent to a small-boat marina and sportfishing center. Boats, kayaks and jet skis are for rent here as well. Another attraction is the family-friendly **Seaside Lagoon** ( ☎ 310-318-0681; 200 Portofino Way at Harbor Dr; adult/child $4.50/3.25; 10am-5:45pm late May–Sep), a large saltwater swimming pool heated by the nearby steam-generating plant and framed by a sandy beach with picnic tables, volleyball courts and a snack bar.

## Palos Verdes Peninsula     Map pp62–3

A rocky precipice rising from the sea and separating Santa Monica Bay from San Pedro Bay, the Palos Verdes Peninsula (PV, for short) is spectacular, conservative and exclusive. People living in the four small, homogenous communities here enjoy some of the highest per capita income in the country. Bridle paths parallel many of the meandering, hilly roads lined by grand old trees and even grander villas and mansions. If you're lucky, you may encounter a few of Palos Verdes' resident peacocks, introduced back in the 1920s by real-estate developers.

Palos Verdes Dr W takes you past cliffs and coves along the largely unspoiled, rugged coastline with sublime views of the ocean and Catalina Island. The only easily accessible sandy beach is **Malaga Cove**; **Abalone Cove** is an ecological reserve with teeming tide pools. There's great surfing at **Lunada Bay**, but unfortunately locals have a bad case of territorialism, and the hostility towards outsiders is rather infamous.

Driving along the coast takes you past the **Point Vicente Interpretive Center** ( ☎ 310-377-5370; 31501 Palos Verdes Dr W; adult/concession $2/1; 1-6pm Mon-Fri, 10am-5pm Sat & Sun), which is a great spot for landlubbers to scan the waters for migrating Pacific gray whales between December and April. A small exhibit enlightens you about these amazing sea mammals and doubles as a local history museum. On a nearby cliff stands the 1926 **Point Vicente Lighthouse** ( ☎ 310-541-0334), which was staffed until 1971. One of the biggest and brightest lights along the coast, it can be seen up to 20 miles out at sea. Free tours are held from 11am to 3pm on the second Saturday of the month.

Continuing down the coast will soon take you to the 1949 **Wayfarers Chapel** ( ☎ 310-377-7919; www.wayfarerschapel.org; 5755 Palos Verdes Dr S; admission free; 8am-5pm), an enchanting hillside structure surrounded by mature redwood trees and gardens. The work of Lloyd Wright, it is almost entirely made of glass and is one of LA's most popular wedding spots.

Before leaving PV, any flower fans should head inland to the **South Coast Botanic Garden** ( ☎ 310-544-6815; www.southcoastbotanicgarden.org; 26300 Crenshaw Blvd; adult/child 5-12/student $7/2.50/5; 9am-5pm), which has been reclaimed from a former landfill. When roaming among the flowering fruit trees, redwoods, roses, dahlias and some other 2000 species, remember you're actually on a huge pile of trash. A tram operates on the weekends, and plant shows and sales take place year-round.

## San Pedro    Map pp62–3

South of Palos Verdes, San Pedro is the burial place of Charles Bukowski but is more commonly known as the slow-paced harbor community on the edge of Worldport LA. Formed by the twin ports of LA and Long Beach, Worldport is the world's third largest port (after Singapore and Hong Kong).

San Pedro's historic downtown area is bracketed by 6th and 7th Sts and Pacific Ave and Harbor Blvd. This is where you'll find such restaurants as Papadakis Taverna (p163), and the **Warner Grand Theater** ( ☎ 310-548-7466; 478 W 6th St), a lovely art deco movie palace. The best time to be in town is on the first Thursday of the month for the **San Pedro Art Walk**, which is really more of a street fair with crafts vendors and entertainment held throughout much of downtown.

Most of San Pedro's attractions, though, are along the waterfront. From 10am to 6pm Friday to Monday, when the cruise ships are in town, all of the major sights are connected by a historic waterfront 'Red Car' trolley and two regular electric-trolley routes (all-day fare $1).

### LOS ANGELES MARITIME MUSEUM & AROUND

In a former Streamline Moderne car-ferry terminal this **museum** ( ☎ 310-548-7618; www.lamaritimemuseum.org; Berth 84; suggested donation $1; 10am-5pm Tue-Sat, noon-5pm Sun) at the bottom of 6th St has enough ship models, figureheads and navigational equipment to keep your imagination afloat for a couple of hours. There are exhibits about battleships, commercial diving, whaling and recreational sailing. A highlight of the passenger-ship section is an 18ft cutaway model of the *Titanic*. The museum is wheelchair accessible.

About 1 mile north of the museum, the **SS Lane Victory** ( ☎ 310-519-9545; www.lanevictory.org; Berth 94; adult/child 5-15 $3/1; 9am-4pm) is an immaculately restored WWII-era cargo ship. Self-guided tours take in the engine room and the cargo holds.

A short walk south of the maritime museum is the touristy **Ports O'Call Village** ( ☎ 310-732-7696; Berth 77; admission free; 24hr). Ignore the kitschy trinket stores and concentrate on enjoying a fresh seafood bonanza at the many casual harbor-view restaurants (see p163). Afterwards, hop on a port cruise or join a whale-watching trip (January to March).

Deep-sea fishing excursions are available also. For details see p134.

### CABRILLO MARINE AQUARIUM

The coastal waters off Southern California teem with the kind of marine life that inhabit the tanks at this small but entertaining **aquarium** ( ☎ 310-548-7562; www.cabrilloaq.org; 3720 Stephen White Dr; admission by donation, suggested adult/child $5/1; noon-5pm Tue-Fri, 10am-5pm Sat & Sun). In a modern seaside structure by Frank Gehry, you can meet the aquatic denizens that live in such habitats as the surf-battered rocky shores, the sandy beaches and mudflats, and the open ocean. Jellyfish, sharks and starfish are among the critters you'll encounter. Curators also run kid-oriented educational programs, whale-watching trips and grunion-watches (April to July). Parking is $7 per car (free Monday to Friday, November to February).

### POINT FERMIN PARK

South of the Cabrillo Marine Aquarium, this coastal park, the southernmost point in LA, is a grassy bluff with great ocean views and access to tide pools and beaches. Bring a picnic or pop into the landmark Walker's Café near the park entrance. The highlight, though, is the newly restored 1874 **Point Fermin Lighthouse** ( ☎ 310-548-7618; admission free; 1-3:30pm Sun), the only remaining wooden lighthouse in the world. Also check out the summer concert series (p171).

### ANGELS GATE PARK & AROUND

Head uphill from Point Fermin to Angels Gate Park to visit the **Korean Friendship Bell**, which was given to the US by South Korea and is fashioned after an 8th-century bronze bell. Northwest of here is the **Fort MacArthur Military Museum** ( ☎ 310-548-2631; 3601 S Gaffey St; donations appreciated; noon-5pm Sat & Sun) inside a battery that was once part of the military harbor defense system that was in place between 1916 and 1945. Photos, paintings and memorabilia document this era.

### WILMINGTON

Just north of San Pedro is the small town of Wilmington, the one-time home of city pioneer Phineas Banning (1830–85), the 'father' of the Los Angeles harbor. His 1864 Greek Revival mansion is now the **Banning Residence Museum** ( ☎ 310-548-7777; www.banningmuseum.org;

401 East M St; admission by donation $3; ☽ tours hourly 12:30-2:30pm Tue-Thu, 12:30-3:30pm Sat-Sun). Packed with period antiques, it is a superb re-creation of how well-heeled 19th-century Angelenos lived.

Two blocks south is the only surviving Civil War–era structure in Southern California, the **Drum Barracks Civil War Museum** ( ☎ 310-548-7509; www.drumbarracks.org; 1052 N Banning Blvd; suggested donation $3; ☽ tours hourly 10am-1pm Tue-Thu, 11:30am-2:30pm Sat & Sun). It is filled with artifacts from the years 1861–6 when this was a training center and supply depot for battlegrounds in Arizona, Southern California and New Mexico.

### Long Beach                                    Map pp62–3
Long Beach, on the border with Orange County, has come a long way from its working-class oil and navy days, but gentrification hasn't completely ruined its relaxed, small-town atmosphere – at least not yet. Much of the spiffing up effort has been concentrated along the waterfront where **Shoreline Village** is a pleasant, if artificial, cluster of touristy shops and restaurants. Harbor and other boat cruises leave from here as well.

Across the water you can spot Long Beach's two flagship attractions, the Aquarium of the Pacific and the majestic *Queen Mary* ocean liner. The waterfront is cut off from the downtown area by a huge convention center and other facilities. The main downtown drag is Pine Ave, which is chockablock with restaurants, nightclubs and bars. About 3 miles east of here are the upscale neighborhoods of Belmont Shore and canal-laced Naples. Every April, Formula 1 fans flood Long Beach, where much of the downtown area is turned into a giant racetrack for the Toyota Grand Prix of Long Beach.

Downtown Long Beach is the southern terminus of the Metro Blue Line. A shuttle service, called Passport, serves all major places of interest on four routes (free within downtown; 90¢ otherwise). Passport bus Nos A and D both go out to Belmont Shore. The **Transit Information Center** ( ☎ 562-591-875; www.lbtransit.com; 223 1st St; ☽ 7:30am-4:30pm Mon-Fri) has details about getting around. Also here is **Bikestation** ( ☎ 562-436-2453; 105 The Promenade N; ☽ 7am-6pm Mon-Fri, 10am-5pm Sat & Sun) which rents bicycles from $8 per hour or $33 per day.

#### AQUARIUM OF THE PACIFIC
One of the largest watery zoos in the country, the **Aquarium of the Pacific** ( ☎ 562-590-3100;

---

**DETOUR: SANTA CATALINA ISLAND**

Mediterranean-flavored Santa Catalina Island is a world removed from the bustle of LA. Known locally as Catalina Island, or simply Catalina, it is part of the Channel Islands, a chain of semi-submerged mountains off the coast of Southern California. Catalina has a unique ecosystem and rather tumultuous history. Before appearing on the radar screen of vacationers in the late 19th century, it went through phases as a hangout for sea-otter poachers, smugglers and Union soldiers. Chewing-gum magnate William Wrigley Jr (1861–1932) purchased the place in 1919 and for a few years brought his baseball team, the Chicago Cubs, here for spring training. The island is now largely owned by the Santa Catalina Island Conservancy, which ensures that most of it remains free of development.

Nearly all tourist activity concentrates in the pint-sized port town of **Avalon**, with the yacht-studded harbor hemming in a cluster of cutesy shops and restaurants. Also here is the Green Pier, home of the **Catalina Visitors Bureau** ( ☎ 310-510-1520; www.catalina.com; ☽ vary). It's a nice stroll along the waterfront to the 1929 art deco **Casino** ( ☎ 310-510-0179; 1 Casino Way), which was never a gambling joint but a dance and concert hall. Today it contains a movie theater and the **Catalina Island Museum** ( ☎ 310-510-2595; adult/child/senior $2.50/1/2; ☽ 10am-4pm, closed Tue Jan-Mar).

Behind the casino, divers and snorkelers frolic in the **Casino Point Marine Park**, where schools of fish flit through thick kelp beds and majestic golden garibaldi cruise serenely. **Catalina Divers Supply** ( ☎ 310-510-0330; www.catalinadiverssupply.com) rents equipment and operates guided dive tours from $85, including all gear. Continuing past the casino takes you to **Descanso Beach** (admission $2), a private beach club with sandy and grassy areas for tanning, and a restaurant. Consuming alcohol is allowed on this beach, a rarity in the US.

www.aquariumofpacific.org; 100 Aquarium Way; adult/child/senior $19/11/15; ⊗ 9am-6pm) is a joyful, high-tech romp through an intriguing underwater world where sharks dart, jellyfish dance and sea lions frolic. The 12,500 creatures that call this grand space home hail from such different habitats as the bays and lagoons of Baja California, the icy waters of the northern Pacific, the Technicolor coral reefs of the tropics and even the rich kelp forests swaying in local waters.

If you've always wanted to pet a predator, make a beeline to the **Shark Lagoon**, where shallow touch pools teem with young zebra, nurse and bamboo sharks. Their fiercer cousins, including sand tiger sharks and adult-sized zebra sharks, patrol a larger tank. Crowds gather for the daily feeding sessions.

Elsewhere, you'll be entertained by the antics of sea otters, spooked by football-sized crabs with spiny 3ft-long arms, and charmed by a fleet of drifting sea dragons cleverly camouflaged like a piece of kelp. It's a wondrous world that'll easily keep you enthralled for hours. For an extra fee, the aquarium offers behind-the-scenes tours and, from late May to early September, ocean boat trips. Parking is $6. The facility is fully accessible to the mobility impaired.

Adjacent to the aquarium is Long Beach's newest development, the **Pike at Rainbow Harbor**, where diversions include an antique carousel, a GameWorks arcade, an all-stadium multiplex movie theater (with tiered seating ensuring everyone can see the screen) and chain restaurants galore.

## QUEEN MARY

The *Titanic* may have captured all the headlines, but the grand dame of ocean liners was actually the **Queen Mary** ( ☎ 310-435-3511; www.queenmary.com; 1126 Queens Hwy; adult/child/senior $23/12/20; ⊗ 10am-6pm, hr vary by season). From 1936 to 1964 the giant vessel crossed the Atlantic exactly 1001 times, carrying celebrities, royalty and regular folks. During WWII, she transported troops to the European battlefields, then returned with shiploads of war brides after the fighting stopped. A Long Beach tourist attraction since 1967, part of the ship houses a hotel (p148), restaurants such as Sir Winston's (p163) and the art deco Observation Bar. The Sunday champagne brunch is among the best in town.

Basic admission includes a self-guided tour as well as the tongue-in-cheek 'Ghosts & Legends' special-effects tour, which takes you down into the ship's underbelly, including

Kayaking is big on Catalina and there's a **rental outfit** ( ☎ 310-510-1226) right at Descanso Beach. Paddling out from here quickly gets you away from the crowds and into the backcountry with its rugged coastline, coves and canyons. This is some of the finest kayaking anywhere in Southern California.

The main inland attraction in Avalon is the **Wrigley Memorial & Botanical Garden** ( ☎ 310-510-2595; 1400 Avalon Canyon Rd; admission $3; ⊗ 8am-5pm), about 1½ miles from the port. The memorial, built with blue flagstone and decorated with glazed tile, overlooks the garden with its impressive cacti groves, succulents and six endemic plant species, including the ultra-rare Catalina mahogany.

The only other island settlement is remote **Two Harbors** in Catalina's largely undeveloped backcountry of sun-baked hillsides, valleys and canyons. A curiosity here is the herd of bison, left behind from a 1924 movie shoot. The island's interior is a protected nature preserve and may only be explored on foot or mountain bike (permits required; call ☎ 310-510-1421) or on an organized tour (from $30) such as those offered by **Discovery Tours** ( ☎ 310-510-8687) or **Jeep Eco-Tours** ( ☎ 310-510-2595).

Catalina's main tourist season is June to September when prices soar and the island seems to sink from the load of day-trippers. Consider spending the night when the ambience goes from frantic to romantic in no time. The visitors bureau can help you find accommodation.

**Catalina Express** ( ☎ 310-519-1212, 800-481-3470; www.catalinaexpress.com; round-trip about $50) operates frequent scheduled ferries to Avalon from San Pedro (Map pp62-3; 1¼ hours), Long Beach (Map pp62-3; one hour) and Dana Point (Orange County, 1½ hours), and to Two Harbors from San Pedro (1½ hours) only. From Newport Beach in Orange County, the **Catalina Flyer** ( ☎ 949-673-5245; www.caladventures.com) also goes to Avalon (round-trip $44, 1¼ hours, once daily).

the first-class swimming pool and the boiler room. Dedicated ghost busters should get the Haunted Encounters Passport (adult/child/senior $28/17/25), which includes a visit to the onboard Paranormal Research Center. For a full Queen Mary immersion, sign up for the First Class Passage (adult/child/senior $28/17/25).

The latter also gives you access to the **Scorpion** (adult/concession $10/9), an authentic Soviet submarine moored right next to the *Queen*. As you scramble around the living quarters or the engine and torpedo rooms, try to imagine how 78 crew members, sharing 27 bunks and two bathrooms, subsisted in here for months at a time.

### MUSEUM OF LATIN AMERICAN ART
Anchoring Long Beach's fledgling East Village Arts District, this fine **museum** ( ☎ 562-437-1689; www.molaa.org; 628 Alamitos Ave; adult/child under 12/student/senior $5/free/3/3, admission free on Fri; ☼ 11:30am-7pm Tue-Fri, 11am-7pm Sat, 11am-6pm Sun) proves that there's more to Latin-American art than Diego Rivera and Frida Kahlo. Selections from the permanent collection and temporary exhibits showcase the wealth of creativity that has come from Mexico, Central and South America and the Caribbean since the end of WWII. The restaurant is a nice lunch spot.

### LONG BEACH MUSEUM OF ART
Sitting pretty on a waterfront bluff, this little **museum** ( ☎ 562-439-2119; www.lbma.org; 2300 E Ocean Blvd; adult/child under 12/student/senior $5/free/4/4; ☼ 11am-5pm Tue & Wed, 11am-8pm Thu, 11am-5pm Fri-Sun) presents a lively schedule of changing exhibitions mostly drawn from its collection of American decorative arts, California Modernism, contemporary art (including video) and early 20th-century European art. It's all housed in a sparkling new pavilion adjacent to a 1912 Craftsman mansion with a fun little store and café.

### NAPLES & BELMONT SHORE
Hugging the Orange County line, the canal-laced elite borough of Naples was the 1903 brainchild of Arthur Parsons, a contemporary of Venice's Abbot Kinney. The best way to enjoy this exclusive neighborhood is by being poled around it aboard an authentic gondola (p135). A bridge connects Naples to almost-as-upscale Belmont Shore, which has great shopping and eating along 2nd St and a fun pier for fishing and sunset watching.

## Downtown Los Angeles    Map pp64–5
Few LA neighborhoods are as densely packed with fun things to see and do as Downtown, a place that's rich in history, architecture, restaurants and cultural institutions. Framed by freeways, the area embraces the entire human experience, from City Hall politicians forging the city's future to upwardly hopeful immigrants working in sweatshops and retail, from captains of industry steering their corporate ships to transients trying to survive on Skid Row.

Sure, not too many people actually live here, but that's a trend that's gradually reversing. A mix of new construction and the conversion of aging warehouses and office buildings into stylish lofts is bringing in adventurous urbanites fed up with suburbia. There's a budding arts district near Little Tokyo, hip new galleries and bars in Chinatown and a trendy new hotel, the Standard Downtown LA (p149), whose rooftop lounge draws hipsters from around town. New public buildings further fuel the buzz, most notably Frank Gehry's Walt Disney Concert Hall (p107), LA's newest landmark and only a short walk away from its oldest, the Avila Adobe in El Pueblo de Los Angeles (p104).

If you're open-minded and don't mind a little grit and grime here and there, Downtown is your oyster. Thanks to its compactness, it's also one of the few LA neighborhoods that's best explored on foot. The walking tour in this guide (p130) offers a good introduction to the area. If you're arriving by car, you can save by parking away from the congested Financial District and Pershing Square areas. There are several lots in South Park and Little Tokyo, for instance, charging only $4 or $5 all day. An excellent way to get around is by DASH shuttle (p195).

### EL PUEBLO DE LOS ANGELES
Compact, colorful and car-free, this vibrant historic district sits near the spot where the first colonists settled in 1781. It preserves LA's oldest buildings, including some from the time when the city was little more than a dusty, lawless outpost. More than anything, though, El Pueblo is a microcosm of LA's multiethnic heritage and the contributions

Mexican dancers, Cinco de Mayo
(p137), Downtown LA

Rose Parade (p137), Pasadena

Volleyball, Hermosa Beach (p100), LA

RICHARD CUMMINS

Getty Center (p91), Brentwood, LA

STUART WASSER

Santa Monica (p95)

Pony rides, Griffith Park (p118), LA

NEIL SETCHFIELD

**BLESSINGS BE UPON YE!**

Catholics tend to be equal opportunity blessers and nowhere are their blessings more quirkily bestowed than in LA. The city boasts not one but two festivals where soul-saving words fly as thick as fishwives' curses. The first, with origins in the 1700s, is the **Blessing of the Animals** and takes place in El Pueblo de Los Angeles the Saturday before Easter. Three-legged pit bulls, whacked-out monkeys, Chihuahuas in sombreros, banty roosters and iguanas: if it slithers, slimes, snarls, flies, crawls or hauls, your pet will receive an abundant blessing here from none other than Cardinal Roger Mahoney himself. Properly honored, it then enjoys the right to parade around with its owner, humbly displaying its feathers, fur and fangs. Artist Leo Politi has captured the goings-on in an endearing mural facing El Pueblo's Old Plaza.

Across town, the San Fernando Valley is the birthplace of the **Blessing of the Cars**, which was dreamed up a little over a decade ago by two Catholic sisters who were inordinately fond of both their cars and blessing things. Taking place in late July, the event has since grown into one of the wildest scenes in LA. There are cars! cars! cars!, rock and roll, hot-rod movies and a priest who will – if presumed upon – place holy water in your radiator. There are more tattoos on display than in the US Navy and more boobs clambering for attention than in the US Senate. Lord help us!

For details about either festival, see p137.

made by immigrants from Mexico, France, Italy and China. A fine way to learn more about this legacy is by joining a **free tour** run by enthusiastic volunteers at 10am, 11am and noon Tuesday through Saturday. Meet up at the Old Plaza Firehouse (p106).

The Pueblo's lifeline, and what most people come to see, is **Olvera St** (www.calleolvera.com), an exuberant brick alley that's like a trip to Mexico without a passport. Sure, the gaudy decorations and kitschy souvenir stalls might scream 'tourist trap,' but there are actually some fairly authentic experiences to be had. You can shop for Chicano art in classy galleries, slurp thick Mexican-style hot chocolate in an artsy café or pick up handmade candles or candy. At lunchtime, a small army of budget gourmets invades the many little eateries for delicious tacos, bulging tortas (sandwiches) and other treats.

Even few Angelenos know that there would be no Olvera Street today without the vision and verve of civic champion Christine Sterling. By the 1920s LA's original business district had devolved into a pitiful slum, which was scheduled to be razed to make room for a railway station. Sterling had a different idea. She wanted to create a bustling marketplace to pay tribute to the city's Spanish and Mexican heritage. With a little help from deep-pocketed friends such as *Los Angeles Times* publisher Harry Chandler, and free prison labor, Olvera St opened to great fanfare in 1930.

There's a small exhibit about Sterling, who's known as the 'mother of Olvera St,' in the **Avila Adobe** ( ☎ 213-680-2525; E-10 Olvera St; admission free; ☉ 9am-3pm), LA's oldest existing building. Built in 1818 by Francisco Avila, a wealthy ranchero and one-time LA mayor, it went through later periods as a military headquarters, a boardinghouse and a restaurant. The restored rooms, comfortably furnished in heavy oak, provide a look at 1840s life and are open for self-guided tours. Sterling herself lived here until her death in 1963.

Nearby is the 1887 **Sepulveda House** ( ☎ 213-628-1274, 213-680-2525; Olvera St; admission free; ☉ 10am-3pm Mon-Sat), a lovely Eastlake Victorian that went from being a boardinghouse (a restored kitchen and bedroom are still there) to puppet theater and WWII United Service Organizations (USO) canteen. It now houses **El Pueblo Visitors Center** where you can view a 20-minute historical video and pick up various kinds of brochures and pamphlets.

A few doors down is the **Italian Hall** ( 644-1/2 Main St) whose upper south facade is adorned by *América Tropical*, a rare **mural** by David Alfaro Siqueiros, one of Mexico's three great 20th-century muralists. The 1932 work was whitewashed almost immediately for its provocative (ie communist-flavored) theme. The Getty Conservation Institute recently cleaned up the mural but subsequently installed a protective cover to prevent deterioration. The building itself might soon house an Italian-American museum.

Olvera St spills into the **Old Plaza**, El Pueblo's central square with a pretty wrought-iron bandstand. This is where families stroll, couples kiss and everyone seeks shade beneath the grand old Australian Moreton Bay fig trees. Sprinkled throughout are sculptures of people instrumental in the founding of LA, including Felipe de Neve, who led the first group of settlers, and King Carlos III of Spain, who financed the venture. The colonists' names are engraved on a nearby bronze plaque. The best time to visit the plaza is during Cinco de Mayo (p137), the Blessing of the Animals (p105) or any other of the many Mexican festivals.

Across the street the little 1822 church affectionately known as **La Placita** ( ☎ 213-629-3101; 535 N Main St; admission free; ⏲ 7am-7pm), meaning 'Little Plaza,' is a sentimental favorite with LA's Latino community. On busy weekends priests go hoarse performing up to a dozen Spanish-language masses and hundreds of baptisms. Peek inside for a look at the gold-festooned altar and nicely painted ceiling.

The majestic building on the plaza's south side is **Pico House** (430 Main St), built in 1870 by Pio Pico, the last Mexican governor of California. It was LA's first three-story building and at one time a glamorous hotel. Next door is the **Old Plaza Firehouse** ( ☎ 213-625-3741; 134 Paseo de la Plaza; admission free; ⏲ 10am-3pm Tue-Sun), the city's oldest fire station from 1884. After incarnations as a saloon, a boardinghouse and stores, it is now a museum of 19th-century fire-fighting equipment and photographs.

Just south of here is the brand-new **Chinese American Museum** ( ☎ 213-485-8567; www.camla.org; 425 N Los Angeles St; adult/student/senior $3/2/2; ⏲ 10am-3pm Tue-Sun) in the 1890 Garnier Building, once the unofficial 'city hall' of LA's original Chinatown. An eclectic assortment of photographs, period clothing, temple accoutrements, jewelry boxes and musical instruments sheds light on the life and hardships endured by the early Chinese immigrants. Many items were donated by members of the local community.

Southeast of El Pueblo is **Union Station** (800 N Alameda St), built in 1939 as the last of the grand railroad stations in the US. It's a glamorous exercise in Spanish Mission and art deco and has a waiting room easily the size of a football field and with the loftiness of a cathedral. The station is often used as a movie location; you may have seen it in *Guilty by Suspicion, Blade Runner* or *The Way We Were*.

The twin domes north of the station belong to the **Terminal Annex**, which until 1994 housed LA's central post office. This is where local 'dirty old man' Charles Bukowski worked for years, inspiring the 1971 novel *Post Office* (p33).

## CHINATOWN

As you walk north from El Pueblo, the aroma of chili and beans gradually gives way to soy and bok choy. Created in 1938, LA's small and compact **Chinatown** ( ☎ 213-680-0243; www.chinatownla.com) is still the Chinese-American community's traditional hub even if most Chinese Americans now live in suburban Monterey Park and San Gabriel east of here. Everyone returns for the Chinese New Year's celebrations (usually in February) when a parade of giant dragons, decorated floats and lion dancers brightens Broadway, the main drag.

All year long, restaurants beckon with dim sum, kung pao and Peking duck, while shops overflow with curios, culinary oddities (live frogs anyone?), ancient herbal remedies and lucky bamboo. Signs of revitalization abound. On once-rundown Chung King Rd, a burgeoning arts scene is luring hipsters from around town, while Quentin Tarantino may breathe new life into the abandoned King Hing movie theater.

There are no essential sights here, but the area, a stop on Metro Gold Line, is still a fun place for casual wandering. Your explorations might start in the **Central Plaza** (900 block of Broadway), a small and unabashedly touristy walking mall presided over by a statue of Sun Yat-sen, the Chinese revolutionary leader and founder of the Republic of China (Taiwan). Some of Chinatown's oldest buildings are here, including a five-tiered pagoda from 1941 that houses **Hop Louie** (p170), a restaurant and bar dripping in noir ambience. Challenge your fate by tossing a coin in the **wishing well**, an endearingly naive piece of chinoiserie that's been around since 1939. To get to the galleries and studios of **Chung King Rd**, cross Hill St to West Plaza, which features in the autobiographical novel *On Gold Mountain* by acclaimed Chinese-American writer Lisa See. For details about individual galleries, see p182.

Back on Broadway, make a quick stop at the legendary **Phoenix Bakery** (p184) before heading south past various shopping malls selling cut-rate clothing, toys and knick-knacks. An exotic **farmers market** (p184) takes place on Thursdays one block west of here (on the corner of Hill and Alpine Sts). The district's nicest temple, the ornate **Ten Ho Temple** (750 Yale St), is another block west of the market.

## DODGER STADIUM

Just north of Chinatown, atop a chaparral-cloaked hilltop across I-110 (Pasadena Fwy), sits one of the country's most beloved baseball parks, **Dodger Stadium** (off Map pp64-5; ☎ 323-224-1448; 1000 Elysian Park Ave; tour adult/child 4-14 $8/4; ☯ 2pm Tue-Fri on nongame days Apr-Sep), home of the Los Angeles Dodgers. The one-hour tour takes you to the press box, the radio and TV booths, the Dodger dugout, the Dugout Club, a luxury suite and other areas. Reservations for the tours are required at least one hour in advance. For information about tickets to see a game, see p181.

## CITY HALL

LA's **City Hall** (☎ 213-485-2121; 200 N Spring St; admission free; ☯ 8am-5pm Mon-Fri) is the shining beacon in a sea of architectural mediocrity that marks the Civic Center area south of El Pueblo across US 101 (Hollywood Fwy). City Hall cameoed as the *Daily Planet* building in the *Superman* TV series, served as Jack Webb's home base in the original *Dragnet* and got blown to bits in the 1953 sci-fi thriller *War of the Worlds*. In real life, though, it serves merely as the nerve center of LA politics.

From its dedication in 1928 until 1966 no building in town stood taller than this gleaming white art deco behemoth whose central tower soars skyward for 28 stories. If the smog isn't bad, it's well worth heading to the wraparound observation deck for great views of Downtown, the surrounding city and the mountains. Right below is a gallery with portraits of all mayors since the city's 1851 founding. Coming back down, stop on the 3rd level for a look at the domed rotunda with a marble floor as intricately patterned as those in Italian cathedrals. Enter on Spring St and be prepared to show ID and have your stuff x-rayed. Free tours run from 9am to 2pm, Monday to Friday.

News junkies can get their fix on a free tour of North America's largest daily newspaper, the **Los Angeles Times** (☎ 213-237-5757; 202 W 1st St; ☯ tours 9:30am, 11am & 1:30pm Mon-Fri), one block southwest of City Hall. Tours offer a close-up look at the inner workings of publishing and the history of this storied paper. Reservations are required at least one week in advance; children under 10 are not permitted.

## GRAND AVE CULTURAL CORRIDOR

Grand Avenue, on the northern edge of the Civic Center area, is being touted as the epicenter of Downtown revitalization with its architectural landmarks, museums and emerging dining scene.

### Walt Disney Concert Hall

The undisputed centerpiece along Grand Ave is the sparkling **Walt Disney Concert Hall** (☎ 323-850-2000; www.laphil.com; 111 S Grand Ave; audio tour adult/student/senior $10/8/8; ☯ 9am-3pm nonmatinee days, 9am-10:30am matinee days), Frank Gehry's latest masterpiece and the new home of the Los Angeles Philharmonic. It's a silvery free-form sculpture of curving and billowing stainless-steel walls which conjures visions of a ship adrift in a rough sea. The exquisite auditorium, though, feels like the inside of a finely crafted instrument, a cello perhaps, clad in walls of smooth Douglas fir. It's an imposing yet intimate hall with a 'vineyard' arrangement that has the audience sitting on terraced blocks wrapped around a central stage. Even seats under the giant pipe organ, which looks like a giant bag of french fries, offer excellent sightlines and still-decent acoustics.

Also part of the complex are the Redcat (p179) theater, the Patina (p165) restaurant, a gift shop and two outdoor amphitheaters. The small garden, with its rose-shaped fountain made of shards of blue-and-white porcelain from Delft, is well worth a spin as well.

Although a huge success, the complex has also proven a little too 'brilliant.' It seems that neighbors and motorists have complained about the pesky glare generated by the building's stainless steel exterior. At press time, sandblasting the metal to create a duller finish seemed to be the likely solution to the problem.

You can rent a self-guided audio tour, which reveals much about the history, architecture and acoustics of the complex but doesn't take you inside the auditorium. For details about the LA Phil, see p178.

### Music Center

The LA Phil's old home, the **Dorothy Chandler Pavilion**, is just northeast of the Walt Disney Concert Hall and is now used for an expanded schedule by the LA Opera (p178). Along with the **Mark Taper Forum** (p178) and the **Ahmanson Theatre** (p179), the pavilion forms the **Music Center** ( ☎ 213-972-7200, tours ☎ 213-972-7483; www.musiccenter.org; 135 N Grand Ave; free guided tours; ✆ 10am-1:30pm Tue-Fri, 10am-noon Sat). Tours, which also make a brief stop in the lobby of the Walt Disney Concert Hall, depart from the pavilion's main entrance.

### Cathedral of Our Lady of the Angels

Another new Downtown landmark is the **Cathedral of Our Lady of the Angels** ( ☎ 213-680-5200; www.olacathedral.org; 555 W Temple St; admission free; ✆ 6:30am-7pm Mon-Fri, 9am-7pm Sat, 7am-7pm Sun; **P** ), the first Roman Catholic cathedral built in the western US in three decades. Spanish architect José Rafael Moneo created a dramatically contemporary structure that is completely without right angles. Behind its austere, ochre mantle awaits a vast room of worship whose monumentalism is tempered by the soft natural light filtering through milky, alabaster windows. It's quite a stunning effect.

Art abounds from the moment you enter through Robert Graham's massive bronze doors guarded by a Madonna sculpture. The walls of the main nave are clad in enormous tapestries as intricate and detailed as a Michelangelo fresco. Designed by John Nava, they depict a procession of 135 saints from around the world and throughout the ages, including Mother Teresa. Their gaze is directed towards the main altar, a massive yet simple slab of red marble pivoting on a pillar festooned with bronze angels. Above it all looms a giant cross framed by windows.

To learn more, join a free guided tour at 1pm, Mondays to Fridays, or pick up a self-guided tour booklet at the cathedral store. Free organ recitals take place at 12:45pm on Wednesdays.

### Colburn School of Performing Arts

On Grand Avenue, strolling south of the Walt Disney Concert Hall takes you past an odd building whose steeply pitched zinc roof looks like an upside-down cake tin. Inside is the **Colburn School of Performing Arts** ( ☎ 213-621-2200; www.colburnschool.edu; 200 S Grand Ave), which is sometimes called the 'Julliard of the West.' Check for student or faculty concerts (sometimes free).

### Museum of Contemporary Art & California Plaza

A must for fans of contemporary art is **MOCA Grand Ave** ( ☎ 213-626-6222; www.moca.org; 250 S Grand Ave; adult/child under 12/student/senior $8/free/5/5; ✆ 11am-5pm Mon, 11am-8pm Thu, 11am-5pm Fri, 11am-6pm Sat & Sun). Its collection of paintings, sculptures and photographs from the 1940s to the present – pop art to minimalism – is considered one of the world's finest for this period. All the heavy hitters are there, from Robert Rauschenberg to Mark Rothko and Jackson Pollock. MOCA has also hosted major touring exhibits, including the acclaimed Andy Warhol retrospective in 2003.

It's all within a building that many consider Arata Isozaki's masterpiece. The Japanese star architect combined cubes, pyramids and cylinders with glass, aluminum and red sandstone to create a bold yet fanciful art space whose whitewashed galleries are flooded with natural light from skylights. Free tours are offered at noon, 1pm and 2pm. There's also a cool bookstore–gift shop and Patinette, an indoor-outdoor café with great lattes and paninis. Wheelchair access is excellent.

MOCA is shadowed by the glistening towers of California Plaza, a vast office complex that hosts the **Grand Performances**, one of the best free outdoor performance arts series held in summer (p171). On the southeastern side of the plaza is **Angels Flight**, a historic funicular that was briefly revived in 1996 only to be mothballed again five years later after a derailed car left one person dead and injured others. There are stairs down to Hill St and the wonderful **Grand Central Market** (p164), although you may have to hopscotch around a few homeless folks to get there.

### Wells Fargo Center

On Grand Ave, pop into the small but intriguing **Wells Fargo History Museum** ( ☎ 213-253-7166; www.wellsfargohistory.com/museums/lamuseum.html; 333 S Grand Ave; admission free; ✆ 9am-5pm Mon-Fri), which relives the gold rush area with all sorts of artifacts. Imagine how the West was won as you walk past an original Concord stagecoach, a 100oz gold nugget and a 19th-century bank office. The friendly staff is only too happy to answer questions or start the 15-minute video about the history of the West and Wells Fargo's role in it.

The museum is part of the **Wells Fargo Center**, another huge office complex that's filled with public art, including numerous nude sculptures by Robert Graham dotted around the glassy atrium and Jean Dubuffet's cartoonish *Le Dandy* in the Hope St entrance vestibule.

### FINANCIAL DISTRICT

LA's traditional business and financial district got its skyscraper-studded skyline during an aggressive building boom in the 1970s and '80s. Its core, which stretches along Figueroa and Flower Sts between 5th and 8th Sts, is compact and of special interest to architecture fans.

The district is home to the **US Bank Tower** (655 W 5th St), which at 1017ft, is the tallest building between Chicago and Hong Kong. Until recently it was called 'Library Tower' because developers had to buy air rights from the adjacent Richard Riordan Central Library (see below) in order to exceed official height limits. Film buffs might remember it being attacked by an alien spaceship in *Independence Day*.

The tower abuts the **Bunker Hill Steps**, an attractive staircase that links 5th St with the Wells Fargo Center (p108) and other hilltop office complexes. At the top is a small fountain featuring a female nude by Robert Graham. En route you pass McCormick & Schmick's (p164), a seafood restaurant with a popular happy hour (p168).

Back on 5th St, across from the steps, is a beloved LA institution, the 1922 **Richard Riordan Central Library** ( ☎ 213-228-7000; www.lapl .org; 630 W 5th St; ☽ 10am-8pm Mon-Thu, 10am-6pm Fri & Sat, 1-5pm Sun), named for a former mayor. You can check email, read magazines and newspapers, browse the stacks, view the latest exhibits at the excellent Getty Gallery or the Photography Gallery, or grab a bite in the cafeteria. Free tours are available at 12:30pm Monday to Friday, 11am and 2pm on Saturday, and 2pm on Sunday.

The historic library is a beautiful building, designed by Bertram Goodhue and topped by a distinctive pyramid. Sphinxes greet you at the 5th St entrance and a colorful 1933 mural showing milestones in LA history swathes a 2nd-floor rotunda. The library's extensive children's section is next door in a room with a stunning Spanish Colonial painted wood-beamed ceiling and another historical mural.

In 1986 two arson fires destroyed or damaged over a million books and large sections of the building. When it reopened – seven years and $214 million later – an eight-story glass-roofed atrium and the **Maguire Gardens** had been added. The latter is a small but lovely spot, filled with benches, meandering paths, fountains and public art, all against a backdrop of cypress, olive and pepper trees. Also here is one of Downtown's finest restaurants, Café Pinot (p165).

Looking north on Flower St from the gardens you can spot the futuristic **Westin Bonaventure Hotel & Suites** (p150), whose glittering quintet of mirror-skinned cylinders might be familiar to moviegoers who've seen *Rain Man* and *In the Line of Fire*. Taking the bubble elevator to the top-floor cocktail lounge gives you a 360-degree view of Downtown LA.

Following Flower St south, past the twin towers of **ARCO Plaza** (515 S Flower St), which is buttressed by an underground shopping mall, takes you to 7th St where you'll find the remarkable **Fine Arts Building** (811 W 7th St), a 1927 structure that is a visual feast inside and out. Two giant figures representing Architecture and Sculpture peer down from the richly ornamented Romanesque facade, while the galleried Spanish Renaissance lobby is covered in lovely tile.

There's good shopping nearby in the **Macy's Plaza** (p191) and **7+Fig** (p191) malls. As you approach the latter, you can contemplate the perils of corporate greed symbolized by the man with his head stuck in the wall, an amusing yet provocative **sculpture** (725 S Figueroa St) by Terry Allen and Philip Levine. The Downtown Los Angeles Visitors Information Center (p57) is here as well.

### PERSHING SQUARE & AROUND

LA's oldest public park, **Pershing Sq** (www .laparks.org), bordered by 5th, 6th, Olive and Hill Sts, has been through several incarnations since being dedicated as Plaza Abaja (Lower Plaza) in 1866. It got its current name in 1918 in honor of WWI general, John J Pershing, and its current appearance in 1994 after a major clean-up and a redesign by Mexican architect Ricardo Legoretta. There's a purple tower and plenty of public art to enliven the square, but hardly any trees. Although it's not quite the urban oasis city planners envisioned, the park draws crowds for its special events, especially during the lunchtime summer concert series (p171) and for the ice-skating rink in December.

If Pershing Sq is a part of LA history, so is the hulking **Millennium Biltmore Hotel** ( ☎ 213-624-1011, 800-245-8673; www.millenniumhotels .com; 506 S Grand Ave), which has flanked its northern side since 1923. LA's oldest and grandest hotel has hosted presidents, kings and celebrities, plus the 1960 Democratic National Convention and eight Academy Awards ceremonies. Its sumptuous interior boasts carved and gilded ceilings, marble floors, grand staircases and palatial ballrooms, many of them decorated by Italian muralist Giovanni Smeraldi (who also did major work in the Washington White House). Afternoon tea is served daily from 2pm to 5pm in the rococo-style Rendezvous Court. See p149 for details about staying at the hotel.

Another graceful throwback to a glamorous past is the nearby 1927 **Oviatt Building** (617 S Olive St), an art deco gem that originally housed a fancy men's store and is now the home of the Cicada (p165) restaurant. After falling in love with art deco on a trip to Paris, store owner James Oviatt had all the fixtures and decorations for his new store shipped straight from France, including lots of exclusive decorative panels by famed glass designer René Lalique.

If architecture leaves you cold, perhaps a new silver bracelet or gold ring will warm your heart. You'll find a dizzying array of these and other baubles south of Pershing Sq throughout the **Jewelry District** (Olive & Hill Sts, btwn 6th & 8th Sts), the country's second-largest after New York.

Quality and styles vary widely and the atmosphere ain't Rodeo Dr, but with prices much lower than anywhere else in town nobody seems to mind. One of the marts occupies the historic **Pantages Theater** (401-21 W 7th St), a hugely popular vaudeville venue in the 1920s.

**BROADWAY THEATER DISTRICT**
Cacophonous, pungent and garish: Broadway between 3rd and 9th Sts pulses with a swirl of urban energy and activity all day long. Now a cut-rate retail strip catering primarily to Latino shoppers, this major thoroughfare is the spine of Downtown's historic core. It may be hard to imagine now, but in the early 20th century this was a glamorous shopping and entertainment district where people came to see vaudeville shows and silent movies. Huge crowds gathered to cheer Mary Pickford, Charlie Chaplin and other megastars of the day as they leapt from limos to attend lavish movie premieres.

Many of the early-20th-century buildings survive, including, most famously, a dozen former theaters built between 1913 and 1931 in dramatic styles of architecture, from beaux arts to East Indian to Spanish Gothic. Collectively they earned Broadway a spot on the National Register of Historic Places.

After WWII, as LA sprouted one suburb after another and Hollywood eclipsed Downtown as the epicenter of filmdom, Broadway plunged into decline. Most theaters closed and some were even gutted and turned into retail space. For the past decade or so, however, restoration-minded developers have slowly begun to reclaim the district block by block, building by building. It's a slow process, to say the least, and success isn't always apparent to outsiders. Judge for yourself.

The best way to get the latest inside scoop is on tours run by the Los Angeles Conservancy (p136), which take you inside some of these amazing theaters. Every June, the conservancy also hosts the Last Remaining Seats film series of Hollywood classics in a couple of these great theaters.

There are parking garages all along Broadway and one-hour free parking at the Grand Central Market (enter on Hill St) with $10 purchase.

**Bradbury Building**
This 1893 **building** ( ☎ 213-626-1893; 304 S Broadway; admission free; �9am-6pm Mon-Fri, 9am-5pm Sat & Sun) is one of LA's undisputed architectural crown jewels. Behind its red-brick facade awaits a breathtaking galleried atrium with inky cast-iron banisters and glazed brick walls; it's all flooded with natural light streaming in through a tent-shaped glass roof. Location

scouts love the place, whose star turn came in the cult flick *Blade Runner.*

The building was commissioned by mining mogul turned real-estate developer Lewis Bradbury who picked George Wyman, an unknown draftsman, to draw up the designs. Wyman allegedly accepted the gig after consulting a Ouija board and drew inspiration from the 1887 Edward Bellamy novel, *Looking Back,* about a utopian civilization in the year 2000. The Bradbury was Wyman's only success. Security staff hand out a free pamphlet with more details and let you go up to the 1st-floor landing.

### Biddy Mason Park

Just south of the Bradbury Building, this pocket-sized **park** ( ⊗ 8am-8pm Mon-Fri, 9am-8pm Sat & Sun) – actually more of courtyard with a few trees – pays homage to one of LA's African-American pioneers. Born a slave in the American South, Biddy Mason (1818–91) arrived in LA after the Civil War and became a property owner, philanthropist and, eventually, founder of the First African Methodist Episcopal Church, LA's first African-American church and still its most influential. An art installation by Betye Saar and Sheila Levrant de Bretteville chronicle Mason's amazing story.

### Grand Central Market

Across the street, in a 1905 beaux arts building where architect Frank Lloyd Wright once kept an office, is the frenzied **Grand Central Market** ( ☎ 213-624-2378; 317 S Broadway; ⊗ 9am-6pm). In business since 1917, this indoor market makes for a great browse. Shuffle along the sawdust-sprinkled aisles beneath old-timey ceiling fans and neon signs, and past stalls artfully arranged with mangoes, peppers, jicamas and other produce. Elsewhere you can stock up on spices, herbs, nuts and dried fruit, or snack on tasty soups, tacos or burritos (see p163). A few steps south, have a look at Johanna Poethig's monumental mural **Calle de la Eternidad** (Street of Eternity). Inspired by pre-Columbian art, it shows two arms reaching towards the heavens.

### Broadway Theaters

The stretch of Broadway between 6th and 9th Sts has the greatest concentration of movie palaces but first up, across from the Bradbury Building (see opposite), is the **Million Dollar Theater** (307 S Broadway), built for – surprise! – exactly $1 million in 1918. Note the frieze with eight exotic statues representing various forms of creativity, from dancing to painting, through the ages. The upper floors, which once housed the headquarters of the Metropolitan Water District, were recently restored as office and living space. The theater itself was most recently used as a church but is now closed. Big bands played here in the '40s and, a decade later, it became the first venue on Broadway to cater to Spanish speakers. Downstairs, the bizarre **Farmacia Million Dollar** (Million Dollar Pharmacy) sells potions and lotions to protect you from the devil and evil spirits.

Further south, the 1931 **Los Angeles Theater** (615 S Broadway) is a wonderfully over-the-top French baroque fantasy. Inside, a stunning three-tiered fountain anchors a sparkling hall of mirrors, elaborate chandeliers, a vaulted coffered ceiling and a grand central staircase. It opened in 1931 with the premiere of Charlie Chaplin's *City Lights,* which was attended by Albert Einstein, among other luminaries. These days it's used for special events and touring shows.

Across the street, the 1911 **Palace Theater** (630 S Broadway) is one of the oldest along here. Behind an exterior inspired by a Florentine palazzo lurks an intimate space filled with garland-draped columns and murals depicting pastoral scenes. It's still in good enough shape to host special events and parties.

In the next block, the 1921 **State Theater** (703 S Broadway), Broadway's biggest theater with almost 2500 seats, is now a Spanish-language church. The auditorium is often open during the day, although it's hard to appreciate the flamboyant ceiling in the dim light.

The 1913 **Globe Theater** (744 S Broadway), one of the oldest on the strip, started out as a live theater but, sadly, has been turned into a swap meet. The nearby 1927 **Tower Theater** (802 S Broadway) premiered the first all-talkie film, *The Jazz Singer.* Its wonderfully baroque interior was inspired by European opera houses and is often used for location shoots.

Next up is the fully restored 1926 **Orpheum Theater** (842 S Broadway), a spectacular space with rich silk tapestries, marble pilasters, a gilded coffered ceiling and even a still-functioning Wurlitzer organ. Judy Garland, George Burns and Nat King Cole were among the entertainers that used to perform here and these days it's often rented out for special events, including film screenings. The upstairs floors now offer stylish loft living.

Across the street, the 1929 **Eastern Columbia Building** (849 S Broadway) is a handsome art deco structure clad in a sparkling turquoise mantle. It's not a movie theater but originally housed a clothing store. Note the gilded sunburst pattern above the entrance and on the tower's clock face.

In the next block you'll see the 1927 Spanish Gothic **United Artists Theater** ( ☎ 818-240-8151, 800-338-3030; www.drgenescott.com; 933 S Broadway) whose construction was bankrolled by Mary Pickford, Douglas Fairbanks Snr and Charlie Chaplin. Now the 'cathedral' of televangelist Dr Gene Scott, it is recognizable from afar for its huge rooftop 'Jesus Saves' neon sign. The only way to get inside is during Sunday services. Reservations are required.

### LITTLE TOKYO

Little Tokyo is the Japanese counterpart to Chinatown, with an attractive mix of traditional gardens, Buddhist temples, outdoor shopping malls and sushi bars. Although the community can trace its roots back to the 1880s, the district now has a distinctly modern look that would feel sterile if it was not enlivened by plenty of public art. Only a few historic buildings remain along E 1st St, their survival ensured since being placed on the National Register of Historic Places in 1996. One of these structures houses a visitors center, the **Little Tokyo Koban** ( ☎ 213-613-1911; 307 E 1st St; ☼ 9am-6pm Mon-Sat). Parking is free for the first hour in the garage at 333 S Alameda St and there are inexpensive lots and metered street parking on 2nd St east of Central Ave.

A few doors down, the **Japanese American National Museum** (JANM; ☎ 213-625-0414; www .janm.org; 369 E 1st St; adult/child under 6/student/senior $8/free/4/5, admission free 5-8pm Thu & on 3rd Thu of month; ☼ 10am-5pm Tue & Wed, 10am-8pm Thu, 10am-5pm Fri-Sun) offers a great introduction to this neighborhood and its people. Equipped with the latest technology, it is the country's first museum dedicated to telling the story of Japanese emigration to, and life in, the US during the past 130 years. The galleries are packed with objects of work and worship, photographs, art, antique ki-

monos and even the uniform worn by *Star Trek* actor George Takei. The gallery dedicated to the painful chapter of the WWII internment camps features an original barrack from the Heart Mountain camp. You can also access the museum's extensive archives, which include books, periodicals and microfilms. Afterwards you can relax in the tranquil garden or café and browse the well-stocked gift shop.

Before moving into its stylish modern digs in 1998, the JANM occupied the 1925 **Nishi Hongwanji Buddhist Temple** next door. In 1942 thousands of Japanese Americans were assembled here before being shipped off to the camps. At the time of writing it was being transformed into the **National Center for the Preservation of Democracy**, a JANM-affiliated, nonprofit educational facility with a mission to promote democracy, diversity and civic involvement. It was set to open in 2005.

Just north of here, the **MOCA Geffen Contemporary** ( ☎ 213-626-6222; www.moca.org; 152 N Central Ave; adult/child under 12/student/senior $8/free/5/5, admission free Thu; ☼ 11am-5pm Mon, 11am-8pm Thu, 11am-5pm Fri, 11am-6pm Sat & Sun) occupies a former police garage cleverly converted into a vast exhibition space by Frank Gehry. It's a subsidiary of the main Museum of Contemporary Art (MOCA) on Grand Ave (p108) and is used primarily for large-scale installations. Tours, which are free with admission, run at noon, 1pm and 2pm. The museum is fully wheelchair accessible.

Just beyond the museum is the **Go for Broke monument** (160 N Central Ave), which honors the Japanese-American soldiers who fought for the USA in WWII, even as their families were interned in the camps.

Across E 1st St from the JANM is the **Japanese Village Plaza** ( ☎ 213-620-8861; btwn 1st & 2nd Sts), a pedestrian mall with gift shops, restaurants and good people-watching. It is overlooked by a **Yagura**, a replica of a traditional fire lookout tower typically found in rural Japan. A few steps west, tucked into a hidden courtyard away from the street, is the **Koyasan Buddhist Temple** ( ☎ 213-624-1267; 342 E 1st St).

Little Tokyo's cultural hub, the **Japanese American Cultural & Community Center** ( ☎ 213-628-2725; www.jaccc.org; 244 S San Pedro St; admission free; ☼ noon-5pm Tue-Fri, 11am-4pm Sat & Sun) is south of here. It features a gallery, library, gift shop and the peaceful **James Irvine Garden** (admission free; ☼ 9am-5pm), a miniature forest complete with a rushing stream and bamboo groves. To get to the gardens, enter the building, take the elevator to the 'B' level and follow the signs. In the adjacent building the **Aratani/Japan America Theater** ( ☎ 213-680-3700) presents everything from Kabuki or No (stylized dance-dramas) to Bunraku (puppet shows).

### ARTS DISTRICT

In the gritty, industrial section southeast of Little Tokyo an increasingly lively arts district has sprung up. It's drawn a young, adventurous and spirited crowd of people who live and work in makeshift studios above abandoned warehouses and small factories. There's enough of them here to support a growing number of cafés, restaurants and shops.

The area got a nod of respectability when the **Southern California Institute of Architecture** (Sci-Arc; ☎ 213-613-2200; www.sciarc.edu; 960 E 3rd St) moved into the former Santa Fe Freight Yard in 2001. It's a progressive laboratory whose faculty and students continually push the envelope in architectural design. You can see some of the results in the **gallery** (admission free; ☼ 10am-6pm) or attend a lecture or film screening; call or see the website for upcoming events.

Northeast, across LA's trickling 'river,' is the **Brewery Art Complex** ( ☎ 323-342-0717; www.breweryart.org; 2100 N Main St), LA's largest artist colony, in a former brewery. There are a few galleries, but studios are generally closed to the public except during the biannual Artwalks (usually in spring and fall; call or check the website for details), though you can wander around to examine the large installations – usually works in progress – scattered throughout.

Near the art complex is the **San Antonio Winery** (Map pp64-5; ☎ 323-223-1401; www.sanantoniowinery.com; 737 Lamar St; admission free; ☼ 10am-6pm Sun-Tue, 10am-7pm Wed-Sat), LA's last remaining historic winery. It was founded in 1917 by Italian immigrant Santo Cambianica whose descendants still make buttery chardonnay, velvety cabernet sauvignon and other vintages. You can sample some of them for free in the tasting room, enjoy a meal at the Italian restaurant or learn more about the noble grape at a wine seminar. Free behind-the-scenes winery tours take place at noon, 1pm and 2pm from Monday to Friday, and on the hour from 11am to 4pm on Saturday and Sunday.

### SOUTH PARK

In the southwestern corner of Downtown, South Park is still a work in progress, although there are pockets of new life here as well. A major catalyst has been the **Staples Center** ( ☎ 213-742-7340; www.staplescenter.com; 1111 S Figueroa St), which opened next to the Los Angeles Convention Center in late 1999. This saucer-shaped sports and entertainment arena features all the latest in top-notch technology, including a Bose sound system. It's home turf for the Los Angeles Lakers, Clippers and Sparks basketball teams, the Kings ice hockey team and the Avengers indoor football team. When major headliners – Bruce Springsteen to Britney Spears – are in town, they'll most likely perform at the Staples.

East of the arena, the **Museum of Neon Art** (MONA; ☎ 213-489-9918; www.neonmona.org; 501 W Olympic Blvd; adult/child/student/senior $5/free/3.50/3.50, ☼ 11am-5pm Wed-Sat, noon-5pm Sun) is a cool gallery highlighting neon, electric and kinetic art, including a serenely smiling Mona Lisa. According to museum staff, this is the only permanent facility of its kind. There's also an outdoor gallery of neon signs on **Universal City Walk** (p121) in Universal City. See p136 for details about MONA's nighttime bus tours.

A few steps north of here is the park that perhaps inspired the district's name, the small and peaceful **Grand Hope Park** (9th St, btwn Grand Ave & Hope Sts). Designed by Lawrence Halprin, one of the country's foremost landscape architects, it was the first of the area's beautification projects which began in the late '80s. It's often filled with students from the adjacent **Fashion Institute of Design & Merchandising** ( ☎ 213-624-1200; 919 S Grand Ave), a private college with an international student body. A gallery and museum display some of their finest work and also host an annual exhibit (usually in spring) of costumes worn in Academy Award–nominated movies.

Many graduates go on to start their own companies in the nearby **Fashion District** ( ☎ 213-488-1153; www.fashiondistrict.org). Bounded by Main and Wall Sts and 7th St and Pico Blvd, this 90-block area is nirvana for bargain hunters, even if shopping around here is more Middle Eastern bazaar than American mall. All in all there are over 800 stores selling casual, career and evening wear for men and women, plus the full range of accessories, textiles and kids' clothing. The vast selection of samples, knockoffs and original designs will make your head spin. Prices are lowest in raucous Santee Alley. For the full lowdown on shopping the district, see p185.

Nearby, LA's **Flower Market** ( ☎ 213-627-3696; Wall St, btwn 7th & 8th Sts; admission Mon-Fri $2, Sat $1; 8am-noon Mon, Wed, Fri, 6am-noon Tue, Thu, Sat) is the largest in the country and dates back to 1913. Flower cultivation in the city began in 1892 when Japanese-American farmers planted fields south of Downtown and in Santa Monica. The market is busiest in the wee hours of the morning, when florists hoist buckets of posies – brimming with flowers from tangy Hawaiian ginger to sweet roses and snapdragons – onto their trucks. Not to worry, though: there's still plenty left by the time the market opens to the public.

Though it looks bleak, the industrial no-man's-land southeast of the Fashion District is worth a detour for a peek at the 1937 **Coca-Cola Bottling Plant** (1334 S Central Ave), which puts the 'fun' in functional. Streamline Moderne doesn't get any sleeker than this classic LA landmark designed by Robert Derrah. Its design was inspired by an ocean liner and features portholes, a catwalk, cargo doors and a bridge. Two giant classic Coke bottles stand guard at the corners.

### KOREATOWN

Koreatown is an amorphous, steadily expanding area west of Downtown. Although dominated by Koreans, it is also home to large numbers of Latino immigrants. Much of it is an undistinguished sprawl of shops and housing tracts sprinkled with a few sightseeing gems, although only the **Korean American Museum** ( ☎ 213-388-4229; www.kamuseum .org; 4th fl, 3727 W 6th St; admission free; 11am-6pm Wed-Fri, 11am-3pm Sat) highlights the history and achievements of the local community with changing art exhibits and cultural events.

The main east–west artery, Wilshire Blvd, offers a number of worthwhile non-Korean landmarks. Coming from Downtown, you'll first hit upon **MacArthur Park**, an expanse of green that's gone from gritty to pretty following a recent refurbishment. Unfortunately, it still attracts a fair number of the down-and-out and, like all LA parks, should be avoided after dark. The main feature is a good-sized lake with an impressive 500ft fountain. (And yes, this is the park Richard

Harris rhapsodized so ludicrously about in the eponymous 1968 Jimmy Webb song.) Don't leave here without sinking your teeth into a pastrami sandwich at Langer's Delicatessen (p164).

Fans of Victoriana will get their fill at the nearby **Grier Musser Museum** ( ☎ 213-413-1814; 403 S Bonnie Brae St; adult/child/student/senior $6/4/5/5; noon-4pm Wed-Sat), an immaculately restored turn-of-the-20th-century Queen Anne home that's stuffed with period antiques and knick-knacks. To keep things dynamic, it presents changing holiday exhibits – from Valentine's Day to Halloween and Christmas.

Continuing west on Wilshire Blvd soon gets you to the beautiful 1929 **Bullocks Wilshire Building** ( ☎ 213-738-8240; www.swlaw.edu /bullockswilshire; 3050 Wilshire Blvd), which was the nation's first department store to cater to customers arriving by car, with a covered driveway and a parking lot, and for decades remained one of the most elegant places in town to shop. Closed after the 1992 riots, it now houses a law school.

A few blocks beyond is the 1922 **Ambassador Hotel** (3400 Wilshire Blvd), one of LA's oldest and grandest hotels and the one-time home of the Cocoanut Grove nightclub, a glitzy Hollywood hangout. Alas, the Ambassador's most lasting legacy is as the place were presidential hopeful Robert Kennedy was assassinated in 1968. The hotel closed in 1990 and has languished ever since, although at press time the plan was to demolish all but the main building in order to build a (badly needed) school on the site.

Further on, at the intersection of Wilshire and Western Blvds, the 1931 art deco **Wiltern Theater** (get it?) struts its stuff clad in a glorious turquoise mantle. It's now primarily a venue for big-name music acts and special events.

In southern Koreatown, **St Sophia Cathedral** ( ☎ 323-737-2424; www.stsophia.org; 1324 S Normandie Ave; admission free; 10am-4pm Tue-Fri, 10am-2pm Sat), the spiritual hub of Southern California's Greek Orthodox community, is well worth a detour. Walking inside the main nave is like stepping into a giant's treasure chest, spilling over with gold, crystal and jewels. Every square inch is swathed with Biblical-themed murals and illuminated by muted light filtering in through radiant stained-glass windows. Cap a visit with a plate of gyros at the adjacent Papa Cristo's (p163).

# East Los Angeles

East of Downtown, the Los Angeles River is a bit like the US–Mexican border without the wall and the guards. Beyond the concrete gulch lies a sprawling neighborhood that's home to the largest concentration of Mexicans outside of Mexico, plus thousands of Latinos from Central and, to a lesser extent, South America. Life in the barrio is tough but lively. People shop and mill about in the streets lined with bakeries *(panaderías)*, convenience stores *(tiendas)*, stores selling herbal cures *(botánicas)* and toy shops. Brightly colored murals adorn many facades, but behind the color, life can look pretty grim. Unemployment is high, incomes low and gang violence and poor schools ubiquitous.

There aren't any major tourist sights in the area, but Boyle Heights, the neighborhood closest to Downtown LA, has a few worthwhile stops. This is where you'll find **Mariachi Plaza** (Map pp64-5; cnr Boyle Ave & 1st St), where traditional Mexican musicians dressed in fanciful suits and wide-brimmed hats mill beneath wall-sized murals waiting to be hired for restaurant or social engagements. In mid-November, the **Mariachi Festival** (p138) brings together hundreds of performers and their fans. For a classy meal, try the nearby **La Serenata de Garibaldi** (p165). Otherwise continue a bit further east to **El Mercado** (3425 E 1st St), a wonderfully boisterous and colorful indoor market, where locals stock up on tortilla presses, pig bellies and toys. The upstairs restaurants are often packed, especially when there's live music.

North of here is one of LA's major Latino arts centers, **Self-Help Graphics & Art** ( ☎ 323-881-6444; www.selfhelpgraphics.com; 3802 Cesar E Chavez Ave; admission free; ☼ 10am-4pm Tue-Sat, noon-4pm Sun) whose colorful facade is a mosaic of pottery and glass shards. It was founded by a Franciscan nun in 1973 and has been nurturing and promoting Latino art ever since. The gift shop and gallery are well worth a visit. Every November 1 and 2, Self-Help hosts as many as 3000 people in what has become the largest Día de los Muertos (Day of the Dead) celebration in Southern California (see p138).

# Exposition Park & South Central

A quick jaunt south of Downtown LA by DASH bus (p195), **Exposition Park** is filled with enough stellar museums, historic sports facilities and green spaces to keep you busy for a day. The sprawling site originally hosted agricultural fairs, then devolved into a magnet for the down-and-out and finally emerged as a public park in 1913. In summer, an array of fragrant blooms in the **Rose Garden** (admission free; ☼ 8:30am-sunset Apr-Dec) makes it a nice picnic spot. Parking at the park is $6.

Nearby, the **Mercado La Paloma** (off Map pp64-5; ☎ 213-748-1963; 3655 S Grand Ave; admission free; ☼ 8am-6:30pm) is worth a quick detour, especially if you're hungry. It's an abandoned warehouse turned into a delightful Mexican marketplace with an art gallery, quality crafts stalls and numerous eateries, including the excellent Chichen Itza (p166).

The area south of Exposition Park is traditionally referred to as **South Central**. Gangs, drugs, poverty, crime and drive-by shootings are just a few of the negative images – not entirely undeserved – associated with this district. Much of the area is bleak and foreboding, but there are also thriving pockets, such as the Leimert Park neighborhood, and world-class sights such as the Watts Towers. Central Ave is a must for anyone interested in LA's African-American heritage.

## NATURAL HISTORY MUSEUM OF LA COUNTY

Take a spin around the world and back in time at this popular **museum** (NAM; ☎ 213-763-3466; www.nhm.org; 900 Exposition Blvd; adult/child 5-12/student/senior $9/2/6.50/6.50; ☼ 9:30am-5pm Mon-Fri, 10am-5pm Sat & Sun) in Exposition Park's northwest corner. Inside a palatial structure that wouldn't look out of place in Renaissance Spain awaits a veritable warren of exhibition halls chronicling the earth's evolution and showcasing life in its mind-boggling diversity.

There are usually some special exhibits going on, but even so don't miss a spin around the permanent halls filled with everything from stuffed African elephants to Tyrannosaurus-rex skulls and a giant megamouth, one of the world's rarest sharks. A highlight among the historical exhibits is the **Times Mirror Hall of Native American Cultures**, with much prized Navajo textiles, baskets, pottery, jewelry and a re-created cliff dwelling. The **Gem & Mineral Hall** is a glittering spectacle with a walk-through gem tunnel and more gold than any other such collection in the US.

The NHM is also a cool spot to take the kids. In the hands-on **Discovery Center** little ones can dig for fossils, meet Cecil the Iguana during an animal presentation, or handle real fur and bones. The **Insect Zoo** with its tarantulas, hissing cockroaches and other creepy crawlies also makes for some unforgettable memories.

### CALIFORNIA SCIENCE CENTER
If your memory of school science makes you groan, then a visit to this imaginative multimedia **museum** ( ☎ 213-744-7400; www.ca sciencectr.org; 700 State Dr; admission free; ☼ 10am-5pm) should convince you that, gee, science *can* be fun. There's absolutely nothing stuffy about this place where you can watch baby chicks hatch in an incubator, test your reaction skills in virtual-reality games and even ride out a simulated earthquake. All throughout, you'll have plenty of buttons to push, lights to switch on and knobs to pull. During the school year, the center usually crawls with school kids on weekday mornings, so plan accordingly if you want a little more quiet.

There are three main exhibition areas. The **World of Life** exhibit focuses mostly on the human body. You can hop on a red blood cell for a computer fly-through of the circulatory system or ask Gertie how long your colon really is. The undisputed star, though, is Tess, a giant animated technodoll billed as '50ft of brains, beauty and biology.' Small children may have trouble understanding the science, but they *will* remember Tess.

Virtual-reality games, high-tech simulations, laser animation and other such gadgetry await in the **Creative World** exhibit, which zooms in on the gadgets and devices humans have invented in order to facilitate communication, transportation and construction.

Spirits will soar at the **Air & Space Gallery** ( ☼ 10am-1pm Mon-Fri, 11am-4pm Sat & Sun), which is all about the principles of flight and space travel. Exhibits include such awesome planes as the pioneering 1902 Wright Glider and the all-titanium A-12 Blackbird. Other highlights include the Gemini 11, the real capsule launched into space in 1966, and a Soviet-made Sputnik, the first human-made object to orbit the earth in 1957.

Back in the main building, you can get the lowdown during science demonstrations, browse the store, grab a bite or get hypnotized by Hypar, a constantly expanding or contracting kinetic sculpture. Junior James Bonds can test their valor while riding a bicycle along a cable suspended three stories above the ground. The adjacent IMAX (p173) is a good place to wind down at the end of an action-filled day.

### CALIFORNIA AFRICAN AMERICAN MUSEUM
This state-run **museum** ( ☎ 213-744-7432; www.caa museum.org; 600 State Dr; admission free; ☼ 10am-4pm Wed-Sat), just emerged from a major renovation, does an excellent job documenting African and African-American art and history, especially as it pertains to California and other western states. The main exhibit skillfully traces an entire people's torturous journey from the African homeland into slavery and eventual freedom. An active lecture and performance schedule brings together the community and those wanting to gain a deeper understanding of what it means to be black in America.

### LOS ANGELES MEMORIAL COLISEUM & SPORTS ARENA
John F Kennedy, Pope John Paul II and the Rolling Stones have all been celebrated by cheering crowds at the monumental **Los Angeles Memorial Coliseum** ( ☎ 213-747-7111; www.la coliseum.com; 3911 S Figueroa St), south of the California Science Center. Built in 1923 it is the world's only facility to have hosted two summer Olympiads (1932 and 1984), two Super Bowls (I and VII) and one World Series (1959). It got its 'memorial' moniker to honor the fallen of WWI. Two idealized bronze nudes, designed by LA artist Robert Graham for the 1984 Olympics, greet visitors approaching the famous art deco eastern entrance.

The adjacent indoor **Los Angeles Memorial Sports Arena** ( ☎ 213-748-6136; 3939 S Figueroa St) dates from 1959 and hosts rock concerts, ice shows, the circus and even the occasional rodeo.

### UNIVERSITY OF SOUTHERN CALIFORNIA (USC)
Immediately north of Exposition Park, **USC** (Map pp60-1; ☎ 213-740-5371, tours ☎ 213-740-6605; www.usc.edu; 3535 S Figueroa St) was founded in 1880 and is one of the oldest private research universities in the American West. The leafy campus has some nice architecture and is

**THE MAGIC TOUCH**

Earvin Johnson got his 'magic' moniker for his extraordinary talents on the basketball court, which the legendary Los Angeles Laker parlayed into five NBA titles and three Most Valuable Player awards. These days, though, Johnson is working his magic in neglected neighborhoods all over the country by bringing brand-name businesses to their streets.

Here in LA, where he lives (albeit in Beverly Hills), Johnson has made the underserved communities of South Central his focus. He's brought Starbucks cafés to Inglewood and Carson, a ritzy Loews multiplex to Baldwin Hills and a TGI Friday's to Ladera Heights. With his winning smile and astute business instincts, he's entered into partnerships with gun-shy corporate executives and developers, and convinced them that the inner cities can be lucrative investing grounds indeed. Magic's winning formula requires outlets to hire locally and to calibrate the menu or movie selection to meet the expectations of the community. By all accounts, it works splendidly, as residents have warmly embraced the new outlets. But hey. That's just Magic. He always does put his money where his mouth is.

a pretty place for a stroll or picnic. Learn more during the free 50-minute campus walking tours, which run from 10am to 3pm, Monday to Friday. See p81 for famous alumni.

The campus' Harris Hall is the home of **USC Fisher Gallery** ( ☎ 213-740-4561; www.usc.edu /fishergallery; 823 Exposition Blvd; admission free; ☉ noon-5pm Tue-Sat Sep-Apr), which presents fine-art exhibits drawn from its ever-expanding permanent collection of American landscapes, British portraits, French Barbizon School paintings and, more recently, Mexican modern masters such as Rufino Tamayo and Gronk (Glugio Nicandro).

### CENTRAL AVE

From the 1920s to the 1960s, Central Ave (about 1½ miles east of Exposition Park) was the lifeblood of LA's African-American community, not by choice but because of segregation laws that kept blacks out of other neighborhoods. Central Ave became a hotbed of jazz, a legacy commemorated every July with the **Central Avenue Jazz Festival** (p137). Legends such as Lena Horne, Count Basie and Duke Ellington all stayed at the 1928 **Dunbar Hotel** (off Map pp64-5; 4225 S Central Ave), which is now a seniors center. A small exhibit in the lobby commemorates the era.

North of here, towards Downtown, is the **African American Firefighter Museum** (Map pp64-5; ☎ 213-744-1730; www.aaffmuseum.org; 1401 S Central Ave; admission free; ☉ 10am-2pm Tue & Thu, 1-4pm Sun) inside a beautifully restored 1913 fire station that served Central Ave. Until 1955 it was one of only two fire stations in town that employed black firefighters.

Exhibits include vintage engines, a 1940 ladder truck, an 1890 hose wagon and various uniforms.

Further south, Central Ave takes you into **Watts**, a neighborhood best known as the epicenter of the LA riots of 1965 and 1992. Large pockets of neglect remain, but there have also been improvements thanks in part to such groups as the **Watts Labor Community Action Committee** (WLCAC; Map pp62-3; ☎ 323-563-5639; www.wlcac.org; 10950 S Central Ave; admission free; ☉ daily) whose headquarters is a great place to learn more about the community. The visual – and spiritual – centerpiece of the complex is the **Mother of Humanity**, a bronze sculpture celebrating womankind's contributions to civilization. The **Civil Rights Museum** takes you into the hull of a slave ship and along a Mississippi Delta dirt road to exhibits on Martin Luther King and the 1960s civil rights movement. For some fine jazz and blues attend the center's **Bones & Blues** concerts held every last Friday of the month (tickets $20). Call the center for opening hours.

### WATTS TOWERS

In 1921 Italian immigrant Simon Rodia set out 'to make something' and then spent 33 years doing just that. The result is one of the world's greatest monuments of folk art, the **Watts Towers** (Map pp62-3; ☎ 213-847-4646; 1765 E 107th St; adult/child under 12/teen/senior $5/free/3/3; ☉ 11am-2:30pm Fri, 10:30am-2:30pm Sat, 12:30-3pm Sun), a wonderful and whimsical free-form sculpture made from a motley assortment of found objects – from green 7-Up bottles to sea shells, and rocks to pottery. The towers were recently restored and are now open for self-guided tours. The adjacent **Watts Towers Art Center** ( ☎ 213-847-4646; admission free; ☼ 10am-4pm Tue-Sat, noon-4pm Sun) sponsors workshops, performances and classes for the community, hosts art exhibits in its gallery and organizes the acclaimed **Watts Towers Day of the Drum** and **Jazz Festival** in September (p138). The towers are about 6 miles south of Downtown LA.

### LEIMERT PARK

About 2½ miles west of Exposition Park, the Leimert (luh-mert) Park neighborhood (Map pp60–1) has emerged as the cultural hub of LA's African-American community. The action is centered in Leimert Park Village, especially along Degnan Blvd between 43rd St and the namesake park. Phillip's Barbecue (p165) has great ribs, the World Stage (p176) is a destination for jazz aficionados, and blues brothers head around the corner to the historic Babe & Ricky's (p175).

Another local hangout is **Lucy Florence's Coffeehouse** ( ☎ 323-293-2395; 4385 Degnan Ave), which usually serves up some cultural event (readings, music, theater) alongside its mocha and sweet potato pie. Also here is the **Museum in Black** ( ☎ 323-292-9528; 4331 Degnan Blvd; admission free; ☼ 10am-6pm Tue-Sat), which combines a commercial African art gallery with a small but unique collection of segregation-era memorabilia that attests both to the humiliation and accomplishments of African Americans (it's in the back, you may have to ask to see it). Call ahead to confirm opening hours.

### FARMER JOHN PIG MURAL

The bleak industrial city of Vernon, about 4 miles east of Exposition Park, is brightened by a lovely **mural** (Map pp60-1; 3049 E Vernon Ave, Vernon) called *Hog Heaven*, which shows happy pigs romping around bucolic farming country. There would be absolutely nothing weird about this were the scene not gracing the very factory where said oinkers are being turned into sausages and pork rinds. The mural dates back to 1957 and is the work of Hollywood set designer Les Grimes.

## Griffith Park
Map p75

Sprawling **Griffith Park** ( ☎ 323-913-4688; www.ci .la.ca.us/RAP/grifmet/gp/index.htm; 4370 Crystal Springs Dr; admission free; ☼ 6am-10pm), just north of Hollywood, is a thick spread of California oak, wild sage and manzanita, and makes for a family-friendly escape from LA's urban velocity. The land was bequeathed to the city in 1896 by Griffith J Griffith, a Welsh immigrant who made millions speculating on gold mines only to spend two years in San Quentin prison for the attempted murder of his wife.

At five times the size of New York's Central Park, Griffith Park embraces an outdoor theater, the city zoo, an observatory, two museums, golf courses, tennis courts, playgrounds, bridle paths, hiking trails and even the Hollywood Sign. A sentimental favorite is the richly festooned 1926 **Griffith Park Merry-Go-Round** ( ☎ 323-665-3051; Park Center btwn LA Zoo & Los Feliz entrance; rides $1; ☼ 11am-5pm daily May-Sep, weekends only Oct-Apr). Each horse is beautifully carved and painted and sports a real horse-hair tail.

Access to the park is easiest via the Griffith Park Dr or Zoo Dr exits off I-5 (Golden State Fwy). Parking is plentiful and free. For information and maps stop by the **Griffith Park Ranger Station** ( ☎ 323-665-5188; 4730 Crystal Springs Dr). Trails close at sunset.

### GRIFFITH OBSERVATORY

On the southern slopes of Mt Hollywood, **Griffith Observatory** ( ☎ 323-664-1181; www.griffith obs.org; 2800 E Observatory Rd) served as the backdrop for James Dean's switchblade fight in *Rebel Without a Cause*. A small bust of the actor stands near the entrance to the classic snowy white, copper-domed landmark which has provided a window on the universe since 1935.

The sweeping views from here alone – across mountains and skyscrapers to the gleaming Pacific – are spectacular, especially on a clear day and at night. Alas, the entire complex is off-limits until at least early 2006 when an exhaustive and much-needed renovation and expansion is expected to be completed.

Until then, stargazers can visit the **Griffith Park Observatory Satellite** (admission free; 4800 Western Heritage Way; ☼ 1-10pm Tue-Fri, 10am-10pm Sat & Sun) near the Los Angeles Zoo. The temporary facility features astronomy exhibits (including meteorites and a Mars rock), planetarium shows and a telescope for viewing the moon and planets.

## LOS ANGELES ZOO & BOTANICAL GARDENS

The **Los Angeles Zoo** ( ☎ 323-644-4200; www.lazoo .org; 5333 Zoo Dr; adult/child/senior $10/5/7; ☽ 10am-5pm late Sep–Jun, 10am-6pm Jul–early Sep) with its 1200 finned, feathered and furry friends rarely fails to enthrall the little ones. What began in 1912 as a refuge for retired circus animals recently also won accreditation as a **botanical garden**, thanks to its amazing wealth of plants and trees. Still, it's definitely the zoo's animal magnetism that brings in over a million visitors each year.

Long-term residents such as the **elephant Gita** and the **alligator Methuselah** are perennial crowd-pleasers. Playful **chimpanzees** live in the Mahale Mountain exhibit, which re-creates their original habitat in Tanzania, while **orangutans** make their home in the Red Ape Rain Forest. A new gorilla reserve was in the works at press time. Elsewhere, cuddly **koalas** reside in a special darkened building designed to give visitors a chance to see these nocturnal animals at their most active. Tots gravitate to **Adventure Island** with its petting zoo and hands-on play stations as well as the brand-new **Children's Discovery Center**.

PS: This is the zoo where a Komodo dragon chewed off part of Sharon Stone's ex-husband's foot.

## MUSEUM OF THE AMERICAN WEST

Those keen on learning how the West was won will hit the mother lode at this excellent **museum** ( ☎ 323-667-2000; www.museumoftheamerican west.org; 4700 Western Heritage Way; adult/child/student/ senior $7.50/3/5/5, admission free after 4pm Thu; ☽ 10am-5pm Tue & Wed, 10am-8pm Thu, 10am-5pm Fri-Sun). Formerly known as the Autry Museum of Western Heritage, this facility was endowed by movie star and America's favorite singing cowboy Gene Autry. Its 10 galleries engagingly combine scholarship and showmanship and are a veritable gold mine of memorabilia.

Star exhibits include Annie Oakley's gold-plated pistols, devices for cheating at saloon gambling, a copy of the guidebook that caused the Donner Party to get lost in the California Sierras and an amazing collection of Colt handguns. One gallery explores how the West was 'discovered' again and again, by everyone from prehistoric tribes to missionaries to gold diggers. Elsewhere, in-depth historical exhibits test romantic myths of the Old West against its harsher realities. Other galleries deal with the clashes between conquerors and Native Americans, including General Custer's (in)famous Last Stand at Little Bighorn, and the roles played by Europeans, Chinese, Mexicans, Mormons, Canadians and other immigrants.

Children can playfully learn about history in the Family Discovery Gallery or at storytelling sessions. Various gallery talks, symposia, film screenings and other cultural events take place throughout the year. In summer, a popular outdoor music series takes place on Thursday nights.

It recently merged with the Southwest Museum of the American Indian (p122) under the umbrella of the Autry National Center. If you're visiting both museums purchase a combination ticket (adult/child 2-12/student/senior $12/5/8/8).

## TRAVEL TOWN MUSEUM & AROUND

Railroad buffs have flocked to this delightful outdoor **museum** ( ☎ 323-662-5874; 5200 W Zoo Dr; admission free; ☽ 10am-4pm Mon-Fri, 10am-5pm Sat & Sun) for over half a century. It preserves dozens of vintage rail cars, including steam locomotives (the oldest from 1864, the 'youngest' from 1925) and two still-functioning diesel locomotives. Kids get all excited when clambering around the old-timey freight and passenger cars or imagining themselves as engineers. Rides around the museum aboard a miniature train generate even bigger smiles. A huge hall holds historical fire engines and a model-train network, which a dedicated local hobby club operates, usually on weekends from 10am to 4pm.

Just east of the museum, the **Los Angeles Live Steamers** ( ☎ 323-664-9678; 5202 Zoo Dr; ☽ 11am-3pm Sun) is a group of local folks with a passion for scale model locomotives. On Sunday afternoons, they offer free rides on their one-eighth-size model trains.

And if that's not enough train stuff for you, head to the park's southeast corner for a ride aboard the **Griffith Park Southern Railroad** ( ☎ 323-664-6903; 4400 Crystal Springs Dr; adult/child/ senior $2/2/1.50; ☽ 10am-4:30pm Mon-Fri, 10am-5pm Sat & Sun). Since 1948, this small fleet of miniature trains has ferried millions of children around a 1-mile loop past pony rides, an old Western town and a Native-American village.

**TOURING THE STUDIOS: MOVIE MAGIC REVEALED**

To see particular TV stars, your best bet is to watch tapings of their shows. **Audiences Unlimited** ( ☎ 818-753-3470, ext 812; www.tvtickets.com) handles ticket distribution for dozens of shows, mostly sitcoms. Production season runs from August to March, and tickets are free. **CBS** (Map pp68-9; ☎ 323-575-2624; www.cbs.com; 7800 Beverly Blvd) also distributes tickets directly (see p190).

**NBC Studios** (Map p75; ☎ 818-840-3537; 3000 W Alameda Ave, Burbank, San Fernando Valley; tour adult/child $7.50/4.50; ☉ 9am-3pm Mon-Fri) runs studio tours with stops at the *Tonight Show* set and such departments as wardrobe, make-up and set construction. Call or check www.nbc.com/nbc /footer/Tickets.shtml for information on how to obtain free tickets to live tapings of the *Tonight Show*.

Close by, **Warner Bros Studios** (Map p75; ☎ 818-972-8687; 4301 W Olive Ave, Burbank, San Fernando Valley; tour $35; ☉ 9am-3pm Mon-Fri Oct-Apr, 9am-4pm Mon-Fri May-Sep) runs 'edu-taining' two-hour tours of its historic studio, still one of the busiest in Hollywood after 80 years or so. You get to watch a video of WB's greatest hits and roam around a memorabilia-filled museum before it's off on a tram tour to sound stages, backlot sets such as 'New York Street,' and technical departments, including props and costumes. Tours leave roughly every half hour. Bring photo ID. Reservations are a good idea during peak times.

South of here, in Culver City, you can tour **Sony Pictures Studios** (Map pp62-3; ☎ 323-520-8687; 10202 W Washington Blvd; tour $24; ☉ Mon-Fri), which was originally the venerable MGM, the studio that gave us *The Wizard of Oz* and *Ben Hur*. Movies and TV shows are still filmed here, including the studio's bread and butter, the game show *Jeopardy*. Despite the historical MGM connection, the two-hour walking tour focuses mostly on Sony productions. Highlights include a visit to the *Jeopardy* set and sound stage 27 where *The Wizard of Oz* was filmed. Call for specific tour times; reservations are mandatory and children under 12 are not permitted. Bring photo ID.

**FOREST LAWN MEMORIAL PARK – HOLLYWOOD HILLS**

The northwestern edge of Griffith Park segues seamlessly into this humongous **cemetery** ( ☎ 323-254-7251; www.forestlawn.com; 6300 Forest Lawn Dr; admission free; ☉ 8am-5pm). A fine catalog of dead celebrities – including Lucille Ball, Bette Davis and Stan Laurel – rests within a bizarre setting that combines pathos, art and patriotism. The carefully manicured grounds are strewn with paeans to early North American history, including a giant mosaic called *The Birth of Liberty,* Boston's re-created Old North Church and bronze statues of Washington, Jefferson and Lincoln. You can even watch a movie about the American Revolution. There's another, similarly over-the-top branch in Glendale (p122).

**BRONSON CAVES**

Scenes from *Batman, Star Trek,* the *Lone Ranger* and many other TV shows and feature films were shot in this former quarry with its steep cliffs and wonderfully spooky caves. It's tucked away in a remote area in the southwest corner of Griffith Park and is a bit tricky to find. Take Canyon Dr north from Franklin Ave and park in the last lot before the locked gate at Woodlandland Camp. Walk back south, then turn left and head past a gate and up a fire road for about a quarter-mile, then turn left when the trail forks and the caves will be right there. The trail continues on the other side of the caves, offering good views of the Hollywood Sign.

**GREEK THEATRE**

Hugging a forested hillside on the southern edge of Griffith Park, the **Greek Theatre** ( ☎ 323-665-1927; www.greektheatrela.com; 2700 N Vermont Ave) is a lovely amphitheater in business since 1930. From May to October, it hosts a stellar roster of talent with a focus on such baby-boomer faves as Aretha Franklin, James Taylor, and Crosby, Stills and Nash. A Wall of Fame features handprints of the stars – including Johnny Mathis, Harry Belafonte and Santana – who have sold more than 100,000 tickets here.

## San Fernando Valley

Just north of the Hollywood Hills, the San Fernando Valley – known simply as 'the

Valley' – is a sprawling grid of suburbia that's also home to most of the major movie studios, including Warner Bros, Disney and, of course, Universal. In addition, the Valley also has the distinction of being the world capital of the porn movie industry. Attractions are few and scattered about, although generally the eastern Valley yields the greater promise. **Burbank** has the movie studios and **Glendale** to the east has good shopping and Armenian restaurants, thanks to a sizable population of immigrants from that country.

West of Burbank, a small but lively arts district has sprung up in **North Hollywood**, which is conveniently served by the Metro Red Line, as is Universal City to the south. **Studio City**, the area west of Universal, has a growing nightlife and restaurant scene, especially along Ventura Blvd, the Valley's main east–west drag. Note that temperatures here are usually 20°F higher – and pollution levels worse – than in areas further south.

## UNIVERSAL STUDIOS HOLLYWOOD & CITY WALK

One of the world's oldest continuously operating movie studios, **Universal** (Map p75; ☎ 818-622-3801; www.universalstudioshollywood.com; 100 Universal City Plaza; admission over/under 48in $53/43; ⏰ vary) was founded by German immigrant Carl Laemmle in 1909 and moved to its current site – on a former chicken ranch – in 1915. To make a little money on the side, Laemmle sold eggs and invited the public to observe filmmaking firsthand. The movie-based theme park, though, didn't start operating until 1964, a quarter century after his death. It's an entertaining mix of fairly tame – and sometimes dated – thrill rides and high-energy live action shows, plus a studio backlot tram tour peppered with special effects. Although Universal is a working studio, you're unlikely to see any action, let alone a star.

You'll probably need to devote a full day to Universal, especially in summer when the park drowns in visitors. To beat the crowds, try to get there before the gates open or invest in the Front of Line Pass ($89.75 to $99.75) or the deluxe guided VIP Experience ($139). Some rides, including the popular Back to the Future and Jurassic Park, have minimum height requirements (usually 40 or 46 inches). The Hollywood CityPass (see p78) is valid for general admission. Also check Universal's website for special promotions. Opening hours vary by day and season; call ahead or check the website for details.

The theme park sprawls across upper and lower sections connected by a quarter-mile-long escalator. Many people head straight for the **Studio Tour**, a 45-minute part-educational, part-thrill narrated ride aboard a rickety tram that – sort of – provides a glimpse behind the scenes of movie-making. You'll travel past working soundstages to outdoor sets used in *Jurassic Park, Back to the Future,* the classic Hitchcock thriller *Psycho* and many others. You'll also face down King Kong, brave a flash flood, and survive a shark attack and an 8.3 magnitude earthquake. It's a bit hokey, but fun.

Of the three thrill rides, the top billing goes to **Jurassic Park**, a seemingly gentle float through a prehistoric jungle with a rather 'raptor-ous' ending. Nearby, also on the lower lot, is the newest ride, the imaginative but much too short **Revenge of the Mummy**, an indoor roller coaster romp through 'Imhotep's Tomb' that at one point has you going backwards. Up on top, the sentimental favorite is **Back to the Future**, where you'll be free-falling into volcanic tunnels, plunging down glacial cliffs and colliding with dinosaurs, all aboard a Delorean.

Of the live shows, **Terminator 2: 3D** is a futuristic romp combining live action stunts with eye-popping digital imaging technology and starring California governor Arnold Schwarzenegger. **Spider-Man Rocks** is a cutesy, fast-paced musical show with dance numbers and aerial acrobatics. The movie may have bombed, but the **Water World** show is a runaway hit with mind-boggling stunts that include giant fireballs and a crash-landing seaplane.

Snack food and drinks, including beer and margaritas, are available throughout the park, although you'll probably do better at the adjacent **Universal City Walk**, an unashamedly commercial strip of restaurants, shops, bars and entertainment venues. It's best at night when clever vintage neon signage on loan from the Museum of Neon Art (p113) creates a bit of Vegas-style glam.

Also here is the **Universal Amphitheatre** (☎ 818-622-4440; www.hob.com; 100 Universal City Plaza), a big venue for headlining rock and pop acts.

## DETOUR: SIX FLAGS MAGIC MOUNTAIN & HURRICANE HARBOR

Velocity is king at **Six Flags Magic Mountain** ( ☎ 661-255-4111, 818-367-5965; www.sixflags.com /parks/magicmountain; 26101 Magic Mountain Pkwy, Valencia; adult/child under 4ft/seniors $48/30/30; ☺ from 10am daily Apr–early Sep, Sat & Sun only mid-Sep–Mar, closing times vary from 6pm-midnight) where you can go up, down and inside out faster and in more baffling ways than anywhere besides a space shuttle.

The ever-growing arsenal of rides, shows and attractions includes 16 roller coasters that literally scare the bejesus out of most of us. Ride the aptly named **Scream**, which goes through seven loops, including a zero-gravity roll and a dive loop with you sitting – feet dangling – in a floorless car. **Flashback** deals you six spiral hairpin drops, while **Viper** drops 188ft into a double-boomerang turn that can be most unpleasant if you're not ready for it. If you've got a stomach of steel, don't miss **X**, where you ride in cars that spin around themselves while hurtling forward and plummeting all at once.

Note that children under 4ft are not allowed on many of the fiercest rides. In fact, in summer, a better place to take the little ones might be right next door to **Six Flags Hurricane Harbor** ( ☎ 661-255-4100, 818-367-5965; www.sixflags.com/parks/hurricaneharborla; 26101 Magic Mountain Parkway; adult/child under 4ft/senior $24/17/17; ☺ from 10am daily Jun-Aug, Sat & Sun only May & Sep, closing times vary). At this jungle-themed water park you can keep cool frolicking in fanciful lagoons and churning wave pools, plunging down wicked speed slides or being pummeled on rafting rides.

Combination tickets to both parks are $57 (no discounts) and can be used on the same day or on separate days.

The parks are about 30 miles north of LA, right off the Magic Mountain Pkwy exit off I-5 (Golden State Fwy). If you don't have your own vehicle, it's easiest to join one of the organized tours. Just look for flyers in your hotel.

## FOREST LAWN MEMORIAL PARK – GLENDALE

Often cheekily called the 'country club for the dead,' this humongous **cemetery** (off Map p75; ☎ 818-241-4151; 1712 S Glendale Ave; ☺ 9am-5pm), is the final resting place of scores of Hollywood legends. Clark Gable, Carole Lombard and Jean Harlow are in the **Great Mausoleum**; Clara Bow, Nat King Cole, Gracie Allen and George Burns can be found in the **Freedom Mausoleum**, and Walt Disney and Errol Flynn rest in the **Court of Freedom**. There's plenty of copied art, such as a version of Michelanglo's *David* and a stained-glass rendition of Leonardo da Vinci's *Last Supper*. For more celebrity corpses, see Forest Lawn Memorial Park – Hollywood Hills (p120).

## MISSION SAN FERNANDO REY DE ESPAÑA

This historic **Spanish mission** (Map pp60-1; ☎ 818-361-0186; 15151 San Fernando Mission Rd, Mission Hills; adult/child/senior $4/3/3; ☺ 9am-4:30pm) was the second built in the LA area (after the one in San Gabriel, p127). The highlight is the 1822 convent, built with 4ft-thick adobe walls and Romanesque arches. Inside is an elaborate baroque altarpiece from Spain. A small museum chronicles the mission's history.

## Highland Park & Mt Washington

The two neighborhoods of Mt Washington and Highland Park wrap around the Arroyo Seco, a rocky riverbed running from the San Gabriel Mountains to Downtown LA. It was flooded with artists and architects in the early 20th century, but lost its idyllic setting with the arrival of I-110 (Pasadena Fwy) in 1940.

Several of its attractions still spotlight a premetropolitan LA.

### SOUTHWEST MUSEUM OF THE AMERICAN INDIAN

Overlooking the historic Arroyo Seco, LA's oldest **museum** (off Map pp64-5; ☎ 323-221-2164; www.southwestmuseum.org; 234 Museum Dr; adult/child 2-12/student/senior $7.50/3/5/5; ☺ 10am-5pm Tue-Sun) was founded in 1907 by Charles Lummis (see Lummis House, opposite) and holds one of the most formidable collections of Native-American art and artifacts in the US. It recently merged with the Museum of the American West (p118) under the umbrella of the Autry National Center. If you're visiting both museums purchase a combination ticket (adult/child 2-12/student/senior $12/5/8/8).

The four permanent galleries focus on the traditions and cultures of Native Americans in California, the Pacific Northwest, the Southwest and the Great Plains. This division lets you compare the traditions, rituals, clothing, crafts, religious ceremonies and social structures that developed in each of these areas. Highlights include magnificent feather headdresses, carved totem poles and jewelry. The museum also owns a prestigious basket collection with over 13,000 items.

### LUMMIS HOUSE
Charles Lummis (1859–1928) was the city's first librarian and a prolific writer and editor, but his true legacy is as a preservationist and founder of the Southwest Museum (see opposite). From 1898 to 1910 he built this modest **home** (off Map pp64-5; ☎ 323-222-0546; 200 E Ave 43 at Carlota Blvd; donations appreciated; ☯ noon-4pm Fri-Sun) almost entirely by hand from boulders, recycled telephone poles and railroad rails. It is also known as El Alisal, the Spanish name for a sycamore tree. The **Historical Society of Southern California** (www.socalhistory.org) is headquartered here today and maintains a small exhibit about Lummis.

### HERITAGE SQUARE MUSEUM
Eight Victorian beauties dating from 1865 to 1914 were saved from the wrecking ball in the late 1960s and literally airlifted to this faux villagelike **outdoor museum** (off Map pp64-5; ☎ 626-449-0193; www.heritagesquare.org; 3800 Homer St; adult/child 6-12/senior $6/3/5; ☯ noon-5pm Fri-Sun), just off the Ave 43 exit of I-110 (Pasadena Fwy).

Highlights include the Italianate Perry House, the Queen Anne/Eastlake-style Hale House and the quirky Longfellow Hastings Octagon House. The grounds are open for self-guided tours, but to marvel at the interiors you'll have to join a tour offered on the hour from noon to 3pm (included in the admission price).

## Pasadena & San Gabriel Valley
Resting beneath the lofty San Gabriel Mountains, northeast of Downtown LA, Pasadena is a leafy city with impressive old-time mansions, superb Craftsman architecture and fine art museums. Every New Year's Day, the country turns its attention to Pasadena as it stages the Tournament of Roses, aka the **Rose Parade** (p137), a tradition dating back to 1890.

The city is also home to two world-famous schools, the California Institute of Technology (Caltech) and the Art Center College of Design, and a pair of excellent **flea markets** (p191). Its main fun zone is **Old Pasadena**, a bustling 20-block shopping and entertainment district set up in beautifully restored historic brick buildings lining Colorado Blvd between Arroyo Parkway (the main road into town coming from Downtown LA) and Pasadena Ave. While here, also swing by the imposing Moorish and Spanish Colonial **Castle Green** (Map p76; ☎ 626-577-6765; 99 S Raymond Ave), which began life in 1898 as Pasadena's poshest luxury resort hotel and is now an apartment building. Call about upcoming tours.

Pasadena is surrounded by the numerous suburban communities of the San Gabriel Valley and is also the gateway to the **Angeles Crest Hwy** (p124).

### NORTON SIMON MUSEUM
Rodin's *The Thinker* in the garden is only an overture to the full symphony of art awaiting inside this exquisite **museum** (Map p76; ☎ 626-449-6840; www.nortonsimon.org; 411 W Colorado Blvd; adult/child under 18/student/senior $6/free/free/3; ☯ noon-6pm Wed & Thu, noon-9pm Fri, noon-6pm Sat-Mon). Norton Simon (1907–93) was an entrepreneur with a Midas touch and an art collector with exquisite taste. In less than three decades, he parlayed his millions into a well-respected collection of Western art from the Renaissance to the 20th century, plus an exquisite sampling of 2000 years of Indian and Southeast Asian sculpture.

Many of history's most skilled and renowned artists are represented here, including Old Masters such as Rembrandt, Raphael and Lucas Cranach the Elder, and French impressionists including Cézanne, Monet, Matisse, Renoir and Gauguin. Other perennial crowd-pleasers include three Van Gogh paintings, several Picassos and paintings and sculptures by Degas. Asian sculpture is in the basement, while Western sculpture graces the gorgeous garden designed in the tradition of Monet's at Giverny, France.

Audioguides with details about 200 works rent for $3.

### GAMBLE HOUSE
A standout among Pasadena's fine private estates, the **Gamble House** (Map p76; ☎ 626-793-3334;

www.gamblehouse.org; 4 Westmoreland Pl; tour $10; ⏰ noon-3pm Thu-Sun) served as the winter residence of the Gamble family of Procter & Gamble fame and is a prime example of Craftsman architecture. Designed in 1908 by the style's prime practitioners, Charles and Henry Greene, it retains its original furnishings and rich decor. One-hour tours of the house give you close-ups of the beautiful woodwork, the iridescent stained glass and clever design features such as outdoor sleeping porches. The house starred as the home of mad scientist Doc Brown (Christopher Lloyd) in the three *Back to the Future* movies.

There are more Greene & Greene homes, including **Charles Greene's private residence** (Map p76; 368 Arroyo Tce), along Arroyo Tce and Grand Ave just south of here. Pick up a self-guided walking tour pamphlet at the Gamble House bookstore. Greene aficionados should also check out the permanent exhibit at the Huntington Library, Art Collections & Botanical Gardens (below).

### PASADENA MUSEUM OF HISTORY

The Feynes Estate, a palatial 1906 beaux arts mansion near the Gamble House is now the setting of this **local history museum** (Map p76; ☎ 626-577-1660; www.pasadenahistory.org; 470 W Walnut St; adult/child museum $5/free, house tour $4/free, combination $7/free; ⏰ noon-5pm Wed-Sun, tours 1:30pm & 3pm). You can take a tour of the house and its ample antiques, oriental carpets and rich wooden floors. Also check out the current historical exhibits and take a spin around the beautiful gardens. A separate building contains a small collection of Finnish folk art, a reminder of the period when this was a Finnish consulate.

### WRIGLEY MANSION & GARDENS

An elegant Italian Renaissance villa, the 1914 **Wrigley Mansion** (Map p76; ☎ 626-449-4100; 391 S Orange Grove Blvd; admission free), with its wood paneling, marble fireplaces and brocade wallpaper, was the winter home of chewing-gum magnate William Wrigley Jr. It is now the headquarters of the Tournament of Roses Association, which organizes the annual Rose Parade on New Year's Day. Tours are offered at 2pm and 3pm on Thursdays from February to August only, but you're free to stroll around the **gardens** (⏰ sunrise-sunset) year-round.

---

#### DETOUR: ANGELES NATIONAL FOREST

The San Gabriel mountain range that hems in the northern edge of urban LA is part of the **Angeles National Forest** (Map p60-1; ☎ 626-574-1613; www.fs.fed.us/r5/angeles) whose creeks, canyons and campgrounds provide quick city getaways year-round. It's great during the spring wildflower season and even gets pretty good fall color. Traffic can be insane on busy weekends, especially in summer with people trying to escape the heat, and after decent snowfall in winter, which brings skiing in the higher elevations.

The easiest, prettiest and closest access road is the **Angeles Crest Hwy** (Hwy 2) which offers spectacular views on its 64-mile meander from La Cañada Flintridge to the resort town of Wrightwood. It's at the foot of LA County's tallest mountain, officially called Mt San Antonio (10,064ft) but better known as **Old Baldy** for its treeless top. There are ranger stations along the way, but it's about 28 miles to the main **Chilao Visitor Center** ( ☎ 626-796-5541; admission free; ⏰ 8am-4pm Wed-Sun), which has exhibits, maps, brochures and helpful staff.

After about 14 miles you will have passed the turnoff to Red Box Rd which, after 5 miles, dead-ends at the famous **Mt Wilson Observatory** (Map p60-1; ☎ 626-793-3100; www.mtwilson.edu; Red Box Rd; admission free; ⏰ 10am-4pm Apr-Oct, weather permitting, check website Nov-Mar) atop 5715ft Mt Wilson. It has offered a window on the universe since 1904 thanks to astronomer George E Hale, and was the world's top astronomical research facility in the early 20th century; research continues here to this day. You can't see through any of the telescopes but are free to walk around the grounds (download a handy self-guided tour from the website) and visit the museum, or to join a free guided tour at 1pm on Saturdays and Sundays.

Note that visiting the Angeles National Forest requires a **National Forest Adventure Pass** (p45). Places to pick one up include **Sport Chalet** (Map p60-1; ☎ 818-790-9800; 920 Foothill Blvd & 951 Foothill Blvd, La Cañada) or **Jay's Shell Station** (Map p60-1; ☎ 818-790-3836; 4530 Angeles Crest Hwy).

## ROSE BOWL STADIUM & BROOKSIDE PARK

Pasadena's most famous landmark, the 1922 93,000-seat **Rose Bowl Stadium** (Map p76; ☎ 626-577-3100; www.rosebowlstadium.com; 1001 Rose Bowl Dr) was designed by Myron Hunt and is where the UCLA Bruins football team plays its home games. Every New Year's Day, the stadium hosts the famed Rose Bowl Game between two top-ranked college football teams. At other times, concerts, special events and, on the second Sunday of each month, a huge **flea market** (p191) bring in the crowds.

The Rose Bowl is surrounded by **Brookside Park**, a broadening of the Arroyo Seco, a now-dry riverbed that runs from the San Gabriel Mountains to Downtown LA. It's a nice spot for hiking, cycling and picnicking. South of the stadium is the new facility of the **Kidspace Children's Museum** (p132). Still beyond are the gracefully arched 1913 **Colorado St Bridge** and the former **Vista del Arroyo Hotel** (Map p76; ☎ 626-441-2797; 125 S Grand Ave), a grand 1903 structure that now houses the Ninth Circuit Court of Appeals. Free tours of the court are available by appointment.

## ART CENTER COLLEGE OF DESIGN

West of the Rose Bowl and overlooking the city and the Arroyo Seco from its ridge-top perch is this world-renowned **arts college** (Map p76; ☎ 626-396-2200; www.artcenter.edu; 1700 Lida St). Free tours run during the school year at 2pm Monday to Thursday and 1pm Friday; reservations are required. The **Williamson Gallery** (admission free; ☽ noon-5pm Tue-Thu, noon-9pm Fri, noon-5pm Sat & Sun) has rotating shows of top-name artists and designers (as well as the usually excellent student work) in various media.

## PASADENA CIVIC CENTER AREA

Pasadena's Civic Center, built in the 1920s along a central axis about ¼-mile northeast of Old Pasadena, is a reflection of the enormous wealth and civic pride that have governed this city since its early days. The eye is immediately drawn to the beautiful Spanish Renaissance–style **City Hall** (Map p76; ☎ 626-744-4000; 100 N Garfield Ave), a 'wedding cake' of a structure with arches, pinnacles, turrets and a grand tiled dome all centered on a lush courtyard garden with fountains; it's under renovation until at least 2007. Across from here, at the corner of Garfield Ave and Union St, the **Jackie Robinson Memorial** (Map p76) honors the Pasadena-born athlete who,

in 1945, became the first African American to play major league baseball when signing with the Brooklyn (now LA) Dodgers.

North of City Hall, the 1927 **Central Library** (Map p76; ☎ 626-744-4066; 285 E Walnut St; admission free; ☽ 9am-9pm Mon-Thu, 9am-6pm Fri & Sat, 1-5pm Sun) represents another work of Rose Bowl architect Myron Hunt. It features noise-absorbing cork floors and elegant oak paneling.

South of City Hall, and separated from the Civic Center area by the Paseo Colorado mall, the 1931 **Pasadena Civic Auditorium** (Map p76; ☎ 626-449-7360; 300 E Green St) boasts an interior swathed in Roman-inspired murals. It hosts concerts, musicals and the annual People's Choice Awards, and in the past, TV's Emmy Awards were presented here.

## PACIFIC ASIA MUSEUM

Pasadena owes its own Chinese imperial–style palace to Grace Nicholson, a local art dealer and huge fan and collector of Asian art and culture. The structure, which features an upward-curved green tile roof and stone dogs to ward off evil, served as Nicholson's private home from 1924 until her death in 1948. The **museum** (Map p76; ☎ 626-449-2742; www.pacificasiamuseum.org; 46 N Los Robles Ave; adult/student/senior $5/3/3; ☽ 10am-5pm Wed & Thu, 10am-8pm Fri, 10am-5pm Sat & Sun), which showcases her collection of five millennia worth of art and artifacts from Asia and the Pacific, opened in 1961. The rotating exhibits include everything from Chinese ceramics to Indian silk paintings and Japanese woodblock prints. The lovely garden with a koi pond is a nice spot for resting weary bones.

## PASADENA MUSEUM OF CALIFORNIA ART

California is a veritable petri dish of creativity, yet few museums are devoted exclusively to showing off the finished product. That's where Bob and Arlene Oltman come in. The art-collecting Pasadena couple is the driving force behind this **museum** (Map p76; ☎ 626-568-3665; www.pmcaonline.org; 490 E Union St; adult/child under 12/student/senior $6/free/4/4; ☽ noon-5pm Wed-Sun), whose exhibits focus on art, architecture and design created by California artists from 1850 to today. It's all in a custom-built venue with a dramatic open staircase leading to the 2nd-floor galleries. The Oltman's live up on top. Ask about access to the rooftop terrace with awesome views of City Hall and, on smog-free days, the San Gabriel Mountains.

**LOS ANGELES**

## CALTECH

With 29 Nobel laureates among its faculty or alumni, it's no wonder that the **California Institute of Technology** (Caltech; Map p76; ☎ 626-395-6327; www.caltech.edu; 551 S Hill Ave) is regarded with awe in academic circles. (Yes, Albert Einstein did sleep here.) One of the world's top scientific research institutes, Caltech actually started in 1891 as an arts and crafts school called Throop University. The science focus didn't come until 1907 at the instigation of board member and astronomer George E Hale, who also founded Mt Wilson Observatory in the mountains nearby (p124).

Free tours of the attractive campus with its many century-old structures leave from the visitors center at 355 S Holliston Ave, which also hands out free self-guided tour maps. Tours depart at 2pm, Monday to Friday, except on holidays or rainy days or during winter break. Architectural tours take place sporadically as well. The famous seismology laboratory can only be seen by reservation.

Caltech also operates the **Jet Propulsion Laboratory** (JPL; Map pp60-1; ☎ 626-354-9314; www.jpl.nasa.gov; 4800 Oak Grove Dr), NASA's main center for robotic exploration of the solar system. It's in La Cañada Flintridge, about 3.5 miles north of Pasadena, but can only be visited on open-house days. Check the website for dates and details about ongoing missions.

## HUNTINGTON LIBRARY, ART COLLECTIONS & BOTANICAL GARDENS

Urban LA feels a world away at the rarefied **Huntington** (Map p76; ☎ 626-405-2100; www.huntington.org; 1151 Oxford Rd; adult/child 5-11/student/senior $15/6/10/12; ☺ 10:30am-4:30pm Tue-Sun Jun-Aug, noon-4:30pm Tue-Fri, 10:30am-4:30pm Sat & Sun Sep-May), the former estate of railroad tycoon Henry Huntington. His private home, a 1910 beaux arts mansion by Myron Hunt, now houses British and French 18th-century paintings including, most famously, Thomas Gainsborough's *Blue Boy*. The nearby **Scott Gallery** houses 200 years' worth of American art, along with period furniture and silver and an exhibit on the Craftsman architects Charles and Henry Greene (also see p123). Beyond here the **Boone Gallery**, originally a garage, presents temporary exhibits.

Highlights from the **library collection**, in darkened galleries near the estate's main en-

---

### DETOUR: BIG BEAR LAKE

Embraced by the San Bernardino National Forest, 110 miles east of LA, Big Bear Lake is a family-friendly four-season playground, drawing ski bums from around mid-December to March, and hikers, mountain bikers and water-sports fans the rest of the year.

The **visitors center** ( ☎ 800-4-244-2327; www.bigbearinfo.com; 630 Bartlett Rd; ☺ 8am-5pm Mon-Fri, 9am-5pm Sat & Sun) is in 'the Village' on the lake's southern shore, where most tourist activity is concentrated.

Big Bear's two ski mountains, Bear Mountain and Snow Summit, are off the main Hwy 18 and jointly managed by **Big Bear Mountain Resorts** ( ☎ 909-866-5766; www.bigbearmountainresorts.com; adult lift ticket half-/full-day $36/48). Bear Mountain is the higher of the two with a vertical drop of 1665ft (vs 1200ft on Snow Summit) and is nirvana for boarders with 117 jumps, 57 jibs and two pipes across 195 acres. At Snow Summit the focus is on traditional downhill with trails for all levels of experience. Altogether the mountains are laced by over 50 runs and served by 23 lifts. Complete ski and boot rentals are about $25.

In summer, Snow Summit issues its siren call to **mountain bikers**. Several pro and amateur races take place here each year. The 13-mile **Grandview Loop** is great for getting your feet in gear. A **chairlift** (half-/full-day pass $15/20; ☺ May–beginning of ski season) provides easy access to the top. Maps, tickets and bike rentals are available from **Team Big Bear** ( ☎ 909-866-4565; www.teambigbear.com; bikes half-/full-day $27/50, helmets $7) at the mountain base.

**Hiking** is another major summer activity, as are swimming, jet skiing, kayaking, boating and fishing. Boating rentals are available along the lakeshore.

To get off the beaten track, take your car for an off-road spin along the **Gold Fever Trail**, a 20-mile self-guided romp on a graded dirt road around an old gold-mining area. If you prefer to let someone else do the driving, contact **Big Bear Off-Road Adventures** ( ☎ 909-585-1036; www.offroadadventure.com) for its tour schedule.

trance, include a 1455 Gutenberg Bible and a 1410 manuscript of Chaucer's *The Canterbury Tales*.

Follow up such cultural delights with a stroll around the botanical gardens, a feast of 15,000 kinds of plants neatly arranged in a dozen themed landscapes. The **Desert Garden** with its giant aloe and golden barrel cacti is a must-see, as is the **Japanese Garden** set within a canyon and anchored by a romantic pond. The **Rose Garden** is best from April to September, while the **Camellia Garden** is a highlight from January to March. For little ones the new, interactive **Children's Garden** yields lots of surprises.

The classic way to cap off a visit to the Huntington is with afternoon tea in the **Rose Garden Tea Room** (reservations ☎ 626-683-8131; $15). Next door is a self-service restaurant. Picnicking is not allowed.

While here, you might as well make a quick detour to **El Molino Viejo** (The Old Mill; Map p76; ☎ 626-449-5458; www.oldmill.info; 1120 Old Mill Rd; admission free; ☺ 1-4pm Tue-Sun), a brick and adobe structure that houses Southern California's first water-powered grist mill, built in 1816 for the San Gabriel Mission (right).

## DESCANSO GARDENS

About 6 miles northwest of central Pasadena, these lovely **gardens** (Map pp60-1; ☎ 818-949-4200; www.descanso.com; 1418 Descanso Dr; adult/child 5-12/student & senior $7/2/5; ☺ 9am-5pm), in La Cañada Flintridge, are famous for their 100,000 or so camellias, which bloom from January through March. Lilacs and orchids are at their best in April, while roses and other annuals start blossoming around May. Wooded sections, streams, a lake and a bird sanctuary form part of the gardens.

## SAN GABRIEL MISSION

About 3 miles southeast of central Pasadena, the city of San Gabriel is home to a **mission** (Map pp60-1; ☎ 626-457-3035; www.sangabrielmission .org; 428 S Mission Dr; adult/child 6-17/senior $5/3/4; ☺ 9am-4:30pm), the fourth of 21 built in California. Established in 1771, it was from this mission 10 years later that a small group of settlers set out on a trek that would end with the founding of Los Angeles near today's El Pueblo de Los Angeles (p104). The mission itself flourished, reaping produce from the fertile land and making soap, candles and wine.

---

Accommodation at Big Bear Lake runs the gamut from snug B&Bs and cabins to lodges, motels and hotels. Staff at the visitors center book accommodation for $10 per reservation. The following places are recommended:

**Honey Bear Lodge & Cabins** ( ☎ 909-866-7825, 800-628-8714; www.honeybearlodge.com; 40994 Pennsylvania Ave; r Sun-Thu $40-100, Fri & Sat $100-190; P ) The loft suites and rooms with private spa are the most charming. Enquire about discounts for multiple-night stays.

**Knickerbocker Mansion Country Inn** ( ☎ 909-878-9190, 877-423-1180; www.knickerbockermansion.com; 869 Knickerbocker Rd; r Mon-Thu $110-200, Fri-Sun $125-225; P 🖳 ) Classy B&B in a hand-built log home from the 1920s. Two-night minimum stay.

**Adventure Hostel** ( ☎ 909-866-8900, 866-866-5255; www.adventurehostel.com; 527 Knickerbocker Rd; dm Mon-Thu $20, Fri-Sun & daily during ski season $25, r $40-120; P 🖳 ) Clean, recently remodeled and friendly hostel on the edge of the Village.

Try the following places for good eats:

**Grizzly Manor Cafe** ( ☎ 909-866-6226; 41268 Big Bear Blvd; meals under $10; ☺ 6am-2am) For bear-sized breakfasts try this quirky locals' hangout.

**Old Country Inn** ( ☎ 909-866-5600; 41126 Big Bear Blvd; mains lunch $8-12, dinner $12-22; ☺ 8am-9pm) Hearty German cooking at night; big salads, sandwiches and burgers at lunchtime.

**Pine Nut Coffee House** ( ☎ 909-866-3537; 535 Pine Knot Ave; dishes under $8) Healthful wraps and chocolate chip cookies to die for.

Big Bear is on the eastern terminus of the Rim of the World Dr (Hwy 18), a panorama-filled mountain road that climbs, curves and meanders for about 40 miles from San Bernardino. A quicker – and almost as spectacular – approach is via Hwy 330, which starts in Highland and intersects with Hwy 18 in Running Springs. **Mountain Area Regional Transit Authority** (Marta; ☎ 909-878-5200; www.marta.cc) buses connect Big Bear with the Greyhound station in San Bernardino ($5).

The church (1805) is a sturdy stone structure with numerous Spanish Moorish design accents, a copper baptismal font, an altar made in Mexico City in 1790 and carved statues of saints. Wandering the grounds takes you past the cemetery, original soap and tallow vats, and fountains. The museum contains Bibles, religious robes and Native-American artifacts.

The historic area surrounding the mission is well worth a quick stroll. Following Mission Dr takes you past the pretty **Plaza Park** and the 1927 **Civic Auditorium** ( ☎ 626-308-2868; 320 S Mission Dr).

### LOS ANGELES COUNTY ARBORETUM & BOTANIC GARDEN

About 5 miles east of central Pasadena, in the city of Arcadia, this sprawling 127-acre **park** (Map pp60-1; ☎ 626-821-3222; www.arboretum.org; 301 N Baldwin Ave; adult/child 5-12/student/senior $7/2.50/5/5, admission free on 3rd Tue of month; ⏰ 9am-5pm) was originally the private estate of Elias 'Lucky' Baldwin, one of LA's early real-estate tycoons. It's a fantastic, rambling space filled with lush vegetation from around the world, a large spring-fed lake and 19th-century buildings, including a Victorian cottage and an adobe. Classes, seminars, lectures and other events keep things lively year-round. The park is also a hugely popular film location; much of John Huston's *African Queen* (starring Humphrey Bogart and Katharine Hepburn) was filmed here. A tram ($3 per person) travels throughout the park.

### SANTA ANITA PARK

Across from the LA Arboretum, the art deco **Santa Anita Park** (Map pp60-1; ☎ 626-574-7223; www.santaanita.com; 285 W Huntington Dr, Arcadia; admission $5, free for child under 17 if accompanied by adult; ⏰ Dec 26–late Apr, late Sep–Oct) is Southern California's oldest and one of its most prestigious thoroughbred racing tracks. This is the home of the legendary Seabiscuit, the rags-to-riches horse whose inspiring story became a major movie in 2003. Tram tours taking you to Seabiscuit's barn, various filming locations, the jockey's room and other sites are offered during racing seasons. Check the recording at ☎ 626-574-6677 for tour times and prices.

The track itself opened in 1934 and pioneered the use of the automated starting gate, the photo finish and the electrical timer. Stars who keep and race their horses here have ranged from Bing Crosby and Errol Flynn to Mark McGrath (of Sugar Ray), Alex Trebek and Burt Bacharach. During WWII, Santa Anita served first as a Japanese-American detention camp and then as a US army base.

## ACTIVITIES
### Cycling

Urban LA isn't exactly a biker's paradise, but there are actually some 200 miles of bike trails. The best is the South Bay Bicycle Trail, a flat 22-mile paved path that follows the beach south from Santa Monica to Torrance Beach, with a detour around the harbor at Marina del Rey. Other trails include the 37-mile San Gabriel River Trail from Azusa to Long Beach and an 8-mile Griffith Park trail that passes the Los Angeles Zoo & Botanical Gardens and the Museum of the American West. Another trip from Griffith Park is along the newly expanded LA River Bikeway, which parallels a surprisingly wild and pleasant 5-mile stretch of the river from Atwater Village to Burbank. A good place to enter the bikeway is where Zoo Dr meets Riverside Dr. Mountain bikers can take to the fire roads and paths of the Santa Monica Mountains.

A good source for specifics is the website of **Los Angeles Bike Paths** (www.labikepaths.com), which has news, maps and referrals. Bikes and in-line skates are available for rent in all the beach towns as well as from such outfits as **Hollywood Pro Bicycles** (Map pp66-7; ☎ 323-466-5890; www.labiketours.com; 6731 Hollywood Blvd, Hollywood; ⏰ 10am-8pm Mon-Sat, 10am-6pm Sun). Rates vary but you should be able to get a decent bike for about $25 per day.

### Gyms

Many mid-range and practically all top-end hotels have small fitness centers but for a full-fledged workout try one of these places: **Gold's Gym** (Map pp72-3; ☎ 310-392-6004; www.goldsgym.com; 360 Hampton Dr, Venice; per day $20; ⏰ 4am-midnight Mon-Fri, 5am-11pm Sat & Sun) Pump it up at the self-proclaimed 'mecca of bodybuilding' where Arnold himself once bulked up for the title of Mr Universe. Call or check the Yellow Pages for other locations.
**Crunch Gym** (Map pp68-9; ☎ 323-654-4550; www.crunch.com; 8000 W Sunset Blvd, West Hollywood; per day $24; ⏰ 5am-midnight Mon-Fri, 7am-10pm Sat & Sun) Work out with the pretty people at this high-tech gym with cutting-edge classes such as cardio striptease and fat-burning Pilates.

**Spectrum Club** (Map pp72-3; ☎ 310-829-4995; www.spectrumclubs.com; 2425 Olympic Blvd, Santa Monica; per day $20; ☼ 5am-10pm Mon-Fri, 7am-8pm Sat & Sun) Good all-round gym.

**24 Hour Fitness** (Map pp70-1; ☎ 310-553-7600; www.24hourfitness.com; 9911 W Pico Blvd, Beverly Hills; per day $10; ☼ 24hr Mon-Thu, 5am-11pm Fri-Sun) Numerous branches around town.

## Horseback Riding

Leave the urban sprawl behind on the forested bridle trails of Griffith Park or Topanga Canyon. Horses rent for about $18 to $20 for the first hour and $12 to $15 for each subsequent hour. All rides are accompanied by an experienced wrangler.

**Bar S Stables** (Map p75; ☎ 818-242-8443; 1850 Riverside Dr, Burbank)

**Escape on Horseback** (Map pp60-1; ☎ 818-591-2032; www.losangeleshorsebackriding.com; 2623 Old Topanga Canyon Rd, Topanga Canyon)

**Sunset Ranch Hollywood** (Map pp66-7; ☎ 323-469-5450; www.sunsetranchhollywood.com; 3400 Beachwood Dr, Hollywood) Besides horse rentals, this outfit operates Friday night dinner rides ($50, plus about $20 for food

and tip). Spaces are filled on a first-come, first-available basis; sign-up starts at 4:30pm, the last horse leaves at 5:30pm.

## Kayaking

**Malibu Ocean Sports** ( ☎ 877-952-9257; www.malibuoceansports.com) operates kayaking tours, including a gentle moonlight paddle around Marina del Rey ($39) and a two-hour Malibu Coastline Kayak Tour ($59). The best kayaking, though, is on Catalina Island (p102).

## Swimming & Surfing

Beaches beckon all along LA's coastline, with Santa Monica, Venice, Hermosa and Manhattan the most popular. Water temperatures become tolerable by late spring and are highest (about 70°F) in August and September. The water quality is mostly good, although the ocean is usually off-limits for three days following a storm because of untreated run-off. The local, nonprofit **Heal the Bay** ( ☎ 310-453-0395; www.healthebay.org) constantly evaluates the water quality and posts its findings on its website. There's good surfing at Malibu

---

**TOP 10 LA BEACHES**

- Leo Carrillo (off Map pp60-1) – Scenic beach with great swimming, surfing and kid-friendly tide pools, cliff caves and a nature trail.

- El Matador (off Map pp60-1) – Small beach hideaway hemmed in by battered rock cliffs and strewn with giant boulders. Wild surf; not suitable for children. Clothing optional.

- Zuma (Map pp60-1) – Gorgeous 2-mile long ribbon of sand with good water quality, excellent swimming and body surfing, and lots of tight bodies.

- Malibu Lagoon/Surfrider (Map pp60-1) – Legendary surf beach with superb swells and extended rides. Water quality is only so-so. The lagoon is great for birders.

- Will Rogers (Map pp60-1) – LA's most cruisey gay beach, especially towards the southern stretch.

- Santa Monica (Map pp72-3) – Extra-wide, hugely popular beach that's packed on weekends with families escaping the inland heat. Besides sand and ocean, attractions include the Santa Monica Pier (p96) and the paved shoreline path for strolling, in-line skating and cycling.

- Venice Beach (Map pp72-3) – LA's most outlandish beach paralleled by the Venice Boardwalk (p97) with its nonstop parade of friends and freaks. Drum circle in the sand on Sundays.

- Manhattan Beach (Map p74) – Quintessential SoCal beach scene where babes and dudes strut their stuff and hardcore surfers hang 10 around the pier, which is also home to a small aquarium, the Roundhouse Marine Studies Lab & Aquarium (p99).

- Hermosa Beach (Map p74) – LA's beach-volleyball capital and frequent tournament host, Hermosa also gets a youthful crowd thanks, in part, to the raucous pub row along Pier Ave.

- Cabrillo Beach (Map pp60-1) – Popular with kids, this beach has great tide pools, a playground, swimming and boat rentals. The Cabrillo Marine Aquarium (p101) is right here. Excellent windsurfing.

---

### HIKING IN THE SANTA MONICA MOUNTAINS

**Malibu Creek State Park** (Map pp60-1) Nature puts on a terrific show in this section of the Santa Monica Mountains. Its streams, thick forests and chaparral-covered hillsides – where Chumash Indians once roamed – have stood in for Wales, the South Pacific and, most famously, for Korea in the hit TV series *M*A*S*H*. Only 5 miles from the Malibu beaches, the park is laced with trails, including one leading to the main filming site of *M*A*S*H*, where an old Jeep and other leftover set pieces rust serenely in the California weather. En route you'll pass a visitors center (open weekends), which displays photographs taken during the shoots. The trailhead is in the park's main parking lot on Malibu Canyon Rd, which is called Las Virgenes Rd if coming from Hwy 101 (Hollywood Fwy). Parking is $8.

**Runyon Canyon** (Map pp66-7) Just a hop, skip and jump from frenzied Hollywood Blvd awaits this surprise slice of wilderness, a favorite playground for hip and fitness-obsessed locals and their dogs, which roam mostly off-leash. You'll have fine views of the Hollywood Sign, the city and, on clear days, all the way to the beach. The southern trailhead is at the end of Fuller St, off Franklin Ave; Mulholland Dr is the park's northern boundary (street parking is available at both). From the Fuller St entrance, the trail meanders past the ruined 1930s estate of famed Irish tenor John McCormack. Plans by a later owner to turn the park into a private country club were foiled by neighbors and it was bought by the city in 1984. For the full low-down, see www.runyon-canyon.com.

**Fryman Canyon** (Map pp60-1) Sweeping views of the San Fernando Valley, deep forest canyons and year-round springs are among nature's gifts to hikers venturing along the Betty B Dearing Trail. Most people start in Fryman Canyon Park at the Nancy Hoover Pohl Overlook off Mulholland Dr. To get to the trailhead, take Laurel Canyon Blvd to Mulholland Dr, turn west and the parking lot will be on your right. The trail also travels through adjacent Wilacre Park. The trailhead is on Fryman Rd, off Laurel Canyon Blvd.

---

Lagoon State Beach, aka Surfrider Beach, and at the Manhattan Beach pier.

If you want to learn surfing, expect to pay about $70 to $100 for a two-hour private lesson or $40 to $60 for a group lesson, including board and wet suit. Instruction takes place at various beaches, including Santa Monica, Hermosa Beach and Malibu. Contact these schools for details.

**Learn to Surf LA** ( ☎ 310-920-1265; www.learntosurf la.com)

**Malibu Long Boards** ( ☎ 818-990-7633; www.malibu longboards.com)

**Malibu Ocean Sports** ( ☎ 877-952-9257; www.malibu oceansports.com)

**Surf Academy** ( ☎ 310-372-1036, 877-599-7873; www .surfacademy.org)

### Yoga

Many Angelenos consider yoga an important part of their routine, as a way to stay physically fit and mentally strong. For a class schedule, call or check the websites of the following studios:

**Yoga Works** (Map pp72-3; ☎ 310-393-5150; www .yogaworks.com; 2215 Main St, Santa Monica; per class $16) Popular place for doing the plough or sun salutation with dozens of classes per week for all levels of expertise, plus one- and two-day intro courses. Call about other branches.

**Bikram Yoga Studio** Mid-City (off Map pp68-9; ☎ 310-854-5800; www.bikramyoga.com/schools/bevhills .htm; 1862 S La Cienega Blvd; per class $20, students under 25 $10); Silver Lake (off Map pp66-7; ☎ 323-668-2500; www.bikramyogasilverlake.com; 3233 Glendale Blvd; per class $15) If you like it hot, try these rigorous 90-minute workouts in a studio heated to 95°F (you'll need to bring your own towel).

**Golden Bridge** (Map pp68-9; ☎ 323-936-4172; www .goldenbridgeyoga.com; 5901 W 3rd St, Mid-City; 1st class $7, otherwise $15) Prenatal and kundalini yoga classes in a total New Age vibe.

## WALKING TOUR: DOWNTOWN LA

Unlike most of LA, Downtown is tailor-made for exploring on foot. Distances are relatively short and streets are lined with everything from blockbuster sights such as the Walt Disney Concert Hall to little-known gems such as the city's most beautiful art deco restaurant. This tour hopscotches around several Downtown districts, allowing you to sample the city's many faces, flavors and personalities.

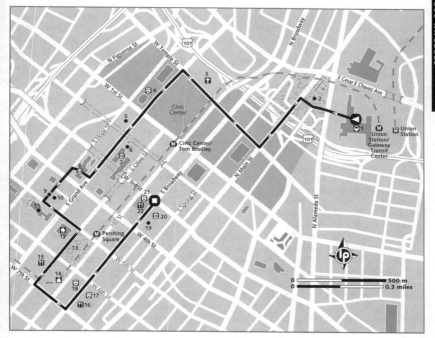

Your journey through Downtown starts, quite appropriately, at LA's major transportation hub, **Union Station** (**1**; p104), an elegant vestige of the era when the railroad was the main method of traveling. Crossing Alameda St quickly takes you to **El Pueblo de Los Angeles** (**2**; p104), the city's historic heart with buildings dating back to the Mexican period. It is also a cultural center of LA's Latino community, especially along festive Olvera St and in the central Old Plaza with its ancient trees and pretty bandstand.

Work your way south along Main St across the Hwy 101 overpass, from where you can already spy your next stop, the **Cathedral of Our Lady of the Angels** (**3**; p108), LA's sparkling new Roman Catholic house of worship on Temple St. The inside of the cathedral is nice, quiet and cool and filled with original art.

Continue a block north, then turn left on Grand Ave, which takes you past the **Music Center** (**4**). This giant entertainment complex consists of two theaters and two concert halls, most famously the sparkling new **Walt Disney Concert Hall** (**5**; p107), Frank Gehry's latest masterpiece and home of the

| Start & finish | Union Station |
|---|---|
| Distance | 3 miles |
| Duration | From two hours to all day |

world-renowned LA Phil. More culture awaits as you head south on Grand Ave passing first the **Colburn School of Performing Arts** (**6**; p108) and then **MOCA Grand Ave** (**7**; p108), Southern California's premier contemporary art museum.

MOCA sits at the edge of the Financial District with its engaging mix of historic office buildings and modern monoliths. On your right is one such worker's beehive, the Wells Fargo Center, where the **Wells Fargo History Museum** (**8**; p108) is worth a look for its fine displays about the stagecoach era. Exit the center on Hope St, along the way noting the tropical indoor garden accented with nude sculptures by local artist Robert Graham. Turn left to get to the top of the attractive **Bunker Hill Steps** (**9**) – marked by another Graham nude – which cascade down to 5th St with LA's tallest building, the **US Bank Tower** (**10**; p109) on your left. In front you is the historic **Richard Riordan Central Library** (**11**; p109) and its modern addition, both worthy of a quick spin. From here head downhill on 5th St, past the grand **Millennium Biltmore Hotel** (**12**; p109) whose public hallways and ballrooms ooze old-time glamour.

The hotel rubs up against **Pershing Square** (**13**; p109), the site of summertime concerts and a holiday-season ice rink. From here, head south on Olive St where you'll be looking at shimmering baubles in the **Jewelry District** (**14**; p109). While strolling down Olive St, also peek inside the handsome **Oviatt Building** (**15**; p109), home to the aforementioned art deco restaurant, then turn left on 7th St for the two-block walk to Broadway. Besides being one of Downtown's busiest (if downmarket) shopping streets, it's also flanked by a dozen historic movie palaces from the silent-movie era, which are collectively known as the Broadway Theater District. Sadly, none of them show movies anymore, but several have been restored as special events and party venues. As you head north on Broadway, you'll pass the endearing **Clifton's Cafeteria** (**16**; p134), one of LA's kookiest eateries. Have a look inside, then continue past the **Palace Theater** (**17**; p111) and, across the street, the magnificent **Los Angeles Theater** (**18**; p111).

As you make your way further north, you'll eventually pass by ittybitty **Biddy Mason Park** (**19**; p111), which honors a prominent African-American Angeleno. Just beyond awaits a Broadway highlight, the ethereal **Bradbury Building** (**20**; p110), which film buffs will remember from *Blade Runner*. Go inside for a look at the stunning lobby. The Bradbury sits right across from the **Million Dollar Theater** (**21**; p111), one of the oldest on Broadway. The tour concludes at the colorful **Grand Central Market** (**22**; p111), where you can rest your feet and have a bite or a cuppa.

To get back to Union Station, walk one block south to the corner of Spring St and 3rd St and board the DASH bus 'D.'

## LOS ANGELES FOR CHILDREN

Traveling to LA with the rug rats tagging along is not a problem. Besides such perennial favorites as Disneyland (p199), Knott's Berry Farm (p211) and Universal Studios Hollywood (p121), there's plenty to explore on the beach, in the mountains and even in the urban core.

Many museums and attractions have special kid-oriented exhibits, activities, workshops and guided tours. For what's on during your visit, call the venue or check out the Calendar section of the *Los Angeles Times'* Sunday edition, which has a special section dedicated to children's activities. A good general source is the monthly *LA Parent* magazine distributed for free in child-oriented places throughout town. Check http://losangeles.parenthood.com for locations. For a selection of shops catering to kids, see p188.

### Sights & Activities

LA offers plenty of diversions for the wee ones. The charming **Zimmer Children's Museum** (Map pp68-9; ☎ 323-761-8989; www.zimmermuseum .org; 6505 Wilshire Blvd, Suite 100, Mid-City; adult/child $5/3; ⊙ 10am-5pm Tue, 12:30-5pm Wed, Thu & Sun), off the lobby of the Jewish Federation Center, brims with interactive exhibits that'll keep kids – Jewish or not – entertained for hours while gently teaching them about tolerance, responsibility, generosity, community spirit and other values. Kids can 'fly' to exotic lands; rescue lives while driving an ambulance; play and even compose music; and stroll along a re-created Main St with a synagogue, and shops selling bagels and books.

Over in Pasadena, the new facility of the **Kidspace Children's Museum** (Map p76; ☎ 626-449-9144; www.kidspacemuseum.org; 480 N Arroyo Blvd; admission $8; ⊙ 9:30am-5pm) opened in December 2004. It's a great place full of hands-on exhibits and outdoor areas and gardens for exploring, with a packed schedule of activities.

Kids love animals, of course, making the sprawling **Los Angeles Zoo & Botanical Gardens** (p119) – home of cuddly koalas, mighty elephants and the new Children's Discovery Center – a sure winner. It's in **Griffith Park** (p118), which is the city's single best family playground. Besides the zoo, it offers picnic areas, a nostalgic merry-go-round, horseback riding, nature walks, miniature train rides and other fun things to do. There are also two kid-oriented museums, the Travel Town train museum (p119) and the Museum of the American West (p119) with its dedicated Family Discovery Gallery.

Dinosaur fans should stop in at the **Natural History Museum of LA County** (p115) in Exposition Park. It also has great exhibits about other critters, including a brigade of creepy crawlies at the Insect Zoo. Budding scientists will have a field day next door at the **California Science Center** (p116) with dozens of interactive stations. Older kids with a science bent are sure to be intrigued by the excavations of fossilized bones at the **La Brea Tar Pits** (p87) in Hancock Park (summer only).

Along the coast, the **Santa Monica Pier** (p96) yields lots of possibilities, from carnival rides to a fanciful carousel and small aquarium. More fishy encounters can be had at the **Roundhouse Marine Studies Lab & Aquarium** (p99) in Manhattan Beach, the **Cabrillo Marine Aquarium** (p101) in San Pedro and the **Aquarium of the Pacific** (p102) in Long Beach, where you can pet sharks. The latter city also has the grand **Queen Mary** (p103), where teens might get a kick out of the ghost tours (these might be too scary for little ones). Boat tours of LA's giant port leave from **Shoreline Village** (p102), also in Long Beach, and from **Ports O'Call Village** (p101) in San Pedro. All along the beach you can rent bicycles and in-line skates. Beaches especially suited for children are **Mother's Beach** (Map pp72–3) in Marina del Rey with its own playground, and the **Seaside Lagoon** (p100) in Redondo Beach.

Urban experiences that kids might enjoy include looking at the 'stars' along Hollywood Blvd's **Walk of Fame** (p59); checking out the street musicians on **Third St Promenade** (p96) in Santa Monica; watching the artists, tarot card readers and bizarre folk along the **Venice Boardwalk** (p97); and browsing for trinkets along colorful **Olvera St** (p105) in Downtown LA.

Also recommended:

**Bright Child Children's Activity Center** (Map pp72-3; ☎ 310-393-4844; 1415 4th St, Santa Monica; adult/child per 2hr $free/10; ✹ 10am-6pm) Indoor playground with slides, swings, a wind tunnel and other fun zones; suitable for children under 10.

**Under the Sea** (adult/child $free/7; ✹ Mon-Fri) Culver City (Map pp72-3; ☎ 310-915-1133; 12211 W Washington Blvd, Suite 120); San Fernando Valley (off Map p75; ☎ 818-567-9945; 2424 W Victory Blvd, Burbank) Ocean-themed indoor playground with a bounce house, climbing structures, a baby corner and other play stations. Call for specific opening hours.

## Entertainment

**Bob Baker Marionette Theater** (Map pp64-5; ☎ 213-250-9995; 1345 W 1st St, near Downtown) Generations of Angelenos have been enthralled with Bob's adorable singing and dancing marionettes and stuffed animals that interact with the young audiences seated on a carpet. It's pure magic.

**Magicopolis** (Map pp72-3; ☎ 310-451-2241; www.magicopolis.com; 1418 4th St, Santa Monica; tickets $17.50-25) Aspiring Harry Potters will enjoy the sleight-of-hand and mind-boggling illusions performed by pros in this intimate space. Shows last about 90 minutes, and there's a great shop for all your wizard supplies.

**Storyopolis** (Map pp68-9; ☎ 310-358-2500; www.storyopolis.com; 116 N Robertson Blvd, West Hollywood; ✹ 10am-6pm Mon-Sat, 11am-4pm Sun) This magical place marries a gallery of original children's art with what many consider the best kids bookstore in town and a packed schedule of family-friendly events. These include book signings, gallery openings and author readings. At 11am on Tiny Tuesdays and Wee Wednesdays are wonderful, free storytelling sessions for the preschool set.

**Puppet & Magic Center** (Map pp72-3; ☎ 310-656-0483; 1255 2nd St, Santa Monica; admission $6.50; ✹ 1pm Wed, 1pm & 3pm Sat & Sun) Steve Meltzer's Puppetolio puppet show (suitable for ages 3 and

---

### BABYSITTING SERVICES

If you need a vacation from your kids or are in the mood for a romantic evening for two, try the following babysitter services or ask at your hotel for a recommendation. Most services prefer at least 24-hour advance notice.

**Babysitters Agency of Santa Monica** ( ☎ 310-306-5437; per hr $12; ✹ 9am-5pm Mon-Sat) In business for almost 50 years. There's a four-hour booking minimum from Sundays to Fridays and a five-hour minimum on Saturdays.

**Babysitters Guild** ( ☎ 310-837-1800; per hr $10-16; ✹ 10am-4pm Mon-Fri) All sitters are screened, over 21 and fluent in English. There's a four-hour booking minimum

**Buckingham Nannies** ( ☎ 310-247-1877, 800-393-4844; per hr $10-15; ✹ 8:30am-5pm Mon-Fri) Uses fully qualified nannies with at least two-years' experience. Fees are in addition to $25 registration fee and $15 daily fee payable to the agency.

**LOONY LOS ANGELES**

Anything goes and anything sells in LA, a city that acts as a magnet for the wacky, the outlandish and the plainly bizarre. Take, for instance, **Angelyne**, a self-styled Hollywood vixen of indeterminate age famous for nothing but tooling around town in a convertible pink Corvette and erecting huge billboards of her scantily clad self. She ran for California governor during the 2003 recall election (as an independent) and got 2536 votes, which put her in 29th place out of field of 135. Across town, the Venice Boardwalk is no slouch in the strangeness department either. Among the many people who uphold the tradition of weirdness is **Harry Perry**, a turbaned, rollerskating 'Kamakosmickrusader' (his word) who showers unsuspecting tourists with some pretty, shall we say, 'unique' guitar riffs. Both, of course, have Web pages (www.angelyne.com and www.venicebeachcalifornia.com, if you must know). But there's lots of stuff crazier in LA than some of its people. Here's a list of out-LA-ndish favorites.

### Sights & Museums

**Museum of Jurassic Technology** (MJT; off Map pp72-3; ☎ 310-836-6131; www.mjt.org; 9341 Venice Blvd, Culver City; adult/child under 12/student/senior $5/free/3/3; ☽ 2-8pm Thu, noon-6pm Fri-Sun) Despite the name, exhibits at the MJT have nothing to do with dinosaurs and you'll find more technology in a bicycle shop. Instead you'll be bumping into displays about Cameroonian stink ants, a tribute to trailer parks and a sculpture of the Pope squished into the eye of a needle. Madness may begin to nibble at your mind as you wander through this dark warren of rooms, trying to comprehend the assemblage of improbably weird, obscure and arcane displays. Little by little, the lines separating reality, imagination and perception become a hazy blur. The MJT may or may not be an actual museum but a mind-bending spoof, an elaborate hoax or a complete exercise in ironic near-hysteria by founder and curator David Wilson. Only two things are certain: the MJT will challenge the way you look at reality and it will stay on your mind for a long, long time. PS: Former *New Yorker* staff writer Lawrence Weschler has even written an entire book about the place called *Mr Wilson's Cabinet of Wonder*.

**Bunny Museum** (off Map p76; ☎ 626-798-8848; www.thebunnymuseum.com; 1933 Jefferson Dr, Pasadena; admission free) Hop on over to this unique collection of 17,000 bunny items (plus six real-life animals) all residing in the home of Candace Frazee and Steve Lubanski ('honey bunny' to each other). It all began with a plush white bunny Steve gave his wife on Valentine's Day in 1992 and quickly grew into an obsession for both. To this day they give each other a bunny-themed item every day as a token of their love. Their cute critters come in all shapes and sizes – as figurines, as toys, on tea cups and plates, on tea towels and egg cups. And keeping an eye on it all is Bonnie Bunny, one of the couple's pets who died of a lung tumor. The museum's even earned an entry in the *Guinness Book of World Records*. It's open on 20 different holidays and by appointment.

**Porno Walk of Fame** (Map pp68-9; 7734 Santa Monica Blvd, West Hollywood) LA's XXX-rated walk of fame is right outside the Tomkat gay movie theater, right in the heart of West Hollywood's 'Borscht Belt' of Russian émigrés. Even those who wouldn't touch a porn movie with a 10-inch pole probably know the names of such legendary hard-core divas and studs as Linda Lovelace and Harry Reems of *Deep Throat* fame. Alas, voyeuristic types expecting cement prints of performers' signature body parts may be disappointed: it's PG-rated hands and feet only.

up) has delighted audiences since 1998. All performances are followed by a tour 'behind the strings' and a visit to the puppet museum. Steve also runs puppet workshops.

# TOURS
## Boat

A lovely way to get away from the hustle of the city for a couple of hours is by taking a boat tour. The following companies offer various types of getaways, including harbor tours, dinner cruises, champagne brunch cruises and whale-watching excursions (January to March). Boats depart from Marina del Rey, San Pedro and Long Beach.

**Hornblower Cruises** ( ☎ 310-301-6000; www.hornblower.com)

**Spirit Cruises** ( ☎ 310-548-8080; www.spiritdinnercruises.com)

**Los Angeles Pet Memorial Park** (Map pp60-1; ☎ 818-591-7037; www.lapetcemetery.com; 5068 N Old Scandia Ln, Calabasas; admission free; ☼ 8am-5pm Mon-Sat, 8am-dusk Sun) At first sight it looks like many other cemeteries with rolling lawns shaded by mature trees, flower-decorated tomb stones and even a mausoleum. More than 40,000 dogs, cats, birds, iguanas and other pets (there's an entire horse section) have found their final rest on these lovely grounds, including such celebrities as Pete from *The Little Rascals* and Hopalong Cassidy's horse Topper. Founded in 1928, this is one of the oldest pet cemeteries in the western US. It's about 20 miles northwest of Hollywood.

### Bars & Restaurants

**CIA** (off Map p75; ☎ 818-506-6353; 11334 Burbank Blvd, North Hollywood) And now from the Ministry of Visual and Moral Atrocities comes…the CIA, aka the California Institute of Abnormal Arts! Described as 'PT Barnum's bad acid trip,' this emporium is a warped celebration of fascinating freakishness with decor that looks like a train wreck of a traveling carnival from Mars. This is where you might catch a band called Ebola Music Orchestra, fronted by a stripper known as Bridget the Midget. It's a circus of the Sinister where girly shows, psycho sword-swallowers and the mortal remains of dead fairies and French clowns will have your skin crawling and your mind reeling.

**Clifton's Cafeteria** (Map pp64-5; ☎ 213-627-1673; 648 Broadway, Downtown; ☼ 6:30am-7pm) This venerable eatery was founded in 1931 by a Salvation Army captain who doled out free grub to starving Angelenos during the Great Depression. 'Grub' is still what is served here, but the ultra-campy setting is what makes it special. Sprawling over several levels, Clifton's is an enchanted forest with fake trees, squirrels and deer. For spiritual sustenance, duck into the diminutive chapel.

### Shops

**Panpipes Magickal Marketplace** (Map pp66-7; ☎ 323-462-7078; www.panpipes.com; 1641 N Cahuenga Blvd, Hollywood; ☼ 10am-7pm Mon-Sat) Modern-day alchemist George Hiram Derby, who sports pentagram tattoos and is trained in voodoo, pagan crafts and other ritualistic and spiritual fields, presides over the nation's oldest occult and pagan supply shop (since 1961). Come here to stock up on your basic powdered lizard, crystal balls and Ouija boards, or to have George mix you up one of his magical potions to help fix whatever ails you. Ingredients, kept in neatly stacked glass vials, can be as common as essential oils and as rare as, yes, mummy dust.

**Necromance** (Map pp68-9; ☎ 323-934-8684; www.necromance.com; 7220 Melrose Ave, Mid-City; ☼ noon-7pm Mon-Sat, 2-6pm Sun) At Nancy Smith's bazaar of the bizarre lots of dead stuff is neatly displayed behind glass and on shelves. The skeletal mouse heads are a steal at $8, but the full-blown human head (about $500) would come in handy for your next Hamlet impression. A frog in formaldehyde for your mantelpiece? Or how about a vampire repellent kit complete with garlic, holy water and a wooden stake? Necromance is full of surprises.

**Skeletons in the Closet** (off Map pp64-5; ☎ 323-343-0760; http://lacstores.co.la.ca.us/coroner; 1104 N Mission Rd, Downtown; ☼ 8:30am-4:30pm Mon-Fri) This ghoulish gift shop, operated by the LA County Coroner's Office, is located two floors above the morgue. Bestsellers include personalized toe-tags, body outline beach towels, even travel garment 'body bags.' Proceeds benefit the Youthful Drunk Driving Visitation Program, an alternative sentencing program.

For a few more suggestions, see p190.

Romantic spirits will love the one-hour **Gondola Getaway** (Map pp62-3; ☎ 562-433-9595; www .gondolagetawayinc.com; 5437 E Ocean Blvd, Long Beach; per couple $65, up to 4 additional persons per person $15; ☼ 11am-11pm) cruises. Board your own private gondola and be piloted by an oar-wielding gondolier around the scenic canals of the Naples neighborhood in Long Beach. Baguette, cheese, salami and an ice bucket are provided (you'll need to bring your own libations).

Reservations are necessary; make them early, especially for the weekend sunset cruises.

PS: Don't forget to kiss your sweetie under each and every bridge.

### Bus

In business since 1935, **Starline Tours** ( ☎ 323-463-3333, 800-959-3131; www.starlinetours.com) is the granddaddy among the city's narrated bus tours. Popular options include the two-hour

---

**TOP 10 FREE TOURS**

- California Institute of Technology (Caltech) campus (Pasadena, p126)
- Cathedral of Our Lady of the Angels (Downtown, p108)
- City Hall (Downtown, p107)
- El Pueblo de Los Angeles & Olvera St (Downtown, p104)
- Getty Center (Brentwood, p91)
- *Los Angeles Times* (Downtown, p107)
- Music Center (Downtown, p108)
- Richard Riordan Central Library (Downtown, p109)
- University of California, Los Angeles (UCLA) campus (Westwood, p90)
- University of Southern California (USC) campus (Exposition Park Area, p116)

---

Movie Star Homes Tour (adult/child $35/36), which departs every 30 minutes from outside Grauman's Chinese Theatre (Map pp66–7) in Hollywood. The 5½-hour Grand City Tour ($51/34) covers all the hot spots in Hollywood, Downtown and in between, and includes pick-up from your hotel. An all-day combination of the two tours costs $72/55. Theme park tours to Universal Studios ($75/59), Disneyland or Disney's California Adventure ($87/72), Knott's Berry Farm ($78/62) and Six Flags Magic Mountain ($51/34) are also available; rates include park admission.

Companies offering similar tours:

**Guideline Tours** ( ☎ 323-465-3004, 800-604-8433; www.guidelinetours.com)

**LA Tours** ( ☎ 323-460-6490, 800-881-7715; www.latours.net)

**LA CityTours.com** ( ☎ 310-581-0718, 888-800-7878; www.lacitytours.com)

### Specialty

The nighttime **Neon Cruises** ( ☎ 213-489-9918; www.neonmona.org; tour $45; ☽ 7:30-10:30pm Sat) bus tour organized by the Museum of Neon Art (p113) in Downtown LA takes you to the best in vintage neon art the city has to offer. Call for tour dates; tours always sell out, so make reservations early.

If architecture is your thing you can tool around town in a 1962 black Cadillac taking in styles from Tudor to utopian with **Architecture Tours Los Angeles** ( ☎ 323-464-7866; www.architecturetoursla.com).

The ecologically-minded should try **LA River Tours** ( ☎ 323-223-0585; www.folar.org; suggested donation $5; ☽ 3rd Sun of month Mar-Nov) where you can discover the history, mystery and ecology of the LA River and find out why it's not just that ugly concrete channel you've been making jokes about. Each tour explores a different section.

### Walking

**Los Angeles Conservancy** ( ☎ 213-623-2489; www.laconservancy.org; ☽ 10am Sat), a nonprofit organization with a mission to preserve LA's historical buildings, now offers 15 entertaining and informative walking tours lasting about 2½ hours and geared toward an adult audience. Most explore various areas of Downtown such as the Broadway Theater District, the Millennium Biltmore Hotel, Little Tokyo or Union Station. In addition, there are tours of other historic districts, such as Highland Park, San Pedro and USC. Call or check the website for tour times and specifics. Reservations are required.

**Red Line Tours** (Map pp66-7; ☎ 323-402-1074; www.redlinetours.com; 6773 Hollywood Blvd; adult/child 9-15/student/senior $10/15/18/18) offers 'edu-taining' walking tours of Hollywood and Downtown using headsets that cut out traffic noise so you can hear your guide perfectly. Guides use a clever mix of anecdotes, fun facts, trivia and historical and architectural data to keep their charges entertained. Call for tour times.

## FESTIVALS & EVENTS

LA has a packed calendar of annual festivals and special events. For even more merriment, see Out & About in Los Angeles (p84), Cool Tunes Below the Moon (p171), Movies Under the Stars (p173) and Top Three Film Festivals (p172).

RICK GERHARTER

Giant Oscars oversee preparations for the Academy Awards, Hollywood (p59)

Santa Monica Pier (p96), Santa Monica

RICHARD CUMMINS

RAY LASKOWITZ

Los Angeles freeway (p193)

DAVID PEEVERS

Hollywood Walk of Fame (p59), Hollywood

JONATHAN SELIG

US Bank Tower (p109) and
Millennium Biltmore Hotel
(p110), Downtown LA

MARY LOU JANSON

Grauman's Chinese Theatre (p78),
Hollywood

LEE FOSTER

Petersen Automotive Museum
(p87), LA

Walt Disney Concert Hall (p107), Downtown LA

EMMANUEL

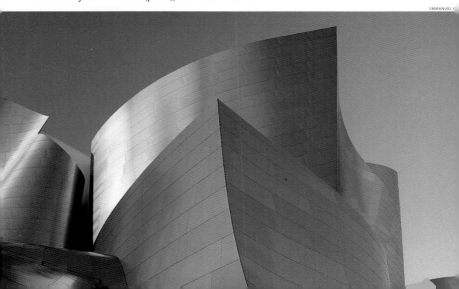

## January & February

**Rose Parade** ( ☎ 626-449-4100; www.tournament ofroses.com) An enormous cavalcade of flower-festooned floats along Pasadena's Colorado Blvd on New Year's Day. Followed by the Rose Bowl football game and postparade viewing of floats at Victory Park.

**Chinese New Year** ( ☎ 213-680-0243, 213-617-0396) Colorful Dragon Parade, plus free entertainment, fireworks, food and games, carnival rides and other traditional revels in the heart of Chinatown during late January or early February.

## March

**LA Marathon** ( ☎ 310-444-5544; www.lamarathon .com) Over 25,000 runners and wheelchair racers turn out on the first Sunday in March for this 26.2-mile race from Figueroa and 6th Sts in Downtown through Chinatown, Hollywood and Echo Park. The Quality of Life Expo runs concurrently.

**Santa Clarita Cowboy Festival** ( ☎ 661-286-4021; www.cowboyfestival.org) Western poets and country music in Santa Clarita (near Six Flags Mountains), in late March.

## April

**Toyota Grand Prix of Long Beach** ( ☎ 888-827-7333; www.longbeachgp.com) A weeklong auto-racing spectacle in mid-April drawing world-class drivers.

**Blessing of the Animals** ( ☎ 213-625-5045; www .cityofla.org/elp/) Brings pets and people from all parts of Southern California to Downtown LA's Olvera St to be blessed on the Saturday before Easter. Also see p105.

**Los Angeles Times Festival of Books** ( ☎ 800-528-4637, ext 72665; www.latimes.com/festivalofbooks) Free fair held the third weekend in April with author readings and discussions, storytelling and children's activities on the UCLA campus in Westwood.

**Fiesta Broadway** ( ☎ 310-914-0015; www.fiestabroad way.la.net) One of the largest Cinco de Mayo street fair celebrations in the world with entertainment from renowned Latino singers along historic Broadway in Downtown. Held on the last Sunday in April.

## May

**Cinco de Mayo** ( ☎ 213-625-5045; www.cityofla.org/elp) Celebrates the Mexican victory over the French at the Battle of Puebla (1862); free festivities around Olvera St in Downtown during early May.

**NoHo Theater & Arts Festival** ( ☎ 818-763-5273; www.nohoartsdistrict.com) One of the largest thespian fests in Southern California with lots of free performances, art, music and dance. Held during mid-May.

**Topanga Banjo Fiddle Contest & Folk Festival** ( ☎ 818-382-4819; www.topangabanjofiddle.org) Bluegrass music festival in mid-May with more than 100 contestants at Paramount Movie Ranch in the Santa Monica Mountains.

## June

**Mariachi USA Festival** ( ☎ 800-6274 2244; www .rodri.com) Four-hour fiesta on the third weekend in June celebrating the finest mariachi music and ballet folklórico at the Hollywood Bowl.

**Long Beach Bayou Festival** ( ☎ 562-427-8834; www .longbeachfestival.com; admission $25) A weekend of Cajun and Zydeco sounds and Creole food against the backdrop of the *Queen Mary*, in late June.

**Absolut Chalk** ( ☎ 626-440-7379; www.absolutchalk .com) A weekend of beautifying Pasadena streets, albeit only temporarily, at the world's largest street painting festival, in late June.

## July

**Lotus Festival** ( ☎ 888-527-2757; www.laparks.org) Celebrates Asian and Pacific Island culture with exotic foods, dragon boat races, a community carnival, fireworks and other festivities. Held on the weekend following July 4.

**Central Avenue Jazz Festival** ( ☎ 213-485-2437; www.culturela.org) Weekend festival in late July celebrates the period from 1920s to '50s when Central Ave was a hotbed of West Coast jazz; music, food, arts and crafts.

**Blessing of the Cars** ( ☎ 323-663-1265; www.blessing ofthecars.com) Thousands turn out to have their classic car, hot rod or motorcycle blessed by a real priest in late July. Plenty of merriment to go along with it. Also see p105.

## August

**Nisei Week Japanese Festival** ( ☎ 213-687-7193; www.niseiweek.org) Free festival in Little Tokyo, with a grand parade, queen coronations, a *taiko* drum gathering, karaoke, food, dancing and crafts. Held from early to mid-August.

**Long Beach Jazz Festival** ( ☎ 562-424-0013; www .longbeachjazzfestival.com) This three-day festival in mid-August usually features top talent such as George Duke, Al Jarreau and Poncho Sanchez.

**Sunset Junction Street Fair** ( ☎ 323-661-7771; www .sunsetjunction.org; admission $10) Multiblock street party with food and knickknack stalls and live-music stages celebrates the cultural wackiness of the neighborhood. Held mid-August.

**LA Greek Fest** ( ☎ 323-737-2424; www.lagreekfest .com) A weekend of ouzo, *sirtaki* (a Greek folk dance) and gyros right next to St Sophia Cathedral brings together the Greek community and their friends in late August.

**Watts Summer Festival** ( ☎ 323-789-7304; www .wattsfestival.orgg) Celebrates African-American culture and heritage through arts, crafts, theater, food and fashion. Held late August.

**African Marketplace & Cultural Faire** ( ☎ 323-734-1164; www.africanmarketplace.org) Series of festivals and events from late August to early September celebrating the African diaspora with hundreds of crafts booths and lots of entertainment and music.

## September

**LA County Fair** ( ☎ 909-623-3111; www.fairplex .com) Huge 18-day fair from mid- to late September with carnival rides, prizes, livestock exhibits and live country entertainment at the LA County Fairgrounds in Pomona.

**Oktoberfest** ( ☎ 310-327-4384; www.alpinevillage.net) Largest Oktoberfest in Southern California with beer, sausages, oompah bands and chicken dancing at the Alpine Village in Torrance, from early September to late October.

**Mexican Independence Festival** ( ☎ 213-625-5045; www.cityofla.org/elp) On Olvera St in Downtown, a free celebration of Mexico's independence from Spain with live performers, food, historic displays and celebrities from Mexico. Held mid-September.

**Abbot Kinney St Festival** ( ☎ 310-396-3772; www .abbotkinney.org) Soak up the groovy Venice vibe at this annual celebration of local arts, crafts, food and eccentrics in late September.

**Watts Towers Day of the Drum Festival & Jazz Festival** ( ☎ 213-847-4646; www.wattstowers.net) One weekend in late September: two back to back events. Drummers from around the world and free jazz, gospel and blues the following day.

## October

**Catalina Island JazzTrax Festival** ( ☎ 760-323-5770; www.jazztrax.com) The best and newest in smooth jazz brings fans from around the country to Catalina during the month of October.

**Edge of the World Theater Festival** ( ☎ 310-281-7920; www.edgeoftheworld.org) Celebrates the diversity of LA's theater community with dozens of plays staged around town throughout October.

**West Hollywood Halloween Carnival** ( ☎ 323-848-6400; www.visitwesthollywood.com) Free rambunctious street fair on October 31 with eccentric, and occasionally X-rated, costumes all along Santa Monica Blvd in West Hollywood.

## November

**Día de los Muertos** (Day of the Dead; ☎ 213-625-5045; www.cityofla.org/elp) A Mexican festival of the return of the dead to Earth for one day each year. Held on November 1 and 2 with a large candlelight procession, decorated altars and skull-shaped candy on Olvera St in Downtown. There's also a big celebration at Self-Help Graphics & Art in East LA (p115).

**Mariachi Festival** ( ☎ 213-466-1156) Free mariachi music and ballet folklórico at Mariachi Plaza in Boyle Heights; mid-November.

**Doo Dah Parade** ( ☎ 626-440-7379; www.pasadena doodahparade.com) Free wacky parody of the traditional Rose Parade, on Colorado Blvd in Pasadena, with such marchers as a precision briefcase drill team, a roving

volleyball game and the West Hollywood Cheerleaders. Held on the Sunday before Thanksgiving.

**Griffith Park Light Festival** ( ☎ 323-913-6488; www .laparks.org) Mile-long stretch of various holiday-themed light displays from 5pm to 10pm daily, late November to December 26. Walk or drive through slowly.

**Hollywood Christmas Parade** ( ☎ 323-469-2337; www.hollywoodchamber.net) Free parade featuring celebrities from film and TV ringing in the season by waving at bystanders from flashy floats along Hollywood Blvd. Held on the Sunday after Thanksgiving.

## December

**Marina del Rey Holiday Boat Parade** ( ☎ 310-670-7130; www.mdrboatparade.org) Beautifully decorated and twinkling yachts illuminate the harbor in Marina del Rey during mid-December; best viewed from Burton Chase Park.

**Las Posadas** ( ☎ 213-625-5045; www.cityofla.org/elp) Free candlelight processions that relive Mary and Joseph's journey to Bethlehem, followed by piñata-breaking for kids on Olvera St and surrounding streets; December 16 to 24.

# SLEEPING

When choosing where to stay in sprawling Los Angeles, think about what type of experience you most want. Urban explorers will probably base themselves in or close to West Hollywood and its trendy nightlife, shopping and dining. Posh and sedate, Beverly Hills is among the safest areas in town and certain to impress your friends back home. Downtown is great for fans of history and architecture and boasts a growing cultural scene, but most people don't feel comfortable walking around after dark. The same is true of Hollywood, although with its easy access to Metro Rail's Red Line, the area is convenient if you don't have your own wheels. The beach towns are great for soaking up the SoCal vibe. Malibu makes for a nice city retreat and offers the prettiest camping options, but Santa Monica is more central and gives you lots to do besides the beach. Marina del Rey and Manhattan Beach are both convenient if you want to camp out near LAX, although both are also worth a stay in their own right. Long Beach is not a bad place to base yourself if you're planning on exploring both LA and Orange County. If Universal Studios is the focus of your visit, check out the accommodations in the San Fernando Valley.

Some bargains notwithstanding, hotel rates in LA are higher than the national average. Expect to pay between $100 and $200 for a mid-range room. Some hotels allow children to stay for free, but be aware that this usually applies only if no extra bedding is required (for instance if the room has two double beds). An occupancy tax of 12% to 14% is added to all room rates; prices listed here do not include tax unless otherwise stated.

## Hollywood                    Map pp66–7
### BUDGET

**USA Hostels Hollywood** ( ☎ 323-462-3777, 800-524-6783; www.usahostels.com; 1624 Schrader Blvd; dm incl tax $22-25, r incl tax $59-65; 🖳 ) This energetic and well-run hostel is great for those keen on plunging headlong into Hollywood's nightlife. It's also close to public transportation and the Greyhound bus station. Meet fellow travelers during barbecues, parties and comedy nights or while whipping up a meal in the well-equipped communal kitchen. All rooms have their own bathroom. Freebies include linen, pancake breakfast and all-day coffee and tea. Enquire about discounted rates from November to May.

**Orange Drive Manor Hostel** ( ☎ 323-850-0350; www.orangedrivehostel.com; 1764 N Orange Dr; dm incl tax $20-24, r incl tax $40-56; (P) $5; 🖳 ) This friendly hostel, mere steps from Hollywood & Highland, is housed in a rambling 1920s mansion and offers plenty of privacy and a peaceful atmosphere. The spruced-up fireplace lounge and outdoor garden are nice gathering spots. It's not signed, so just look for the house number.

**Hollywood Celebrity Hotel** ( ☎ 323-850-6464, 800-222-7017; www.hotelcelebrity.com; 1775 Orchid Ave; r $80-120; (P) 🖳 ) The sleek new art deco–style lobby is a promising overture, but it contrasts with the rooms which are a bit long in the tooth. Still, most are fairly large and those with full kitchens are ideal for self-caterers. Days start with a free continental breakfast and newspaper. No wheelchair access.

**Dunes Inn Sunset** ( ☎ 323-467-5171, in California ☎ 800-443-8637, outside California ☎ 800-452-3863; www.dunesla.com; 5625 W Sunset Blvd; r $80-100, children stay free; (P) ) You won't feel like a star in this run-of-the-mill motel but everything's clean and rooms have space aplenty if only basic amenities. The on-site retro café-bar is convenient for fueling up but other simple eateries – and the subway station – are within walking distance.

**Liberty Hotel** ( ☎ 323-962-1788, 800-750-6561; 1770 Orchid Ave; one/two/three/four persons $75/85/90/120;

(P) 🖳 ) The flowery carpets and patterned bedspreads here are at no risk of ending up on the pages of *House Beautiful* but the renovated rooms are quite comfortable. All have private bathroom and TV and some feature a microwave and refrigerator, but so does the small communal kitchenette just off the lobby. No wheelchair access.

### MID-RANGE

**Magic Castle Hotel** ( ☎ 323-851-0800, 800-741-4915; www.magiccastlehotel.com; 7025 Franklin Ave; r incl breakfast $130-240, children stay free; (P) $8; 🐛 ) A recent makeover has moved this longtime standby out of the budget category. Rooms now feature trendy blond-wood furniture and attractive art, and families will love the full-kitchen suites sleeping up to six people. Start your day with fresh croissants and gourmet coffee on your balcony (some rooms) or by the pool. Staying here also gets you into the adjacent Magic Castle, a fabled private magic club in a Victorian mansion.

**Hollywood Hills Hotel & Apartments** ( ☎ 323-874-5089, 800-615-2224; www.hollywoodhillshotel.com; 1999 N Sycamore Ave; r incl breakfast $100-160, children stay free; (P) $8; 🐛 ) Breathtaking city views, a curvy pool guarded by a Shinto shrine, and roomy digs with balcony and kitchen are among the assets at this older but well-kept property. It's up in the hills (just below Yamashiro, p169) yet still within walking distance of the Hollywood Blvd action. Check-in is at the Magic Castle Hotel (above).

**Best Western Hollywood Hills Hotel** ( ☎ 323-464-5181, 800-287-1700; www.bestwestern.com; 6141 Franklin Ave; r $90-160, children under 15 stay free; (P) 🐛 ) Not all rooms are created equal at this family-run

---

**TOP FIVE HOTEL BARS**

- Convivial – Veranda Bar, Figueroa Hotel (p149)

- Divey – Hank's, Stillwell Hotel (p149)

- Historic – Observation Bar, Queen Mary (p103)

- Romantic – Bar at the Hotel Bel-Air (p144)

- Trendy – Cameo Bar, Viceroy Hotel (p145)

---

hotel, with some still awaiting a face-lift. For more space and quiet get a room in the back facing the sparkling tiled pool. Self-caterers will welcome the refrigerator and microwave, although you'll find plenty of filling sustenance at the on-site coffee shop, a popular hipster spot that's open until 3am.

**Hollywood Orchid Suites** ( ☎ 323-874-9678, 800-537-3052; www.orchidsuites.com; 1753 N Orchid Ave; r $80-210, children under 16 stay free; P ⬚ ⬚ ) Self-caterers can whip up entire turkeys in the fully-equipped kitchens in this old-fashioned, all-suite establishment within a hop, skip and jump of Hollywood & Highland. During downtime, catch some rays poolside or on the sundeck on the roof.

**Highland Gardens Hotel** ( ☎ 323-850-0536, 800-404-5472; www.highlandgardenshotel.com; 7047 Franklin Ave; r $70, ste $100-200; P ⬚ ⬚ ) In the heart of Hollywood, this '50s hotel is retro without even trying. Some rooms are a bit worn but all are good-sized and many face the lush garden with a heated outdoor pool. The suites with one, two and three bedrooms and full kitchens can easily accommodate families and small groups. Finally, a piece of sad trivia: Janis Joplin overdosed in room 105 in 1970. The hotel has no wheelchair access. Enquire about discounted rates from October to April.

**TOP END**

**Hotel Bamboo** ( ☎ 323-962-0270; www.athomela.com /property; 2528 Dearborn Dr; r $195-450; P $21) Zen goes high-tech at this unmarked Hollywood Hills hideaway embraced by a lush bamboo grove. The five rooms and suites each have a private entrance, stark yet stylish decor (platform beds, granite bathrooms), views of the hotel's Japanese gardens or the Holly-

wood Sign, plus a veritable alphabet soup of entertainment devices: TV, CD, MP3, DVD, VCR and DSL. Smoking is a no-no.

**Hollywood Roosevelt Hotel** ( ☎ 323-466-7000, 800-950-7667; www.hollywoodroosevelt.com; 7000 Hollywood Blvd; r $200-400, children under 10 stay free; P $18; ⬚ ⬚ ) This historic hotel with its doesn't-get-more-central location has been completely redone, with most rooms now sporting a sleek Asian contempo look and a bevy of stylish amenities. Only the poolside cabana rooms still wear that genuine retro look. The handsome lobby retains the original Spanish flair. For more on its history, see p78.

**Renaissance Hollywood Hotel** ( ☎ 323-856-1200, 888-236-2427; www.renaissancehollywood.com; 1755 N Highland Ave; r $190-250; P $10; ⬚ ⬚ ) If you fancy sipping your mai tai poolside with a view of the Hollywood Sign, this deluxe hotel right next to the Hollywood & Highland complex fits the bill. Gear up for a day of sightseeing in spacious, amenity-laden rooms drenched in mid-century cool. For the best views, get one above the 10th floor. Original art sets accents throughout, starting in the lobby, which is adorned by a bright abstract canvas by LA's own Charles Arnoldi.

## West Hollywood
**BUDGET**

Map pp68–9

**Banana Bungalow Hollywood** ( ☎ 323-655-1510, 800-446-7835; www.bananabungalow.com; 7950 Melrose Ave; dm incl tax & breakfast $21, r incl tax & breakfast $59-89; ⬚ ) This convivial hostel puts the 'mod' in modern. The boldly colored retro decor and the location near LA's epicenter of hipness make it a standout on LA's budget scene. Dorms sleep six in full-size beds and have lockers, while the good-sized private rooms come with TV; some even have balconies. All rooms have a private bathroom. Other perks: free linen and a lounge, café and outdoor patio perfect for striking up friendships. Self-caterers, though, will only find a microwave to work with. Enquire about discounted rates from October to May.

**Alta Cienega Motel** ( ☎ 310-652-5797; 1005 N La Cienega Blvd; r $60, r No 32 $70, children under 16 stay free; P ⬚ ) Nothing distinguishes this basic motel from dozens of others in town, yet for Doors fans it is a place of pilgrimage. The 'Lizard King' Jim Morrison himself boozed and snoozed in room No 32 back in the late 1960s after finding himself without a driver's license following a DUI charge.

## MID-RANGE

**Secret Garden B&B** ( ☎ 323-656-3888, 877-732-4736; www.secretgardenbnb.com; 8039 Selma Ave; r $95-165; **P** **☐**) This pink Spanish Moorish jewel with its romantic Rapunzel tower is tucked away in a dreamy garden, a mere block away from the velocity of the Sunset Strip. All five rooms bulge with character and eclectic furnishings. Each has its own bathroom, but only two are en-suite (the rest require a short walk down the hall). For a treat book the separate guesthouse with slate floor, sleigh bed and Jacuzzi.

**Grafton on Sunset** ( ☎ 323-654-4600, 800-821-3660; www.graftononsunset.com; 8462 W Sunset Blvd; r $165-300, children under 18 stay free; **P** $20; **☐** **☂**) We like this charismatic boutique hotel for its feng shui aesthetic, enormous swimming pool and rooms sporting such nifty touches as organic bath amenities and plush robes. Staying here puts you within a whisker of the strip's high-velocity club scene (ask the concierge about VIP access). The on-site Balboa steak house is popular with nonguests as well.

**Standard Hollywood** ( ☎ 323-650-9090; www.standardhotel.com; 8300 W Sunset Blvd; r $100-225, ste $450; **P** $18; **☐** **☂**) This *über*-hip hotel seems stuck in perpetual party mode, so don't come here for a quiet night's sleep. Instead, expect a dose of boundary-pushing surprises, including a pool fringed by Smurf-blue astroturf, a barber who doubles as a tattoo artist, and condoms in the minibar. At night the lobby morphs into a chic club lounge. The 24-hour coffee shop is a scene in itself.

**Le Montrose Suite Hotel** ( ☎ 310-855-1115, 800-776-0666; www.lemontrose.com; 900 Hammond St; ste $165-550; **P** $22; **☐** **☂**) Time at this stylish hideaway seems to move a bit slower than in the rest of LA. The spruced-up suites have living rooms with gas fireplaces, and the larger ones also have a kitchenette and balcony. Feast on gourmet fare at the guest-only restaurant, then work off the indulgence in the rooftop pool (great views), the health club or by taking a spin on a bicycle. Renovation of the public areas has been slated for around May 2005.

**Best Western Sunset Plaza Hotel** ( ☎ 323-654-0750, 800-421-3652; www.bestwestern.com; 8400 W Sunset Blvd; r incl breakfast $100-150, children under 12 stay free; **P** $10; **☐** **☂**) This place, which puts you right into the Sunset Strip party scene, pairs high energy and cosmopolitan flair with reasonable prices. It has 100 nicely decorated rooms

plus suites with kitchens that are perfect for small groups or families. Rates includes lots of free stuff, including breakfast, newspaper, local calls and high-speed Internet access.

**Summerfield Suites by Wyndham** ( ☎ 310-657-7400; www.wyndham.com; 1000 Westmount Dr; ste incl breakfast $140-190, children under 18 stay free; **P** $18; **☂**) Handily located near nightlife and restaurants, yet on a quiet, residential street, this all-suite property may score low on the hipness scale but it's outfitted with everything you'll need for a pleasant stay. The rooftop pool makes for a nice postsightseeing hangout, and the nearby Trader Joe's supermarket comes in handy if you're in a kitchen unit.

**Ramada Plaza Hotel & Suites** ( ☎ 310-652-6400, 800-272-6232; www.ramada.com; 8585 Santa Monica Blvd; r $130-200, ste $185-350, children under 18 stay free; **P** $22; **☐** **☂**) Smack-bang in the heart of 'Boystown' this friendly complex is a perfect base for those keen on making an in-depth study of West Hollywood's nightlife. Restore energies poolside while working on your tan or surfing the Web, wirelessly, of course. Rooms have a vaguely art deco vibe and all the usual amenities.

**Valadon Hotel** ( ☎ 310-854-1114, 800-835-7997; www.valadonhotel.com; 8822 Cynthia St; ste $120-190; **P** $16.50; **☐** **☂**) This is a pleasant all-suite hotel with rooms that lay on the flower decor a bit thick but are perfectly fine in the amenities department. People on business will appreciate the multiline phones, high-speed Internet and in-room fax machines, although the high phone charges may not look good on your expense statement. Nice rooftop pool.

## TOP END

**Mondrian** ( ☎ 323-650-8999, 800-525-8029; www.morganshotelgroup.com; 8440 W Sunset Blvd; r $310-385, ste $370-570; **P** $24; **☐** **☂**) Like the gates to heaven, two giant metal doors, but no marquee, signal your arrival at LA's beacon for the rich and beautiful. The Philippe Starck–designed public spaces – the sleek lobby, the restaurant, the open-air Sky Bar (p169), the sexy pool – are like stages where the auditioning never stops. Rooms are top-notch, the service only so-so. But heck, even the valets look like Calvin Klein models.

**Sunset Marquis Hotel & Villas** ( ☎ 310-657-1333, 800-858-9758; 1200 N Alta Loma Rd; www.sunsetmarquishotel.com; ste $340, villas $800-1000; **P** $22; **☐** **☂**)

---

**THE AUTHOR'S CHOICE**

**Chateau Marmont** (Map pp68-9; ☎ 323-656-1010, 800-242-8328; www.chateaumarmont.com; 8221 W Sunset Blvd; r $295, ste $350-$510, bungalow $1500; P $25; 🖳 🕱 ) This swank 1927 hangout whose design takes its cue from a French castle is a fixture in Hollywood lore. Practically every luminary in celluloid history – from Greta Garbo to Jimmy Dean to Gwyneth Paltrow – has enjoyed breakfast or drinks in its lobby-bar, trysted in a bungalow or swum laps in its pool. Howard Hughes used to spy on bikini beauties from the balcony of his suite, which these days is Bono's favorite. Naturally, rooms here are immaculate, service is flawless and ultradiscreet, and everyone's treated like a celebrity. The superstitious might want to stay clear of Bungalow No 2 where John Belushi set his final speedball in 1982.

---

This discreet retreat is a favorite with visiting rock-and-roll royalty (there's even a recording studio on the premises). Eric Clapton, U2 and Bruce Springsteen are among those who regularly check into the luxurious villas surrounded by tropical gardens. The suites are slightly less impressive but who cares if you could rub elbows with Mick Jagger in the hotel's chic Whiskey Bar.

**Argyle** ( ☎ 323-654-7100, 800-225-2637; www.argyle hotel.com; 8358 W Sunset Blvd; r $250, ste $300, children under 18 stay free; P $22; 🖳 🕱 ) This art deco marvel began life in 1931 as the Sunset Towers apartment building, home to such stars as John Wayne, Jean Harlow and Errol Flynn. Its streamlined facade is matched by a beautifully detailed interior and rooms furnished with period reproductions. They're pretty small, though, so get a suite if you need more room, preferably one with Sunset Blvd views.

## Mid-City                    Map pp68–9
**Farmer's Daughter** ( ☎ 323-937-3930, 800-334-1658; www.farmersdaughterhotel.com; 115 S Fairfax Ave; r $115-125; P $7; 🖳 🕱 ) After an extreme makeover, this LA fixture has catapulted from shabby to chic, sporting a sleek new 'urban cowboy' look that is an amazing alchemy of styles. Denim bedspreads and rocking chairs team up with original art, shiny plank floors and high-speed and wireless Internet access. The staff is ultrahelpful and happy to share their favorite spots at the Farmers Market and Grove mall across the street.

**Beverly Laurel Hotel** ( ☎ 323-651-2441, 800-962-3824; 8018 Beverly Blvd; r $90-105, with kitchenette extra $15; P 🕱 ) Those wanting to ride the retro wave on a slim budget should check out this venerable 1950s motel near the Farmers Market. Rooms, which wrap around a

well-kept swimming pool, have modern furnishings and more than a modicum of style, including framed black-and-white photographs. The attached Swingers (p155) diner crawls with hipsters until the wee hours. Pet-friendly.

**Elan Hotel Modern** ( ☎ 323-658-6663, 888-611-0398; www.elanhotel.com; 8435 Beverly Blvd; r $135-215, children stay free; P $14.50) Close to some of LA's best shopping and dining, the Elan flaunts a subdued urban feel. The standard rooms may be a bit too snug to fit tons of luggage, so opt for a junior suite if space is an issue. All sport a bevy of amenities more typical of pricier properties, including Egyptian cotton sheets and goose-down comforters and pillows.

**Sofitel Los Angeles** ( ☎ 310-278-5444, 800-521-7772; www.hotelsofitel.com; 8555 Beverly Blvd; r $165-230, children under 12 stay free; P $18.50; 🖳 🕱 ) If you're in the mood for a little French-flavored indulgence, give this property a try. Standing sentinel over the giant Beverly Center shopping mall, this is a full-service hotel with a restaurant-bar, a business center and rooms decked out in cheerful blues and yellows. The 24-hour room service is convenient in case you get the midnight munchies. This hotel caters well to the needs of the disabled.

## Beverly Hills                 Map pp70–1
### BUDGET & MID-RANGE
**Beverly Hills Reeves Hotel** ( ☎ 310-271-3006; 120 S Reeves Dr; r without/with bathroom $60/80) Budget and Beverly Hills don't usually mix, except at this faded but fairly well run property on a quiet side street. With these prices you know you're not getting the Ritz, but rooms are comfortable enough and come with a microwave. The cheapest ones share a bathroom.

**Maison 140** ( ☎ 310-281-4000, 800-432-5444; www .maison140.com; 140 S Lasky Dr; r incl breakfast $160-225; P $16; 🖵 ) This sensuous gem in the former home of silent-movie siren Lillian Gish cleverly marries French frivolity and Asian understatement. Cap your day with a French Kiss champagne cocktail in the intimate Bar Noir before retiring to your stylish, if fairly small, room filled with vintage furnishings and little luxuries such as Frette linens and flat screen TVs. Rates include an evening wine reception and pool privileges at the Avalon Hotel (right).

**Crescent** ( ☎ 310-247-0505; www.crescentbh.com; 403 N Crescent Dr; r $145-225; P $18; 🖵 ) New owners have spun this once dowdy property into a mod hot spot with a buzzing lobby-lounge-bar (ask for a room on the 2nd floor and in back if you're bothered by noise) and stylish indoor-outdoor restaurant, Boe. The chic rooms tend to be on the small side but the flat screen TV, iPod ministereos and free wireless Internet access are all welcome hipster touches.

**Best Western Beverly Pavilion** ( ☎ 310-273-1400, 800-441-5050; www.bestwestern.com; 9360 Wilshire Blvd; r $130-150, children under 17 stay free; P $18; 🏊 ) This nicely decorated property puts you in the poshest part of Beverly Hills yet with a price tag that is surprisingly modest. The rooftop pool is a stand-out, while rooms – mostly sheathed in pink and peach pastels – provide plenty of space and amenities.

**Beverly Terrace Hotel** ( ☎ 310-274-8141, 800-421-7223; www.beverlyterracehotel.com; 469 N Doheny Dr; r incl breakfast $105-145; P 🏊 ) This older property may not be in the trendiest part of Beverly Hills, but it certainly sits near plenty of good shopping, dining and partying and has decent-sized rooms recently redone in a fresh Asian style. The on-site restaurant, Trattoria Amici (p156) does great Italian and is a locals' hangout. Rates include continental breakfast, best enjoyed poolside.

## TOP END

**Avalon Hotel** ( ☎ 310-277-5221, 800-535-4715; www .avalonbeverlyhills.com; 9400 W Olympic Blvd; r $200-250, ste $350; P $22; 🖵 🏊 ) Mid-century modern meets amenities fit for the new millennium at this stylish boutique hotel. Rooms vamp it up with vintage Nelson bubble lamps and Eames cabinets; the pool is in the shape of a figure eight. Marilyn Monroe once lived in this building and Lucy and Desi came and went as well. The celeb quotient is still high today, especially at the ultracool Blue on Blue restaurant-bar.

**Regent Beverly Wilshire** ( ☎ 310-275-5200, in California ☎ 800-427-9354, outside California ☎ 800-421-4354; www.regenthotels.com; 9500 Wilshire Blvd; r $365-395, ste $560-900, children stay free; P $29; 🖵 🏊 ) The Regent is one of LA's most illustrious defenders of the grand tradition. With front-row vistas of Rodeo Dr and a sumptuous historical aura, this elegant full-service property leaves no wish unfulfilled. And yes, this is the hotel from which Julia Roberts first stumbled, then sashayed, in *Pretty Woman*.

**St Regis Los Angeles** ( ☎ 310-277-6111, 888-625-4988; www.stregis.com; 2055 Ave of the Stars; r $329-485, ste $550-700; P $18; 🏊 ) The moment you step into the lobby of this swank Century City hotel, you know it's luxury all the way to the top. The rooms, oversized and classically furnished in soothing earth tones, come with sweeping views and a plethora of playful perks such as monogrammed slippers and a remote lighting system. The pool and spa are great relaxation spots. The St Regis has the questionable honor of having LA's most expensive digs: the Penthouse Suite, which goes for $10,000 per night.

**Beverly Hills Hotel** ( ☎ 310-276-2251, 800-283-8885; www.beverlyhillshotel.com; 9641 Sunset Blvd; r $380-470, ste & bungalows $820-5000; P $25; 🖵 🏊 ) If you fancy (and can afford) dwelling in the utmost of luxury in an ambience oozing

---

### THE AUTHOR'S CHOICE

**Mosaic Hotel** (Map pp70-1; ☎ 310-278-0303, 800-463-4466; www.innatbeverlyhills.com; 125 Spalding Dr; r $269-600; P $20; 🖵 🏊 ) Known as the Beverly Hills Inn in an earlier incarnation, the Mosaic lets you feed luxury cravings without eviscerating your bank account. Some rooms are a bit on the small side but the stylish furnishings, Frette robes, Bvlgari soaps and wireless Internet access put a smile on most people's faces. The little restaurant-bar which spills out into the pool and garden area serves tasty nibbles, but being steps away from hot eateries and the neighborhood's other tony delights certainly doesn't hurt.

opulence and infused with historical charm, this is your place. For historical background, see p143.

**Le Meridien** ( ☎ 310-247-0400, 800-543-4300; www .lemeridien.com; 465 S La Cienega Blvd; r $190-220, ste $240-600, children under 18 stay free; **P** $24; **🖳 🖭** ) After an extreme makeover by big-name French architect Pierre Yves Rochon, this hulking hotel flaunts its rejuvenated look with pride. It's a big, full-service house with upscale international flair and various-sized rooms outfitted with lots of communication gadgets in case you're in town to ink that deal. Nice touch: bathrooms with deep, stress-melting tubs.

## Westwood, Bel Air & Brentwood                Map pp70–1
**MID-RANGE**

**Luxe Hotel Sunset Boulevard** ( ☎ 310-476-6571; www.luxehotels.com; 11461 Sunset Blvd, Brentwood; r $150-300, children under 18 stay free; **P** $18; **🖳 🖭** ) Despite its location right next to the 405 Fwy, this property feels a world removed from the bustle thanks to nicely landscaped, sprawling gardens. Rooms are spacious and comfortable and sport a slew of modern amenities. It's just a short drive away from the Getty Center and UCLA.

**Century Wilshire Hotel** ( ☎ 310-474-4506, 800-421-7223; www.centurywilshirehotel.com; 10776 Wilshire Blvd, Westwood; r incl breakfast $115-195, ste incl breakfast $225-375; **P** **🖭** ) Converted from an old apartment building, this good-value hotel has a homey feel and 99 differently decorated rooms facing either a courtyard or a swimming pool. The one- and two-bedroom suites have full kitchens.

**Hilgard House Hotel** ( ☎ 310-208-3945, 800-826-3934; www.hilgardhouse.com; 927 Hilgard Ave, Westwood; s/d incl breakfast $160/170, ste incl breakfast $180-290; **P** ) This snug boutique hotel has Old World charm and is mere steps from UCLA and Westwood Village, making it popular with visiting parents and professors. Rooms are traditionally furnished and on the small side, although there are also a few one- and two-bedroom suites with full kitchen.

**Brentwood Motor Hotel** ( ☎ 310-476-9981, 800-840-3808; www.bmhotel.com; 12200 Sunset Blvd; r incl breakfast $120-200; **P** **🖳** ) In the age of chain motels, this little 20-unit inn run by friendly family folks is a breath of fresh air. The decent-sized rooms have been put through

a recent face-lift and now feature free high-speed Internet access. All have a small refrigerator and coffee maker.

### TOP END
**Hotel Bel-Air** ( ☎ 310-472-1211, 800-648-4097; www .hotelbelair.com; 701 N Stone Canyon Rd; r $400-575, ste $850-3500; **P** $20; **🖳 🖭** ) An urge to splurge would be well directed towards this peaceful hideaway where every detail speaks of refinement and discretion is key. Rooms, each with private entrance and classy French country furnishings, are embraced by romantic gardens where white swans preen. If the price tag is too steep, come for afternoon tea or drinks in the fireplace bar.

## Culver City
**Villa Brasil Motel** (off Map pp72-3; ☎ 310-636-0141; www.villabrasilmotel.com; 11740 Washington Blvd; r $56-66; **P** ) With a facade splashed in orange, blue and green, this newly spruced up little motel is quite literally a bright spot on otherwise drab Washington Blvd, not far from the Sony Studios. The tropical looks continue in the rooms, which are a tad twee but come with cable TV, ceiling fans and kitchenette.

**Culver Hotel** (off Map pp72-3; ☎ 310-838-7963, 888-328-5837; www.culverhotel.com; 9400 Culver Blvd; r $90-300, children stay free; **P** **🖳** ) This venerable 1924 property has hosted many classic stars – Clark Gable, John Wayne and the munchkins from the Wizard of Oz among them – while they were shooting films at the nearby MGM Studios (now Sony Pictures Studios). A gracious lobby gives way to comfortable, if not luxurious, rooms furnished with antiques and sporting marble bathrooms. The on-site restaurant serves global cuisine (mains $8 to $12).

## Malibu                                        Map pp60–1
**BUDGET**

**Leo Carrillo State Beach Campground** ( ☎ 818-880-0350, reservations ☎ 800-444-7275; 35000 W Pacific Coast Hwy; sites $13-20) This shady, kid-friendly site, about 28 miles northwest of Santa Monica, is extremely popular and fills up quickly during the warmer months. It has 135 sites, flush toilets and coin-operated hot showers. A long sandy beach, offshore kelp beds and tide pools are all great places for exploring. Reservations recommended May to October.

**Malibu Beach RV Park** ( ☎ 310-456-6052, 800-622-6052; www.maliburv.com; 25801 Pacific Coast Hwy; tent/partial/full RV sites with ocean view $26/48/62, with mountain view $22/39/52) This popular oceanside park is well-maintained and safe and has 150 sites with full and partial hookups, plus 52 tent spaces. Rates include showers and outdoor spa access. Reserve as early as possible. It's about 20 miles up the coast from Santa Monica. Enquire about discounted rates from October to April.

**Malibu Creek State Park Campground** ( ☎ 818-880-8367; www.reserveamerica.com; sites $13-20) Camp in the park that once served as the movie set for *M*A*S*H* and *Planet of the Apes*. Sites for tents, trailers and RVs are available. The park is about 5 miles north of the Pacific Coast Hwy via Malibu Canyon Rd. The turnoff is 1½ miles past the Malibu Pier.

### MID-RANGE

**Casa Malibu Inn** ( ☎ 310-456-2219, 800-831-0858; casamalibu@earthlink.net; 22752 Pacific Coast Hwy; r $100-350; P ) This ultimate 'California Dreamin' getaway overlooks its own beach that's perfect for having lots of 'Fun Fun Fun.' It has 21 delightfully appointed rooms that are wrapped around a vine-festooned inner courtyard, with about half of them enjoying ocean views. The nicest ones have private decks, fireplaces or kitchenettes. Lana Turner fans should book the Catalina Suite where the glamour queen once stayed for 18 months.

**Malibu Country Inn** ( ☎ 310-457-9622, 800-386-6787; www.malibucountryinn.com; 6506 Westward Beach Rd; r Sun-Thu $140-230, Fri & Sat $180-265; P ☀ ) This nicely restored 1943 Cape Cod–style inn is a quiet bluff-top retreat near Zuma Beach, about 7 miles north of the Malibu Pier. The owners have put some imagination toward decorating the rooms, the nicest of which have a fireplace and private patio. The inn's cute Hideaway Café is a pretty spot for a meal any time of day.

### TOP END

**Malibu Beach Inn** ( ☎ 310-456-6444, 800-462-5428; www.malibubeachinn.com; 22878 Pacific Coast Hwy; r $360-390, ste $510-530; P ) This breezy hotel is right on a tranquil swimming beach near the Malibu Pier. Rooms are decorated hacienda-style and have nice bathrooms sheathed in colorful hand-painted tiles. Most have a patio

that's great for breakfast, whale-watching or sunset drinks. On chilly nights you can curl up inside in front of your fireplace.

## Santa Monica
Map pp72–3

### BUDGET

**Sea Shore Motel** ( ☎ 310-392-2787; www.seashoremotel.com; 2637 Main St; r $75-95, children stay free; P ) This little motel is one of a dying breed: a clean, budget-priced place mere steps from the beach, bars, boutiques and restaurants. The newly slicked-up rooms have tile floors, refrigerators, data-port phones and cable TV, and breakfast is available at the next-door café (separate charge). Rooms don't have air-con.

**Travelodge Santa Monica** ( ☎ 310-450-5766, 800-231-7679; www.travelodge.com; 3102 W Pico Blvd; r incl breakfast $64-104, children stay free; P ) There's plenty to like about this chain entry next to a Trader Joe's supermarket and steps from restaurants and a funky coffee shop. Rooms are large and spotless (many have kitchenettes) and there's a courtyard with gas barbecue and picnic tables. The beach is about 2½ miles away.

**HI-Los Angeles/Santa Monica** ( ☎ 310-393-9913, 800-909-4776, ext 137; www.lahostels.org; 1436 2nd St; members/nonmembers dm $28/31, r with shared bathroom $69/72; ⌨ ) Wedged between the beach and Third St Promenade, this hostel has a location that's the envy of much fancier places. The 200 beds are spread over four- to 10-bed dorms and a few charmless doubles without bathrooms. Hook up with fellow travelers in the kitchen, library or movie room, or on guided tours offered through the adjacent HI Travel Center.

### MID-RANGE

**Loews Santa Monica Beach Hotel** ( ☎ 310-458-6700, 800-235-6397; www.loewshotels.com; 1700 Ocean Ave; r $250-450, ste $675-2600; P $25; ⌨ ☀ ) The first in the phalanx of luxury beach hotels in Santa Monica has an attractive atrium lobby accented with two rows of soaring palm trees. The lovely pool faces out over the ocean, as do many of the good-sized rooms. This is one of the most family-friendly hotels in town with a special family concierge, kids-oriented activities and DVD and Gameboy loans for teens.

**Viceroy** ( ☎ 310-260-7500, 800-622-8711; www.viceroysantamonica.com; 1819 Ocean Ave; r $110-150, ste $200-500; P $18; ☀ ) The bland exterior belies the fact that this relatively new arrival has brought a touch of Hollywood glamour to the sea. Owned by the same people that are behind the Avalon Hotel (p143) and Maison 140 (p143) in Beverly Hills, this outpost sports a campy British Colonial theme and an unusual color palette that includes a grassy green. The Cameo Bar (p170) and Whist restaurant draw socialites from across town.

**Ambrose** ( ☎ 310-315-1555, 877-262-7673; www .ambrosehotel.com; 1255 20th St; r incl breakfast $165-225, children stay free; **P** 🖳 ) This blissful boutique hotel about 20 blocks from the beach beautifully blends Craftsman and Asian aesthetics. Nice places to lounge about include the library with lusty fireplace and the tranquil garden with koi pond. The spic-and-span rooms have high ceilings, dark-wood furniture and the latest in entertainment and communication devices. Some have balconies with teak furniture and fireplaces. Rates include gym access.

**Channel Road Inn B&B** ( ☎ 310-459-1920; www .channelroadinn.com; 219 W Channel Rd; r incl breakfast $165-375, children under 14 stay free; **P** 🖳 ) This is an upscale and romantic B&B with sumptuous, amenity-laden rooms facing either the ocean or the lovely garden. Breakfasts are gourmet affairs, especially when the apple French toast is served. Meet fellow guests during afternoon tea or at the evening wine and cheese gathering. Bicycles for taking a spin along the beach are available for free.

**Embassy Hotel Apartments** ( ☎ 310-394-1279; www.embassyhotelapts.com; 1001 3rd St; r $130-300; **P** ) If you like quirk and old-timey character, you'll be charmed by this 1926 Spanish Colonial–style gem. From the beautiful lobby with beamed ceiling, grand piano and colorful tile work, a rickety elevator takes you to your spacious period-furnished room or suite. The beach is two blocks away, as are the shops and restaurants of swank Montana Ave.

**Cal Mar Hotel Suites** ( ☎ 310-395-5555, 800-776-6007; www.calmarhotel.com; 220 California Ave; ste $110-180; **P** 🖳 ) The looks of this place may be hopelessly stuck in the disco decade, but who's to complain if a moderate tariff buys you a large suite with kitchen and a supercentral, yet quiet location? It's a great choice for families and anyone in need of plenty of elbow room. The heated pool comes in handy if the ocean's too cold for a swim.

**Best Western Ocean View Hotel** ( ☎ 310-458-4888, 800-452-4888; www.bestwestern.com; 1447 Ocean Ave; r $140-230, children under 18 stay free; **P** $15; 🖳 ) A standard affair in a terrific location. Rooms are pleasingly furnished and those with ocean view have petite balconies perfect for watching the sun drop into the Pacific. Light sleepers should get a room away from noisy Ocean Ave.

**Bayside Hotel** ( ☎ 310-396-6000, 800-525-4447; www.baysidehotel.com; 2001 Ocean Ave; r $110-150, children stay free; **P** ) This aptly named property literally puts you within earshot of the waves. The ocean-view rooms are well worth the extra expense, especially when watching the sunset, cold beer in hand, after a hard day on the beach. Some have a kitchen or a small refrigerator; those in back come with air-con.

### TOP END

**Hotel Casa del Mar** ( ☎ 310-581-5533, 800-898-6999; www.hotelcasadelmar.com; 1910 Ocean Front Walk; r $405-650; **P** $26; 🖳 🏊 ) If you wish to relive the grandeur of a 1920s beach resort, book yourself into this posh player right next to the sand. Wallow in style and luxury in ultracomfortable rooms that get a fresh, Mediterranean feel from gold, green and sandy hues. Not only the romantically inclined will appreciate the opulent beds, extra-large Jacuzzis and sunset views.

**Hotel California** ( ☎ 310-393-2363, 866-571-0000; www.hotelca.com; 1670 Ocean Ave; r $180-280; **P** $15; 🖳 ) Everything's just peachy at this beachy abode, a Frisbee throw from the sand. Sunny rooms come with sparkling hardwood floors, heavenly beds where surfboards double as headboards, and fridges. Be sure to ask for a room facing the nicely landscaped courtyard as the street-side ones can get pretty noisy. No air-con, but you'll rarely miss it.

## Venice & Marina del Rey    Map pp72–3
### BUDGET

**Cadillac Hotel** ( ☎ 310-399-8876; www.thecadillachotel .com; 8 Dudley Ave, Venice; dm $30, r $100-110, ste $110-160; **P** 🖳 ) Charlie Chaplin used to spend summers at this flashy pink and turquoise art deco landmark on Venice's funky Ocean Front Walk. These days a mostly youthful clientele sets up quarters in the well-priced dorms and private rooms, all with ocean views. The sundeck is conducive to striking up friendships, and on cloudy days you can work up a sweat in the gym or sauna. The area, alas, gets a bit dodgy after dark. Enquire about discounted rates from October to May.

### MID-RANGE & TOP END

**Inn at Venice Beach** ( ☎ 310-821-2557, 800-828-0688; www.innatvenicebeach.com; 327 Washington Blvd, Venice; r incl breakfast $110-180; P ) Close to the beach, the Venice canals, and bars and restaurants, this pleasant inn sports fresh and cheerful decor and rooms with a good range of amenities. All wrap around a central courtyard perfect for munching your morning muffins on a warm summer day.

**Venice Beach House** ( ☎ 310-823-1966; www.venice beachhouse.com; 15 30th Ave, Venice; r with shared bathroom $130, private bathroom $170-195; P $10) A block from the beach, this ivy-draped B&B in a 1911 Craftsman bungalow (listed on the National Register of Historic Places) is a welcoming old-California retreat with nine cozy rooms, some of them with shared bathrooms. The romantically inclined should book the James Peasgood room with its lofty wood ceiling and double Jacuzzi.

**Best Western Jamaica Bay Inn** ( ☎ 310-823-5333, 888-823-5333; www.bestwestern.com; 4175 Admiralty Way, Marina del Rey; r $130-200, children under 17 stay free; P $3; 🐾 ) Fronting sheltered Mother's Beach, this property is great for families and even has its own playground. Palm trees add a tropical touch and the rooms have cheerful bedspreads, framed art and private balconies (ask for one with ocean views). You can walk to restaurants and Venice Beach.

**Best Western Marina Pacific Hotel & Suites** ( ☎ 310-452-1111, 800-421-8151; www.bestwestern.com; 1697 Pacific Ave, Venice; r incl breakfast $120-160, incl breakfast ste $170-250; P $9) This hotel is a pleasant island of quiet in freaky Venice. After a day on the beach, return to good-sized rooms decked in beachy colors and all mod cons. The nicest have balconies with at least partial ocean views, and the full-kitchen suites are great for families. Free shuttle to Santa Monica and Marina del Rey.

**Inn at Playa del Rey B&B** ( ☎ 310-574-1920; www.innatplayadelrey.com; 435 Culver Blvd, Playa del Rey; r incl breakfast $175-245, ste incl breakfast $295-365; P 💻 ) Close to LAX, this adorable inn is a charming alternative to the airport-area chain hotels. You'll sleep like a baby in the sumptuous beds in airy and, for the most part, spacious rooms overlooking a bird sanctuary or the marina. Some have a bal-

cony or fireplace. Rates include a hot buffet breakfast, afternoon tea and cookies, and an evening wine reception.

## South Bay Beaches
Map p74

### BUDGET

**Surf City Hostel** ( ☎ 310-798-2323; www.surfcityhostel .ws; 26 Pier Ave, Hermosa Beach; dm incl breakfast $19, r incl breakfast $48; 💻 ) Right on Hermosa's Pier Ave and steps from the sand, this hostel puts the 'fun' in funky and is a great base for those wanting a full-time immersion into the SoCal beach scene. Halls, dorms and rooms are splashed with colorful murals and bathrooms were recently remodeled. Rates include tea and coffee and airport pick ups.

### MID-RANGE

**Hawthorn Suites** ( ☎ 310-546-8942, 888-5465-1819; www.hawthornsuites-lax.com; 1817 N Sepulveda Blvd, Manhattan Beach; r incl breakfast $125-150, children under 12 stay free; P 💻 ) This newish place gets top marks for its spacious and nicely appointed studio and one-bedroom suites wrapping around a greenery-filled courtyard. Some have full kitchens in case you feel the urge to whip up a meal. Other notable features include the hot breakfast buffet, supercomfortable mattresses and wireless high-speed Internet access.

**Hotel Hermosa** ( ☎ 310-318-6000, 800-331-9979; www.hotelhermosa.com; 2515 Pacific Coast Hwy, Hermosa Beach; r $70-350; P 💻 🐾 ) Sitting pretty in pink right on a busy thoroughfare, this sprawling good-value inn has a dozen room types catering to everyone from trysting couples to fun-loving families and no-nonsense business folks. Depending on which room you pick, you'll enjoy ocean views, a Jacuzzi or double-shower, kitchenette, fireplace or other nifty amenities. The decor is an acquired taste but the Japanese garden is a nice touch.

**Sea View Inn** ( ☎ 310-545-1504; www.seaview-inn .com; 3400 N Highland Ave, Manhattan Beach; r $105-345; P 🐾 ) Located close to the beach, this friendly property offers different room and suite categories, including some with ocean-facing balconies perfect for breezy alfresco breakfasts or sunset drinks. Traffic noise can be a factor in some, so light sleepers may prefer a quieter alley-facing room. The free bike, beach chair and boogie board rentals are a welcome bonus.

**LOS ANGELES**

**Best Western Sunrise Hotel** ( ☎ 310-376-0746, 800-334-7384; www.bestwestern.com; 400 N Harbor Dr, Redondo Beach; r incl breakfast $120-150; P 🖳 🕱 ) This sprawling place near the King Harbor marina has cheerfully decorated rooms that come with handy refrigerators and coffee-makers. It breaks through the standard motel mould by offering make-your-own fresh waffles at breakfast, cookies and punch during the afternoon and free bicycle rentals. There's also a good-sized swimming pool.

**Sea Sprite Motel & Apartments** ( ☎ 310-376-6933; www.seaspritemotel.com; 1016 The Strand, Hermosa Beach; r $95-295; P 🕱 ) It's pretty noisy, rooms could use a sprucing up and some of the staff is attitudinous, but the right-next-to-the-sand location is clearly the trump card of this property. Units are basic and vary in size, but many have full kitchens and balconies. Bonus: a nicely kept pool overlooking the beach. In an earlier life, famous folks, including Dizzy Gillespie and Tito Puente, stayed here while performing at the nearby Lighthouse Café (p175). Enquire about discounts from mid-September to mid-May.

**TOP END**

**Beach House at Hermosa** ( ☎ 310-374-3001, 888-895-4559; www.beach-house.com; 1300 The Strand, Hermosa Beach; r incl breakfast $210-360, children stay free; P $20) Whatever you've heard about California's laid-back lifestyle, this sparkling beachfront inn epitomizes it. Fall asleep to the sound of the waves in large, lofty suites with full or partial ocean views, private balconies and wood-burning fireplaces. The paved bikeway is right outside and restaurants and nightlife are a quick stroll away.

## San Pedro & Long Beach   Map pp62–3

**BUDGET**

**HI-Los Angeles/South Bay** ( ☎ 310-831-8109, 800-909-4776; www.lahostels.org; 3601 S Gaffey St, No 613, San Pedro; member/nonmember dm $17/20, tr per person $20/22, d $40/42; ☽ May-Sep; P ) You'll enjoy sweeping Pacific views from this bluff-top hostel right in San Pedro's Angels Gate Park (p101). The dorms and public areas sport themed decor from African jungle to American jazz and Native-American culture. The facilities include a big kitchen, a TV room and a guest laundry. Metro Bus No 466 stops just outside.

**MID-RANGE**

**Hotel Queen Mary** ( ☎ 562-435-3511; www.queen mary.com; 1126 Queens Hwy, Long Beach; r $110-220, ste $450-650, children under 17 stay free; P $10) There's an irresistible romance to ocean liners like the *Queen Mary*, a nostalgic retreat that time-warps you back to a long-gone, slower-paced era. The 1st-class staterooms have been nicely refurbished and brim with original art deco details (avoid the cheapest ones, which are on the inside). Staying overnight gives you the full run of the boat and includes admission to guided tours. For additional details, see p103.

**Coast Hotel Long Beach** ( ☎ 562-435-7676, 800-716-6199; www.coasthotels.com; 700 Queensway Dr, Long Beach; r $100-170, children stay free; P 🖳 🕱 ) Palm trees, a scenic waterfront location and a nice, spacious layout imbue this hotel with a relaxed resort feel. The larger premium rooms with harbor-facing patio are well worth the extra expense. It's close to the *Queen Mary*, the cruise ship terminal and the Catalina Island ferry; downtown Long Beach is just a quick ride away on the free city shuttle.

**Turret House** ( ☎ 562-624-1991, 888-488-7738; www .turrethouse.com; 556 Chestnut Ave, Long Beach; r incl breakfast $80-120) The new owners Brian and Jeff (and their adorable dogs) have poured their hearts and cash into turning this little B&B into an oasis of charm. The stately Victorian has five cozy rooms, each with fireplace, TV and bathroom with clawfoot tub. Rates include a generous continental breakfast spread and passes to a nearby gym, and there's a hot tub on the premises, too. Pet-friendly.

**Lord Mayor's B&B Inn** ( ☎ 562-436-0324; www .lordmayors.com; 435 Cedar Ave, Long Beach; r incl breakfast $95-175; P 🖳 ) The 1904 Edwardian house was the home of the city's first mayor and has been meticulously restored by community preservationists Reuben and Laura Brasser. If possible, stay in the main house where rooms are decorated in old-fashioned style and filled with antiques. The adjacent cottages are big enough for families. All rooms have wireless Internet access.

**TOP END**

**Dockside Boat & Bed** ( ☎ 562-436-3111, 800-436-2574; www.boatandbed.com; Rainbow Harbor, Dock 5, 316 E Shoreline Dr, Long Beach; r incl tax & breakfast $190-250, extra person $25; P $12) This unique floating hostelry should appeal to salty types with a sense of romance. Let the waves rock you to sleep as you snuggle up aboard your own private motor yacht, sailboat or 50ft Chinese junk. All of the boats are moored close to downtown Long Beach and enjoy views of the *Queen Mary*. Breakfast is delivered to your vessel.

## Downtown Los Angeles    Map pp64–5

### BUDGET

**Stillwell Hotel** ( ☎ 213-627-1151, 800-553-4774; www .stillwell-la.com; 838 S Grand Ave; r $70, children under 11 stay free; 💻 ) Nearly a century old, the Stillwell offers clean and no-nonsense rooms, good security and Hank's (p171), a wonderfully dark and divey bar. It's within walking distance of the Staples Center and the Los Angeles Convention Center.

**Ritz Milner Hotel** ( ☎ 213-627-6981, 877-645-6377; www.milner-hotels.com; 813 S Flower St; r incl breakfast $80-100, children under 11 stay free; P $10) The Ritz it ain't, but the Milner – across from the Stillwell – is still a solid, central and safe budget choice. A recent renovation both modernized many of the rooms while restoring some of their historical features. The staff is multilingual and the on-site pub a convivial spot.

### MID-RANGE

**Figueroa Hotel** ( ☎ 213-627-8971, 800-421-9092; www .figueroahotel.com; 939 S Figueroa St; r $100-140; P $8; 💢 ) It's hard not to be charmed by this Downtown favorite with its striking, Spanish-style lobby that gives way to gorgeous guest rooms with a splashy Moroccan theme. Feel like a pasha in your wrought-iron bed or sipping tea while reclining on big pillows. This is an older property, so not all rooms are equal; ask to see a couple before deciding. The pool and outdoor Veranda Bar are perfect for getting off your feet after a day of sightseeing. Rooms are not wheelchair-friendly.

**Standard Downtown LA** ( ☎ 213-892-8080; www .standardhotel.com; 550 S Flower St; r from $135; P $25; 💻 💢 ) So LA it's almost a cliché, this hotel – magically converted from the former Superior Oil headquarters – goes after the same young, hip and shag-happy crowd as its older Sunset Strip sister (p141). Leave the kids at home when booking yourself into a room with platform bed, peek-through shower and little else in the way of furniture. The rooftop pool-bar (p170) has one of the city's most intense pick-up scenes.

**Omni Los Angeles Hotel** ( ☎ 213-617-3300, 800-843-6664; www.omnihotels.com; 25 S Olive St; r $110-210; P $24; 💻 💢 ) Modern and efficient, the Omni puts you within steps of the Walt Disney Concert Hall, the Museum of Contemporary Art and other cultural hubs. The oversized rooms lack no amenities but can't quite shake that generic, if comfortable, business hotel feel. Welcome assets include a rooftop pool and gourmet fare at Noé (p165). Weekend rates sometimes drop below $100 (check the website).

**Hilton Checkers** ( ☎ 213-624-0000, 800-423-5798; www.checkershotel.com; 535 S Grand Ave; r $120-210, ste from $250; P $21; 💢 ) Radiant rooms in soothing natural colors form a relaxing antidote to busy days on the tourist track at this classy 1927 boutique hotel. Other places to unwind include the rooftop pool and the elegant restaurant. Extra amenities include free newspaper and shoe shine.

**Miyako Hotel Los Angeles** ( ☎ 213-617-2000, 800-228-6596; www.miyakoinn.com; 328 E 1st St; r $100-150, children under 12 stay free; P $9; 💻 ) This modern Little Tokyo hotel is just steps from good eats and is well equipped to meet the demands of business travelers, families and couples on a quick city getaway. You'll find all the usual big-hotel trappings – from voicemail to coffeemakers – as well as a lovely spa with Jacuzzi, sauna and optional shiatsu massage ($60 for one hour).

**Best Western Dragon Gate Inn** ( ☎ 213-617-3077, 800-282-9999; www.dragongateinn.com; 818 N Hill St; r incl breakfast $80-180, ste incl breakfast $160-200, children under 18 stay free; P $15; 💻 ) In the heart of Chinatown, this friendly place scores big with amenity fans on a budget. Sparkling rooms come with such useful extras as refrigerators and coffeemakers. Enjoy breakfast (try the scrumptious muffins) in the café in the atrium, where you can also consult an English-speaking herbalist and acupuncturist.

### TOP END

**Millennium Biltmore Hotel** ( ☎ 213-624-1011, 800-245-8673; www.millenniumhotels.com; 506 S Grand Ave; r $150-200, ste from $300; P $24; 💻 💢 ) This 1923 Pershing Sq landmark exudes the grandeur of a European palace, and has lured a galaxy of presidents, royalty and celebrities. Rooms, sheathed in soothing gold and blue hues, feature all the trappings, although some are surprisingly small. The art deco health club is so gorgeous, it takes the work out of workout. For more details, see p110.

**Westin Bonaventure Hotel & Suites** (☎ 213-624-1000, 888-625-5144; www.starwood.com/westin; 404 S Figueroa St; r $260-340, children under 12 stay free; **P** $22; **🖳 🌊** ) Sleek, cool and space-agey, the Bonaventure's five glass cylinders contain LA's largest hotel with over 1200 rooms, 20 restaurants and 40 stores. The labyrinthine interior is perfect for playing hide-and-seek, while the revolving rooftop lounge is a popular trysting retreat.

## San Fernando Valley             Map p75

**Safari Inn** (☎ 818-845-8586, 800-716-6199; www.coast hotels.com; 1911 W Olive Ave, Burbank; r $90-130, f $170, children under 12 stay free; **P 🖳 🌊** ) The classic 1950s neon sign is the only throwback to a bygone era at this friendly motel. Cheerful bed spreads and framed poster art add splashes of color to the nicely renovated rooms, including the family-friendly one-bedroom suites with full kitchens. Rates include local calls and wireless high-speed Internet access. It's reasonably close to Universal Studios and NBC Studios.

**Coast Annabelle Hotel** (☎ 818-845-7800, 800-716-6199; www.coasthotels.com; 2011 W Olive Ave, Burbank; r $130-170, children under 12 stay free; **P 🌊** ) The Annabelle is the Safari's more grown-up sister hotel, right across the street. The rooms are larger and everything is a bit nicer here, from the art to the furniture to the mattress. The large desk and dual-line telephones will come in handy for those who are here on business.

**Beverly Garland's Holiday Inn** (☎ 818-980-8000, 800-476-9981; www.beverlygarland.com; 4222 Vineland Ave, North Hollywood; r $130-150, ste $220-275; **P** $9; **🌊** ) Operated by Beverly Garland of TV and movie fame (she even has a star on the Walk of Fame), this is a sprawling and nicely landscaped property close to Universal Studios (free shuttles) and with its own pool and tennis courts. Families should ask about the kids' suites.

**Sportsmen's Lodge Hotel** (☎ 818-769-4700, 800-821-8511; www.slhotel.com; 12825 Ventura Blvd, Studio City; r $125-175, children stay free; **P 🖳 🌊** ) Emulating a British country estate, this lovely lodge is surrounded by a handsome garden complete with waterfalls and swan pond. Rooms ooze Old World charm, and there's a clubby restaurant and pub to continue the theme. Facilities include a fitness center and

large pool. All rooms have a private patio. Free shuttle service to/from Universal Studios and the Bob Hope Airport.

If Universal Studios is the focus of your visit, you won't get any closer to the gate than by staying at the **Sheraton Universal Hotel** (☎ 818-980-1212, 800-325-3535; www.starwood.com /Sheraton; 333 Universal Hollywood Dr, Universal City; r $300-1000, children under 18 stay free; **P** $14; **🖳 🌊** ) or the **Hilton Los Angeles/Universal City** (☎ 818-506-2500, 800-445-8667; www.hilton.com; 555 Universal Hollywood Dr, Universal City; r $150-210, children under 18 stay free; **P** $11; **🖳 🌊** ). Both of these monolithic glass towers have nicely appointed rooms with great city views from the upper floors, and shuttle service to the theme park entrance.

## Pasadena                        Map p76
### BUDGET

**Saga Motor Hotel** (☎ 626-795-0431, 800-793-7242; www.thesagamotorhotel.com; 1633 E Colorado Blvd; r incl breakfast $77-92, f incl breakfast $110-130; **P 🌊** ) This well-kept vintage inn is a great base for exploring Los Angeles, provided you have your own car. Rooms, though nothing special, are spotless and well kept. The nicest are near the good-sized pool orbited by plenty of chaises and chairs for soaking up the sun. Families should ask about the extra-large rooms.

### MID-RANGE

**Bissell House B&B** (☎ 626-441-3535, 800-441-3530; www.bissellhouse.com; 201 S Orange Grove Blvd; r incl breakfast $150-225; **P 🌊** ) Sumptuous antiques, sparkling hardwood floors and a crackling fireplace make this 1887 Victorian B&B on 'Millionaire's Row' a bastion of warmth and hospitality. The romantic hedge-framed garden feels like a sanctuary, and there's a pool for cooling off on hot summer days. If you don't like flowery decor, book the Prince Albert room. The Garden Room comes with a double Jacuzzi.

**Artists' Inn & Cottage B&B** (☎ 626-799-5668, 888-799-5668; www.artistsinns.com; 1038 Magnolia St; r incl tax & breakfast $120-205; **P 🖳** ) Each of the six rooms and four suites in this lovely Victorian farmhouse in South Pasadena has decor inspired by Degas, Gauguin and other artists or artistic periods. Rooms in the cottage are quieter, and most suites have fireplaces and canopy beds. Days start with a scrumptious breakfast and wind down with port and chocolates in the comfort of your room.

**Sheraton Pasadena Hotel** ( ☎ 626-449-4000, 800-457-7940; www.sheraton.com; 303 Cordova St; r $130-265, children under 12 stay free; P $7; 🖳 🐾 ) Since it's a Sheraton, you pretty much know that you're going to get a fairly high level of comfort and service, room decor unlikely to offend anyone, and a full range of facilities. The suit brigade invades during the week, making weekend bargains quite common. The free shuttle whisking you to area restaurants is an unexpected perk.

Also recommended:

**Pasadena Inn** ( ☎ 626-795-8401, 800-577-5690; www.pasadena-inn.com; 400 S Arroyo Parkway; r $100-110; P 🐾 ) Newly renovated standard property within walking distance to Old Pasadena.

**Hilton Pasadena** ( ☎ 626-577-1000, 800-445-8667; www.hilton.com; 150 S Los Robles Ave; r $100-250; P 🐾 ) Full-service high-rise hotel with warmly furnished rooms.

**TOP END**

**Ritz-Carlton Huntington Hotel & Spa** ( ☎ 626-568-3900, 800-241-3333; www.ritzcarlton.com/hotels/huntington; 1401 S Oak Knoll Ave; r $265-395, children under 18 stay free; P $24; 🖳 🐾 ) If it weren't for the palm trees, you'd half expect this ultraposh hostelry to be a French country estate complete with rambling gardens, a huge swimming pool and even a covered picture bridge. A recent renovation has dressed rooms in regal reds or blues and outfitted them with elaborate drapery, sparkling furniture and, as a nod to the 21st century, a flat screen TV. The Sunday brunch ($55) is pricey but legendary and the overall service is impeccable.

## EATING

One of the great delights of visiting LA is eating out in one of the cities that, back in the 1980s, gave birth to California cuisine. While healthily prepared dishes revolving around fresh, seasonal ingredients are still in vogue, other recent trends have included Nuevo Latino, which draws from various Latin-American food cultures, and the good old-fashioned steak house.

West Hollywood, Beverly Hills, Santa Monica and Downtown LA have the most innovative restaurants, but there's plenty of tasty cooking going on beyond the culinary temples. After all, LA's motley mélange of ethnicities allows for authentic and often excellent food from around the world.

There are options galore for vegetarians and vegans, some of which are included here. For more choices, check www.veg paradise.com. For more of the lowdown on LA's cuisine scene, see p48.

Reservations are a good idea at dinnertime. To score a table at the trendiest places, call several days ahead or opt for an early or late-ish slot on a weekday.

### Hollywood, Los Feliz & Silver Lake
Map pp66–7

**BUDGET**

**Yuca's** ( ☎ 323-662-1214; 2056 Hillhurst Ave, Los Feliz; mains $3-6; 🕚 11am-6pm Mon-Sat; P ) Fresh ingredients, clever spicing and rock-bottom prices are what keep business constant at this tiny hut with a few parking-lot tables. Burritos, tacos and tortas all fly nonstop through the service window. Grab a cold one at the liquor store next door and dig in.

**Mel's Drive-in** ( ☎ 323-465-2111; 1660 N Highland Ave, Hollywood; mains $7-10; 🕚 24hr) Catch that *American Graffiti* vibe at this fun '50s diner, located in the same building as the Hollywood Museum (p79). It does burgers best, but salads and sandwiches are also good refueling options. Fun factor: table-side miniature jukeboxes. There's another location nearby in **West Hollywood** (Map pp68-9; ☎ 323-464-3243; 8585 W Sunset Blvd).

**Birds** ( ☎ 323-465-0175; 5925 Franklin Ave, Hollywood; mains $6-12) This coffee shop in the hipster block of Franklin Ave is famous for marinated chicken sent through the rotisserie for that light and crispy tan. For a full meal, pair it with the zesty dipping sauces and homemade sides. Otherwise content your tummy with sandwiches, salads, burgers and other staples.

**Sanamluang** ( ☎ 323-660-8006; 5176 Hollywood Blvd, Hollywood; mains $5-10; 🕚 9am-4am; P ) After the bars close flocks of starving night owls descend upon this no-nonsense Thai eatery

---

**TOP FIVE VEGETARIAN PICKS**

- Annapurna (Culver City, p158)
- Native Foods (Westwood, p157)
- Real Food Daily (Santa Monica, p159)
- Green Temple (Redondo Beach, p162)
- Spot (Hermosa Beach, p162)

which is tucked into a nondescript strip mall. The dish of choice seems to be the sinus-clearing General's noodle soup, although the garlic and pepper shrimp also fill the belly nicely. It's cash only and no alcohol.

**Fred 62** ( ☎ 323-667-0062; 1850 N Vermont Ave, Los Feliz; mains $2.62-13.62; ☼ 24hr) This updated '50s-style diner in the heart of Los Feliz Village serves up polyethnic sandwiches, salads and noodles to hungry hipsters on small budgets. All prices end in '62' – cute.

**Scooby's** ( ☎ 323-468-3647; 6654 Hollywood Blvd, Hollywood; hot dogs $2.30-3.70; ☼ noon-10pm Sun-Thu, noon-2:30am Fri & Sat) Dressed in cheerful red, this new hot-dog den has got the goods to challenge the supremacy of the venerable Pink's Hot Dogs (p155). Scooby's gourmet wieners are great, but it's the fries – fresh, nicely crispy and served with a mayo-based dipping sauce – that give this place an edge. Fresh lemonade, too.

For Zankou Chicken see p166.

### MID-RANGE

**Madame Matisse** ( ☎ 323-662-4862; 3536 W Sunset Blvd, Silver Lake; mains breakfast & lunch $6-9, dinner $10-18; ☼ 7:30am-9:30pm) This bustling, pocket-sized bistro is a charming slice of Provence right on the Silver Lake strip. Originally known as a breakfast place, chef Olivier Bouillot's skill truly shines when it comes to soul-warming country dishes such as coq au vin or duck breast. BYOB at dinner (no corkage).

**Rambutan Thai** ( ☎ 213-273-8424; 2835 W Sunset Blvd, Silver Lake; mains $8-15; ☼ lunch Mon-Sat, dinner daily; Ⓟ ) By painting the walls a passionate red and dimming the lights, Rambutan's owners have turned this mini-mall venue into a place stylish enough to take a date. The usual hit parade of Thai favorites is supplemented by an interesting menu of 'Thai tapas' that's perfect for grazers or those wishing to keep their slim figure.

**Carousel** ( ☎ 323-660-8060; 5112 Hollywood Blvd, Hollywood; mains $8-20; ☼ closed Mon; Ⓟ ) The aroma of garlic and lemon hangs in the air at this small strip-mall Lebanese-Armenian eatery. You could easily make a meal from such addictive meze (appetizers) as smoky hummus or flaky *fatayer* (cheese-stuffed puff pastry), but then you'd miss out on the succulent kebabs or roasted quail. The Glendale branch in the **San Fernando Valley** ( ☎ 818-246-7775; 304 N Brand Blvd) is considerably more formal.

**Ammo** ( ☎ 323-871-2666; 1155 N Highland Ave, Hollywood; mains lunch $9-18, dinner $14-25; ☼ lunch Mon-Fri, dinner Mon-Sat) At this recently restyled hole-in-the-wall, the menu is loaded with the ultimate culinary oxymoron: healthy comfort food. Regulars hanker after chef Amy Sweeney's turkey meat loaf, roast organic chicken and double-cut pork chops. Vegetarians have fresh pastas, salads and a toothsome risotto *verde* to salivate over.

**Cheebo** ( ☎ 323-850-7070; 7533 W Sunset Blvd, Hollywood; mains breakfast $5-9, lunch $8-14, dinner $10-26; ☼ 8am-11:30pm) With its pumpkin-colored walls, paper-covered tables and cups of crayons, this low-key eatery screams 'tots-friendly.' Yummy organic pizzas – from classic pepperoni to gourmet goat cheese and artichoke – are delivered piping hot on wooden boards. Lots of choices for vegetarians, and killer chocolate soufflé.

**Cafe Stella** ( ☎ 323-666-0265; 3932 W Sunset Blvd, Silver Lake; mains $14-24; ☼ dinner Tue-Sat; Ⓟ ) Were it not for the eclectic patrons, this darling bistro, tucked away in a secluded courtyard at Sunset Junction (look for the red star on the rooftop), would not look out of place on Paris' Left Bank. The menu, scribbled on a blackboard, features mostly classics such as tarragon chicken, escargot or onion soup.

**Palermo** ( ☎ 323-663-1178; 1858 N Vermont Ave, Los Feliz; dishes $7-13; ☼ Wed-Mon) A little pizza, a little red wine, laughter and good company – what more do you need to feel good about life? Cops to rockers, families to gays, everyone flocks to Tony the owner and his classic pizzas smothered in cheese. Wine is a steal at 75¢ per glass. It's *la dolce vita*, Los Feliz style.

**El Conquistador** ( ☎ 323-666-5136; 3701 W Sunset Blvd, Silver Lake; mains $9-13.50; ☼ lunch Wed-Sun, dinner daily) This wonderfully campy Mexican cantina – festooned year-round with twinkling lights – is perfect for launching yourself into a night on the razzle. One margarita is all it takes to drown your sorrows, so be sure to fill the belly with tasty nachos, *chiles rellenos* (stuffed peppers, usually with cheese, but anything goes) and quesadillas to sustain your stamina through the night.

**Vert** ( ☎ 323-491-1300; 4th fl, 6801 Hollywood Blvd, Hollywood; mains $10-26; Ⓟ ) Upstairs at Hollywood & Highland, Vert is Wolfgang Puck's paean to the Parisian brasserie with occasional flavor excursions to Italy and California.

**THE LA FOOD SCENE** *Rose Dosti*

A friend who had been out of the country for some time returned to Los Angeles and almost fainted at the sight of a city that had turned from a sleepy, sprawling metropolis into the hippest and most vibrant restaurant city in the country. 'What happened?' she asked.

Well, LA didn't become a food capital of the world overnight. It took a convergence of factors, such as an Asian and Latino population explosion, the end result being unparalleled ethnic diversity. Neighborhoods now bulge with restaurants, cafés and markets where you can get Central American *pupusas*, Korean *bulgogi*, Chaozhou-style noodles, Japanese sushi, Middle Eastern kebabs, Indian tandoori, Vietnamese *pho* and Thai pad Thai, and, of course, regional Mexican cooking styles from the Yucatán to Oaxaca. There are Moroccan, Russian, Romanian, Israeli, Cuban, Ethiopian and Afghani restaurants that make dining an adventure on the cheap. Great restaurants are clustered all over LA, but in particular Little Tokyo (Downtown), Chinatown (Monterey Park), Little Armenia and Koreatown (Wilshire Center), Little India and Little Saigon (Artesia).

New food safety and transportation technologies developed since the 1960s brought the world's products to our shores overnight. Health awareness of the '70s created a vegetarianism that has morphed into several cuisines, including macrobiotic, vegan and the latest – raw food – at places such as Juliano's Raw, Real Food Daily and Urth Caffe.

A thriving global economy of the late '70s and '80s allowed modern European and Asian chefs to flock to California. Masters such as Wolfgang Puck (Spago Beverly Hills), Joachim Splichal (Patina), Celestino Drago (Drago), Hans Röckenwagner (Röckenwagner/Brasserie), together with the Japanese kaiseki artists – Katsu Michite (Katsu), Susumi Fukui (Chaya Brasserie) and Nobu Matsuhisa (Matsuhisa) – brought virtuoso cooking to LA. The early crop of liberated American male and female chefs – Mary Sue Milliken and Susan Feniger (Border Grill and Ciudad), Michael McCarty (Michael's) and Bruce Marder (Capo) – inspired innovative, experimental cooking using ingredients in ways never imagined. The result? The creation of a new California cuisine and its offshoots: Cal-Asian, Cal-Eclectic, Pan-Asian, Cal-French and Franco-Japanese. The legacy is found among today's top restaurants, including Joe's, Josie's, Lucques, Linq, Vida, Chinois on Main, White Lotus, Koi, Blowfish, Campanile, La Cachette, and Water Grill. It's at the numerous cafés spawned from big-time eateries (Café Pinot and the Puck cafés). It's at the moderately priced chains, such as California Pizza Kitchen, at the prepared food eateries, such as Julienne and Marmalade, and even at hotel restaurants, such as the Belvedere at the Peninsula and at the Hotel Bel-Air. Many of the hippest restaurants and cafés are clustered in the vicinities of West Hollywood and Venice.

Even celebrities have gotten into the act. Once hidden behind velvet curtains while sipping martinis, today's stars freely slurp lattes at Starbucks, stop at the many spas for an elegant salad and a scrub, or nibble on tapas in the growing number of hip late-night hangouts such as Cobras & Matadors, Dolce and Minibar, or at their favorite steak houses (Morton's, Lincoln's, Balboa or the Palm). Or, most likely, they preside over restaurants they've bankrolled: Madre's (Jennifer Lopez), Ago (Robert De Niro) and the Continental (Ben Affleck and Matt Damon), among others.

So where do you go? Take your pick. From stargazing at the Ivy to enjoying a delicious Korean barbecue at Soot Bull Jeep (one of more than 200 Korean restaurants), in Los Angeles the culinary world is at your fingertips.

Settle into a stylish turquoise booth, order the signature Bellini (prosecco and green apple juice), then look forward to steak au poivre, pan-roasted pork chop or even a classic Puck pizza. Portions are generous.

For Cobras & Matadors see p155.

**TOP END**

**Musso & Frank Grill** ( ☎ 323-467-7788; 6667 Hollywood Blvd, Hollywood; mains $20-35; ☾ Tue-Sat) Holly-

wood history hangs thickly in the air at the boulevard's oldest eatery and still – or perhaps again – one its hippest. Red-jacketed waiters balance platters of steaks, chops, grilled liver and other dishes that originated in the days when cholesterol wasn't part of our vocabulary. For breakfast, which is served all day, try the signature flannel cakes (thin pancakes; $6). Service is smooth, and so are the martinis. See also p80.

**TOP FIVE BREAKFAST SPOTS**

- Griddle Café (West Hollywood, p154)
- Hugo's (West Hollywood, p154)
- Marston's (Pasadena, p166)
- Omelette Parlor (Santa Monica, p159)
- Uncle Bill's Pancake House (Manhattan Beach, p162)

**Vermont** ( ☎ 323-661-6163; 1714 N Vermont Ave, Los Feliz; mains lunch $9-16, dinner $13-28; ☽ lunch Mon-Fri, dinner daily; P ) This is a smart, grown-up spot with an elegant, white dining room punctuated by pillars and palmetto palms. The updated versions of American comfort food remind us of the simple goodness of a slow-roasted lamb shank, grilled sea bass or pan-seared beef fillet. Reservations recommended.

For Xiomara see p168.

## West Hollywood                    Map pp68–9
### BUDGET
**Griddle Café** ( ☎ 323-874-0377; 7916 W Sunset Blvd; dishes $6-9; ☽ 8am-3pm) If you greeted the day by peeling your lids back from crusty, bloodshot eyes, a trip to this scenester joint may be just what the doctor ordered. Start with an infusion of high-octane coffee, then slowly restore balance to brain and stomach with wagon-wheel-sized pancakes or a legendary Tequila Sunrise, their own tasty spin on *huevos rancheros* (a tortilla topped with red salsa and fried eggs).

**Tail O' the Pup** ( ☎ 310-652-4517; 329 N San Vicente Blvd; hot dogs $2.30-4.25; ☽ 6:30am-5pm) One look at Eddie Blake's little roadside shack near the Beverly Center and you know what's cooking here. Shaped like a giant hot dog, this place has been around since 1938 and was once a favorite of Orson Welles. The tasty dogs continue to attract a loyal following to this day, although the burgers ain't bad either.

For Le Pain Quotidien see p156; for Mel's Drive-in see p151; and for Real Food Daily see p159.

### MID-RANGE
**Alto Palato** ( ☎ 310-657-9271; 755 N La Cienega Blvd; mains $14-28; ☽ dinner Tue-Sun; P ) The menu at this comfortable trattoria hopscotches from one Italian region to the next, mostly with convincing results and at reasonable prices. The thin-crust pizza is superb as is the whole roasted sea bass and the creamy gelato. Budget gourmets descend on Wednesdays when a three-course meal costs a mere $28. Happy hour (5pm to 7pm Tuesday to Friday) brings $4 martinis and $6 pizzas.

**Hugo's** ( ☎ 323-654-3993; 8401 Santa Monica Blvd; mains $9-14; ☽ 7:30am-10pm) This nondescript coffee shop may not look an Industry magnet but it does lure its share of famous faces, especially at breakfast time. The menu is mostly of the healthy soul-food variety, with the Tantric veggie burger and the tofu vegetable grill being popular meatless staples. Tea fans will rejoice at the selection of quality brews.

**Urth Caffe** ( ☎ 310-659-0628; 8565 Melrose Ave; mains $7-15; ☽ 6am-midnight) This megahip hangout near the Pacific Design Center has been packed with hotties, producers and gawkers for more than a decade. The organic teas and coffees are all primo quality but it's the see-and-be-seen patio that gives this place its edge. For sustenance, try its pastries, salads and sandwiches. Also in **Beverly Hills** (Map pp70-1; ☎ 310-205-9311; 267 S Beverly Dr).

### TOP END
**Chaya Brasserie** ( ☎ 310-859-8833; 8741 Alden Dr; mains lunch $8-17, dinner $9-32; ☽ lunch Mon-Fri, dinner daily; P ) Chaya's menu is as tantalizing as the Zen-meets-industrial dining room where a small bamboo grove tickles the skylights. Chef Shigefumi Tachibe gives the culinary lead to Mediterranean cuisine with supporting roles assigned to Japan, China and other Asian countries. The selection changes with the seasons but typical dishes include duck spring rolls, miso-bronzed sea bass and roast venison. Reservations advised. Also in **Venice** (Map pp72-3; ☎ 310-396-1179; 110 Navy St).

**Koi** ( ☎ 310-659-9449; 730 N La Cienega Blvd; mains $8-24; ☽ lunch Mon-Fri, dinner daily; P ) There's no question, this trendy restaurant is a winner in the looks department with its bamboo-fringed patios, votive candles and sexy fireside lounge. A-listers from George Clooney to Madonna have all been spotted picking over plates of sushi, sashimi and such Japanese-inspired mains as albacore tuna with basil *ponzu* (citrus-infused soy sauce).

## Mid-City
Map pp68–9

### BUDGET

**Swingers** ( ☎ 323-653-5858; 8020 Beverly Blvd; dishes $4-10; ⏰ 6:30am-4am) If you're after Americana with a dollop of Hollywood, this diner is the genuine article. Its red plastic booths often fill with kool kids combating hunger pangs or hangovers, depending on the time of day. Servers in fishnet stockings and a certain, shall we say, sassy charm balance heaping platters of energy-restoring goodies while Little Richard makes the jukebox hop. Also in **Santa Monica** (Map pp72-3; ☎ 310-393-9793; 802 Broadway).

**Pink's Hot Dogs** ( ☎ 323-931-4223; 709 N La Brea Ave; dishes $2.50-5.40; ⏰ 9:30am-2am Sun-Thu, 9:30am-3am Fri & Sat) Lines outside this landmark 'doggeria' can be discouragingly long, but hang in there: their famous all-beef dogs slathered with tasty chili are well worth the wait. Plus who knows? You might meet someone nice in line. In the wee weekend hours, Pink's gets mobbed by clubbers.

**Canter's Deli** ( ☎ 323-651-2030; 419 N Fairfax Ave; mains $6-15; ⏰ 24hr) To satisfy a hankering for chicken soup or gefilte fish, head to this landmark Jewish diner, in business since 1948. The Kibitz Room lounge gets its share of celebrity drop-ins.

The original **Farmers Market** (6333 W 3rd St) is a great spot for a casual meal any time of day, especially if the rug rats are tagging along. Favorite belly-filling stations include the following:

**Gumbo Pot** ( ☎ 323-933-0358; mains $4-8) Southern food so fingerlickin' good, Blanche Dubois might approve.

**Lotería! Grill** ( ☎ 323-930-2211; dishes $2.50-9) Handmade, back-to-basics Mexican.

**Singapore's Banana Leaf** ( ☎ 323-933-4627; mains $5-8) Southeast Asian perfumed with peanut, mango, tamarind and other exotic flavors.

### MID-RANGE

**Cobras & Matadors** ( ☎ 323-932-6178; 7615 Beverly Blvd; tapas $4-12; ⏰ dinner; **P** ) Tables at this trendy tapas bar are squished together as tight as lovers, but scoring one can still be a tall order. It's worth a wait though for waist-friendly portions of perfectly cured *jamón serrano* (cured ham), oven-roasted mussels or garlic-sautéed mushrooms. If you pick up a bottle of vino at the shop next door, you'll pay no corkage fee. The branch in **Los Feliz** (Map pp66-7; ☎ 323-669-3922; 4655 Hollywood Blvd) serves wine and beer.

**Pastis** ( ☎ 323-655-8822; 8114 Beverly Blvd; mains $13-20; ⏰ dinner; **P** ) The menu is constantly on the go at this relaxed bistro that seems plucked straight out of Provence. It's the kind of place where waiters converse in fluent French with expats and Francophiles, and where meals become culinary celebrations that comfortably stretch out over an entire evening. The bouillabaisse simply rocks.

**Angelini Osteria** ( ☎ 323-297-0070; 7313 Beverly Blvd; mains $10-34; ⏰ lunch Tue-Fri, dinner Tue-Sun; **P** ) Conversation flows as freely as the wine at this convivial eatery whose eclectic clientele shares a passion for great Italian food with owner-chef Gino Angelini. Celebs from Pavarotti to the Pope have savored his soulful risottos, pungent pastas and delightful lamb chops with price tags to match all budgets.

**Surya** ( ☎ 323-653-5151; 8048 W 3rd St; mains $9-22; ⏰ lunch Mon-Fri, dinner daily; **P** ) Curries are like culinary poetry at this upscale Indian restaurant dedicated to Surya, the Hindu god of the sun, which might explain the saffron-colored walls. Friendly waitstaff will happily help you navigate the menu, although your bill should always include an order of steamy naan and anything out of the tandoor (clay oven).

**Buddha's Belly** ( ☎ 323-931-8588; 7475 Beverly Blvd; mains $8-16; ⏰ lunch Mon-Sat, dinner daily; **P** ) An appetizing aroma steaming from the open kitchen envelops you as soon you step inside this pretty space accented with colorful paper lanterns. The menu takes a trip around Asia with Thai curry, Vietnamese *pho* (noodle soup; rhymes with paw) and Japanese-style cod all making appearances. If you don't watch it, you risk leaving with a belly as big as the eponymous Buddha serenely watching over the pandemonium.

For Natalee Thai Cuisine see p158.

### TOP END

**A.O.C.** ( ☎ 323-653-6359; 8022 W 3rd St; dishes $4-14; ⏰ dinner; **P** ) This hugely popular stomping ground of the rich, lithe and silicone-enhanced offers a rare fusion of substance and style. The small-plate menu will have you noshing happily on sweaty cheeses, homemade charcuterie and richly nuanced hot dishes such as braised pork cheeks. The selection of 50 wines by the glass offers a perfect complement for each morsel.

**LOS ANGELES**

**Campanile** ( ☎ 323-938-1447; 624 S La Brea Ave; mains brunch $8-15, lunch $12-18, dinner $24-36; ☺ brunch Sat & Sun, lunch Mon-Fri, dinner Mon-Sat; ℗ ) Campanile has occupied a spot in LA's culinary pantheon for nearly 15 years. Chef Mark Peel knows how to turn market-fresh ingredients into beautiful dishes that will linger in your memory long after you've paid the bill. Monday nights' $35 three-course meals offer the best value. Partner Nancy Silverton reigns as the city's bread and dessert queen.

### Beverly Hills                    Map pp70–1
**BUDGET**
**Mulberry Street Pizzeria** ( ☎ 310-247-8100; 240 S Beverly Dr; pizza $2.50-25) Owned by Bronx-born actress Cathy Moriarty *(Raging Bull, Kindergarten Cop)*, this pint-sized joint delivers New York–style pizza that's like little slices of heaven. The crust is crispy, the tomato sauce has just the right amount of tang and the toppings are piled on generously. A great spot for lunch or a snack.

**Le Pain Quotidien** ( ☎ 310-859-1100; 9630 S Santa Monica Blvd; dishes $7-17; ☺ 7:30am-7pm) The name is French for 'daily bread' but you don't need to be religious to worship at this great, if pricey, *boulangerie* (bakery). The baguettes here are as good as they get without taking a flight to Paris and the pastries will tempt even the staunchest low-carb devotees. You can take out or stay to enjoy soups, salads or sandwiches on the patio. Also in **West Hollywood** (Map pp68-9; ☎ 310-854-3700; 8607 Melrose Ave).

For Real Food Daily see p159.

**MID-RANGE**
**Nate 'n Al's** ( ☎ 310-274-0101; 414 N Beverly Dr; dishes $8-15; ☺ 7:30am-8:45pm Sun-Fri, 7:30am-9:30pm Sat) It's not much to look at, but this landmark deli will have you gobbling what may quite

---

**TOP FIVE PICKS FOR CELEBRITY-SPOTTING**

- A.O.C. (Mid-City, p155)
- Crustacean (Beverly Hills, opposite)
- Koi (West Hollywood, p154)
- Nate 'n Al's (Beverly Hills, above)
- Spago Beverly Hills (Beverly Hills, opposite)

---

possibly be the best pastrami on rye, lox on bagels and chicken soup this side of Manhattan. If you're lucky, your visit may even come with a free side of star sightings.

**Il Pastaio** ( ☎ 310-205-5444; 400 N Cañon Dr; mains $15-21; ☺ lunch Mon-Sat, dinner daily; ℗ ) Spaghetti, capellini, pappardelle – they're all handmade and fresh at this bustling shoe box–sized trattoria. Chef Celestino Drago finds endless ways to pair his product with vegetables, meats, fish and inventive sauces. The appetizers, risottos and salads are all tops too, but the noise can be a distraction.

**Mako** ( ☎ 310-288-8338; 225 S Beverly Dr; mains lunch $10-13, dinner small plates $4-13; ☺ lunch Wed-Fri, dinner Mon-Sat; ℗ ) Champion chef Makoto Tanaka perfected his craft at Spago Beverly Hills (p157) and Chinois on Main (p161) before wowing patrons at his own minimalist-chic restaurant. The small plate menu is ideal for sampling flavors and textures, from snow crab tempura to Asian risotto or chicken salad. At lunch most people order the 'Bento Box' filled with whatever inspires Makoto that day.

**Il Cielo** (Map pp70-1; ☎ 310-276-9990; 9018 Burton Way; mains $12-30; ☺ closed Sun) Candles, Chianti and a courtyard table are all you need for a romantic night out with your significant other at this classy yet cozy ristorante. The food is solid, not exceptional, but the attentive waitstaff and the setting ensure an unforgettable night.

**Trattoria Amici** ( ☎ 310-858-0271; 469 N Doheny Dr; mains $10-23; ☺ lunch Mon-Fri, dinner daily; ℗ ) The romantic garden patio is the place to be for languid alfresco dinners with your sweetie. Although ensconced within the rather unglam Beverly Terrace Hotel (p143), this charming eatery gets high marks from locals and even has an occasional celebrity popping in for a plate of pasta.

**Gyu-Kaku** ( ☎ 310-659-5760; 163 N La Cienega Blvd; mains lunch $9-13, dinner $15-30; ☺ lunch Wed-Sun, dinner daily; ℗ ) If you like a do-it-yourself approach to dining, give this popular Japanese chain a try. Specializing in *yakiniku*, which translates as 'grilled meats,' it requires you to cook your own slabs over a belching charcoal brazier set right into your table. The dessert of choice is classic s'mores. Kids love it. There is another branch in **Westwood** (Map pp68-9; ☎ 310-234-8641; 10925 W Pico Blvd).

For Cheesecake Factory see p161; for McCormick & Schmick's see p164; for Urth Caffe see p154; and for Versailles see p158.

## TOP END

**Spago Beverly Hills** ( ☎ 310-385-0880; 176 N Cañon Dr; mains lunch $14-27, dinner $26-36; ☽ lunch Mon-Sat, dinner daily; ℗ ) Wolfgang Puck's flagship emporium has long been tops for A-list celebrity-spotting and fancy eating. Try to score a table on the lovely patio and prepare for your taste buds to do cartwheels as chef Lee Hefter digs deep into his repertory to give pork chops, porcini or pasta the gourmet treatment. Even dessert is worth the hip-expanding indulgence. Reservations essential.

**Crustacean** ( ☎ 310-205-8990; 9646 S Santa Monica Blvd; mains lunch $12-16, dinner $20-39; ☽ lunch Mon-Fri, dinner Mon-Sat; ℗ ) At this tony Euro-Vietnamese restaurant, you can literally walk on water – on top of a floor-sunken koi stream, that is. The menu here is as intriguing as the sultry French Colonial decor, with top honors going to the whole roasted Dungeness crab and the garlic noodles, both bathed in owner-chef Elizabeth An's 'secret spices.' Reservations essential.

**Matsuhisa** ( ☎ 310-659-9639; 129 N La Cienega Blvd; mains lunch $10-25, dinner $20-30, tasting menu from $100; ☽ lunch Mon-Fri, dinner daily; ℗ ) Despite ho-hum decor, Nobu Matsuhisa's outpost has long been one of the top restaurants in town. You might well be rubbing elbows with Madonna or Tom Cruise as you savor superfresh sushi, feather-light tempura, halibut cheeks in pepper sauce or any other dish from the epic menu. Food fanciers with deep pockets order the *omakase* (chef's choice) menu. Reservations essential.

## Westwood, Bel Air & Brentwood
Map pp70–1

### BUDGET

**Native Foods** ( ☎ 310-209-1055; 1110-1/2 Gayley Ave, Westwood; dishes $5-10; ☽ 11am-10pm) Pizzas, burgers, sandwiches, salads – the menu reads like those at your typical California café, yet there is one notable difference: no animal products will ever find their way into this vegan haven. Tempeh and seitan are homemade and turned into such globally inspired fare as Jamaican jerk salad and Ghandi curry. Popular for takeout, too.

**Ambala Dhaba** ( ☎ 310-966-1772; 1781 Westwood Blvd, Westwood; mains $6-12) At this traditional North Indian eatery you could stick to chicken tandoori or fish tikka but then you'd miss out on the more exotic specialties. Instead, start out with *gol gappe* (vegetable-stuffed golf ball–sized breads), move on to fiery *bakra* (goat) curry or *saag makki di roti* (pancake with spinach) and finish up with an almond saffron *kulfi* (ice cream).

**Sunnin Lebanese Cafe** ( ☎ 310-477-2358; 1779 Westwood Blvd, Westwood; mains $7-12) An appetizing aroma streaming from the twee open kitchen greets you as soon as you enter this Middle Eastern eatery, which gets an F for decor and an A for the cooking. You can't go wrong by ordering the meze – smoky baba ghanouj to habit-forming hummus – although the falafel, all crispy on the outside, moist on the inside, are as good as it gets.

### MID-RANGE

**Zen Grill & Sake Lounge** ( ☎ 310-209-1994; 1051 Broxton Ave, Westwood; mains $8-20; ☽ lunch Tue-Fri, dinner Tue-Sun) Restaurant designer du jour Dodd Mitchell has dreamed up a high-tech Far Eastern look for this vibrant eatery which serves up inspired pan-Asian fusion. From Korean-style short ribs to Thai green curry, Mongolian lamb to Indonesian satay, it's all mouthwateringly good.

**Tanino** ( ☎ 310-208-0444; 1043 Westwood Blvd, Westwood; mains $10-25; ☽ lunch Mon-Fri, dinner daily; ℗ ) Italian restaurants may be a dime a dozen in Los Angeles but at Tanino the decor, menu and service all blend together as perfectly as a rich Sicilian stew. Sun-baked Sicily just happens to be where the eponymous chef hails from and the region's cuisine, with its feisty flavors, provides inspiration for many of the delicious pastas and risottos on the menu here.

**Taiko** ( ☎ 310-207-7782; 11677 San Vicente Blvd, Brentwood; mains $7-20; ℗ ) This prim Japanese café inside a stylish Brentwood mall is the place to slurp succulently flavored soba and udon soups, either hot or cold, or dig into delectable rice bowls topped with a variety of meats and vegetables. Prepare for a wait: low prices and top quality are an irresistible combo.

For Gyu-Kaku see p156; for La Serenata de Garibaldi see p165.

## TOP END

**Restaurant** ( ☎ 310-472-5234; 701 N Stone Canyon Rd, Bel Air; breakfast $25, mains lunch $18-28, dinner $29-42; ⊙ breakfast & lunch Mon-Sat, brunch Sun, dinner daily) The restaurant at the exquisite Hotel Bel-Air scores a perfect 10 on the 'romance-meter.' Even getting there has that fairytale feel as you sashay past preening swans along flower-festooned paths and a perpetually crackling fireplace. Impeccable service, a superb farm-fresh Cal-French menu and out-of-this-world prices make eating here even more memorable. Reservations are de rigueur.

## Culver City

### BUDGET

**Tacomiendo** (off Map pp72-3; ☎ 310-915-0426; 4502 Inglewood Blvd; dishes $2-5; ⊙ 9:30am-10pm) This little Mexican eatery is unlikely to make it into the food guides, but it should. For the price of a Starbucks latte, you can feast on tortas, tacos and other staples, all prepared fresh, quickly and using only quality meats (and no lard). The free condiment bar features hot pinto beans and three types of salsa. Great *aguas* (fresh fruit drinks), too.

**Annapurna** (off Map pp72-3; ☎ 310-204-5500; 10200 Venice Blvd; mains $5-9; P ) Bollywood musicals flickering on flat screens are only a minor distraction from the delightful food at this brightly lit, all-vegetarian restaurant specializing in South Indian fare. Despite the strip-mall setting, the quality is here top-notch. Try the *dosas* (stuffed lentil crepes) or the *uthappams* (rice pancakes) with various toppings. The daily lunch buffet is especially good value.

### MID-RANGE

**Natalee Thai Cuisine** (off Map pp72-3; ☎ 310-202-7003; 10101 Venice Blvd; mains $6-10; P ) This stylish eatery has long been a neighborhood darling for top Thai. The kitchen dishes up all the traditional staples, healthily prepared and wittily introduced on the extensive menu. The chicken satay appetizer and the pad Thai are recommended. Also in **Beverly Hills** (Map pp70-1; ☎ 310-855-9380; 998 S Robertson Blvd).

**Café Brasil** (off Map pp72-3; ☎ 310-837-8957; 10831 Venice Blvd; mains $5-18, set lunch $7; P ) On Venice Blvd's 'Little Rio,' this urban beach shack serves some of the best Brazilian food in town. Meats are grilled to perfection and paired with rice, black beans, fresh salsa

and fried plantains. On weekend, expats descend for the hearty *feijoada*, a traditional pork stew. You're free to bring your own beer or wine.

**Versailles** (off Map pp72-3; ☎ 310-558-3168; 10319 Venice Blvd; mains $6-11; P ) A haze of heavenly smells greets you as you step into this casual Cuban eatery whose lip-smacking roast lemon chicken will make you cluck with delight. Other regulars are partial to the succulent roast pork, but everyone agrees it's the black beans, rice, sweet onions and fried plantains that add a special touch. Also in **Manhattan Beach** (Map p74; ☎ 310-937-6829; 1000 N Sepulveda Blvd) and near **Beverly Hills** (Map pp70-1; ☎ 310-289-0392; 1415 S La Cienega Blvd).

**Beacon** (off Map pp72-3; ☎ 310-838-7500; 3280 Helms Ave; mains lunch $5-20, dinner $20-30) LA foodies know chef Kazuto Matsusaka as one of the city's prime interpreters of fusion cuisine, but at his new outpost in the old Helms Bakery his focus is more on Asian flavors and textures. The miso-marinated black cod is succulent and the crispy oysters are nicely adventuresome. Leave room for the green-tea cheesecake.

## Malibu                          Map pp60–1

### BUDGET

**Howdy's Taqueria** ( ☎ 310-456-6299; 3835 Cross Creek Rd, Malibu Country Mart; dishes $5-9; ⊙ 9am-9pm) A favorite with beach bums and Pepperdine students, Howdy's makes Mexican food catering to most diets and food neuroses. Choose from tofu tacos, vegetarian chorizo burritos and grilled veggie salads or go traditional with *huevos rancheros* or chicken enchiladas.

**Neptune's Net** ( ☎ 310-457-3095; 42505 Pacific Coast Hwy; meals $6-10; ⊙ 10:30am-8pm Apr-Oct, 10:30am-7pm Nov-Mar, 10:30am-9pm Fri year-round; P ) This landmark shack with an ocean-view patio serves up delicious shrimp, crab, oysters and other seafood straight from the sea tank. Fans include everyone from Harley riders to beach bums and families. It's way up the coast, just shy of the Ventura County line.

### MID-RANGE

**Taverna Tony** ( ☎ 310-317-9667; 23410 Civic Center Way; mains $10-23; P ) This lively Greek spot fronted by a flowery terrace packs them in day after day with fingerlickin' fare that feeds both the soul and belly. For a serious indulgence, loosen your belt and order the Greek Feast (lunch/dinner $19/28 per person; two-person minimum) with 15 different dishes (12 at lunchtime). Reservations advised.

**Allegria** ( ☎ 310-456-3132; 22821 Pacific Coast Hwy; mains $11-23; P ) This convivial trattoria near the Malibu Pier is often filled with patrons lusting after the pizzas tickled by wood fire just long enough to produce perfectly crispy, and thin, crusts. Other dishes beckon too, including pretty pastas, tender osso buco and crispy fried calamari paired with a tomato sauce that's got some kick.

**TOP END**

**Geoffrey's** ( ☎ 310-457-1519; 27400 Pacific Coast Hwy; mains lunch $14-24, dinner $18-36; P ) This posh player in northern Malibu possesses just the right mix of assets to ensure it'll never go out of style: the Pacific Ocean as a front yard, nicely executed Cal-Asian cuisine, and a regular clutch of celebrity patrons. In short, it's the perfect date spot, especially at night when it is oh-so romantic.

**Inn of the Seventh Ray** ( ☎ 310-455-1311; 128 Old Topanga Canyon Rd; lunch $10-14, dinner $20-36; ☽ brunch Sun, lunch Mon-Sat, dinner daily; P ) An idyllic canyon setting and a karmically correct menu (main courses are listed 'in order of esoteric vibration') are among the main draws of this out-of-the-way place. All of the food is organic and much is meat-free. Five-course tasting dinners are $60 ($50 for the vegetarian version). Great vegan duck.

## Santa Monica         Map pp72–3

**BUDGET**

**Omelette Parlor** ( ☎ 310-399-7892; 2732 Main St; dishes under $7; ☽ 6am-2:30pm Mon-Fri, 6am-4pm Sat & Sun) This place has been whipping up some of the best egg dishes and breakfasts in town since opening during the 'Summer of Love' in 1967. Omelettes are industrial-weight, and the beefy sandwiches pack a punch. Expect a line, especially on weekend mornings.

**Real Food Daily** ( ☎ 310-451-7544; 514 Santa Monica Blvd; mains $6-12) Tempted by tempeh? Salivating for seitan? Vegan cooking queen Ann Gentry sure knows how to give these meat subs the gourmet treatment. Start things off with lentil-walnut pâté, move on to the vegan club sandwich with Caesar salad, then finish up with a rich tofu cheesecake. There are other branches in **West Hollywood** (Map pp68-9; ☎ 310-289-9910; 414 N La Cienega Blvd)

**TOP FIVE ROMANTIC SPOTS**

▪ Inn of the Seventh Ray (Malibu, left)

▪ Geoffrey's (Malibu, left)

▪ Il Cielo (Beverly Hills, p156)

▪ Michael's (Santa Monica, p160)

▪ Restaurant (Bel Air, opposite)

and **Beverly Hills** (Map pp70-1; ☎ 310-858-0880; 242 S Beverly Dr). The latter is certified kosher.

**Lemon Moon** ( ☎ 310-442-9191; 12200 W Olympic Blvd; meals $5-12; ☽ 8am-3:30pm; P ) Gourmet food in an office park? The two tend to be mutually exclusive, but not here. In a setting of postmodern sleekness, you can enjoy freshly baked pastries or inspired egg dishes for breakfast, and panini, salads and soups at lunchtime. There's patio seating or lug your loot to the beach or a park for a picnic.

**Ye Olde King's Head** ( ☎ 310-451-1402; 116 Santa Monica Blvd; mains $6.50-13) This is the unofficial HQ of Santa Monica's huge British expat population, and if you don't mind the fusty odor of 25-years' worth of deep-fried fish and chips, you'll feel quite Piccadilly here. Bangers and mash or steak-and-kidney pie go quick, but the King's fish and chips are the best in town.

If you're looking for quick food fix, check out the options at Eatz, the food court on the ground floor of Santa Monica Place (p191), which has everything from pizza to pot stickers. Better yet, head up Third St for a couple of blocks to the bilevel food court at No 1315 where options range from Chinese (on the ground floor, try the roast pork) to **Wolfgang Puck Express** ( ☎ 310-576-4770; 1315 Third St Promenade; mains $7-10), where best-sellers include the Chinese chicken salad and wood-fired pizza.

For Swingers see p155.

**MID-RANGE**

**Border Grill** ( ☎ 310-451-1655; 1445 4th St; bocaditos $3-9, mains lunch $8-14, dinner $12-26; ☽ brunch Sat & Sun, lunch Tue-Sun, dinner daily; P ) We like building our meals by ordering a few of the tasty *bocaditos* (little bites) at this bustling up-scale Mexican cantina, the original outpost of TV chefs Susan Feniger and Mary Sue Milliken. The rock shrimp ceviche never disappoints and neither do the wild mushroom

**LOS ANGELES**

---

**TOP FIVE SPOTS FOR TOTS**

- Bob's Big Boy (San Fernando Valley, p166)
- Cheebo (Hollywood, p152)
- Gyu-Kaku (Beverly Hills, p156)
- Mel's Drive-in (Hollywood, p151)
- Sidewalk Café (Venice, opposite)

---

quesadillas. Bigger dishes range from *carnitas* (braised pork) to cinnamon brine-marinated pork chops.

**Rocca** ( ☎ 310-395-6765; 1432 4th St; mains $6-12; ☿ dinner) Just one block from bustling Third St Promenade is this two-story gem of a trattoria with a wall of wine and a Romeo and Juliet–style balcony. Chef Don Dickman finds endless ways to spin fresh ingredients into tasty dishes ranging from the rustic (gnocchi with oxtail ragout) to the refined (slow-roasted salmon). There's a new menu daily.

**17th Street Cafe** ( ☎ 310-453-2771; 1610 Montana Ave; breakfast $6-10, mains lunch $9-13, dinner $10-20; ☿ 8am-9pm) At this popular post-Montana-shopping noshing nook the emphasis is on fresh, wholesome and organic ingredients. The kitchen staff is happy to customize dishes to the latest diet fad, religious requirements or food intolerances. The weekend brunch offers great people-watching and might even net the occasional celebrity.

**Lares** ( ☎ 310-829-4559; 2909 Pico Blvd; mains $5-23; P ) With its subdued Spanish Colonial looks, this popular Mexican restaurant far off the tourist track is more festive than fiesta and filled with art work to boot. The slow-cooked *carnitas* – juicy and easily pulled apart – are a specialty, as are the sizzling fajitas. Good margaritas, too.

**Röckenwagner/Brasserie** ( ☎ 310-399-6504; 2435 Main St; mains $12-22; ☿ brunch Sun, dinner Tue-Sat) To experience the true genius of chef Hans Röckenwagner book a table in the intimate dining room where you can choose from two tasting menus. For more plebeian fare, some of it with a southern German inflection (veal goulash, Weisswurst, strudel), head to the brasserie in front.

**Mr Cecil's California Ribs** ( ☎ 310-442-1550; 12244 Pico Blvd; dishes $10-24) You'll have a fine time sending your cholesterol levels through the roof at this quirky circular joint with its beamed ceiling and patio facing away from the traffic. The ribs – marinated for a day, then barbecued to perfection – are fall-off-the-bone delicious. For an extra kick, slather on one of their homemade sauces.

**Café Bizou** ( ☎ 310-582-8203; Water Garden, 2450 Colorado Ave; mains lunch $11-16, dinner $13-20; ☿ brunch Sun, lunch Mon-Fri, dinner Tue-Sun) As dependable as April rain in Paris, this French bistro is on the speed dial of many local budget gourmets. The menu is more country than haute with tender roast chicken, steak au poivre and veal sweetbreads all jockeying for your attention. Add soup or salad for just a $1 more. Corkage fee is $2. Also in **Pasadena** (Map p76; ☎ 626-792-9923; 91 N Raymond Ave).

**Father's Office** ( ☎ 310-393-2337; 1018 Montana Ave; tapas $3.50-5, mains $10-15; ☿ dinner) This tunnel-shaped restaurant-bar is famous for its hamburger slathered with blue cheese, applewood-smoked bacon and caramelized onions. These go well with any of the dozens of quality microbrews available here – if you can get the bartender's attention, that is. For grazers there's a respectable array of tapas.

For La Serenata de Garibaldi see p165.

**TOP END**

**Mélisse** ( ☎ 310-395-0881; 1104 Wilshire Blvd; mains $25-40; ☿ dinner; P ) A fixture on any number of prestigious 'best of' lists, Mélisse wows a Rolls-Royce crowd of diners with Oscar-worthy food, impeccable service and an elegant, European-style dining room. Owner-chef Josiah Citrin's endless imagination results in such market-fresh palate-teasers as roast calamari stuffed with shrimp ratatouille or king salmon with pole-bean ragout. Exquisite cheese tray, too.

**JiRaffe** ( ☎ 310-917-6671; 502 Santa Monica Blvd; mains dinner $18-28; ☿ dinner; P ) Owner-chef Raphael Lunetta is an avid surfer who learned his culinary craft in Paris and now regales diners with caramelized pork chops, his signature roast-beet salad and other flavor-intensive dishes. Walnut furniture, crystal chandeliers and original art give the dining room a private-mansion feel.

**Michael's** ( ☎ 310-451-0843; 1147 3rd St; mains lunch $15-25, dinner $25-40; ☿ lunch Mon-Fri, dinner Mon-Sat; P ) This charming restaurant has been a highlight on the foodie map for over a quarter of a century. It scores big for the exquisitely prepared California cuisine, which tastes even better if you manage to snag a table in the idyllic garden. Reservations essential.

**Chinois on Main** (☎ 310-392-9025; 2709 Main St; mains $20-36; lunch Wed-Fri, dinner daily; P) Wolfgang Puck's pioneering French-Asian outpost never seems to go out of style. Sure, the food's expensive, the portions smallish and the din annoying, but food fans keep coming back for such delights as succulent barbecue baby pork ribs, crispy Cantonese duck, classic Chinese chicken salad and, of course, the ultimate indulgence, the crème brûlée trio.

## Venice & Marina del Rey — Map pp72–3

### BUDGET

**Abbot's Pizza** (☎ 310-396-7334; 1407 Abbot Kinney Blvd, Venice; slices $2.50-3, pizzas $12.50-20) Join the leagues of surfers, students and urbanites at this little walk-in joint for its addictive bagel-crust pizzas. Go classic with pepperoni and sausage or gourmet with wild mushroom, barbecue chicken or olive pesto.

**Pam's Place** (☎ 310-301-8002; 636 S Venice Blvd, Venice; mains $9-20; closed lunch Sun; P) This popular neighborhood Thai eatery is as comfortable as a hug from an old friend. Against a backdrop of bucolic murals the kitchen churns out tastebud-tempting pad Thai, flaming chicken or beef, and intricately spiced curries. Service is friendly and won't rush you.

### MID-RANGE

**Hal's Bar & Grill** (☎ 310-396-3105; 1349 Abbot Kinney Blvd, Venice; mains lunch $8-14, dinner $13-30; brunch Sat & Sun, lunch Mon-Fri, dinner daily, bar to 2am; P) The name may evoke brass and wood, but Hal's dining room is all cool industrial loft brightened by revolving art from local artists such as Laddie John Dill. The menu, put together from farm-fresh ingredients, changes seasonally but always features such reliable classics as grilled chicken, Caesar salad and ice-cream sundaes. Free jazz on Sunday and Monday.

**Piccolo Cipriani** (☎ 310-314-3222; 5 Dudley Ave, Venice; mains $10-14; P) The decor of this teensy spot, mere steps from the sand, pays homage to the 'real' Venice with its vintage black-and-white photos of the canal city and Carnevale masks. The gracious proprietors too hail straight from Italy and, after doing stints at prestigious LA restaurants, they now shower patrons with handmade pastas, flavor-packed meats and delightful desserts. *Perfetto!*

**Antica Pizzeria** (☎ 310-577-8182; Villa Marina Marketplace, 13455 Maxella Ave, Marina del Rey; pizzas $8.50-11; P) As the founder of the North American chapter of the Associazione Vera Pizza Napoletana, owner-chef Peppe Miele knows a thing or two about making the perfect pizza. If the mall setting doesn't transport you to the Boot, his margherita with its wafer-thin crust and fresh tomato topping just might.

**Rose Café** (☎ 310-399-0711; 220 Rose Ave, Venice; mains $9-12; 7am-5:30pm; P) This popular Euro-feel place often crawls with laptop-toting writers, chatty artists and beefcakes from the nearby Gold's Gym. Dig into fresh salads, light pastas or seafood in the restaurant's hedge-framed outdoor dining room, or nibble on yummy baked goods in the more casual café section. Afterwards browse for unique knickknacks in the little gift shop.

**Sidewalk Café** (☎ 310-399-5547; 1401 Ocean Front Walk, Venice; mains $9-14; 8am-11pm) This tried-and-true spot is hands-down the most popular place to grab a bite along the Venice Boardwalk. The menu plays it safe with burgers, salads, sandwiches and other feel-good food, but it's all delicious and served in huge, satisfying portions. There's even free entertainment provided by the steady stream of bizarre humanity parading by. It's all but dead after dark.

**Cheesecake Factory** (☎ 310-306-3344; 4142 Via Marina, Marina del Rey; mains $6-27; P) The nicest branch of this small chain snuggles into a placid cove right on the harbor. On balmy nights, the wait for an outdoor table is well worth it, but no matter where you sit you'll find plenty of all-American favorites great for lining the stomach. Top it all off with a slice of their famous cheesecake. They also do a popular Sunday brunch. The original branch is in **Beverly Hills** (Map pp70-1; ☎ 310-278-7270; 364 N Beverly Dr).

### TOP END

**Joe's** (☎ 310-399-5811; 1023 Abbot Kinney Blvd, Venice; mains lunch $10-14, dinner $21-26, 4- or 5-course menus $50-60; closed Mon; P) Like a good wine, this stylish but charmingly unpretentious restaurant only seems to get better with age. Owner-chef Joe Miller consistently serves up great and gimmick-free Cal-French food. The menu changes frequently but if halibut with pink turnip puree or warm calamari salad are featured, go for it. The choicest tables are out on the patio with its waterfall fountain.

For Chaya Brasserie see p154.

## South Bay Beaches                        Map p74
### BUDGET
**Uncle Bill's Pancake House** ( ☎ 310-545-5177; 1305 N Highland Ave, Manhattan Beach; mains $3-7.50; ☺ closes at 2pm) Despite the name, this South Bay breakfast legend serves much more than just pancakes (although they're great; try the macadamia nut version). Grab a table on the ocean-view patio, then ponder whether to go for classic eggs and bacon or the Istanbul omelette (made with turkey – get it?).

**El Sombrero** ( ☎ 310-374-1366; 1005 N Manhattan Ave, Manhattan Beach; mains $3-9.50) This longtime locals' favorite with its comfy booths is a great place for a Mexican food fix. The burritos, tacos and enchiladas may not give you fits of euphoria, but they'll still put your belly into a state of happiness.

**Green Temple** ( ☎ 310-944-4525; 1700 S Catalina Ave, Redondo Beach; mains $5-10; ☺ closed Mon) The decor at this meat-free café is funky Asian dreamscape, but the food is considerably more down-to-earth. Good choices include the three-bean soup and the savory steamers, a successful marriage of tofu or tempeh with rice and veggies perfumed by a mysterious, but delicious, sauce.

**Spot** ( ☎ 310-376-2355; 110 2nd St, Hermosa Beach; mains $6-11) This stalwart of healthy eating has been offering topflight vegan and vegetarian food in a laid-back, unpretentious setting for a quarter century. The menu ranges from standards such as veggie burgers and salads to the more fanciful mushroom-walnut loaf. Portions are big, prices are not.

In Hermosa Beach, a time-honored way to start the day is with pancakes, waffles or omelettes from the **Backburner Cafe** ( ☎ 310-372-6973; 87 14th St, Hermosa Beach) mains $2.25-7.25; ☺ closes around 2pm) or **Beach Hut No 2** ( ☎ 310-376-4252; 1342 Hermosa Ave, Hermosa Beach; mains $3-6; ☺ closes around 2pm).

### MID-RANGE
**Chez Mélange** ( ☎ 310-540-1222; 1716 S Pacific Coast Hwy, Redondo Beach; mains lunch $9-16, dinner $10-30; ☺ breakfast & lunch Mon-Fri, brunch Sat & Sun, dinner v; (P) ) Even picky eaters should be pleased the vast and daily-changing menu at popular brasserie. The kitchen staff

gets most things right, although the Cajun meat loaf and the Rabbit Three Ways get especially high marks from loyal patrons. If you like the food, learn how to make it at the attached cooking school (p52).

**Gina Lee's Bistro** ( ☎ 310-375-4462; Riviera Plaza, 211 Palos Verdes Blvd, Redondo Beach; mains $8-21; ☺ dinner Tue-Sun; (P) ) The strip-mall location may not dazzle but Gina's imaginative Asian fusion fare does. Dishes borrow from the flavors of China, Japan and Korea but are prepared California-style with little fat, superfresh ingredients and robust flavors. This results in plump wontons, juicy *ponzu* catfish, spinach salad dressed in coconut vinaigrette and other intriguing palate pleasers.

**Zazou** ( ☎ 310-540-4884; 1810 S Catalina Ave, Redondo Beach; mains lunch $9-15, dinner $12-24; ☺ lunch Tue-Sat, dinner daily; (P) ) This humming place is the darling of South Bay foodies who flock here for creative meals inspired by several countries hemming the Mediterranean. The accent is on fresh fish, seafood and meats, which turn up in such dishes as lamb osso buco, seafood risotto and roast duck. On a balmy night, the patio tables are the most desirable.

**Bluewater Grill** ( ☎ 310-318-3474; King Harbor Marina, 665 N Harbor Dr, Redondo Beach; mains $11-26; (P) ) Dock-fresh fish and seafood are the stars of this stylish restaurant with front-row views of yachts bobbing gently in the harbor. The menu even reveals the origin of the finny treats (Alaskan halibut, Fijian ahi, Costa Rican mahimahi). From the chowder to the fish and chips and mesquite-grilled sea bass, it's all excellent. It also serves brunch on Sunday.

**Mamma D's** ( ☎ 310-456-1492; 1125 N Manhattan Ave, Manhattan Beach Blvd; mains lunch $5-7, dinner $8.50-16) This neighborhood Italian fits like a well-worn shoe and is much liked for its friendly service, build-your-own pastas and crunchy thin-crust pizzas. Expect a wait.

For Versailles see p158.

### TOP END
**Christine** (Map pp62-3; ☎ 310-373-1952; Hillside Village, 24530 Hawthorne Blvd, Torrance; mains lunch $10-15, dinner $15-26; ☺ lunch Mon-Fri, dinner daily; (P) ) The flavors of Italy, France and the Far East are expertly woven together at this hospitable neighborhood restaurant, a top pick in the South Bay. The chef gets especially creative with the appetizer menu, which may include lobster macaroni with cognac-chive cream sauce or the crayfish and avocado tower.

## San Pedro & Long Beach   Map pp62–3

### BUDGET

**Taco Surf** ( ☎ 562-434-8646; 5316 E 2nd St, Long Beach; dishes $5-12) This is a spit-and-sawdust cantina seemingly airlifted straight from Baja. Seating is inside in oversized wooden booths or on the sidewalk patio. If you don't like crowds, avoid happy hour (2pm to 5pm Monday to Friday) with its $1 tacos and beers.

**Egg Heaven** ( ☎ 562-433-9277; 4358 E 4th St, Long Beach; mains $4-9; ☽ breakfast & lunch) This old-fashioned diner in Belmont Heights does scrumptious breakfasts and lunches

### MID-RANGE

**Alegria** ( ☎ 562-436-3388; 115 Pine Ave, Long Beach; tapas $6-11, mains $15-20; P ) The trippy, Technicolor mosaic floor, an eccentric art nouveau bar and trompe l'oeil murals form an appropriately spirited backdrop to Alegria's fresh and vivid Latino cuisine. The tapas menu is great for grazers and the paella a feast for both eyes and stomach. There's even live flamenco on some nights.

**Belmont Brewing Company** ( ☎ 562-433-3891; 25 39th Pl, Belmont Shore; mains $10-20) This bustling brewpub has a great outdoor deck overlooking the Belmont Pier (perfect for watching sunsets), fresh and handcrafted brews, and a well-priced menu that goes far beyond pub grub. Make a meal of the appetizers or go haute with such dishes as seafood Leo, a fishy bonanza packaged in filo dough.

**Christy's** (Map pp62-3; ☎ 562-433-7133; 3937 E Broadway, Long Beach; mains lunch $10-20, dinner $18-30; ☽ lunch Mon-Fri, dinner daily; P ) With its four intimately lit rooms, this cozy ristorante is not a bad place for a languid dinner for two. Owned by Christy Bono, daughter of the late Sonny Bono, it serves solid Italian fare, including better-than-average salads and a great marinated veal chop coupled with fresh porcini mushrooms. Great wine list, too.

### TOP END

**Sir Winston's** ( ☎ 562-435-3511; Queen Mary, 1126 Queen Mary's Hwy, Long Beach; mains $22-38; ☽ dinner; P ) This elegant dining room with its complexion-friendly lighting time-warps you back to the days when the *Queen* was the vessel of choice of the rich and royalty. The chef pairs first-rate ingredients and classic cooking techniques into such menu headliners as prime beef tenderloin and lobster crab cakes. Dress nicely. Reservations required.

**Papadakis Taverna** ( ☎ 310-548-1186; 301 W 6th St, San Pedro; mains $16-25; ☽ dinner; P ) The gods have been smiling upon this earthy Greek restaurant for over three decades. Tables fill up nightly with patrons hankering for moussaka, spanakopita (spinach-stuffed filo pastries), succulent lamb and fragrant fowl. Owners Tom and John are usually on hand to meet, greet and seat old hands and newcomers. Belly dancing, glass-smashing and other riotous rituals are just part of the fun.

## Downtown Los Angeles & Around   Map pp64–5

### BUDGET

**Angélique Cafe** ( ☎ 213-623-8698; 840 S Spring St; dishes $6-10; ☽ 7am-4pm Mon-Sat) After you've finished browsing the Fashion District, lug your bags to this charming French café to refuel on crispy salads, bulging sandwiches and classic bistro fare. Owner-chef Bruno's pâtés, sold here for a few dollars per pound, pop up at premium prices in swank restaurants around town.

**Philippe the Original** ( ☎ 213-628-3781; 1001 N Alameda St; sandwiches $5; ☽ 6am-10pm) From cops to couples, they all flock to this legendary 'home of the French dip sandwich' with a pedigree going back to 1908. Do as millions have done before you and order a crusty roll filled with pork, lamb, turkey, beef or ham, pair it with a side of coleslaw or potato salad and hunker down at the long tables parked on the sawdust-covered floor. Coffee is just 9¢ (and that's no misprint). Cash only.

**Señor Fish** ( ☎ 213-625-0566; 422 E 1st St; mains $5.50-12.50; ☽ 8am-9pm) Treat your taste buds to tasty scallop burritos, ceviche, garlic shrimp or other Mexican-style seafood dishes served at this unassuming Little Tokyo eatery.

**La Luz del Día** ( ☎ 213-628-7495; 1 Olvera St; dishes $3-9; ☽ Tue-Sun) At lunchtime, there's always a line snaking out onto the plaza at this self-service venue in the historic El Pueblo. The habit-forming *carnitas* are the biggest lure, but adventurous eaters might find the spunky *nopales* (cactus) salad to their liking. Cash only.

**Papa Cristo's** ( ☎ 323-737-2970; 2771 W Pico Blvd, Koreatown; mains $5-10; ☽ 9am-8pm Tue-Sat, 9am-4pm Sun) You'll kick up your heels like Zorba himself after a meal of Greek eats at this frenzied bistro in the shadow of St Sophia Cathedral. The rack of lamb is a steal at $10 and the sizzling feta or grilled octopus will make your taste buds dance. At 6:30pm on Thursday nights it's 'big fat family dinners' ($19) when tables bend with nibbles and belly dancers tickle patrons' fancy.

**Tamales Liliana's** (off Map pp64-5; ☎ 323-780-0829; 3448 E 1st St, East LA; dishes $2-6; ☷ 9am-9pm Mon-Fri, 7am-9pm Sat & Sun) Liliana's makes tamales the way they ought to be: light, yet tight and generously stuffed with pork, chicken or beef drenched in wondrous sauces. We also like the *huevos divorciados*, a cheeky spin on *huevos rancheros* where rice and beans separate the eggs.

**Grand Central Market** (☎ 213-624-2378; 317 S Broadway; ☷ 9am-6pm; meals $2-7; **P**) This historic indoor market is perfect for sopping up Downtown's mélange of ethnicities, languages and cuisines. Just wander along the aisles and pick a place that looks good or head straight to **Maria's Pescado Frito** (central aisle) for great fish tacos and ceviche tostadas; **Gaucho** (facing Broadway) for lobster empanadas and bulging sandwiches; or **China Café** (upper level, near Hill St) for sinus-clearing chicken soup or heaping plates of chow mein.

### MID-RANGE

**Yang Chow** (☎ 213-625-0811; 819 N Broadway; mains $8-15; **P**) Don't let the ugly storefront exterior be a turnoff to entering this popular Chinatown dining parlor. Regulars drool over the 'slippery shrimp' (actually a mountain of breaded sweet and slightly spicy shrimp), but other dishes are just as convincing. The dried sautéed string beans with pork and the platters of toothsome pan-fried noodles are both good choices.

**Pete's Café & Bar** (☎ 213-617-1000; 400 S Main St; mains lunch $9-17, dinner $10-24; ☷ lunch Mon-Fri, dinner daily; **P**) In a handsomely restored historic building, Pete's is a lofty lunchtime hot spot for hip office folk, City Hall politicos and *Los Angeles Times* journos. The menu is modern American feel-good food, including inventive salads, sandwiches and a mean burger doused in fontina and tomato aioli. After dark, it has more of bar vibe, but food's served until at least midnight.

**Langer's Delicatessen** (☎ 213-483-8050; 704 S Alvarado St, Koreatown; pastrami sandwich $9, mains $8-20; ☷ 8am-4pm Mon-Sat) Generations of smoked-meat lovers have flocked to this iconic Jewish deli (in business since 1947) right next to spruced up but still dodgy MacArthur Park

(p114) for some of the best pastrami in town. If you don't want to bother with parking, you can call your order in, pull up to the curb and have it brought to your car. The Metro Red Line subway stop is right outside.

**McCormick & Schmick's** (☎ 213-629-1929; 4th fl, 633 W 5th St; mains $6-26; ☷ lunch Mon-Fri, dinner daily; **P**) Ultrafresh fish prepared in umpteen ways and served in an elegant and traditional setting at reasonable prices – no wonder this place gets a steady crowd. Its twice-daily happy hours are among the best in town (p168). Access is via the Bunker Hill Steps. Also in **Beverly Hills** (Map pp70-1; ☎ 310-859-0434; Two Rodeo Dr).

**Oomasa** (☎ 213-623-9048; 100 Japanese Village Plaza; mains lunch $9-13, dinner $10-20; ☷ closed Tue) The antithesis of trendy, this Little Tokyo restaurant with its giant horseshoe-shaped bar is a haven for sushi purists. From dark-red tuna to marbled salmon, it's all super-fresh, expertly cut, affordably priced and best enjoyed while snuggled into one of the old-timey booths.

**Empress Pavilion** (☎ 213-617-9898; 3rd fl, Bamboo Plaza, 988 N Hill St; dim sum per plate $2-5, dinner $20-25; ☷ dim sum & lunch 9am-3pm, dinner 3-10pm; **P**) Other Chinatown places do dim sum, but regulars swear by this Hong Kong–style banquet hall with seating for a small village (500 people, to be exact). Translucent dumplings, wontons, pot stickers, barbecued pork and other delicacies just fly off the carts wheeled right to your table by a small army of servers.

**Café Metropol** (☎ 213-613-1537; 923 E 3rd St; mains $7-15; ☷ 8am-10pm Mon-Sat; **P**) You'll have to get off the beaten path to track down this Euro-flavored Arts District bistro, but the gourmet sandwiches, organic salads and yummy pizzas make the trip well worth your while. Buzziest at lunchtime, it's an airy space of industrial elegance where bold canvases adorn the brick walls.

**Ciudad** (☎ 213-486-5171; 445 S Figueroa St; mains lunch $9-19, dinner $15-26; ☷ lunch Mon-Fri, dinner daily; **P**) Bold Latin fare has been the recipe for success at this Downtown outpost of TV chefs Susan Feniger and Mary Sue Milliken. The spirited decor is perfect for such perky dishes as Peruvian ceviche and wild mushroom empanadas. Great desserts and even better caipirinhas.

**Taylor's Steak House** (☎ 213-382-8449; 3361 W 8th St; mains $13-27; ☷ lunch Mon-Fri, dinner daily; **P**) This Raymond Chandler–esque chophouse in Koreatown was retro long before retro became hip. Settle into a shiny red faux-leather booth and start things off healthily with a signature Molly salad (named for a longtime waitress). Then surrender helplessly to your inner carnivore with big, yummy cuts costing less than a plate of pasta at fancier places. Pure bliss.

**Soot Bull Jeep** ( ☎ 213-387-3865; 3136 W 8th St, Koreatown; mains $13-15; P ) Everyone enjoys barbecue but have you ever had yours *bulgogi*-style? You will at this Koreatown cauldron where smoke shrouds diners as they grill slabs of marinated beef, pork or other meats on coal-fired braziers set into each table. It's exotic, chaotic and lots of fun. Just don't count on wearing the same clothes the following day.

**La Serenata de Garibaldi** ( ☎ 323-265-2887; 1842 E 1st St, East LA; breakfast $7-9, mains lunch $9-15, dinner $10-22; ☺ breakfast Sat & Sun, lunch & dinner daily; P ) Occupying a pretty hacienda close to Mariachi Plaza, this sophisticated restaurant puts the accent on fresh fish and giant shrimp paired with tantalizing sauces. Try the pungent green cilantro or the mellow mushroom in white wine. The menu also features a surprising number of meatless choices. The Westside spin-offs in **Santa Monica** (Map pp72-3; ☎ 310-656-7017; 1416 4th St) and near **Westwood** (off Map pp70-1; ☎ 310-441-9667; 10924 W Pico Blvd) are good but lack the authenticity of the flagship.

**Teresitas** ( ☎ 323-266-6045; 3826 E 1st St, East LA; mains $6-13; ☺ 10am-8pm Tue-Thu, 10am-4pm Fri, 8am-9pm Sat, 8am-5pm Sun) Teresa Campos Hernandez has been serving up her unique brand of delicious *comida* (food) to cops, council members and locals for over two decades. This is Mexican home-cooking at its finest: the richly flavored *albóndigas* soup with golf-ball-sized meat balls, refreshing *nopales* (prickly pear cactus) salad and pork ribs smothered in soulful chili sauce all have their aficionados.

### TOP END

**Patina** ( ☎ 213-972-3331; 141 S Grand Ave; mains lunch $18-30, dinner $33-40; ☺ lunch Mon-Fri, dinner daily; P ) The restaurant empire of culinary wunderkind Joachim Splichal has been growing steadily, but Patina, now in stunning new digs at the Walt Disney Concert Hall, remains his flagship. Tantalize your tongue with such unique compositions as blue-

crab mango cannelloni or Peking duck with caramelized Belgian endives. For the ultimate splurge, order the chef's menu (lunch/dinner $50/100).

**R-23** ( ☎ 213-687-7178; 923 E 2nd St; mains lunch $10-15, dinner $40-60; ☺ lunch Mon-Fri, dinner daily; P ) R-23 is a fantasy come true for serious sushi aficionados. Not even the bold art and bizarre Frank Gehry–designed corrugated-paper chairs can distract from the exquisite and ultrafresh piscine treats prepared by a team of sushi masters who aren't chintzy with the smiles – or the cuts. The green-tea cheesecake makes for a fitting finish.

**Noé** ( ☎ 213-356-4100; 251 S Olive St; mains $10-30, 6-/9-course tasting menu $65/95; ☺ dinner; P ) Master chef Robert Gadsby, a longtime fixture in LA's top kitchens, cooks up a storm at this stylish outpost inside the Omni Los Angeles Hotel (p149). His restless palate results in what he calls 'progressive American' cuisine, which translates into such dishes as seared yellow fin tuna, duck with parsnip puree and periwinkle chowder. Reservations required.

**Water Grill** ( ☎ 213-891-0900; 544 S Grand Ave; mains $25-40, ☺ lunch Mon-Fri, dinner daily; P ) Only the brisk ocean breeze is missing from this first-rate seafood restaurant. Start with the 'fruits of the sea platter' – bonanza of oysters, clams, crab, shrimp and lobster ($20) – then move on to such piscatorial delights as ahi tuna tartare or dock-fresh Alaskan halibut. Try to leave room for the signature chocolate bread pudding.

**Nick & Stef's Steakhouse** ( ☎ 213-680-0330; 330 S Hope St; mains lunch $12-20, dinner $19-32; ☺ lunch Mon-Fri, dinner daily; P ) You'll have a fine time sending your cholesterol count through the roof with the flavorful, melt-in-your-mouth meats served in this *très moderne* dining shrine. And, damn the torpedoes, finish with the lemon meringue pie.

Also recommended:

**Cicada** ( ☎ 213-488-9488; 617 S Olive St; mains $14-34; ☺ lunch Mon-Fri, dinner Mon-Sat; P ) Northern Italian fare in the sumptuous art deco Oviatt Building (p110).

**Café Pinot** ( ☎ 213-239-6500; 700 W 5th St; mains lunch $14-23, dinner $17-31; ☺ lunch Mon-Fri, dinner daily; P ) Joachim Splichal outpost does sophisticated Cal-French; pretty patio facing tiny Maguire Gardens (p109).

### Exposition Park & South Central

**Phillip's Barbecue** (Map pp60-1; ☎ 323-292-7613; 4307 Leimert Blvd, Leimert Park Village, South Central; meals $5-12; P ) Banish any worries about love handles or clogged arteries before coming to this smoky and soulful hole-in-the-wall on the edge of Leimert Park Village. The pork and beef ribs are fall-off-the-bone tender, the sausage nicely crispy and the sauce addictive. The latter comes with various degrees of heat, so go easy unless you're auditioning as a fire-eater. Finish up with the unusual 7-Up cake. Cash only.

**Chichen Itza** (off Map pp64-5; ☎ 213-741-1075; 3655 S Grand Ave; dishes $5-10; 🕑 6:30am-8:30pm) Part of the Mercado La Paloma, an old warehouse turned Mexican marketplace and community center, this little eatery near Exposition Park serves some of LA's best and most authentic food from Mexico's Yucatán peninsula. Try such flavor bombs as the intriguingly spiced *cochinita pibil* (pork steamed in banana leaves) or crispy *panuchos* (deep-fried stuffed tortillas).

## San Fernando Valley
### BUDGET
**Bob's Big Boy** (Map p75; ☎ 818-843-9334; 4211 Riverside Dr, Burbank; meals $6-9; 🕑 24hr; P ) For a genuine slice of Americana (or apple pie, for that matter), swing by this landmark 1950s coffee shop featured in such movies as *Heat* and *Austin Powers: The Spy Who Shagged Me*. On Friday and Sunday nights, the car-hop service (alas without the roller skates) lets you catch that *American Graffiti* vibe. Friday is classic-car night. Breakfast is served anytime.

**Zankou Chicken** (off Map p75; ☎ 626-405-1502; 1296 E Colorado St, Glendale; dishes $2.40-7.50; 🕑 10am-midnight; P ) Even Armenian-food virgins are likely to become instant fans of Zankou's lip-smacking rotisserie chicken with its perfect golden tan. Slather on some of the vampire-repelling garlic sauce and you've tasted a bit of heaven. Half a bird costs just $6 and comes with creamy hummus, salad and pita bread. Cash only. Also in eastern **Hollywood** (Map pp66-7; ☎ 323-655-7845; 5065 W Sunset Blvd).

For some of the best Texas-style barbecue this side of Dallas, head to **Dr Hogly Wogly's Tyler Texas Bar-B-Que** (Map pp60-1; ☎ 818-780-6701; 8136 N Sepulveda Blvd, Van Nuys).

For Carousel see p152.

### MID-RANGE & TOP END
**Minibar** (Map p75; ☎ 323-882-6965; 3413 Cahuenga Blvd W, Universal City; plates $5-13; 🕑 dinner; P ) Not far from Universal Studios, this fun restaurant-lounge with back-to-the-future decor churns out small plates with big flavor. Join the plugged-in crowd feasting on a global piñata of flavors, from Thai ceviche to salmon-brie strudel to Moroccan-spiced chicken wings.

**Mandaloun** (off Map p75; ☎ 818-507-1900; 141 S Maryland St, Glendale; mains $10-22; P ) Everything at this upscale Lebanese restaurant happens on a grand scale. Owner Ara Kalfayan greets you with a *big* smile, seats you in a *big* dining room and brings you a *big* menu. Before long, you're devouring *big* portions of sublime kebabs, lamb chops, tabouli and other tasty fare. It has belly dancing on weekends and water pipes on the patio.

**Ca' del Sole** (Map p75; ☎ 818-985-4669; 4100 Cahuenga Blvd, North Hollywood; mains $10-20; 🕑 lunch Sun-Fri, dinner daily; P ) Near Universal Studios, the 'house of the sun' is one of the Valley's most attractive restaurants, a veritable slice of Venice complete with fireplaces and romantic patio. Much of the chef's imagination has gone into the tantalizing antipasto menu, which may feature pan-roasted quail, homemade pork-and-fennel sausage, or octopus salad.

**Saddle Peak Lodge** (Map p60-1; ☎ 818-222-3888; 419 Cold Canyon Rd, Calabasas; brunch $14-17, dinner mains $25-38; 🕑 brunch Sun, dinner Wed-Sun; P ) Tucked into the Santa Monica Mountains, this award-winner may be a bit remote, but deep-pocketed meat lovers especially will find the inspired menu worth the drive. As rustic as a Colorado mountain lodge, this rural oasis serves up elk, venison, buffalo and other game in a setting watched over by mounted versions of the same. Reservations are recommended, dress smart.

## Pasadena & San Gabriel Valley
Map p76
### BUDGET
**Europane** ( ☎ 626-577-1828; 950 E Colorado Blvd; pastries, sandwiches $6-8; 🕑 7am-5:30pm Mon-Sat, 7am-2pm Sun) Crispy croissants, crunchy biscotti and sizable sandwiches with interesting fillings are the bread-and-butter of this delightful café-bakery. They make great stuff to take out for a picnic or stay put to mingle with moms, students and writers. Cash only.

**Marston's** ( ☎ 626-796-2459; 151 E Walnut Ave; mains breakfast & lunch $4-10, dinner $15-25; 🕑 breakfast & lunch Tue-Sat, dinner Wed-Sat; P ) Marston's serves lunch and dinner, but it's the prospect of the scrumptious all-American breakfasts that helps us get out of bed. But no matter when you get there, this diminutive cottage with its sunny porch is likely packed to the rafters.

## MID-RANGE

**Bar Celona** ( ☎ 626-405-1000; 46 E Colorado Blvd; tapas $4-7, mains lunch $5-14, dinner $16-23; **P** ) The Rioja-tinted walls offer a fiery backdrop for the taste-bud teasers streaming from the kitchen at this classy newcomer. Pick your way around the tapas menu or dig into big platters of paella or slow-cooked boneless short ribs. Either way, your belly will think it's fiesta time.

**Saladang Song** ( ☎ 626-793-5200; 383 S Fair Oaks Ave; mains $6-17; ☯ 6:30am-10pm) Soaring concrete walls with artsy, cutout steel insets hem in the outdoor dining room of this modern Thai temple. Even simple curries become extraordinary here, while the unusual breakfast soups offer a nice change from the eggs-and-bacon routine. Some people prefer the original Saladang next door, which has a more traditional menu.

**Burger Continental** ( ☎ 626-792-6634; 535 S Lake Ave; breakfast/lunch buffet $5/8, all-you-can-eat Sunday brunch $14, dishes $5-15; ☯ 7am-11pm; **P** ) What sounds like a patty-and-bun joint is in reality Pasadena's most beloved Middle Eastern nosh spot. Nibble on classic hummus, dig into sizzling kebab dinners or go adventurous with the Moon of Tunis platter (chicken, gyros and shrimp in filo). Live bands and belly dancers provide candy for ears and eyes. Great patio.

**Mission 261** ( ☎ 626-588-1666; 261 S Mission Dr, San Gabriel; dim sum each $2-7; ☯ dim sum 10:30am-3pm Mon-Fri, 9am-3pm Sat & Sun, dinner daily; **P** ) There's no shortage of people who think that Mission 261 is the best Chinese restaurant in

Southern California. It's certainly one of the biggest, occupying a warren of banquet rooms inside a century-old adobe near the San Gabriel Mission (p127). Its dim sum is a veritable holy grail of dumplings, pot stickers and other delicacies, many of them fashioned into artistic shapes. Order by filling out a form as you would in a sushi restaurant rather than selecting from passing carts.

**Yujean Kang's** ( ☎ 626-585-0855; 67 N Raymond Ave; mains $8-18; **P** ) Don't expect kung pao or chow mein at this popular Chinese outpost where the eponymous chef constantly pushes the culinary envelope with unusual flavor pairings. Recommended dishes include Chinese polenta with plump shrimp and mushrooms, hearty wonton soup, and prawns teamed with fava beans. The wine list is tops.

**Twin Palms** ( ☎ 626-577-2567; 101 W Green St; mains brunch $7-16, lunch $8-15, dinner $11-28; ☯ brunch Sun, lunch Mon-Sat, dinner daily) This humming eatery is easy to spot thanks to the namesake pair of palms towering above its huge canopied patio. The kitchen staff serves up delicious California cuisine, with fish, lean meats and pasta all making appearances. On weekends the place morphs into a dance club after 10pm. The daily happy hour and $9 express lunches are additional assets.

**Madre's** ( ☎ 626-744-0900; 897 Granite Dr; mains $10-28; ☯ closed Mon; **P** ) J Lo's joint is a shabby-chic Latin restaurant filled with flowers, chandeliers, etched mirrors and lacy tablecloths. The food blends robust Cuban and Puerto Rican classics such as empanadas, *ropa vieja* (slow-cooked, spicy beef) and *churrasco* (flank steak). Prices are high, portions large and the mojitos magic.

For Café Bizou see p160.

---

### THE AUTHOR'S CHOICE

**Nonya** (Map p76; ☎ 626-583-8398; 61 N Raymond Ave; mains lunch $7-10, dinner $15-28; ☯ lunch Sun-Fri, dinner daily; **P** ) If you've never had Peranakan food (and who has?), this is the place to try it. Peranakans are Singaporeans descended from Chinese settlers and the local Malays going back as far as the 15th century. The intriguing cuisine fuses flavors, ingredients and cooking techniques from both cultures into dishes so perky they might get you off your Prozac. Exotic ingredients such as tamarind, sambal and galangal find their destiny in such dishes as *ayam limau parut* (tamarind curry chicken) and *otak-otak* (sole in spicy coconut sauce). It's all beautifully presented in an elegant dining room with the sophistication of a Chinese mansion and the tranquility of a tea house. For a teaser, try lunch or the appetizers offered during happy hour (4pm to 7pm Monday to Friday).

**LOS ANGELES**

## TOP END

**Parkway Grill** ( ☎ 626-795-1001; 510 S Arroyo Parkway; mains lunch $9-20, dinner $19-32; ☯ lunch Mon-Fri, dinner daily; Ⓟ ) This is a Pasadena classic where the chef grows his own herbs and vegetables and then turns them into glorious Cal cuisine. Get an order of flatbread sprinkled with blue cheese, pears and walnuts while pondering the virtues of the mesquite-grilled filet mignon over the slow-roasted Long Island duck or the pan-seared lobster. Vegetarian choices, alas, are limited.

**Xiomara** ( ☎ 626-796-2520; 69 N Raymond Ave; mains lunch $8-16, dinner $17-29; ☯ lunch Mon-Fri, dinner daily; Ⓟ ) The restrained decor is the perfect foil for the flavor explosions arriving on your plate at this humming Nuevo Latino bistro. It's easy to dream of faraway places while nursing a signature mojito (here called Mambo's), but the food – spiced with attitude – will quickly give you a reality check. The poblano risotto is a great meatless choice. Also near **Hollywood** (Map pp68-9; ☎ 323-461-0601; 6101 Melrose Ave).

## DRINKING

LA is prime sipping territory, whether your taste runs toward Budweiser or three-olive martinis. From funky beachside watering holes to elegant hotel bars and historic dives where Bogie and Bacall used to knock 'em back, you're rarely far from your favorite libation. The cocktail boom has spawned a new generation of stylish places, mostly in a lounge style, often with DJs at the decks. Hollywood Blvd and the Sunset Strip are classic bar-hopping grounds, but there's plenty of good drinking going on in the beach cities, Downtown and Koreatown as well.

## Hollywood, Los Feliz & Silver Lake    Map pp66-7

**Formosa Cafe** ( ☎ 323-850-9050; 7156 Santa Monica Blvd, Hollywood) The one-time watering hole of Bogart, Monroe and Gable is a cool place to sop up some Hollywood nostalgia along with your cocktail. Mai tais and martinis are beverages of choice. Smoking patio.

**4100 Bar** ( ☎ 323-666-4460; 4100 W Sunset Blvd, Silver Lake) A serene Buddha looks out over a crowd that's unpretentious, omnisexual and artsy; in short, classic Silver Lake. The bartenders have been around the block once or twice.

**Good Luck Bar** ( ☎ 323-666-3524; 1514 Hillhurst Ave, Los Feliz) The clientele is cool, the jukebox loud and the drinks seductively strong at this cultish watering hole decked out in Chinese opium den–inspired carmine red. Yee Mee Loo Blue and a Chinese herb-based whisky are popular choices.

**Tiki Ti** ( ☎ 323-669-9381; 4427 W Sunset Blvd, Silver Lake) This garage-sized tropical tavern packs in showbiz folks from neighboring KCET TV station, blue-collar types and local scenesters for sweet and wickedly strong drinks

---

## TOP FIVE HAPPY HOURS

■ **Border Grill** (p159; ☯ 4-7pm Mon-Fri, after 10pm Fri & Sat, 11:30am-4pm Sun) Knock back $3 margaritas or mojitos while staying stable with such 'border bites' as plantain empanadas, green-corn tamales and poblano quesadilla, also $3 each.

■ **Ciudad** (p164; ☯ 3-7pm Mon-Fri) You'll be happy in no time with the $4 drinks and *cuchifritos* (appetizers) served in the bar of this spunky Latin restaurant. The mojitos are great but for a change try a piscorita made with potent Peruvian schnapps.

■ **McCormick & Schmick's** (p164; ☯ 3:30-7pm & 9-11pm Mon-Thu, 3-11pm Fri) This serial fish house keeps you happy not once but twice daily. Drinks are full price but such belly-fillers as fish tacos, teriyaki beef skewers and the incredible cheeseburger are just $1.95 each.

■ **Tengu** (Map pp70-1; ☎ 310-209-0071; 10853 Lindbrook Dr, Westwood; ☯ 5:30-7:30pm daily) This trendy spot serves great sushi and innovative appetizers whose normally stratospheric price tag is cut in half during the daily happy hour in the bar.

■ **Toppers** (Map pp72-3; ☎ 310-393-8080; 1111 2nd St, Santa Monica; ☯ 4-7pm daily) Enjoy knock-out sunset views, potent margaritas and a tasty selection of $2.50 appetizers at this penthouse bar atop the Radisson-Huntley Hotel. Getting up there aboard a glass-encased outside elevator is half the fun. Women: check out the restroom with its surreal 'toilet-with-a-view.'

(try a Rae's Mistake, named for the bar's founder). The under-the-sea decor is surreal. Credit cards are not accepted and – damn the torpedoes! – smoking is permitted.

**Yamashiro** ( ☎ 323-466-5125; 1999 N Sycamore Ave, Hollywood) Sure, this landmark Japanese palace is also a restaurant, but we think the stylish bar is simply the perfect spot for romantic tête-à-têtes, with the entire city glittering below.

**Frolic Room** ( ☎ 323-462-5890; 6245 Hollywood Blvd, Hollywood) This quintessential noir dive in the dark heart of Hollywood announces itself with a blazing neon sign. Drinks are cheap, and there's a cool jukebox and a wall of Hirschfeld-style caricatures of Hollywood legends.

**Bigfoot Lodge** ( ☎ 323-662-9227; 3172 Los Feliz Blvd, Los Feliz) Smokey the Bear presides over this laid-back log cabin, a cool spot to camp out for a drink or two (try the Girl Scout Cookie cocktail). The action heats up when there's live music or the DJ hits the decks.

**Three Clubs** ( ☎ 323-462-6441; 1123 N Vine St, Hollywood) Hard-to-spot drinking parlor with low-key vibe despite the velvet rope. It's between the gas station and the mini-mall on the northwest corner of Santa Monica Blvd and Vine St.

**Cat & Fiddle Pub** ( ☎ 323-468-3800; 6530 W Sunset Blvd, Hollywood) Order up a pint, grab an outdoor table in the fountain courtyard and enjoy Sunday twilight jazz radio broadcasts at this ever-popular pub, a favorite among expat Brits.

**Beauty Bar** ( ☎ 323-468-3800; 1638 N Cahuenga Blvd, Hollywood) At this pint-sized cocktail bar, decorated with hair-salon paraphernalia from the Kennedy era, you can sip your martini, get your nails done or peruse the hipster crowd while seated in swivel chairs beneath plastic hair dryers.

**Red Lion Tavern** (Map 000-03; ☎ 323-662-5337; 2366 Glendale Blvd, Silver Lake) Expat Germans, Downtown attorneys and Silver Lake socialites congregate here for quality German brews on tap (including Spaten, Dortmunder and Warsteiner) which are delivered to the beer garden by waitresses strapped into dirndls.

Also recommended:

**Daddy's** ( ☎ 323-463-7777; 1610 N Vine St, Hollywood) Pick-up joint with sensuously curved booths (and hips).

**Lava Lounge** ( ☎ 323-876-6612; 1533 N La Brea Ave, Hollywood) Tiki-themed bar, often with live music.

## West Hollywood & Mid-City
Map pp68–9

**Bar Marmont** ( ☎ 323-650-0575; 8171 Sunset Blvd, West Hollywood) Everything drops into place as smoothly as an ice cube at this chic boîte flanking the equally superlative Chateau Marmont. Despite its A-lister caché, the vibe here is surprisingly toned-down. Sip your cosmo at the bar underneath the butterfly ceiling or repair to the patio teeming with babes and beaus.

**El Coyote** ( ☎ 323-939-2255; 7312 Beverly Blvd, Mid-City) It's always fiesta time at this been-there-forever cantina whose stiff margaritas pretty much guarantee a cheap buzz. Service is swift and sweet but the food only so-so, although you may need some to keep your brain in balance.

**Sky Bar** ( ☎ 323-848-6025; 8440 W Sunset Blvd, West Hollywood) The poolside bar at the Mondrian (p141) has made a virtue out of snobbery. Unless you're exceptionally pretty, rich or are staying at the hotel, chances are relatively slim that you'll be imbibing expensive drinks (from plastic cups no less, because of the pool) with the ultimate in-crowd.

**El Carmen** ( ☎ 323-852-1552; 8138 W 3rd St, Mid-City) A pair of mounted bull heads and Lucha Libre (Mexican wrestling) masks create an over-the-top 'Tijuana North' look at LA's ultimate tequila tavern (over a hundred to choose from).

## Santa Monica & Venice
Map pp72–3

**Voda** ( ☎ 310-394-9774; 1449 2nd St, Santa Monica) Voda is chic, small and filled with flattering candlelight, making it a top date spot, especially if you can snag one of the leather booths. The house beverage – vodka – turns up in any number of fruit-infused drinks capably mixed by a crew of congenial barkeeps.

**Circle Bar** ( ☎ 310-450-0508; 2926 Main St, Santa Monica) This former dive bar has been reincarnated as a sizzling 'meet' market that's almost always packed to the rafters with fun-seeking, hormone-happy singles. Strong drinks, loud music and a seductive red-on-black decor further loosen inhibitions, although waiting in line to get past the bouncers can be a turnoff.

**Bar Copa** ( ☎ 310-452-2445; 2810 Main St, Santa Monica) Stylish without the pretense, this low-lit mellow lounge is a chill spot for a cocktail and a chat and attracts a suitably hip crowd.

Later at night, tables disappear to reveal an intimate dance floor where the music tends towards hip-hop, R&B and soul.

**Library Alehouse** ( ☎ 310-314-4855; 2911 Main St, Santa Monica) This no-nonsense taproom will have your head spinning with its 29 micro-brews and imports on tap, including Paulaner Hefeweizen straight from Munich and some bizarre brew called the Arrogant Bastard Ale. Keep it all down with the designer pub grub, all best consumed on the packed patio.

**Liquid Kitty** ( ☎ 310-473-3707; 11780 Pico Blvd, near Santa Monica) If you're in the mood for a purrrr-fect martini, stop by this laid-back lounge bathed in bat-cave darkness. There's live music on Sundays and a different DJ three nights a week. On Monday the karaoke crooners take over the microphone. Don't look for a name out front, just for the twinkling martini glass.

**Brig** ( ☎ 310-399-7537; 1515 Abbot Kinney Blvd, Venice) Old timers remember this place as a divey pool hall (the mural outside shows the one-time owners). Now it's an up-to-the-minute-design den vibrating with electronica and attracting an appealing mix of grown-up beach bums, arty professionals and professional artists.

**Cameo Bar** ( ☎ 310-451-8711; 1819 Ocean Ave, Santa Monica) This trendy bar off the lobby of the ultrachic Viceroy (p145) hotel brings the velvet rope routine to the ocean. The silver and green color scheme is stunning in a gaudy sort of way, but most of the beautiful people mingle poolside anyway, preferably in a semiprivate cabana.

If you like bars that ooze history, pop into **Chez Jay** ( ☎ 310-395-1741; 1657 Ocean Ave, Santa Monica) or the **Galley** ( ☎ 310-452-1934; 2442 Main St, Santa Monica), both low-key, classic watering holes with campy nautical themes.

## South Bay Beaches          Map p74

**705 Bar** ( ☎ 310-372-9705; 705 Pier Ave, Hermosa Beach) More sophisticated than most beachside watering holes, 705 combines a lounge, sushi bar (but eat elsewhere) and live music club under one roof.

**Aloha Sharkeez** ( ☎ 310-374-7823; 52 Pier Ave, Hermosa Beach) It's always fiesta time at this '*Animal House* by the sea,' where potent libations and an abundance of bare skin help fan the party. There's another one just like it in Manhattan Beach, called **Baja Sharkeez** ( ☎ 310-545-6563; 3801 Highland Ave).

**Side Door** ( ☎ 310-372-1684; 900 N Manhattan Ave, Manhattan Beach) What it lacks in size, this twee lounge makes up for in ambience, which is cool and mellow, yet pretense-free. The overstuffed couches are perfect for posing, martini in hand – if you can snag a space.

**Mangiamo** ( ☎ 310-318-3434; 128 Manhattan Beach Blvd, Manhattan Beach) The Italian fare here gets a thumbs up, but we also like this place for its classy, quiet ambience, good selection of quality wines and perfectly poured martinis.

## Long Beach          Map pp62–3

**Alex's Bar** ( ☎ 562-434-8292; 2913 E Anaheim St) This punk hole is as alternative as it gets in Long Beach. Cheap drinks, free wireless Internet access with purchase and occasional live bands. Enter from the back.

**Yard House** ( ☎ 562-628-0455, 401 Shoreline Village Dr) The bartenders here command an oval bar that looks like a spaceship helm and serve some 250 beers on tap, connected to 5 miles of beer lines and 27 pumps. Serious boozers consume their brew from yard-long beer glasses.

Also see the Belmont Brewing Company (p163).

## Downtown Los Angeles & Around          Map pp64–5

**Rooftop Bar @ Standard Downtown LA** ( ☎ 213-892-8080; 550 S Flower St) The scene at this outdoor lounge, swimming in a sea of skyscrapers, is libidinous, intense and more than a bit surreal. There are vibrating waterbed pods for lounging, hot-bod servers and a pool for cooling off if it gets too steamy. Velvet rope on weekends.

**Mountain** ( ☎ 213-625-7500; 473 Gin Ling Way; ☾ Wed-Sun) Downtown dwellers and East-side hipsters gather at this artsy Chinatown bar, which is perfect for capping off a session of gallery-hopping on nearby Chung King Rd. The Kool Aid–orange decor makes you feel like you're sitting inside a volcano.

**Hop Louie** ( ☎ 213-628-4244; 950 Mei Ling Way) If the Mountain is too crowded, head to this classic restaurant-bar that wears its patina of age with pride. It's inside a landmark China-town pagoda. Skip the food.

**Golden Gopher** ( ☎ 213-614-8001; 417 W 8th St) Downtown hipsters are the core clientele of this campy glamour lounge in a somewhat scary neighborhood. Gopher lamps provide the kind of mellow lighting that makes everyone look good and there's lots of couches for relaxing in case your brain isn't handling that third martini. Those who haven't had enough at closing time can stock up at the in-house liquor store.

**HMS Bounty** ( ☎ 323-385-7275; 3357 Wilshire Blvd, Koreatown) This barely-lit tavern has poured oceans of cheap and strong liquor since it started sailing in 1947. These days a new generation of hipsters, mostly of the pierced and tattooed persuasion, rubs elbows with hooch-loving geezers that look like they've been there since day one.

**Prince** ( ☎ 213-389-2007; 3198 W 7th St, Koreatown) Of the same vintage as the HMS Bounty, this one goes for the British bordello look (think red everything, framed oil paintings and superkitschy lamps with figurines for pedestals). The crowd is a potpourri of ethnicities united by a penchant for stiff drinks at civilized prices.

**Hank's** ( ☎ 213-623-7718; 838 S Grand Ave) Dark, divey and filled with everyone from lowlifes to suits, this classic 1940s watering hole in the Stillwell Hotel (p149) is so noir you feel like you've stepped into a Raymond Chandler novel. The bartenders pour with a generous elbow while the jukebox plays Sinatra and Cash.

**Gallery Bar** ( ☎ 213-624-1011; 506 S Grand Ave) If you like to unwind in a sophisticated way, you'll find a five-star ambience at this posh bar in the Millennium Biltmore Hotel (p149). The signature drink is the Black Dahlia, named for infamous 1947 murder victim Elizabeth Short who was last spotted alive at the hotel. Her death remains a mystery.

**Weiland Brewery** ( ☎ 213-680-2881; 400 E 1st St; ☽ 11am-2am Mon-Fri, 5pm-2am Sat) This low-key pub near Little Tokyo serves grub until the wee hours and gets busy during the two daily happy hours. Good chili.

**Brass Monkey** ( ☎ 213-381-7047; 3440 Wilshire Blvd; ☽ 10am-2am) With its tacky decor and Koreatown setting, it's hard to imagine that this karaoke joint counts celebs such as Jack Black and David Arquette among its regulars. Crooners can choose from a library of 15,000 songs in six languages. Get here early to stake out a spot before the action starts at 9pm (4pm on Friday).

## ENTERTAINMENT

LA's party scene is lively, edgy and multifaceted. You can hobnob with hipsters at a trendy Hollywood dance club, groove to experimental sounds in a Silver Lake music venue, or catch a concert on the pier, a movie in a cemetery or a multimedia event at an abandoned warehouse.

---

### COOL TUNES BELOW THE MOON

Summer is a great time to visit LA, not in the least because of all the free concert series that are offered all over town. Most take place weekly. Check the websites listed here or the listings magazines (p172) for details.

One of the most popular concert series is the **Twilight Dance Series** (www.twilightdance.org), whose eclectic, multicultural lineup turns the Santa Monica Pier into a weekly dance and party zone. Up the road, in Brentwood, the **Sunset Concert Series** (www.skirball.org), at the beautiful Skirball Cultural Center, is another place to catch quality world-music acts performing on a stage surrounded by a lily pond.

Down the coast, you can listen to classical and pop music against the backdrop of sailboats at the **Marina del Rey Summer Concerts** (www.visitthemarina.com) in Burton Chace Park or enjoy an ocean-view picnic during **Music by the Sea** (www.musicbythesea.org) concerts in San Pedro's Point Fermin Park. Art and jazz make for an irresistible combination during **Friday Night Jazz** (www.lacma.org/art/music/music.htm) concerts at the Los Angeles County Museum of Art (this series goes year-round).

Downtown LA has two great series, most notably the **Grand Performances** (www.grandperformances.org), which brings top-caliber music, dance and theater acts to the fabulous California Plaza Watercourt. Nearby, the **Pershing Square Summer Concert Series** (www.laparks.org /pershingsquare/concerts.htm) gets big crowds for its lunchtime concerts. Last but not least, Pasadena has the **One Colorado Summer Series** (www.onecolorado.net) featuring jazz, salsa, blues and classical music.

LA also has plenty in store for fans of highbrow pursuits, including a world-class philharmonic orchestra and an opera led by Plácido Domingo, one third of the original Three Tenors. Mainstream, offbeat and fringe theater and performance art all thrive, as do the comedy clubs. Seeing a movie, not surprisingly, has become a luxe event in this town with a new generation of stadium-style multiplex theaters offering giant screens, total surround-sound, and comfy tiered leather seats.

### LISTINGS

These publications will help you plug into the local scene in no time:

**ArtScene** (www.artscenecal.com) Monthly freebie listing art-gallery shows.

**Flavorpill** (www.flavorpill.com) Online magazine spotlights offbeat happenings; sign up for its free weekly emails.

**LA Alternative Press** (www.laalternativepress.com) Biweekly with an Eastside focus.

**LA City Beat & LA Valley Beat** (www.lacitybeat.com) Not as comprehensive as the *LA Weekly*, but currently the only all-city alternative; published free every Thursday.

**LA Magazine** (www.lamagazine.com) Monthly glossy features 'The Guide,' a highly selective what's-on section.

**LA Weekly** (www.laweekly.com) The single best source for keeping the finger on the pulse of what's happening in LA; published free every Friday and distributed through bars, cafés, shops and newspaper boxes.

**Los Angeles Times** (www.latimes.com) Has useful weekend events preview in Thursday edition and a comprehensive Calendar section on Sundays.

### TICKETS

Tickets for most events are available from individual venues by phone, in person and sometimes also online. For information on half-price theater tickets, see p178. For hard-to-get tickets or 'sold-out' shows, try the following:

**Al Brooks Ticket Agency** ( ☎ 213-626-5863)

**Barry's Ticket Service** ( ☎ 818-990-8499; www .barrystickets.com)

**Ticketmaster** ( ☎ 213-480-3232; www.ticketmaster.com)

### Cinemas

Not surprisingly, cinemas abound in the capital of celluloid. The newest generation of multiplexes has ultradeluxe, stadium-style theaters with comfortable leather chairs and ear-popping surround sound. Ticket prices have soared as a result, with Saturday night screenings now fetching as much as $14, although $11 ($7.50 for children or seniors) is more typical. You can save a few dollars by seeing flicks during the week or before 6pm. Tickets for most theaters can be pre-booked through **Moviefone** (from any LA area code ☎ 777-3456).

**ArcLight & Cinerama Dome** (Map pp66-7; ☎ 323-464-4226; www.arclightcinemas.com; 6360 W Sunset Blvd, Hollywood) This ultramodern multiplex is attached to the now fully restored 1963 geodesic Cinerama Dome. Pick your flick from the airport-style 'departure board,' then report to your assigned seat in one of the 14 theaters. There's an edgy bar for pre- or post-show libations or nosh, and ages 21+ screenings where you can enjoy a beer or martini along with your popcorn. It's also an occasional film festival venue.

**El Capitan Theatre** (Map pp66-7; ☎ 323-347-7674; 6838 Hollywood Blvd, Hollywood) The most beautiful theater in Hollywood features first-run Disney movies, often preceded by live show extravaganzas. Also see p79.

---

**TOP THREE FILM FESTIVALS**

In LA, it's not love or money but movies that make the world go round. Besides churning out blockbuster productions, the city also hosts dozens of film festivals, including such highly specialized ones as the Festival of Science Fiction, Fantasy & Horror and the Pan African Film & Art Festival. We've picked through the pile for our faves:

**AFI Fest** ( ☎ 866-234-3378; www.afi.com) One of the longest running film festivals in LA (since 1986), this November festival is a showcase for international films by everyone from emerging to master filmmakers. This is the festival that premiered *Monster*, *The Cider House Rules* and other Academy Award winners.

**Los Angeles Film Festival** ( ☎ 866-345-6337; www.lafilmfest.com) This June festival strives to present the best in indie movies from around the world, from shorts and music videos to documentaries and full features. In 2004 it hosted the US premiere of *Fahrenheit 911*.

**Outfest** ( ☎ 213-480-7088; www.outfest.org) The biggest and foremost among the many festivals showcasing gay, lesbian, bisexual and transgender film and video with more than 200 shorts and features. It's held every July.

## MOVIES UNDER THE STARS

Angelenos love their movies and their fine weather, so it should be no surprise that viewing films alfresco has become a popular fad. During the warmer months (roughly May to October), classic and contemporary films spool off at various venues around town, but four standout series command record turnouts.

Taking the cake for most unusual screening location is **Cinespia** (www.cinespia.org; admission $10; ☼ some Sat May–Oct), which projects movies such as Robert Altman's *The Long Goodbye* onto a mausoleum wall at the Hollywood Forever Cemetery (p81), the place of perpetual slumber for a galaxy of old-time movie stars. Crowds descend early for prescreening picnics and cocktails while a DJ spins old soundtracks.

If that's too morbid for you, head on over to the **Santa Monica Drive-In** ( ☎ 310-458-8901; www.smff.com; admission free; ☼ some Tue Aug & Sep), which gets crowds of up to 5000 for free family-friendly flicks presented right on the Santa Monica Pier (the name is misleading as you can't take your car; bring pillows, chairs or blankets). Tickets are free but must be picked up in advance at the Santa Monica Visitors Center (p58) and other venues.

If a day at Universal Studios hasn't left you exhausted, stick around for the **Universal City Walk Summer Drive-In** ( ☎ 818-622-4455; www.citywalkhollywood.com; Universal City Walk; admission free; ☼ Thu Jun–Aug). No cars here either, just good old and new classics, produced by Universal of course, and presented on a giant screen right on the Universal City Walk.

Burbank in the San Fernando Valley also gets in on the act with its **Outdoor Picture Show** ( ☎ 818-566-8617; www.mediacitycenter.com; admission free; ☼ Wed late Jun–mid-Aug). It's in the giant Media City Center mall next to IKEA.

**Grauman's Chinese Theatre** (Map pp66-7; ☎ 323-464-8111; 6925 Hollywood Blvd, Hollywood) This is an Industry favorite for glitzy movie premieres, so you never know which famous bottom may have graced the seat before you. Make sure you buy tickets for the historic theater, not the unspectacular Mann Chinese 6 multiplex next door. Also see p78.

**American Cinematheque** ( ☎ 323-466-3456; www.americancinematheque.com) Hollywood (Map pp66-7; 6712 Hollywood Blvd); Santa Monica (Map pp72-3; 1328 Montana Ave) Serious cinephiles flock to this nonprofit venue presenting eclectic film fare – from classics to cutting-edge experimental – in two rescued and restored historic venues: the Egyptian Theatre and the Aero Theatre. Some screenings are followed by discussions with actors or directors associated with the movie. Also see p80 for additional information.

**Pacific Theatres at the Grove** (Map pp68-9; ☎ 323-692-0829; www.thegrovela.com; 189 The Grove Dr, Mid-City) Lean back in a reclining seat as you take in the latest Hollywood release flickering before you on a wall-to-wall screen. All of the 14 theaters offer stadium seating and a top-notch sound system.

**Silent Movie Theatre** (Map pp68-9; ☎ 323-655-2520; www.silentmovietheatre.com; 611 N Fairfax Ave, Mid-City; admission varies, usually adult/student $15/10)

'Silents are golden' at this unique theater, the last in the nation exclusively devoted to the early films of Charlie Chaplin, Lillian Gish, Valentino and other stars of the silent age. Screenings are accompanied by live music and often preceded by cartoons or shorts. Check the website or listings magazines for upcoming shows.

**Cecchi Gori Fine Arts Theatre** (Map pp70-1; ☎ 310-281-8223; www.landmarktheaters.com; 8556 Wilshire Blvd, Beverly Hills) This art-house cinema occupies a gorgeous 1936 art deco movie palace and is one of the last single-screen venues in town. Fully restored and updated, it shows mostly indies and restored classics.

**Nuart Theatre** (off Map pp70-1; ☎ 310-478-6379; www.landmarktheaters.com; 11272 Santa Monica Blvd, near Westwood) This hip art house presents the best in offbeat and cult flicks, including the camp classic, *The Rocky Horror Picture Show* every Saturday at midnight.

**Bridge** (off Map pp72-3; ☎ 310-568-3375; www.thebridgecinema.com; 6081 Center Dr, Culver City) This self-titled 'cinema de lux' shows up to 19 blockbuster movies simultaneously in state-of-the-art theaters with stadium seating and wide screens. One of them is IMAX-style.

**California Science Center IMAX** ( ☎ 323-724-3623; www.californiasciencecenter.org/Imax/Features/Features.php; Exposition Park, 700 State Dr, near Downtown; adult/

child/student/senior $7.50/4.50/5.50/5.50) It takes a 3-D projector the size of a Volkswagen to project the high-tech IMAX movies on a screen soaring seven stories tall and stretching 90ft wide. Most of the nature-themed films are family friendly.

## Live Music

Big-name acts appear at several venues around town, including the **Staples Center** (p113), the **Universal Amphitheatre** (p121) next to Universal Studios Hollywood, the historic **Wiltern Theater** (p114) near Downtown and, in summer, the **Hollywood Bowl** (p82) and the **Greek Theatre** (p120) in Griffith Park. For world music, check out what's playing at the **John Anson Ford Theatre** (p82), also in Hollywood.

Listed following are some of our favorite live-music clubs. Cover charges vary widely – some gigs are free, but most average between $5 and $10. Unless noted, venues are open nightly and only open to those 21 or older. Also check the listings mags for free concerts playing at **Amoeba Music** (p189). For the lowdown on the numerous free summer concert series, see p171.

### ROCK & ALTERNATIVE
**Knitting Factory Hollywood** (Map pp66-7; ☎ 323-463-0204; 7021 Hollywood Blvd, Hollywood; all ages) The schedule at this bastion of indie bands isn't quite as out there as at the New York City mother club, but there's still plenty of top-notch world music, progressive jazz and other alterna-sounds to be enjoyed. Headliners take the main stage, the rest make do with the intimate AlterKnit Lounge.

**King King** (Map pp66-7; ☎ 323-960-9234; 6555 Hollywood Blvd, Hollywood) This is an edgy musicians' hangout in the heart of Hollywood yet far removed from the glam circuit. Often excellent local talent holds forth in a lofty industrial-chic warehouse filled with sofas for snuggling and a central bar on wheels. Tuesday concentrates on salsa and Wednesday is a no cover charge rock night.

**Gig** (Map pp66-7; ☎ 323-936-4440; 7302 Melrose Ave, Hollywood) Most of the bands playing at this un-showy place will never hit the big time, but that doesn't stop them from wailing their hearts out. With up to five acts nightly, you know it's hit-or-miss, but as long as you're lolling on the comfy couches, beer in hand, life's pretty good.

**Spaceland** (Map pp66-7; ☎ 323-661-4380; 1717 Silver Lake Blvd, Silver Lake) At the epicenter of Silver Lake's underground rock scene, local alt-rock, indie, skate-punk and electrotrash bands take the stage in the hope of making it big (Beck and the Eels played some early gigs here). Between sets, the crowd mingles in the upstairs smoking lounge. There's usually no cover on Mondays.

**House of Blues** (Map pp68-9; ☎ 323-848-5100; www.hob.com; 8430 W Sunset Blvd, West Hollywood; no cover for restaurant; Ⓟ $15) Top talent of all stripes, not just the blues, performs at this faux–Mississippi Delta shack, the original branch of this wildly successful chain. Great sound, neat folk art and a bar that morphs into a stage make for a memorable experience, even if the Southern food is only so-so. The Sunday gospel brunch (seatings at 10am and 1pm; adult/child $35/18.50), however, is an institution.

**Troubadour** (Map pp68-9; ☎ 310-276-6168; 9081 Santa Monica Blvd, West Hollywood; all ages; ☙ closed Sun) Back in the '60s and early '70s, the Troub did its part in catapulting the Eagles and Tom Waits to stardom, and it's still a great place to catch tomorrow's headliners. The all-ages policy ensures a mixed crowd that's refreshingly low on attitude. If you don't snag one of the seats up on the balcony, you'll be standing all the way. Mondays are free.

**Cat Club** (Map pp68-9; ☎ 310-657-0888; 8911 W Sunset Blvd, West Hollywood) Ex–Stray Cat drummer Slim Jim Phantom owns this narrow, long and intimate Sunset Strip rock den with its cozy sofa loft and smoking patio. Slim Jim usually makes an appearance on 'The Star Fuckers' Thursdays, sometimes joined by Guns N' Roses guitarist Gilby Clarke or other rock friend regulars.

**Roxy** (Map pp68-9; ☎ 310-276-2222; 9009 W Sunset Blvd, West Hollywood; all ages) A Sunset fixture since 1973, the Roxy once managed to lure legends such as Bruce Springsteen but lately has featured mostly upwardly hopeful unsigned bands. A sleek new look may restore a measure of hipdom, as should regular Monday gigs by Metal Skool, a fun '80s-metal parody band with a cultlike following.

**Whisky-a-GoGo** (Map pp68-9; ☎ 310-652-4202; 8901 W Sunset Blvd, West Hollywood; all ages) After more than 40 years on the rock circuit, this historic fixture may no longer be the hippest joint on the Sunset Strip, but it'll always be the place that launched Jim Morrison and fine art of go-go dancing back in the '60s. These days a roster of pay-for-play hard rockers often takes the stage.

**Largo** (Map pp68-9; ☎ 323-852-1073; 432 N Fairfax Ave, Mid-City; all ages; ☯ closed Sun) This low-key space is loved by dedicated acoustic musicians and their audiences. Friday nights with Jon Brion, who has produced for Aimee Mann and Fiona Apple, are standing-room only. There's a strict no-chattering policy during show time. Make dinner reservations (mains $12 to $14) or be prepared to stand.

**Joint** (Map pp70-1; ☎ 310-275-2619; 8771 W Pico Blvd, near Beverly Hills) This tiny venue has a solid track record of pulling in pretense-free music lovers with the finest rock, alternative and eclectic beats. What it lacks in size it makes up for with superb sound, great sight lines and stylish red and black decor. Keith Richards and Robert Plant are known to pop in on occasion.

**Temple Bar** (Map pp72-3; ☎ 310-393-6611; 1026 Wilshire Blvd, Santa Monica) This candlelit place scores high on the groove-meter for its unique Buddha-meets-beach decor and quality cross-cultural lineup from edgy jazz to upbeat Latin and funky hip-hop. The crowd's relaxed, the air incense-laden and the food spicy. Also check out the monthly film and poetry nights.

**14 Below** (Map pp72-3; ☎ 310-451-5040; 1348 14th St, Santa Monica) No one would accuse this club of trendsetting, but that's just fine with the laid-back local crowd. Those not listening to the roster of wanna-be rock stars can hang by the fireplace, shoot pool in back or settle into a couch for a spot of people-watching.

**Smell** (Map pp72-3; ☎ 213-625-4325; 247 S Main St, Downtown; all ages; ℗) An artsy underground vibe rules at this club in the dark belly of Downtown. Bands are mostly of the up-and-coming indie variety, sometimes with a radical political bent. They have a vegan snack bar but no liquor license. The entrance is in the back of an alley.

Also recommended:

**Lighthouse Cafe** (Map p74; ☎ 310-372-6911; 30 Pier Ave, Hermosa Beach) A major jazz venue in the '50s and '60s, today's musical menu goes from punk to '80s pop, sometimes in seconds.

**Viper Room** (Map pp68-9; ☎ 310-358-1880; 8852 W Sunset Blvd, West Hollywood) Celebrity-heavy.

## BLUES

For smooth blues and jazz, also check out the monthly **Bones & Blues** concerts that are held at the Watts Labor Community Action Committee (p117).

**Babe & Ricky's** (Map p60-1; ☎ 323-295-9112; www.bluesbar.com; 4339 Leimert Blvd, Leimert Park Village, South Central; ☯ Thu-Mon) 'Mama' Laura Gross has presided over this venerable blues joint for over four decades, nursing along new talent and even hosting legends such as Eric Clapton and BB King. The Monday night jam sessions (cover $5, includes Mama's famous fried-chicken buffet) often bring the house down.

**Harvelle's** (Map pp72-3; ☎ 310-395-1676; www.harvelles.com; 1432 4th St, Santa Monica) The Chicago vibe at this dark and timeless hole-in-the-wall blues joint is so real, you can almost see the Sears Tower in the distance. Harvelle's has been packing 'em in since 1931 but somehow it still manages to feel like a well-kept secret. There are no big-name acts here, but the quality is high nevertheless.

**Blue Cafe** (Map p62-3; ☎ 562-983-7111; www.thebluecafe.com; 210 The Promenade, Long Beach; ☯ closed Mon) Bands perform most nights – plus Saturday afternoons – at this raucous tavern with its chatty sidewalk terrace. Tuesday night is open mike, while the college crowd invades Wednesdays lured by drinks specials beckon. Upstairs, a dozen full-size billiard tables beckon.

**Cafe Boogaloo** (Map p74; ☎ 310-318-2324; www.cafeboogaloo.com; 1238 Hermosa Ave, Hermosa Beach) Live blues is featured at this relaxed joint, where you can also enjoy two dozen microbrews on tap and a Southern-influenced menu.

**BB King's Blues Club** (Map p75; ☎ 818-622-5464; Universal City Walk, Universal City; ℗ $8) If you find yourself up on tourist-saturated Universal City Walk, you could check if any of the local or touring acts appearing here are worth your time and money.

## JAZZ

LA hosts a couple of California's top jazz parties, the **Long Beach Jazz Festival** (p137) in August and the **Catalina Island JazzTrax Festival** (p138) in October. In summer, you can catch free jazz every Friday at the Los Angeles County Museum of Art in the Miracle Mile District (p171). The jazz series at Walt Disney Concert Hall (p107), under the direction of Dianne Reeves, is superb as well. For boning up on the local scene, read **All About Jazz** (www .allaboutjazz.com/losangeles). Note that some venues impose a drinks' minimum (usually two, nonalcoholic ones are fine) in addition to or in place of the cover charge.

**Catalina Bar & Grill** (Map pp66-7; ☎ 323-466-2210; 6725 W Sunset Blvd, Hollywood; cover $10-18, plus dinner or 2 drinks; ☉ closed Mon) LA's premier jazz club has moved into new, slicker and more spacious digs but nothing's changed about Catalina Popescu's top-notch booking policy. All the jazz greats have graced her stage over the years, from Dizzie Gillespie to the Marsalis brothers and Chick Corea. Two shows nightly.

**World Stage** (Map pp60-1; ☎ 323-293-2451; www .theworldstage.org; 4344 Degnan Blvd, Leimert Park Village, South Central; ☉ varies) This no-nonsense space was founded by the late jazz drummer Billy Higgins. There's no food or drink, just good music from some of the finest talent around. The Thursday jam session has people grooving until 2am.

**Jazz Bakery** (off Map pp72-3; ☎ 310-271-9039; www.jazzbakery.org; 3233 Helms Ave, Culver City; cover $25-30; P ) This nonprofit hardcore jazz hangout in the former Helms Bakery complex pulls in some pretty heavy hitters – Dave Grusin and brother Don and the Wallace Roney Quintet among them. You can bring your own drinks (but no food) inside. Two shows nightly: 8pm and 9:30pm. Half-price rush tickets are available for students under 21 for any seats still free at show time.

**Vibrato Grill & Jazz** (off Map pp70-1; ☎ 310-474-9400; 2930 Beverly Glen Circle, Bel Air; usually no cover, 2-drink minimum; all ages) None other than trumpet legend Herb Alpert is behind this posh new supper club ensconced in a Bel Air shopping center. Come for the cool West Coast jazz, the American chophouse menu, or both. Bright abstract paintings, also by

---

**TOP FIVE LATE-NIGHT NOSH SPOTS**

- Coffee shop at Best Western Hollywood Hills Hotel (Hollywood, p139)
- Fred 62 (Hollywood, p152)
- Pink's Hot Dogs (Mid-City, p155)
- Sanamluang (Hollywood, p151)
- Swingers (Mid-City, p155)

---

Alpert, adorn the walls, while bronze busts of Louis Armstrong & Co preside over the sleek wood and granite bar.

### LATIN & WORLD

For the latest hot spots, also check out www .planetsalsa.com/clubscene/laclubs.htm.

**El Floridita** (Map pp66-7; ☎ 323-871-8612; 1253 N Vine St, Hollywood; cover $10, free with dinner; ☉ Mon, Wed, Fri & Sat) The original Floridita in Havana was Hemingway's favorite hangout and the Hollywood version is *the* place to go *cubano* in LA. Order a mojito and watch the beautiful dancers do their thing (or join in if you feel you've got the moves). The Monday night jams are legendary; make reservations at least a week in advance (for any day, for that matter).

**Conga Room** (Map pp68-9; ☎ 323-938-1696; www .congaroom.com; 5364 Wilshire Blvd, Miracle Mile District; cover $20, $10 with dinner; ☉ Thu-Sat) Watch ladies in spiky heels and nattily dressed gents whirl around to the salsa beat at this upscale club with the slightly decadent feel of prerevolution Havana. Come early for dance lessons or dinner at La Boca restaurant.

**Zabumba** (off Map pp72-3 ☎ 310-841-6525; 10717 Venice Blvd, Culver City; cover $3-8; ☉ closed Mon) See if you can keep your hips from moving while being doused with bossa nova, jazz, *axé*, samba and salsa at this Brazilian restaurant-bar-club right on LA's 'Little Rio' strip.

## Dance Clubs

If you want all your clichés about LA confirmed, look no further than a nightclub in Hollywood or West Hollywood. Come armed with a hot bod, a healthy attitude or a fat wallet in order to impress the armoire-sized goons deciding on who gets to go past the velvet rope. Even making it onto the 'guest list' (for instance by signing up for it online) does not guarantee that you'll be spared a long wait, rejection, or both. Clubs in other parts of town are considerably more laid-back, but almost all require you to be at least 21 (bring picture ID). Cover ranges from $5 to $20. Doors are usually open from 9pm and close around 2am.

**Ivar** (Map pp66-7; ☎ 323-465-4827; 6356 Hollywood Blvd, Hollywood) Don't be deceived by the prisonlike exterior of this sizzling dance spot; inside it's all plush and posh, albeit in an industrial minimalist sort of way. Four bars, a smoking patio, a good-sized dance floor and a catwalk with go-go dancers are there for your entertainment.

**White Lotus** (Map pp66-7; ☎ 323-463-0060; 1743 N Cahuenga Blvd, Hollywood; mains $20-30; ☉ restaurant 6-11pm Tue-Sat, club 9pm-2am Tue-Sat) This stylish restaurant-club combo – done up feng shui–style – is great if you're not into switching venues halfway through a night of partying. Build your stamina by scarfing up sushi and other protein bombs, then report next door to the red-hot dance floor (access is guaranteed with dinner) to mingle with the pretty people.

**Highlands** (Map pp66-7; ☎ 323-461-9800; 6801 Hollywood Blvd, Hollywood) The mall-setting of this club could be a turnoff if the mall wasn't the splashy Hollywood & Highland fun complex. It's a huge place with seven bars, a restaurant and lots of shiny, happy and barely legal people. The multiple balconies are perfect for smoking, stargazing and scanning the LA skyline.

**Nacional** (Map pp66-7; ☎ 323-962-7712; 1645 Wilcox Ave, Hollywood; ☉ closed Mon) Another entry in Hollywood's growing cadre of megaclubs, this one has a seductive prerevolution-Cuba theme with fiery mood lighting and loungy Bauhaus-style furniture. A picky door policy keeps out weekend warriors that don't fit the profile (whatever that may be). Different sounds nightly.

**Boardner's** (Map pp66-7; ☎ 323-462-9621; 1652 N Cherokee Ave, Hollywood; ☉ 11am-2am) This Hollywood legend, in the party business since 1942, is a refreshing break from the velvet-rope brigade. It's been featured in *LA Confidential*, *Leaving Las Vegas* and other movies and even appears on the radar screen of such celebs as Ben Affleck and Nicole Kidman. There's DJs on the decks most nights spinning everything from electro to indie and '80s punk. Saturday it's Goth night.

**Garden of Eden** (Map pp66-7; ☎ 323-465-3336; 7080 Hollywood Blvd, Hollywood; ☉ usually Fri-Sun) No, it's not a nudist club but there's certainly no shortage of skin-baring temptresses at this fashionable hip-hop haven. The exotic Casbah look of this double-decker venue attracts its share of A-listers, including Hugh Hefner and local athletic royalty. Dress to impress, or forget about it.

**Gabah** (Map pp66-7; ☎ 323-664-8913; 4658 Melrose Ave, Hollywood; ☉ Wed-Sun) This dark and edgy club in a gritty section of Melrose is a world removed from the pseudo-glamour of central Hollywood. A no-nonsense crowd sweats it out on the dance floor framed by leopard-spotted walls (gabah means 'jungle' in Arabic). A roster of progressive local DJs spin a mix of urban sounds, from hip-hop and groove to reggae and acid jazz. Cash only.

**El Cid** (Map pp66-7; ☎ 323-668-0318; 4212 W Sunset Blvd, Silver Lake) This traditional flamenco show venue has spawned a second identity as a hipster dance club with a rotating roster of DJs. It's inside a rambling hillside hacienda that actually began as a soundstage for pioneering movie director, DW Griffith. Flamenco dinner shows still take place earlier in the evening on weekends.

**Parlour Club** (Map pp68-9; ☎ 323-650-7968; 7702 Santa Monica Blvd, West Hollywood) We can't guarantee that, as you're reading this, this cozy dive still does Punk Rock Karaoke, the men-only Dirty Dirty House Club and Bricktops!, a cabaret hosted by Vaginal Davis, LA's fave drag queen, but it's sure to be something similarly wacky. This one's straight out Twin Peaks (and we mean that in a nice way).

**Club Sugar** (Map pp72-3; ☎ 310-899-1989; 814 Broadway, Santa Monica; ☉ Tue & Thu-Sat) You can keep it casual in the dress department at this incense-laced venue with a solid track record of pulling in an eclectic, energetic crowd with cutting-edge house and electro. There's no sign, so look for the door right next to Swingers (p155). Try one of their drinks made with *soju* (vodkalike Korean hooch).

**Zanzibar** (Map pp72-3; ☎ 310-451-2221; 1301 5th St, Santa Monica; ☉ Wed-Sun) Electronica spinmeisters Jason Bentley and Garth Trinidad work their turntable magic on throngs of hipsters at this hot new Santa Monica boîte with sensuous African-themed decor. The wraparound bar is great for socializing, while the comfy couches invite canoodling. Show up early to avoid the inevitable line.

**Mayan Theater** (Map pp64-5; ☎ 213-746-4674; 1038 S Hill St, Downtown; ☉ 9pm-3am Fri & Sat) If you're into salsa, this is *the* place to shake your bootie on Saturday nights. The sexy templelike setting of this 1927 ex–movie palace provides almost as much eye candy as do the young things gyrating on the triple dance floors. Come at 8pm for dance lessons ($18, including admission). On Fridays the focus is on house and Spanish rock. It's extremely dressy – call or check the website for dress-code details.

**Muse** (Map p76; ☎ 626-793-0608; 54 E Colorado Blvd, Pasadena) Old Pasadena's premier club lets you match your mood to three levels of dance-floor action. Downstairs the DJ provokes movement with hip-hop and R&B, while one level up the taste goes to alternative and Top 40. The top level has couches and pool tables for resting feet and ear drums.

Also recommended:

**Dragonfly** (Map p66-7; ☎ 323-466-6111; 6510 Santa Monica Blvd, Hollywood) Hardcore party chamber with theme nights ranging from laid-back reggae to sexy sounds for the fetish set.

**Echo** (Map pp66-7; ☎ 213-413-8200; 1822 W Sunset Blvd, near Silver Lake) Divey hangout that's a favorite with Eastside hipsters hungry for an eclectic alchemy of sound.

**Avalon** (Map pp66-7; ☎ 323-462-3000; 1735 N Vine St, Hollywood) Megasized, megahip venue in an old theater; concerts during the week, disco on Saturday.

**Little Temple** (Map pp66-7; ☎ 323-660-4540; 4519 Santa Monica Blvd, Silver Lake; ⊙ closed Mon) The Eastside cousin of Santa Monica's Temple Bar (p175), this lounge is perfect for anyone with a yen for Zen and soulful sounds.

## Classical Music & Opera

**Los Angeles Philharmonic** (☎ 323-850-2000; www .laphil.org; tickets $35-120) One of world's finest orchestras, the LA Phil has been ably led by Esa-Pekka Salonen, a youthful and charismatic Finn, since 1992. Works by contemporary composers (including himself), celebrity recitals, world music and jazz along with the masters of yore – Beethoven to Sibelius – make up his progressive programming. Concerts take place at the Walt Disney Concert Hall (p107) from October to June and at the Hollywood Bowl (p82) from June to September.

For some Disney concerts, 'choral bench' tickets behind the orchestra are available for $15. They are released at noon on the Tuesday two weeks before the week of the concert and are available in person at the box office or by phone. Be warned: they go quicker than a Porsche.

**Los Angeles Opera** (☎ 213-972-8001; www.laopera .com; tickets $30-190) Since 2000, star tenor Plácido Domingo has presided over the LA Opera with Kent Nagano as music director. The varied and high-caliber productions range from sonic crowd-pleasers such as *Carmen* and *Aida* to lesser known works such as Samuel Barber's *Vanessa*. Performances take place at the Dorothy Chandler Pavilion (p108).

**Los Angeles Master Chorale** (☎ 800-787-5262, 213-972-7282; www.lamc.org; tickets $19-79) From October to June, this critically acclaimed 120-voice choir presents stand-alone recitals and also performs with the LA Phil and the LA Opera. Its base is at the Dorothy Chandler Pavilion (p108).

**Los Angeles Chamber Orchestra** (☎ 213-622-7001, ext 215; www.laco.org; tickets $17-75) LA's top chamber ensemble specializes in a wide repertory of music from the 17th century to the present. Performances take place at UCLA's **Royce Hall** (Map pp70-1; 405 Hilgard Ave, Westwood), the **Alex Theater** (off Map p76; 216 N Brand Blvd) in Glendale, west of Pasadena, and the Zipper Concert Hall at the Colburn School of Performing Arts (p108).

Also recommended:

**Da Camera Society** (☎ 310-440-1351; www.dacamera .org; tickets $34-84) Chamber music in historic venues around town.

**Pasadena Symphony** (☎ 626-584-8833; www.pasa denasymphony.org; 300 E Green St, Pasadena; tickets $15-69, student & senior rush on day of performance $12) Concerts at the historic Pasadena Civic Auditorium (p125).

## Theater

Glitzy Broadway shows to gritty one-act dramas, live theater is thriving in LA, thanks to a limitless talent pool and a willingness to push the creative envelope. On dozens of stages you can watch budding talent hamming it up or seasoned thespians such as John Lithgow or Richard Dreyfuss getting back to their roots.

Many theaters now sell tickets through their websites. If you have online access, you can also get half-price tickets to many shows through **LAStageTIX** (www.theatrela.org), an alliance of 210 performance arts organizations around town.

LA hosts several theater festivals, including the **NoHo Theater & Arts Festival** (p137) in May and the **Edge of the World Theater Festival** (p138) in October. In summer check the listings mags for performances by **Shakespeare Festival LA** (www.shakespearefestivalla.org), which presents the best of the Bard in changing venues around town. Tickets are free with a canned-food donation for charity. See the website for full details.

### LARGER STAGES

**Mark Taper Forum** (Map pp64-5; ☎ 213-628-2772; www.taperahmanson.com; Music Center, 135 N Grand Ave,

Downtown; tickets $40-60) The Mark Taper is the home base of the Center Theatre Group, one of SoCal's leading resident ensembles. It has developed numerous new plays, most famously Tony Kushner's *Angels in America*, which went on to win Tony, Pulitzer and Emmy Awards. Public rush tickets ($12; cash only; two tickets maximum per person) are available at the box office two hours before curtain (except on Saturday nights, Sunday matinees and opening nights).

**Ahmanson Theatre** (Map pp64-5; ☎ 213-628-2772; www.taperahmanson.com; Music Center, 135 N Grand Ave, Downtown; tickets $20-80) Next to the Mark Taper Forum, this grand space is also used by the Center Theatre Group, primarily for big-time Broadway-style musicals and visiting blockbusters from around the world. See Mark Taper Forum (opposite) for rush ticket information.

**Redcat** (Map pp64-5; ☎ 213-237-2800; www.redcat .org; 631 W 2nd St, Downtown) Since opening in 2003, Redcat (which stands for Roy and Edna Disney Cal Arts Theater) has quickly emerged as the city's finest venue for avant-garde and experimental theater, performance art, dance, readings, film and video. The large gallery showcases cutting-edge local and international talent.

**Pantages Theatre** (Map pp66-7; ☎ 323-468-1770; www.broadwayla.org; 6233 Hollywood Blvd, Hollywood; tickets vary) This flamboyant art deco venue (also see p80) is a fittingly dramatic setting for the megabucks musicals that often draw nightly capacity crowds of nearly 3000 people. The menu ranges from popular staples such as *Oklahoma* and *Evita*, to more contemporary fare such as *The Lion King* and *The Producers*.

**Will Geer Theatricum Botanicum** (Map pp60-1; ☎ 310-455-3723; www.theatricum.com; 1419 N Topanga Canyon Blvd, northwest of Santa Monica; tickets adult $15-25, student & senior $11-15) This magical natural outdoor amphitheatre was founded by Will Geer (TV's Grandpa Walton) during the 1950s McCarthy era as a refuge for blacklisted actors and folk singers like himself. Now under his daughter Ellen's direction, summer repertory takes on Shakespeare, Dylan Thomas, Tennessee Williams and other American and European writers from June to mid-October. To get there, head north on Pacific Coast Hwy, turn inland on Topanga Canyon Blvd and proceed for 6 miles; the theater will be on your left.

**Kirk Douglas Theatre** (off Map pp72-3; ☎ 213-628-2772; www.taperahmanson.com; 9820 Washington Blvd, Culver City; tickets $19-40) What used to be a historic movie house is now a 300-seat theater, thanks to a generous cash infusion from the Douglas family. Opened in the fall of 2004, it is the newest venue of the Center Theatre Group (see Mark Taper Forum, opposite) and primarily a showcase of new plays by LA writers, and theater by and for children and teens.

**East West Players** (Map pp64-5; ☎ 213-625-4397; www.eastwestplayers.org; 120 N Judge John Aiso St, Little Tokyo, Downtown; tickets $23-38) Founded in 1965, this pioneering Asian-American ensemble performs at the David Henry Hwang Theater at the Union Center for the Art, which began as Little Tokyo's first Christian church. Its repertory of Broadway to modern classics takes a backseat to acclaimed premieres by local playwrights. Alumni have gone on to win Tony, Emmy and Academy awards.

**Pasadena Playhouse** (Map p76; ☎ 626-356-7529; www.pasadenaplayhouse.org; 39 S El Molino Ave, Pasadena; tickets $45-55) In business since 1924, this venerable theater underwent a serious sprucing up in the '80s and has been thriving ever since. Shows are a mix of the tried-and-true (Sondheim, Coward) and new writers such as Bronx-boy John Patrick Shanley.

## SMALLER STAGES

**Actors' Gang Theatre** (Map pp66-7; ☎ 323-465-0566; 6209 Santa Monica Blvd, Hollywood; tickets $20-25) The 'Gang' was founded in 1981 by Tim Robbins and other renegade UCLA acting-school grads. Its daring and offbeat reinterpretations of classics have a loyal following, although it's the bold new works developed at ensemble workshops that give the troupe its edge.

**Coronet Theatre** (Map pp68-9; ☎ 310-657-7377; www.coronet-theatrela.com; 366 N La Cienega Blvd, West Hollywood; tickets $10-25) Ever since it premiered Bertolt Brecht's *Galileo Galilei* starring Charles Laughton in 1947, this small theater has repeatedly managed to capture the limelight with daring productions, including the unlikely smash hits *The Puppetry of the Penis* and *Menopause: The Musical*. Glenn Close and Woody Harrelson are among the actors who have trod the boards here.

**Hudson Theatres** (Map pp66-7; ☎ 323-856-4249; www.hudsontheatre.com; 6539 Santa Monica Blvd, Hollywood; tickets $10-25) This quartet of stages (plus a cute café) has catapulted a number of productions to Broadway, TV and the big screen, including Nia Vardalos' *My Big Fat Greek Wedding*, which had its world premiere right here.

**MET Theatre** (Map pp66-7; ☎ 323-957-1152; www.themettheatre.com; 1089 N Oxford Ave, Hollywood; tickets $20) It never hurts to have friends in high places. Holly Hunter and Ed Harris have strutted their stuff on the MET's stage and other Hollywood bigwigs – from Dustin Hoffman to Angelina Jolie – have helped out with some cash. The fare here runs from edgy to traditional and has included the premiere of Sam Shepard's *Curse of the Starving Class*.

**Odyssey Theatre** (off Map pp70-1; ☎ 310-477-2055; www.odysseytheatre.com; 2055 S Sepulveda Blvd, near Westwood; tickets $20-25) This well-respected ensemble presents new work, updates the classics and develops its own plays in a ho-hum space that houses three 99-seat theaters under one roof. British enfant terrible Steven Berkoff occasionally guest stars in his provocative one-man shows.

**Edgemar Center for the Arts** (Map pp72-3; ☎ 310-399-3666; www.edgemarcenter.org; 2437 Main St, Santa Monica; tickets vary) This state-of-the-art two-theater and gallery space counts Steven Spielberg and Neil Simon among its board members. It's in a landmark building by Frank Gehry and also hosts acting workshops for adults and kids.

**Highways Performance Space & Gallery** (Map p76; ☎ 310-315-1459; www.highwaysperformance.org; 1651 18th St, Santa Monica; tickets mostly $15-18) Provocative, often shocking, performance art is what socially progressive artists cook up in this cutting-edge lab of creativity. The schedule is a multicultural, all-embracing mosaic of cabaret, music, readings, dance recitals, mixed-media shows and plays that continually push the envelope of expression.

**Deaf West Theatre** (Map p75; ☎ 818-762-2773; www.deafwest.org; 5112 Lankershim Blvd, North Hollywood; tickets vary) Bridging the gap between deaf and hearing-impaired artists and their audiences, Deaf West, founded in 1991, was the first professional sign language theater west of the Mississippi. Its repertory includes classic revivals, contemporary and original works, all performed in sign language with voice interpretation and/or supertitles. The theater is about two blocks south of the Metro Red Line's North Hollywood station.

## Comedy

On any given night, comedy stars – some of them very famous – may be polishing their chops in one of LA's many comedy clubs. Make reservations or show up early for decent seats. At clubs serving full menus, the best seats are reserved for dinner patrons. If you're not eating, you'll find that many clubs require a two-drink minimum order on top of the cover charge (usually $10 to $20). With few exceptions, noted following, you must be 21 or older to get in.

**Comedy & Magic Club** (Map p74; ☎ 310-372-1193; www.comedyandmagicclub.com; 1018 Hermosa Ave, Hermosa Beach; over 18) Headliners such Bill Maher and Bob Saget serve up yucks at this fine South Bay venue, although it is best known as the place where Jay Leno fine-tunes his *Tonight Show* most Sunday nights. Reservations required.

**Comedy Store** (Map pp68-9; ☎ 323-656-6225; www.thecomedystore.com; 8433 W Sunset Blvd, West Hollywood) There's hardly a famous comic alive that hasn't at some point performed in this venerable onetime gangster hangout, from Chris Tucker to Andrew 'Dice' Clay and Whoopi Goldberg. Pauly Shore's mom, Mitzi, has presided over the joint's trio of rooms for about three decades. The upstairs Belly Room sometimes has no cover charge.

**Groundlings** (Map pp68-9; ☎ 323-934-4747; www.groundlings.com; 7307 Melrose Ave; all ages) This improv school and company has tickled people's funny bones for over 30 years and has launched the careers of Lisa Kudrow, Jon Lovitz, Will Ferrell and other top talent. Improv night on Thursday brings together the main company, alumni and surprise guests.

**Ice House** (Map p76; ☎ 626-577-1894; www.icehousecomedy.com; 24 N Mentor Ave, Pasadena; over 18) This place morphed from folk to comedy club in the '70s and still has people in stitches today. Performers include former contestants from the popular TV show *Last Comic Standing*.

**Improv Olympic West** (Map pp66-7; ☎ 323-962-7560; www.iowest.com; 6366 Hollywood Blvd, Hollywood) This is the home of 'The Harold,' a 30-minute improv technique pioneered by the late Del Close at the club's Chicago mother ship. Some shows are free.

**Hollywood Improv** (Map pp68-9; ☎ 323-651-2583; www.improv.com; 8162 Melrose Ave, Hollywood) Jokemeister Drew Carry shows up several times monthly at this venerable haunt, which is equal-opportunity funny with its Mo' Better Mondays, Chopshticks and Gender Blender shows, featuring African-American, Asian and lesbigay comics, respectively.

Also recommended:

**Laugh Factory** (Map pp68-9; ☎ 323-656-1336; www .laughfactory.com; 8001 W Sunset Blvd, West Hollywood; over 18) Long-standing high-tech club with multicultural programming: Asian Saturdays (midnight), African-American Sundays and Latino Mondays.

**Bang Improv Studio** (Map pp68-9; ☎ 323-653-6886; www.bangstudio.com; 457 N Fairfax Ave; cover $5-10; all ages) You'll get lots of bang – and laughs – for your buck at this pint-sized improv stage.

**M Bar & Restaurant** (Map pp66-7; ☎ 323-856-0036; www.thembar.com; 1253 N Vine St; cover up to $10; over 18) This mini-mall bar has over-the-top decor, a casual vibe and comedy nights with offbeat jokesters.

## Sports
### BASEBALL
Since moving here from Brooklyn in 1958, the Dodgers have become synonymous with LA baseball. The team plays from April to October at Dodger Stadium (p107) just north of Downtown. Tickets cost $6 to $60 and are usually available at the box office on game day.

### BASKETBALL
For a while they seemed unbeatable: from 2000 to 2002, the **Los Angeles Lakers** (www.nba .com/lakers; tickets $10-400) took three NBA (National Basketball Association) championships in a row, ably guided by 'Zen coach' Phil Jackson and led on the field by superstars Shaquille O'Neal and Kobe Bryant. Defeat hit hard in 2003 and again in 2004, resulting in Jackson's and O'Neal's departure. With the Lakers in a lull, Angelenos are wondering if LA's second men's NBA team, the historically mediocre **Los Angeles Clippers** (www.nba.com /clippers; tickets $10-285) will step up their game.

Meanwhile, on the women's side, the **Los Angeles Sparks** (www.wnba.com/sparks; tickets $5-120) won WNBA (Women's National Basketball Association) championships in 2001 and 2002 but couldn't continue their winning streak. Their star player is Lisa Leslie, the first woman to dunk a basket, who has also earned three gold medals as part of the last three US Olympic teams.

All three teams play at the Staples Center (p113). The WNBA season (late May to August) follows the regular men's NBA season (October to April). Lakers tickets are hardest to come by and mostly sold through Ticketmaster (p172).

You can also catch great hoops action with the **UCLA Bruins** (☎ 310-825-2101; www.ucla bruins.com) at Pauley Pavilion (Map pp70–1) on the campus in Westwood.

### FOOTBALL
Despite occasional rumblings, as of this writing LA does not have a professional football team, so fans have to make do with the college teams competing in the Pacific 10 (Pac-10) Conference. The **UCLA Bruins** (tickets ☎ 310-825-2101; www.uclabruins.com; adult/child $12/4) play at the Rose Bowl (p125), while the **USC Trojans** (☎ 213-740-4672; www.usctrojans .com; tickets $40) are based at the Los Angeles Memorial Coliseum (p116) in Exposition Park south of Downtown. The season runs from September to November.

Die-hard football fans can also feed their habit by watching the **Los Angeles Avengers** (tickets ☎ 213-742-7340; www.laavengers.com) of the Arena Football League (AFL) fight it out at the Staples Center (p113) from February to June.

### HORSE RACING
LA County has two major thoroughbred racing tracks:

**Santa Anita Park** (Map pp60-1; ☎ 626-574-7223; www.santaanita.com; 285 W Huntington Dr, Arcadia; admission $5; season Christmas–mid-Apr, late Sep–early Nov) Horse racing enthusiasts consider this one of the best tracks in America. Also see p128.

**Hollywood Park** (Map pp62-3; ☎ 310-419-1500; www .hollywoodpark.com; 1050 S Prairie Ave, Inglewood; admission $7; season Apr-Jul, Nov-Dec) About 3 miles east of LAX.

### ICE HOCKEY
The **Los Angeles Kings** (tickets ☎ 213-742-7340; www.lakings.com; tickets $25-115) play in the National Hockey League (NHL) whose regular season runs from October to April, followed by the play-offs. Despite an enthusiastic fan base, the team has never won the Stanley Cup in its over 30 years of existence, although it reached the final in 1993 led by great Wayne 'The Great' Gretzky. The Kings play at the Staples Center (p113).

### SOCCER
Major League Soccer (MLS) may not yet be huge with general audiences but *futból*

definitely enjoys a passionate following among LA's Latino population. Since the league's 1995 inception, the **Los Angeles Galaxy** ( ☎ 310-630-2200; www.lagalaxy.com; tickets $15-45) has been putting on quite an impressive show. Since 2003 it plays in the sparkling new **Home Depot Center** (Map pp62-3; 18400 Avalon Blvd), which also serves as the US national soccer training headquarters. The stadium is in the southern LA suburb of Carson; get there by taking the Avalon exit off I-405. Things are set to heat up in 2005, when LA will be getting a second MLS soccer team, resulting in the league's first intracity rivalry. The season runs April to October.

## SHOPPING

LA is a great place to shop, and we're not just talking malls (although there are plenty of good ones around). The city's zest for life, envelope-pushing energy and entrepreneurial spirit translate into a cosmopolitan cocktail of unique boutiques that are a joy to explore. For many Angelenos shopping is one of life's great pleasures, a benign diversion that's as much about visual and mental stimulus as it is about actually buying stuff. Whether you're a penny-pincher or a power-shopper, you'll find plenty of opportunities to drop some cash in the city's hodgepodge of neighborhoods.

If money is no object, Beverly Hills beckons with international couture, jewelry and antiques, especially along Rodeo Dr, one of the world's most expensive shopping strips. Fashionistas in search of cutting-edge designs with that sassy LA edge should travel east to the urban designer boutiques lining Robertson Blvd between Beverly Blvd and 3rd St, Melrose Ave between San Vicente Blvd and Fairfax Ave, and Sunset Plaza in the 8600 and 8700 blocks of Sunset Blvd, just west of La Cienega Blvd. The area around the Pacific Design Center (dubbed the 'Avenues of Art & Design') yields some great finds on trendy home furnishings, furniture and art.

Further east, in Hollywood, La Brea Ave between Santa Monica and Wilshire Blvds is flanked by an eclectic mix of shops selling vintage clothing, art, home accessories and a global potpourri of tchotchkes. Sunset Blvd has plenty of music stores, including the famous Amoeba. On the Eastside, Los Feliz' Vermont Ave offers a happening blend of bookshops, hipster street-fashion

boutiques and punk record stores. At Sunset Junction in nearby Silver Lake, gradual gentrification has given birth to a schizophrenic commercial mix where a gourmet cheese shop shares a block with a Goth supply den, a mid-century furniture store and a lowbrow art gallery.

South of here, Downtown's Fashion District can yield great bargains if you're willing to brave the sensorial onslaught and dig through a lot of cheap junk. Downtown is also great for exotic souvenirs. Head to Olvera St or El Mercado in East LA for handcrafted Mexican leather goods, toys and piñatas. Chinatown has many shops selling imported porcelain, furniture and silk clothing, as well as chopsticks and soapstone Buddhas. Little Tokyo's main shopping center is the Japanese Village Plaza, between 1st and 2nd Sts. Look for imported kimonos, anime, origami art and fine spun pottery. For African art – masks, sculptures, paintings and crafts – head to Degnan Ave in Leimert Park Village.

Of the beach towns, the shopping is best in Santa Monica, which has three distinct shopping areas. Third St Promenade and the adjacent Santa Monica Place mall are mostly the purview of upscale chains, from Banana Republic to French Connection. For more interesting shopping head north to tony Montana Ave, which is chockablock with one-of-a-kind boutiques between 9th and 17th Sts. Main St in southern Santa Monica is another fun shopping zone, although less upscale and pricey.

Cheap and crazy knickknacks are what you'll find along the Ocean Front Walk in Venice Beach. This is the place to come if you're in the market for a spiked leather hat for your dog or a spiked leather bikini for your sister (or vice versa). If that's not your thing, head inland where Abbot Kinney Blvd has emerged as one of the Westside's most eclectic and interesting shopping strips with a great mix of art, fashion and New Age emporiums.

## Art

Unless noted, galleries are open from 10am to 5pm Tuesday to Saturday.

**Chac-Mool Gallery** (Map pp68-9; ☎ 310-550-6792; 8920 Melrose Ave, West Hollywood; ✆ 10am-6pm Tue-Fri, 11am-5pm Sat) This gallery may be small and stark but the canvases and sculptures on view often pack a provocative punch. The emphasis is on contemporary (read: abstract) Americans, including big names such as Robert Graham, Roy Thurston, Alison Van Pelt and Kenneth Noland.

**Fahey/Klein Gallery** (Map pp68-9; ☎ 323-934-2250; 148 S La Brea Ave, Mid-City) If a picture says a thousand words, this fine-art photography gallery is among the most eloquent in the field. Monthly rotating shows present both vintage and contemporary works in genres ranging from portraiture to landscapes and still lifes. Only the top names are here, including Annie Leibovitz, Herb Ritts and jazz scene photographer William Claxton.

**La Luz de Jesus** (Map pp66-7; ☎ 323-666-7667; 4633 Hollywood Blvd, Silver Lake; ☺ 11am-7pm Mon-Wed, 11am-9pm Thu-Sat, noon-6pm Sun) For a sneak peek at what might well be tomorrow's hot new artists, pop into Billy Shire's counterculture emporium. Shire, who's been dubbed the 'Peggy Guggenheim of lowbrow,' puts on monthly changing shows of edgy postpop works in genres ranging from folk and religious to pin-up and comic art. Manuel Ocampo, Neon Park, Robert Williams and others got their start here.

**Iturralde Gallery** (Map pp68-9; ☎ 323-937-4267; 2nd fl, 116 S La Brea Ave, Mid-City) At this spacious gallery the spotlight is firmly trained on contemporary Latin-American art. Run by sisters Ana and Teresa Iturralde, this space often serves as a launch pad to the North American market for south-of-the-border artists. Recently, the roster has included Cubans, and featured Raul Cordero and Jose Bedia.

**Margo Leavin Gallery** (Map pp68-9; ☎ 310-273-0603; 812 N Robertson Blvd, West Hollywood) Claes Oldenburg's *Knife Slicing Through Wall* sculpture provides a dramatic welcome to this well-established gallery, which specializes in contemporary paintings, drawings and sculpture.

**LA Louver Gallery** (Map pp72-3; ☎ 310-822-4955; 45 N Venice Blvd, Venice) Mere steps from the beach, this highfalutin gallery is known for its choice contemporary American and European art, including works by Tony Berlant, David Hockney, and Edward and Nancy Reddin Kienholz.

**Blum & Poe** (off Map pp72-3; ☎ 310-453-8311; 2754 S La Cienega Blvd, Culver City) One of LA's top contemporary art galleries anchors Culver City's emerging gallery district on La Cienega Blvd. The roster of high-profile art-

ists that have exhibited here includes Dave Muller, Sharon Lockhart and Sam Durant.

**Copro/Nason Gallery** (off Map pp72-3; ☎ 310-398-2643; 11265 Washington Blvd, Culver City; ☺ 1-6pm Wed-Sat) Like La Luz de Jesus, this is another great space for drawing a bead on LA's alternative art scene. Founders Joe Copro and Douglas Nason have funneled their shared passion for 'Kustom Kulture' art into a publishing company and gallery space. In a similar vein as La Luz de Jesus, exhibits often teeter on the surreal, outlandish and utterly bizarre. Niagara, Shag, Skot Olsen and Jolanda Olie have all been exhibited here.

**LMAN Gallery** (Map pp64-5; ☎ 213-628-3883; 949 Chung King Rd, Downtown; ☺ noon-6pm Wed-Sat) This is one of the few galleries on Chinatown's Chung King Rd that actually presents art by contemporary Asian artists, both local and from overseas.

**Mary Goldman Gallery** (Map pp64-5; ☎ 213-617-8217; 932 Chung King Rd, Downtown; ☺ noon-6pm Wed-Sat) This well-established gallery represents contemporary artists from LA, New York and Europe working in all types of media.

## Drinks & Eats

Traveling gourmets should have no problem stocking up on the familiar and the exotic in LA. For details about LA's oldest winery, see San Antonio Winery (p113).

**Cheese Store of Beverly Hills** (Map pp70-1; ☎ 310-278-2855; 419 N Beverly Dr, Beverly Hills; ☺ closed Mon) Mimolette and Raclette are not characters from a French romantic novel but just two of the hundreds of cheeses temptingly displayed at this little store. Take your pick from fragrant goat cheeses, creamy bries, crumbly blues, smoky goudas and other familiar and exotic cheeses, most of them handcrafted. The staff will happily advise.

**Cheese Store of Silver Lake** (Map pp66-7; ☎ 323-644-7511; 3926 W Sunset Blvd, Silver Lake) This place (not affiliated with the Beverly Hills store) has a smaller but also high-quality selection.

**La Brea Bakery** (Map pp68-9; ☎ 323-939-6813; 624 S La Brea Ave, Mid-City) It's been over 15 years since Nancy Silverton introduced her wholesome, flavorful and nutrition-packed loaves to the land of presliced Wonderbread. Now her handcrafted products are served at restaurants and sold in supermarkets (including Trader Joe's and Whole Foods, see p191) around town. This little store, though, is where it all started.

**Le Palais des Thés** (Map pp70-1; ☎ 310-271-7922; 401 N Cañon Dr, Beverly Hills; ☺ closed Sun) If you consider fine tea one of life's great pleasures, you'll find kindred spirits at this exquisite boutique, the first US branch of this small Paris-based chain. There are some 250 varieties from 30 countries to choose from, plus tea pots, tea cups, caddies, infusers and other accoutrements.

**Sorrento Italian Market** (off Map pp72-3; ☎ 310-391-7654; 5518 S Sepulveda Blvd, Culver City; ☺ 7am-7pm Mon-Sat, 7am-4pm Sun) Craving cannoli? Mad for mortadella? Salivating over salami? Head over to this old-world deli and market packed to the rafters with everything from wine to vinegar and pasta. Locals in the know come for the eggs and other products right from the local farm of owner Albert Vera, a former Culver City mayor.

**Comparte's of California** (off Map pp72-3; ☎ 310-826-3380; 912 S Barrington Ave, Brentwood; ☺ closed Sun) The Dom Perignon among candy stores, Comparte's has supplied mouthwatering truffles, toffees and chocolates to connoisseurs for over half a century. Their specialty, though, are hand-dipped fruits, with apricots drenched in rich dark chocolate being the perennial favorite. Free samples.

**Galco's** (off Map pp64-5; ☎ 323-255-7155; 5702 York Blvd, Highland Park; ☺ 9am-6:30pm Mon-Sat, 9am-4pm Sun) If Coca-Cola and Dr Pepper don't do it for you, why not try a Bireley's, Boylan, Faygo or any of the other 400 or so old-time soda pops that line the shelves of John Nese's unassuming corner store near Downtown. His Plantation Style Mint Julep is a cool drink on a hot day.

**Phoenix Bakery** (Map pp64-5; ☎ 213-628-4642; 969 N Broadway, Downtown) This bustling Chinatown bakery has been making fanciful cakes and cookies since 1938. It's especially famous for its strawberry-and-cream cakes.

## Farmers Markets
California is famous for its year-round produce, and vendors at weekly neighborhood farmers markets offer the best in quality and selection, much of it certified organic. Besides fruit and vegetables, there's usually a smattering of stalls selling flowers, crafts, and ready-made food such as French pastries, tamales or fresh pasta. Some even have live entertainment. Santa Monica is the undisputed market leader, with four of them taking place year-round, but there are

literally dozens more citywide. For a full list see www.cafarmersmarkets.com or www .farmersmarkets.org.

**Beverly Hills** (Map pp70-1; Civic Center Dr; ☺ 9am-1pm Sun)
**Culver City** (off Map pp72-3; Main St; ☺ 2-7pm Tue)
**Downtown/Chinatown** (Map pp74; cnr Hill & Alpine Sts; ☺ 4-8pm Thu)
**Hermosa Beach** (Map p74; Valley Dr btwn 10th & 8th Sts; ☺ noon-4pm Fri)
**Hollywood** (Map pp66-7; Ivar & Selma Aves btwn Sunset & Hollywood Blvds; ☺ 8am-1pm Sun)
**Santa Monica** (Map pp72-3) airport (Airport Ave, off Bundy Dr; ☺ 8am-1pm Sat); downtown (Arizona Ave & 3rd St; ☺ 8:30am-2pm Wed, 8:30am-1pm Sat); Main St (at California Heritage Museum; ☺ 9:30am-1pm Sun)
**Silver Lake** (Map pp66-7; Sunset Blvd btwn Edgecliff Dr & Maltman Ave; ☺ 8am-noon Sat)
**West Hollywood** (Map pp68-9; Plummer Park, 1200 N Vista St; ☺ 9am-2pm Mon)
**Westwood** (Map pp70-1; Weyburn Ave; ☺ 1-7pm Thu)

## Fashions
### DESIGNER
**Kristin Londgren** (Map pp68-9; ☎ 323-653-9200; 8308 W 3rd St, Mid-City; ☺ closed Sun & Mon) Londgren's original designs may not resonate with everyone (hand-knit tank top with separate neck cowl anyone?) but there's no denying that they have a unique edge. There's plenty of beaded jewelry to match, plus an assortment of acrylic home accessories by modernist maven Alessandro Albrizzi.

**Curve** (Map pp68-9; ☎ 310-360-8008; 154 N Robertson Blvd, West Hollywood) Fashionistas from around town make the pilgrimage to this stylish stretch of Robertson Blvd where Delia Seaman and Nevena Borissova present sexy, sassy and sometimes even sensible designer wear in their minimally furnished boutique. Don't even think about shopping here if you're size six or higher.

**Kitson** (Map pp68-9; ☎ 310-859-2652; 115 N Robertson Blvd, West Hollywood) If you like to stay ahead of the fashion curve, pop into this hip haven chock-full of tomorrow's outfits and accessories, many of them by local labels. A routine stop for celebs on a shopping prowl, Kitson also has stuff designed by the famous, such as girlish bags by Nicky Hilton who happens to be a fan of the ultracool King Baby sterling silver jewelry also sold here.

**American Apparel** (www.americanapparel.com; ☺ 11am-10pm Mon-Thu, 11am-11pm Fri & Sat, noon-8pm Sun) Downtown (Map pp64-5; ☎ 213-687-0467; 374 E 2nd

St, Little Tokyo); Los Feliz (Map pp66-7; ☎ 323-661-1407; 4665 Hollywood Blvd) Brand-name bunnies probably won't appreciate AA's stylish but logo-free T-shirts, tank tops, skirts and shorts available in a rainbow of colors. Everything is cut and sewn from high-quality cotton right here in Downtown LA in what the company says is a sweatshop-free facility. Check the website for locations of the other five branches around town.

**Lisa Kline** (Map pp68-9; ☎ 888-547-2554; 136 N Robertson Blvd, West Hollywood) A pioneer on the Robertson fashion strip, Lisa Kline has kept nubile young things looking good since 1995. Vamp it up with tops, skirts, dresses and pants from such hot labels as Juicy Couture, Ella Moss, Rebecca Taylor or Avitar. Women with real curves, alas, will find little selection. There's also a **men's store** (123 S Robertson Blvd) and a brand-new **outlet store** (Map pp68-9; 7207 Melrose Ave) with discounts of up to 75%.

**Last Chance** (off Map pp72-3; ☎ 310-287-2333; 8712 Washington Blvd, Culver City; ⊙ closed Sun) Label lovers on a budget make a regular beeline to this store to sieve through the latest shipment of last-season garments or overstock by Diesel, Seven, Prada, Ella Moss and many other designers, all sold at up to 75% off retail. There's also a good assortment of shoes, accessories and jewelry to complete the look.

**Fred Segal** West Hollywood (Map pp68-9; ☎ 323-651-4129; 8100 Melrose Ave); Santa Monica (Map pp72-3; ☎ 310-458-9940; 500 Broadway) Cameron and Gwyneth are among the stars getting kitted

---

### LA'S FASHION DISTRICT DEMYSTIFIED

Bargain hunters from throughout the city flock to this frantic 90-block warren of fashion in southwestern Downtown every day of the week (also see p113). Shopping here can be a lot of fun but first-timers often find the district bewildering and overwhelming. For orientation, you can print out a self-guided tour of the area from www.fashiondistrict.org. Serious shoppers can contact **Urban Shopping Adventures** ( ☎ 213-683-9715) for a guided tour led by people who know the district inside-out.

Basically, the area is subdivided into several distinct retail areas:

- Women – Los Angeles St between Olympic and Pico Blvds; 11th St between Los Angeles and San Julian Sts
- Children – Wall St between 12th St and Pico Blvd
- Men & bridal – Los Angeles St between 7th & 9th Sts
- Textiles – 8th St between Santee and Wall Sts
- Jewelry & accessories – Santee St between Olympic Blvd and 11th St
- Designer knockoffs – Santee Alley and New Alley (enter on 11th St between Maple and Santee Aves)

Shops with signs reading 'Wholesale Only' or 'Mayoreo' are off-limits to the public. Leave your credit cards at home because most vendors will only accept cash. Haggling is OK, but don't expect to get more than 10% or 20% off. There are usually no refunds or exchanges, so choose carefully and make sure the item is in good condition (many items sold here are 'seconds,' meaning they're slightly flawed). Most stores don't have dressing rooms. Hours are generally 9am to 5pm Monday to Saturday. Many stores are closed on Sunday except those on Santee Alley.

Clued-in fashionistas in town on the last Friday of the month can snap up amazing deals when dozens of designer showrooms – Betsey Johnson to Von Dutch – open to the public for just a few hours to unload samples and overstock. Prices are below wholesale and sometimes bargaining can yield extra savings. Sales take place from 9am to 3pm at the **New Mart** (Map pp64-5; ☎ 213-627-0671; 127 E 9th St), which specializes in contemporary and young designers, and across the street at the **California Mart** (Map pp64-5; ☎ 213-630-3600; 110 E 9th St), which is one of the largest apparel marts in the country with 1500 showrooms. Come early and bring cash. Not all showrooms are open every time, but there's always plenty to browse through. Note that sales are sometimes cancelled during fashion trade shows or around holidays. Always call ahead to confirm.

LOS ANGELES

out at this kingpin of LA fashion boutiques that doubles as a launch pad for new designers. Besides casual wear, you can stock up on beauty products, sunglasses, gifts and other essentials. Cash-strapped fashionistas invade during the two-week sale, usually in late September.

**DNA** (Map pp72-3; ☎ 310-399-0341; 411 Rose Ave, Venice) Tiny DNA is jam-packed with a small but choice assortment of hip garb for men and women, much of it with a stylish European flair, by local and national designers.

**Turtle Beach Swimwear** (Map pp68-9; ☎ 310-652-6039; 320 N La Cienega Blvd, West Hollywood) This little shop will have you looking good poolside with its big selection of mix-and-match tops and bottoms. Tankinis to push-ups, thongs to boy shorts in nylon, cotton, velvet, crochet – you name it, it's here. They even do custom work and can also reproduce your beloved but worn-out suit.

### LINGERIE

**Under G's** (Map pp70-1; ☎ 310-273-9333; 417 N Bedford Dr, Beverly Hills) This pretty store stocks the full assortment of underwear from G-rated boy shorts to revealing G-strings for women in all shapes or sizes. The winsome staff will help even the most body-conscious find a flattering fit. Labels includes La Perla, Harno, Aubade and Cosabella.

**Trashy Lingerie** (Map pp68-9; ☎ 310-652-4543; 402 N La Cienega Blvd, Mid-City; ⚇ closed Sun) Those who worship at the altar of hedonism should check into this cluttered store, stocked with everything girls and boys with imagination might need for a night of naughtiness. The assortment ranges from barely-there bikinis to complete school-girl outfits and, of course, bras and panties galore. To keep out looky-loos, you must pay $5 for an 'annual membership' at the door.

**Agent Provocateur** (Map pp68-9; ☎ 323-653-0229; 7961 Melrose Ave, Mid-City; ⚇ closed Sun) Currently the hottest ticket in seductive playwear, this British designer chain specializes in stylish, often provocative, but never sleazy, undergarments for adventurous women. The huge selection includes cleavage-enhancing bustiers and translucent baby dolls.

**Frederick's of Hollywood** (Map pp66-7; ☎ 323-466-8506; 6608 Hollywood Blvd, Hollywood) This is one of the oldest lingerie stores and still among the most popular. These are the people that gave us push-up bras and G-

strings. The assortment runs from the mainstream to the professional but it's all displayed tastefully with no need to blush. Also check out the collection of celebrity undies in the little museum in the back of the store (p80).

### VINTAGE & SECONDHAND

**Decades & Decades Two** (Map pp68-9; ☎ 323-655-0223, 323-655-1960; 8214 Melrose Ave, Mid-City; ⚇ closed Sun) Cameron Silver has a passion for '60s and '70s couture and accessories and keeps his gorgeous style emporium stocked with Pucci, Courrèges, Paco Rabanne, Chanel and other design legends. The top quality attracts Industry stylists and even the occasional celebrity. Downstairs at Decades Two, you can stock up on barely worn contemporary styles that may include Jimmy Choo heels, Marc Jacobs skirts and Fendi totes.

**Wasteland** (Map pp68-9; ☎ 323-653-3028; 7428 Melrose Ave, Mid-City; ⚇ 11am-8pm Mon-Sat, 10am-7pm Sun) This huge warehouse-sized space has glamour gowns, velvet suits and other vintage outfits going back to the '40s, plus rows of racks packed with contemporary styles, all in great condition and reasonably priced. You can even sell or trade your cast-offs, although the buyers here are pretty picky.

**Colleague Gallery** (Map pp72-3; ☎ 310-828-1619; Bergamot Station, 2525 Michigan Ave, Santa Monica; ⚇ 11am-3pm Mon & Thu, 1st Sat of month) Despite its location in the arty enclave of Bergamot Station, this nonprofit 'gallery' hawks not paintings but secondhand designer fashions, often at rock-bottom prices. Racks are filled with everything from couture to casual wear by Armani, Chanel, YSL, Ralph Lauren and other labels. Proceeds benefit Children's Institute International.

**Jet Rag** (Map pp68-9; ☎ 323-939-0528; 825 N La Brea Ave, Mid-City) Missiles crash into the facade and animal skeletons double as mannequins at this warehouse-sized store with quality retro clothing and accessories. During the Sunday parking-lot sales, you can do battle with thrifty hipsters foraging for treasures among the bales of used clothing – just $1 a piece.

**Squaresville** (Map pp66-7; ☎ 323-669-8464; 1800 N Vermont Ave, Los Feliz) High quality at low prices is the magic formula that's kept this bilevel vintage store in business for many years. It's a veritable gold mine for clothes and accessories from all phases of fashion since the 1940s, including some we'd rather forget.

## SHOES

**Camille Hudson Shoes** (Map pp68-9; ☎ 323-953-0377; 4685 Hollywood Blvd, Los Feliz) Discerning 'foot-ishistas' regularly make the pilgrimage to this *über*-cool boutique for Camille's own line of immaculately crafted flats in vibrant colors (canary yellow to hot pink). She also stocks a choice selection of rare imports.

**Remix Vintage Shoes** (Map pp68-9; ☎ 323-936-6210; 7605 Beverly Blvd, Mid-City) This handsome store is stocked with never-worn vintage footwear from the 1920s to the '70s. If you need a pair of wingtips or wedgies to complete your retro look, this is where you'll find them. They also reproduce the most popular lines.

**Debout Shoes** (off Map p75; ☎ 818-906-7761; 13023 Ventura Blvd, Studio City, San Fernando Valley) Discover your inner Imelda at this irresistible store where you'll find all the latest foot fashions, mostly from Europe. Fashionable designs include maryjanes by Chie Mihara, flip-flops by Havaiana and supercomfy Puma sneakers.

## Gifts & Souvenirs

**Paper Source** (Map p76; ☎ 626-577-3825; 163 W Colorado Blvd, Pasadena) Letter writing may be a dying art in the age of emails and text messages, but this store still caters to traditionalists. Besides stationery in all shades of the rainbow it also stocks the most exquisite wrapping paper and all manner of accessories.

**Anime Jungle** (Map pp64-5; ☎ 213-621-1661; 319 E 2nd St, Downtown) Fans of anime, *tokusatsu* (live action heroes) and Japanese independent films will be well taken care of at this store, which brims with imported and domestic DVDs, VHS and CDs, plus all manner of accessories. It's right inside the Little Tokyo Mall (between the Cal Fed bank and the Miyako Hotel Los Angeles). Also check out nearby **Kamikaze Anime** (Map pp64-5; ☎ 213-626-2915; 329 E 2nd St).

**Hustler Hollywood** (Map pp68-9; ☎ 310-860-9009; 8920 Sunset Blvd, West Hollywood; ☺ 10am-2am) 'Relax – it's just sex' is the motto of this emporium of erotica run by the daughter of porno purveyor Larry Flynt. Lots of logo wear, books and magazines, toys, love lotions and lingerie orbit the 'inner sanctum' where you can purchase XXX-rated videos starring some of the people who might be standing next to you in the checkout line.

**Pleasure Chest** (Map pp68-9; ☎ 323-650-1022; 7733 Santa Monica Blvd, West Hollywood; ☺ 10am-mid-night Sun-Wed, 10am-1am Thu, 10am-2am Fri & Sat) LA's kingdom of kinkiness is filled with sexual hardware catering to every conceivable fantasy and fetish, though more of the naughty than the nice kind.

**Just Tantau** (Map pp72-3; ☎ 310-392-9878; 1353 Abbot Kinney Blvd, Venice) One of the oldest businesses on this funky-chic shopping strip, Tantau has great gifts for your hard-to-please friends. There's plenty of classy jewelry, alongside cotton clothing, handcrafted picture frames and other home accessories.

**La Plata Cigar Company** (Map pp64-5; ☎ 213-747-8561; 1026 S Grand Ave, Downtown) LA's only cigar factory has been rolling its aromatic smokes right in the back of this diminutive store since 1947. The tobaccos are primarily Dominican, Honduran and Ecuadorian, and up to nine kinds of leaf may find their way into each cigar.

## Health & Beauty

**Kiehl's** (Map pp72-3; ☎ 310-255-0055; 1516 Montana Ave, Santa Monica) Kiehl's body and skincare products are as coveted today as they have been for the past 150 years. This beautiful store, designed to look like an old-time apothecary, stocks the entire product palette, face creams to lip balm to sunscreen. Ask for free samples.

**Palmetto** Fairfax District (Map pp68-9; ☎ 323-653-2470; 8321 W 3rd St); Santa Monica (Map pp72-3; ☎ 310-395-6687; 1034 Montana Ave) This pretty store caters to your femme pampering needs, from soothing bubble baths to shimmering body creams and karma-cleansing candles, plus lots of unique knickknacks that make great gifts for the folks back home.

**Beauty Collection Apothecary** (Map pp68-9; ☎ 323-930-0300; 110 S Fairfax Ave, Mid-City) Both boys and gals love the huge selection of brands – from Ahava to Zirh – at this sleek beauty boutique at the Farmers Market. Look no further if you're in the hunt for Tweezerman nail clippers, infant shampoo by California Baby or the locally made Brave Soldier skincare 'for athletes.'

## Jewelry

**Jewelry District** (Map pp64-5; ☎ 213-622-3335; Olive & Hill Sts btwn 6th & 8th Sts, Downtown) For bling bling at a bargain head to the epicenter of LA's jewelry industry (the district is second in size only to New York's) where you can save up to 70% over retail on watches, gold, silver and gemstones. Quality varies and the mostly traditional designs are unlikely to make the glossy fashion magazines, but the selection is certainly huge. Some stores sell only to 'the trade.'

You're guaranteed superior quality, with corresponding price tags, at any of the shops on Rodeo Dr in Beverly Hills, where you can buy upscale and one-of-a-kind baubles. For those of us who failed to triple our net worth during the '90s, even a pair of tiny diamond stud earrings remains elusive at $4000. Others might actually find something to buy at this trio of treasure chests: **Tiffany** (Map pp70-1; ☎ 310-273-8880; 210 N Rodeo Dr), **Van Cleef & Arpels** (Map pp70-1; ☎ 310-276-1161; 300 N Rodeo Dr) and **Cartier** (Map pp70-1; ☎ 310-275-4272, 220 & 370 Rodeo Dr). If you're ready to seriously swoon, hit the buzzer to enter the emporium of **Harry Winston** (Map pp70-1; ☎ 310-274-8554; 371 N Rodeo Dr), the ultimate diamond purveyor to the stars.

**Moondance Jewelry Gallery** (Map pp72-3; ☎ 310-395-5516; 1530 Montana Ave, Santa Monica) You'd never know it from just walking past, but this little store is the go-to place for unique items by some of the hottest contemporary designers du jour, including Jeanine Payer, Ten Thousand Things and Me & Ro.

**Accents Jewelry** (Map pp72-3; ☎ 310-396-2284; 2900 Main St, Santa Monica) Pretty baubles to adorn just about every body from ears to toes fill the glass vitrines at this friendly little store on bustling Main St. Besides owner Steven Hanna's own creations, you'll be tempted by dozens of other lines, most of them in sterling silver and many designed by his former students.

**Maya** (Map pp68-9; ☎ 323-655-2708; 7452 Melrose Ave; Mid-City) Wallets of all sizes will find something affordable here. This eclectic store stocks a huge selection of funky silver jewelry – including toe rings, waist chains and ear curls – alongside an equally impressive collection of imported Asian and African masks, fertility figures and other carved items.

## Kids' Stuff

**Wound & Wound Toy Co** (Map pp68-9; ☎ 323-653-6703; 7374 Melrose Ave, Mid-City; ☉ 11am-8pm Mon-Thu, 11am-10pm Fri & Sat, noon-7pm Sun) Even adults can't resist fiddling with the wild universe of wind-up toys found at this fun store. Each costs just a few dollars, even the tiny human brain that hops along the counter.

They also sell hurdy-gurdy music boxes and tin toys; look for not-for-sale shelves of retired collectibles by the front door. Also at **Universal City Walk** (Map p75; ☎ 818-509-8129).

**La La Ling** (Map pp66-7; ☎ 323-664-4400; 1810 N Vermont Ave, Los Feliz) Babies and toddlers keen on making a fashion statement in kindergarten should drag their hip parents to this self-proclaimed 'baby lifestyle boutique.' A recent browse turned up C&C California T-shirts, faded jeans by Paper Denim & Cloth and a cashmere poncho by Claude. Owner Ling Chan also runs art, music and language classes so your bambinos can tell you *'merci beaucoup'* for their cool new stuff.

**Flap Happy Outlet Store** (Map pp72-3; ☎ 310-453-3527; 2330 Michigan Ave, Santa Monica) Tucked into an unspectacular corner of Santa Monica near the Bergamot Station gallery complex, this is where you can stock up on last season's play clothes, swim diapers, onesies, T-shirts and other apparel and accessories for kids ages zero to eight. Discounts up to 70%.

**Munky King** (Map pp64-5; ☎ 213-620-8787; 441 Gin Ling Way, Downtown; ☉ noon-7pm Sun-Thu, noon-8pm Fri & Sat) Part of the Chinatown art renaissance, this is a toy temple with a twist and an inventory more suitable to teens (and their hip parents) than tots. Specialized in independent designer toys from around the world, it features urban vinyl toys (a trend originating in Hong Kong), bizarre stuffed animals called Ugly Dolls, Kubricks from Japan and other alternative playthings.

**Puzzle Zoo** (Map pp72-3; ☎ 310-393-9201; 1413 Third St Promenade, Santa Monica; ☉ 10am-10pm Sun-Thu, 10am-midnight Fri & Sat) Growing minds will find plenty to like when perusing the over-stuffed shelves of this venerable toy store. Low-tech dolls, Lego and wooden trains will tempt the little ones, while the older set can drool over the action figures (Austin Powers to Lord of the Rings) or the mind-bending 3-D puzzles. Also in the **Beverly Center** (p190; ☎ 310-659-6829).

**Meltdown Comics & Collectibles** (Map pp68-9; ☎ 323-851-7283; 7522 W Sunset Blvd, West Hollywood; ☉ noon-7pm Sun & Mon, noon-9pm Tue, Thu-Sat, 10am-10pm Wed) LA's coolest comics store beckons with indie and mainstream books, from Japanese manga to graphic novels by Daniel Clowes of *Ghost World* fame. Also part of the store is Baby Melt with a great if small-ish selection of offbeat books, clothing and toys for kids, including Hello Kitty goods,

Roman Dirge's mix-and-match Halfsies minifigures, and reprints of Tin Tin in several languages.

## Kitchen & Home

**Le Sanctuaire** (Map pp72-3; ☎ 310-581-8999; 2710 Main St, Santa Monica) Cooking is one of life's great pleasures but for Jing Tio it's an obsession. He constantly scours the earth for the best in artisanal products that'll turn even simple meals into culinary celebrations. Only the finest oils, vinegars, teas, pastas and so on grace his shelves, along with Christofle stemware, Laguiole knives and Hermes porcelain.

**Surfas** (off Map pp72-3; ☎ 310-559-4770; 8825 National Blvd, Culver City; ⌚ closed Sun) The ultimate chef's playground, this giant warehouse is stuffed with kitchen tools and gadgets ranging from the essential to the ridiculous, plus a rich assortment of hard-to-find gourmet foods, all at very reasonable prices. From pepper mills to paella pans, duck bacon to Beluga caviar, you'll find them here.

## Music

**Amoeba Music** (Map pp66-7; ☎ 323-245-6400; 6400 W Sunset Blvd, Hollywood; ⌚ 10:30am-10pm Mon-Sat, 11am-9pm Sun) Hailing from San Francisco, independent Amoeba has made a big splash in Hollywood. All-star staff and listening stations help you sort through over half a million new and used CDs, DVDs, videos and vinyl. Price tags can be high, but in-store live shows are free (call the store or check the *LA Weekly* for the lineup).

**Vinyl Fetish** (Map pp66-7; ☎ 323-957-2290; 1614 N Cahuenga Blvd, Hollywood; ⌚ noon-9pm) Just up the street from Amoeba, this store is nirvana for the turntable brigade with classic and hot new releases in dance music, Goth, industrial, new wave and other esoteric sounds. The in-the-know staff will happily help you source a new favorite, and a handful of players stand by for easy prepurchase listening.

**Aron's Records** (Map pp66-7; ☎ 323-469-4700; 1150 N Highland Ave, Hollywood; ⌚ 10am-10pm Mon-Thu, 10am-midnight Fri & Sat) Since 1965 Aron's has been pleasing alpha-male customers with racks of used vinyl and CDs from the lands of punk, hard-core, obscure electronica and beyond. World beat and jazz selections are equally well-priced. For collectors, the Rare Room might yield some quality finds. The quarterly parking-lot sales, where everything is under $3, are legendary.

**Tower Records** (Map pp68-9; ☎ 310-657-7300; 8801 W Sunset Blvd, West Hollywood; ⌚ 9am-midnight) Chart hounds, import freaks, classical connoisseurs – they all will find their fill at this chain music store. The service is only so-so, but the selection is great, especially for mainstream stuff. Check the Yellow Pages for other branches around the city.

**Rockaway Records** (Map pp66-7; ☎ 323-664-3232; 2395 Glendale Blvd, Silver Lake; ⌚ 10am-9:30pm Mon-Sat, noon-8pm Sun) Rockaway buys, sells and trades all types of great music. Used CDs are fairly priced and there are plenty of booths for prepurchase listening. Collectors can forage through the rare-music section or stock up on posters, magazines and memorabilia.

**Rhino Records** (off Map pp70-1; ☎ 310-474-8685; 2028 Westwood Blvd, Westwood; ⌚ 10:30am-10pm Mon-Sat, noon-5:30pm Sun) With a pedigree going back over three decades, this legendary store gives serious collectors itchy fingers. Its selection of new and used vinyl and CDs includes hard-to-find treasures from all genres – rock, soul, blues, folk, jazz etc. Since it moved into much larger digs, you'll also find videos, DVDs, books, magazines and even a comics store. Great parking-lot sales.

**Hear Music** (Map pp72-3; ☎ 310-319-9527; 1429 Third St Promenade, Santa Monica; ⌚ 11am-11pm Sun-Thu, 11am-midnight Fri & Sat) This former indie store is now in cahoots with Starbucks but still specializes in grown-up sounds – from electronica to blues, world music to jazz – you're unlikely to find just anywhere. Test-listen over 10,000 CDs at ubiquitous PC stations or make your own customized compilation at the Listening Bar aided by friendly and knowledgeable staff members.

**Groove Riders** (off Map pp70-1; ☎ 818-981-3366; 14566 Ventura Blvd, Sherman Oaks; ⌚ noon-9pm) This DJ favorite in the San Fernando Valley is one of the best-stocked stores for the latest electronic club sounds from drum 'n' bass and techno to breakbeat and trance. There's also a library of rare and out-of-print titles, new and used DJ equipment and some pretty nifty street fashions and accessories. It also operates the Institute of Mixology for budding DJs.

**Head Line Records** (Map pp68-9; ☎ 323-655-2125; 7706 Melrose Ave, Mid-City; ⌚ noon-8pm) This is one of the best places in town for punk and hardcore, both domestic and rare imports, including limited editions. The owner is a good source for plugging into the scene.

**TINSELTOWN TREASURES**

So you've stood in Tom Cruise's footsteps at Grauman's Chinese Theatre, sat at the table at Koi once occupied by Britney Spears, and seen Ashton Kutcher in the flesh during a taping of the *Tonight Show*. But now the end of your LA trip is sadly in sight and Kansas City, Canberra or Nottingham just don't seem as glam as the City of Angels. To keep the tinsel glittering for a bit longer, pick up a souvenir from one of these stores, all of which stock a bit more than plastic Oscar statuettes and Hollywood Sign fridge magnets.

**Baby Jane of Hollywood** (Map pp68-9; ☎ 323-848-7080; 7985 Santa Monica Blvd, West Hollywood; ☺ noon-8pm) Fancy a Burt Lancaster autograph, vintage movie poster, or topless picture of Dame Julie Andrews? Then swing by this little store in the French Quarter Market Place (p85), which gained notoriety when hawking rubble from celebrity homes after the 1994 Northridge earthquake (half of the proceeds went to charity).

**It's a Wrap** (off Map p75; ☎ 818-567-7366; 3315 W Magnolia Ave, Burbank) Items from tank tops to tuxedos worn by actors, extras and cameos working on TV or movies is also the bread-and-better of this outfit. Everything, including designer clothes, is sold at steep discounts. Tags tell you the name of the show and sometimes that of the actor, so you'll know what to brag about.

**Larry Edmunds Bookshop** (Map pp66-7; ☎ 323-463-3273; 6644 Hollywood Blvd, Hollywood) The small storefront belies the great stuff that can be unearthed at this longtime purveyor of scripts, posters, stills and books about films, theater and TV.

**Reel Clothes & Props** (off Map p75; ☎ 818-508-7762; 5525 Cahuenga Blvd, North Hollywood; ☺ closed Sun) Besides wardrobe from such movies as *Men in Black* and *Monster's Ball*, Reel also has truckloads of props, including lamps, picture frames and ashtrays. Many of their higher-priced collectibles are also sold at www.reel clothes.com and on eBay. The store is about half a mile north of the North Hollywood subway station.

## Offbeat Items

**Wacko** (Map pp66-7; ☎ 323-663-0122; 4633 Hollywood Blvd, Silver Lake) Billy Shire's emporium of camp and kitsch has been a fun browse for over three decades. Pick up hula-girl swizzle sticks, a Frida Kahlo mesh bag, an inflatable globe or other, well, wacky, stuff. In back is La Luz de Jesus (p183), one of LA's top lowbrow art galleries.

**Hollywood Toys & Costumes** (Map pp66-7; ☎ 323-465-5555; 6600 Hollywood Blvd, Hollywood) Fancy strutting around in a Catwoman suit or a pair of feathery angel wings? For over half a century, this Walk of Fame store has catered to every whim and fantasy, not to mention countless film, TV and stage productions. Check out the 'monster pit' in the floor by the entrance and the gallery of the masks.

**Ozzie Dots** (Map pp66-7; ☎ 323-663-2867; 4637 Hollywood Blvd, Silver Lake) You'll need a wacky sense of aesthetics paired with a good dose of humor to put together a winning outfit from this shop's outrageous assortment of retro fashions, costumes and bizarre accessories such as paper soda jerk hats or sock garters.

**Audrey's Good Vibrations** (Map pp72-3; ☎ 310-664-1180; 1204 Abbot Kinney Blvd, Venice) At this quintessentially Venice store, you can have your chakra tested (free) before stocking up on organic oils, gem elixirs and flower essences to purge yourself of negative energy and restore karmic balance.

**Koma Books** (Map pp64-5; ☎ 213-239-0030; 1228 W 7th St, Downtown) Koma owner Dan specializes in the most warped, bizarre, sleazy, controversial and anarchic material ever committed to print. Murderers' diaries, Japanese porn, the history of LSD; nothing is off-limits. Call for opening hours.

## Shopping Malls

**Beverly Center** (Map pp70-1; ☎ 310-854-0071; 8500 Beverly Blvd, West Hollywood) Despite the bunker-like looks, this is LA's glamour mall, the place you're most likely to spot a celebrity prowling for kitten heels or a skimpy sundress. Macy's and Bloomingdale's anchor about 160 boutiques. There's a food court, restaurants (including the Hard Rock Café) and a California Welcome Center (p57).

**Westfield Shoppingtown Century City** (Map pp70-1; ☎ 310-277-3898; 10250 Santa Monica Blvd) If you prefer to do your shopping alfresco, this is your kind of mall. Godiva chocolates, Hugo Boss and Abercrombie & Fitch are just three of the 140 mostly high-end stores offering plenty of opportunity for parting with your cash. Bloomingdale's and Macy's anchor. Nice food court, too.

**Santa Monica Place** (Map pp72-3; ☎ 310-394-5451; 395 Santa Monica Place, Santa Monica) Frank Gehry designed this midsize mall with ocean views, which has featured in such movies as *Terminator II*. Besides Robinsons-May and Macy's, it's filled with designer stores, the Santa Monica Visitors Center (p58) and a huge, global food court with some more-than-decent eating options. Visitors can get discount coupons by calling ☎ 310-394-1049 or through www.santamonicaplace.com.

**Grove** (Map pp68-9; ☎ 323-900-8080; 189 The Grove Dr, Mid-City) LA's newest retail hub is a Euro-style outdoor mall rubbing up against the historic Farmers Market (p86). Besides a Nordstrom department store there's the usual bevy of chain stores flanking and a central 'main street' and circular plaza.

**Westside Pavilion** (off Map pp70-1; ☎ 310-474-6255; 10800 W Pico Blvd, Westwood) With its glass-covered atrium, three floors of boutiques and a pair of department stores (Nordstrom and Robinsons-May), this is a pleasant indoor mall where shoes and jewelry are special strengths.

**Citadel Outlets** (Map pp60-1 ☎ 323-888-1724; 5675 E Telegraph Rd, City of Commerce) LA County's only major outlet mall is concealed by a movie-set-like castle facade some 9 miles south of Downtown, right off I-5 Washington exit.

Ann Taylor, Eddie Bauer, Old Navy, Nine West and Benetton are among the 50 retailers selling seconds and last season's leftovers, often at amazing discounts.

Also recommended:

**Macy's Plaza** (Map pp64-5; ☎ 213-624-2891; 700 S Flower St, Downtown)

**7+Fig** (Map pp64-5; ☎ 213-755-7150; Figueroa & 7th Sts, Downtown) Attractive mall with popular food court and lunchtime piano player.

**Glendale Galleria** (Map p75; ☎ 818-240-9481; 2148 Glendale Galleria)

## Supermarkets

Ralphs, Vons, Pavilions and Albertsons are all variations on the good-old typical supermarket. No matter in which part of town you find yourself, you're never more than a few blocks away from one or the other.

**Trader Joe's** ( ☎ 800-746-7857) Santa Monica (Map pp72-3; ☎ 310-581-0253; 3212 Pico Blvd); West Hollywood (Map pp68-9; ☎ 310-657-0152; 8611 Santa Monica Blvd) Ask Angelenos what they would most miss if they left LA and many will blurt out 'Trader Joe's' in the same breath as 'sunshine' and 'beach.' That's because TJ's (as they say) has the most amazing selection of quality foods, including great wines, cheeses and prepared foods such as salads, at prices that make budget gourmets cluck with

---

### TOP FIVE FLEA MARKETS

Flea markets are like urban archaeology: you'll need plenty of patience and luck when sifting through other people's trash and detritus, but oh the thrill when finally unearthing a piece of treasure! We've rounded up the best of LA's many hunting grounds, so arrive early, bring small bills, wear those walking shoes and get ready to haggle.

**Rose Bowl Flea Market** (Map p76; Rose Bowl, 1001 Rose Bowl Dr, Pasadena; admission $7-20; ☯ 5am-4:30pm 2nd Sun of the month) The mother of all flea markets with over 2200 vendors. True pros show up at 5am (when admission is $20), flashlight in hand, to ferret out the best stuff.

**Pasadena City College Flea Market** (Map p76; 1570 E Colorado Blvd, Pasadena; admission free; ☯ 8am-3pm 1st Sun of the month) A favorite among thrifty treasure hunters. With about 450 vendors it's less overwhelming than the Rose Bowl and is famous for its music section. Proceeds help finance scholarships and student activities.

**Melrose Trading Post** (Map pp68-9; 7850 Melrose Ave; admission $2; ☯ 9am-5pm Sun) Small but choice, this market has about 100 purveyors feeding the current retro frenzy with funky and often quite bizarre stuff – from '40s glamour gowns to mermaid swizzle sticks.

**Santa Monica Outdoor Antique & Collectible Market** (Map pp72-3; Airport Ave, off Bundy Ave, Santa Monica; admission 6am-8am $7, 8am-3pm $5; ☯ 6am-3pm 4th Sun of the month) Victorian armoires, porcelain chamber pots, antique vases – there's enough stuff here to furnish an entire village of B&Bs. Quality is generally high, and so are the prices. It's at the Santa Monica Airport.

**Long Beach Outdoor Antique & Collectible Market** (Map pp62-3; Veteran's Memorial Stadium, Conant St btwn Lakewood Blvd & Clark Ave; admission $5; ☯ 6:30am-3pm 3rd Sun of the month) Bargains abound at this sprawling market with over 800 stalls hawking everything from vintage postcards to pottery, fur to furniture. Near Long Beach Airport.

**LOS ANGELES**

delight. For additional branches, phone the toll-free number above, then punch in your zip code.

**Whole Foods Market** (www.wholefoods.com) Fairfax District (Map pp68-9; ☎ 323-964-6800; 6350 W 3rd St); Redondo Beach (Map p74; ☎ 310-376-6931; 405 N Pacific Coast Hwy); West Hollywood (Map pp68-9; ☎ 323-848-4200; 7871 Santa Monica Blvd) This is an excellent, comprehensive natural foods store with humungous fresh produce, meat and fish counters and shelves upon shelves of vitamins. Check the website or the Yellow Pages for additional chains.

**Bristol Farms** Manhattan Beach (Map p74; ☎ 310-474-4317; 1570 Rosecrans Ave); West Hollywood (Map pp68-9; ☎ 323-845-1699; 7860 W Sunset Blvd) This small chain of gourmet supermarkets has attractive presentation, stellar selection and out-of-this-world prices.

**Gelson's** Marina del Rey (Map pp72-3; ☎ 310-306-2952; 13455 Maxella Ave); West Hollywood (Map pp68-9; ☎ 323-656-5580; 8330 Santa Monica Blvd) Gelson's excels at anything fresh – produce, meat, fish, flowers, baked goods etc – and is dependable in all other departments. Prices are rather high.

Other natural food stores include **Erewhon Natural Foods Market** (Map pp68-9; ☎ 323-937-0777; 7660 Beverly Blvd, Mid-City), which gets a good celebrity following, and **Wild Oats Natural Marketplace**, with several branches around town, including one in downtown **Santa Monica** (Map pp72-3; ☎ 310-395-4510; 500 Wilshire Blvd).

## GETTING THERE & AWAY
### Air

The main gateway to LA is the **Los Angeles International Airport** (LAX; Map pp62-3; ☎ 310-646-5252; www.lawa.org) right on the coast between Marina del Rey and Manhattan Beach. It has eight terminals situated around a two-level, central traffic loop. Ticketing and check-in are on the upper (departure) level, while baggage-claim areas are on the lower (arrival) level. The hub for most international airlines is the Tom Bradley International Terminal.

To travel between terminals, board the free Shuttle A beneath the 'Shuttle' sign outside each terminal on the lower level. Hotel courtesy shuttles stop here as well. A free minibus for the disabled can be ordered by calling ☎ 310-646-6402.

Domestic flights operated by Alaska, Aloha, America West, American, Southwest and United also arrive at **Bob Hope Airport** (Map pp60-1; ☎ 818-840-8840, 800-835-9287; www.burbankairport.com) in Burbank in the San Fernando Valley, which is handy if you're headed for Hollywood, Downtown or Pasadena.

To the south, on the border with Orange County, **Long Beach Airport** (Map pp62-3; ☎ 562-570-2600; www.longbeach.gov/airport) is convenient for Disneyland and is served by Alaska, American, America West and Jet Blue.

Another option is **Ontario International Airport** (Map pp60-1; ☎ 909-937-2700; www.lawa.org/ont), about 35 miles east of Downtown LA. It handles flights by 13 airlines, including Alaska, America West, American, Delta, Southwest and United.

### Bus

The main bus terminal for **Greyhound** (Map pp64-5; ☎ 213-629-8421; 1716 E 7th St) is in a grimy part of Downtown, so try not to arrive after dark. Bus No 58 makes the 10-minute trip to the transit plaza at Union Station with onward service around town, including Metro Rail's Red Line to Hollywood and Gold Line to Pasadena. Some Greyhound buses go directly to the terminal in **Hollywood** (Map pp66-7; ☎ 323-466-6381; 1715 N Cahuenga Blvd) and a few also pass through **Pasadena** (Map p76; ☎ 626-792-5116; 645 E Walnut St) and **Long Beach** (Map pp62-3; ☎ 562-218-3011; 1498 Long Beach Blvd). For general information about traveling aboard Greyhound, including sample fares, see p364 and p366.

### Car & Motorcycle

If you're driving into LA, there are several routes by which you might enter the metropolitan area.

From San Francisco and Northern California, the fastest route to LA is on I-5 through the San Joaquin Valley. Hwy 101 is slower but more picturesque, while the most scenic – and slowest – route is Hwy 1 (Pacific Coast Hwy).

From San Diego and other points south, I-5 is the obvious route. Near Irvine, I-405 branches off I-5 and takes a westerly route to Long Beach and Santa Monica, bypassing Downtown LA entirely and rejoining I-5 near San Fernando.

From Las Vegas or the Grand Canyon, take I-15 south to I-10, then head west into LA. I-10 is the main east–west artery through LA and continues on to Santa Monica.

## Train

Downtown's historic Union Station is the home of **Amtrak** (Map pp64-5; ☎ 800-872-7245; 800 N Alameda St). Interstate trains stopping in LA are the *Coast Starlight* to Seattle, the *Southwest Chief* to Chicago and the *Sunset Limited* to Orlando. The *Pacific Surfliner* travels daily between San Diego and Santa Barbara via LA. See p369 for full details.

## GETTING AROUND
### To/From the Airports
#### LAX

Door-to-door shuttles operate from the lower level of all terminals beneath the signs marked 'Shuttle.' Three companies dominate: **Prime Time** (☎ 800-473-3743), **Super Shuttle** (☎ 310-782-6600) and **Xpress Shuttle** (☎ 800-427-7483). You can expect to pay $14 to Downtown, $23 to Hollywood and $18 to Santa Monica. Practically all airport-area hotels have arrangements with shuttle companies for free or discounted pick-ups.

Curbside dispatchers will summon a taxi for you. Fares average $20 to $25 to Santa Monica, $25 to $35 to Downtown or Hollywood and up to $80 to Disneyland, plus a $2.50 airport surcharge.

You can also make the trip on public transportation, which is less convenient but cheaper. From outside any terminal catch a free Shuttle C bus to the LAX Transit Center at 96th St and Vicksburg Ave, the hub for buses serving all of LA, including the following:

**Culver City** Culver City bus No 6; about 20 minutes; $0.75
**Downtown** Metro Bus Nos 42a West; about 1¼ hours; $1.25
**Hollywood** Metro Bus No 42a West to Overhill/La Brea, transfer to Metro Bus No 212 North; about 1½ hours; $2.50
**South Bay cities** Metro Bus No 439; ½–1 hour; $1.25
**Venice and Santa Monica** Big Blue Bus No 3 East; about 50 minutes; $0.75
**West Hollywood** Metro Bus No 220 West; about 1¼ hours; $1.25
**Westwood** Culver City bus No 6; about 1 hour; $0.75

#### BOB HOPE AIRPORT

For door-to-door shuttle companies, see LAX above. Typical shuttle fares to Hollywood, Downtown or Pasadena are $20, $24 and $22. Cabs charge about $20, $30, $40, respectively. Metro Bus No 163 South goes to Hollywood (40 minutes), while Downtown is served by Metro Bus No 94 South (one hour).

#### LONG BEACH AIRPORT

Shuttle service (see LAX earlier for contact information) costs $34 to Disneyland, $51 to Downtown LA and $28 to Manhattan Beach. If you're using a cab, expect to pay $45, $65 and $40, respectively. By public transportation, Long Beach Transit Bus No 111 South makes the trip to the Transit Mall in downtown Long Beach in about 45 minutes. From here you can catch the Metro Blue Line to Downtown LA.

### Bicycle

Most buses are equipped with bike racks and bikes ride for free, although you must securely load and unload your bike yourself. Bicycles are also allowed on Metro Rail trains except during rush hour (6:30am to 8:30am and 4:30pm to 6:30pm Monday to Friday). See p128 for tips on where to hire a bike.

### Car & Motorcycle

Unless time is no factor – or money extremely tight – you're going to want to spend some time behind the wheel. The worst thing about driving is the sheer volume of traffic, especially during the morning (7am to 9am) and afternoon (3:30pm to 6pm) commutes.

Santa Monica, Beverly Hills and West Hollywood have public parking garages where the first two hours are free and rates low thereafter. Private lots and garages, especially in office districts, can cost an

---

#### FREEWAY LOGIC

Angelenos live and die by their freeways and sooner or later you too will end up part of this metal cavalcade. It helps to know that most freeways have both a number and a name which corresponds to where they're headed. However, to add to the confusion, freeways passing through Downtown LA usually have two names. The I-10, for instance, is called the Santa Monica Fwy west of the central city and the San Bernardino Fwy east of it. The I-5 heading north is the Golden State Fwy, heading south it's the Santa Ana Fwy. And the I-110 is both the Pasadena Fwy and the Harbor Fwy. Generally, freeways going east–west have even numbers, those running north–south have odd numbers.

exorbitant $3.50 for each 20-minute period. See individual neighborhood sections under Sights (p58) for local parking tips. Parking at motels and cheaper hotels is usually free, while fancier ones charge anywhere from $8 to $25 for the privilege. Valet parking at nicer restaurants and hotels is commonplace.

All the major international car-rental agencies have branches at LAX and throughout LA (see p367 for toll-free reservation numbers). If you don't have a booking use the courtesy phones in the arrival areas at LAX to phone car-rental companies for quotes or reservations. Office and lots are outside the airport, but each company has free shuttles to take you there.

For Harley rentals, go to **Eagle Rider** (Map pp62-3; ☎ 310-536-6777; www.eaglerider.com; 11860 S La Cienega Blvd, Hawthorne; ☸ 9am-5pm), just south of LAX, or **Route 66** (Map pp72-3; ☎ 310-578-0112, 888-434-4473; 4161 Lincoln Blvd, Marina del Rey; ☸ 9am-6pm Tue-Sat, 10am-5pm Sun & Mon). Rates range from $75 to $135 a day, with discounts for longer rentals.

## Public Transportation
### METRO BUS & RAIL

Most public transportation is handled by **Metro** ( ☎ 800-266-6883; www.metro.net; ☸ 6:30am-7pm Mon-Fri, 8am-4:30pm Sat & Sun). To find out how to get from point A to point B, call Metro's toll-free number or use its website's trip planner.

The regular base fare is $1.25 per boarding with a surcharge of 50¢ to $1 for freeway express buses. Day passes are $3 and good for unlimited travel on all Metro Bus and Metro Rail lines. Weekly passes are $14 and valid from Sunday to Saturday. Monthly passes are $52 and valid for one calendar month. You can also save by buying a bag of 10 tokens for $11; you'll need one token per boarding.

Metro Bus drivers sell single tickets (exact fare required), while Metro Rail tickets are available from ticket vending machines at each station. Day passes are also available from drivers and the machines, but weekly or monthly passes and tokens must be bought at one of 850 locations around town, including Ralphs and Pavilions supermarkets (call or see the website for the one nearest you).

### Metro Buses
Metro operates about 200 bus lines, most of them local routes stopping every few blocks. Metro Rapid buses stop less frequently and have special sensors that keep traffic lights green when a bus approaches. Commuter-oriented express buses connect communities with Downtown and other business districts and usually travel via the freeways.

### Metro Rail
This is a network of four rail lines, three of them converging in Downtown (see Map p77). All of the stations are served by Metro buses.
**Blue Line** Downtown to Long Beach; connects with the Red Line at 7th St/Metro Center station and the Green Line at the Imperial/Wilmington stop.
**Gold Line** Downtown's Union Station to Pasadena via Chinatown, Mt Washington and Highland Park; connects with the Red Line at Union Station.
**Green Line** Norwalk to Redondo Beach; connects with the Blue Line at Imperial/Wilmington.
**Red Line** Subway going from Downtown's Union Station to North Hollywood (San Fernando Valley) via central Hollywood and Universal City; connects with the Blue Line at the 7th St/Metro Center station in Downtown.

### MUNICIPAL BUSES
Santa Monica–based **Big Blue Bus** (BBB; ☎ 310-451-5444; www.bigbluebus.com) serves much of western LA, including Santa Monica, Venice, Westwood and LAX (75¢). Express bus No 10 runs from Santa Monica to Downtown ($1.75). The BBB also operates the electric Tide Shuttle, which connects Third St Promenade with Main St (25¢).

---

### SIGHTSEEING (ALMOST) ON A DIME

For a cheap sneak peek at some of the city's major neighborhoods, hop on Metro Bus No 720. For little more than the price of a candy bar, you can sit back in its air-conditioned comfort as it barrels along Wilshire Blvd all the way from Santa Monica to Downtown via Westwood, Beverly Hills, Fairfax District, Miracle Mile District and Koreatown. If you get a day pass, you're free to get on and as often as you wish. If you don't interrupt your trip, the one-way journey takes about 90 minutes.

The **Culver CityBus** ( ☎ 310-253-6500; www .culvercity.org) provides service throughout Culver City and the Westside, including LAX (75¢).

### DASH BUSES

These small clean-fuel shuttle buses, run by the **LA Department of Transportation** (LADOT; ☎ your area code + 808-2273; www.ladottransit.com), operate along 30 routes serving local communities (25¢ per boarding). Here are some of the most useful lines:

**Beachwood Canyon Route** Useful for close-ups of the Hollywood Sign, runs from Hollywood Blvd up Beachwood Dr.

**Downtown Routes** Six separate routes, actually, hitting all the hot spots, including Chinatown, City Hall, Little Tokyo, the Financial District and Exposition Park.

**Fairfax Route** Makes a loop taking in the Beverly Center mall, the Pacific Design Center, the Farmers Market and LACMA and other museums on the Miracle Mile.

**Hollywood/West Hollywood Route** Connects Hollywood & Highland with the Beverly Center along Sunset Blvd (including Sunset Strip) and La Cienega Blvd.

## Taxi

Except for those lined up outside airports, train stations, bus stations and major hotels, cabbies only respond to phone calls. Fares are metered and cost $2 at flag fall plus $1.80 a mile. Companies include the following:

**Checker** ( ☎ 800-300-5007)

**Independent** ( ☎ 800-521-8294)

**Yellow Cab** ( ☎ 800-200-1085)

# Orange County

Mention Orange County and most people think only of Disneyland, tract homes, traffic jams and Republicans. But there's more 'beyond the Orange Curtain' than Mickey Mouse, Stepford Wives and Hummer-driving neo-cons. California's surf culture was born in the town of Huntington Beach, one of a string of famous beach communities on the 42-mile-long Orange County coast. Inland towns have large Latino populations whose ancestors came here when orange crops were the main source of income. And a burgeoning Vietnamese community has transformed the city of Westminster into 'Little Saigon.'

Although it's a mosaic of 34 independent cities with three million inhabitants, Orange County identifies itself as a 'county' more than any other in Southern California, with county-wide publications, such as the daily newspaper *Orange County Register* and the *Orange County Weekly,* for entertainment reviews and listings. Thanks to a hit TV show, 'OC' has become the shorthand by which people refer to the county, cementing its identity as a single place in the minds of American TV viewers.

The biggest problem tourists face in Orange County is finding cultural texture. This is a hodgepodge of suburbs after all, not a giant city. OC fashion comes from the malls, and most restaurants are chains. But don't forget, when too much commercialism gets you down, there's always the glorious beach to rejuvenate the spirit. Just don't try to drive there during rush hour.

---

### HIGHLIGHTS

- Paying a visit to the Mouse at **Disneyland** (p199) and lingering for brilliant fireworks over **Sleeping Beauty Castle** (p204)

- Sunning on the fine, white sand of Orange County's **Huntington Beach** (p215) and watching sexy surfers ply the crashing waves

- Stepping back in time at the gorgeous **Mission San Juan Capistrano** (p231), one of the best preserved of the famous California missions

- Gazing from the bluff-top Heisler Park out at the churning aquamarine waters off the coast of **Laguna Beach** (p227), a breathtaking sliver of California Riviera

- Meditating at the **Crystal Cathedral** (p212), a sparkling house of worship by master-architect Philip Johnson

| | |
|---|---|
| ORANGE COUNTY POP: 3 MILLION | AVERAGE TEMPS: JAN 44/65°F, JUL 61/80°F |

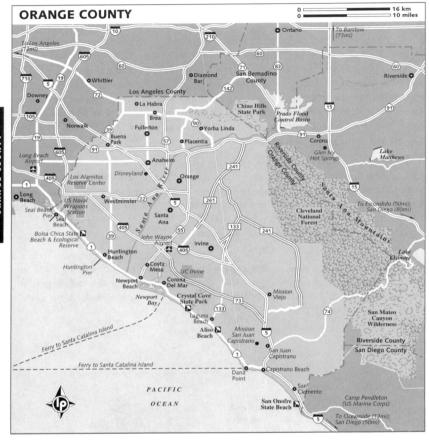

# ORANGE COUNTY

## GETTING THERE & AROUND
### Air

Coming from overseas, you'll change flights – and clear US Customs – at one of the major western US gateway airports, such as LA, San Francisco, Chicago or Dallas. Airlines serving Orange County include Alaska, Aloha, America West, American, Continental, Delta, Frontier, Midwest, Northwest, Southwest and United.

If you're heading to Disneyland or the Orange County beaches, you can avoid the always-busy Los Angeles International Airport (LAX) by flying into the easy-to-navigate **John Wayne Airport** (SNA; ☎ 949-252-5200; www.ocair.com) in Santa Ana. If you want restaurants and duty-free shopping, stick to

LAX, but for get-in, get-out domestic travel, SNA is ideal. The airport is inland 8 miles from Newport Beach, via Hwy 55, near the junction of I-405 (San Diego Fwy).

**Long Beach Airport** (LGB; ☎ 562-570-2600; www.longbeach.gov/airport), to the north just across the county line, is a handy alternative.

See p210 for details of the Airport Bus from LAX to Disneyland.

### Bus

For getting around by public transportation, the **Orange County Transportation Authority** (OCTA; ☎ 714-636-7433; www.octa.net; info line 5am-10pm Mon-Fri, 7am-7pm Sat & Sun) operates a fleet of buses serving towns and destinations throughout the county. The fare is $1 per ride or $2.50 for a day pass. Both types of tickets are sold aboard and you'll need exact change. Free OCTA bus system maps and schedules are available at train stations, most chambers of commerce and online. You can get schedule information by phone, but there is no after-hours automated phone service, so call before it closes.

## Car

The easiest way to get around Orange County is by car – but try to avoid driving on the freeways during morning and afternoon rush hours (7am to 10am and 3pm to 7pm).

## Train

Fullerton, Anaheim, Orange, Santa Ana, Irvine and San Juan Capistrano are all on Amtrak's *Pacific Surfliner* train route (p369) and are also linked by the **Metrolink** ( ☎ 800-371-5465; www.metrolinktrains.com) commuter trains from downtown LA (p369).

---

**TOP THREE SPOTS TO POSE FOR A PHOTO**

■ Disneyland – In front of the floral **Mickey Mouse** (p202), just inside the entrance gate

■ Newport Beach – **Lookout Point** (p221) in Corona del Mar, high above Newport Harbor

■ Laguna Beach – **Heisler Park** (p227), in front of the sculptures atop the bluffs overlooking the churning waves

---

# DISNEYLAND & ANAHEIM

**pop 328,000**

When Walt Disney trotted out his famous mouse in 1928, it triggered a commercial bonanza that's been relentlessly expanding ever since. Fueled by the dreams of children worldwide, Disney has become a legend of corporate success – and excess – in virtually every medium it has touched: film, TV, publishing, music, merchandising and, of course, theme parks.

Opened in 1955 by Walt Disney himself, Disneyland has been carefully 'imagineered'

and perfectly crafted to ensure every visitor a wonderful time. Everything is impeccable, from the pastel sidewalks to the behavior and personal hygiene of the roughly 21,000 park employees, called 'cast members' in Disney-speak. But it's not without shortcomings. Some cast members are aggressive with their too-happy world view; it can be creepy. And the Disneyland of old had none of the product placement that exists here today. You can hardly walk anywhere without spotting a strategically placed corporate logo from a major company. There's a lot to criticize, but there's a lot to praise, too, making Disneyland an essential stopover on a tour of Southern California.

The surrounding city of Anaheim recently completed a staggering $4.2 billion revamp and expansion, cleaning up rundown stretches where hookers once roamed, and establishing the first police force in the US specifically to guard tourists (they call it 'tourist-oriented policing'). The cornerstone of the five-year effort was the addition of a second theme park in February 2001, Disney's California Adventure (DCA). It's adjacent to the original park, and designed to pay tribute to the state's most famous natural landmarks and cultural history. Also new is Downtown Disney, an outdoor pedestrian mall lined with corporate-owned chain stores, restaurants and entertainment venues. The ensemble is called the 'Disneyland Resort.' In Anaheim park, access roads have been widened and attractively landscaped, and the whole area has been given the lofty name 'The Anaheim Resort.'

## INFORMATION
### Internet Access

Unless you're staying at a Disneyland hotel, there is no Internet access in any of the parks.

**Anaheim Visitors Center** ( ☎ 714-765-8888; www .anaheimvisitorscenter.com; cnr Harbor Blvd & Orangewood Ave; ☻ 7:30am-7:30pm Mon-Sat, 9am-6pm Sun) The closest place to check email.

**Kinko's** ( ☎ 714-703-2250; 700 W Convention Way; per min 40¢; ☻ 7am-10pm Mon-Fri, 9am-5pm Sat & Sun) In the Anaheim Marriott, at the convention center near the corner of Harbor Blvd and Katella Ave.

### Lockers

You can check items in lockers, which cost $5 to $7 per day, depending on the locker's

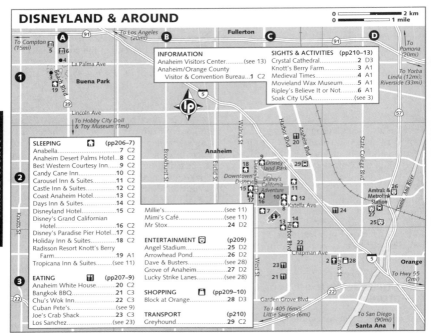

## DISNEYLAND & AROUND

0 ——— 2 km
0 ——— 1 mile

**INFORMATION**
Anaheim Visitors Center..........(see 13)
Anaheim/Orange County
  Visitor & Convention Bureau...**1** C2

**SIGHTS & ACTIVITIES** (pp210–13)
Crystal Cathedral..................**2** D3
Knott's Berry Farm................**3** A1
Medieval Times.....................**4** A1
Movieland Wax Museum.......**5** A1
Ripley's Believe It or Not.......**6** A1
Soak City USA.....................(see 3)

**SLEEPING** (pp206–7)
Anabella...............................**7** C2
Anaheim Desert Palms Hotel...**8** C2
Best Western Courtesy Inn......**9** C2
Candy Cane Inn....................**10** C2
Carousel Inn & Suites............**11** C2
Castle Inn & Suites...............**12** C2
Coast Anaheim Hotel............**13** C2
Days Inn & Suites.................**14** C2
Disneyland Hotel..................**15** C2
Disney's Grand Californian
  Hotel...............................**16** C2
Disney's Paradise Pier Hotel...**17** C2
Holiday Inn & Suites.............**18** C2
Radisson Resort Knott's Berry
  Farm...............................**19** A1
Tropicana Inn & Suites........(see 11)

**EATING** (pp207–9)
Anaheim White House...........**20** C2
Bangkok BBQ......................**21** C3
Chu's Wok Inn.....................**22** C3
Cuban Pete's.......................(see 9)
Joe's Crab Shack..................**23** C3
Los Sanchez.......................(see 23)
Millie's..............................(see 11)
Mimi's Café.........................(see 11)
Mr Stox.............................**24** D2

**ENTERTAINMENT** (p209)
Angel Stadium.....................**25** D2
Arrowhead Pond..................**26** D2
Dave & Busters....................(see 28)
Grove of Anaheim................**27** D2
Lucky Strike Lanes...............(see 28)

**SHOPPING** (pp209–10)
Block at Orange...................**28** D3

**TRANSPORT** (p210)
Greyhound.........................**29** C2

---

size. All have in-and-out privileges. There are lockers on Main St, but don't confuse these with the package-check areas for purchases made at the park's shops (shoppers can store items purchased in the park for free at these areas; ask for details at the register).

### Lost & Found
Lost & found ( ☎ 714-817-2166)

### Medical Services
**Western Medical Center Anaheim** ( ☎ 714-533-6220; 1025 S Anaheim Blvd; ⏱ 24hr) Urgent medical attention available 24/7.

### Money
In Disneyland, the Bank of Main Street has foreign currency exchange and basic services. In Disney's California Adventure park, head to the Guest Relations lobby.
**Bank of America** ( ☎ 714-533-4470; 2260 S Harbor Blvd) In Anaheim.
**Travelex** ( ☎ 714-502-0811; 1565 S Disneyland Dr; ⏱ 9am-5pm Mon-Fri) In Downtown Disney; change foreign currency here.

### Post
**Holiday Station post office** ( ☎ 714-533-8182; www .usps.com; 1180 W Ball Rd; ⏱ 8:30am-5pm Mon-Fri) Mail packages and letters at this full-service post office.

### Smoking
Most of the park is nonsmoking, but look for special areas where you can light up; they're marked on park maps.

### Tickets & Opening Hours
Both parks are open 365 days a year. You can access the **current schedule** (recorded info ☎ 714-781-4565, live assistance ☎ 714-781-7290; www .disneyland.com) by phone or online. Park hours vary, depending on the marketing department's forecasted attendance numbers. During peak season (mid-June to early September) Disneyland's hours are usually 8am to midnight; the rest of the year, 10am to 8pm or until 10pm. DCA closes at 10pm in summer, earlier in the off-season.

One-day admission to *either* Disneyland or DCA costs $50 for adults, $40 for children aged three to nine. To visit *both* parks in one day costs $70/60 per adult/child. Multi-

Day Park Hopper Tickets cost $98/78 for two days, $129/99 for three days, $159/129 for four days, and $184/149 for five days of admission within a two week period. Ticket prices increase annually; check the website for the latest information or to buy tickets.

You can also purchase a Southern California CityPass for $179/129, which permits three-day admission to Disneyland and DCA, as well as one-day admission to Knott's Berry Farm (p211), the San Diego Zoo (p253) and SeaWorld (p278); the total savings is roughly $70 per person.

Disney introduced the free Fastpass system, which pre-assigns you specific boarding times for selected attractions, thereby significantly cutting wait times. Look for ticket machines near the entrances to the rides. Simply show up at the time printed on the ticket and go straight to the Fastpass line instead of the regular line. There's still a wait, but it'll be much shorter. You can only get one Fastpass at a time.

Better yet, if you're alone, ask the attendant at the entrance to each attraction if there's a single-rider line; often you can head right to the front of the queue.

## Tourist Information

**Anaheim Visitors Center** ( ☎ 714-765-8888; www.ana heimvisitorscenter.com; cnr Harbor Blvd & Orangewood Ave; ☼ 7:30am-7:30pm Mon-Sat, 9am-6pm Sun) Just south of DCA, with information on countywide lodging, dining and transportation, as well as Internet kiosks. The staff will help you book lodging and will answer questions via telephone. For a primer on OC's car culture, pick up the *Orange County Area Driving Guide*; it has simple directions and maps to nearby attractions. The visitors center is operated by the **Anaheim/Orange County Visitor & Convention Bureau** ( ☎ 714-765-8888; www.anaheimoc.org).

## Travel Agencies

**Walt Disney Travel Company** ( ☎ 714-520-5060, 800-828-0228; www.disneytravel.com) You can save substantially by booking your trip to Disneyland through this agent, which sells packages that include air, hotel and park tickets.

ORANGE COUNTY

---

### DOING DISNEY RIGHT

Here are some tips to help you make the most of your visit:

■ Plan on at least one day for each park, more if you want to go on all the rides. Lines are longest during summer and around major holidays. In general, visiting midweek is better than Friday, Saturday or Sunday, and arriving early in the day is best. If you really want to avoid crowds, come in spring or fall or right after Labor Day. Nobody's here in February. However, in December and the first week of January crowds pack the resort to see the holiday decorations.

■ In summer bring a hat, suntan lotion, patience and – if cutting costs is important – bottled water.

■ Many rides have minimum age and height requirements; avoid tantrums by prepping the kids.

■ When you arrive at the park, expect to have your bags searched before passing through the turnstiles (looking for bombs and knives, etc; you're allowed to bring in food).

■ Plan your time carefully. As you enter, pick up a park map and a show schedule to help you prioritize. You can also find out about temporary closures of attractions, check show times and get information at the Disneyland Information Board in City Hall, on the left as you arrive inside the park. At Disney's California Adventure (DCA), inquire at the Guest Relations Lobby, just inside the gate.

■ In order for Disneyland to be the happiest place on Earth, you'll need some small window into someone else's misery. You'll find it on the faces of exhausted parents moping down Main St. Don't make the same mistake. During the heat of the day, if possible, go back to your hotel. The kids can frolic in the pool while you doze with a book on your face. Come 9pm, while you're standing around waiting for the fireworks display, you'll be glad you did. *Really* glad.

■ See Tickets & Opening Hours (p200) for tips on reducing the wait time for attractions.

ORANGE COUNTY

**TOP FIVE MUST-SEE ATTRACTIONS**

- Space Mountain (Tomorrowland, p203)
- Pirates of the Caribbean (New Orleans Square, p203)
- Haunted Mansion (New Orleans Square, p203)
- Indiana Jones (Adventureland, p203)
- It's a Small World (Fantasyland, p203)

## SIGHTS & ACTIVITIES
### Disneyland Park

Like it or not, welcome to the 'happiest place on Earth.' As you walk through the gates of **Disneyland** (recorded info ☎ 714-781-4565, live assistance ☎ 714-781-7290, switchboard ☎ 714-781-4000; www.disneyland.com) and along the red-brick path – suggestive of a red carpet – a giant floral Mickey Mouse blooms before you. A sign above the nearby archway reads 'Here you leave today and enter the world of yesterday, tomorrow and fantasy' – a disconcerting notion to Buddhists and philosophers, but a delight to the millions of children who visit every year. This is their park, but adults who can willingly suspend disbelief and give in to the 'magic of Disney' will have just as much fun.

Notice that there are no outside visual intrusions. You can't see out, and nobody can see in. The Disneyland Railroad and the wall of foliage mark 'the berm' between the inside and outside worlds. There are over 40,000 shrubs and perennial flowers, and more than 5000 trees throughout the park to achieve the overall effect. Disney even has its own genetically modified rose; look for it at the base of the flag pole as you enter.

What amusement parks call 'rides,' Disneyland calls 'attractions.' A ride, say, on a roller coaster, is little more than a quick thrill. An attraction is a journey into a narrative. At Disneyland there are *only* attractions; pay attention to the details you start to see as soon as you queue up. You can visit the same attraction several times and still miss something. The real magic of Disney lies in its meticulous and extensive production values.

### MAIN STREET USA

Upon entering the park, you're funneled onto Main St USA, which was fashioned after Walt's hometown of Marcilene, Missouri, and resembles the classic turn-of-the-20th-century all-American town, before the advent of the mall. Everything here is designed to celebrate an idealized vision of the USA. The music playing in the background is from American musicals. There's a flag-retreat ceremony every afternoon. And the main attraction is about Abraham Lincoln. **Great Moments with Mr Lincoln** is a 15-minute audio-animatronic (an eerily lifelike talking mannequin) presentation on Honest Abe in which you wear headsets that deliver sound so stellar you'll mistakenly feel someone breathing down your neck.

Have your picture taken with Mickey or Minnie or any of the other oversized characters prancing around here. You can also pick up the **Disneyland Railroad**, a steam train that makes a loop around the park and stops at four different stations.

There's plenty of shopping, but wait until the end of the evening; Main St's stores remain open after the park's attractions close.

Main St ends in the **Central Plaza**, the center of the park and the point from which all the 'lands' extend (eg Frontierland and Tomorrowland). Lording over the plaza is the **Sleeping Beauty Castle**. Inside the iconic structure (which was fashioned after a real castle in southern Germany), dolls and big books tell the story of Sleeping Beauty.

**WHERE'S MICKEY?**

As you wander through the Disneyland Resort, try and find the 'hidden Mickeys.' Throughout the parks and in Downtown Disney, the distinctive outline of Mickey Mouse's head and ears is hidden in unexpected places. Atop flag poles, on painted signs, in filigree, at entrance gates – they're everywhere, you just have to train your eye to find them. Here's one to get you started: After you pass through the turnstiles at Disneyland, turn right and look at the fanciful woodwork in the white-washed sign atop the stroller- and wheelchair-rental station. The distinctive three circles are carved out of the wood.

Pay attention to the wonderful **optical illusion** along Main St. As you look from the entrance, up the street toward Sleeping Beauty Castle, everything looks far away and big. When you're at the castle looking back, everything looks closer and smaller. Welcome to Disneyland.

## TOMORROWLAND

Fetishization of modern technology at the time of the park's opening in 1955 inspired Tomorrowland, which sought to provide a glimpse into the future – evidence the retro-high-tech **Monorail** (which you can ride to Downtown Disney). The freeway system had not yet been built, which explains why **Autopia** was such a hit 50 years ago. Today young kids who don't yet have their driver's license love operating the miniature cars around the looping 'highway,' but adults – who are probably just as happy *not* to be driving right now – should skip the attraction. Instead take **Star Tours**, in which you find yourself clamped into a StarSpeeder vehicle piloted by a dysfunctional android on a wild and bumpy ride through deep space. **Space Mountain**, one of the park's signature attractions and one of the best roller coasters in America, will take your head off as you hurtle into complete darkness at frightening speed – you *will* scream long and loud. The Disneyland Railroad also stops here.

## FANTASYLAND

At the core of the park, behind Sleeping Beauty Castle, Fantasyland is filled with the characters of classic children's stories, such as Dumbo the Elephant and Peter Pan. Little kids and romantic adults love the **King Arthur Carousel**. Children also like whirling around the **Mad Tea Party** tea-cup ride. **Peter Pan's Flight**, one of the park's original attractions, takes you floating through the air in a galleon. If you only see one attraction in Fantasyland, visit **It's a Small World**, a boat ride past hundreds of animatronic children from all of the world's cultures singing the song of the same name. Young children go nuts for this musical voyage, but be warned: days after you've left the park, this maddening little ditty will play on and on in your head (the only sure antidote: Led Zeppelin). Another classic, the **Matterhorn Bobsleds** is a steel-frame roller coaster that mimics a bobsled ride down a mountain.

## MICKEY'S TOONTOWN

At the northern end of the park, beyond Fantasyland, Mickey's Toontown is the province of the elementary-school set. This is where Mickey and Minnie make their home (separately, of course; this *is* Disneyland), where Donald keeps his boat, Goofy has a Bounce House and Chip 'n Dale tree house. Little ones who enjoy motion will love **Roger Rabbit's Cartoon Spin**, a miniature car ride you can spin on its tracks, and **Gadget's Go Coaster**, a roller coaster sized perfectly for tots. The Disneyland Railroad also stops here.

## FRONTIERLAND

Frontierland gives a nod to the rip-roarin' Old West, when cowboys made their own kind of law and order. This is a low-key are a of the park, and even small children will emerge unshaken after a ride on the **Big Thunder Mountain Railroad** roller coaster. **Rivers of America** pays tribute to 19th-century river culture, with **Tom Sawyer's Island** in the middle of the water. Take **Tom Sawyer's Raft** to the island, where kids can play in the woods.

## ADVENTURELAND

Dedicated to exploration and adventure, Adventureland loosely derives its style from Southeast Asia and Africa. The hands-down highlight is the jungle-themed **Indiana Jones Adventure**. Enormous HumVee-type vehicles lurch and jerk through the wild for spine-tingling encounters with creepy crawlies and scary skulls in re-creations of stunts from the famous film trilogy. (Look closely at Indie during the ride: is he real or animatronic?) Nearby, little ones love climbing the stairways of **Tarzan's Treehouse** and imagining what it would be like to live in the trees. If all this jungle leaves you hot and tired, head to the air-conditioned retro-Polynesian **Enchanted Tiki Room**, Walt's first foray into audio-animatronics.

## NEW ORLEANS SQUARE

Adjacent to Adventureland, New Orleans Square has all the charm of that city's French Quarter, but none of the marauding drunks. New Orleans was Walt's and his wife Lilian's favorite city, and Walt paid tribute to it by building this stunning square. **Pirates of the Caribbean**, the longest ride in Disneyland (17 minutes), opened in 1967 and was the first addition to the original park. You'll float through the subterranean haunts of tawdry pirates, where buccaneers' skeletons perch atop their mounds of booty. This is the only ride in the park that addresses sex ('Buy a Bride') – blame it on the '60s. At the **Haunted Mansion**, '999 happy haunts' – spirits and goblins, shades and ghosts – evanesce and disappear while you ride in a cocoonlike car through web-covered graveyards of dancing skeletons. The Disneyland Railroad also stops at New Orleans Square.

### CRITTER COUNTRY

Winnie the Pooh makes his home here. Tucked behind the Haunted Mansion, Critter Country's main attraction is **Splash Mountain**, a flume ride through the story of Brer Rabbit and Brer Bear, based on the controversial film *Song of the South*. Stuffed-animal characters sing and dance as you float by. Right at the big descent, a camera snaps your picture. Some visitors to the park lift their shirts, earning the ride the nickname 'Flash Mountain.' Alas, hi-tech imaging now allows the park's cast members to cover up the offending breasts with a digitally placed Mickey Mouse T-shirt. (But you can find lots of images on the Internet from the old days.)

### SHOWS & PARADES

Verify all show times once you arrive in the park; also see p206 for events at DCA.

In summer look for **fireworks** above the park, nightly around 9:30pm. (In winter, snow falls after the fireworks; check schedules for locations.) The **Parade of the Stars** starring famous Disney characters takes place twice daily in high season.

**Snow White**, the musical, tells the famous story on stage, several times daily in the Fantasyland Theatre. No tickets necessary; line up 15 to 30 minutes before show time for good seats.

**Fantasmic!**, an outdoor extravaganza of huge proportions on Rivers of America across from New Orleans Square, may be the best show of all. It pulls out all the stops, using full-size ships, lasers, pyrotechnics (at one point the water catches fire), and over-the-top production values that define the Disney magic. Arrive early to scope a spot – the best are down the front by the water – or splurge and reserve the oh-so-civilized balcony seating upstairs in New Orleans Square, which

includes premium show seating, coffee and desserts. **Premium seating tickets** ( ☎ 714-781-4400; adult/child $50/40) can be reserved up to 30 days in advance. Ordinary seats are included in the price of park admission.

### TOURS

One of the best ways to get the most out of Disneyland is to take a **guided tour** (info ☎ 714-817-2299). Prices are the same for adults and children, and don't include park admission.

**Welcome to Disneyland Tour** ( ☎ 714-781-4400; 3hr tour $25) Gives the best overview and helps you plan your visit. Includes lunch.

**Walk in Walt's Footsteps** ( ☎ 714-781-7290; 3½hr tour $50) Visits all of the mastermind's favorite spots in the park, including his apartment in New Orleans Square. Includes sit-down lunch.

**Premier Tour** ( ☎ 714-300-7710; tour per hr $75-95) Hire a personal guide for a custom tour for up to 10 people. Four hour minimum.

## Disney's California Adventure

Whereas Disneyland is all about fantasy and make-believe, Disney's California Adventure (DCA) is about California geography and history – or at least a sanitized version of it. DCA covers more acres than Disneyland and feels less crowded, even on summer afternoons. If the other park leaves you feeling claustrophobic and jostled, you'll enjoy this one better, though it lacks the density of attractions and depth of imagination. Unlike Disneyland, DCA was built in conjunction with other major corporations, and it has a more brittle veneer because of it. Parts feel like a shopping mall more than a unified theme park, but it's still a work in progress. Disney parks are ever-changing, always evolving.

---

### TOP FIVE DCA ATTRACTIONS

- California Screamin' (Paradise Pier, p205)
- Soarin' Over California (Golden State, p205)
- Tower of Terror (Hollywood Pictures Backlot, p205)
- Grizzly River Run (Golden State, p205)
- It's Tough to be a Bug (A Bug's Land, p205)

Note that at DCA there's a mix of attractions and straightforward amusement park–style rides, such as the roller coaster and Ferris wheel, neither of which have any significant narrative. (But you can drink alcohol at DCA, which can help you invent your own stories.) Unlike at Disneyland, you can see outside the park to the *real* California beyond the gates.

### SUNSHINE PLAZA

The entrance to DCA sits directly opposite the entrance to Disneyland and was designed to look like an old-fashioned painted-collage postcard. As you pass through the turnstiles, note the gorgeous mosaics on either side of the entrance. One represents Northern California, the other Southern California. After passing under the Golden Gate Bridge, you'll arrive at Sunshine Plaza, where a 50ft-tall sun made of gold titanium 'shines' all the time because heliostats direct the rays of the real sun onto the Disney sun. Close your eyes and stand in the plaza, and you'll hear – over the blaring beach music (licensed by Disney, of course) – the simulated sound of the surf as produced by the plaza's fountain, a neat trick.

### HOLLYWOOD PICTURES BACKLOT

Designed to look like the back lot of a Hollywood studio, there's a mishmash of building styles here, with everything from a Frank Lloyd Wright knock-off to a Pantages-style theater. If you're early, you'll have an unobstructed look at the forced-perspective mural at the end of the street, a sky-and-land backdrop that looks, at least in photographs, like the street keeps going. Very cool. In the air-conditioned **Animation Building**, which most people pass by, you can put your voice into a Disney film and find out which Disney character you're most like, perfect for little ones. Across the street see Kermit at **Muppet Vision 3D**. The big attraction, though, is the 183ft-tall **Twilight Zone Tower of Terror**, which is essentially a drop down an elevator chute in a haunted hotel. The attraction opened in 2004, three years after September 11, 2001, causing some controversy about the choice of names.

### A BUG'S LAND

Kids love the scale of things at a Bug's Land, where you can get the perspective of a bug.

The attractions were designed in conjunction with Pixar Studios after its film *A Bug's Life*. Little ones have a great time splashing in the 'irrigation systems' at **Bountiful Valley Farm** – come during the heat of the day so they don't get too cold afterward – but the best attraction is the 3-D **It's Tough to Be a Bug**. Hilarious and oddly touching, it packs some unexpected tactile surprises. Other good rides include **Heimlich's Chew Chew Train** and the **Drive 'em Buggies** bumper cars.

### GOLDEN STATE

Broken into sections that recognize California's cultural achievements, the Golden State has several distinct areas. **Condor Flats** recognizes the state's aerospace industry. Its main attraction, **Soarin' Over California**, is a virtual hang-gliding ride using IMAX technology; it's sure to give you 'bird-envy' as you float over the state's most beautiful landscapes and sights, including the Golden Gate Bridge and, of course, Disneyland itself. Keep your nostrils open for the smell of the sea, orange groves and pine forests blowing in the wind. **Grizzly River Run** takes you 'rafting' down a faux Sierra Nevada river; you *will* get wet so come when it's warm. Raise a glass to Napa at the **Golden Vine Winery**. At the Palace of Fine Arts in 'San Francisco,' check out **Golden Dreams**, where an eerie embodiment of Whoopi Goldberg takes you on a 22-minute film journey through California history. The movie doesn't shy away from prejudice and race – most notably the exploitation of Chinese railroad workers – but it sanitizes other details, such as how LA really got its water (William Mulholland was no saint, see p41).

### PARADISE PIER

If you like rides, you'll love Paradise Pier, which is supposed to look like a combination of all the beachside amusement piers in California, such as the Santa Monica Pier and the Balboa Fun Zone in Newport Beach, all surrounding a Tidy Bowl–blue lagoon signifying the ocean. The state-of-the-art **California Screamin'** roller coaster occupies 10 acres and resembles an old wooden coaster, but it's got a smooth-as-silk steel track; the beginning of the ride feels like you're being shot out of a cannon. Awesome. For more birds-eye views of the park, head to the **Sun Wheel**, a giant Ferris wheel where each of the gondolas pitches and yaws as it makes its grand circuit. If you have tots with you, take them on **Mulholland Madness**, a mini coaster. If you have a steel stomach, the **Mailboomer** launches you straight up a whopping 180ft.

### SHOWS & PARADES

The premier show at DCA is **Aladdin**, a 40-minute one-act musical extravaganza, based on the movie of the same name. It's in the Hyperion Theater on the Hollywood Studios Backlot. Arrive 30 to 60 minutes early to get good seats. Sit in the mezzanine for the best view of the flying carpet.

In the evening the **Electrical Parade** ends the day at DCA, with thousands of tiny colored chase lights blinking on fabulous floats. If you're here in summer and have a park hopper ticket, first see the Electrical Parade, then head to Disneyland to watch the fireworks.

## Downtown Disney

The quarter-mile-long pedestrian mall that is Downtown Disney feels longer than it is, mostly because it's packed with stores, restaurants, entertainment venues and, in summer, hordes of people. Though there are no mom-and-pop shops with individual character here, there's a lot of good window shopping. For specific recommendations, see p210. On summer evenings musicians play outside.

## SLEEPING

Anaheim gets most hotel business from Disneyland tourism, but the city is also a year-round convention destination, and room rates spike accordingly. Most properties offer packages combining lodging with tickets to Disneyland or other area attractions. Some operate shuttles to the parks; inquire when you book. Many hotels and motels have family rooms that sleep up to six people.

## Budget

**Days Inn & Suites** ( ☎ 714-535-3200, 800-416-7583; www.daysinnanaheimresort.com; 2029 S Harbor Blvd; r $69-89; **P** 🖳 🐾 ) Built in 2003, this well-maintained modern motel has fridges and microwaves in every room, plus on-site laundry facilities. Rates include continental breakfast. You can walk to Disneyland in 20 minutes.

**Best Western Courtesy Inn** ( ☎ 714-772-2470, 800-233-8062; www.bestwestern.com/courtesyinn; 1070 W Ball Rd; r $65-80; **P** 🐾 ) Rooms all have fridges and microwaves. Could use some upgrades, but it's clean and reasonably priced. Walk to Disneyland in 10 minutes.

**HI Fullerton** ( ☎ 714-738-3721, 800-909-4776, ext 138; www.hiusa.org; 1700 N Harbor Blvd, Fullerton; dm members/nonmembers $19/22; 🕑 Jun-Sep) About 5 miles north of Disneyland, this clean and friendly summer-only facility is inside a Mediterranean home with just 20 beds in three dorms (no private rooms). There's a nice porch, Internet access and kitchen facilities. The office closes at 11pm but 24-hour access is available. Bus No 47 runs to the hostel from the Anaheim Greyhound station; from the Amtrak station, take bus No 43. To/from Disneyland also take bus No 43.

## Mid-Range

**Candy Cane Inn** ( ☎ 714-774-5284, 800-345-7057; www.candycaneinn.net; 1747 S Harbor Blvd; r $97-149; **P** 🐾 ) This oh-so-cute motel has welcoming grounds bursting with blooming flowers. Rooms have all mod-cons, plus down comforters and plantation shutters. The hotel is adjacent to the main gate to Disneyland. Top choice.

**Carousel Inn & Suites** ( ☎ 714-758-0444, 800-854-6767; www.carouselinnandsuites.com; 1530 S Harbor Blvd; r $79-99, ste $99-189; **P** 🐾 ) Just over the berm from Disneyland, this otherwise standard four-story motel makes an effort to look good, with upgraded furniture and pots of flowers hanging from its exterior corridors' wrought-iron railings. The rooftop pool has great views of Disneyland's fireworks. Suites sleep four to eight people.

**Anabella** ( ☎ 714-905-1050, 800-863-4888; www.anabellahotel.com; 1030 W Katella Ave; r $90-189; **P** 🖳 🐾 ) Right across the street from DCA, this hotel covers seven acres next to the convention center. It was built in the late 1990s and has rooms decorated in Spanish Colonial style, with extras such as granite bathroom counters, fridge and Web TV.

**Coast Anaheim Hotel** ( ☎ 714-750-1811, 800-663-1144; www.coasthotels.com; 1855 S Harbor Blvd; r $69-129; **P** 🖳 🐾 ) You can see the fireworks over Disneyland from some upper-floor rooms at this 13-story hotel with a hot tub and large pool surrounded by palm trees. There's also a bar, restaurant and coffee shop. It's a 10-minute walk to the park.

**Radisson Resort Knott's Berry Farm** ( ☎ 714-995-1111; www.radisson.com/buenaparkca; 7675 Crescent Ave, Buena Park; r $89-140; P ☐ ☒ ) If you want a theme-park vacation for less money, and you have non-brand-sensitive kids who won't squawk if you don't stay next to Disneyland, this eight-story resort hotel at Knott's Berry Farm is a great alternative.

**Anaheim Desert Palms Hotel** ( ☎ 714-535-1133, 800-635-5423; www.anaheimdesertpalm.com; 631 W Katella Ave; r $79-109; P ☐ ☒ ) A five-story all-suites hotel, the Desert Palms has rooms with microwaves and fridges; downstairs there's a bar, restaurant, fitness center, hot tub and continental breakfast in the morning. Some rooms sleep six.

**Holiday Inn & Suites** ( ☎ 714-876-2609, 800-824-5459; www.holidayinn-anaheim.com; 1240 S Walnut St; r $89-109; P ☒ ) There are extra touches such as comfy furniture and granite bathroom counters at this well-kept mid-range cookie-cutter hotel with an on-site restaurant. Take a short shuttle to the park.

Also consider these standard motels:

**Tropicana Inn & Suites** ( ☎ 714-635-4082, 800-828-4898; www.tropicanainn-anaheim.com; 1540 S Harbor Blvd; r $90-140; P ☐ ☒ ) Big pool, across from Disneyland.

**Castle Inn & Suites** ( ☎ 714-774-8111, 800-227-8530; www.castleinn.com; 1734 S Harbor Blvd; r $92-132; P ☐ ☒ ) Plain rooms, turreted facade; across from Disneyland.

## Top End

For the full Disney experience, stay in one of the three hotels in the **resort** (reservations ☎ 714-956-6425, 800-225-2024; www.disneyland.com). One-night stays are expensive, but rates fluctuate almost daily. Save money by booking multi-night stays and vacation packages. Standard rates are listed following. Each hotel has at least two restaurants and two bars.

**Disney's Grand Californian Hotel** ( ☎ 714-635-2300; 1600 S Disneyland Dr; r $275-400; P ☐ ☒ ) Giant timber beams rise six stories in the cathedral-like lobby of the Grand Californian, a monument to the American Arts and Crafts movement and the top choice for lodging at Disneyland. Rooms have cushy amenities, such as triple-sheeted beds, down pillows and all-custom furnishings, from bedspreads to bathrobes. Outside there's a redwood water slide into the pool. At night kids wind down with bedtime stories by the lobby's giant stone hearth. Even if you're not

staying here, take a look inside; enter from Downtown Disney or DCA.

**Disneyland Hotel** ( ☎ 714-778-6600; 1150 Magic Way; r $225-300; P ☒ ) Built in 1955, the year Disneyland opened, the park's original hotel hasn't lost its sleek appeal, only now its two towers feel retro-mod. Turn off the lights in your room and Tinkerbell's pixie dust glows in the dark on the walls. Geared especially toward families, the hotel has good-sized rooms, some of which sleep four or more. Downstairs there's a steakhouse. Outside there's a great pool – the best of the three hotels – with a 110ft waterslide. The monorail stops outside.

**Disney's Paradise Pier Hotel** ( ☎ 714-999-0990; 1717 S Disneyland Dr; r $175-225; P ☒ ) The budget property of the three on-site hotels, this one has fewer amenities, but the largest water-slide of all – a thrilling 186ft. Rooms are just as spotlessly kept as at the others; they're decorated with colorful fabrics and custom furniture. There's a good but pricey Japanese restaurant, too. The hotel connects directly to DCA; request a room overlooking the park.

## EATING

At both Disneyland and DCA, park maps indicate restaurants and cafés where you can find healthy foods and vegetarian options; look for the red apple icon. Call **Disney Dining** ( ☎ 714-781-3463) if you have dietary restrictions.

If you're traveling with children, call Disney Dining to inquire about character dining, meals during which Disney characters work the dining room and greet the kids. If you're here for a birthday, call and ask about decorate-your-own-cake parties and birthday meals (order 48 hours ahead). Every restaurant at Disneyland Resort has a kids' menu.

### Disneyland Park

In the park itself, each 'land' has several places to eat. The following are some spots for sit-down dining.

**Blue Bayou** ( ☎ 714-781-3463; New Orleans Square; mains lunch $12-18, dinner $23-37) Surrounded by the 'bayou' inside Pirates of the Caribbean, this is the top choice for sit-down dining in Disneyland Park. With the sets, humidity and low lighting, it really does feel like New Orleans. Famous for its Monte Cristo

ORANGE COUNTY

sandwiches at lunch, and Creole and Cajun specialties at dinner. Make reservations or wait in line.

**Carnation Cafe** ( ☎ 714-781-3463; Main St; mains $8-12; ☺ 8am-9pm) Good sandwiches and hot main courses – try the chicken pot pie or the steak melt. Sit outside or inside; both have table service.

**River Belle Terrace** ( ☎ 714-781-3463; Frontierland; mains under $10; ☺ 10am-3pm Mon-Thu, 9am-9pm Fri-Sun) Kids love the Mickey Mouse pancakes at breakfast, served until 11:30am.

There's also cafeteria- and buffet-style dining. Our picks:

**French Market Restaurant** ( ☎ 714-781-3463; New Orleans Square; mains under $10; ☺ noon-7pm Mon-Thu, 11am-8pm Fri-Sun) Southern-style cookin'; good veggie gumbo.

**Plaza Inn** ( ☎ 714-781-3463; Main Street USA; mains under $10; ☺ breakfast, lunch & dinner) Home-style American comfort food; come at 8:30am to 10:30am for character breakfasts.

**Rancho del Zocalo** ( ☎ 714-781-3463; Frontierland; mains $7-13; ☺ 11am-3pm Mon-Thu, 11am-8pm Fri-Sun) Mexican and barbecue.

## Disney's California Adventure

**Trattoria at Golden Vine Winery** ( ☎ 714-781-3463; mains $7-11; ☺ 11am-6pm) DCA's best place for a sit-down lunch serves surprisingly inexpensive and wonderfully tasty Italian pasta, salads and gourmet sandwiches.

**Vineyard Room** ( ☎ 714-781-3463; kids' meals $6-8, 3-/4-course prix fixe $43/56; ☺ dinner Fri-Sun) DCA's white-tablecloth dining room serves contemporary Cal-Italian cuisine in three- or four-course set menus, from polenta and portobello to prosciutto and veal. If you want to splurge but can't quite swing the Napa Rose, this is a fine backup.

There's a food court at Pacific Wharf.

## Downtown Disney

Downtown Disney has lots of restaurants. Call ahead for priority seating or bookings.

**Catal & Uva Bar** ( ☎ 714-774-4442; mains breakfast $5-7, lunch $11-17, dinner $18-20; ☺ breakfast, lunch & dinner) The chef cooks up a fusion of California and Mediterranean cuisines – lamb sandwich with tapenade, paella, chipotle ribs – at this airy two-story restaurant decorated in sunny Mediterranean-Provençal style with exposed beams and lemon-colored walls. Sit on the balcony for downtown's best mid-range dining.

**Napa Rose** ( ☎ 714-300-7170; Grand Californian Hotel, 1600 S Disneyland Dr, Downtown Disney; mains $27-38, 4-course prix fixe $65; ☺ dinner) There are echoes of Frank Lloyd Wright in the stunning white-tablecloth dining room of the Grand Californian Hotel, where soaring windows, high-back Arts and Crafts–style chairs, and towering ceilings befit Disney's – and possibly all of Orange County's – finest restaurant. On the plate, the contemporary 'California Wine Country' (read: Northern California) cuisine is as impeccably crafted and visually stunning as Sleeping Beauty Castle. Make reservations, and bring your checkbook.

Other choices worth considering:

**La Brea Bakery** ( ☎ 714-781-3463; mains breakfast $6-7, lunch & dinner $7-18; ☺ breakfast, lunch & dinner) Good sandwiches and salads.

**Rainforest Café** ( ☎ 714-772-0413; mains $10-25) Kids love the tropical-jungle theme.

**Tortilla Joe's** ( ☎ 714-535-5000; mains $11-22) Mexican specialties.

## Around Disneyland

**Bangkok BBQ** ( ☎ 714-534-4490; 12541 S Harbor Blvd, Garden Grove; mains lunch $5, dinner $7-10; ☺ lunch Mon-Fri, dinner daily) A bowl of soup and rice plate at lunch costs just $5 at this strip-mall Thai joint; dinners don't cost much more.

**Los Sanchez** ( ☎ 714-971-5883; 12151 S Harbor Blvd, Garden Grove; mains $4-10; ☺ 9am-10pm Sun-Thu, 9am-11pm Fri & Sat) The cooking is fiery and delicious at this big, family-owned Mexican joint. Try the *carne asada*, shrimp *rancheros* or seafood *tostada*. If you don't recognize the names, there's a picture of every dish on the wall. It's one block south of Chapman Ave.

**Chu's Wok Inn** ( ☎ 714-750-3511; 13053 Chapman Ave, Garden Grove; dinner $9-13) There's table service at this family-run hole-in-the-wall Mandarin Chinese strip-mall restaurant near the Crystal Cathedral. It's one block east of Harbor Blvd at Haster St.

**Mimis Café** ( ☎ 714-956-2223; 1400 S Harbor Blvd; meals $7-15; ☺ 7am-11pm) The New Orleans–style decor is cheery and the service perky at this chain restaurant that serves large portions of inspired coffee-shop fare. There's an espresso bar and good pastries, too.

**Millie's** ( ☎ 714-535-6892; 1480 S Harbor Blvd; mains $5-11; ☺ 6am-midnight) If lines at Mimi's are too long, walk next door to this chain diner decorated with fake plants. Great banana splits.

**Cuban Pete's** ( ☎ 714-490-2020; 1050 W Ball Rd; mains lunch $5-11, dinner $11-20; ☺ lunch Thu-Sun, dinner daily) Outside it looks like a witch's castle, but inside it's all woodsy and decorated with photos of Old Havana. The Cuban and Caribbean cooking is richly spiced, but there's also a kids' menu. There's live music Thursday to Saturday nights; call ahead to confirm.

**Joe's Crab Shack** ( ☎ 714-703-0505; 12011 Harbor Blvd, Garden Grove; mains $9-19; ⏲ 11am-10pm Sun-Thu, 11am-11pm Fri & Sat) There's tons of stuff hanging from the corrugated-metal ceiling at Joe's, an ersatz dockside fish house that's pretty good for a chain seafood restaurant.

If you want to splurge on a fancy dinner and escape Disneyland, Anaheim has two top-end choices:

**Anaheim White House** ( ☎ 714-772-1381; 887 S Anaheim Blvd; mains lunch $13-22, dinner $22-36; ⏲ lunch Mon-Fri, dinner daily) Tuxedoed waiters serve stylized contemporary Franco-Italian cuisine on glittering china in the dining room of an elegant 1910 mansion that's entirely decked out in white and gold. Great for an anniversary or your mom's birthday. Make reservations and get gussied up.

**Mr Stox** ( ☎ 714-634-2994; 1105 E Katella Ave; mains lunch $15-25, dinner $25-35; ⏲ lunch Mon-Fri, dinner daily) Mr Stox serves some of Anaheim's best Cal-American cooking in a clubby atmosphere with oval booths and thick carpeting. The chef bakes five different breads daily. Prime steaks. Great seafood. Pricey. Wear nice shoes and make reservations.

## DRINKING

Unfortunately, you can't buy any alcohol in Disneyland Park, only at DCA and in Downtown Disney.

**Uva Bar** ( ☎ 714-774-4442; Downtown Disney) Sip wine while munching on garlic fries at Downtown Disney's best outdoor spot for drinks and people-watching.

**ESPN Zone** ( ☎ 714-300-3776; Downtown Disney) You can rent a recliner with your own remote control and waitress service at this vast sports and drinking emporium with 175 TV monitors – there are even screens above the men's room urinals. Only dedicated sports fans will be able to tolerate the visual and aural onslaught.

**Hook's Point** ( ☎ 714-781-3463; Disneyland Hotel; ⏲ closed Sun & Mon in winter) A great alternative to the frat-boy joints, this quiet wine bar in the Disneyland Hotel has good fruit-and-cheese platters and sparkling wine by the glass.

## ENTERTAINMENT
### Downtown Disney

**AMC Theatres** ( ☎ 714-769-4262, show times ☎ 714-769-4262) Pick from 12 screens of current-release movies; every theater has love-seat stadium seating.

**Ralph Brennan's New Orleans Jazz Kitchen** ( ☎ 714-776-5200; Downtown Disney; ⏲ 4-10pm) You can hear New Orleans–style jazz on the weekends and piano jazz weeknights at this bar and restaurant. The food quality is erratic, but sometimes good.

**ESPN Zone** ( ☎ 714-300-3776; Downtown Disney; ⏲ 11am-midnight) Upstairs above the restaurant (skip the food), adults and kids who are accompanied by someone over 21 can play interactive sports games, from rock-climbing to air hockey. If you don't like sports, don't even think of setting foot here.

**House of Blues** ( ☎ 714-778-2583; www.hob.com; Downtown Disney) The best place for rock and blues, HOB occasionally gets some heavy-hitters on its rotating calendar; call or check online for show times and tickets. On Sunday there's a fun gospel brunch; make reservations. Come for the music, not the food.

### Around Disneyland

**Grove of Anaheim** ( ☎ 714-712-2700; www.thegrove ofanaheim.com; 2200 E Katella Ave) Headliners, such as BB King, Alice Cooper, Nancy Sinatra and Tom Jones, have all played at this moderately small concert venue in Anaheim; call for current schedules. Sight lines are great, and no seat too far away.

**Angel Stadium** ( ☎ 888-796-4256; www.angels baseball.com; 2000 Gene Autry Way, Anaheim; tickets $9-44) The Anaheim Angels play major-league baseball from May to October.

**Arrowhead Pond** ( ☎ 877-945-3946; www.mighty ducks.com; 2695 E Katella Ave, Anaheim) The Mighty Ducks play hockey from September to May.

See p213 for entertainment venues at the Block at Orange, a mega-sized mall 6 miles southeast of Disneyland.

## SHOPPING

Each 'land' has its own shopping, appropriate to its theme.

### Disneyland Park

**Emporium** ( ☎ 714-781-7290; Main St) The biggest store in Disneyland has the largest variety of souvenirs, clothing and Disneyana, from T-shirts to mouse ears.

**China Closet** ( ☎ 714-781-7290; Main St) This shop sells classic porcelain Disney figurines and snow globes.

## Downtown Disney

Most shops in Downtown Disney open and close with the parks.

**Basin** ( ☎ 714-808-9293) Buy fizzy bath balls and body lotion here.

**Build-a-Bear Workshop** ( ☎ 714-776-5980) Make your own teddy bear here.

**Compass Books & Cafe** ( ☎ 714-502-9999) For summer reading and newspapers.

**Department 56** ( ☎ 714-772-6828) Buy a miniature village for under the Christmas tree.

**Lego Imagination Center** ( ☎ 714-991-6512) This is the place to come and buy the famous building blocks that kids love so much; there's lots of hands-on in-store play, too.

**Marceline's Confectionery** ( ☎ 714-300-7922) For fantastic fudge and great hand-dipped caramel apples, you can't beat Marceline's; there's a hidden Mickey in the sign out front!

**Sephora** ( ☎ 714-254-7028) A huge line of mid- to high-end cosmetics.

## GETTING THERE & AWAY
### Air

See p198 for information on air connections. The **Airport Bus** (info ☎ 714-938-8900, dispatch ☎ 714-938-8937, 800-938-8933, 800-772-5299; www.airportbus.com) runs between Los Angeles International Airport (LAX) and Disneyland-area hotels at least hourly ($16/25 one way/round-trip to LAX, $11/18 to John Wayne Airport; SNA).

### Bus

**Greyhound** ( ☎ 714-999-1256; www.greyhound.com; 100 W Winston Rd) has frequent departures to/from Downtown Los Angeles ($9.50, 1½ hours) and San Diego ($15, 2¼ to three hours).

### Car

The Anaheim Resort is just off I-5 on Harbor Blvd, about 30 miles south of Downtown LA. The park is roughly bordered by Ball Rd, Disneyland Dr, Harbor Blvd and Katella Ave.

Arriving at Disneyland and DCA is like arriving at an airport. Giant easy-to-read overhead signs indicate which ramps you need to take for the theme parks, hotels or Anaheim's streets. The system is remarkably ordered.

### PARKING

All-day parking costs $9, cash only. Enter the 'Mickey & Friends' parking structure from southbound Disneyland Dr at Ball Rd. (It's the largest car park in the world, with a capacity of 10,300 vehicles.) Take the tram to reach the parks; follow signs. The lots stay open until two hours after the parks close.

The lots for Downtown Disney are reserved for shoppers and have a different rate structure: the first three hours are free, with an additional two more free hours if you have a validation from a table-service restaurant or the movie theater. After that you'll pay $6 per hour, up to $30 a day. Downtown Disney also has valet parking for an additional $6, plus tip. Cash only.

### Train

The depot next to Angels Stadium is where **Amtrak** ( ☎ 714-385-1448; 2150 E Katella Ave) trains stop. Tickets to/from LA's Union Station are $8.50 (45 minutes), to San Diego it's $17 (two hours).

## GETTING AROUND
### Bus

The bus company **Anaheim Rapid Transit** (ART; ☎ 714-563-5287, 888-364-2787; www.rideart.org) provides frequent service to/from Disneyland from hotels in the immediate area, saving headaches parking and walking. An all-day pass costs $3 per day. You must buy the pass before boarding; pick one up at one of a dozen kiosks or online; call for details. Otherwise it's $3 per one-way trip.

Many hotels and motels have free shuttles to Disneyland and other area attractions.

### Monorail

Take the monorail from Tomorrowland to the Disneyland Hotel, across from Downtown Disney, and save about 20 minutes of walking time.

# AROUND DISNEYLAND

Orange County sprawls. One city blends into the next as you drive the wide boulevards that extend outward from Disneyland, and though the entire area looks at first like one giant suburban strip, there are a number of interesting places to visit outside Disneyland. You need only know where to look.

# KNOTT'S BERRY FARM

Though Disneyland gets all the accolades, **Knott's** ( ☎ 714-220-5200; www.knotts.com; 8039 Beach Blvd, Buena Park; adult/child 3-11 $45/15) was the first theme park in America. Just 4 miles north-west of Anaheim off the I-5, Knott's is smaller and less frenetic than the Disneyland parks, but it's lots of fun, especially for families with pre-teen children. The atmosphere isn't as sanitized as Disney – Knott's attractions occasionally address sex and death – and nobody demands you be happy. The service isn't as good, but prices for food and souvenirs are more reasonable.

Most people manage to see Knott's in one day, though if you want to stay overnight there's a reasonably priced resort hotel here (p206), and you can spend day two at the adjacent water park (p212). Some rides have minimum height restrictions. Opening hours vary seasonally, so call ahead; on days that the park is open past 6pm special admission prices apply for entry after 4pm (adult/child $22/15). Bring dry clothes and bathing suits for the kids. Parking costs $9.

The park opened in 1932, when Mr Knott's boysenberries (a blackberry-raspberry hybrid) and Mrs Knott's fried-chicken dinners attracted crowds of local farmhands. Mr Knott built an imitation ghost town to keep them entertained, and eventually hired local carnival rides and charged admission. Mrs Knott kept frying the chicken, but the rides and Old West buildings became the main attraction.

Today the park keeps the Old West theme alive at **Ghost Town**, which features weathered historic buildings brought from real mining towns in California and other western states. There are staged gun fights, and gold-panning and glass-blowing demonstrations. Ride around the park on the **Calico Railroad**, which came from the Silverado goldfields of Colorado; it's pulled by an original 1881 Baldwin steam engine. Knott's also acknowledges pre-gold-rush history with Aztec dancers and a California missions exhibit – there's even mariachi music in **Fiesta Village**.

But it's the thrill rides that draw most people to Knott's. The newest of the bunch is 'Xcelerator,' a '50s themed roller coaster that blasts you, as if from a cannon, from 0mph to 82mph in only 2.3 seconds. Before you can even scream, your skin gets pulled back on your face; and there's a hair-raising twist at the top. Awesome.

The teeth-chattering **GhostRider** is one of the best wooden roller coasters in California. It hurtles you along a neck-breaking 4530ft track, at one point plunging you 108ft with a G-force of 3.14. Expect long lines.

The **Perilous Plunge** is the tallest water ride in the world. It catapults you up 127ft, then drops you down a 115ft-long water chute at an insane 75-degree angle. You *will* get soaked. **Supreme Scream** drops you 25 stories at 50mph with a G-force of four, bouncing back upward with a G-force of -1.5, all in about 45 seconds.

For a tamer adventure, **Big Foot Rapids** sloshes down a faux white-water river, leaving you drenched (unless they turn the waterfalls off, as happens in colder weather). **Camp Snoopy** is a kiddy wonderland populated by Snoopy, Charlie Brown, Lucy, Linus and all the other Peanuts characters.

In October Knott's hosts what is regarded as SoCal's best and scariest Halloween party. Professional costumed performers haunt the park, special rides and attractions

**ORANGE COUNTY**

---

### DETOUR: RICHARD NIXON LIBRARY

Ever wonder just who Richard Nixon really was? You may not find a satisfactory answer, but you'll certainly gain new insight into the man at the **Richard Nixon Presidential Library & Birthplace** ( ☎ 714-993-3393; www.nixonlibrary.org; 18001 Yorba Linda Blvd, Yorba Linda; adult/child 7-11/student/senior $8/3/5/6; ☼ 10am-5pm Mon-Sat, 11am-5pm Sun), which displays everything from the dress that Pat wore at the 1973 inaugural to the pistol given to Nixon by Elvis Presley. You can watch a film called *Never Give Up: Richard Nixon in the Arena,* listen to carefully edited White House tapes from the Watergate era, and view the telephone used to communicate with Apollo 11 astronauts while they were on the moon. There's also a 70ft-long doll-house-like replica of the Nixon White House, as well as a re-creation of the Lincoln Sitting Room, Nixon's favorite room in the house. The library is located in Yorba Linda, in northeastern Orange County. To get there, exit east on Yorba Linda Blvd from Hwy 57 and continue straight to the library.

go up for the occasion, and park lights are dimmed or turned off entirely.

There are plenty of eateries within the park, but the classic meal is the button-busting fried-chicken-and-mashed-potato dinner at **Mrs Knott's Chicken Dinner Restaurant** (mains $15-20). It's in the California Market-place, a shopping and dining mall just outside the park's main gate.

Next to Knott's is the affiliated water park **Soak City USA** ( ☎ 714-220-5200; www.knotts.com; adult/child 3-11 $25/13, after 3pm $15/10; ☺ summer), with high-speed slides, tubes and flumes. You must have a bathing suit without rivets or metal pieces to go on some slides. Bring a towel.

## MEDIEVAL TIMES DINNER & TOURNAMENT

A perfect follow-up to a day at a theme park, **Medieval Times** ( ☎ 714-523-1100; www.medievaltimes.com; 7662 Beach Blvd; adult/child under 12 $46/32) pulls out all the stops in presenting its medieval dinner and show. You sit surrounding an arena in which knights show off their horsemanship (on real live Andalucian horses), then joust and fence in a battle to protect the honor of the kingdom and the beautiful blonde princess. It's all very grand and great fun, especially for families. Dinner is OK – roasted chicken and spare ribs that you eat with your hands – but the show's the thing. Make reservations.

## RIPLEY'S BELIEVE IT OR NOT! & MOVIELAND WAX MUSEUM

A block north of Knott's, these 'museums,' are pretty hokey, although they're fun if you're in a wacky mood. The more interesting of the two is **Ripley's** ( ☎ 714-522-1152; www.ripleysbuenapark.com; 7850 Beach Blvd; adult/child 4-11/senior $9/5.25/7; ☺ 11am-5pm Mon-Fri, 10am-6pm Sat & Sun). Adventurer, reporter and collector Robert L Ripley traveled the globe in the 1920s and 1930s in search of curiosities. His folk memorabilia and documentation of human oddities provide twisted entertainment.

**Movieland Wax Museum** ( ☎ 714-522-1155; www.movielandwaxmuseum.com; 7711 Beach Blvd; adult/child 4-11/senior $13/7/11; ☺ 10am-7:30pm Mon-Fri, 9am-8:30pm Sat & Sun), across the street from Ripley's, has the usual dizzying maze of wax figures of celebrities, politicians and religious figures. The ticket office closes 90 minutes before the museum does.

Combination tickets to both places cost $17/10/14 per adult/child aged four to 11/senior.

## HOBBY CITY DOLL & TOY MUSEUM

A bit of Americana kitsch 2 miles south of Knott's, Hobby City is a cluster of 20 specialty art and craft shops, including a Native-American store in a log cabin and shops that sell stuffed bears, model trains and model cars; there's even one that sells reptiles. The **Doll & Toy Museum** ( ☎ 714-527-2323; 1238 S Beach Blvd; adult/child $2/1; ☺ 10am-5pm), housed in a half-scale model of the White House, offers the best entertainment value here. Along with every type of Barbie doll ever made, the museum has Russian dolls from the 1800s. Its toy replicas of TV, movie and sports personalities, rock stars and presidents present an interesting survey of pop culture in the US over the last 60 years.

## BOWERS MUSEUM OF CULTURAL ART & KIDSEUM

In a gracious 1932 mission-style complex in Santa Ana, this exquisite **museum** ( ☎ 714-567-3600; www.bowers.org; 2002 N Main St; permanent collection $5, major shows adult/student/senior $14/8/8; ☺ 11am-4pm Tue-Sun) has a rich permanent collection of pre-Columbian, African, Oceanic and Native American art, but gets its biggest crowds with its tantalizing and high-quality special exhibits (which require separate tickets; call ahead). A recent example is 'Treasures from the British Museum.'

The Bowers has a great indoor-outdoor restaurant called **Tangata** ( ☎ 714-550-0906; mains $8-17; ☺ lunch Tue-Sun). It features a Mediterranean menu masterminded by LA star chef Joachim Splichal.

The **Kidseum** ( ☎ 714-480-1520; www.bowers.org/kidseum/kidseum.asp; 1802 N Main St; admission $5; ☺ 11am-4pm Sat & Sun), one block south, keeps youngsters entertained with 11,000 sq ft of hands-on exhibits on world cultures. The museum is also open weekdays in summer – call ahead for details.

## CRYSTAL CATHEDRAL

You needn't agree with televangelist Robert Schuller's teachings or be an 'Hour of Power' fan to appreciate the architecture of the **Crystal Cathedral** ( ☎ 714-971-4000; www.crystalcathedral.org; 12141 Lewis St), in Garden Grove, about 2 miles southeast of Disneyland. A cross between an office complex and a science-fiction movie set, the cathedral is built in the shape of a four-pointed star and boasts 10,661 windows, seating for 3000 and a 16,000-pipe organ.

Designed by Cleveland-born Philip Johnson, international-style architect turned postmodernist, the church anchors a vast campus of gardens, reflecting pools, fountains and sculpture. Explore on your own or take a free 30-minute tour (offered regularly from 9am to 3:30pm Monday to Saturday). Don't miss the freestanding modern Gothic prayer chapel on the cathedral's north side; its pillars are made of eight different types of Italian marble and inside is a five-piece lead crystal cross that weighs 200lb.

Schuller's congregation is part of the protestant Reform Church of America, which originally worshipped at the Orange County drive-in movie theater with Schuller preaching from atop the snack stand. His 'Hour of Power' is now broadcast on TV networks around the world.

The **church productions** ( ☎ 714-544-5679) of the Glory of Christmas and the Glory of Easter are major fund-raisers. These are staged spectaculars re-enacting Biblical stories, using live camels, flying angels and other theatrics. Call for tickets.

# ORANGE
**pop 127,000**

The city of Orange, about 6 miles southeast of Disneyland, is home to the mega-sized mall **Block at Orange** ( ☎ 714-769-4000; www.theblock atorange.com; 20 City Blvd West), where you'll find all the latest OC chain-store fashion, plus restaurants, movie theaters and a skateboarding park. But you'll find more charm in the town's historic center, called **Old Towne Orange**. It was originally laid out by Alfred Chapman and Andrew Glassell who, in 1869, received the 1 sq mile piece of real estate in lieu of legal fees. Here, surrounding a **plaza** (cnr Chapman & Glassell Sts), is the best and most concentrated collection of antiques, collectibles and consignment shops in Orange County. Though it's fun to browse, real bargains are rare. Unfortunately, some dealers may try to pass off replicas as antiques: caveat emptor!

Recharge on coffee in Plaza Sq at **Diedrich Coffee** ( ☎ 714-288-6221; 44 Plaza Sq; ☾ 5:30am-10pm). Next door **Felix Continental Cafe** ( ☎ 714-633-5842; 36 Plaza Sq; mains lunch $7-11, dinner $15-25), an Orange institution, serves Caribbean, Cuban and Spanish dishes, in a no-frills diner setting with mirrored walls.

**Citrus City Grille** ( ☎ 714-639-9600; 122 N Glassell St; mains lunch $9-14, dinner $14-27) is pricey and noisy, but the food's terrific at this Cal-American grill. It specializes in comfort food, from pot roast with Burgundy-wine sauce to ravioli with gorgonzola alfredo.

For entertainment, try **Lucky Strike Lanes** ( ☎ 714-363-4300; Block at Orange, 20 City Blvd West; ☾ 11am-2am), a stylin' bowling alley and pool hall as could only exist in SoCal. The place is decked out with low-slung Naugahyde sofas, Chinese lanterns and halogen-spot lighting.

ORANGE COUNTY

---

### DETOUR: GLEN IVY HOT SPRINGS

Soak away your troubles at this lovely **day spa** ( ☎ 888-258-2683; www.glenivy.com; 25000 Glen Ivy Rd; admission Mon-Thu $30, Fri-Sun & holidays $42; ☾ 9:30am-6pm Apr-Oct, 9:30am-5pm Nov-Mar). Nicknamed 'Club Mud,' it has 15 pools and spas filled with naturally heated mineral water, surrounded by five acres of landscaped grounds profuse with bougainvillea, eucalyptus and palm trees. You can wallow in the water, lounge in the saunas or steam rooms, take an aqua aerobics class, treat yourself to a massage (for an extra fee), or swim some laps in a larger swimming pool.

The best thing, though, is the red-clay mud pool. Like some prehistoric animal wandering into the tar pits, you first soak yourself in muck. Then, apply what amounts to a full-body mask by grabbing chunks of clay and smearing them all over your body before lounging in the sun until it's baked on to your skin. Whether this treatment truly has therapeutic effects is debatable, but it's certainly fun. And here's a tip for photos: you can shape the mud on your head into fantastic masks, horns and sci-fi shapes. Bring an old swim suit, as the clay does stain a little. Minimum age for entry is 16.

The spa is in Corona, technically just east of Orange County in Riverside County. To get there, exit I-15 at Temescal Canyon Rd, turn right and drive 1 mile to Glen Ivy Rd, then right again and go straight to the end.

On weekends call to reserve a table or lane. Bowling costs $7 per game, plus $4 shoe rental. It also serves bar food and burgers.

At **Dave & Busters** ( ☎ 714-769-1515; Block at Orange, 20 City Blvd West; ☽ 11:30am-midnight Sun-Thu, 11:30am-1:30am Fri & Sat) you can chug-a-lug while playing Ms Pacman, billiards, shuffleboard, or video and simulator games. It's a huge bar and arcade frequented not by marauding youths, but by adults who wear khakis.

## LITTLE SAIGON

The city of Westminster, southwest of Anaheim near the junction of I-405 and Hwy 22, is home to a large Vietnamese population, which has carved out its own vibrant commercial district around the intersection of Bolsa and Brookhurst Aves. At its heart is the **Asian Garden Mall** ( ☎ 714-842-8018; 9200 Bolsa Ave), a behemoth of a structure packed with 400 ethnic boutiques, including herbalists and jade jewelers.

One of the best of the many casual eateries here is **Pho 79** ( ☎ 714-893-1883; dishes $4-15), on the lower level toward the mall's north entrance, which has a great variety of noodle and vegetable dishes. The *pho ga* (chicken noodle soup) is superb, especially on a cold day.

Across the street, the **New Saigon Mall Cultural Court** marries commercialism and spirituality with its impressive display of statues and murals.

# ORANGE COUNTY BEACHES

Surfers, artists and retirees set the tone for Orange County's beach towns, which are distinct from the rest of the county. Strung along the Pacific Coast Hwy (PCH; Hwy 1), each community has its own flavor. But they're all very relaxed, despite the area's rapid development. Oil rigs sit about a mile offshore all along the coast and scattered among inland houses and businesses, lending a surreal quality to the landscape.

Accommodations in summer get booked far in advance; prices rise and some properties impose minimum two- or three-night stays. You can stay in one town and take day trips to the others. From Seal Beach in the north to Laguna Beach in the south, the drive takes about 45 minutes to an hour.

## SEAL BEACH
**pop 24,100**

Refreshingly noncorporatized Seal Beach has a great beach and an inviting downtown area. The town stretches along a few blocks of Main St, between Ocean Ave, which skirts the beach, and Pacific Coast Hwy. Along Main, you'll find restaurants and some interesting mom-and-pop antique and consignment clothing stores. Like most SoCal towns, Seal Beach has a split personality: aside from being a carefree little beach community, it's also home to a huge US naval weapons station and to Leisure World, one of SoCal's first and most exclusive retirement communities.

### Information

Seal Beach's **chamber of commerce** ( ☎ 562-799-0179; www.sealbeachchamber.org; 201 8th St, Suite 120; ☽ 12-3pm Mon, Wed, Fri, 10am-noon Thu) dispenses lodging and other information, but only about its members. You can mail letters and buy stamps on Main St at the **US Post Office** ( ☎ 562-598-6915; www.usps.com; 221 Main St, CA 90740; ☽ 9am-5pm Mon-Fri).

### Sights & Activities

Main St spills into the **Seal Beach Pier**, which extends 1885ft over the ocean. The current pier, built in 1985, replaced the 1906 original, which fell victim to winter storms in the early 1980s, but it has been rebuilt with a wooden boardwalk so wear shoes (not high heels!) or you'll get splinters in your feet. Carry a few quarters to feed the mounted binoculars, which give you a close-up view of the hotties in the lifeguard towers and of the Port of LA in Long Beach to the north.

At the **beach**, which faces south here, families spread out on blankets, build sandcastles and play in the water. The gentle waves make it a great place to learn to surf. Surfers and boogie boarders are segregated; read the signs or ask lifeguards. Though there's a hideous oil derrick just off shore, if you take off your glasses and focus on what's immediately in front of you, it's lovely. At the end of the day, there are cold-water outdoor showers to rinse off the sand and salt. You may have a difficult time parking in summer; be patient. You might have to park inland.

Rent a bicycle at **Main St Cyclery** ( ☎ 562-430-3903; 135 Main St; per hr/day $10/40; ☽ closed Wed). Learn to surf with **M&M Surfing School** ( ☎ 714-846-7873; www.mmsurfingschool.com), which offers five-day-long surf intensives for about $225; it also leads single-day instruction for $60 to $80, which includes the board and wet suit. Or you can just rent a soft (foam) board for $25 per day. You can rent hard (fiberglass) and soft boards from **Bruce Jones Surfboards** ( ☎ 562-592-2314; 16927 PCH), just south of Seal Beach, which start at $20 per half-day.

Jazz, folk and bluegrass bands play on Wednesday evenings in summer from 6pm to 8pm as part of **Summer Concerts in the Park** ( ☎ 562-799-0179; Eisenhower Park), by the pier at the foot of Main St.

## Sleeping

There are no budget accommodations in Seal Beach; head inland and south along Pacific Coast Hwy toward Huntington Beach (see p217).

**Pacific Inn** ( ☎ 562-493-7501, 866-466-0300; www .pacificinn-sb.com; 600 Marina Dr; r $110-150; P ⬜ ⬜ ) The only motel near town that's within walking distance of the beach (two blocks) has rooms with extras such as down comforters and comfy mattresses.

**Seal Beach Inn & Gardens** ( ☎ 562-493-2416, 800-443-3292; www.sealbeachinn.com; 212 5th St; r $140-180; P ⬜ ) The mature landscaping surrounding this 1924 inn complements the coziness and charm of the antique-filled rooms, which are in small casitas surrounding a central courtyard. There's chess in the library, tea in the parlor and a pool in the small backyard. One block from the beach.

## Eating

**Ruby's** ( ☎ 562-431-7829; 900a Ocean Blvd; most mains under $10; ⏰ 7am-10pm, 7am-9pm winter) At the end of the pier, this '50s-theme diner serves up pretty good burgers and shakes; the ocean views are fantastic.

**Grandma's Cookies & Ice Cream** ( ☎ 562-596-8580; 210 Main St; ⏰ 10am-10pm) Kids go nuts for the ice cream and jars of candy, while adults prefer the homemade chocolates and fresh-baked cookies at this super-cute old-fashioned candy store.

**Taco Surf** ( ☎ 562-594-0600; 115 Main St; mains under $10; ⏰ 11am-9:30pm) There's sawdust on the floor at this Baja-style Mexican cantina that serves yummy fish tacos and homemade salsa. There's beer and wine margaritas, but no tequila.

**O'Malley's on Main** ( ☎ 562-430-0631; 140 Main St; mains breakfast & lunch $5-9, dinner $9-19; ⏰ 7am-2am) At breakfast there's eggs and pancakes, at lunch good sandwiches, and at dinner corned beef, bangers and mash, and fish and chips. The bar gets hoppin' and has 12 beers on tap.

**Walt's Wharf** ( ☎ 562-598-4433; 201 Main St; mains lunch $8-15, dinner $12-25) Everybody's favorite for fresh fish – some people even come from LA – Walt's gets packed on weekends, and you can't make reservations. But it's worth the long wait for the oak-fire-grilled seafood and steaks, served with delicious sauces. There's a huge selection of wines by the glass. If you can't wait for a table, eat at the bar.

For quick eats try the following:

**A Slice of New York Pizza** ( ☎ 562-493-4430; 142 Main St; pizza slices $2.50; ⏰ 11am-10pm) Good pizza.

**Old Town Café** ( ☎ 562-430-4377; 137 Main St; mains under $10; ⏰ breakfast & lunch daily, dinner Fri & Sat) Eggs and sandwiches.

## Drinking & Entertainment

**Bogart's Coffeehouse** ( ☎ 562-431-2226; 905 Ocean Blvd; ⏰ 6am-10pm) Sip espresso on the sofa and play Scrabble with an ocean view; on Saturday it sometimes hosts live music.

**Bay Theatre** ( ☎ 562-431-9988; www.baytheatre .com; 340 Main St) This historic cinema revives great films on the big screen, from the Marx Brothers to the *Exorcist*, and it occasionally hosts concerts performed on the theater's mighty Wurlitzer organ.

## Shopping

Be sure to walk the full three blocks of Main St to see all the little shops.

**Up, Up & Away** ( ☎ 562-596-7661; 139-1/2 Main St) Pick up a kite to fly on the beach.

**Sideboard** ( ☎ 562-594-8159; 322 Main St) Cooking buffs should visit this indie culinary specialty store.

**Seal Beach Music** ( ☎ 562-430-0594; 118 Main St) Musicians will dig this great, old-fashioned small-town musical instrument shop.

## HUNTINGTON BEACH

pop 190,000

Ever since Hawaiian-Irish surfing star George Freeth (brought to California by pioneer developer, Henry Huntington; p99) gave demonstrations here in 1914, Huntington Beach (HB) has been one of SoCal's major surf destinations. In fact, it earned the title 'Surf City, USA' from the song by rock-and-roll surf daddies Jan and Dean. (The song's refrain: 'two girls for every boy.' Remember it?) Today surfing is big business. Buyers for major retailers come to Huntington Beach to see what surfers are wearing, then market the look for mass consumption.

Once the least polished and most low-key of Orange County's beach towns, gentrification has definitely arrived here. Shopping centers and housing are going up north and south of Main St at a furious pace. Along lower Main St, old-fashioned surf culture meets new-millennium cookie-cutter architecture that houses numerous cafés, bars and casual restaurants.

## Orientation

The Pacific Coast Hwy runs along the coast; Main St runs perpendicular to PCH and ends at the pier. Inland, Main St ends at Hwy 39 (Beach Blvd), which connects to I-405.

Coming from I-405, take Hwy 39 to PCH and turn right (north). Once in town, you won't need a car.

## Information

**Huntington Beach Hospital** ( ☎ 714-842-1473; www.hbhospital.com; 17772 Hwy39) There's a 24-hour emergency room and urgent-care clinic here.
**Post office** ( ☎ 714-536-4973; 316 Olive Ave; ✆ 8:30am-5pm Mon-Fri) Buy stamps and mail packages near Main St at the Beach Center branch of the post office. There's a self-service stamp machine available 6:45am to 6pm weekdays, and 6:45am to 4:30pm Saturday.
**Public library** ( ☎ 714-375-5071; 525 Main St; Internet access per hr $3; ✆ 10am-7pm Tue-Fri, 9am-5pm Sat) Offers Internet access.
**Visitors Bureau** ( ☎ 714-969-3492, 800-729-6232; www.hbvisit.com; 301 Main St, Suite 208; ✆ noon-7pm Mon-Fri, 11am-7pm Sat & Sun) For maps and information.

## Sights

Look for the **Surfing Walk of Fame** (cnr PCH & Main St), which immortalizes local legends.

### THE BEACH

One of SoCal's best beaches, the sand here gets packed on summer weekends with surfers, volleyball players, swimmers and families. The beach is the reason most people live here.

**Huntington City Beach** ( ☎ 714-536-5281) surrounds the pier at the foot of Main St. Further south, **Huntington State Beach** ( ☎ 714-536-1454) extends from Beach Blvd (Hwy 39) to the Santa Ana River and the Newport Beach boundary.

If you forgot to pack beach gear, you can rent umbrellas, volleyballs, towels and even swim suits at **Zack's** ( ☎ 714-536-0215; www.beachfoodfun.com; Zack's Pier Plaza, cnr PCH & Main St). In the evening, volleyball games give way to beach bonfires. If you want to build one or have a barbecue, stake out one of the 1000 cement fire rings early in the day, especially on holiday weekends, when you should plan to arrive when the beach opens. To indicate that it's taken, surround the ring with your gear. You can get wood from concessionaires on the beach.

Bathrooms and showers are located north of the pier at the back of the snack-bar complex. The beach closes at 10pm and reopens at 5am; the pier closes at midnight. Parking lots by the beach – when you can get a spot – cost $1.50 per hour or $9 per day. Otherwise you can park at the municipal lots along Pacific Coast Hwy or on the street further inland.

Dogs play in the surf at **Dog Beach**, north of Golden West St, south of Seapoint Ave, between Huntington City and Bolsa Chica State Beaches.

### HUNTINGTON PIER

The 1853ft Huntington Pier has been here – in one form or another – since 1904. The mighty Pacific has damaged giant sections of it half a dozen times and completely demolished it twice since then. The current concrete structure was built in 1983. You can rent a fishing pole for $3 per hour at the **bait and tackle shop** ( ☎ 714-960-1392). About half way up the pier, there are two tiny stores in trailers. The **Surf City Store** ( ☎ 714-374-0277) is the only shop in town licensed to use the name 'Surf City' on its merchandise; pick up a T-shirt. Across the way, consider buying a kite at the **Kite Connection** ( ☎ 714-536-3630).

### INTERNATIONAL SURFING MUSEUM

One of the few of its kind in California, this small **museum** ( ☎ 714-960-3483; 411 Olive St; adult/concession $2/1; ✆ noon-5pm Wed-Sun), off Main St, is an entertaining mecca for surf-culture enthusiasts. Exhibits chronicle the sport's history with photos, early surfboards, surf wear, and surf music recordings by the Beach Boys, Jan and Dean, and the Ventures. There's also an interesting display about the women of surf.

## BOLSA CHICA STATE BEACH

The 3-mile stretch of Pacific Coast Hwy north of Huntington toward Seal Beach is flanked on one side by Bolsa Chica State Beach, which has dark and dusty sand facing a monstrous oil rig half a mile off shore. On the other side of the highway is the **Bolsa Chica State Ecological Reserve**, which looks rather desolate (especially with the few small oil wells scattered about), but actually teems with bird life. Terns, mergansers, pelicans, pintails, grebes and endangered Belding's savannah sparrows congregate among the pickleweed and cordgrass in a restored salt marsh. A 1.5-mile loop trail starts from the parking lot on Pacific Coast Hwy. Parking costs $10.

## Activities

### SURFING

Surfing in HB is competitive. Control your longboard or draw ire from the local dudes who pride themselves on being agro (surf-speak for aggressive). Surf north of the pier.

If you're a novice, it's a good idea to take lessons. Try the following:

**M&M Surfing School** ( ☎ 714-846-7873; www.mmsurfingschool.com) Offers five-day surf intensives for about $225; it also gives single-day instruction for $60 to $80.

**Zack's** ( ☎ 714-536-0215; www.beachfoodfun.com; Zack's Pier Plaza, cnr PCH & Main St) Offers instruction for $60; if you just want to rent a board, you'll pay $8 per hour or $25 per day.

**HB Wahine** ( ☎ 714-596-2696; www.hbwahine.com) A great women-only surf school.

### CYCLING & SKATING

One of the best ways to explore the coast is by riding a bicycle or skating on the 8.5-mile bike path that runs from Huntington State Beach in the south to Bolsa Chica State Beach. Rent skates and bikes at **Zack's** ( ☎ 714-536-0215; www.beachfoodfun.com; Zack's Pier Plaza, cnr PCH & Main St) for about $10 per hour or $25 per day; the shop is by the foot of the pier.

## Festivals & Events

HB loves a good party, from the **Paintball World Series** to 25km marathons and skateboard competitions. For a current list of events, contact the HB **Visitors Bureau** ( ☎ 714-969-3492, 800-729-6232; www.hbvisit.com; 301 Main St, Suite 208; ☼ noon-7pm Mon-Fri, 11am-7pm Sat & Sun).

Professional volleyball players come for the **Pro Beach Volleyball Tournament** in May.

In late July to early August look for the **US Open of Surfing**. In October HB throws a big **Oktoberfest** and a fun **Halloween** party.

## Sleeping

### BUDGET

**Colonial Inn Hostel** ( ☎ 714-536-3315; www.huntingtonbeachhostel.com; 421 8th St; dm per night/week $21/130, d $50; 🖳 ) In a 1906 home three blocks from the beach, the area's only hostel is a peach of a place. Dorms sleep three to eight people, and communal areas include a nice kitchen, a living room and a backyard. There's a laundry, and free surfboard and bike rentals.

There are three budget motels north of town, halfway to Seal Beach on the busy four-lane Pacific Coast Hwy.

**Pacific View Inn & Suites** ( ☎ 714-592-4959, 800-726-8586; 16220 PCH; r $90-120; P ) The best of the three; if you're polite and well groomed there's a good chance you can negotiate the price.

**Oceanview Motel** ( ☎ 562-592-2700; www.oceanviewmotel-hb.com; 16196 PCH; r $65-115; P ) Lower-mid-range, standard-issue rooms.

**777 Motor Inn** ( ☎ 714-846-5561; 16240 PCH; r $48-75; P ) Very divey, very cheap, probably only good for surfer dudes.

### MID-RANGE

If you can't find a room, head inland along Hwy 39 toward I-405; there are several average motels with mid-range prices. Other options near the beach:

**Sun 'n' Sands Motel** ( ☎ 714-536-2543; www.sunnsands.com; 1102 PCH; r $120-230; P 🐾 ) Rates spike absurdly high in summer for this nothing-special, mom-and-pop motel, but its location across from the beach lets them get away with it.

**Best Western Huntington Beach Inn** ( ☎ 714-536-7500; www.bestwestern.com; 800 PCH; r $130-210; P ) The well-kept, cookie-cutter rooms are standard-issue at this beachside hotel.

**Huntington Surf Inn** ( ☎ 714-536-2444; www.huntingtonsurfinn.com; 720 PCH; r $110-130; P ) Expect a surly reception from a humorless innkeeper, but the location of this clean motel – near Main St and the beach – is great. Don't ask for a refund; you won't get it.

You'll save money by staying inland near the freeway. Try these places:

**Hotel Huntington Beach** ( ☎ 714-891-0123, 877-891-0123; www.hotelhb.com; 7667 Center Ave; r $100-125; P 🖳 🐾 ) This eight-story hotel, which looks like an office building, is decidedly sans personality, but the clean rooms are perfect for get-up-and-go travelers. The hot tub is a perk.

**Comfort Suites** ( ☎ 714-841-1812; 800-714-4040; www.comfortsuites.com/hotel/ca102; 16301 Hwy 39; r $90; P 🖳 🖳 ) There's nothing special about this place, but the rates are reasonable.

### TOP END
There are two upper-end hotels situated south of Main St that cater to the business-class bourgeoisie.

**Hyatt Regency Huntington Beach** ( ☎ 714-698-1234, 800-233-1234; www.huntingtonbeach.hyatt.com; r $205-305; P 🖳 🖳 ) It looks like an ersatz Spanish-style condo complex on steroids, but the deluxe rooms are inviting and impeccably maintained; there's also a good spa.

**Hilton Waterfront Beach Resort** ( ☎ 714-845-8000, 800-445-8667; www.waterfrontbeachresort.hilton .com; 21100 PCH; r $250-350; P 🖳 🖳 ) The giant tower of this hotel stands in blatant disregard for the town's low rooflines, but if you want an ocean view from up high, this is the only place.

## Eating
### BUDGET
**Wahoo** ( ☎ 714-536-2050; 120 Main St; mains under $7; 🕑 10:30am-9:30pm) The fish is served flame-broiled or spicy-blackened at HB's favorite for cheap eats. Order at the counter, chow down beneath fluorescent lights.

**Ruby's Diner** ( ☎ 714-969-7829; mains $5-15; 🕑 7am-9pm) At the end of the pier, you can sip milk-shakes and watch the waves at Ruby's.

**Longboard** ( ☎ 714-960-1896; 217 Main St; mains $6-11; 🕑 11am-11pm Sun-Thu, 11am-2am Fri & Sat) For beer and a sandwich – try the cheese steak – head to Longboard, which occupies the oldest building in HB (1904).

**Sugar Shack** ( ☎ 714-536-0355; 213 Main St; mains $4-6; 🕑 breakfast & lunch) Get here at 6am to see the surfer dudes as they don their wet suits. Breakfast served all day. Expect a wait for this HB institution.

### MID-RANGE
**Red Pearl Kitchen** ( ☎ 714-969-0224; 412 Walnut Ave; mains $13-22; 🕑 dinner) A pressed-tin ceiling and orange-and-red paper lanterns add style to this sexy industrial-chic Southeast Asian eatery off Main St, whose fiery and flavor-packed cooking draws inspiration

from the cuisine of Thailand, Vietnam, Malaysia and Japan. Plan to share plates. Full bar available.

**Spark** ( ☎ 714-960-0996; 300 PCH; mains $11-22; 🕑 dinner) Come before dark to this 2nd-floor Cal-Mediterranean, and watch the sun set over the water while dining on hickory- and oak fire–grilled steaks, chops and seafood, as well as crispy-thin pizza from the wood-fired oven. Try the grilled-chicken polenta with goat cheese.

**Inka** ( ☎ 714-374-3399; 301 Main St; mains $9-21) Garlic, cilantro, chilies and lime are the dominant ingredients at this casual Peruvian restaurant where the bar gets jumpin,' especially when there's live music.

**Coach's** ( ☎ 714-969-2233; 200 Main St, Suite 105; mains $13-20; 🕑 11am-10pm) If you're craving shish kebab or falafel, this indoor-outdoor Turkish-Mediterranean won't leave you feeling transported to Istanbul, but the simple dishes hit the spot.

## Drinking
It's easy to find a bar in HB. Walk up Main St and you'll spot them all.

**Huntington Beach Beer Co** ( ☎ 714-960-5343; 201 Main St, 2nd fl) This cavernous brew pub specializes in ales and has eight giant, stainless-steel kettles brewing it all the time. There's also good pub grub. On weekend nights DJs and bands play.

**Perqs** ( ☎ 714-960-9996; 117 Main St) Live bands usually play on Friday and Saturday nights; weeknights it's a quasi-sports bar.

**Killarney Pub & Grill** ( ☎ 714-536-7887; 209 Main St) It bills itself as an Irish pub, but the profusion of plasma TV screens makes it a sports bar with green-painted walls. Rollickin' good fun for beer-drinking sports enthusiasts.

**Shorehouse Cafe** ( ☎ 714-960-8091; 520 Main St) Drink whiskey and shoot pool with HB's rough-cut crowd.

## Entertainment
**Mann Theatres Pierside Pavillion 6** ( ☎ 714-969-3151; 300 PCH) Shows first-run movies at the corner of Main St.

**Bulldog Hookah and Havana Corner Smoke Lounge** ( ☎ 714-267-4569; 417 Main St; 🕑 2-11:30pm Sun-Thu, 1pm-1:30am Fri & Sat) Finally a place for smokers. HB's mellowest crowd lazes on sofas, puffing on cigars and toking on hookahs while watching the *Simpsons* and playing chess. Choose from 46 flavors of molasses-sweetened, shredded tobacco, but there's no alcohol. The Bulldog is *not* a front for stoners – it's just a singular hangout that you won't find anywhere else in OC. You must be 18 to enter.

**Streetlight Cafe** ( ☎ 714-969-7336; 201 Main St) An indie coffeehouse with sofas for lounging, it also has live bands on Friday and Saturday evenings. Enter off Walnut St.

## Shopping

Most stores stay open until 8pm, some until 10pm on weekends.

**Tipsy Gipsy** ( ☎ 714-969-6660; 324 Main St) Come here for Goth-by-the-beach and Hollywood-gypsy fashions.

**American Vintage Clothing** ( ☎ 714-969-9670; 201-C Main St) Thrift and vintage hounds should check out this one. Enter off Walnut St.

**Jack's Surf Boards** ( ☎ 714-536-4516; 101 Main St) For surfwear, this is the obvious place.

**Wiskers** ( ☎ 714-969-8478; 301 Main St) Pick up all manner of dog-fetishist items and pet supplies here.

**Jax Bicycle Center** ( ☎ 714-969-8684; 401 Main St) See the latest in cool-dude bicycle designs.

**Electric Chair** ( ☎ 714-536-0784; 410 Main St) Get pierced at this subversive shop for f*@k-the-man accessories.

## NEWPORT BEACH

pop 72,000

The most sophisticated of Orange County's beach towns, Newport Beach also has one of the biggest pleasure-craft harbors in the US and the highest-volume of Mercedes-Benz dealerships in the world. If you like retail shopping, you'll love Newport: not only are there inviting areas you can meander on foot, but just east of town lies Fashion Island, one of the county's major shopping centers.

But it's the sights and sounds of the coast that captivate the imagination in Newport – the light shimmering on the water, the ballet of yachts in the harbor, the thundering roar of the open ocean's waves.

The citizens of the town are fresh-faced and bronze-skinned and wear the latest in resort-wear fashions; many sport silicone breasts and Botoxed brows. You'll be hard-pressed to find even one brooding, pimply faced smoker in a too-large sweater. Not that you have to be dolled up and rich to enjoy a

visit here, but it certainly helps to have cash in your pocket (and maybe a little bronzer and face powder, too). Though Newport retains some of its modest mid-century appeal in many of its small, villagelike neighborhoods, it has lately become a magnet for the parvenu: get ready to witness some of the most conspicuous consumption anywhere in California.

If you dislike consumer culture you might get prickly in Newport, but if you focus your attention on the hypnotic beauty of the coast, the near-perfect weather and the joy of being on vacation, you're sure to have a lovely time.

### Orientation

Hwy 55 (Newport Blvd) is the main access road from I-405. It intersects with Pacific Coast Hwy, then merges with Balboa Blvd leading to the eastern tip of the Balboa Peninsula. Hwy 73 (Corona del Mar Fwy) also connects I-405 with Newport Beach (via MacArthur Blvd), before continuing as a toll road to Laguna Beach and beyond.

Pacific Coast Hwy skirts the harbor on its route through town; though the highway runs north–south through the state, in Newport it cuts east–west. It's called 'PCH' generally, but in town it's called West Coast Hwy and East Coast Hwy, depending on which side of the bay it's on. Numerous boat dealerships, charter outfits, yacht clubs and seafood restaurants sit clustered in buildings that once served as shipping warehouses for the Irvine Ranch, the large sheep-raising and tenant-farming operation that was part of the original Spanish land grant on which the inland city of Irvine – and much of Orange County – was built.

South of Pacific Coast Hwy via Balboa Blvd, the Balboa Peninsula makes a natural 6-mile barrier between Newport Harbor and the ocean. Most tourist activity is centered here, including beaches and the Balboa Fun Zone. Six of the seven harbor islands are man-made, the result of dredging (Bay Island is naturally occurring and allows no vehicular traffic).

Balboa Island is the biggest, and has fun boutiques and eateries stretched out along Marine Ave. The remaining islands are exclusively residential.

There's more shopping north of Pacific Coast Hwy at Fashion Island (p224).

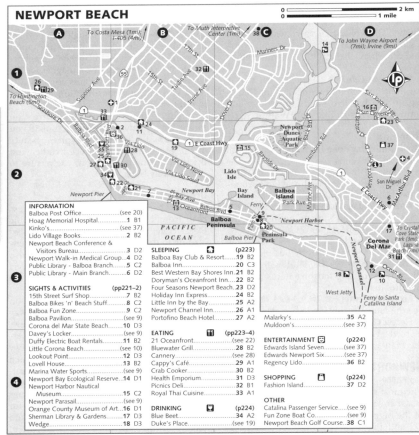

# NEWPORT BEACH

0 _____ 2 km
0 _____ 1 mile

# Information

## BOOKSTORES

Fashion Island has chain bookstores.
**Lido Village Books** ( ☎ 949-673-2549; 3424 Via
Oporto) On the Balboa Peninsula, near the Newport Blvd
bridge, look for this small bookstore.

## INTERNET ACCESS

**Kinko's** ( ☎ 949-760-1595; 230 Newport Center Dr; per
hr $12; ☼ 24hr)
**Public Library** main branch ( ☎ 949-717-3800; www
.newportbeachlibrary.com; 1000 Avocado Ave; ☼ 9am-
9pm Mon-Thu, 9am-6pm Fri & Sat, noon-5pm Sun); Balboa
branch ( ☎ 949-644-3076; 100 E Balboa Blvd; ☼ 9am-
9pm Mon-Thu, 9am-6pm Fri & Sat) The main branch is
open on Sunday, but it's near Fashion Island. The Balboa
branch is closer to the beach.

## MEDICAL SERVICES

**Hoag Memorial Hospital Presbyterian** ( ☎ 949-
764-4624; www.hoaghospital.org; cnr Hwys 1 & 55)
Emergency room operating 24/7.
**Newport Walk-in Medical Group** ( ☎ 949-760-9222;
360 San Miguel Dr; ☼ 8am-9pm Mon-Fri, 9am-6pm Sat &
Sun) For non-emergency urgent care.

## MONEY

**Travelex** ( ☎ 714-751-1203; South Coast Plaza, Costa
Mesa; ☼ 10am-9pm Mon-Fri, 11am-6pm Sat & Sun)
Change money at the giant mall in Costa Mesa (see p225).

## POST

**Balboa post office** ( ☎ 949-675-2469; 204 Main St,
Balboa Peninsula; ☼ 9am-4pm Mon-Fri) Convenient to
the beach.

**ORANGE COUNTY**

## TOURIST INFORMATION

**Newport Beach Conference & Visitors Bureau**
( ☎ 949-719-6100, 800-942-6278, 24hr recorded info
☎ 949-729-4400; www.newportbeach-cvb.com; 110
Newport Center Dr, Suite 120) Located on the road that
loops around Fashion Island. The bureau stocks good
lodging and dining guides, and a detailed town map.

## Sights

### BALBOA PENINSULA & ISLAND

Six miles long and 0.25 miles wide, the Balboa Peninsula has a white-sand beach on its ocean side and countless stylish homes, including the 1926 **Lovell House** (1242 W Ocean Front). Designed by Rudolph Schindler, one of Southern California's most seminal modernist architects, it was built using site-cast concrete frames with wood.

Hotels, restaurants and bars cluster around the peninsula's two piers: **Newport Pier**, near its western end, and **Balboa Pier** at the eastern end. The oceanfront strip teems with beachgoers, and the people-watching is great. Particularly near Newport Pier, you'll find rental shops that carry umbrellas, beach chairs, boogie boards and other necessities for a day by the water. Park anywhere on the residential side streets and walk to the sand.

Opposite the Balboa Pier on the harbor side of the peninsula, the **Balboa Fun Zone** ( ☎ 949-673-0408; www.thebalboafunzone.com; ☉ 11am-8pm Mon-Thu, 11am-9pm Fri, 11am-10pm Sat) has delighted locals and visitors since 1936. There's a small Ferris wheel, arcade games, touristy shops and restaurants, as well as the landmark 1905 **Balboa Pavilion**, which is beautifully illuminated at night. Look for stands selling the local delicacy: frozen bananas. Dipped in chocolate and rolled in nuts, they're fab.

The Fun Zone is also the place to catch a harbor cruise, fishing or whale-watching excursion (see p222), or the ferry (p224) to Balboa Island just across the channel. The ferry lands at Agate Ave, about 11 blocks west of Marine Ave, the main drag lined with cute shops, cafés and restaurants. For close-ups of the island's many beautiful homes, take a stroll along its shoreline; it's about 1.5 miles around.

At the very tip of the peninsula, by the West Jetty, the **Wedge** is a bodysurfing and knee-boarding spot famous for its perfectly hollow waves that can get up to 30ft high. The waves are shore-breakers. They crest on the sand, not out to sea, so you can easily slam your head. This is *not* a good place for learning how to handle the currents; newcomers should head a few blocks west for calmer water.

## MUSEUMS

Near Fashion Island, the **Orange County Museum of Art** ( ☎ 949-759-1122; www.ocma.net; 850 San Clemente Dr; adult/child under 12/student $7/free/5; ☉ 11am-5pm Tue-Sun, to 8pm Thu) provides a survey of California art and has cutting-edge contemporary exhibits. A sculpture garden, gift shop, and a theater screening classic, foreign and art-related films round out the facility.

The **Newport Harbor Nautical Museum** ( ☎ 949-673-7863; www.nhnm.org; 151 E Coast Hwy; admission free; ☉ 10am-5pm Tue-Sun), housed in a stern-wheeler, documents the region's maritime heritage through old-time photographs, ships' models, paintings and memorabilia.

## CORONA DEL MAR

A ritzy bedroom community with elegant stores and restaurants favored by the skirt-and-sweater crowd, Corona del Mar stretches along Pacific Coast Hwy and hugs the eastern flank of the Newport Channel. There's good window shopping.

**Corona del Mar State Beach** ( ☎ 949-644-3151; ☉ 5am-10pm) lies at the foot of rocky cliffs. Children love the tide pools at the beach's east end at **Little Corona Beach** (but the pools are being loved to death – don't yank anything from the rocks and tread lightly; light, oxygen and heavy footsteps can kill the critters). There are restrooms, fire rings (arrive early to snag one) and volleyball courts. Parking costs $8/10 per vehicle on weekdays/weekends; arrive by 9am on weekends to get a space. You may be able to find free parking atop the cliffs behind the beach along Ocean Blvd.

**Lookout Point** sits above the beach along Ocean Blvd. People practically throw cocktail parties here, mostly because of the fantastic views overlooking the mouth of the harbor. Conceal your chardonnay: technically you can't drink here, though many people do. Take the stairs to **Pirate's Cove**, a great waveless beach, which is good for families. Some of the scenes for *Gilligan's Island* were shot in the cove.

Corona del Mar's prize attraction is the **Sherman Library & Gardens** ( ☎ 949-673-2261; www.slgardens.org; 2647 E Coast Hwy; adult/child $3/1, Mon free; ☉ gardens 10:30am-4pm daily, library 9am-4:30pm

Tue-Thu). The gardens are manicured and lush, with profuse orchids, a koi pond and a garden for the visually impaired. The small research library holds a wealth of California historical documents, as well as paintings by early California landscape artists.

### CRYSTAL COVE STATE PARK

The 3.5 miles of open beach and 2000 acres of undeveloped woodland at this state **beach** (☎ 949-494-3539, 949-492-0802; www.parks.ca.gov; PCH) let you forget you're in a crowded metropolitan area, at least once you get past the parking lots and stake out a place on the sand.

You can mountain bike and hike on the inland side; however, the once-pristine rolling hills and sweeping ridgelines have been sullied in recent years. Everyone thought the hilltops were part of the state park until the Irvine Company, the actual landowner, bulldozed and leveled them to make room for Newport Coast, a hideous development of McMansions – tract homes inhabited by the nouveau riche. Take heart: starting in 2005, you can rent your own discreet little cottage on the beach. To reserve cabins and inland campsites, and check the cabin rates, contact **ReserveAmerica** (☎ 800-444-7275; www .reserveamerica.com; campsites $10-14).

### NEWPORT BAY ECOLOGICAL RESERVE

Inland from the harbor, where run-off from the San Bernardino Mountains meets the sea, the brackish water of the Newport Bay Ecological Reserve supports more than 200 species of birds. This is one of the few estuaries in Southern California that has been preserved, and it's an important stopover on the Pacific Flyway (see p40).

The wildlife viewing is great. The **Muth Interpretive Center** (☎ 949-923-2290; 2301 University Dr; ☽ 10am-4pm Tue-Sun) has displays and information about the 752-acre reserve; call for directions, it's on the corner of Irvine Ave. For guided tours with naturalists (including kayak and canoe tours), contact the **Newport Bay Naturalists & Friends** (☎ 949-640-6746, 949-923-2269; www.newportbay.org).

## Activities

### BOATING

The best thing about Newport Beach is its harbor and beaches. Make sure that you at least take a harbor tour (see opposite), but better yet rent your own watercraft.

Kayak, sail or motor around the harbor with an outboard motorboat from **Marina Water Sports** (☎ 949-673-3372; 600 E Bay Ave) at the Fun Zone on Balboa Peninsula. Kayaks cost $12 per hour, sailboats $35 per hour and motorboats start at $50 per hour.

Rent a flat-bottomed electric boat that you pilot yourself, and take a cruise with up to 12 friends. Boats have heat and closeable canopies. Bring CDs, food and beer, and make an evening or afternoon of it. Reserve one with **Duffy Electric Boat Rentals** (☎ 949-645-6812; www.duffyboats.com; 2001 West Coast Hwy). Rates are about $75 per hour and require a two-hour minimum. Marina Water Sports rents them for a little less (about $60 per hour), but they're not as cushy.

### PARASAILING

Try parasailing (flying alone, 600ft above the water, with a parachute that's tethered to a speed boat) with **Newport Parasail** (☎ 949-723-3166; ☽ summer), which has trips for $69. It's next door to Marina Water Sports; call to confirm the location.

### CYCLING & SKATING

Ride a bike along the dedicated path that runs the length of the Balboa Peninsula. Inland, you can ride in a loop on the paved road that encircles the Upper Newport Bay and Ecological Reserve (in the afternoon the reserve gets breezy and cool; carry a sweater). There are lots of places to rent bikes, skates and surreys (with the fringe on top) at the Newport and Balboa Piers. Near the Fun Zone, head to **Balboa Bikes 'n' Beach Stuff** (☎ 949-723-1516; 601 E Balboa Blvd; bikes per hr/day $9/25; ☽ closed Tue & Wed in winter) on the corner of Palm. For bikes near Newport Pier, visit **15th Street Surf Shop** (☎ 949-673-5810; 103 E 15th St; bikes per hr/day $5/17).

## Tours

One of the best way to see Newport Beach is on a boat. Several companies offer narrated harbor tours from near the Balboa Pavillion. The **Fun Zone Boat Co** (☎ 949-673-0240) operates 45/90-minute trips ($7/10) from Balboa Peninsula near the Fun Zone. **Catalina Passenger Service** (☎ 949-673-5245; 400 Main St, Balboa Peninsula) has 45-minute (adult/child $7/3) and 90-minute cruises (adult/child $10/3) that leave hourly from Balboa Pavillion. Both run extra boats during the Christmas Boat Parade festival; make reservations.

Take a whale-watching trip from December 26 through to March; contact **Davey's Locker** ( ☎ 949-673-1434; www.daveyslocker.com; 400 Main St, Balboa), also at the Balboa Pavilion, which offers trips for $20/15 per adult/child. It also operates sport-fishing trips out to sea, including half-day ($30) and overnight ($105) excursions. You can also ride with them in the Christmas Boat Parade ($18/14 adult/child).

## Festivals & Events

For details on local events, contact the visitors bureau.

The week before Christmas brings thousands of spectators to Newport Harbor to watch the nightly **Christmas Boat Parade**, a tradition that began in 1919. The 2½-hour parade of lighted and decorated boats begins at 6:30pm. You can watch it all for free from the Fun Zone or Balboa Island or on a harbor tour (see p222).

## Sleeping

Rates drop by as much as 50% in winter. Rates listed are for high season. If you want to rent a house for a week, expect to pay about $2000, but if you're traveling with other families, you can come out ahead. Contact the visitors bureau for a list of realtors.

**Newport Channel Inn** ( ☎ 949-642-3030, 800-255-8614; www.newportchannelinn.com; 6030 W Coast Hwy; r $79-139; P ) Right on the busy highway but just one block from the beach, this spotless motel has large rooms that sleep from two to seven people. Great service, friendly owners. Top budget choice.

**Best Western Bay Shores Inn** ( ☎ 949-675-3463, 800-222-6675; www.thebestinn.com; 1800 W Balboa Blvd; r $159-230; P ⛱ ) The nautical-theme rooms are surprisingly attractive, given that the place is essentially a motel. Rates include breakfast, in-room movies and beach gear. Some rooms have partial ocean views. You're paying for the location.

**Little Inn by the Bay** ( ☎ 949-673-8800, 800-438-4466; www.littleinnbythebay.com; 2627 Hwy 55; r $109-179; P ) This pretty good motel has a great location, within walking distance of the beach. Bikes, boogie boards and beach chairs are available for rent.

**Holiday Inn Express** ( ☎ 949-722-2999, 800-633-3199; www.hiexpress.com; 2300 W Coast Hwy; r $120-170; P ⛱ ) Brand new in 2004, its spotless rooms have up-to-date furnishings and extras such

as microwaves and fridges. For a mid-range chain property, it's great.

**Portofino Beach Hotel** ( ☎ 949-673-7030, 800-571-8749; www.portofinobeachhotel.com; 2306 W Oceanfront; r $160-350; P ) You can't beat the location of this small, old-fashioned beachside hotel decorated with cabbage-rose wallpaper. Rooms, all with marble baths, are a bit stuffy, especially those with fireplaces; some have ocean views, but the quietest ones are in back.

**Balboa Bay Club & Resort** ( ☎ 949-645-5000, 888-445-7153; www.balboabayclub.com; 1221 W Coast Hwy; r $295-450; P 🖥 ⛱ ) Humphrey Bogart courted Lauren Bacall at this harborside, full-service luxury resort, back when it was still a private yacht club. Now there's a new hotel attached to the historical building, and its discreet architecture complements the craftsmanship of the yachts moored outside. Rooms have topflight amenities; book one on the waterside. It's pricey, but perfect for a kiss-and-make-up splurge. Good restaurant, too.

Other options:

**Doryman's Oceanfront Inn** ( ☎ 949-675-7300; www.dorymansinn.com; 2102 W Oceanfront; r $195-365; P ) Second-floor oceanfront B&B, good for couples and antiques lovers; great location.

**Balboa Inn** ( ☎ 949-675-3412, 877-225-2629; www.balboainn.com; 105 Main St; $170-250; P ⛱ ) Lovely 1929 landmark building near Balboa Pier.

**Four Seasons Newport Beach** ( ☎ 949-759-0808, 800-819-5053; www.fourseasons.com; 690 Newport Ctr Dr; r from $325; P 🖥 ⛱ ) Perfect service; great for a luxury shopping-weekend getaway (it's near Fashion Island); tallest building in town.

## Eating

**Cappy's Café** ( ☎ 949-646-4202; 5930 W Coast Hwy; mains $5-13; 🕓 6am-3pm) Locals give Cappy's an enthusiastic thumbs-up for its tasty omelettes and cholesterol-heavy breakfasts.

**Picnics Deli** ( ☎ 949-722-7200; 435 E 17th St; mains $7-11, meals $15-20; 🕓 11am-6pm Tue-Sat) Two San Francisco–trained chefs make the best to-go food in OC at this small deli in a strip mall. From succulent sandwiches of perfectly seasoned fresh-grilled meat, fish or veggies on house-baked bread, to full dinners as gorgeous as those in the windows of Fauchon in Paris (at half the price), everything is made with a soulful sophistication rarely found in chain-restaurant-ravaged Orange County. Don't miss the cheese case.

**Health Emporium** ( ☎ 949-673-2244; 3347 E Coast Hwy; mains under $10; 🕓 7am-10pm) Besides being a good grocery store, this place has a fine prepared-food counter with lots for vegetarians and vegans; there are also homemade soups and a grill menu you can enjoy in the small **café** ( 7am-3pm & 4-9:30pm).

**Crystal Cove Shake Shack** ( ☎ 949-497-9666; 7703 E Coast Hwy) Stop for a date shake on your way to the park. They're delish.

**Crab Cooker** ( ☎ 949-673-0100; 2200 Hwy 55; mains $9-17; 11am-10pm) Expect a wait at this always-busy fish joint, which serves great seafood and fresh crab on paper plates to an always-appreciative crowd in flip-flops and jeans. Good chowder, too.

**Royal Thai Cuisine** ( ☎ 949-645-8424; 4001 West Coast Hwy; mains $8-18) Gracious service, a smartly decorated dining room, and consistently delicious cooking distinguish this as the top Thai eatery in Newport. At lunch there's a good $9 special.

**Bluewater Grill** ( ☎ 949-675-3474; 630 Lido Park Dr; mains $11-24; 11am-10pm) Sit on the wooden deck and watch the boats at this polished harborside restaurant/oyster-bar that serves off-the-boat-fresh fish. Great for bloody Marys and a leisurely seafood-and-coleslaw lunch.

**Cannery** ( ☎ 949-566-0060; 3010 Lafayette Rd; mains lunch $12-20, dinner $19-35) The joint gets jumpin' on weekends at this steak-and-seafood, two-story former cannery across from Bluewater. Upstairs there's a sushi bar. Downstairs there's valet *boat*-parking service. Reservations essential.

**21 Oceanfront** ( ☎ 949-673-2100; 2100 W Ocean-front; mains $23-42; dinner) Prime steaks and off-the-dock seafood, served in a dimly lit Victorian-style dining room, make this refined oceanfront restaurant a favorite for birthdays and anniversaries. Don't forget your wallet.

## Drinking

**Blue Beet** ( ☎ 949-675-2338; 107 21st Pl) Young singles carouse on the rooftop patio or at the long wooden bar of this brick-walled saloon near the Newport Pier. Live music most nights means an occasional cover charge. At midnight it serves tacos. Earlier there's pizza and burgers.

**Malarky's** ( ☎ 949-675-2340; 3011 Hwy 55) Hunky-lifeguard bartenders pour tequila for sorority girls and their frat-boy suitors from USC. Bring ID; you *will* get carded.

**Muldoon's** ( ☎ 949-640-4110; 202 Newport Ctr Dr, Fashion Island) If you've been shopping or to the movies at Fashion Island and you're looking for a pint and a bite, this is one of the only spots open past 11pm for the beyond-30 set. Ten beers on tap. Good – if pricey – Irish pub grub. The crowd wears khakis and shops retail.

**Duke's Place** ( ☎ 949-645-5000; 1221 W Coast Hwy) Don white linen, valet the car and sip margaritas while tapping your toe to piano jazz and watching the yachts at the high-style Balboa Bay Beach Club & Resort.

## Entertainment

**Regency Lido** ( ☎ 949-673-8350; 3459 Via Lido) Shows independent films and has glow-in-the-dark murals on the walls. On the corner of Hwy 55.

See first-run mainstream films at either of these two multiplexes at Fashion Island:

**Edwards Island Seven** ( ☎ 949-640-1971; 999 Newport Ctr Dr)

**Edwards Newport Six** ( ☎ 949-640-4600; 300 Newport Ctr Dr)

## Shopping

There's good shopping in Newport Beach. Window-shop the tony boutiques along Pacific Coast Hwy in Corona del Mar. On Balboa Island, Marine Ave is lined with cute shops in a village atmosphere, a good place to pick something up for the kids. The cobblestone streets of Lido Marina Village and the nautical-theme Cannery Village have several good shops, including a small indie bookstore (p220).

**Fashion Island** ( ☎ 949-721-2000; 550 Newport Ctr Dr; 10am-9pm Mon-Fri, 11am-7pm Sat, 11am-6pm Sun) This is the real draw for serious shopping. It's an indoor-outdoor mall of over 200 mid- to upper-end retail stores, among them Bloomingdale's, Neiman Marcus, Macy's Women and Robinsons-May.

## Getting There & Away

The catamaran to Catalina Island (p102) departs daily at 9am; from here it's a $44 round-trip.

## Getting Around

OCTA bus No 71 stops at the corner of Pacific Coast Hwy and Hwy 55 and goes south to the end of the Balboa Peninsula. Bus No 57 goes north to South Coast Plaza in Costa Mesa.

The Balboa Fun Zone is connected to Balboa Island (p221) via a tiny car and passenger

## DETOUR: COSTA MESA

Orange County prides itself on being SoCal's shopping capital. The area brims with enormous, attractively designed malls, complete with fountains, restaurants, movie theaters, shops and entertainment. No other mall defines the county's shopping scene more than **South Coast Plaza** (☎ 800-782-8888) in Costa Mesa (exit I-405 at Bristol). But don't call it a mall, or you'll get rapped on the knuckles. They call it a 'shopping resort.' Disagreements over nomenclature aside, one thing's for sure: South Coast Plaza grosses more than any other shopping center in the USA. Boutiques by the likes of Chanel and Ralph Lauren do their part to keep the numbers high. Bigger stores include Saks Fifth Avenue, Nordstrom, Macy's, Crate & Barrel and even lowly Sears.

If this is too much mall – er, shopping resort – for you, consider a visit to the **Lab** (2930 Bristol St, Costa Mesa). Conceived in 1993 to bring 'urban culture' to quintessentially suburban Orange County, the so-called anti-mall occupies a refurbished factory filled with 'alternative,' youth-oriented stores. But whaddya know? OC alternative culture also manifests itself in chains – Na Na, Urban Outfitters, etc. Still, they've got some fun stuff, and it's certainly edgier than Polo or Sears.

If you hate to shop, don't write off Costa Mesa as Costa Misery just yet. Believe it or not, the city is the cultural center of Orange County. The **Orange County Performing Arts Center** (☎ 714-556-2787; www.ocpac.org; 600 Town Center Dr, Costa Mesa) draws international performing-arts luminaries and professional Broadway road shows. Check the calendar before you head to Southern California, and you might get to see the American Ballet Theater, Dianne Reeves or the resident **South Coast Repertory** (SCR; ☎ 714-708-5555; www.scr.org), the latter of which merits the respect of anyone who loves the stage. In 1988 the company won a Tony Award for 'distinguished achievement,' no small feat in a county that's often laughed at or ignored by the East Coast elite. SCR stages plays fall through spring.

For a pre-theater flute of champagne or *sole meunière*, or if you're just looking for an appropriate venue in which to show off your new little black dress, head to **Chat Noir** (☎ 714-557-6647; 655 Anton Blvd, Costa Mesa; mains lunch $12-20, dinner $20-30; ⏰ lunch Mon-Fri, dinner daily). There's lots of silicone and lacquered hair at this giant French brasserie, but the food is consistently terrific, and the bar gets packed; make reservations for peak times. Live jazz plays Tuesday to Saturday evenings after 8pm.

Costa Mesa is the next city inland from Newport Beach, via Hwy 55. Take the Del Mar Ave/Fair Dr exit; continue straight along Hwy 55 for a mile, then turn left on Bristol to South Coast Plaza.

ferry, which operates around the clock (60¢ per person or $1.50 for car and 60¢ per vehicle occupant); in winter it stops for a couple of hours in the middle of the night.

## LAGUNA BEACH

**pop 25,000**

Secluded beaches, low cliffs, glassy waves, waterfront parks and eucalyptus-covered hillsides imbue Laguna Beach with a Riviera-like feel, and make it one of SoCal's most cultured and charming seaside resorts. A refreshing change from the rest of Orange County's beige-box architecture, Laguna has cute cottages from craftsman to contemporary in design, a perfect backdrop for a downtown stroll. One of the earliest incorporated cities in California, Laguna has

a strong and long tradition in the arts, and is the home of several renowned festivals (see p228). Public art abounds and there are several dozen galleries, a renowned art museum and a popular art walking tour on the first Thursday evening of the month. Laguna swells with tourists on summer weekends, but away from the downtown village (the central business district) and Main Beach (where the downtown village meets the shore), there's plenty of uncrowded sand and open water.

Laguna's earliest inhabitants, the Ute-Aztecas and Shoshone tribes, called the area 'Lagonas' because of two freshwater lagoons in what is now Laguna Canyon. The name endured until 1904, when it was changed to Laguna. At roughly the same

ORANGE COUNTY

time, San Francisco artist Norman St Claire came to Laguna to paint watercolors of the surf, cliffs and hills. His enthusiasm attracted other artists who were influenced by French impressionism and were known as the 'plein air' (as in 'open air' or 'outdoors') school. The Laguna Beach Art Association was founded in 1918, and by the late '20s more than half of the town's 300 residents were artists.

The most lasting development began in Laguna Beach in 1926, when Pacific Coast Hwy between Newport Beach and Dana Point opened, giving Laguna three access routes. Mary Pickford, Douglas Fairbanks, Mickey Rooney and Bette Davis vacationed here regularly, and helped establish the highly regarded Laguna Playhouse and the Festival of the Arts, both of which you can visit today.

Hwy 1 goes by several names in Laguna Beach. South of Broadway, downtown's main street, it's called South Coast Hwy; north of Broadway it's North Coast Hwy. And you'll hear locals call it Pacific Coast Hwy or simply PCH.

## Orientation

Laguna stretches for about 7 miles along Pacific Coast Hwy. Shops, restaurants and bars are concentrated along a 0.25 mile stretch in the Village, along three parallel streets: Broadway, Ocean and Forest. The town gets packed in summer.

## Information
### BOOKSTORES
**Barnaby Rudge Bookseller** ( ☎ 949-497-4079; www.barnabyrudge.com; 1445 Glenneyre St) Wonderful antiquarian book shop. Sells maps and prints, too.
**Latitude 33** ( ☎ 949-494-5403; 311 Ocean Ave) Good independent, generalist bookstore. It's also a great camera-repair shop.

### INTERNET ACCESS
**Laguna Beach Visitors & Conference Bureau**
( ☎ 949-497-9229, 800-877-1115; www.lagunabeachinfo .org; 252 Broadway; ☻ 9am-5pm Mon-Fri, 11am-3pm Sat Sep-Jun, 9am-5pm Mon-Fri, 11am-3pm Sat, 11am-3pm Sun Jul & Aug) You can check your email free for 15 minutes here.
**Public library** ( ☎ 949-497-1733; www.ocpl.org; 363 Glenneyre St; ☻ 10am-8pm Mon-Wed, 10am-6pm Thu, 10am-5pm Fri & Sat) A maximum of one hour's use per day; make a donation. It's at the corner of Laguna.

### MEDICAL SERVICES
**Sleepy Hollow Medical Group** ( ☎ 949-494-3740; 364 Ocean Ave; ☻ 8am-6pm Mon-Sat, to noon Sun) For non-emergency urgent care.
**South Coast Medical Center** ( ☎ 949-499-1311; www.southcoastmedcenter.com; 31872 Coast Hwy) For a 24-hour hospital emergency room, head 5 miles south of the downtown village along Hwy 1 to this center. It's in South Laguna Beach at 7th Ave.

### MONEY
**Travelex** ( ☎ 714-751-1203; South Coast Plaza, Costa Mesa; ☻ 10am-9pm Mon-Fri, 11am-6pm Sat & Sun) Change money at the giant mall in Costa Mesa (see p225).

### POST
**Post office** ( ☎ 949-362-8306; 350 Forest Ave; ☻ 8:30am-5pm Mon-Fri) The Playa Branch sits at the corner of Beach St in the downtown village.

### TOURIST INFORMATION
**Laguna Beach Visitors & Conference Bureau**
( ☎ 949-497-9229, 800-877-1115; www.lagunabeach info.org; 252 Broadway; ☻ 9am-5pm Mon-Fri, 11am-3pm Sat Sep-Jun, 9am-5pm Mon-Fri, 11am-3pm Sat, 11am-3pm Sun Jul & Aug) Helpful staff, bus schedules, copies of local restaurants' menus and pamphlets on everything from hiking trails to self-guided public-art walks. The free weekly *Coastline Pilot* is a good source for local news and events.

## Dangers & Annoyances
Fire is a particular danger in Laguna. The canyons act like chimneys, and small grass fires quickly become infernos. Use extreme caution with matches and cigarette butts, especially if you're hiking in the canyons. And never throw lit cigarettes out of car windows.

## Sights
### LAGUNA ART MUSEUM
This breezy **museum** ( ☎ 949-494-8971; 307 Cliff Dr; adult/child under 12/student $9/free/7; ☻ 11am-5pm) has changing exhibits usually featuring one or two California artists, and a permanent collection heavy on California landscapes, vintage photographs and works by early Laguna artists. The museum also makes an effort to support new artists. There are free docent tours at 2pm daily, and an interesting gift shop.

### BEACHES
Laguna Beach has 30 public beaches and coves, but many are hidden from view by multimillion-dollar homes. However, most beaches are accessible by stairs off Pacific Coast Hwy; just look for the 'beach access' signs. Be prepared to pass through people's backyards to reach the sand.

**Main Beach** has volleyball and basketball courts, and is the best beach for swimming. North of Main Beach, it's too rocky to surf; tidepooling is best. Pick up a tide table at the visitors bureau. (Tidepool etiquette: Tread lightly and don't pick anything up that you find living in the rocks.)

Just north of Main Beach, stroll the grassy, bluff-top **Heisler Park** for sweeping views of the craggy coves and deep-blue sea. Bring your camera. Drop down below the park to **Diver's Cove**, a deep, protected inlet popular with snorkelers and, of course, divers. North of town, **Crescent Bay** has big hollow waves good for bodysurfing, but parking is difficult here; try the bluffs atop the beach.

About 1 mile south of the Village, **Victoria Beach** has volleyball courts and **La Tour**, a Rapunzel's towerlike structure from 1926. Take the stairs down Victoria Dr; there's limited parking on Pacific Coast Hwy. Nearby **Aliso Beach** has a fair amount of parking and is popular with surfers, as is **Salt Creek Beach** in Laguna Niguel.

You can rent beach chairs, umbrellas and boogie boards from **Main Beach Toys** ( ☎ 949-494-8808; 150 Laguna Ave at PCH).

## PUBLIC ART

Laguna is full of public art, from well-placed murals to free-standing sculptures in unlikely places. Pick up the self-guided *Public Art Brochure* from the visitors bureau. It shows color photos of all 41 of Laguna's public art pieces, as well as a bulleted map to help you navigate. Stop by **Heislers Park** to see almost a dozen sculptures.

Also check out **Browns' Park** (cnr Legion St & S Coast Hwy), a tiny clifftop 'pocket park' no wider than 25ft across; the views to sea are mesmerizing. Read the meditative passage fashioned out of wrought-iron below the railing. Lovely.

## PACIFIC MARINE MAMMAL CENTER

A nonprofit organization dedicated to rescue and rehabilitate injured or ill marine mammals, the **mammal center** ( ☎ 949-494-3050; www.pacificmmc.org; 20612 Laguna Canyon Rd; admission by donation; 10am-4pm) has a small staff and many volunteers who help nurse the ailing sea lions and seals back to health.

You can visit, but remember, this is a rescue center, not SeaWorld. Still, it's educational and heart-warming. And you can buy a stuffed animal in the gift shop to benefit the center.

## Activities

### HIKING

Surrounded by a green belt – a rarity in SoCal – Laguna has some good areas preserved for hiking. You'll find two marked trails at **Alta Laguna Park**, a hidden park up-canyon from town; few people ever visit. Inside the park the moderate **Park Avenue Nature Trail**, a 1.25-mile one-way hike, takes you through fields of wild flowers in spring.

The 2.5-mile **West Ridge Trail** follows the ridgeline of the hills above Laguna for stunning ocean views; it's open to hikers and mountain bikers. The visitors bureau stocks a fold-out trail guide. Take Park Ave from town to its end at Alta Laguna Blvd; turn left to the park, where there are restrooms and telephones. Both trails are in-and-out trails, not loops.

### KAYAKING

Take a guided sea-kayaking tour of the craggy coves of the Laguna coast with **North Laguna Float Company** ( ☎ 949-494-5910; 2hr guided floats $25), a good company with reasonable prices that operates seven days. On weekends, consider the also-good **La Vida Laguna** ( ☎ 949-275-7544; www.lavidalaguna.com; 2hr guided floats $59). Make reservations for both.

---

### LAGUNA ART FESTIVALS

Laguna Beach's landmark event is the **Festival of the Arts** (650 Laguna Canyon Rd; 10am Jul & Aug; adults/students/seniors $5/3/3), a seven-week juried exhibit of 160 artists whose work varies from paintings to handcrafted furniture to scrimshaw. Begun in 1932 by local artists who needed to drum up buyers, the festival now attracts patrons and tourists from around the world. In addition to the art, there are free daily artists' workshops, a children's art gallery and live entertainment. Closing hours vary.

The most thrilling part of the fair, a tremendous experience that will leave you rubbing your eyes in disbelief, is the **Pageant of the Masters** ( ☎ 949-497-6582, 800-487-3378; www.foapom .com; admission $15-65), where human models are blended seamlessly into re-creations of famous paintings. It began in 1933 as a sideshow to the main festival. Tickets are hard to secure, unless you order weeks or months in advance – though you may be able to snag last-minute cancellations at the gate. Nightly performances begin at 8:30pm.

In the '60s Laguna Beach artists who didn't make the grade for the juried exhibition started their own festival to take advantage of the art seekers passing through town. They set up directly across from the festival, mocking its formal atmosphere by scattering sawdust on the ground. Thus, the so-called **Sawdust Festival** ( ☎ 949-494-3030; www.sawdustfestival.org; 935 Laguna Canyon Rd; adult/child/senior $6.50/2/5.50; 10am-10pm) was born. Ironically enough, it's juried now, but you can still find arts and crafts that are both utilitarian and affordable.

A third art happening, the **Art-A-Fair Festival** ( ☎ 949-494-4514; 777 Laguna Canyon Rd; adult/ student/senior $5/3/3; 10am-9pm Sun-Thu, 10am-10pm Fri & Sat) runs simultaneously. It's a nationally juried show, focused mainly on watercolors, pastels and oil paintings, but expect to see some photography, jewelry, ceramics and other arts and crafts, too.

## CYCLING

Laguna Beach isn't the greatest for road biking. Drivers along the always-busy Pacific Coast Hwy are distracted by the view, so pay attention if you head out on that road.

Up in the hills, you can have a blast mountain biking; there are also paved off-road trails. Rent a bike and get trail information at **Laguna Cyclery** ( ☎ 949-494-1522; lagunacyclery.net; 240 Thalia St) or **Rainbow Bicycle Co** ( ☎ 949-494-5806; www.teamrain.com; 485 N Coast Hwy). The cost of 24-hour rental is about $35 for road bikes and $30 to $40 for mountain bikes.

## SURFING

Because of the coves in Laguna, the surfing isn't as stellar as it is further north in places such as Huntington Beach or even Newport Beach. However, if you have your heart set on it, you can rent a board or get instruction from **Costa Azul Surf Co** ( ☎ 949-497-1423; www.costaazul.net; 689 S Coast Hwy). Rental boards cost $20, wet suits $15. Lessons include board rental and cost $75 per hour. Also consider classes with **Aloha School of Surfing** ( ☎ 949-415-0644; www.alohaschoolofsurfing.com; 31306 Brooks St), which cost $75 per hour.

## Tours

Stop by the visitors bureau to pick up brochures detailing self-guided tours you can take of Laguna. The **Heritage Walking Companion** is a tour of the town's architecture; the **Self-Guided Tour Laguna by Bus** gives a more general overview. Each involves riding public transportation (see p231), which is a relief: if you tried to take the tours using your own car, you'd go nuts trying to find parking, especially on weekends.

On the first Thursday of the month, **First Thursdays Gallery Art Walk** ( ☎ 949-683-6871; www.firstthursdaysartwalk.com) makes the rounds of local galleries from 6pm to 9pm, then ends the evening with free admission to the museum from 9pm to 10pm.

For guided tours for the athletically inclined, call **La Vida Laguna** ( ☎ 949-275-7544; www.lavidalaguna.com), which offers docent-led nature hikes, guided mountain-bike outings and city tours on electric bicycles.

## Sleeping

There are no budget lodgings in Laguna in summer. Listed here are summer rates; come fall, they drop significantly.

**Crescent Bay Inn** ( ☎ 949-494-2508, 888-494-2508; www.crescentbayinn.com; 1435 N Coast Hwy; r $65-135; Ⓟ ) What this vintage-'50s motel lacks in amenities it makes up for in value. Some units have kitchenettes. And some even have ocean views! Cheapest place in town.

**Best Inn** ( ☎ 949-494-6464, 877-363-7229; 1404 N Coast Hwy; r $105-180; Ⓟ ⊠ ) About 1 mile northwest of the Village, this is a friendly, better-than-average motel with good prices – for Laguna at least. Take the shuttle to downtown.

**Vacation Village** ( ☎ 949-494-8566, 800-843-6895; www.vacationvillage.com; 647 S Coast Hwy; r & ste $92-339; Ⓟ ⊠ ) Southeast of the Village, this 130-unit complex has motel rooms in several satellite buildings, about half of them with kitchens. This is a family-friendly place. Two pools and a whirlpool round out the appeal.

**By the Sea Inn** ( ☎ 949-497-6645, 800-297-0007; www.bytheseainn.com; 475 N Coast Hwy; r $129-209; Ⓟ ⊠ ) For its proximity to the water and the downtown village, this three-story motel is a relative bargain in pricey Laguna. A hot tub, steam room, sauna and in-room VCRs add to the value.

**Casa Laguna Inn** ( ☎ 949-494-2996, 800-233-0449; www.casalaguna.com; 2510 S Coast Hwy; r $160-290; Ⓟ 🖳 ⊠ ) Laguna's B&B gem is built around a historic 1920s Mission Revival house surrounded by lush plantings. Rooms are inside former artists' bungalows built in the 1930s and '40s; all have delicious beds, some have Jacuzzis. There's full breakfast, evening wine and cheese. Wonderful.

**Manzanita Cottages** ( ☎ 949-661-2533, 877-661-2533; www.manzanitacottages.com; 732 Manzanita Dr; cottages $135-250; Ⓟ ) These oh-so-cute bungalows, up the hill from downtown, were designed in the 1920s by a Hollywood producer, and they retain all their original romantic charm. Each has a gas fireplace and full kitchen. Lovely gardens, too. Reserve in advance. There's always a minimum two-night stay, in summer it's longer.

**Hotel Laguna** ( ☎ 949-494-1151, 800-524-2927; www.hotellaguna.com; 425 S Coast Hwy; r $120-300; Ⓟ ) Laguna's only historic hotel was built in 1930 and has none-too-special rooms overlooking South Coast Hwy (loud) or the beach (expensive) – but it's long on nostalgia and has a private beach adjoining Main Beach. Great bar downstairs.

**Best Western Laguna Reef Inn** ( ☎ 949-499-2227, 800-528-1234; www.lagunareefinn.com; 30806 S Coast Hwy; r $150-235; Ⓟ 🖳 ⊠ ) Rates are better than average for what you get at this lushly landscaped motel at the south end of town. Its spotless rooms have comfortable furnishings, microwaves and fridges.

**Surf & Sand Resort** ( ☎ 949-497-4477, 800-524-8621; www.surfandsandresort.com; 1555 S Coast Hwy; r $260-515; P ⌨ ☕ ) All but three of the 165 rooms at this great-for-a-splurge, sparkling seaside resort have full ocean views – you'll be lulled to sleep by the crashing of waves. Rooms sport a soothing natural color scheme and ultra-comfy beds. There's a full-service spa.

**Inn at Laguna** ( ☎ 949-497-9722, 800-544-4479; www.innatlagunabeach.com; 211 N Coast Hwy; r $189-500; P ☕ ) At the north end of Main Beach, this three-story white concrete hotel has some rooms with balconies overlooking the water. All have a fresh, clean look complete with French blinds and thick featherbeds. Extras include VCRs, stereos, bathrobes and a continental breakfast delivered to your room.

**Montage Resort & Spa** ( ☎ 949-715-6000, 866-271-6953; www.montagelagunabeach.com; 30801 S Coast Hwy; r $500-750; P ⌨ ☕ ) If you've come crawling back to your lover and must now demonstrate your new-found devotion with great fanfare, you'll find nowhere more indulgent on the coast than this over-the-top luxury resort. Even if you're not staying here, come for a spa treatment or a cocktail so you can espy the art in the lobby and the spectacular inlaid sunburst in the swimming pool. At the south end of the resort, there's underground public parking (25¢ for 15 minutes) and a public-access walkway that loops around the grounds, atop the bluffs overlooking the sea, and provides free entry to the sandy shore.

## Eating

Laguna Beach has too many Mexican restaurants. Among the listings that follow, you'll find the south-of-the-border standouts.

**Zinc Café** ( ☎ 949-494-6302; 350 Ocean Ave; dishes $4-7; ☾ breakfast & lunch) Ground zero for Laguna's see-and-be-seen vegetarians, Zinc has a hedge-enclosed patio where you can munch on tasty veg meals (yes, it serves eggs). Order at the counter.

**La Sirena** ( ☎ 949-497-8226; 347 Mermaid St; dishes $3-10; ☾ 11am-9pm) In pricey Laguna, hole-in-the-wall La Sirena shines for its bargain-basement prices and knockout contemporary Mexican specialties (think crunchy jicama and zingy salsa, not fat-laden refries with melted yellow cheese). Grab one of the cov-

eted sidewalk tables or stand at the counter while you feast on blackened-salmon salad, tacos with house-made tortillas, or herb-cheese-stuffed grilled-pasilla chilies with *carnitas*. Top pick for cheap eats.

**Taco Loco** ( ☎ 949-497-1635; 640 S Coast Hwy; dishes $3-9; ☾ 11am-midnight Sat-Thu, 11am-2am Fri & Sat) Throw back Coronas with the surfers while watching the passersby on Pacific Coast Hwy at this fantastic self-service, traditional Mexican sidewalk café. On Tuesday come for dollar tacos.

**Las Brisas** ( ☎ 949-497-5434; 361 Cliff Dr; mains lunch $9-17, dinner $19-29) Come here for one of the best views you'll ever have of Laguna, and sip margaritas while you stare at the crashing waves from the glassed-in patio on the bluff, or book a table in the dining room. After leaving, you won't long remember your Mexican-seafood meal, but the image of the coast will leave an indelible impression. Cocktail hour gets packed. Don't come if it's dark outside. Make reservations.

**Cottage** ( ☎ 949-494-3023; 208 N Coast Hwy; mains breakfast & lunch $5-10, dinner $17-21; ☾ breakfast, lunch & dinner) It feels like grandma's living-room inside this cute spot for breakfast and lunch, where great cranberry-orange pancakes are served until 3pm. There's dinner, too, but breakfast is the big reason to come.

**242 Café Fusion Sushi** ( ☎ 949-494-2444; 242 N Coast Hwy; dinner $18; ☾ dinner Tue-Sun) One of the only female sushi chefs in Orange County slices and rolls Laguna's hands-down-best sushi. The place seats maybe 20 people at a time, so expect a wait. Great sake and beer.

**French 75** ( ☎ 949-494-8444; 1464 S Coast Hwy; ☾ dinner) Rekindle your romance at this cozy, candlelit French charmer, *the* spot in Laguna for high heels and champagne. The hearty preparations of provincial-style cooking don't rival the haute-cuisine restaurants of LA, but the low ceilings, hidden nooks, and swingin' jazz combo make for a *très* sexy evening. Bring your credit card.

**Wild Oats** ( ☎ 949-376-7888; 283 Broadway; ☾ 7am-11pm) Pick up groceries, meats, organic produce and grab-and-go picnic foods here.

Also check out the following:

**Salerno** ( ☎ 949-494-5000; 220 Beach St; mains $12-24; ☾ lunch Wed-Sun, dinner Tue-Mon) Locally owned hearty, old-school Italian – like Mama used to make.

**Sundried Tomato** ( ☎ 949-494-3312; 361 Forest Ave; mains lunch $6-13, dinner $16-27) Chopped salads, sun-dried tomato soup, pasta and sandwiches.

## Drinking

**Terrace** ( ☎ 949-452-1151; Hotel Laguna, 425 S Coast Hwy; ❨ 11am-11pm) Watch bathing beauties from a plastic lawn chair while downing pricey beers, right above Main Beach.

**Splashes** ( ☎ 949-497-4477; Surf & Sand Resort, 1555 S Coast Hwy) This bar feels like Hawaii because it's the only place in Laguna you can drink right on the beach (don't forget your wallet).

**White House** ( ☎ 949-494-8088; 340 S Coast Hwy) Serves OK food early, but come for the nightly entertainment and drink until 2am.

**Woody's at the Beach** ( ☎ 949-376-8809; 1305 S Coast Hwy) Laguna Beach has the only gay venues for miles around, and there's surprisingly great food and a fun bar scene for the OC gay-on-the-go set.

**Boom Boom Room** ( ☎ 949-494-7588; ❨ Tue-Sun) Across the street from Woody's, at the Coast Inn, this place is a dance club on Wednesday, Friday and Saturday, and charges $5 after 9pm.

For pub grub and microbrews head to **Laguna Beach Brewing Company** ( ☎ 949-494-2739; 422 S Coast Hwy), which has live music Thursday to Sunday, and the **Ocean Ave Brewing Company** ( ☎ 949-497-3381; 237 Ocean Ave; ❨ Tue-Sun).

## Entertainment

**Laguna Playhouse** ( ☎ 949-497-2787; www.laguna playhouse.com; 606 Laguna Canyon Rd) The oldest continuously operating theater on the West Coast stages lighter plays in summer, heavier works in winter.

## Shopping

Laguna's downtown village is a shopper's paradise, with hidden courtyards and funky little shacks that beg exploration. Forest Ave downtown has the highest concentration of chic boutiques.

**Shelby's Foot Jewelry** ( ☎ 949-494-7992; 577 S Coast Hwy; ❨ 10am-9pm) All the jewelry is handcrafted for toes, ankles, feet, thumbs and waists; it's in a courtyard called Laguna Village.

Satisfy a chocolate craving at **La Rue du Chocolat** ( ☎ 949-494-2372; 448 S Coast Hwy), inside the Peppertree Lane shopping courtyard, where you'll also find **Cecile Brunner** ( ☎ 949-464-9141), a custom millinery shop.

## Getting There & Around

To reach Laguna Beach from the I-405, take Hwy 133 (Laguna Canyon Rd) southwest.

Laguna is served by OCTA bus No 1, which runs along the coast.

Laguna is hemmed in by steep canyons, and parking is a perpetual problem. Pack quarters to feed the meters. If you're spending the night, leave your car at the hotel and ride the local bus. Parking lots in the village charge $10 or more per entry and fill up early in the day in summer. Pacific Coast Hwy through town moves slowly in summer, especially in the afternoon on weekends; allow extra time. If you can't find parking downtown, drive to the north end of town by the beach and ride the bus.

**Laguna Beach Transit** ( ☎ 949-497-0746; 300 block of Broadway) has its central bus depot on Broadway, just north of the visitors bureau in the heart of the village. It operates three routes at hourly intervals (no service between noon and 1pm or on Sunday or holidays). Routes are color-coded and easy to follow, but they're subject to change. For tourists, the most important route is the one that runs north–south along Pacific Coast Hwy. Pick up a brochure and schedule at your hotel or the visitors bureau. Rides cost 75¢.

## AROUND LAGUNA BEACH
### Catalina Island

If you're planning a trip to Catalina Island (p102), you can pick up the ferry 8 miles south of Laguna Beach in Dana Point.

### San Juan Capistrano

Known the world over for its famous swallows that fly back to town every year on the same date, San Juan Capistrano is also home to the 'jewel of the California missions.' It's a little town, about 10 miles south and inland of Laguna Beach, but the beautiful **Mission San Juan Capistrano** ( ☎ 949-234-1300; www.missionsjc.com; 31882 Camino Capistrano; adult/child $6/4; ❨ 8:30am-5pm) draws visitors from around the world. The charming Serra Chapel – whitewashed and decorated with colorful symbols – is believed to be the oldest building in California. It's the only one still standing in which Father Junípero Serra gave Mass. Serra founded the mission on November 1, 1776, and tended it personally for many years. With access to San Clemente harbor, and as the only development between San Diego and LA, this was one of the most important missions in the chain. Like many others, it was largely self-sustaining, and had its own mills, granaries, livestock and crops, as well as other small industries.

Plan on spending at least an hour poking around the sprawling grounds – lush gardens, fountains and courtyards – and mission structures – including the padre's quarters, soldiers' barracks, cemetery and Great Stone Church. The gift shop has books on early California and mission history, as well as trinkets to take home.

San Juan Capistrano is also where the legendary swallows return each year to nest – on March 19, the feast of Saint Joseph – after wintering in South America, just as the song says. The **Festival of the Swallows** is the highlight of the mission's active year-round events schedule. The birds hang around until October 23 and are best observed at feeding time, usually early in the morning and late afternoon to early evening.

Camino Capistrano, leading up to the mission, is lined with souvenir shops, galleries and restaurants. One block west, next to the Capistrano train depot, the **Los Rios Historic District** is a cutesy assemblage of 31 historic cottages and adobes that now mostly house cafés and gift shops. For breakfast or lunch near the mission, the best spot is the 1881 **Ramos House Café** ( ☎ 949-443-1342; 31752 Los Rios St; mains $6-11; ☺ breakfast & lunch Tue-Sun), famous for its earthy comfort food that's flavored with herbs from the garden 'round back. The **Coach House** ( ☎ 949-496-8930; www.thecoachhouse.com; 33157 Camino Capistrano) is a well-known entertainment venue featuring a roster of local and regional rock and alternative bands; expect a cover of $10 to $30, depending on who's playing.

From Laguna Beach, take OCTA bus No 1 south to K-Mart Plaza, then connect to bus No 191/A in the direction of Mission Viejo, which drops you near the mission ($2, one hour).

The Amtrak depot is one block south and west of the mission; it would be perfectly reasonable to arrive by train from LA or San Diego in time for lunch, visit the mission, and be back in the city for dinner.

Drivers should exit I-5 at Ortega Hwy and head west for about 0.25 miles.

RICHARD CUMMINS

1950s-style diner, Laguna Beach (p225), Orange County

Lifeguard tower, Newport Beach
(p219), Orange County

RICHARD CUMMINS

RICHARD CUMMINS

Aliso Beach (p227), Laguna Beach,
Orange County

STEPHEN SAKS

Serra Chapel, Mission San Juan
Capistrano (p231), Orange County

EDDIE BRADY

Paragliding, Torrey Pines Gliderport (p282), La Jolla, San Diego

RICHARD CUMMINS

Piñatas for sale, Old Town
State Historic Park (p256),
San Diego

House detail, Hillcrest (p257), San Diego

RICHARD C

RICHARD CUMMINS

Gaslamp Quarter (p236), downtown
San Diego

# San Diego

It's easy to fall in love with San Diego. What's not to like? When much of the USA shivers under blankets of rain and snow, San Diegans picnic in the park and slice through waves on surfboards. The city's downtown skyline stands sentinel over one of the world's great natural harbors, home to the US Naval fleet. Beneath the high-rises, the brick buildings of the historic Gaslamp Quarter – the city's center for dining and nightlife – exude an early-20th-century charm. Add to this Balboa Park – the country's largest urban park – the world-famous zoo and miles of beaches, and it's hard to dispute the locals' claim of San Diego as 'America's Finest City.'

People looking for a laid-back California lifestyle will find it in San Diego County's beach towns more than in any other part of the state. A dozen small communities from Coronado to Oceanside each has its own flavor and flair, from bohemian to bourgeois. As corny as it sounds, San Diego indeed has something for everyone, from museums and military ships to shopping and shell-collecting.

Still, detractors point out a complacency that all this perfection inspires: the words 'dynamic' and 'San Diego' are rarely uttered in the same sentence. A city shaped by the military, it lacks the sophistication and urban energy of Los Angeles or San Francisco, and even though San Diego has a sizable immigrant population, it has little cosmopolitan flair and has adopted a 'no-growth' and 'no-change' attitude. In the end, however, it's hard to fault San Diego for its smugness. As the saying goes, 'If it ain't broke, don't fix it.' Whether you swim at the cove in La Jolla, stare mesmerized at the city skyline bathed in the glow of the setting sun, or quaff a cold brewski in Pacific Beach, you'll find that America's Finest City is mighty fine indeed.

## HIGHLIGHTS

- Museum-hopping in **Balboa Park** (p248)
- Swilling margaritas in **Old Town** (p266) and pub-crawling downtown's **Gaslamp Quarter** (p266)
- Ambling across Uptown's **Spruce St Footbridge** (p257)
- Skating seaside in **Pacific Beach** (p277)
- Cooing at koalas at the **San Diego Zoo** (p253) in Balboa Park
- Hang-gliding over **La Jolla** (p282) and kayaking the surf off **La Jolla Shores** (p275)
- Shopping for vintage drag in **Hillcrest** (p270)
- Swimming the surf at Coronado's **Silver Strand** (p280)

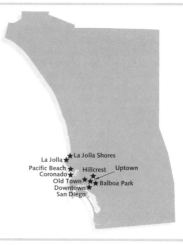

| SAN DIEGO POP: 1.2 MILLION | AVERAGE TEMPS: JAN 45/65°F, JUL 63/75°F |

# DOWNTOWN & AROUND

The city of San Diego has lots to offer land-lubbers, from diverse museums and a world-class zoo, to eye-popping architecture and toe-tapping music. The coastal communities, including La Jolla, Coronado, Ocean Beach, Mission Beach and Pacific Beach, are covered in the Coastal San Diego section (p273).

## ORIENTATION
It's easy to find your way around downtown. The airport, train station and Greyhound terminal are all in or near downtown, a compact grid east of San Diego Bay. The I-5 is the main north–south freeway; I-8 runs east from Ocean Beach, up the valley of the San Diego River (called Mission Valley) and eventually into Arizona.

Waterfront attractions along the Embarcadero lie just west of the downtown grid. Balboa Park, with its many museums and famous zoo, is in the northeastern corner of the city. Old Town, San Diego's original town site, is a couple of miles northwest of downtown. Above Old Town, the Presidio hill overlooks Mission Valley, now a freeway (I-8) and a commercial corridor, and just to the east is Hillcrest, the center of the city's gay and lesbian community and the heart of Uptown.

## INFORMATION
### Bookstores
Every shopping mall in San Diego has at least one bookshop, usually of the large, chain-owned variety. Bookhounds should peruse the offerings of bookstores on Fifth Ave between University and Robinson Aves in Hillcrest.

**Le Travel Store** (Map pp240-1; ☎ 619-544-0005; 745 Fourth Ave) Excellent selection of maps, travel guides and accessories. Helpful staff.
**Obelisk Bookstore** (Map pp242-3; ☎ 619-297-4171; 1029 University Ave) Caters particularly to gay, lesbian, bisexual and transgender readers.

### Internet Access
All public libraries provide free Internet access; no library card required. You can make reservations one day in advance by calling the main library (right). There are also 15-minute express terminals available if you don't have a reservation.

You can pay to log on at Kinko's copy stores throughout the city; check a telephone directory for the nearest location. Or try the following:
**David's Coffeehouse** (Map pp242-3; ☎ 619-296-4173; 3766 Fifth Ave; ☼ 7am-11pm Sun-Thu, to midnight Fri & Sat) Access email at this Hillcrest coffeehouse (p266).
**Internet Cafe** (Map pp240-1; ☎ 619-702-2233; 800 Broadway at Eighth Ave; per hr $8) Downtown.
**Living Room Coffeehouse** (Map pp242-3; ☎ 619-295-7911; 1417 University Ave; ☼ 6am-midnight) Another Hillcrest coffeehouse (p266) offering email facilities.

### Left Luggage
**Greyhound Station** (Map pp240-1; ☎ 619-239-3266; 120 W Broadway) Luggage storage costs $2 for the first three hours with a $4 maximum the first day; each successive day costs $5. You may leave bags up to 30 days.

### Libraries
**Main library** (Map pp240-1; ☎ 619-236-5800; www .sannet.gov/public-library; 820 E St; ☼ noon-8pm Mon & Wed, 9:30am-5:30pm Tue & Thu-Sat, 1-5pm Sun ) About two blocks east of the Gaslamp Quarter. There are smaller branch libraries (check the Yellow Pages).

### Media
**San Diego Reader** For information on what's happening in town, particularly on the active music, art and theater scenes, pick up a free copy at convenience stores and cafés. It comes out every Thursday.
**San Diego Union-Tribune** Reasonably good local daily.

### Medical Services
**Scripps Mercy Hospital** (Map pp242-3; ☎ 619-294-8111; 4077 Fifth Ave) Urgent medical attention available 24/7; an urgent-care clinic operates in addition to emergency room. For non-emergencies, call the clinic and inquire about wait times.

### Money
You'll find ATMs throughout San Diego.
**Travelex** (Map pp240-1; ☎ 619-235-0901; 177 Horton Plaza; ☼ 10am-6pm Mon-Fri, 10am-4pm Sat, 11am-4pm Sun) For foreign-currency exchange.

### Post
For local post office locations, call ☎ 800-275-8777 or log on to www.usps.com.
**Downtown Post Office** (Map pp240-1; ☎ 619-232-8612; 815 E St; ☼ 8:30am-5pm Mon-Fri)
**Midway Postal Station** (Map pp242-3; ☎ 619-758-7101; 2535 Midway Dr, San Diego, CA 92138; ☼ 7am-5pm Mon, 8am-5pm Tue-Fri, 8am-4pm Sat) Receives poste-restante (general delivery) mail.

SAN DIEGO

## Toilets

San Diego has few public toilets. Head to shopping centers, such as Horton Plaza, and to hotel lobbies. If you're discreet and well dressed, you can usually walk undetected into a crowded bar or restaurant and use its bathroom.

## Tourist Information

**International Visitors Information Center**
(Map pp240-1; ☎ 619-236-1212; 1040-1/3 W Broadway at Harbor Dr; ☺ 9am-5pm Mon-Sat, 10am-5pm Sun) The on-site official visitors center for the city sits across from Broadway Pier, along the Embarcadero.

**Old Town State Historic Park Visitor Center**
(Map pp242-3; ☎ 619-220-5422; www.parks.ca.gov; ☺ 10am-5pm) For in-person information about state parks in San Diego County, head to the Robinson-Rose House at the end of the plaza in Old Town.

**San Diego Convention & Visitors Bureau**
(Map pp240-1; ☎ 619-236-1212; www.sandiego.org) The city's official visitor information source will send a complimentary vacation-planning guide anywhere in the world, and provides on-line hotel reservations and discount vacation packages through its website.

# SIGHTS
## Downtown          Map pp240–1

San Diego's downtown is adjacent to the waterfront in the area first acquired, subdivided and promoted by Alonzo Horton in 1867. Most of the land on the waterside of the trolley line is landfill: until the mid-1920s the southern end of Fifth Ave was the main dock for unloading cargo ships; and junkets and fishing boats were once moored where the Convention Center now rises, its design a nod to the neighborhood's maritime history.

No longer the combination of bland office developments and creeping inner-urban dereliction it was in the 1960s, downtown nonetheless lacks the urban energy of, say, San Francisco or even Seattle, both smaller cities than San Diego. Still, a visit to Horton Plaza and the Gaslamp Quarter – the primary hubs for shopping, dining and entertainment – will make you feel like you're in a happening metropolitan area. And the Embarcadero is good for a harbor-side stroll.

In the northwestern corner of downtown, Little Italy is a vibrant Italian-American neighborhood close to the freeway, within walking distance of the harbor, and full of good eats.

### HORTON PLAZA CENTER

The centerpiece of San Diego's downtown redevelopment, **Horton Plaza** ( ☎ 619-238-1596; ☺ 10am-9pm Mon-Fri, 10am-7pm Sat, 11am-6pm Sun; P ) occupies seven city blocks and includes a five-level complex with 2300 parking spaces. It has a multiscreen cinema, two live theaters, restaurants, cafés and 140 shops lining an open courtyard. It was designed by Jon Jerde, a controversial California-based urban architect, using the 'festival-marketplace' concept of urban renewal, in which a congregation of vendors with separate facades and entrances set up shop in one unified space.

From the outside the plaza is not very inviting (critics say it 'turns its back on downtown,' which, at the time of construction in 1985, was as-yet ungentrified and rundown). Inside, the toy-town arches and balconies typical of postmodernism make it feel slightly as if you're walking through an MC Escher drawing. The top-floor food court is not cheap, but it's the best of its kind in San Diego and is great for people-watching, too.

Some shops and restaurants operate with extended hours. The main pedestrian entrance is on Broadway. Parking is validated with purchase.

### GASLAMP QUARTER

When Horton first established New Town San Diego in 1867, Fifth Ave was its main street and home to its main industries – saloons, gambling joints, bordellos and opium dens. While more respectable businesses grew up along Broadway, the Fifth Ave area became known as the Stingaree, a notorious red-light district. By the 1960s it had declined to a skid row of flophouses and bars, but its seedy atmosphere made it so unattractive to developers that many of its older buildings survived when others around town were being razed. In the early 1980s, when developers started thinking about demolition and rebuilding, local protests and the Gaslamp Quarter Council saved the area.

Wrought-iron street lamps, in the style of 19th-century gas lamps, were installed, along with trees and brick sidewalks (the 'gas lamps' are really translucent globes with fluorescent bulbs, not flickering flames). Restored buildings dating from the 1870s to the 1920s now house restaurants, bars, galleries and theaters. The 16-block area south of Broadway between Fourth and Sixth Aves is designated a National Historic District, and development is strictly controlled. There's still a bit of sleaze though, with a few 'adult entertainment' shops and some fleabag hotels, but they lend texture to the area, which might otherwise have become gentrified beyond recognition. Visit on a warm summer evening when people throng the streets and crowd the outdoor tables (see p262 and p266, for suggestions). To get a feel for Gaslamp Quarter architecture and history, come during the day.

**William Heath Davis House** ( ☎ 619-233-4692; www.gaslampquarter.org; 410 Island Ave at Fourth Ave; admission $3; ⏱ 11am-6pm Mon-Sat, 11am-3pm Sun) is one of nine prefabricated houses that Davis brought from Maine in 1850. This one contains a small museum with 19th-century furnishings. At 11am each Saturday, the Gaslamp Quarter Historical Foundation leads a two-hour guided walking tour from here (adults/students/seniors $8/6/6), but the tour's risqué topics and stop-and-go walking aren't appropriate for children.

**Gaslamp Books & Antiques** ( ☎ 619-237-1492; 413 Market St; admission free; ⏱ hours vary) doubles as a museum, since the owner, a Western history expert, displays all sorts of memorabilia that he's collected during his 50-plus years in San Diego. The sign outside says 'Wyatt Earp Museum.' Call for opening hours.

The heart of San Diego's China Town has always been on Third Ave (although it has spread out considerably in recent years). At the corner of J St, the Chinese Mission Building was designed by Louis J Gill (minimalist San Diego architect Irving Gill's nephew) and houses the **San Diego Chinese Historical Museum** ( ☎ 619-338-9888; 404 Third Ave; admission free; ⏱ 10:30am-4pm Tue-Sun). Built in the 1920s, this small, white stucco building has red tiles decorating the roofline, hardwood floors and an inviting backyard. Displays include Chinese-American artifacts and art objects specific to San Diego.

### MUSEUM OF CONTEMPORARY ART DOWNTOWN

Opposite the train station and adjacent to the San Diego Trolley stop, this **museum** ( ☎ 619-234-1001; www.mcasd.org; 1001 Kettner Blvd; admission free; ⏱ 11am-5pm Thu-Tue) is the downtown branch of the La Jolla-based institution (p274), which has brought innovative artwork to San Diegans

since the 1960s. The downtown branch has ever-changing exhibits of painting and sculpture that are widely publicized (see the *San Diego Reader* or call the gallery). Guided tours start at 2pm on Saturday and Sunday.

### SAN DIEGO CHILDREN'S MUSEUM

This interactive children's **museum** (Museo de los Niños; ☎ 619-233-8792; www.sdchildrensmuseum.org; 200 Island Ave) was undergoing expansion at the time of writing and will be closed to the public during construction of its new facility; check the website for further details. At the original museum young children enjoyed giant construction toys, spaces for painting and modeling, and a stage with costumes for impromptu theater, as well as storytelling, music, activities and exhibits. The new museum will include improved versions of the old favorites in a dramatic new building with indoor-outdoor exhibition space.

## Little Italy                           Map pp240–1

Bounded by Hawthorn and Ash Sts on the north and south, and Front St and the waterfront on the east and west, San Diego's Little Italy was settled in the mid-19th century by Italian immigrants, mostly fishermen and their families, who created a cohesive and thriving community. They enjoyed a booming fish industry and whiskey trade (which some claim was backed by local Mafia).

When the I-5 was completed in 1962, the heart (and, many say, soul) of the area was destroyed. Buildings were condemned and entire blocks were demolished for the freeway's construction. After its completion, increased traffic turned pedestrian streets and harbor access routes into busy thoroughfares. Over the past several years, however, redevelopment has brought exciting contemporary architecture to the area, making Little Italy one of the hippest places to live and eat downtown. And the area (especially along India St) is still a good place to find imported foods (p263).

Built in 1925, **Our Lady of the Rosary Catholic Church** (cnr State & Date Sts) is still a hub of Little Italy activity. Its rich ceiling murals, painted by an Italian who was flown over to do the work, are among San Diego's best pieces of religious art. Across the street in Amici Park, locals play bocce, an Italian form of outdoor bowling.

# METROPOLITAN SAN DIEGO

0 — 5 km
0 — 3 miles

Torrey Pines
State Reserve

Torrey Pines
City Beach
Black's
Beach

Scripps
Pier

UCSD

To Solana Beach
(13mi);
Encinitas
(16mi); Carlsbad (26mi);
Oceanside (29mi)

Miramar Rd

To Escondido

La Jolla Village Dr

US Marine Corps
Air Station Miramar

La Jolla
Shores

La Jolla

Windansea
Beach

Soledad
Mtn
(822ft) ▲

Nautilus St

Pacific
Beach

Clairemont Mesa Blvd

San Diego River

To Santee

San Diego M, orge Rd

Wuring Ave

Navajo Rd

Jackson Dr

Lake
Murray

To El
Cajon

Tourmaline
Surf Beach

Crystal Pier

Garnet Ave
Grand Ave

Mission
Bay

Balboa Ave

Tecolote
Canyon
National
Park

San Diego
State University

Montezuma Rd

El Cajon Blvd

University Ave

La Mesa

Mission
Beach

University
of San Diego

Mission Valley Rd
Friars Rd

College Ave

East
San Diego

Lemon Grove Ave

Lemon
Grove

Mission Bay
Park

University
Heights

Normal
Heights

El Cajon Blvd

54th St

Ocean Beach
Park

Ocean
Beach Pier

Old
Town

Hillcrest

Washington St

University Ave

Fairmount Ave

San Diego
Trolley

Point Loma
Ave

Ocean
Beach

San Diego
International
Airport

San
Diego

Balboa
Park

94

30th St

Paradise Valley Rd

Sunset Cliffs
Park

Harbor Dr

Harbor Island

Shelter
Island

Broadway
Market St
Imperial Ave

Akins Ave

San Diego
Trolley

North Island
US Naval
Air Station
Coronado

National Ave

Coronado
Bay Bridge

Harbor Dr

Sweetwater River

Point Loma

Cabrillo Memorial Dr

San Diego
Bay

National
City

Chula
Vista

Telegraph Canyon Rd

PACIFIC
OCEAN

Silver Strand
State Beach

Silver Strand Blvd

US Naval
Communication
Station

Main St

Otay River

Otay Valley Rd

To Mes
de Ota
Border
Crossin

Palm Ave
Imperial
Beach

South
San Diego

Beyer Way

905

Beyer Blvd

San
Ysidro

Imperial
Beach
Pier

Border
Field
State
Park

Tijuana River

California (USA)
Baja California (MEXICO)

Border
Crossing

Tijuana

## INFORMATION
Travelex....................................(see 25)

## SIGHTS & ACTIVITIES
Cabrillo National Monument........**1** A4
H&M Landing.........................(see 19)
Harbor Sailboats.......................(see 6)
Mission San Diego de Alcalá......**2** C2
Old Point Loma Lighthouse........**3** A4
Point Azura...........................(see 15)
Point Loma Sport Fishing...........**4** B3
San Diego Sports Arena.............**5** B3
San Diego Yacht Charters...........**6** B3
SeaWorld................................**7** B3
Shelter Island Sailing................**8** B3

## SLEEPING
est Western Island Palms Hotel.**9** B3
Coronado Inn.........................**10** B4
Coronado Village Inn.................**11** B4
Crown City Inn......................(see 11)
l Cordova Hotel.....................**12** B4
l Rancho Motel......................(see 11)
Glorietta Bay Inn....................(see 12)
Hotel del Coronado.................**13** B4
Humphrey's Half Moon Inn.......(see 9)
KOA.....................................**14** C4
a Avenida............................(see 12)
Loews Coronado Bay Resort......**15** C5
heraton Harbor Island..............**16** B3

## EATING
134 Cafe.............................(see 12)
Chez Loma..........................(see 20)
Coronado Brewing Co.............**17** B4
Mc P's...............................(see 12)
Nite & Day Café.....................**18** B4
Point Loma Seafoods...............**19** B3
Prince of Wales.....................(see 13)
Rhinoceros Cafe & Grill..........(see 12)

## ENTERTAINMENT
Lamb's Players Theater............**20** B4
Qualcomm Stadium.................**21** C2

## SHOPPING
Fashion Valley.......................**22** B3
Hazard Center.......................**23** B3
Mission Valley Center..............**24** C3
University Towne Centre..........**25** B1

## TRANSPORT
Bikes & Beyond......................**26** B4
Holland's Bicycles..................**27** B4

A · B · C · D

**1**

Harbor Dr
Ivy St
To Casbah (0.5mi)
Hawthorn St
46
73
69
Grape St
55
Little Italy
Fir St
39
45
Elm St
24
51
Date St
13
33
8
County Center/
Little Italy
44

Grape St
2nd Ave
Columbia St
5

**2**

San Diego Bay

**3**

11
49
31  N Harbor Dr
Pacific Hwy
Kettner Blvd
India St
Columbia St
State St
Union St
Front St
1st Ave
2nd Ave
A St
Cruise Ship Terminal
Santa Fe
Depot
B St
52  29
56
74
75
Santa Fe Depot
San Diego Trolley
American Plaza Terminal
C St
70  Broadway Pier
2
12  19
See Enlargement
Broadway

**4**

Navy Pier
E St
E St
14
US Naval
Supply
Center
F St
F St
Hort
Plaz
40
G St
Pantoja
Park
G St
Tuna Lane
G St
Downtown

**5**

Tuna
Harbor
Seaport Village
Market St
15
Island Ave
San Diego Trolley
23
San Diego – Coronado Ferry
Market Pl
Harbor Dr
2nd Ave
Conventic
Center We

**6**

Seaport Village
Embarcadero
Marina Park
San Diego
Convention
Center
17

0 ——— 500 m
0 ——— 0.3 miles

**INFORMATION**
Downtown Post Office.................................1 F4
International Visitors Information
　Center................................................2 B4
Internet Cafe..........................................3 F4
Le Travel Store.......................................4 H5
Main Library...........................................5 F4
San Diego Convention & Visitors
　Bureau...........................................(see 2)
Travelex.................................................6 G5

**SIGHTS & ACTIVITIES** (pp236–48)
Copley Symphony Hall............................7 E3
Firehouse Museum..................................8 C2
Gaslamp Books & Antiques.....................9 H6
Horton Plaza.........................................10 G5
Maritime Museum.................................11 B3
Museum of Contemporary Art
　Downtown........................................12 C4
Our Lady of the Rosary Catholic
　Church.............................................13 C2
San Diego Aircraft Carrier Museum...14 B4
San Diego Children's Museum/
　Museo de los Niños...........................15 D5
San Diego Chinese Historical
　Museum.............................................16 D5
San Diego Convention Center.............17 D6
USS Midway........................................(see 14)
William Heath Davis House..................18 E5

**SLEEPING** (pp260–1)
500 West Hotel....................................19 C4
Bristol Hotel.........................................20 G4
HI San Diego Downtown
　Hostel...............................................21 H6
Horton Grand Hotel.............................22 E5
J Street Inn...........................................23 D5
La Pensione Hotel................................24 C2
Prava Hotel..........................................25 H4
Staybridge Suites.................................26 F3
US Grant Hotel.....................................27 G4
USA Hostels San Diego.........................28 H5
W Hotel...............................................29 C3
Westgate Hotel....................................30 G4

**EATING** (pp262–4)
Anthony's Fishette...............................31 B3
Bandar.................................................32 C2
Buon Appetito......................................33 C2
Cafe Lulu.............................................34 H5
Café Sevilla..........................................35 H6
Cheese Shop........................................36 H6
Chive...................................................37 H6
Dick's Last Resort................................38 E6
Filippi's Pizza Grotto............................39 C1
Fish Market..........................................40 A5
Gaslamp Strip Club..............................41 E5
Ghirardelli Soda Fountain &
　Chocolate Shop................................42 H6
Greystone............................................43 H5
Indigo Grill...........................................44 C2
Mimmo's Italian Village........................45 C1
Mona Lisa............................................46 C1
Royal Thai............................................47 E5
Star of India.........................................48 H5
Star of the Sea.....................................49 B3

**DRINKING** (p266)
Bitter End.............................................50 H5
Caffe Italia...........................................51 C2
Karl Strauss Brewery & Grill.................52 C3
Moose McGillycuddy's..........................53 E5
Red Circle Bar......................................54 H5
Star Bar...........................................(see 54)
Waterfront...........................................55 C1

**ENTERTAINMENT** (pp267–9)
Civic Theater........................................56 D3
Croce's Restaurant & Jazz
　Bar...................................................57 H5
Croce's Top Hat Bar &
　Grille.................................................58 H5
Horton Grand Theatre..........................59 E5
Olé Madrid...........................................60 H5
On Broadway........................................61 E4
Onyx Room..........................................62 H5
Pacific Gaslamp 15...............................63 H5
Petco Park...........................................64 F6
Regal United Artists Horton Plaza
　14.....................................................65 H5
San Diego Repertory
　Theater.............................................66 G5
San Diego Symphony........................(see 7)
Spreckels Theater.................................67 G4
Thin................................................(see 62)
Times Arts Tix......................................68 G4

**TRANSPORT** (pp270–3)
California Rent a Car.............................69 B1
Ferry Landing.......................................70 A4
Greyhound Station...............................71 F4
Transit Store.........................................72 G4
West Coast Rent a Car..........................73 C1

**OTHER**
Hornblower Cruises..............................74 B3
San Diego Harbor
　Excursion..........................................75 B4

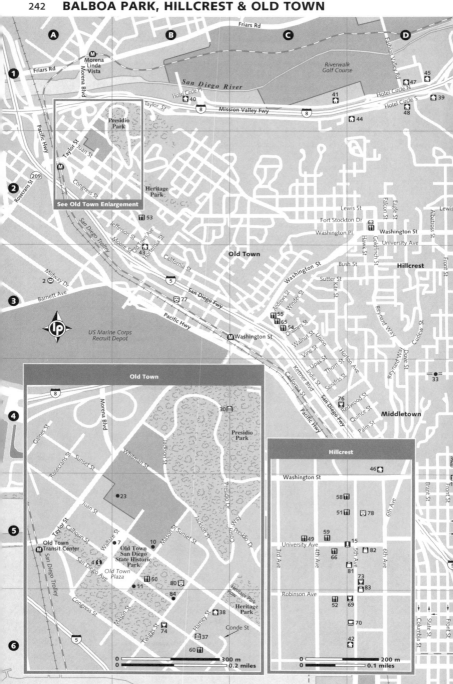

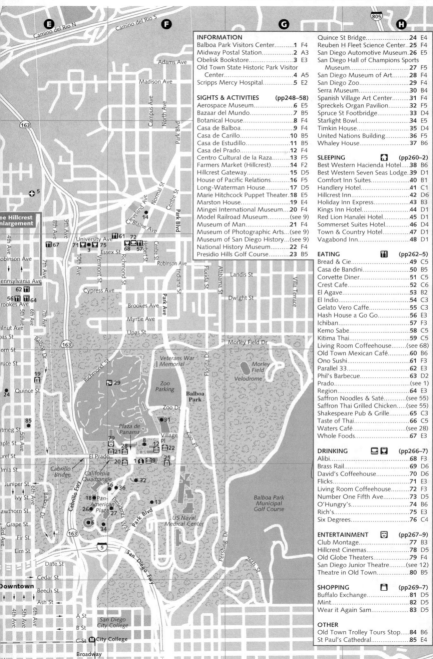

| | | |
|---|---|---|
| 0 | | 1 km |
| 0 | | 0.5 miles |

**INFORMATION**
Balboa Park Visitors Center...........**1** F4
Midway Postal Station...................**2** A3
Obelisk Bookstore.........................**3** E3
Old Town State Historic Park Visitor
 Center.......................................**4** A5
Scripps Mercy Hospital..................**5** E2

**SIGHTS & ACTIVITIES** (pp248–58)
Aerospace Museum........................**6** E5
Bazaar del Mundo.........................**7** B5
Botanical House............................**8** F4
Casa de Balboa.............................**9** F4
Casa de Carillo............................**10** B5
Casa de Estudillo.........................**11** B5
Casa del Prado............................**12** F4
Centro Cultural de la Raza...........**13** F5
Farmers Market (Hillcrest)............**14** F2
Hillcrest Gateway.........................**15** D5
House of Pacific Relations.............**16** F5
Long-Waterman House..................**17** D5
Marie Hitchcock Puppet Theater...**18** E5
Marston House..............................**19** E4
Mingei International Museum........**20** F4
Museum of Man...........................**21** F4
Museum of Photographic Arts.....(see 9)
Museum of San Diego History.....(see 9)
National History Museum.............**22** F4
Presidio Hills Golf Course............**23** B5

Quince St Bridge..........................**24** E4
Reuben H Fleet Science Center.....**25** F4
San Diego Automotive Museum....**26** E5
San Diego Hall of Champions Sports
 Museum.....................................**27** F5
San Diego Museum of Art............**28** F4
San Diego Zoo............................**29** E4
Serra Museum..............................**30** B4
Spanish Village Art Center............**31** F4
Spreckels Organ Pavilion..............**32** F5
Spruce St Footbridge....................**33** D4
Starlight Bowl..............................**34** E5
Timkin House..............................**35** D4
United Nations Building.................**36** F5
Whaley House..............................**37** B6

**SLEEPING** (pp260–2)
Best Western Hacienda Hotel........**38** B6
Best Western Seven Seas Lodge.....**39** D1
Comfort Inn Suites.......................**40** B1
Handlery Hotel............................**41** C1
Hillcrest Inn................................**42** D6
Holiday Inn Express......................**43** B3
Kings Inn Hotel............................**44** D1
Red Lion Hanalei Hotel.................**45** D1
Sommerset Suites Hotel................**46** D4
Town & Country Hotel..................**47** D1
Vagabond Inn..............................**48** D1

**EATING** (pp262–5)
Bread & Cie................................**49** C5
Casa de Bandini...........................**50** B5
Corvette Diner............................**51** C5
Crest Cafe..................................**52** C6
El Agave.....................................**53** B2
El Indio......................................**54** C3
Gelato Vero Caffe........................**55** C3
Hash House a Go Go.....................**56** E3
Ichiban......................................**57** F3
Kemo Sabe..................................**58** C5
Kitima Thai.................................**59** C5
Living Room Coffeehouse...........(see 68)
Old Town Mexican Café................**60** B6
Ono Sushi....................................**61** F3
Parallel 33..................................**62** E3
Phil's Barbecue............................**63** D2
Prado........................................(see 1)
Region......................................**64** E3
Saffron Noodles & Saté.............(see 55)
Saffron Thai Grilled Chicken.......(see 55)
Shakespeare Pub & Grille.............**65** C3
Taste of Thai...............................**66** C5
Waters Café...............................(see 28)
Whole Foods...............................**67** E3

**DRINKING** (pp266–7)
Alibi..........................................**68** F3
Brass Rail....................................**69** D6
David's Coffeehouse.....................**70** D6
Flicks.........................................**71** E3
Living Room Coffeehouse.............**72** F3
Number One Fifth Ave..................**73** D5
O'Hungry's..................................**74** B6
Rich's.........................................**75** E3
Six Degrees.................................**76** C4

**ENTERTAINMENT** (pp267–9)
Club Montage..............................**77** B3
Hillcrest Cinemas.........................**78** D5
Old Globe Theaters......................**79** F4
San Diego Junior Theatre............(see 12)
Theatre in Old Town.....................**80** B5

**SHOPPING** (pp269–7)
Buffalo Exchange.........................**81** D5
Mint..........................................**82** D5
Wear it Again Sam.......................**83** D5

**OTHER**
Old Town Trolley Tours Stop.....**84** B6
St Paul's Cathedral.......................**85** E4

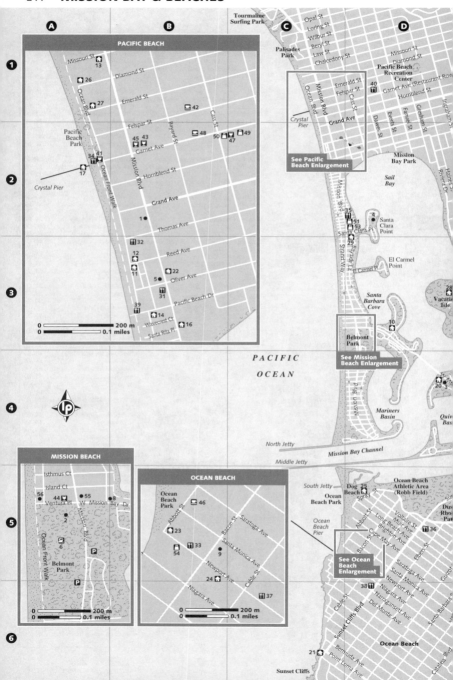

0 | 2 km
0 | 1 mile

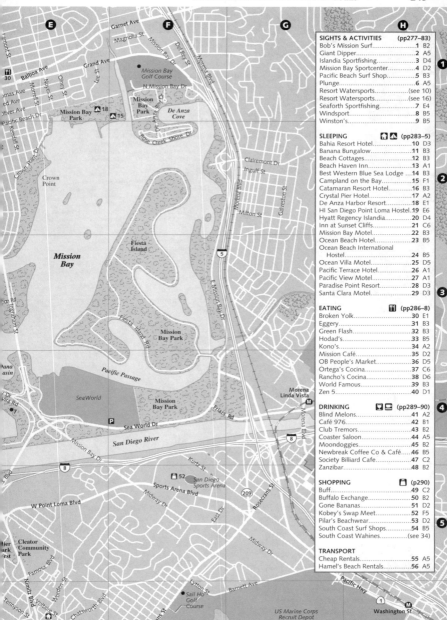

| SIGHTS & ACTIVITIES | (pp277–83) | |
| --- | --- | --- |
| Bob's Mission Surf | 1 | B2 |
| Giant Dipper | 2 | A5 |
| Islandia Sportfishing | 3 | D4 |
| Mission Bay Sportcenter | 4 | D2 |
| Pacific Beach Surf Shop | 5 | B3 |
| Plunge | 6 | A5 |
| Resort Watersports | (see 10) | |
| Resort Watersports | (see 16) | |
| Seaforth Sportfishing | 7 | E4 |
| Windsport | 8 | B5 |
| Winston's | 9 | B5 |

| SLEEPING | (pp283–5) | |
| --- | --- | --- |
| Bahia Resort Hotel | 10 | D3 |
| Banana Bungalow | 11 | B3 |
| Beach Cottages | 12 | B3 |
| Beach Haven Inn | 13 | A1 |
| Best Western Blue Sea Lodge | 14 | B3 |
| Campland on the Bay | 15 | F1 |
| Catamaran Resort Hotel | 16 | B3 |
| Crystal Pier Hotel | 17 | A2 |
| De Anza Harbor Resort | 18 | E1 |
| HI San Diego Point Loma Hostel | 19 | E6 |
| Hyatt Regency Islandia | 20 | D4 |
| Inn at Sunset Cliffs | 21 | C6 |
| Mission Bay Motel | 22 | B3 |
| Ocean Beach Hotel | 23 | B5 |
| Ocean Beach International Hostel | 24 | B5 |
| Ocean Villa Motel | 25 | D5 |
| Pacific Terrace Hotel | 26 | A1 |
| Pacific View Motel | 27 | A1 |
| Paradise Point Resort | 28 | D3 |
| Santa Clara Motel | 29 | D3 |

| EATING | (pp286–8) | |
| --- | --- | --- |
| Broken Yolk | 30 | E1 |
| Eggery | 31 | B3 |
| Green Flash | 32 | B3 |
| Hodad's | 33 | B5 |
| Kono's | 34 | A2 |
| Mission Café | 35 | D2 |
| OB People's Market | 36 | D5 |
| Ortega's Cocina | 37 | C6 |
| Rancho's Cocina | 38 | D6 |
| World Famous | 39 | B3 |
| Zen 5 | 40 | D1 |

| DRINKING | (pp289–90) | |
| --- | --- | --- |
| Blind Melons | 41 | A2 |
| Café 976 | 42 | B1 |
| Club Tremors | 43 | B2 |
| Coaster Saloon | 44 | A5 |
| Moondoggies | 45 | B2 |
| Newbreak Coffee Co & Café | 46 | B5 |
| Society Billiard Cafe | 47 | C2 |
| Zanzibar | 48 | B2 |

| SHOPPING | (p290) | |
| --- | --- | --- |
| Buff | 49 | C2 |
| Buffalo Exchange | 50 | B2 |
| Gone Bananas | 51 | D2 |
| Kobey's Swap Meet | 52 | F5 |
| Pilar's Beachwear | 53 | D2 |
| South Coast Surf Shops | 54 | B5 |
| South Coast Wahines | (see 34) | |

| TRANSPORT | | |
| --- | --- | --- |
| Cheap Rentals | 55 | A5 |
| Hamel's Beach Rentals | 56 | A5 |

0 |=========| 10 km
0 |=========| 6 miles

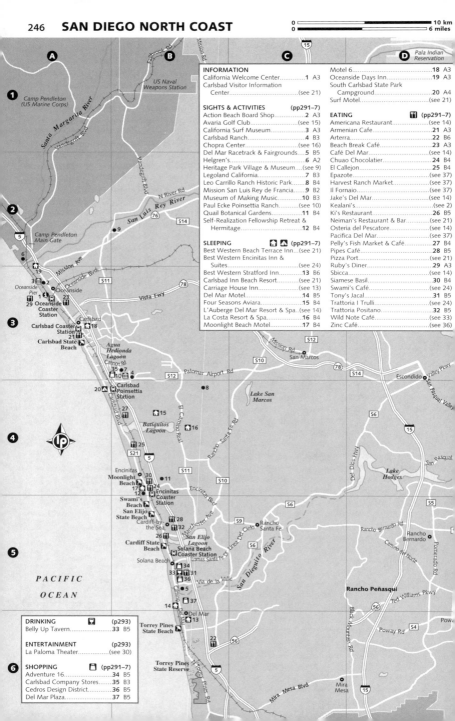

**INFORMATION**
California Welcome Center...............**1** A3
Carlsbad Visitor Information
    Center...............................(see 21)

**SIGHTS & ACTIVITIES**          (pp291–7)
Action Beach Board Shop...............**2** A3
Avaria Golf Club..........................(see 15)
California Surf Museum..................**3** A3
Carlsbad Ranch.............................**4** B3
Chopra Center.............................(see 16)
Del Mar Racetrack & Fairgrounds...**5** B5
Helgren's....................................**6** A2
Heritage Park Village & Museum...(see 9)
Legoland California.......................**7** B3
Leo Carrillo Ranch Historic Park...**8** B4
Mission San Luis Rey de Francia...**9** B2
Museum of Making Music.............**10** B3
Paul Ecke Poinsettia Ranch...........(see 10)
Quail Botanical Gardens................**11** B4
Self-Realization Fellowship Retreat &
    Hermitage.............................**12** B4

**SLEEPING**                       (pp291–7)
Best Western Beach Terrace Inn...(see 21)
Best Western Encinitas Inn &
    Suites...................................(see 24)
Best Western Stratford Inn...........**13** B6
Carlsbad Inn Beach Resort............(see 21)
Carriage House Inn.......................(see 13)
Del Mar Motel.............................**14** B5
Four Seasons Aviara......................**15** B4
L'Auberge Del Mar Resort & Spa...(see 14)
La Costa Resort & Spa..................**16** B4
Moonlight Beach Motel.................**17** B4

Motel 6......................................**18** A3
Oceanside Days Inn......................**19** A3
South Carlsbad State Park
    Campground...........................**20** A4
Surf Motel..................................(see 21)

**EATING**                    🍴 (pp291–7)
Americana Restaurant...................(see 14)
Armenian Cafe.............................**21** A3
Arterra........................................**22** B6
Beach Break Café.........................**23** A3
Café Del Mar...............................(see 14)
Chuao Chocolatier........................**24** B4
El Callejon..................................**25** B4
Epazote......................................(see 37)
Harvest Ranch Market...................(see 37)
Il Fornaio...................................(see 37)
Jake's Del Mar............................(see 14)
Kealani's....................................(see 2)
Ki's Restaurant............................**26** B5
Neiman's Restaurant & Bar............(see 21)
Osteria del Pescatore....................(see 14)
Pacifica Del Mar..........................(see 37)
Pelly's Fish Market & Café.............**27** B4
Pipes Café..................................**28** B5
Pizza Port...................................(see 21)
Ruby's Diner...............................**29** A3
Sbicca.......................................(see 14)
Siamese Basil...............................**30** B4
Swami's Café..............................(see 24)
Tony's Jacal................................**31** B5
Trattoria I Trulli...........................(see 24)
Trattoria Positano........................**32** B5
Wild Note Café............................(see 33)
Zinc Café...................................(see 36)

**DRINKING**                    🍸 (p293)
Belly Up Tavern...........................**33** B5

**ENTERTAINMENT**                (p293)
La Paloma Theater........................(see 30)

**SHOPPING**                   🛍 (pp291–7)
Adventure 16..............................**34** B5
Carlsbad Company Stores..............**35** B3
Cedros Design District..................**36** B5
Del Mar Plaza.............................**37** B5

# LA JOLLA

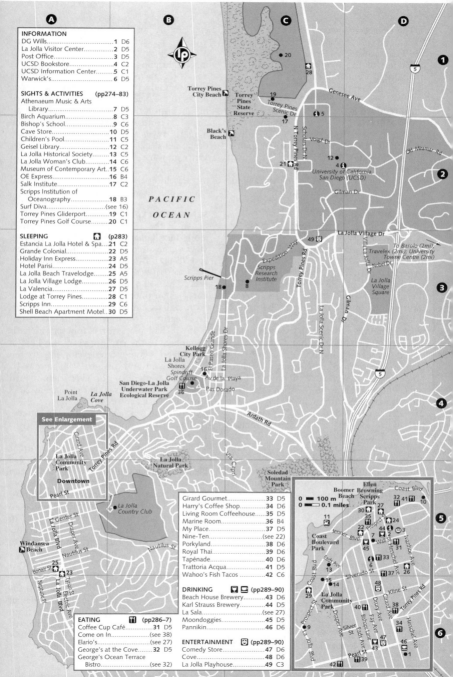

The **Firehouse Museum** ( ☎ 619-232-3473; 1572 Columbia St at Cedar St; admission $2; ⏲ 10am-2pm Thu & Fri, 10am-4pm Sat & Sun) preserves a historical collection of fire-fighting equipment and has exhibits depicting some of San Diego's 'hottest' moments.

## Embarcadero & the Waterfront
Map pp240–1

San Diego's waterfront, built almost entirely on landfill, is about 500 yards wider than it was in the late 1800s. Its well-manicured waterfront promenades, perfect for strolling, stretch along Harbor Dr. The following sights are laid out in north–south order.

### MARITIME MUSEUM

Just north of Ash St, this **museum** ( ☎ 619-234-9153; www.sdmaritime.org; 1492 N Harbor Dr; adult/child $8/6; ⏲ 9am-8pm) is easy to find: look for the 100ft-high masts of the iron-hulled square-rigger *Star of India*. Built on the Isle of Man and launched in 1863, the tall ship plied the England–India trade route, carried immigrants to New Zealand, became a trading ship based in Hawaii and, finally, worked the Alaskan salmon fisheries before winding up here. She's a handsome vessel, but don't expect anything romantic or glamorous on board: this is an old workhorse, not the *Love Boat*. Also moored here: the *California*, California's official tall ship; the century-old steam yacht *Medea*; and the *Berkeley*, an 1898 ferry boat that originally ferried passengers across San Francisco Bay to connect with the terminus of the transcontinental railroad. You can also take a 20-minute narrated ride in a 1914 harbor-pilot boat (adult/child $12/9, which includes admission to the museum). In summer nautical-themed movies are shown aboard the *Star of India*; call the museum for times and information.

### SAN DIEGO AIRCRAFT CARRIER MUSEUM

The giant aircraft carrier **USS Midway** ( ☎ 619-544-9600; www.midway.org; 910 N Harbor Dr; adult/child $13/7; ⏲ 10am-5pm) was one of the Navy's major flagships from 1945–91, last playing a combat role in Gulf War I. On the flight deck of the hulking vessel, walk right up to four aircraft, including an F-14 Tomcat and F-4 Phantom jet fighter. Below, on the hangar deck, at **Mach Combat** ( ☎ 619-544-9600, ext 277; www.machcombat-midway.com; admission per hr $20-40),

you can 'fly' an F-4 in a mini-simulator at a desk, or get the full cockpit experience in which you wear a flight suit, receive a mission briefing, close down the canopy and 'take off'; make reservations. Tour guides lead you to the narrow confines of the upper decks to the bridge and to 'pri-fly' (primary flight control, the carrier's equivalent of an airport's control tower), but lines can be long. If crowds are thin when you arrive, see the upper decks first. Some inside areas get stuffy on warm summer days: come early to avoid midday heat and crowds. There's also a café selling $6 sandwiches. Plan to spend two to four hours on board.

### SEAPORT VILLAGE & AROUND

South of the USS *Midway*, you can stroll along **Tuna Harbor**, where you can get a long view of the aircraft carrier and walk to **Seaport Village** ( ☎ 619-235-4014; ⏲ 10am-10pm summer, 10am-9pm winter). Neither port nor village, this collection of novelty shops and restaurants has an unconvincing maritime theme with faux, early-20th-century seafront architecture. It's touristy and twee, but is not a bad place for a spot of souvenir shopping. In coming years the Port of San Diego is going to redevelop this stretch of waterfront and Seaport Village may be drastically altered – or even demolished entirely – as early as 2006 or as late as 2018 when its lease expires.

Wrapping southeast along the **Embarcadero Marina Park** – where there's a public fishing pier and an open-air amphitheater, which presents free concerts on summer evenings – you'll see the 'sails' of the **San Diego Convention Center** ( ☎ 619-525-5000; Harbor Dr). Built in a successful attempt to promote the city as a site for major conventions, this unusual-looking complex opened in 1989 and gets booked solid five years in advance. The design, by Canadian avant-garde architect Arthur Erickson, was said to have been inspired by an ocean liner.

## Balboa Park
Map pp242–3

With its museums, gardens and world-famous zoo, Balboa Park tops the list of what to see in San Diego. Maps dating from 1868 show that Alonzo Horton's planned additions to San Diego included a 1400-acre City Park at the northeastern corner of what was to become downtown. Ever

## THE LEGACY OF KATE SESSIONS

Kate O Sessions graduated with a degree in botany from the University of California at Berkeley in 1881, a time when few women attended college and even fewer studied the natural sciences. She came to San Diego as a schoolteacher, but soon began working as a horticulturist, establishing gardens for the fashionable homes of the city's emerging elite. In 1892, in need of space for a nursery, she proposed an unusual deal to city officials: she would have the use of 30 acres of city-owned Balboa Park for her nursery in return for planting 100 trees per year and donating 300 others for placement throughout San Diego. The city agreed to the arrangement, and Kate Sessions more than fulfilled her side of the bargain. Within 10 years, Balboa Park had shade trees, lawns, paths and flower beds. Grateful San Diegans soon began referring to her as 'The Mother of Balboa Park.'

the businessman, Mr Horton enhanced the value of the land in his subdivision by restricting future development. It looked good on paper, but in reality it was all bare hilltops, chaparral and steep-sided arroyos (water-carved gullies). Enter Kate Sessions, the UC Berkeley botany graduate, who in 1892 started her nursery on the site, paying rent to the city in trees (see above).

By the early 1900s, Balboa Park had become a well-loved part of San Diego. Its name honors the Spanish conquistador believed to be the first European to sight the Pacific Ocean.

Following the success of San Francisco's world-renowned Panama-Pacific International Exposition (1914), San Diego, in a burst of self-promotion, held its own two-year fair from 1915–16 and dubbed it the Panama-*California* Exposition. Much of it took place in Balboa Park. Exposition buildings were designed in romantic, Spanish Colonial style that endures today.

In the planning of the 1915–16 Panama-California Exposition, Irving Gill's modern, minimalist architecture was rejected in favor of the beaux arts style and baroque decoration of New Yorkers Bertram Goodhue and Carlton Winslow. The exposition buildings were meant to be temporary, and were constructed largely of stucco, chicken wire, plaster, hemp and horsehair. The buildings proved so popular, however, that many of them continued to be used. As the originals deteriorated, they were replaced with durable concrete structures. These buildings now house the museums along **El Prado**, the main pedestrian thoroughfare in the park.

In 1935 the Pacific-California Exposition brought new buildings southwest of El Prado

around the Pan-American Plaza. Architecturally the Spanish Colonial theme was expanded to include the whole New World, from indigenous styles (some of the buildings had Pueblo Indian and even Mayan influences) through to the 20th century. Most of these buildings have been preserved, as well and now house other exhibits, museums and theaters.

The San Diego Zoo (p253) occupies 100 acres in the north of Balboa Park, and the eastern third is occupied by the sports facilities of Morley Field, with tennis courts, a swimming pool, a velodrome, nine- and 18-hole golf courses, and even a 'disc golf' course, which is designed for playing with Frisbees. About a quarter of the original 1400 acres has been given over to the Cabrillo Fwy, the US Naval Hospital and other non-park uses.

### ORIENTATION & INFORMATION

If you want simply to enjoy the gardens and architecture, you can stroll around Balboa Park any time, but be cautious after dark. To visit all the museums and attractions would take days, so it's a good idea to plan your time. Start at the **Balboa Park Visitors Center** ( ☎ 619-239-0512; www.balboapark.org; 1549 El Prado; ☯ 9:30am-4:30pm), in the House of Hospitality, where you can pick up a good park map ($1) and buy admission passes. If you're going to spend time here, consider purchasing the Balboa Passport ($30; good for one-time entry to the park's 13 museums within one week of purchase) or the Combo Pass ($55; passport plus zoo admission).

Many museums are closed Monday, and several (on a rotating basis) are free Tuesday, so before you buy a pass, determine on which days you're going to visit the park.

Balboa Park is easily reached from downtown on bus Nos 7, 7A or 7B along Park Blvd. By car, Park Blvd provides easy access to free parking areas near most of the exhibits, but the most scenic approach is over the Cabrillo Bridge. From the west, El Prado is an extension of Laurel St, which crosses Cabrillo Bridge with the Cabrillo Fwy 120ft below. Make a point of driving this stretch of freeway (State Hwy 163): the steep roadsides, lush with hanging greenery, look like a rain-forest gorge.

The free Balboa Park Tram stops at various points on a continuous loop through the main areas of the park. (It's actually a bus and shouldn't be confused with the Old Town Trolley tour bus.) However, it's easiest and most enjoyable to walk.

If you're here in winter, the first Friday and Saturday in December bring **Christmas on the Prado**, a showcase of performance art, crafts and international food; museum admission is free during the event.

### CALIFORNIA BUILDING & MUSEUM OF MAN

El Prado passes under an archway and into an area called the California Quadrangle, with the **Museum of Man** ( ☎ 619-239-2001; www.museumofman.org; adult/child $5/3, free on 3rd Tue of month; ☉ 10am-4:30pm), in classical revival style, on its northern side. Figures on either side of the arch represent the Atlantic and Pacific Oceans, while the decoration of the arch itself symbolizes the Panama Canal linking the two. This was the main entrance for the 1915 exposition, and the building was one of Goodhue's most ornate Spanish Colonial revival creations, said to be inspired by the churrigueresque church of Tepotzotlán near Mexico City. The single **Tower of California**, richly decorated with blue and yellow tiles, is an architectural landmark of San Diego.

Originally, the building displayed more than 5000 ethnographic artifacts, including some that were specially made for the exposition – the cast concrete reproductions of Mayan carvings are still on display. The museum now specializes in Native American artifacts from the American Southwest, and has an excellent display of baskets and pottery from the San Diego area. The museum shop sells good handicrafts from Central America and elsewhere.

### PLAZA DE PANAMA

In the middle of El Prado, Plaza de Panama was the center of the Panama-California Exposition. The equestrian statue on the southern side is of **El Cid**, who led the Spanish revolt against the Moors in the 11th century. On the plaza's southwestern corner, next to a rare New Zealand agathis tree (a small, fragrant evergreen with flat leaves), the **House of Charm** was the Indian Arts building for the Panama exposition, but got its present name during the 1935 fair as a souvenir market. It was recently rebuilt to its original form and now houses the **Mingei International Museum** ( ☎ 619-239-0003; www.mingei.org; adult/child $6/3, free on 3rd Tue of month; ☉ 10am-4pm Tue-Sun), which has an excellent permanent collection of folk art, costumes, toys, jewelry, utensils and other handmade objects from traditional cultures around the world.

### SAN DIEGO MUSEUM OF ART

Built in 1924, the **SDMA** ( ☎ 619-232-7931; www.sdmart.org; adult/child/youth 18-24/senior $9/4/7/7, free on 3rd Tue of month; ☉ 10am-6pm Tue-Sun, 10am-9pm Thu) was designed by San Diego architect William Templeton Johnson in the 16th-century Spanish plateresque style, so named because it features heavy ornamentation resembling decorated silverwork. The facade is particularly ornate, with sculptures depicting Spanish artists, most of whom have pieces inside the museum. Important traveling exhibits are shown here with increasing frequency. The permanent collection has a number of fine European paintings (though no major works), some worthwhile American landscape paintings and several fantastic pieces in the Asian galleries. The **Sculpture Garden** has pieces by Alexander Calder and Henry Moore, and a great outdoor eatery – Waters Café (p264).

### TIMKEN MUSEUM OF ART

Don't skip the Timken. Distinctive for *not* being in imitation Spanish style, this **museum** ( ☎ 619-239-5548; www.timkenmuseum.org; 1500 El Prado; admission free; ☉ closed Mon, Sun morning & Sep), built in 1965, houses the Putnam collection, a small but impressive group of paintings, including works by Rembrandt, Rubens, El Greco, Cézanne and Pissarro. There's also a wonderful selection of Russian icons. The Timken ranks among the best of San Diego's free activities.

## BOTANICAL BUILDING

The **Botanical Building** (admission free; ⊙ Fri-Wed) looks lovely from El Prado, where you can see it reflected in the large lily pond that was used for hydrotherapy in WWII when the Navy took over the park. The building's central dome and two wings are covered with redwood lathes, which let filtered sunlight into the collection of tropical plants and ferns. The planting changes every season; in December there's a particularly beautiful poinsettia display.

## CASA DEL PRADO

This is one of the most handsome buildings along El Prado, but there is little to draw the visitor inside. It was built as a temporary structure for the 1915 exposition, but an earthquake in 1968 caused so much damage that the building was condemned. It was rebuilt with the support of community arts groups, who now use it for theater and dance performances.

## CASA DE BALBOA

The House of Commerce & Industry was designed by Goodhue in the imitation Spanish Colonial style for the 1915 exposition and later used for a variety of purposes until it burned down in 1978. The original building was faithfully reconstructed, including concrete decorations cast from pieces of the original. It now houses three museums, each with its own shop, and a small café.

The highlight is the **Museum of Photographic Arts** ( ☎ 619-238-7559; www.mopa.org; admission adult/child $7/6, free 2nd Tue of month; ⊙ 10am-5pm Fri-Wed, 10am-9pm Thu), expanded recently by La Jolla architect David Singer. International exhibits range from wildlife shots to what-the-heck-is-that art pieces.

The **Museum of San Diego History** ( ☎ 619-232-6203; www.sandiegohistory.org; admission adult/child $6/2, free 2nd Tue of month; ⊙ 10am-5pm) covers the American period of San Diego from about 1848.

Kids and model-train buffs love the **Model Railroad Museum** ( ☎ 619-696-0199; www.sdmodelrailroadm.com; adult/child under 15 $5/free, free 1st Tue of month; ⊙ 11am-4pm Tue-Fri, 11am-5pm Sat & Sun), the largest in the world. It has working models of actual railroads in Southern California, both historical and contemporary. Be sure to see the Lionel display in back.

## REUBEN H FLEET SPACE THEATER & SCIENCE CENTER

One of Balboa Park's most publicized venues, this one features a hands-on **science museum** ( ☎ 619-238-1233; www.rhfleet.org; adult/child $6.75/5.50; ⊙ 9:30am-8pm, shorter in winter) with interactive displays, and a huge-screen **IMAX theater** (adult/child $11.75/8.75, additional films $3.25; ⊙ 11am to close of museum) that shows several films. The hemispherical, wrap-around screen and 152-speaker state-of-the-art sound system create sensations ranging from pretty cool to mind-blowing, depending on what film is playing. The Science Center is included in the theater price, but can be visited by itself. Admission to the center includes the Deep Sea exhibit, a simulated motion ride through the ocean.

## NATURAL HISTORY MUSEUM

A recent face-lift of William Templeton Johnson's 1933 original has brought a beautiful space and giant-screen cinema to this **museum** ( ☎ 619-232-3821; www.sdnhm.org; adult/child $9/5, free 1st Tue of month; ⊙ 10am-5pm) at the eastern end of El Prado. The feature movies change, but always focus on the natural world; kids love them. The museum houses 7.5 million specimens, including rocks, fossils and taxidermy animals, as well as an impressive dinosaur skeleton and a California fault-line exhibit. Children's programs are held most weekends. The museum also arranges field trips and nature walks in Balboa Park and further afield.

## SPANISH VILLAGE ART CENTER

Behind the Natural History Museum is a grassy square with a magnificent Moreton Bay fig tree (sorry, no climbing). Opposite the square stand, an enclave of small tiled cottages (billed by park authorities as 'an authentic reproduction of an ancient village in Spain') that are rented out as **artists' studios** ( ☎ 619-233-9050; admission free; ⊙ 11am-4pm), where you can watch potters, jewelers, glass blowers, painters and sculptors churn out their crafts. North of the Spanish Village there's a 1924 **carousel** and a **miniature railroad** (admission $1.75; ⊙ 11am-5:30pm Sat, Sun & school holidays, daily in summer), which charge $1 per ride.

## SPRECKELS ORGAN PAVILION

Going south from Plaza de Panama, you can't miss the circle of seating and the

SAN DIEGO

curved colonnade in front of the bandshell housing the organ said to be the world's largest outdoor musical instrument. Donated by the Spreckels family of sugar fortune and fame, the pipe organ came with the stipulation that San Diego must always have an official organist. Make it a point to attend the free **concerts** (☎ 619-702-8138; www.sosorgan.com), held throughout the year from 2pm to 3pm Sunday and 7:30pm Monday from mid-June to August.

#### PAN-AMERICAN PLAZA

The plaza is now simply a large parking lot southwest of the Spreckels Organ. As you approach it from the organ, the **UN Building** is on your right. Its **Unicef International Gift Shop** (☎ 619-233-5044; 10am-4:30pm) has a good selection of stationery, jewelry and candy, and donates its profits to world children's causes. Nearby, the **House of Pacific Relations** (☎ 619-234-0739; admission free; noon-4pm Sun) is actually 15 cottages from the 1915 exposition, inside which you will find furnishings and displays from various countries. When the cottages are open, they often have crafts and food for sale.



Nearby in the Palisades Building, the **Marie Hitchcock Puppet Theater** (☎ 619-685-5990; www.balboaparkpuppets.com; adult/child $3/2) puts on terrific hand- and rod-puppet shows (11am, 1pm and 2:30pm Wednesday to Sunday), and also has puppet-making workshops – great for the kids. The **San Diego Automotive Museum** (☎ 619-231-2886; www.sdautomuseum.org; adult/child $7/3, free 4th Tue of month; 10am-5pm) has a collection of more than 60 cars and motorcycles, perfectly restored and well displayed, with classic cars and motorcycles, such as a 1933 Duesenberg Roadster and a classic motorcycle by Indian.

The round building at the southern end of the plaza houses the excellent **Aerospace Museum** (☎ 619-234-8291; www.aerospacemuseum.org; adult/child $9/4, free 4th Tue of month; 10am-4:30pm), with an extensive display of aircraft – originals, replicas, models and Charles Lindbergh memorabilia. From 2004–07, don't miss the Apollo 9 command module, which is on loan from the Smithsonian. You can also ride in a flight simulator ($4). In the courtyard a Phantom jet pursues a Russian MiG-17 between art deco lamp standards.

At the adjacent Starlight Bowl, the **Starlight Opera** (☎ 619-544-7800; www.starlighttheatre.org) presents a summer season of musicals and light opera.

The Federal Building was built for the 1935 exposition and now holds the **San Diego Hall of Champions Sports Museum** (☎ 619-234-2544; www.sdhoc.com; adult/child $6/3, free 4th Tue of month; 10am-4:30pm), which has exhibits and a hall of fame of San Diego sports figures, including baseball legend Ted Williams and skateboarder Tony Hawk. There's also a 'media center,' in which kids can call the commentary on a game.

#### CENTRO CULTURAL DE LA RAZA

The **center** (☎ 619-235-6135; www.centroraza.com; donation requested; noon-5pm Thu-Sun) hosts powerful exhibitions of Mexican and Native American art, including temporary exhibits of contemporary indigenous artwork. The round, steel building, which is actually a converted water tank, sits way out on the edge of the main museum area; easiest access is from Park Blvd.

#### MARSTON HOUSE

In the far northwestern corner of Balboa Park, is the former home of George Marston, philanthropist and founder of the San Diego Historical Society. Built in 1904, **Marston House** (☎ 619-298-3142; 3525 Seventh Ave; adult/child $5/2; 10am-4:30pm Fri-Sun) was designed by noted San Diego architects William Hebbard and Irving Gill, and is a fine example of the American Arts and Crafts style. The **Historical Society** (☎ 619-232-6203; www.sandiegohistory.org) has restored the interior as a showplace for Arts and Crafts furnishings and decorative objects. To see them, you must take the 45-minute guided tour.

#### GARDENS OF BALBOA PARK

Balboa Park includes a number of distinct gardens, reflecting different horticultural styles and environments. To learn more about them, take one of the free weekly Offshoot Tours, conducted by park horticulturists from mid-January to Thanksgiving. The **Park & Recreation Department** (☎ 619-235-1114) has more information. Reservations are not required – be at the front of the Botanical Building (p251) by 10am.

If you're exploring on your own, visit the **Alcazar Garden**, a formal, Spanish-style garden; **Palm Canyon**, which has more than 50 species of palms; the **Japanese Friendship Garden**

( ☎ 619-232-2780; www.niwa.org; admission $3, free 3rd Tue of month; ☽ 10am-5pm Mon-Fri, 10am-4pm Sat & Sun); the **Australian Garden**; the **Rose Garden**; the **Desert Garden**, which is best in spring; **Florida Canyon**, which gives an idea of the San Diego landscape before the Spanish settlement; and the **Natural History Museum** ( ☎ 619-232-3821; www.sdnhm.org), which leads walks in the canyon.

## SAN DIEGO ZOO

The San Diego Zoo is one of the city's biggest attractions, and anyone at all interested in the natural world should allow a full day to see it. More than 3000 animals, representing over 800 species, are exhibited in a beautifully landscaped setting, typically in enclosures that replicate their natural habitats.

The zoo dates back to the Panama-California Exposition of 1915–16, which featured an assortment of animals in cages along Park Blvd. Local legend has it that Dr Harry Wegeforth, hearing the roar of one of the caged lions, exclaimed, 'Wouldn't it be wonderful to have a zoo in San Diego? I believe I'll build one!' He started his campaign in 1916 in the newspaper and soon formed the Zoological Society of San Diego. By pulling a few strings, Dr Wegeforth then ensured that quarantine requirements made it almost impossible to remove exotic animals from the county, so the society was able to acquire much of the menagerie left over from the exposition.

As a private organization, the Zoological Society could not be given a site on public land, but in 1921 Wegeforth came up with a clever solution. The society donated all the animals and facilities to the city, and the city provided 100 acres of Balboa Park to use as a zoo, which would then be administered by the society. Although the site was bisected by canyons and largely barren, these problems were turned to their advantage: canyons provided a means of separating different groups of animals to prevent the spread of disease, and they could be individually landscaped to simulate appropriate natural settings.

Wegeforth had a talent for extracting money from wealthy benefactors – John Spreckels, the millionaire sugar king, warned that the wily surgeon would 'cut you off at the pockets.' One of the first big

donations was from newspaper magnate and philanthropist Ellen Browning Scripps who paid for a perimeter fence, which was to enforce the payment of admission fees as much as to keep the animals in.

Locals loved it. They brought in various finds, such as seals and rattlesnakes, which were often profitably traded for animals from other zoos. In one exchange, the zoo provided fleas for a New York flea circus. The US Navy unofficially contributed an assortment of animals that had been adopted as mascots but could no longer be kept on ships. US Marines landing in Nicaragua were offered prizes if they captured beasts for Dr Wegeforth. During the 1930s Wegeforth himself traveled the world, collecting jaguars from Venezuela, orangutans from Borneo and marsupials from Australia. On a trip to India, Wegeforth contracted pneumonia and malaria; he died in 1941. His final contributions to the zoo were three elephants, which arrived in San Diego two months after his death.

By the end of WWII the San Diego Zoo had a worldwide reputation, and it helped to rebuild the collections of European zoos that had been devastated by the war. The Zoological Society continued at the forefront of zoo management with the introduction of 'bioclimatic' habitats, which allowed a number of different types of animals to share a simulated natural environment. In the 1960s the society started work on a 2000-acre Wild Animal Park (p254), 32 miles north of the city, which now provides free-range areas for many large animals.

### Information

The **San Diego Zoo** ( ☎ 619-231-1515; www.sandiego zoo.org; regular admission adult/child $21/14, deluxe admission package $32/20; ☽ vary; Ⓟ ) is located in the northern part of Balboa Park and has a large free parking lot off Park Blvd. The parking lot and the zoo fill up on weekends. Bus No 7 will get you there from downtown. Call for opening hours before you visit, since they vary seasonally. If you would like to leave the zoo and return the same day, get a hand stamp from the information booth near the entrance.

The 'deluxe admission package' includes a 40-minute guided bus tour, which otherwise costs $5 per adult and $3.50 per child, as well as a round-trip aerial tram ride on the Skyfari cable car. Discount coupons for the zoo are widely available from San Diego magazines, weekly newspapers and coupon books at hotels and information centers. A combined ticket to visit both the San Diego Zoo and the Wild Animal Park within a five-day period costs $56/38 per adult/child.

Arrive early, as many of the animals are most active in the morning – though many perk back up in the afternoon. Start with the guided double-decker bus tour, which gives a good overview of the zoo with informative commentary; sitting downstairs puts you closer to the animals. Once you've made the loop, your ticket remains good for express bus service in the park, a big help if you're out of shape. Either way, you're going to do a lot of walking; carry quarters for the electric foot massagers located around the park.

Animal shows are held in the two amphitheaters (no extra charge), and they're usually entertaining, especially for kids. The Skyfari cable car goes right across the park and can save you some walking time, though there may be a line to get on it. From June to September, the zoo is open until 10pm and has special exhibits that focus on nocturnal creatures.

Facilities are provided for disabled visitors; call the **zoo** ( ☎ 619-231-1515 ext 4526) for specifics.

**Sights**

The zoo and the Wild Animal Park share an active program of breeding endangered species in captivity for reintroduction into their natural habitats. This has been done with a number of species, including the Arabian oryx, the Bali starling and the California condor.

The **zoo gardens** are renowned and some of the plants are used for the specialized food requirements of particular animals. Just inside the entrance gate, pick up the brochure for the self-guided botanical gardens tour.

The zoo has also expanded its entertainment and educational role in the com-

---

**DETOUR: SAN DIEGO WILD ANIMAL PARK**

Since the early 1960s, the San Diego Zoological Society has been developing the **Wild Animal Park** ( ☎ 760-747-8702; www.sandiegozoo.org; adult/child 3-11 $27/20; ⏰ gates open 9am-8pm summer, 9am-4pm rest of year), an 1800-acre, open-range zoo where herds of giraffes, zebras, rhinos and other animals roam the open valley floor. To see them, visitors take a 50-minute ride around the preserves on the Wgasa Bush monorail (actually an open-sided electric tram), which gives great views of the animals and includes interesting commentary. The animals look wonderful in the wide, open spaces, though often you can't get as close to them as you can in a regular zoo. Since the monorail makes a loop, sit on the right side (inside the loop) for the best viewing.

Over 500 animals are born here every year. At the Petting Kraal you can touch some of the youngest. Animal shows are held in a number of areas, between 11am and 4:30pm daily; pick up a map and a schedule as you enter.

The park has all services, from souvenir shops to places to eat (including choices for vegetarians). It's just north of Hwy 78, five miles east of I-15 from the Via Rancho Parkway exit. Plan 45 minutes transit by car, except in rush hour when that figure doubles. Bus No 386 will get you there from the Escondido Transit Center, Monday to Saturday, but it's a long, involved process getting back; you're better off going by car. For bus information contact **North San Diego County Transit District** ( ☎ 619-233-3004, 800-266-6883 from northern San Diego County; www.gonctd.com).

The park remains open an hour after the gates close. Admission includes the monorail and all shows. Discount coupons are widely available. A combined ticket to visit the San Diego Zoo and Wild Animal Park within a five-day period costs $56/38 per adult/child. Parking is $6 extra. For a real safari experience, photo caravan tours go right among the animals, but they're pricey, and reservations are required; there are also night tours available at different times of year – call the park to inquire. There are also facilities for disabled visitors; call ☎ 760-738-5067 for information. Excluding transit time, plan on spending 2½ to five hours at the park, longer if you're *really* into animals.

munity with the opening of a **children's zoo exhibit** (where youngsters can pet small critters) and of outdoor theaters for animal shows. Both children and adults will enjoy the animal nursery, where you can see the zoo's newest arrivals. Babies are born every spring and summer.

Most visitors will have their own favorites. The **koalas** are so popular that Australians may be surprised to find them a sort of unofficial symbol of San Diego. The **Komodo dragon**, an Indonesian lizard that can grow up to 10ft long, not only looks fearsome, but strides around the reptile house in a very menacing manner.

The park's bioclimactic environments include **Tiger River**, a realistic, re-created Asian rain forest; **Gorilla Tropics**, an African rain forest; and the **Sun Bear Forest**, where the Asian bears are famously playful.

**Absolutely Apes**, is devoted to the apes of Indonesia, including orangutans and siamangs climbing in lush forests. The large, impressive **Scripps Aviary** and **Rainforest Aviary** have well-placed feeders to allow some close-up viewing. And you can walk right beneath 100 species of winged creatures inside the **Owens Aviary**. Finally, don't miss the Chinese **giant pandas** and **African Rock Kopje** (outcrop), where klipspringers (small antelopes) demonstrate their rock-climbing abilities.

## Mission Valley                    Map p239

Although it would often dry up in late summer, the San Diego River was the most reliable source of freshwater for the crops and the livestock of the early missions. The river valley, now called Mission Valley, was frequently flooded until dams were completed upstream in the mid-1950s. The I-8 now runs its length, and is dotted with hotels and shopping centers. Some green, open space remains, much of it at golf courses and country clubs. The restored Mission San Diego de Alcalá is definitely worth a visit, but Mission Valley's most touted feature is its triad of **shopping centers**: Fashion Valley, the Hazard Center and Mission Valley Center.

The San Diego Trolley runs the length of the valley, from downtown to the mission, with stops at Qualcomm Stadium and all the shopping centers. The trolley's route cuts through a scenic corridor of riparian land (and golf courses) not seen from the freeway. You could make a day of trolley-shopping,

getting off at each of the big shopping centers. **Fashion Valley** (☎ 619-297-3381; 7007 Friars Rd) has a premier selection of retailers, including Tiffany & Co, Enzo Antolini and Restoration Hardware, as well as biggies such as Saks Fifth Ave, Macy's and Nordstrom; many stay open to 10pm. **Mission Valley Center** (☎ 619-296-6375; 1640 Camino del Rio N) houses upscale discount outlets, including Nordstrom Rack and Saks Off Fifth Ave; both malls have some good restaurants and multiplex movie theaters. The **Hazard Center** (☎ 619-543-8111; 7676 Hazard Center Dr) has a large Barnes & Noble bookstore, a seven-screen multiplex cinema and several restaurants.

### MISSION SAN DIEGO DE ALCALÁ

Although the first California mission was established on Presidio hill, Padre Junípero Serra decided in 1773 to move it a few miles upriver, closer to a better water supply and more arable land. In 1784 the missionaries built a solid adobe and timber church, but it was destroyed by an earthquake in 1803. The church was promptly rebuilt, and at least some of it still stands on a slope overlooking Mission Valley. With the end of the mission system in the 1830s, the buildings were turned over to the Mexican government and fell into disrepair. Some accounts say that they were reduced to a facade and a few crumbling walls by the 1920s.

Extensive restoration began in 1931, with financial support from local citizens and the Hearst Foundation, a philanthropic organization funded by one of California's most influential families. The pretty white church and buildings you see now are the fruits of the thorough restoration.

The **visitors center** (☎ 619-281-8449; www.missionsandiego.com; 10818 San Diego Mission Rd at Friars Rd; adult/child $3/2; ☉ 9am-5pm) inside the mission has a friendly and informative staff, some good books and tacky souvenirs. The mission sits two blocks north of I-8, between I-15 and Mission Gorge Rd; from the Mission trolley stop, walk two blocks north and turn right onto San Diego Mission Rd.

### Old Town                    Map pp242–3

Under the Mexican government, which took power in 1821, any settlement with a population of 500 or more was entitled to become a 'pueblo.' Since the Presidio's population was about 600, soldiers from the garrison

SAN DIEGO

**SAN DIEGO**

---

**CONVERSION & REVENGE**

The first missionaries visited Native-American settlements with gifts and promises, and their first converts, whom they called 'neophytes,' were encouraged to move into the mission compound on the Presidio, where they lived and worked – and contracted European diseases. The Spanish soldiers in the Presidio garrison abused the mission neophytes and also raided Native-American villages. According to Padre Serra's reports, soldiers would chase their victims on horseback and 'catch an Indian woman with their lassos, to become prey for their unbridled lusts.' So, in 1774 the priests left the Presidio and started their new mission near a large Kumeyaay village, away from the influence of the military.

Unfortunately, they were also away from the protection of the military, and in November 1775 the increasingly resentful Kumeyaay made a concerted attack on the mission and burned it to the ground. One of the priests, Luis Jayme, appealed to the attackers with arms outstretched, crying 'Love God, my children!' He was dragged away and beaten to death, becoming California's first martyr. The survivors retreated to the Presidio, and the Spanish authorities captured, flogged and executed the leaders of the attack. After a few months, the missionaries returned to their site in the valley and built a second mission, with a tiled roof to resist the flaming arrows of Native-American attacks – this type of roof became a standard feature of mission architecture.

---

were able to cultivate and partition the land below Presidio hill, and make it the first official civilian Spanish settlement in California – the Pueblo de San Diego. A plaza was laid out around Casa Estudillo, home of the pueblo's commandant, and within 10 years it was surrounded by about 40 huts and several houses. This square mile of land (roughly 10 times what remains today) was also the center of American San Diego until the fire of 1872, after which the city's main body moved to the new Horton subdivision.

John Spreckels built a trolley line from Horton's New Town to Old Town in the 1920s and, to attract passengers, began restoring the old district. In 1968 the area became **Old Town State Historic Park**, archaeological work began, and the few surviving original buildings were restored. Other structures were rebuilt, and the area is now a pedestrian district (with parking lots around the edges) of shade trees, a large open plaza, and a cluster of shops and restaurants.

In an attempt to emphasize Old Town's historical significance – it has become primarily a shopping and eating destination – the Park Service has hired interpretive rangers to give tours and has expanded the visitors center to include an excellent American-period museum (Native-American pieces are in the Museum of Man at Balboa Park). The **Old Town State Historic Park Visitor Center** ( ☎ 619-220-5422; www.parks.ca.gov; ☼ 10am-5pm) is in the Robinson-Rose House at the southern end of the plaza. The center has a California history slide show, memorabilia and an educated staff. You'll also find good history books for sale and a diorama depicting the original pueblo. If you're particularly interested in history, pick up a copy of the *Old Town San Diego State Historic Park Tour Guide & Brief History* ($2), or take a guided tour, which leaves from the visitor center at 11am and 2pm daily.

Across from the center is **Casa de Estudillo**, a restored adobe home filled with authentic period furniture. It's worth a look and has a self-guided tour map, available from a tour guide at the house's northwestern entrance.

The **Bazaar del Mundo**, just off the plaza's northwestern corner, is a colorful collection of import shops and restaurants, which are open late and definitely worth passing through. If you want to pick up Mexican souvenirs, but don't want to go to Tijuana, come here. Along San Diego Ave, on the southern side of the plaza, there's a row of small, historical-looking buildings (only one is authentically old), some of which house more souvenir and gift shops. Two blocks from the Old Town perimeter sits **Whaley House** ( ☎ 619-298-2482; www.whaleyhouse.org; 2482 San Diego Ave; adult/child $5/3; ☼ 10am-4:30pm Wed-Mon), the city's oldest brick building, which was *officially certified* as haunted by the US Department of Commerce in the early 1960s. Check out the collection of period furniture and clothing from when the house served as courthouse, theater and private residence.

Just north of Old Town, **Casa de Carillo** dates from about 1820 and is said to be the oldest house in San Diego. It is now the pro shop for the public 18-hole **Presidio Hills Golf Course** ( ☎ 619-295-9476; www.golfsd.com; greens fee $10).

The Old Town transit center, on the trolley line at Taylor St at the northwestern edge of Old Town, is a stop for the *Coaster* commuter train, the San Diego Trolley (orange and blue lines), and bus Nos 4 and 5 from downtown; Old Town Trolley tours stop southeast of the plaza on Twiggs St.

### PRESIDIO HILL

In 1769 Padre Junípero Serra and Gaspar de Portolá established the first Spanish settlement in California on Presidio hill, overlooking the valley of the San Diego River. You can walk up from Old Town along Mason St for excellent views of San Diego Bay and Mission Valley. Atop the hill, **Presidio Park** has several walking trails and shaded benches. A large cross, made with tiles from the original mission, commemorates Padre Serra. American forces occupied the hill in 1846, during the Mexican-American War, and named it Fort Stockton, for American commander Robert Stockton. A flagpole, cannon, some plaques and earth walls now form the **Fort Stockton Memorial**. The nearby **El Charro Statue**, a bicentennial gift to the city from Mexico, depicts a Mexican cowboy on horseback. Nothing remains of the original Presidio structures, but there are archaeological digs under way.

The **Serra Museum** ( ☎ 619-297-3258; 2727 Presidio Dr; adult/child $5/2; 🕑 10am-4:30pm Tue-Sun, shorter winter hours) has a small but interesting collection of artifacts and pictures from the Mission and rancho periods, and gives a good sense of the earliest days of European settlement. It would be easy to mistake it for a well-preserved Spanish Colonial style structure, but in fact it was designed by William Templeton Johnson in 1929. Call the museum in advance to confirm hours.

## Uptown & Hillcrest
Map pp242–3

Uptown is roughly a triangle north of downtown, east of Old Town and south of Mission Valley. In the late 19th century it was fashionable to live in the hills north of

downtown, since only those who owned a horse-drawn carriage could afford it. Called Bankers Hill after some of the wealthy residents – or Pill Hill, because of the many doctors there – the upscale heights had unobstructed views of the bay and Point Loma before I-5 was built. A few of the ornate Victorian mansions survive, most notably the 1889 **Long-Waterman House** (2408 First Ave). Easily recognized by its towers, gables, bay windows and veranda, it was once the home of former California governor Robert Waterman. Also notable is the **Timkin House**, one block to the north.

A favorite pastime of residents old and new is crossing the 375ft **Spruce St Footbridge** that hangs over a deep canyon between Front and Brant Sts. The **Quince St Bridge**, between Third and Fourth Aves, is a wood-trestle bridge built in 1905 and refurbished in 1988 after its slated demolition was vigorously protested by community activists.

At the corner of Washington and India Sts stands a shingled complex once known as the **India Street Art Colony**. Opened in the 1970s by architect and artist Raoul Marquis, the art studios, import shops and theaters that originally occupied it are gone. They have been replaced by an excellent café and some first-rate inexpensive eateries.

At the heart of Uptown is **Hillcrest** (bus Nos 1, 3 and 25 go to/from downtown along Fourth and Fifth Ave), the first suburban real-estate development in San Diego. If you drive around, you'll see the work of many of San Diego's best-known architects from the early 20th century, including Irving Gill and William Templeton Johnson. The Mediterranean and Spanish Mission styles, and the influence of the Arts and Crafts movement, are also evident. But the real attraction of Hillcrest is its lively street life, due in part to its status as the center of San Diego's gay and lesbian community.

Explore the neighborhood by beginning at the **Hillcrest Gateway**, a lighted electric sign that arches over University Ave at Fifth Ave. Around the corner, on Fifth Ave between University Ave and Washington St, you'll find the **Village Hillcrest Center**, with its colorful, boxy postmodern architecture. There's a **multiplex cinema** ( ☎ 619-299-2100), as well as restaurants, shops, and a great newsstand. East on University Ave at No 535, look for the 1928 **Kahn Building**, an original commercial

SAN DIEGO

building with architectural elements that border on kitsch. South of University Ave along Fifth Ave, there's a variety of new and used bookstores, many with a good selection of non-mainstream publications.

Hillcrest's **farmers market** ( Fifth Ave, cnr Normal & Lincoln Sts; 9am-1pm Sun) is a good place to people-watch and buy fresh produce.

## TOURS

To get the lay of the land begin your visit with a tour, then return to the sights that interest you most.

**Old Town Trolley Tours** (Map pp242-3; ☎ 619-298-8687, 800-868-7482; www.historictours.com; adult/child 4-12 $15/25) loops around the main attractions near downtown and in Coronado inside an open-air trolley. Best of all, you can get on or off at any number of stops, staying to look around as long as you wish. Not to be confused with the Metropolitan Transit System's trolleys, which run on rails, the Old Town Trolley is a green and orange bus styled after an old-fashioned streetcar. Tickets are good for unlimited all-day travel. Tours start at 9am and run every 30 minutes or so until 7pm. You can start at any trolley stop (they're well marked with orange and are usually next to a regular San Diego Transit bus stop), though the official trolley stand is in Old Town (which is convenient for parking) on Twiggs St. The tours are a great introduction to city, and the commentary is entertaining. Save 10% by purchasing tickets online. Kids like the Seal Tour, which includes a trip around San Diego Bay in an amphibious vehicle – but you may do better taking a harbor cruise with a company that operates regular passenger boats instead (opposite).

**San Diego Scenic Tours** ( ☎ 858-273-8687; www .sandiegoscenictours.com; adult $28-56, child 3-11 $14-28) leads half- and full-day bus tours around San Diego and Tijuana, some of which build in time to shop and dine. You can combine some tours with a harbor cruise.

---

### SAN DIEGO IN 48 HOURS  *Marisa Gierlich*

When I was living in La Jolla, a friend from France called: he was coming to visit, for 48 hours. Despite my insistence that there is just too much to see in San Diego to only spend two days, it was all the time he had. I was determined to show him the best of it. Here was our schedule:

**Day 1**

| | |
|---|---|
| 8am | Breakfast at the Pannikin (La Jolla; p289) |
| 9-11:30am | Walk through La Jolla, along the cove, to the Museum of Contemporary Art and down to Windansea Beach (p274) |
| Noon | Lunch at Kono's (Pacific Beach; p287) |
| 1-5pm | Rent bikes and ride south, along the boardwalk and over to Ocean Beach; look in tattoo parlors, shop for antiques and have a beer (p279) |
| 6pm | Walk around the Gaslamp Quarter (p236) and dine at Bandar (p263) |
| 8pm | See *Love's Labours Lost* at the Old Globe Theater (p268) |
| 11pm | Stop for gelato at Gelato Vero Caffe on the way home (p265) |

**Day 2**

| | |
|---|---|
| 7:30am | Hike through Torrey Pines State Reserve (p275) |
| 9am | Walk through UCSD, look at the Stuart Collection and stop in at the Geisel Library (p276) |
| 11:30am | Lunch at Bread & Cie (Hillcrest; p265) |
| 12:30pm | Shop for books and tchotchkes (trinkets) in Hillcrest (p257) |
| 1-4pm | Explore Balboa Park (p248) |
| 4:30pm | Have a drink at the Hotel del Coronado (Coronado; p280) |
| 6:30pm | Dinner at Mona Lisa (Little Italy; p263) |
| 8pm | See a reggae show at the Belly Up Tavern (Solana Beach; p293) |

My friend didn't see the San Diego Zoo or SeaWorld (next time, with the kids), but man-oh-man did he have fun!

**Contactours** ( ☎ 800-235-5393, 619-477-8687; www
.contactours.com; adult $27-55, child 3-11 $13-25) is a
larger outfit that offers tours of the zoo,
the Wild Animal Park, SeaWorld, Legoland
and Disneyland, in addition to its city tours
and trips to Tijuana.

**Original Bike Cab Co** ( ☎ 888-245-3222, 619-245-
3222; www.bikecab.com) offers a fun way to see
downtown. San Diego's version of a rick-
shaw is the pedicab, a carriage pulled behind a bicycle that carries up to four people.
The drivers (pedalers?) often have tips on
what's happening around town. Flag an
empty pedicab, or call and one will pick
you up. Pedicabs run 10am to midnight
on weekdays, 10am to 3am Saturday and
Sunday. One-way downtown trips cost
$5 per person to get from, say, the Em-
barcadero to Horton Plaza. The same company offers downtown pedicab tours and
trips to other parts of San Diego (from $25
per half-hour).

For a boat tour of San Diego Harbor,
contact **San Diego Harbor Excursion** (Map pp240-1;
☎ 800-442-7847, 619-234-4111; www.sdhe.com; adult $15-
20, child $7.50-10) or **Hornblower Cruises** (Map pp240-1;
☎ 619-725-8888; www.hornblower.com; adult $15-20, child
$7.50-10). Each operates one- and two-hour
sight-seeing tours from the Embarcadero
(near the *Star of India*). Both also have
nightly dinner-dance cruises for about $55
per person ($60 on Saturday) and whale-
watching excursions in season.

Increased national security has limited the
visitation of **military facilities** in San Diego;
however, you can still tour surface ships and
aircraft carriers when they're in port. Call
in advance to determine if there are any
ships available to tour. For aircraft carriers,
call ☎ 619-545-1133; for surface ships call
☎ 619-437-5260.

# FESTIVALS & EVENTS
The calendar is chockfull of community,
cultural and sporting events. Some of the
most interesting and unusual are listed in
this section. For the most current list, contact the San Diego Convention & Visitors
Bureau (p236).

## March
**Ocean Beach Kite Festival** ( ☎ 858-274-2016)
Aficionados of kites come together on the first Saturday in
March for kite making, decorating, flying and competitions
at Ocean Beach.

## April
**San Diego Crew Classic** ( ☎ 619-225-0300; www.crew
classic.org) The national college rowing regatta takes
places in early April at Crown Point Shores Park in
Mission Bay.

## June
**San Diego County Fair** ( ☎ 858-755-1161; www.sd
fair.com) Huge county fair held from mid-June to July 4;
features headline acts and hundreds of carnival rides and
shows at the Del Mar Fairgrounds in Del Mar.

## July
**US Open Sandcastle Competition** ( ☎ 619-424-6663;
www.usopensandcastle.com) You won't believe what can
be made out of sand at the amazing sandcastle-building
competition held mid-July in Imperial Beach, south of
Coronado.
**Del Mar Horse Racing** ( ☎ 858-755-1141; www.dmtc
.com) The well heeled bet on the horses, 'where the turf
meets the sea,' at Del Mar Fairgrounds, from mid-July to
early September.
**San Diego Gay Pride** ( ☎ 619-297-7683; www.sdpride
.org) The city's gay community celebrates in Hillcrest and
Balboa Park at the end of July.

## August
**Summerfest Chamber Music Festival** ( ☎ 858-459-
3728; www.ljcms.org) La Jolla hosts this two-week series
with international performers.
**Old Globe Festival** ( ☎ 619-239-2255; www.oldglobe
.org) This renowned Shakespeare festival at the Old Globe
Theatre in Balboa Park performs both the popular and
lesser-known plays.
**San Diego Street Scene** ( ☎ 800-260-9985; www
.street-scene.com) California's largest music festival
takes place in late August downtown, and features music
performed on outdoor stages and lots to eat.

## September
**Thunderboat Regatta** ( ☎ 619-225-9160; www
.thunderboats.net) Some of the fastest boats in the world
compete on Mission Bay in mid-September.
**Fleet Week** ( ☎ 800-353-3793; www.fleetweeksandiego
.org) The US military shows its might in a parade of ships
and the signature Blue Angels air show from mid- to late
September.

## December
**December Nights** ( ☎ 619-239-0512; www.balboapark
.org) Call in advance for the schedule of events in Balboa
Park; the festival includes crafts, carols and a candlelight
parade in the park.
**Harbor Parade of Lights** ( ☎ 619-224-2240 Oct-Dec
only; www.sdparadeoflights.org) Dozens of decorated,

**SAN DIEGO**

---

### SAN DIEGO FOR CHILDREN

San Diego is a great city for kids, from tots to teens.

#### Saturday in the Park

Don't miss **Balboa Park** (p248). Little kids love the **Marie Hitchcock Puppet Theater** (p252) and the **Model Railroad Museum** (p251); follow up with a ride on the carousel and miniature railroad at the **Spanish Village Art Center** (p251). Older kids go nuts for the **IMAX theater** (p251) at the Reuben H Fleet Space Theater & Science Center; then take a walk through the **Aerospace Museum** (p252) or the **San Diego Hall of Champions Sport Museum** (p252).

#### Animal Antics

Even the most apathetic teenager lights up at the sight of the koalas and pandas at the **San Diego Zoo** (p253). In summertime the zoo hosts special activities for kids, from hula-hooping contests to bungee-trampoline jumping; call for current options. Take a half-day excursion to the **Wild Animal Park** (p254) to see animals roam free.

#### Surf's Up

From riding bicycles or learning to **surf** (p280) to attending the **US Open Sandcastle Competition** (p259) or building your own sandy fortress, there's always something fun to do at the beach. Lifeguards ensure safety, and there are usually showers to rinse off at the end of the day. Once you're dry, head to **Cabrillo National Monument** (p279) for a look at the lighthouse.

#### A Day on the Bay

Spend an afternoon by the waterfront. Take a tour of **San Diego Harbor** (p259), or rent **kayaks** (p282) together. If you like boats but tend to get seasick, stay in port and tour the **USS Midway** (p248) or the tall ships of the **Maritime Museum** (p248).

#### Keeping them Amused

Consider a day at a theme park. Go see Shamu at **SeaWorld** (p278) or ride the wooden roller coaster at **Belmont Park** (p277). For kids under 12, **Legoland** (p294) is a must-see.

#### Soup's On

When it's time for dinner, make a bee line to the **Corvette Diner** (p265), where you're encouraged to whoop it up at the dinner table (don't worry; there's a full bar for grown-ups). Afterward take the whole gang for ice cream at the **Ghirardelli Soda Fountain** (p263).

---

illuminated boats float in procession on the harbor on two Sunday evenings in December.

**Las Posadas and Luminaries** ( ☎ 619-291-4903; www .oldtownsandiego.org) This traditional Latin Christmas celebration in Old Town re-enacts Mary and Joseph seeking shelter.

## SLEEPING

High-season summer rates for double-occupancy rooms are listed here; suites cost more. Prices drop significantly between September and June.

For details of coastal San Diego lodgings, see p283.

### Downtown                    Map pp240–1
**BUDGET**

Some of the cheapest downtown hotels are single-room-occupancy hotels (SROs);

they rent basic rooms, by the day, week or month, to people who might otherwise be homeless. Low-budget travelers often stay in these places and find them acceptable, though some regular guests can be, well, colorful characters, to say the least. In the cheapest rooms, you share a hall bathroom. With one exception, the following hotels are *not* SROs.

**500 West Hotel** ( ☎ 619-234-5252; www.500west hotel.com; 500 W Broadway; s/d $70/80; **P** ) Located at the YMCA but not affiliated with it, 500 West has small but unexpectedly stylish rooms with shared bathrooms. Staying here provides easy access to the Amtrak and Greyhound stations, and to the trolley to Tijuana. It's a top money-saving option. No air-con.

**La Pensione Hotel** ( ☎ 619-236-8000, 800-232-4683; www.lapensionehotel.com; 1700 India St; r $75) Rooms have a queen-size bed and private bathroom at this four-story hotel in Little Italy, in walking distance to most downtown attractions. Great bargain. No air-con.

**J Street Inn** ( ☎ 619-696-6922; www.thejstreetinn .com; 222 J St; per night/week $90/250) All of the rooms have fridge, microwaves and private bathroom at this well-run SRO that rents for the night or longer term. The beds are way too soft, but the place is clean and safe, and the price is right.

**HI San Diego Downtown Hostel** ( ☎ 619-525-1531; www.sandiegohostels.org; 521 Market St; dm members/ nonmembers $20/23, f without bathroom $53-62, with bathroom $74-83; 🖳 ) Centrally located in the Gaslamp Quarter, this HI facility is handy to public transportation and nightlife. It provides basic dorm rooms, and has good kitchen facilities. Includes breakfast. No lock-out times. No air-con.

**USA Hostels San Diego** ( ☎ 619-232-3100, 800-438-8622; www.usahostels.com; 726 Fifth Ave; dm $21, d $54; 🖳 ) A Victorian-era hotel refitted with six-bed dorms and some doubles, this hostel's lounge and kitchen areas are quite nice, and its rates include a hot breakfast. Free shuttles to the beach or to area attractions are offered sporadically, as are day tours, in-house parties and beach barbecues. It's right in the Gaslamp Quarter and so can be a bit noisy, but the crowd doesn't seem to mind. No air-con.

### MID-RANGE

Ask about specials and package deals; you can sometimes get lower rates.

**Prava Hotel** ( ☎ 619-233-3300; www.pravahotel.com; 911 Fifth Ave; r $140-190; P 🕿 ) Rooms are huge at this boutique hotel with pull-out sofas for extra guests, kitchenettes with blenders for cocktails, and king-size beds made up with Egyptian cotton sheets. Downstairs you'll find a happening restaurant and a fitness center.

**Bristol Hotel** ( ☎ 619-432-6141, 800-662-4477; www .thebristolsandiego.com; 1055 First Ave; r $150-180; P 🖳 ) Decorated in snappy pop-art colors, this eight-story high-end-tourist-class hotel looks great and has in-room extras, such as bathrobes and minibars.

**Staybridge Suites** ( ☎ 619-759-4000; www.stay bridge.com; 1110 A St; ste $170-200; P ) Every room is a suite and includes a pull-out sofa and full

kitchen at this upper-mid-range corporate downtown hotel near Balboa Park. Rooms have extras such as DVD players. There's also a rooftop sundeck.

**Horton Grand Hotel** ( ☎ 619-544-1886, 800-542-1886; www.hortongrand.com; 311 Island Ave; r $170; P ) Some rooms in this turn-of-the-century brick hotel have wrought-iron balconies on the street, but the quietest face the inner courtyard. All are decorated in Victoriana and have gas fireplaces.

### TOP-END

**W Hotel** ( ☎ 619-231-8220, 888-625-5144; www.whotels .com; 421 West B St; r from $230; P 🖳 🕿 ) The sexiest, most stylin' hotel in San Diego, the W is aggressively decked out in a sky-sand-and-sea theme, with deep blues and shades of grey and gold. Every room comes with luxury amenities, there's a roof-top sand beach, and a DJ spins house music in the lobby on weekends. Full-service spa. Also see p266.

**Westgate Hotel** ( ☎ 619-238-1818, 800-221-3802; www.westgatehotel.com; 1055 Second Ave; r from $215; P 🖳 ) If you prefer white-glove service, handcrafted European furniture, high tea and harp music, the Westgate is San Diego's top traditional luxury hotel, where every detail is perfect.

**US Grant Hotel** ( ☎ 619-232-3121, 800-237-5029; www.wyndham.com; 326 Broadway; r from $210; P 🖳 ) Given a facelift in 2005, this 1910 hotel was built with a nod to the Hotel del Coronado (p286), a straight three-mile shot from the lobby's front door; this was the fancy city hotel to complement the fanciful beach resort. The US Grant has since hosted everyone from Albert Einstein to Harry Truman. Today it's primarily a business-luxury hotel. Ask about packages.

## Mission Valley                    Map pp242–3

There are several dozen properties along Hotel Circle, which makes an oblong loop on the north and south sides of I-8. You can usually find a room in summer for $80 on weeknights, $130 on weekends. Negotiate prices when occupancy is low and you arrive late in the evening, but expect rates to spike when there's a big convention in town. For properties other than those listed, view the room before you decide to stay, especially if it's cheap, since some of the older motels are run-down. There are no bona-fide luxury hotels on Hotel Circle, though there are several business-class properties.

**Vagabond Inn** ( ☎ 619-297-1691, 800-522-1555; 625 Hotel Circle S; r $90-150; **P** **ℛ** ) Pay $10 more than the dives charge, and you'll get a cleaner room and better service. Two pools and a hot tub. Top choice for value.

**Kings Inn Hotel** ( ☎ 619-297-2231, 800-785-4647; www.kingsinnsandiego.com; 1333 Hotel Circle S; r $80-150; **P** **▢** **ℛ** ) This hotel has mushy beds but clean rooms.

**Handlery Hotel** ( ☎ 619-298-0511, 800-843-4343; www.handlery.com; 950 Hotel Circle N; r $120-160; **P** **▢** **ℛ** ) A step up from the budget hotels, the Handlery has more attractive furnishings (read: wooden armoires and writing desks) and firmer mattresses.

**Town & Country Hotel** ( ☎ 619-291-7131, 800-772-8527; www.towncountry.com; 500 Hotel Circle N; r $120-190; **P** **▢** **▢** **ℛ** ) Four swimming pools, tropical landscaping, and a 10-story tower make the Town & Country feel like a Honolulu hotel. It's popular for business gatherings, shopping trips (there's a bridge to Fashion Valley out back), and family vacations (kids love it). Price specials keep rooms filled off-season.

**Red Lion Hanalei Hotel** ( ☎ 619-297-1101, 800-882-0858; www.hanaleihotel.com; 2270 Hotel Circle N; r $150-240; **P** **ℛ** ) A convention-class hotel with a Polynesian-theme, the Red Lion Hanalei has rooms with super-comfy mattresses, but the hotel is rather expensive for its location. If you can score a good rate, it's worth a visit.

Also recommended:
**Best Western Seven Seas Lodge** ( ☎ 619-291-1300, 800-328-1618; www.bw7seas.com; 411 Hotel Circle S; r $100-150; **P** **▢** )
**Comfort Inn Suites** ( ☎ 619-291-7700, 800-647-1903; www.comfortinnzoo.com; 2485 Hotel Circle Pl; r $100-150; **P** **ℛ** )

## Old Town                    Map pp242–3
If you have a car and want to stay near Old Town but you don't want to pay top dollar, consider staying in neighboring Mission Valley (p261).

**Holiday Inn Express** ( ☎ 619-299-7400, 800-451-9846; www.hiexpress.com/ex-oldtown; 3900 Old Town Ave; r $140-160; **P** **▢** **ℛ** ) Right at the edge of Old Town, its rooms are clean, spacious and up-to-date, and have extras such as microwaves and refrigerators. Good value.

**Best Western Hacienda Hotel** ( ☎ 619-298-4707, 800-888-1991; www.haciendahotel-oldtown.com; 4041 Harney St; r from $150; **P** **ℛ** ) All the rooms are shaped differently at this all-suites hotel, which has a workout room, Jacuzzi and nightly cocktail hour. Rates fluctuate wildly; ask for the American Automobile Association (AAA) discount when you book. Most accommodations are spacious, but avoid Room 313: it's a closet.

## Hillcrest                    Map pp242–3
If you don't like to drive, you can stay in Hillcrest, where there are lots of restaurants, shops and nightlife within walking distance. But bear in mind that it's predominantly gay.

**Hillcrest Inn** ( ☎ 619-293-7078, 800-258-2280; www.hillcrestinn.com; 3754 Fifth Ave; r $60-80) Given its location in a super-fun neighborhood, the Hillcrest Inn offers great value. Its motel rooms surround a central courtyard and there's a Jacuzzi, but neither air-con nor a swimming pool. It's primarily a gay hotel that also welcomes straight guests, but not children.

**Sommerset Suites Hotel** ( ☎ 619-296-2101, 800-962-9665; www.sommersetsuites.com; 606 Washington St; r $140-170; **ℛ** **P** ) Originally built as condominiums in the 1980s, all rooms have full kitchens; many units are two-room suites. In the evening there's complimentary beer and wine.

## Chula Vista
**KOA** (Map p239; ☎ 619-427-3601, 800-562-9877; www.koa.com; 111 N 2nd Ave; tent $34-38, RV sites $43-47, cabins $59-65; **P** **ℛ** ) In Chula Vista, about eight miles southeast of downtown San Diego, the KOA has good camping facilities for families.

# EATING
Make reservations whenever possible, especially on weekends.

## Gaslamp Quarter              Map pp240–1
There are more than 90 restaurants in the Gaslamp Quarter, many of them very good. But because of their proximity to the convention center, they cater to an expense-account crowd and can be overpriced at dinner time. Some are mainly daytime operations, while others provide entertainment well into the night.

## BUDGET

**Cafe Lulu** ( ☎ 619-238-0114; 419 F St; light meals $4-8; ⏰ 9am-1am Sun-Thu, to 2:30am Fri & Sat) Linger over lattes or merlot at this hip café, and re-fuel on sandwiches, cheese boards and cakes. Open late. Outside seating.

**Cheese Shop** ( ☎ 619-232-2303; 627 Fourth Ave; dishes $5-8; ⏰ breakfast & lunch) Breakfasts are good here, but come for the overstuffed sandwiches at lunch – never mind the apathetic service. Try the house-roasted pork loin.

**Dick's Last Resort** ( ☎ 619-231-9100; 345 Fourth Ave; mains $6-12; ⏰ 11am-1:30am) At Dick's, a legendary place with a riotously fun atmosphere, you can carry on in full voice while guzzling beer and chowing down fried food, and none of the other revelers on the giant patio will care a whit.

**Royal Thai** ( ☎ 619-230-842; cnr Fifth & Island Aves; dishes $7-13, lunch specials $8) A casually elegant eatery inside a building that's been an Asian restaurant ever since it opened its doors as Nanking Cafe in 1912. It has another branch in **La Jolla** (Map p247; ☎ 858-551-8424; 757 Pearl St).

**Ghirardelli Soda Fountain & Chocolate Shop** ( ☎ 619-234-2449; 643 Fifth Ave; ice cream $3-6; ⏰ 11am-11pm Sun-Thu, 11am-midnight Fri-Sun) Get jacked on sugar at this old-fashioned ice-cream parlor.

## MID-RANGE & TOP END

**Gaslamp Strip Club** ( ☎ 619-231-3140; 340 Fifth Ave; mains $10-20; ⏰ dinner) Pull your own bottle from the wine vault, then char your own rib eye on the open grills in the retro-Vegas dining room at downtown's best bargain for steak. No bottle costs more than $36, no steak more than $20. Fab martinis. Tons of fun. No one under 21 allowed.

**Bandar** ( ☎ 619-238-0101; 825 Fourth Ave; mains lunch $8-14, dinner $14-26) Exotic spices and fragrant cooking make this white-tablecloth Persian-Middle Eastern a favorite for giant kebabs and salads that zing with flavor. Come hungry: portions are huge, even at lunch, when you can save a bundle.

**Star of India** ( ☎ 619-544-9891; 423 F St; lunch buffet $9, mains $13-18) Delectable North Indian food at this downtown favorite, where you'll find flavorful curries, tandoori specialties and an all-you-can-eat buffet lunch. Lots for vegetarians, too.

**Café Sevilla** ( ☎ 619-233-5979; 555 Fourth Ave; tapas $5-8, mains $15-23; ⏰ dinner ) The tapas and Spanish food are good, but the truly delicious

thing at Sevilla is its live tango and flamenco performances, which include a three-course meal for $40 per person, Friday to Sunday. Book in advance. Otherwise, there's music (and sangria) nightly in the tapas bar.

**Greystone** ( ☎ 619-232-0225; 658 Fifth Ave; mains $27-36; ⏰ dinner) If the ritual of dining on a great steak is a cornerstone of your vacation, look no further than Greystone, where you can indulge in the best all-prime, 21-day dry-aged beef. Bring your credit card.

**Chive** ( ☎ 619-232-4483; 558 Fourth Ave; mains $19-29; ⏰ dinner) Consider the Cal-cuisine at this stylish (but loud) eatery.

## Little Italy                      Map pp240-1

**Mimmo's Italian Village** ( ☎ 619-239-3710; 1743 India St; meals under $10; ⏰ Mon-Sat 8am-4pm) In a cavernous building decorated to the hilt, Mimmo's deli serves salads, hot and cold sandwiches, and lunch specials, such as lasagna and eggplant parmigiana.

**Filippi's Pizza Grotto** ( ☎ 619-232-5094; 1747 India St; dishes $6-11) Chianti bottles hang from the ceiling of this red-and-white-checked-tablecloth old-school Italian that makes fantastic pizza, spaghetti and ravioli.

**Mona Lisa** ( ☎ 619-234-4893; 2061 India St; mains $9-16; ⏰ lunch Mon-Sat, dinner daily) Aside from delicious and hearty meals (try the can-nelloni), Mona Lisa also makes some of the best sandwiches in town, and sells imported Italian specialty foods at its market and deli.

**Buon Appetito** ( ☎ 619-238-9880; 1609 India St; mains lunch $7-12, dinner $10-19) The pasta and salads are simple, straightforward and fresh at this down-to-earth café. (There are other dishes, too, but the pasta is best.)

---

### TOP CHEAP EATS

- Waters Café (Balboa Park, p264)
- Bread & Cie (Hillcrest, p265)
- Saffron Thai (Washington St, p265)
- Phil's Barbecue (Mission Hills, p265)
- Filippi's Pizza Grotto (Little Italy, below)
- Girard Gourmet (La Jolla, p286)
- Point Loma Seafoods (Shelter Island, p288)
- Hodad's (Ocean Beach, p288)

---

**SAN DIEGO**

**Indigo Grill** ( ☎ 619-234-6802; 1536 India St; mains $18-28; 🕑 lunch Mon-Fri, dinner daily) Chef Deborah Scott has catapulted San Diego's culinary scene forward with her stylized, bold and adventurous Oaxacan-Alaskan cooking – as in Mexican-Arctic. (Think fire and ice, spicy and sweet.) The vibe is convivial and relaxed, perfect for lingering. Dinner portions are enormous: you could make a meal of two appetizers. Sharing encouraged, especially at the bar. Make reservations.

## Embarcadero & the Waterfront   Map pp240–1

**Anthony's Fishette** ( ☎ 619-232-5105; 1360 N Harbor Dr; dishes $5-8; 🕑 11am-10pm) On a nothing-fancy patio next to the Maritime Museum, you can dine on great fish and chips with coleslaw, and have a view of the tall ships in the harbor.

**Fish Market** ( ☎ 619-232-3474; 750 N Harbor Dr; mains lunch $13-20, dinner $17-25; 🕑 11am-10pm) For straightforward chowder, shellfish and grilled fish with a harbor view, walk to Tuna Harbor, opposite the port side of the USS *Midway*. Upstairs there's a more formal dining room that serves the same fish, but with sauce; stay downstairs. Snag a window table if you can. No reservations downstairs.

**Star of the Sea** ( ☎ 619-232-7408; 1360 N Harbor Dr; mains $26-36; 🕑 dinner) Windows line the walls of San Diego's top special occasion seafood restaurant, where artful French-California presentations of expertly prepared fish are complemented by an elegant white-tablecloth dining room and mesmerizing water views. Reserve in advance; request a window table.

## Balboa Park   Map pp242–3

You don't have to settle for hot dogs while you're museum-hopping at the park.

**Waters Café** ( ☎ 619-237-0675; 1450 El Prado; mains $6-9; 🕑 11am-3pm Tue-Fri, 9am-3pm Sat & Sun) Savory homemade soups, grilled veggie salads, and baguette sandwiches are typical dishes at this not-to-be-missed outdoor café in the courtyard of the San Diego Museum of Art. Save room for the rich chocolate brownies and the mouth-puckering lemon squares.

**Prado** ( ☎ 619-557-9441; 1549 El Prado; mains lunch $14-18, dinner $17-24; 🕑 lunch daily, dinner Tue-Sun) Dine on Cal-Latin cooking beneath the gorgeous painted ceiling of the Hospitality Building in one of San Diego's most beautiful

dining rooms. The Prado is also perfect for a civilized lunch on the veranda or for afternoon cocktails and appetizers in the bar. Make reservations.

## Old Town   Map pp242–3

Most Old Town eateries serve Mexican and Southwestern cooking in contrived atmospheres (think mariachi bands cruising the tables), but the food is good and you can have a lovely evening enjoying margaritas and a meal on an outdoor patio.

**Casa de Bandini** ( ☎ 619-297-8211; 2660 Calhoun St; meals $8-17; 🕑 11am-9:30pm Sun-Thu, 11am-10pm Fri & Sat) Sit by the babbling fountain at one of Old Town's best, most established places, which serves delicious, reasonably priced meals, such as *pollo asado* (roast chicken) or enchiladas.

**Bazaar del Mundo** (Old Town Plaza) At the northwestern corner of the plaza, the bazaar has three restaurants with a lively atmosphere and pretty good food (meals are $6 to $12, appetizers around $5) – they're especially great for drinks and people-watching.

**Old Town Mexican Cafe** ( ☎ 619-297-4330; 2489 San Diego Ave; dishes around $8; 🕑 7am-midnight) There's nothing like the flavor of freshly made tortillas, and this place makes the best – watch the staff turn them out in the window while you wait to be seated. In addition to breakfast, there's a big bar and dining room serving excellent food; its *machacas* (shredded pork with onions and peppers) are famous.

**El Agave** ( ☎ 619-220-0692; 2304 San Diego Ave; mains lunch $10-18, dinner $18-27) Candlelight flickers on the bottles adorning the walls of this 2nd-floor, white-tablecloth, high-end Mexican that serves real Mexican to the cognoscenti. The mole – a spicy sauce made with chilies and chocolate – is superb, and there are a whopping 1200 different tequilas to choose from. Make reservations.

## Hillcrest   Map pp242–3

Hillcrest provides a good selection of fun, good-value restaurants. On Tuesday night (from 5pm to 8pm) some places have specials ranging from a free appetizer to a buy-one-meal-get-one-free (call ahead to inquire).

### BUDGET & MID-RANGE

**Whole Foods** ( ☎ 619-294-2800; 711 University Ave; 🕑 8am-10pm) For the best groceries and deli items, come to this place, east of Fifth Ave.

RICHARD CUMMINS

Rock formation, Joshua Tree National
Park (p314)

JOHN ELK III

Ocotillo in bloom, Anza-Borrego
Desert State Park (p319)

Bouldering, Joshua Tree National Park (p317)

COREY RICH

LEE FOSTER

Anacapa Island, Channel Islands
National Park (p346)

RICHARD CU

Paseo Nuevo shopping mall (p337),
Santa Barbara

Leadbetter Beach (p330), Santa Barbara

STEPHAN

**Bread & Cie** ( ☎ 619-683-9322; 350 University Ave; pastries $2-4, sandwiches $5-8; ☻ 7am-7pm Mon-Fri, 7am-6pm Sat & Sun) Aside from crafting some of San Diego's best bread (including anise and fig, kalamata and black olive, and three-raisin), this bakery cum deli makes fabulous sandwiches with fillings such as curried-chicken salad. Boxed lunches cost $9. Great pastries, too.

**Kitima Thai** ( ☎ 619-298-2929; 406 University Ave; mains lunch $6-8, dinner $9-16; ☻ 11am-10:30pm) Delicious Kitima diverges from the standard Thai menu and serves inventive, fragrant specialties, such as baked whole basil fish. Tasty lunch specials, too.

**Taste of Thai** ( ☎ 619-291-7525; 527 University Ave; dishes $6-11; ☻ lunch Mon-Sat, dinner daily) Try here for less-stylized fare.

**Corvette Diner** ( ☎ 619-542-1001; 3946 Fifth Ave; mains $7-11; ☻ 11am-10pm Sun-Thu, 11am-midnight Fri & Sat) Your kids will love you for bringing them to this over-the-top '50s-theme diner, where a DJ spins rock-and-roll classics, waiters dance in the aisles, and kids wear drinking straws in their hair. See ya later Chuck E Cheese. (Oh, and the food is good, too. Try the meatloaf.)

**Hash House a Go Go** ( ☎ 619-298-4646; 3628 Fifth Ave; breakfast mains $5-13; ☻ breakfast, lunch & dinner) Serving possibly the best – and certainly the biggest – breakfasts in San Diego, Hash House makes biscuits and gravy as good as in the Carolinas, towering benedicts, pancakes as large as your head, and, of course, hash six different kinds. Come hungry. It serves dinner, too, but breakfasts are best.

**Crest Cafe** ( ☎ 619-295-2510; 425 Robinson Ave; dishes $7-12; ☻ 7am-midnight) Soulful preparations of down-to-earth cooking make this place worth seeking out when you're craving comfort food. Try the herb-crusted chicken, garlic-butter burger or chopped salad. At breakfast, the scrambles are delish.

**Ono Sushi** ( ☎ 619-298-0616; 1236 University Ave; mains $11-15; ☻ lunch Sat & Sun, dinner daily) Ono bucks tradition with its specialty rolls and Pacific Rim–style appetizers. Expect a wait at peak times, but it's worth it.

Also recommended:

**Ichiban** ( ☎ 619-299-7203; 1449 University Ave; dishes $6-9; ☻ 11am-9:30pm) Bargain Japanese, such as teriyaki-chicken bento boxes.

**Phil's Barbecue** ( ☎ 619-688-0559; 4030 Goldfinch St; ☻ 11am-9:30pm Tue-Sun) Mesquite-grilled baby-back ribs, in Mission Hills.

**TOP END**

**Region** ( ☎ 619-299-6499; 3671 Fifth Ave; mains lunch $6-10, dinner $17-24; ☻ lunch Wed-Sat, dinner Tue-Sat) Ground zero for the 'slow food movement' in San Diego, Region's cooking is all about tasting the freshness of the menu's just-off-the-farm organic ingredients. Everything is made in-house, from mozzarella to sorbet. Flavors are pure, clean and simple. Pastries are some of the best in town. If you're a foodie, don't miss this place.

**Parallel 33** ( ☎ 619-260-0033; 741 W Washington St; mains $18-27; ☻ dinner Mon-Sat) The invigorating flavors dance on the palette at this smart and casual neighborhood spot, where the chef skillfully fuses the cuisines of the globe's 33rd-north latitude. Expect savory and sweet combinations from Morocco, Lebanon, India, China, Japan – and San Diego, which also lies at this latitude. Seek this one out.

**Kemo Sabe** ( ☎ 619-220-6802; 3958 Fifth Ave; mains $13-26; ☻ dinner) The fiery cooking draws together elements of Southwestern American and Southeast Asian cooking.

## Washington Street    Map pp242–3

Further north from Little Italy on India St, where it meets Washington St, there's a block of well-known casual eateries.

For some of the best food in town under $10, make a beeline to Saffron, which has two separate sections: **Saffron Thai Grilled Chicken** ( ☎ 619-574-0177; 3731 India St; dishes $4-7; ☻ 10:30am-9pm Mon-Sat, 10:30am-8pm Sun), which specializes in charcoal-grilled chicken served with a choice of sauces, salad and jasmine rice; and **Saffron Noodles & Saté** ( ☎ 619-574-7737; 3737 India St; mains $5-9; ☻ 10:30am-9pm Mon-Sat, 10:30am-8pm Sun), where you can dig into big bowls of steaming noodle soup or order a plate of stir-fried noodles paired with various ingredients.

**El Indio** ( ☎ 619-299-0333; 3695 India St; dishes $2-5; ☻ 7:30am-9pm) Famous since 1940 for its tacos, tamales and excellent breakfast burritos.

**Shakespeare Pub & Grille** ( ☎ 619-299-0230; 3701 India St; dishes $7-13; ☻ 10am-midnight Sun-Thu, 10am-1am Fri & Sat) One of San Diego's most authentic English ale houses, Shakespeare's the place for darts, beer on tap and pub grub, including fish and chips, and bangers and mash.

**Gelato Vero Caffe** ( ☎ 619-295-9269; cnr Washington & India Sts; gelato per ounce $0.59; ☻ 6am-midnight Sun-Thu, 7am-1am Fri & Sat) San Diego's best Italian-style ice cream comes in 16 different flavors.

SAN DIEGO

# DRINKING

There's no shortage of bars in San Diego, but the city is fairly quiet compared to LA. People don't go out late on weeknights, but you can always find someplace to hang out until 1:45am, when bartenders shout 'last call!'

## Coffeehouses

Coffeehouses in San Diego are popular hangouts as well as nighttime venues; often they have live music.

**David's Coffeehouse** (Map pp242-3; ☎ 619-296-4173; 3766 Fifth Ave; ☺ 7am-11pm Sun-Thu, 7am-midnight Fri & Sat) Hang out inside or out on the patio, check your email, and play chess or the baby grand piano at David's, the hub of social activity in Hillcrest, especially for the arty crowd and 12-steppers.

**Living Room Coffeehouse** (Map pp242-3; ☎ 619-325-4445; 2541 San Diego Ave; ☺ 6am-midnight) One of a chain of five locations in San Diego, the Living Room in Old Town is a good place to hang out when you don't want to drink margaritas, but instead have coffee and chat or surf the Internet. There's another **branch** (Map pp242-3; ☎ 619-295-7911; 1417 University Ave; ☺ 6am-midnight) in Hillcrest that's popular with gay boys too young for the bars.

Also check out **Cafe Lulu** (Map pp240-1; ☎ 619-238-0114; 419 F St; ☺ 9am-1am Sun-Thu, 9am-2:30am Fri & Sat), or Little Italy's **Caffe Italia** (Map pp240-1; ☎ 619-234-6767; 1704 India St).

## Bars

### GASLAMP QUARTER    Map pp240-1

The center of the city's straight nightlife, the Gaslamp has the highest concentration of bars and nightclubs in San Diego. The line between restaurants, bars and clubs is sometimes fuzzy in this lively neighborhood.

**Bitter End** ( ☎ 619-338-9300; 770 Fifth Ave) The crowd wears khakis and drinks martinis at this former brothel that has been turned into an atmospheric watering hole. There's an extensive selection of beers on tap. Dancing downstairs.

**Moose McGillycuddy's** ( ☎ 619-702-5595; 535 Fifth Ave) The college crowd shoots pool and gets rowdy at this fun frat-boy bar.

**Red Circle Bar** ( ☎ 619-234-9211; 420 E St) Order a martini, raise your pinkie, and peruse the Soviet-era memorabilia and lissome crowd bathed in sexy red lighting at this trendy Russian-themed boîte. The bar serves more than 100 varieties of vodka.

**Star Bar** ( ☎ 619-234-5575; 423 E St) When you've had it with gentrified style and you're looking for a dive, head to this old-school bar decorated year-round with Christmas lights.

### DOWNTOWN & LITTLE ITALY    Map pp240-1

**Waterfront** ( ☎ 619-232-9656; 2044 Kettner Blvd) The bar was literally on the waterfront until the harbor was filled and the airport built. San Diego's first liquor license was granted to this place in the 1930s, and it's still owned by the same family. Besides being chock full of historic bric-a-brac, this is one of the best places to spend the afternoon or evening. It has a big window that opens onto the street, $5 bar food and live music on weekends.

**Karl Strauss Brewery & Grill** ( ☎ 619-234-2739; 1157 Columbia St) If you like buying your beer at the source, Karl Strauss makes some of San Diego's best. The grill serves food to 10pm weeknights, 11pm weekends.

**W Hotel** ( ☎ 619-231-8220; 421 West B St) The silicone set twirls in Vuitton on the catwalk of the W Hotel (p261) on Thursday, Friday and Saturday nights, but the best night is Thursday, when there's usually not a long line to get inside to stand around on the rooftop sand beach and poolside bar.

### OLD TOWN    Map pp242-3

Most of Old Town's nightlife takes place in the margarita restaurants; see p264.

**O'Hungry's** ( ☎ 619-298-0133; 2547 San Diego Ave) Despite its name, O'Hungry's is more for drinking than for eating. It serves beer by the yard glass, occasionally has live music and can sometimes be lots of fun.

**Six Degrees** ( ☎ 619-296-6789; 3175 India St) San Diego's best lesbian bar has a different theme every night, from football to Goth. It's famous for its Sunday barbecues with cheap burgers and beer on the patio. Call ahead to see what's doing.

### HILLCREST    Map pp242-3

Most of the bars in Hillcrest are gay. For a complete list, check out *Buzz* and the *Gay and Lesbian Times,* both widely available in the neighborhood.

**Brass Rail** ( ☎ 619-298-2233; 3796 Fifth Ave) The city's oldest gay bar has a different music theme nightly, from Latin to African to Top 40. It also gets its share of straight folk and has lots of games to play, including pinball, pool and darts.

**Number One Fifth Ave** (☎ 619-299-1911; 3845 Fifth Ave) If you're looking for a friendly neighborhood joint, this is the place.

**Flicks** (☎ 619-297-2056; 1017 University Ave) A few doors down from Rich's (right), Flicks is a conventional video bar dominated by big screens. It's mostly a place to hang out and nurse a drink, sort of like Starbucks with booze.

**Alibi** (☎ 619-295-0881; 1403 University Ave) All the straight people in Hillcrest who go out drinking – young, old, rich and poor – pass through the doors of Alibi, earning it the nickname the 'Star Wars Bar.'

## ENTERTAINMENT

The free weekly *San Diego Reader* and *San Diego Union Tribune*'s Night & Day section hit the stands each Thursday; both have comprehensive listings, and reviews of movies, theater, galleries and music gigs. The nightlife scene for gay men and lesbians is small but lively, and, predictably, concentrated in Hillcrest.

The San Diego Performing Arts League operates **Times Arts Tix** (Map pp240-1; ☎ 619-497-5000; www.sandiegoperforms.com), which sells half-price tickets for same-day evening or next-day matinee performances of theater, music and dance, as well as full-price tickets to most major events in the area. You'll find its booth in the little Horton Plaza park on Broadway. Call **Ticketmaster** (☎ 619-220-8497; www.ticketmaster.com) for other event information and to book tickets; it handles mid-size and major productions.

### Nightclubs & Live Music

**Casbah** (Map pp240-1; ☎ 619-232-4355; 2501 Kettner Blvd) Near Little Italy and the airport, this is a good place to see alternative rock bands. It has couches, pinball machines and dimly lit alcoves if you don't feel like dancing. Call ahead to learn who's playing. There's usually a $5 to $12 cover charge.

**Croce's Restaurant & Jazz Bar** and **Croce's Top Hat Bar & Grille** (Map pp240-1; ☎ 619-233-4355; 818 Fifth Ave) Both Gaslamp venues are operated by singer Jim Croce's widow, who has made her own mark as one of San Diego's top club owners. Aside from hosting great nightly jazz, blues and R&B performers, both bars serve good food (mains $15 to $25).

**Café Sevilla** (Map pp240-1; ☎ 619-233-5979; 555 Fifth Ave) If you like Latin music, Sevilla has

live performers and dancing most nights. It also has flamenco and tango dinner shows (p263).

**Olé Madrid** (Map pp240-1; ☎ 619-557-0146; 751 Fifth Ave) Another Spanish-style restaurant, this one has DJs spinning music varying from funk to acid jazz; call ahead.

**On Broadway** (Map pp240-1; ☎ 619-231-0011; 615 Broadway) Open to the public only on Friday and Saturday nights, this nightclub occupies a former bank building, and is the place to go when you're dressed up and want to impress your date on a big dance floor.

**Onyx Room** and **Thin** (Map pp240-1; ☎ 619-235-6699; 852 Fifth Ave) The candle-lit Onyx is a downstairs jazz lounge; Thin is an upstairs bar that's contemporary, sleek and minimalist in design, great for cocktails and conversation. Wear nice shoes.

**Club Montage** (Map pp242-3; ☎ 619-294-9590; 2028 Hancock St; ⓨ Fri & Sat) Just southwest of Old Town, Montage is one of San Diego's hippest cathedrals of dance, with a crowd that's young, trendy, good-looking and gay on Saturdays, straight on Fridays. It's possibly the biggest club in San Diego, with three floors, three bars, two dance floors and a rooftop sushi bar. Closed weeknights.

**Rich's** (Map pp242-3; ☎ 619-295-2195; 1051 University Ave; ⓨ Tue-Sun) DJs shower the crowd with Latin, techno, pop and house at one of San Diego's biggest gay dance clubs, in Hillcrest.

### Classical Music & Opera

When you've tired of the beach, trade surf and sand for Bach and Beethoven at the San Diego Symphony. Also see p290.

**San Diego Symphony** (Map pp240-1; ☎ 619-235-0804; www.sandiegosymphony.com; 750 B St; tickets $15-60) The city's accomplished orchestra presents classical and family concerts, as well as the innovative Light Bulb Series, an interactive program intended to demystify classical music; both take place at the Civic Center in **Copley Symphony Hall** (Map pp240-1; 750 B Street). In summer the symphony moves outdoors to the **Navy Pier** (Map pp240-1; 960 N Harbor Dr) for its more light-hearted Summer Pops season.

**San Diego Chamber Orchestra** (☎ 888-848-7326, 760-753-6402; www.sdco.org; tickets $20-35) High-caliber performances of small orchestral works are the hallmarks of the chamber ensemble, whose season runs from October to April. Venues range from **St Paul's Cathedral** (2728 Sixth Ave) on the western edge of Balboa

Park to the Sherwood Auditorium at the **Museum of Contemporary Art** (Map p247; 700 Prospect St) in La Jolla, and even a country club in Rancho Santa Fe, an hour north of downtown.

**San Diego Opera** (SDO; ☎ 619-570-1100; www.sd opera.com; seats $20-160) Known to rival its LA counterpart for high-quality, eclectic programming, the SDO has hosted such stars as Placido Domingo, José Carreras and Cecilia Bartoli. Its season runs from January to May, with performances at the **Civic Theater** (Map pp240-1; ☎ 619-570-1100; 202 Third Ave at B St, Community Concourse). Discount tickets are occasionally available from Times Arts Tix.

For light opera and musical theater pieces, check out the reasonably priced **Lyric Opera San Diego** ( ☎ 619-239-8836; www.lyricoperasandiego .com; tickets $17-27), which performs at the Casa del Prado in Balboa Park.

## Cinemas

Check local papers or call theaters for show times. The main downtown cinemas are the **Regal United Artists Horton Plaza 14** (Map pp240-1; ☎ 619-234-8602), at Horton Plaza, and **Pacific Gaslamp 15** (Map pp240-1; ☎ 619-232-0400; 701 Fifth & G Sts). Both show current release movies.

**Hillcrest Cinemas** (Map pp242-3; ☎ 619-819-0236; 3965 Fifth Ave), in Hillcrest, shows new independent films and European releases.

## Theater

Theater thrives in San Diego and is one of the city's greatest cultural attractions. Book tickets from the theater or with one of the agencies listed in the introduction to this section. Venues include:

**Civic Theater** (Map pp240-1; ☎ 619-570-1100; 202 Third Ave at B St, Community Concourse)

**Horton Grand Theatre** (Map pp240-1; ☎ 619-234-9583; 444 Fourth Ave)

**La Jolla Playhouse** (Map p247; ☎ 619-550-1010; www.lajollaplayhouse.com; UCSD)

**Lamb's Players Theater** (Map p239; ☎ 619-437-0600; www.lambsplayers.org; 1142 Orange Ave, Coronado)

**San Diego Junior Theatre** (Map pp242-3; ☎ 619-239-8355; www.juniortheatre.com; Casa del Prado, Balboa Park)

**San Diego Repertory Theatre** (Map pp240-1; ☎ 619-231-3586; www.sandiegorep.com; 79 Horton Plaza)

**Spreckels Theater** (Map pp240-1; ☎ 619-235-9500; www.spreckels.net; 121 Broadway)

**Theatre in Old Town** (Map pp242-3; ☎ 619-688-2494; www.theatreinoldtown.com; 4040 Twiggs St)

Worth a special mention are Balboa Park's **Old Globe Theaters** (Map pp242-3; ☎ 619-239-2255, 619-234-5623; www.theglobetheaters.org; tickets $22-60), where visitors to the 1935–36 Pacific-California Exposition enjoyed 40-minute renditions of Shakespeare's greatest hits. Saved from demolition in 1937, the theaters became home to a popular summer series of Shakespearian plays, which were performed in full. In 1978 the whole complex was destroyed by an arson fire, but was rebuilt in the style of the original 17th-century Old Globe in England. It reopened in 1982, winning a Tony award in 1984 for its ongoing contribution to theater arts. Between the three venues here – Old Globe, Cassius Carter Stage and the outdoor Lowell Davies Festival Theater – there are performances most evenings and matinees on weekends.

## Sports

The San Diego Padres Major League Baseball team began the 2004 season in the new **Petco Park** (Map pp240-1; ☎ 619-795-5000, 888-697-2373, for tickets 877-374-2784; www.padres.com; 100 Park Blvd; tickets $6-49) stadium right in the middle of downtown San Diego. Despite the obvious potential for traffic snarls, the city has embraced the park and even begun calling the surrounding neighborhood the 'Ballpark District.' The season runs from April to September. Tickets are usually available at the gate unless it's a game crucial to the standings, or the LA Dodgers are in town on a Friday or Saturday night. You can buy tickets by phone, online, or in person (no service charge) from 8:30am to 5pm Monday to Friday, 10am to 4pm Saturday on nongame days; if there's a game, the box office remains open until an hour into play.

The San Diego Chargers National Football League team share **Qualcomm Stadium** (Map p239; ☎ 619-280-2121; www.chargers.com; 9449 Friars Rd; tickets from $25), in Mission Valley (there's a San Diego Trolley stop right in front). It was originally named for sports journalist Jack Murphy, who was instrumental in getting the park built. He also worked to bring the Chargers football team to town in 1961 and the Padres baseball team in 1968. Football season lasts from August to January. Buy tickets through Ticketmaster, by phone, online, or in person (no service charges) at the stadium, Gate C,

**DETOUR: TIJUANA, MEXICO**

Rita Hayworth was discovered here. Carlos Santana began his career in its nightclubs. And one of the world's great culinary inventions, the Caesar salad, hails from nowhere other than – drum roll please – yes, Tijuana, that grubby, noisy, frenzied, but oh-so-tantalizing city of two million souls, just a hop, skip and a jump from San Diego.

During Prohibition in the 1920s, Tijuana (TJ, for short) was the darling of the Hollywood crowd. These days, tequila and beer exert their siren song to college students, sailors and other revelers who, each weekend, descend upon the rollicking bars and nightclubs of Avenida Revolución (La Revo), the main tourist strip. By day, the shops attract bargain hunters for everything from liquor to shoes to pharmaceuticals. Competition is fierce, and the constant hustle from storefront vendors can quickly grate on your nerves. No need to change your money, though: nearly all businesses accept US dollars. A good place for quality crafts is **Pasaje Mexico** (Avenida Revolución, btwn 5th & 6th next to the boot shop).

Once you've 'done' La Revo, be sure to venture beyond for a more interesting and often surprisingly sophisticated side of Tijuana. Pick up a map from a **visitors center** ( ☎ 664-683-1405; www.tijuanaonline.org) that shows the precise locations of everything listed here; you'll find branches right by the pedestrian and car border crossings, as well as on La Revo between Calles 3a and 4a. You can also take a one-hour guided walking tour ($5), led by guides from the visitors center. Tours visit markets and historical sights, and provide a good overview of TJ's history and culture. Sign up at any visitors center.

Wine aficionados should head to **Vinícola LA Cetto** ( ☎ 664-685-3031; Avenida Cañon Johnson 2108) for a chance to sample vintages from the nearby Valle de Guadalupe rarely available outside of Mexico. Architecture fans may want to visit the **Catedral de Nuestra Señora de Guadalupe** (Avenida Niños Héroes & Calle 2a), Tijuana's oldest church. For a cultural fix, make a beeline to the excellent **Museo de las Californias** ( ☎ 664-687-9600; Paseo de los Héroes & Miña; admission $2; ☷ 10am-6pm Tue-Fri, 10am-7pm Sat & Sun), which has engaging exhibits chronicling the intriguing history of Baja California from prehistoric times to the present. The museum is part of the **Centro Cultural de Tijuana**, which has a schedule of classical concerts, theater and dance recitals that undermine TJ's popular image as a cultural wasteland. Nearby, the locals stock up on rice, beans and powdered chili – from pussycat mild to hellishly hot – at the indoor-outdoor market **Mercado Hidalgo**, a colorful, fun place to poke around.

TJ also has a surprisingly interesting dining scene. Good choices on La Revo include the old-time **Café La Especial** ( ☎ 664-685-6654; Avenida Revolucíon 18; breakfast & lunch $5, dinner $10-15), in a shopping arcade below Hotel Lafayette, where you can enjoy Mexican classics in the cavernous, woodsy setting. **Chiki Jai** ( ☎ 664-685-4955; Avenida Revolucíon & Calle 7a; mains around $10), in business since 1947, used to be the hangout of jai alai players and specializes in Spanish food. Beyond the tourist strip, excellent choices include the classy **La Espadaña** ( ☎ 664-634-1488; Blvd Sánchez Taboada 10813; mains $8-20) and the high-end **Cien Años** ( ☎ 664-634-7262; Avenida José María Velasco 1407; mains from $15; ☷ dinner), which has more than 100 tequilas, and recipes going back to the Aztecs and Mayans. It's dressy and requires reservations.

For details about traveling between San Diego and Tijuana, see p270.

from 9am to 6pm Monday to Friday, 10am to 4pm Saturday.

The **San Diego Sports Arena** (Map p239; ☎ 619-224-4176; www.sandiegoarena.com; 3500 Sports Arena Blvd) is where the San Diego Sockers play soccer and the San Diego Gulls play ice hockey. Call Ticketmaster for event tickets or visit the online box office (no fee; call for hours). It's also the venue for any big rock concerts visiting town. Be aware that the neighborhood may be a little rough after dark.

## SHOPPING

Every museum and visitor attraction has a gift shop: souvenir hunters will find a stuffed Shamu at SeaWorld, a realistic-looking rubber snake at the zoo, or a reprinted historical photo at the Museum of San Diego History. The Spanish Village area of Balboa Park is a good place to find paintings (mostly watercolors) of the San Diego area.

Horton Plaza Center (p236) has the highest concentration of shops, most of them chain

SAN DIEGO

**SAN DIEGO**

---

**CROSSING THE US-MEXICAN BORDER**

Every day an average of 226,000 people and 82,000 cars cross the US-Mexican border at San Ysidro, making it the world's busiest border crossing. Open 24 hours per day, the border is about 20 miles south of downtown San Diego and a 10-minute walk from Avenida Revolución, Tijuana's main tourist drag. You can cross the San Ysidro border on foot, by car or by bus from either side. The alternative crossing at Mesa de Otay, 5 miles east of San Ysidro, is open 6am to 10pm. There is no public transportation to Mesa de Otay.

US citizens or permanent residents not intending to go past the border zone (in other words, beyond Ensenada), or to stay in the border zone for more than 72 hours, don't need a visa to enter Tijuana. The same is true for citizens of western EU countries, as well as Australia and New Zealand. However, due to increased security, US citizens are required to carry proof of citizenship, such as a passport, a certified copy of a birth certificate and photo ID, or US naturalization papers and photo ID. A driver's license is no longer sufficient proof, but a valid license can serve as photo ID. Non-citizens or permanent residents can be subject to the full immigration procedure upon returning to the US, so bring your passport and USA visa (if you need one, see p356).

The easiest way to get to Tijuana from San Diego is to take the San Diego Trolley and walk across the border. Due to heightened security, expect delays (10 to 40 minutes) when returning to the US on foot.

**San Diego Trolley**

The San Diego Trolley Blue Line is the cheapest, easiest and most efficient way to travel to the border from central San Diego. Trolleys leave every 15 or 30 minutes from early morning to late at night and around the clock on Saturday ($2, 45 minutes). The terminus is on the US side of the border, from where you continue on foot.

---

stores and many of them pricey. The major department stores – Macy's, Nordstrom, Robinsons-May Neiman-Marcus, Saks Fifth Ave – are at Fashion Valley shopping center (see p255).

For the best hipster, vintage and thrift shopping, head to Hillcrest.

**Mint** (Map pp242-3; ☎ 619-291-6468; 525 University Ave) Shoe fetishists love this stylin' shoe store, where you can find up-to-the-minute footwear for $30 to $130. It's open to 10pm Friday and Saturday.

**Wear It Again Sam** (Map pp242-3; ☎ 619-299-0185; 3823 Fifth Ave) There are several cool thrift stores on Fifth Ave, but this place sells the best vintage gear – and it's well organized.

**Buffalo Exchange** (Map pp242-3; ☎ 858-273-6227; 3862 Fifth Ave) Buffalo stocks both vintage and contemporary fashions, including designer name brands. If you're out of money and want to sell your Prada shoes for cash, this is the place.

**Adams Avenue** (store directory ☎ 619-282-7329; www.gothere.com/AdamsAve) San Diego's main 'antique row,' Adams Ave cuts across some of San Diego's less-visited neighborhoods. The greatest concentration of shops is in Normal Heights between I-805 and I-15. The area has dozens of shops, with furniture, art and antiques from around the world.

**Kobey's Swap Meet** (Map pp244-5; ☎ 619-523-2700, 619-224-4176; admission Fri 50¢, Sat & Sun $1; ☼ 7am-3pm Fri-Sun; Ⓟ) A massive flea market in the parking lot of the San Diego Sports Arena, this is the place to get really cheap stuff. On sale are new and used items, including sunglasses, clothing, jewelry, produce, flowers and plants, tools and furniture.

## GETTING THERE & AWAY
### Air

Because of the limited length of runways (which you will notice as you land), most flights to **San Diego International Airport-Lindbergh Field** (SAN; ☎ 619-231-2100; www.san.org) are domestic. The airfield sits right in the middle of the city, three miles west of downtown. Coming from overseas, you'll change flights – and clear US Customs – at one of the major US gateway airports, such as LA, Chicago, New York or Miami.

The standard one-way fare between LA and San Diego is about $100. The flight from LA takes only about 35 minutes – but

## Car & Motorcycle

Unless you're planning an extended stay or thorough exploration of Tijuana, taking a car across the border is probably more hassle than it's worth. If you do decide to drive, though, the most important thing to do is get Mexican car insurance either beforehand – for instance through your local American Automobile Association (AAA) office – or at the border crossing (available in numerous offices right at the Via de San Ysidro and Camino de la Plaza exits off I-5; from about $8 per day, depending on the age and make of your car). Cars rented in the US may not be driven into Mexico. Heightened post 9/11 border security has made the long waits upon returning to the US even worse. Pack plenty of patience. The alternative crossing at Mesa de Otay is much less congested, but further from town.

The best thing may be to leave your car on the US side of the border and either walk or take a shuttle across. Several parking lots are located just off the Camino de la Plaza exit (the last US exit) off I-5.

A popular lot is **Border Station Parking** (4570 Camino de la Plaza), which charges $7 per day. Also here is a small tourist information kiosk with maps and pamphlets.

## Walking

To cross the border on foot from San Ysidro, simply take the pedestrian bridge, then pass through the turnstiles and you're on Mexican soil. There's a tourist office about 150ft along the walkway and another by the yellow taxi stand.

To reach Avenida Revolución, turn right just before the taxi stand, then continue west past souvenir hawkers and taco stands to a large outdoor mall called Plaza Viva Tijuana. From its far end, another pedestrian bridge leads across the Río Tijuana. From here continue west along Calle 1a (Calle Comercio), past countless more souvenir shops, to the foot of Avenida Revolución. The entire walk takes 10 to 15 minutes.

SAN DIEGO

by the time you drive to the airport, check in, clear security and board the flight, you could have made the two-hour drive (except during rush hour).

If you're flying to/from other US cities, it's nearly as cheap to fly directly in and out of San Diego as it is to LA. Airlines serving San Diego include Aeromexico, Alaska, America West, American, Continental, Delta, Frontier, Jet Blue, Northwest, Southwest, United and US Airways.

## Bus

For bus travel, **Greyhound** (Map pp240-1; ☎ 619-239-3266; 120 W Broadway) serves San Diego from cities across North America. The station has lockers and telephones.

The standard one-way/round-trip fare to/from LA is $16/27; buses depart almost every half hour and the journey takes 2¼ to 2½ hours, depending on the number of stops en route. There is a bus to Anaheim (location of Disneyland) that runs seven times per day for about the same prices (and about the same trip duration).

Services between San Francisco and San Diego require a transfer in LA and cost

$61/120 one-way/round-trip. The journey takes 11 hours, and there are eight departures daily. There are two direct buses to Las Vegas and seven more that require you to change in either LA or San Bernardino. The trip takes 8½ to 12 hours and costs $51/92 one-way/round-trip, with a special half-price 'casino-rate' round-trip; call for details.

Greyhound also offers direct services from San Diego to Tijuana, across the border in Mexico, where you can connect to other buses serving destinations throughout Mexico. There are nine buses daily to Tijuana; the trip takes just over an hour and costs $5/8 one-way/round-trip (see p269).

## Car & Motorcycle

Car-rental prices are about the same in LA and San Diego, usually $35 to $40 per day. From LA, take I-5, the San Diego Fwy, south to downtown. Rush-hour traffic gets heavy on the freeways around LA and San Diego between 7am and 10am and 3pm to 7pm.

## Train

Amtrak (p369) trains arrive and depart from the **Santa Fe depot** (Map pp240-1; 1050 Kettner

Blvd) at the western end of C St. The *Pacific Surfliner* makes up to 11 round-trips to LA; up to five trains continue on to Santa Barbara. Transfer in LA for trains to other US destinations (p365).

Standard coach fares between San Diego and LA are $26 each way and the trip takes 2¾ hours. Trips to/from Santa Barbara also cost $26 each way (5½ hours).

## GETTING AROUND

Many people get around by car, but you can reach most places on public transportation. Metropolitan buses and the trolley lines are run by Metropolitan Transit Service (MTS), and several other bus companies serve surrounding areas. All sorts of local public transportation tickets, maps and information are available from the **Transit Store** (Map pp240-1; ☎ 619-234-1060; 102 Broadway at 1st Ave; ☺ 9am-5pm Mon-Fri). It sells the Day Tripper Transit Pass (one day $5, four consecutive days $15), which is good for unlimited travel on local buses and the trolley.

### To/From the Airport

Bus No 992 – nicknamed The Flyer – operates at 10- to 15-minute intervals between the airport and downtown ($2.25). Buses leave between 4:58am and 12:40am and make several stops along Broadway (beginning at First and Broadway) before heading north on Harbor Dr to the airport.

Several companies operate door-to-door shuttles from all three airport terminals. Per-person fares depend on the distance traveled; figure about $12 to Mission Valley's Hotel Circle, $10 to Old Town or downtown, and $13 to La Jolla. For some of the shorter trips, taxis charge only slightly more and may therefore be preferable, especially if there's more than one of you traveling.

If you're going to the airport, call the shuttle company a day or two ahead to make arrangements for a pick-up time and location. **Cloud 9 Shuttle** ( ☎ 619-505-4950, 800-974-8885; www.cloud9shuttle.com) is the most established company; others include **Xpress Shuttle** ( ☎ 619-295-1900; www.xpressshuttle.com), **Airport Shuttle** ( ☎ 619-234-4403) and **Access Shuttle** ( ☎ 619-282-1515, 800-690-9090; www.access-shuttle.com).

### Boat

San Diego Harbor Excursion operates the **Coronado Ferry** (Map pp240-1; ☎ 619-234-4111, 800-

442-7847; www.sdhe.com; 1050 N Harbor Dr at Broadway). Ferries depart every hour on the hour from 9am to 9pm Sunday to Thursday, to 10pm Friday and Saturday ($2.25 one-way). Ferries leave Coronado on the half hour.

The same company operates a **water taxi** ( ☎ 619-235-8294; ☺ 2-10pm Mon-Fri, 11am-11pm Sat & Sun). It makes a regular connection between Seaport Village and Coronado ($6), where it stops at the Ferry Landing Marketplace and Glorietta Bay. It also makes on-call trips to Shelter Island, Harbor Island, Chula Vista and South Bay.

### Bus

The MTS network covers most of the metropolitan area, North County, La Jolla and the beaches, and is most convenient if you're going to/from downtown and not staying out late at night. Pick up the *Regional Transit Map* from the Transit Store (left).

For route and fare information, call ☎ 619-233-3004 or 800-266-6883; operators are available 5:30am to 8:30pm Monday to Friday, 8am to 5pm Saturday and Sunday (note that the 800-number works only within San Diego; otherwise you'll get LA bus information). For 24-hour automated information, call ☎ 619-685-4900. For online route planning, visit www.sdcommute.com.

Fares cost $2.25 for most trips, including a transfer that is good for up to two hours; express routes cost $2.50. Local buses with limited service cost $1.75. Exact fare is required on all buses.

Useful routes to/from downtown include the following:

**No 3** Balboa Park, UCSD
**No 4** National City
**No 5** Old Town, Little Italy
**No 7** Seaport Village, Balboa Park and Zoo
**No 11** Hillcrest, Adams Ave Antique Row
**No 25** Hillcrest, Fashion Valley
**No 30** Pacific Beach, University Towne Centre
**No 34** Old Town, Mission Bay, Sports Arena, Mission Beach, Belmont Park, Pacific Beach, Birch Aquarium, UCSD, University Towne Centre
**No 35** Old Town, Ocean Beach
**No 901** Coronado

### Car

All the big-name car-rental companies have desks at the airport, but the lesser-known ones are cheaper. Shop around – prices vary widely, even from day to day within the same company. The western terminal at the airport has free direct-phones to a number of car-rental companies – you can call several and then get a courtesy bus to the agency. Also, car rentals are as cheap or cheaper in LA, so you may want to get one there.

If you plan to visit Tijuana, check with the car-rental company to make sure the insurance will cover the car in Mexico. Most policies do not.

For contact information on the big-name companies, including Avis, Budget and Hertz, see p367. Some of the smaller, independent companies have lower rates, such as **California Rent a Car** (Map pp240-1; ☎ 619-238-9999; www.californiarent-a-car.com; 904 W Grape St) and **West Coast Rent a Car** (Map pp240-1; ☎ 619-544-0606; www.westcoastrentacar.net; 834 W Grape St), both in Little Italy. Also consider **Fox Rent a Car** ( ☎ 619-692-0300, 800-225-4369; www.foxrentacar.com), at the airport.

### Taxi
Fares cost an initial $1.70, then $2 per subsequent mile. Established companies include the following:

**American Cab** ( ☎ 619-234-1111)
**Orange Cab** ( ☎ 619-291-3333; www.orangecabsandiego.com)
**Yellow Cab** ( ☎ 619-234-6161; www.driveu.com)

### Train
A commuter rail service, the *Coaster,* leaves the Santa Fe train depot downtown and runs up the coast to North County, with stops in Solana Beach, Encinitas, Carlsbad and Oceanside. In the metropolitan area, it stops at the Sorrento Valley station (where there's a connecting shuttle to the University of California at San Diego; UCSD) and Old Town. Tickets are available from vending machines at stations and must be validated prior to boarding. Fares cost $3.75 to $5.25; machines give change.

There are 11 daily trains in each direction Monday to Friday; the first trains leave Oceanside at 5:23am and the Santa Fe depot downtown at 6:33am; the last ones depart at 5:28pm and 6:42pm, respectively. On Saturday, there are four trains only. There's no service on Sunday. For information, contact **North San Diego County Transit District** ( ☎ 619-233-3004, 800-266-6883 from North County; www.gonctd.com).

### Trolley
Two trolley lines run to/from the downtown terminal near the Santa Fe train depot. The Blue Line goes south to the San Ysidro (Mexico) border and north to Old Town, then continues east through Mission Valley to Qualcomm Stadium and as far as the Mission San Diego de Alcalá. The Orange Line goes east, past the Convention Center to El Cajon and Santee. Trolleys run between 4:20am and 11pm daily at 15-minute intervals during the day, and every 30 minutes in the evening. The Blue Line continues limited all-night service on Saturday, one every two hours or so; call for schedules. Fares vary with distance, but peak at $3. Tickets are dispensed from vending machines on the station platforms and are valid for three hours from the time of purchase. Machines give change.

# COASTAL SAN DIEGO

Waves crash against the white-sand beaches of coastal San Diego, perfect for surfing, sunning, swimming or just gazing at the horizon. Don't expect any surprises: it looks just like it does in the movies.

San Diego's beach communities feel a world away from the office towers of downtown. Coronado, with its famous 1888 Hotel del Coronado, sits across San Diego Bay, accessible via a long bridge or a short ferry ride. At the entrance to the bay, Point Loma has great views of sea and city from the Cabrillo National Monument. Mission Bay, northwest of downtown, has lagoons, parks and facilities for recreational activities from water skiing to camping. The nearby coast – with Ocean Beach, Mission Beach and Pacific Beach – epitomizes the SoCal beach scene, while La Jolla, a little further north, is an upscale seaside community, popular with the skirt-and-sweater set and home of the University of California at San Diego (UCSD).

San Diego's downtown sights are covered in the previous Downtown & Around section, as are information, tours, and festivals and events that encompass all of San Diego.

## INFORMATION
### Bookstores
These two La Jolla bookstores not only have good selections, they also host readings and author events; call for schedules.

**DG Wills** (Map p247; ☎ 858-456-1800; 7461
Girard Ave)
**Warwick's** (Map p247; ☎ 858-454-0347; 2812 Girard
Ave) For the latest titles on everything.

## Money

You'll find ATMs in the business districts
of San Diego's beach towns.
**Travelex** (Map p239; ☎ 858-457-2412; University
Towne Centre; ☺ 10am-6pm Mon-Fri , 10am-4pm Sat,
11am-4pm Sun) Foreign currency exchange at an inland La
Jolla shopping mall.

## Post

**Post office** (Map p247; ☎ 858-459-5476; www.usps
.com; 1140 Wall St; ☺ 7:30am-5pm Mon, 8:30am-5pm
Tue-Fri, 9am-1pm Sat) Main branch.

## Tourist Information

**La Jolla Visitor Center** (Map p247; ☎ 619-236-
1212; www.sandiego.org; 7966 Herschell; ☺ 9am-5pm
Mon-Sat, 10am-5pm Sun) Operated by the San Diego
Convention & Visitors Bureau, this is the secondary branch
of the official downtown visitor center.

# SIGHTS

There's so much to see and do, but where to
begin? We've organized this section heading
from north to south.

## La Jolla                       Map p247

Immaculately landscaped parks, white-
sand coves, upscale boutiques and a perfect
location atop cliffs that drop to deep, clear
blue waters make it easy to understand
why 'La Jolla' translates from Spanish as
'the jewel.' But Native Americans who
inhabited the area from 10,000 years ago
to the mid-19th century called the place
'mut la Hoya, la Hoya' – the place of many
caves. Regardless of the name's origin it's
pronounced 'la *hoy*-ya,' and it's a lovely
place to spend the day. Bus No 34 connects
La Jolla to downtown via the Old Town
transit center.

The area was subdivided in the 1880s, but
started developing when Ellen Browning
Scripps moved here in 1897. The newspaper
heiress acquired much of the land along
Prospect St, which she subsequently donated
to various community uses. Not only did
she support local institutions, such as the
**Bishop's School** (cnr Prospect St & La Jolla Blvd) and
the **La Jolla Woman's Club** (715 Silverado St), she also
had them designed by Irving Gill, who set

the architectural tone of the community –
an unadorned Mediterranean style char-
acterized by arches, colonnades, palm trees,
red-tile roofs and pale stucco.

The surrounding area is home to UCSD,
several renowned research institutes and
a new-money residential area called the
Golden Triangle, bounded by I-5, I-805
and Hwy 52. The space-age church in this
area, which you see from I-5, is a Mormon
Temple, completed in 1993.

### DOWNTOWN LA JOLLA

The compact downtown area sits atop
cliffs surrounded on three sides by the
ocean. Although you catch views of the
Pacific's blue waters here and there between
buildings, there is little aesthetic interaction
between the heart of downtown and the
sea. The main crossroads, Prospect St
and Girard Ave, are known for the 'three
Rs' – restaurants, rugs and real estate. La
Jolla is San Diego's best place for boutique
shopping: galleries sell paintings, sculpture
and decorative items, and small shops fill
the gaps between Banana Republic, Armani
Exchange and Saks Fifth Avenue, which is
on Wall St near Herschel Ave. Look for big
names in fashion along Silverado St west
of Girard Ave.

For a bit of old La Jolla, head southwest
from Girard Ave along Prospect St. Number
780 Prospect St, aka Wisteria Cottage, was
originally Ellen Browning Scripps guest
cottage and has been faithfully renovated
to Irving Gill's original design.

Around the corner from the cottage, the
**La Jolla Historical Society** ( ☎ 858-459-5335; 7846 Eads
Ave; ☺ noon-4:30pm Tue & Thu) has vintage photos
and beach memorabilia (think old bathing
costumes and lifeguard buoys). Further
southwest on Prospect St, you'll find St James
Episcopal Church, the La Jolla Recreation
Center and the Bishop's School, which were
all built in the early 20th century.

La Jolla's **Museum of Contemporary Art**
( ☎ 858-454-3541; www.mcasd.org; 700 Prospect St; admission $4; free 1st Tue & 3rd Sun of month; ☺ 11am-7pm
Thu, 11am-5pm Fri-Tue) gets world-class exhibitions. Originally designed by Irving Gill in
1916 as the home of Ellen Browning Scripps,
the building has been renovated by Phila-
delphia-born postmodern architect Robert Venturi and has an Andy Goldsworthy
sculpture out front.

Read daily newspapers from around the globe at the quiet and civilized **Athenaeum Music & Arts Library** ( ☎ 858-454-5872; 1008 Wall St at Girard Ave; ☯ 10am-5:30pm Tue-Sat, 10am-8:30pm Wed), which also displays small art exhibits. Lovely.

### THE COAST
Private property along the coast of La Jolla restricts coastal access, and parking is very limited in places, but there is a wonderful walking path that skirts the shoreline for half a mile. The path's western end begins at the **Children's Pool**, where a jetty (funded by none other than Ellen Browning Scripps) protects the beach from big waves.

Originally intended to give La Jolla's youth a safe place to frolic, the beach is now more popular with sea lions, which you can view up close as they lounge on the shore. Kids love it. East of the Children's Pool, La Jolla's only 'skyscraper' – the infamous, ugly, mid-1960s-vintage 939 Coast Building – stands in blatant disregard for its neighbors and forever blocks their views of the sea. The apartment building's construction sparked the implementation of current city codes, which limit new structures west of I-5 to a height of 30ft.

Atop Point La Jolla, at the path's eastern end, **Ellen Browning Scripps Park** is a tidy expanse of green lawns and palm trees of **La Jolla Cove** to the north. The cove's gem of a beach provides access to some of the best snorkeling around; it's also popular with rough-water swimmers.

Look for the white buoys offshore from Point La Jolla north to Scripps Pier (visible to the north) that mark the **San Diego-La Jolla Underwater Park**, a protected zone with a variety of marine life, kelp forests, reefs and canyons (see Diving & Snorkeling, p281). Waves have carved a series of caves into the sandstone cliffs east of the cove. The largest is called Sunny Jim Cave, which you can access for a fee of $4 from the **Cave Store** ( ☎ 858-459-0746; 1325 Cave St; ☯ 9am-5pm).

If you like to surf and know what you're doing, head to **Windansea Beach**, two miles south of downtown (take La Jolla Blvd south and turn west on Nautilus St). However, some of the locals at Windansea are aggressive toward outsiders. If you do come, the surf's consistent peak (a powerful reef break that's not for beginners) works best at medium to low tide. You'll find a more civilized welcome immediately south, at the foot of Palomar St, **Big Rock**, California's version of Hawaii's Pipeline, which has steep, hollow, gnarly tubes. The name comes from the large chunk of reef protruding just offshore – a great spot for **tidepooling** at low tide.

### LA JOLLA SHORES
Called simply 'the Shores,' the area northeast of La Jolla Cove is where La Jolla's cliffs meet the wide, sandy beaches that stretch north to Del Mar (p291). Primarily residential, the Shores is home to the members-only La Jolla Beach and Tennis Club (its orange tile roof is visible from La Jolla Cove) and Kellogg City Park, whose beachside playground is good for families. To reach the beach, take La Jolla Shores Dr north from Torrey Pines Rd and turn west onto Ave de la Playa. The waves here are gentle enough for beginner surfers, and kayakers can launch from the shore without much problem.

Some of the best **beaches** in the county are north of the Shores in **Torrey Pines City Park**, which covers the coastline from the Salk Institute (p276) up to the Torrey Pines State Reserve (p276). At extreme low tides (about twice per year), you can walk from the Shores north to Del Mar along the beach. Hang-gliders and paragliders launch into the sea breezes rising over the cliffs at **Torrey Pines Gliderport**, at the end of Torrey Pines Scenic Dr. It's a beautiful sight – tandem flights are available if you can't resist trying it (p282). Down below at **Blacks Beach**, bathing suits are technically required but essentially absent at this predominantly gay beach.

### BIRCH AQUARIUM AT SCRIPPS
Marine scientists were working at the Birch Aquarium at Scripps Institution of Oceanography (SIO) as early as 1910 and, helped by donations from the ever-generous Scripps family, the institute has grown to be one of the world's largest marine research institutions. It is now a part of UCSD, and its pier is a landmark on the La Jolla coast.

A public education project of SIO, **Birch Aquarium** ( ☎ 858-534-3474; www.aquarium.ucsd.edu; 2300 Exhibition Way; adult/child $10/6.50; ☯ 9am-5pm),

**SAN DIEGO**

off N Torrey Pines Rd, has brilliant displays on the marine sciences and of marine life. The Hall of Fishes has more than 30 fish tanks, simulating marine environments from the Pacific Northwest to tropical seas. For $4 extra, you can take Morphis: Movieride, a hydraulic-motion ride with accompanying video that simulates swimming with dolphins; it's really cool if you're 12. If you're interested in studying oceanography or seeing the campus, pick up the self-guided campus-tour brochure. To get to the aquarium, take bus No 34 from downtown and La Jolla.

The SIO is not to be confused with the **Scripps Research Institute** (10550 Torrey Pines Rd), a private, nonprofit biomedical research organization.

### SALK INSTITUTE
In 1960 Jonas Salk, the polio-prevention pioneer, founded the **Salk Institute** ( ☎ 858-453-4100 ext 1200; www.salk.edu; 10010 N Torrey Pines Rd) for biological and biomedical research. San Diego County donated 27 acres of land, the March of Dimes provided financial support and Louis Kahn designed the building. Completed in 1965, it is regarded as a modern masterpiece, with its classically proportioned travertine marble plaza and cubist, mirror-glass laboratory blocks framing a perfect view of the Pacific, and the fountain in the courtyard symbolizing the River of Life. The Salk Institute attracts the best scientists to work in a research-only environment. The facilities have been expanded, with new laboratories designed by Jack McAllister, a follower of Kahn's work. You can tour the Salk Institute free with a volunteer guide at 11am and noon Monday to Friday; call in advance. Bus Nos 41 and 301 go along N Torrey Pines Rd.

### TORREY PINES STATE RESERVE
Encompassing the land between N Torrey Pines Rd and the ocean from the Torrey Pines Gliderport to Del Mar, this **reserve** ( ☎ 858-755-2063; www.torreypine.org; ☼ 8am-sunset) preserves the last mainland stands of the Torrey pine (Pinus torreyana), a species adapted to sparse rainfall and sandy, stony soils. Steep sandstone gullies are eroded into wonderfully textured surfaces, and the views over the ocean and north to Oceanside are superb, especially at sunset.

The main access road, Torrey Pines Scenic Dr, off N Torrey Pines Rd (bus Nos 41 and 301) at the reserve's northern end, leads to a simple adobe – built as a lodge in 1922 by who else but Ellen Browning Scripps. The lodge now serves as a **visitors center** with good displays on the local flora and fauna. Rangers lead **nature walks** from here at 10am and 2pm on weekends and holidays.

Parking costs $6 per car, but admission is free if you arrive on foot. Several walking trails wind through the reserve and down to the beach. If you want to hike, park near the driving range on N Torrey Pines Rd and take the paved path northwest until you reach a box of trail maps at the beginning of the Broken Arrow Trail.

### UNIVERSITY OF CALIFORNIA, SAN DIEGO
A campus of the University of California, **UCSD** ( ☎ 858-534-2230; www.ucsd.edu) was established in 1960, and now has more than 18,000 students and an excellent academic reputation, particularly for mathematics and science programs. It lies on rolling coastal hills in a parklike setting, surrounded by tall, fragrant eucalyptus trees. Its most distinctive structure is the **Geisel Library**, an upside-down pyramid of glass and concrete, whose namesake, children's author Theodor Geisel, is better known as Dr Seuss, creator of the Cat in the Hat. He and his wife have contributed substantially to the library, which exhibits a collection of his drawings and books on the ground floor.

From the eastern side of the library's second level, an allegorical snake created by artist Alexis Smith winds down a native California plant garden past an enormous marble copy of John Milton's Paradise Lost. The piece is part of the **Stuart Collection** of outdoor sculptures spread around campus. Other works include Niki de Saint Phalle's Sun God, Bruce Nauman's Vices & Virtues (which spells out seven of each in huge neon letters), Robert Irwin's very blue Fence and a forest of talking trees. Most installations are near the Geisel Library, and details are available from the Visual Arts Building or the Price Center, where the **UCSD bookstore** ( ☎ 858-534-7323) has excellent stock and helpful staff. Inside the Mandell Weiss Center for the Performing

Arts, the **La Jolla Playhouse** ( ☎ 858-550-1010; www.lajollaplayhouse.com) is known for its high-quality productions.

The best access to campus is off of La Jolla Village Dr or N Torrey Pines Rd (bus Nos 41 and 301 from downtown); parking is free on weekends.

### SOLEDAD MOUNTAIN

For a 360-degree view of La Jolla, take Nautilus St east from La Jolla Blvd, turn left on La Jolla Scenic Dr and follow it to Soledad Mountain Park. The large cross on top was the subject of an unsuccessful lawsuit in the late 1960s – residents objected to the sectarian religious symbol on publicly owned land.

## Mission Beach & Pacific Beach    Map pp244–5

Lovers of the sea come every day to watch and cheer the setting sun at these perfect sand beaches. No place in San Diego County feels more like the SoCal of the movies than here. Buffed surfers and bronzed bohemians pack the three-mile-long stretch from the South Mission Jetty at the southern end of Mission Beach to Pacific Beach Point at the northern end of Pacific Beach (PB). **Ocean Front Walk**, the beachfront boardwalk that connects the beaches together, gets crowded with joggers, in-line skaters and cyclists anytime of the year, and it's one of the best people-watching venues in San Diego. On a warm summer weekend, oiled bodies, packed like sardines, cover the beach from end to end. Forget about parking around noon; it's not gonna happen. The main north–south road, Mission Blvd, can get so crowded that the police simply close it down.

To get around, consider renting a bike or in-line skates (see Getting Around, p290). **Cheap Rentals** ( ☎ 858-488-9070, 800-941-7761; 3221 & 3685 Mission Blvd at Santa Clara St) has low prices and rents everything from bikes and skates to baby joggers; it also accepts advance reservations, which are crucial in summer if you sleep late. Also check out **Hamel's Beach Rentals** ( ☎ 858-488-5050; 704 Ventura Pl) near the Giant Dipper roller coaster in Mission Beach, but it doesn't accept reservations; arrive early. Rentals cost about $10 for two hours, $20 all day; both companies open at 9am.

Down at Mission Beach at the southern end, many small houses and apartments are rented out for the summer season; the kick-back scene is concentrated in a narrow strip of land between the ocean and Mission Bay. Up in PB the activity extends inland, particularly along Garnet Ave, which is lined with bars, restaurants and used-clothing stores. At the ocean end of Garnet Ave, the Crystal Pier is a mellow place to fish or gaze out to sea.

The surf at Mission Beach is a beach break, making it good for beginners, body boarders and bodysurfers. Things are more demanding around Crystal Pier, where the waves are steep and fast. Tourmaline Surfing Park, at the far northern end of the beach, is especially popular with long boarders. For information about equipment rentals, see p280.

### BELMONT PARK

This family-style **amusement park** ( ☎ 858-488-0668; www.belmontpark.com; admission free) in the middle of Mission Beach has been here since 1925. When it was threatened with demolition in the mid-1990s, concerted community action saved the large indoor pool, known as the Plunge, and the Giant Dipper, a classic wooden **roller coaster** ( ☎ 858-488-1549; admission $4; ☿ from 11am) that'll shake the teeth right out of your mouth. More modern attractions include Flowrider, a wave machine for simulated surfing; the Pirates Cove children's play zone; and Venturer II, which features amusement machines that combine video games with virtual reality technology. There are also bumper cars, a carousel, beachwear boutiques, a bar and several places to eat. It's free to enter Belmont Park; you pay for the rides individually ($2 to $4).

### MISSION BAY

In the 18th century, the mouth of the San Diego River formed a shallow bay when the river flowed, and a marshy swamp when it didn't – the Spanish called it False Bay. After WWII an extraordinary combination of civic vision and coastal engineering turned the swamp into a 7-sq-mile playground, with 27 miles of shoreline and 90 acres of public parks. With financing from public bonds and expertise from the Army Corps of Engineers, the river was channeled to the sea, the bay was dredged, and millions of tons of sludge were used to build islands, coves and peninsulas. A quarter of the land created has been leased to hotels, boatyards and other businesses, providing ongoing revenue for the city.

The attractions of Mission Bay run the gamut from luxurious resort hotels to free outdoor activities. Kite flying is popular in Mission Bay Park, beach volleyball is big on Fiesta Island, and there's delightful cycling and in-line skating on the miles of smooth bike paths. Sailing, windsurfing and kayaking dominate the waters in northwest Mission Bay, while water-skiers zip around Fiesta Island. For information about equipment rentals, see p280.

You can avoid adrenaline overload and still have a lovely time on the bay aboard the **Bahia Belle** ( ☎ 858-539-7779; 998 West Mission Bay Dr; adult/kids $6/3), a floating bar disguised as a stern-wheeler paddleboat. It cruises between two resort hotels, the Catamaran and the Bahia, on Friday and Saturday evenings year-round, Wednesday to Saturday in June, and daily in July and August. Cruises start at 6:30pm; call for exact departure times.

### SEAWORLD

One of San Diego's best-known and most popular attractions, **SeaWorld** ( ☎ 619-226-3901, 800-380-3203; www.seaworld.com/ca; adult/child $57/47; ⏲ 9am-11pm summer, 10am-6pm rest of year) opened here in 1964. Shamu, the park's killer whale, has become an unofficial symbol of the city.

SeaWorld's highlights are its live shows, which feature trained dolphins, seals, sea lions and killer whales. **Shamu Adventure** is the most visually spectacular program, the one you won't want to miss. Throughout the 30-minute show, the three star performers – Shamu, Baby Shamu and Namu – glide, leap, dive and flip through the water while interacting with each other, the audience and their trainers. On hot days, kids love to sit in the 'splash zone' of the stadiums, where they're guaranteed to get wet.

There are numerous other aquarium-like installations where you can see and learn about underwater creatures, as well as petting pools where you can touch the slippery surface of a dolphin or manta ray. In **Penguin Encounter**, several penguin species share a habitat that faithfully simulates Antarctic living conditions. The temperature behind the glass-enclosed space is a constant 25°F, but light conditions change with the seasons, just as nature dictates. So, if you're visiting in July (which is winter in Antarctica), expect to catch them waddling and swimming in near-darkness in the middle the day. You'll see dozens of sharks as you walk through a 57ft acrylic tube at **Shark Encounter**. Species include blacktip and whitetip, reef and sand tiger sharks, some of them impressively large.

Several amusement park–style rides include **Journey to Atlantis**, a combination flume ride and roller coaster; and **Wild Arctic**, a simulated helicopter flight, that's followed by a walk past beluga whales and polar bears, eventually winding up in a giant gift shop. Expect long waits for rides, shows and exhibits during peak seasons.

The park is shamefully commercial – you'll be subjected to deafeningly loud advertisements, broadcast on a Jumbotron, while you wait to see Shamu, and there's a corporate logo on everything in sight. Still, SeaWorld manages to do its share for animal conservation, rescue, rehabilitation, breeding and research. But if you don't want to subject your children to countless advertisements which are carefully crafted to get their attention, don't bring them to SeaWorld.

If you pay the regular admission price, you're going to have an expensive day, especially if you're with kids to whom you can't say no. During summer call the park to find out about special promotions. Extras add up fast – parking costs $7, food is expensive (a 20-ounce bottle of water costs $3), and the park bars coolers and picnic lunches (stash a sandwich in your purse anyway).

Few people escape from SeaWorld without spending something on the ubiquitous souvenirs. Ways to save include getting a re-entry stamp, which lets you leave for a break and return later, good during summer when the park is open late; buying a discounted combination ticket, which allows admission to Universal Studios (in LA) and/or Disneyland; or buying a two-day ticket, which costs only $4 more than a regular one.

The park is easy to reach by car. Take SeaWorld Dr off I-5 less than a mile north of where it intersects with I-8. By bus, take No 9 from downtown. Ticket booths close 1½ hours before closing time. Plan to spend at least three hours, though seeing everything will take most of the day.

## Ocean Beach                         Map pp244–5

If you're a hippie at heart, you'll love OB, San Diego's most bohemian seaside community, where you can get tattooed, shop for antiques, and walk into a restaurant barefoot and shirtless without anyone batting an eye. **Newport Ave** is the main drag, and runs perpendicular to the beach through a compact business district of bars, surf shops, music stores, used-clothing stores and, in the 4800 and 4900 blocks, antiques consignment stores. Bus No 23 connects OB to downtown.

The 0.5-mile-long **Ocean Beach Pier** has all the architectural elegance of a freeway ramp. Primarily a fishing pier, it's a good place to stroll; at its end, you'll have a great perspective on the coast. There's also a greasy-spoon **café** (OB Pier Café; ☎ 619-226-3474; ☼ 7am-10pm) for French fries and fishing-pole rentals ($14 per day).

Just north of the pier, near the end of Newport Ave, you'll find the beach scene's epicenter, with volleyball courts and sunset barbecues. Further north on **Dog Beach**, pups chase birds around the marshy area where the San Diego River meets the sea. Head a few blocks south of the pier to **Sunset Cliffs Park**, where surfing and sunsets are the main attractions.

There are good surf breaks at the cliffs and, to the south, off Point Loma. Under the pier, hot surfers slalom the pilings, but unless you know what you're doing, the rips and currents can be deadly.

If you're here on Wednesday afternoon, stop by the OB **farmers market** (☎ 619-279-0032; 4900 Block of Newport Ave; ☼ 4-7pm Wed, 4-8pm Jun-Sep) to see street performers and sample fresh food.

## Point Loma                         Map p239

On maps Point Loma looks like an elephant's trunk guarding the entrance to San Diego Bay. **Cabrillo National Monument** (☎ 619-557-5450; admission $5 per car; ☼ 9am-sunset) sits at the very tip. Aside from being San

Diego's finest locale for history and views, it's also the best place in town to see the gray whale migration (January to March) from land. After a few minutes on the windswept hills you may forget you're in a major metropolitan area.

The **visitors center** (☎ 619-557-5450; ☼ 9am-5:15pm) at the monument has an excellent presentation on Portuguese explorer Juan Rodríguez Cabrillo's 1542 voyage up the California coast, plus good exhibits on the native inhabitants and the area's natural history. The 1854 **Old Point Loma Lighthouse**, atop the point, is furnished with typical pieces from the late 19th century, including lamps and picture frames hand-covered with hundreds of shells – testimony to the long, lonely nights endured by lighthouse keepers. On the ocean side of the point, you can drive or walk down to the **tide pools** (at low tide) to look for anemones, starfish, crabs, limpets and dead man's fingers (thin, tubular seaweed). To reach the monument, take bus No 26 from downtown.

San Diego's first fishing boats were based at Point Loma, and in the 19th century whalers dragged carcasses onto its shores to extract the whale oil. Chinese fishermen settled on the harbor side of the point in the 1860s, but were forced off in 1888 when the US Congress passed the Scott Act prohibiting anyone without citizenship papers from entering the area. Coming home from a normal day's run outside the international waters boundary (30 miles offshore), the Chinese were met by officials who prohibited them from re-entering the harbor. Portuguese fishing families arrived about 50 years later and established a permanent community around the same time that Italian immigrants settled on the other side of the harbor. Many inhabitants of Point Loma are of Portuguese descent, and the **Portuguese Hall** remains a hub of activity for locals.

Charles Lindbergh tested his *Spirit of St Louis* airplane in 1927 on the tidal flats of **Loma Portal**, where Point Loma joins the mainland (at the elephant's neck). The following year a functioning airport was established at his airstrip; it was named Lindbergh Field. The airfield has expanded beyond recognition and now bears the name San Diego International Airport at Lindbergh Field.

SAN DIEGO

## Coronado                                    Map p239

Coronado is compact and densely populated with clean-cut military families, retirees and other folks who depend on resort hotels for their paychecks. Directly across the bay from downtown San Diego, Coronado is, administratively, a separate city that's known for closely guarding its tone and quality of life. Sit up straight and mind your Ps and Qs, and don't cruise **Orange Ave**, the main drag, blaring chassis-buzzing thump-thump music from your SUV, or you'll earn a $100 fine.

The spectacular 2.12-mile-long **Coronado Bay Bridge** opened in 1969 and joins Coronado to San Diego; Silver Strand, a long, narrow sand spit, runs south to Imperial Beach and connects Coronado to the mainland. Nevertheless, Coronado is often incorrectly referred to as 'Coronado Island'; the locals like to call it 'the Rock.' The large North Island Naval Air Station occupies a big chunk of land that was indeed once an island. (The real Coronado Islands are offshore, visible on clear days; they belong to Mexico.)

In 1888 Elisha Babcock and Hampton Story opened the **Hotel del Coronado** (see following), the showy centerpiece of a new resort, and by 1900 they were broke. John D Spreckels, the millionaire who bankrolled the first rail line to San Diego, took over Coronado and turned the whole island into one of the most fashionable getaways on the West Coast.

The **Coronado Visitors Center** ( ☎ 619-437-8788; www.coronadovisitorcenter.com; 1100 Orange Ave;  9am-5pm Mon-Fri, 10am-5pm Sat, 11am-4pm Sun) doubles as the **Coronado Museum of History and Art**. On Wednesday at 2pm and Friday at 10:30am you can take a walking tour ($8) from the visitors center.

On Tuesday, Thursday and Saturday, the tour starts from the **Glorietta Bay Inn** (1630 Glorietta Blvd), near Silver Strand Blvd. The 90-minute route takes in many of Coronado's most interesting sights.

Use the electric Coronado Shuttle to get around (free). Alternatively, bus Nos 901, 902 and 903 from downtown run the length of Orange Ave to the Hotel del Coronado. The Old Town Trolley tour (p258) stops in front of Mc P's Irish Pub, on Orange Ave at 11th St. For information on ferries, water taxis and bike rentals, see p291.

Four-and-a-half miles south of Coronado, the white-sand **Silver Strand State Beach** ( ☎ 619-435-5184; www.parks.ca.gov;  P  $6) has warm, calm water, perfect for swimming and good for families.

### HOTEL DEL CORONADO

Commonly known as the **Hotel Del** ( ☎ 619-435-6611, 800-582-2595; www.hoteldel.com), few hotels in the world are as easily recognized or as much loved as this San Diego icon. Architecturally quirky, with conical towers, cupolas, turrets, balconies and dormer windows, the Del is an all-timber building, and the cavernous public spaces reflect the background of their designers, railroad-depot architects James and Merritt Reed. The acres of polished wood give the interior a warm, old-fashioned feel that conjures daydreams of Panama hats and linen suits.

Edward (then Prince of Wales) first met Mrs Simpson (then Mrs Spenser) at the Del in 1920, though the two did not become an item until some years later. Other famous guests include many US presidents and other dignitaries – pictures and mementos are displayed in the hotel's history gallery. The hotel achieved its widest exposure in the 1959 movie *Some Like It Hot*, which earned it a lasting association with Marilyn Monroe. Pick up a brochure on the history of the hotel and take a self-guided tour. There's an interesting resident ghost story, too, about a jilted woman who haunts the hotel; some claim she silently appears in hallways and on the TV screen in the room where she had her heart broken.

For a taste of the Del without staying here, consider splurging on Sunday brunch in the spectacular Crown Room ($50), where the enormous ceiling resembles an upside-down wooden ship's hull. For more details on the hotel, see p286, and the Prince of Wales, p286.

## ACTIVITIES

If you love surf and sky, you'll go nuts in Coastal San Diego. Carry your swim suit at all times; you never know when the beach will beckon. For information on biking, see p290.

### Surfing

A good number of San Diegans moved here for the surfing, and boy is it good. But the water can get crowded. Several spots, particularly Sunset Cliffs and Windansea, are somewhat 'owned' by locals – which means they'll heckle you to death unless you're an awesome surfer – but in general, San Diego is a great place for surfers of any skill level.

Fall brings strong swells and offshore Santa Ana winds. In summer swells come from the south and southwest, and in winter from the west and northwest. Spring brings more frequent onshore winds, but the surfing can still be good. For the latest beach, weather and surf reports, call **City Lifeguard** ( ☎ 619-221-8824).

Beginners looking to rent surfing equipment should head to Mission or Pacific Beaches, where the waves are gentle. North of the Crystal Pier, Tourmaline Surf Beach is an especially good place to take your first strokes. **Pacific Beach Surf Shop** (Map pp244-5; ☎ 858-373-1138; www.pacificbeachsurfshop.com; 4150 Mission Blvd, Suite 161, Pacific Beach) provides instruction through its Pacific beach Surf School. It has friendly service, and also rents wetsuits and both soft (foam) and hard (fiberglass) boards. Call ahead. Also check out **Bob's Mission Surf** (Map pp244-5; ☎ 858-483-8837; www.missionsurf.com; 4320 Mission Blvd, Pacific Beach). Rental rates at both vary depending on the quality of the equipment, but generally soft boards cost about $10 to $16 per half-day, $15 to $25 per full day; wet suits cost $5. For 90-minute lessons expect to pay $70 (including equipment) for one person, with discounts for additional people.

In La Jolla, head to **OE Express** (Map p247; ☎ 858-454-6195; www.oeexpress.com; 2158 Avenida de la Playa), in La Jolla Shores, which offers lessons for $75 (reduced rate for two or more people), including equipment.

Next door to OE Express, in addition to regular classes, the wonderful women at **Surf Diva** (Map p247; ☎ 858-454-8273; www.surfdiva.com; 2160 Avenida de la Playa) offer two-day weekend workshops for gals (only) of all ages for $95 to $130.

The best surf breaks, from south to north, are at Imperial Beach (especially in winter); Point Loma (reef breaks, which are less accessible but less crowded; best in winter); Sunset Cliffs in Ocean Beach; Pacific Beach; Big Rock (California's Pipeline); Windansea (hot reef break, best at medium to low tide); La Jolla Shores (beach

break, best in winter); and Blacks Beach (a fast, powerful wave). Further up, in North County, there are breaks at Cardiff State Beach, San Elijo State Beach, Swami's, Carlsbad State Beach and Oceanside.

**Body surfing** is good at Coronado, Pacific Beach, Boomer Beach near La Jolla Cove (for the experienced only, best with a big swell) and La Jolla Shores. To get into the whomp (the forceful tubes that break directly onshore), know what you're doing and head to Windansea or the beach at the end of Sea Lane (both in La Jolla).

## Diving & Snorkeling

Off the coast of San Diego County, divers will find kelp beds, shipwrecks (including the *Yukon,* a WWII destroyer), and canyons deep enough to host bat rays, octopus and squid. For current conditions, call ☎ 619-221-8824. Some of California's best and most accessible (no boat needed) diving is in the **San Diego-La Jolla Underwater Park**, accessible from the La Jolla Cove. With an average depth of 20ft, the 6000 acres of look-but-don't-touch underwater real estate is great for snorkeling, too. Ever-present are the spectacular, bright orange Garibaldi fish – California's official state fish and a protected species (there's a $500 fine for poaching one). Further out, you'll see forests of giant California kelp (which can increase its length by up to 3ft per day) and the 100ft-deep La Jolla Canyon.

A number of commercial outfits conduct scuba-diving courses, sell or rent equipment, fill tanks, and conduct boat trips to nearby wrecks and islands. A snorkel and fins cost around $10; scuba-gear rental packages cost about $75; and certification and open-water dives run about $375 for the first person, with discounts for additional people. Closest to the water, **OE Express** (Map p247; ☎ 858-454-6195; www.oeexpress.com; 2158 Avenida de la Playa) is a full-service PADI dive shop in La Jolla Shores that provides rentals and instruction.

## Fishing

A state fishing license is required for people over 16 years old. A **recorded service** ( ☎ 619-465-3474) provides fishing information.

The most popular public fishing piers are Imperial Beach Municipal Pier, Embarcadero Fishing Pier, Shelter Island

Fishing Pier, Ocean Beach Pier and Crystal Pier at Pacific Beach. The best time of year for pier fishing is from about April to October. Offshore catches can include barracuda, bass and yellowtail. In summer albacore is a special attraction. A license is not required for fishing off any of these piers.

Many companies run daily fishing trips year-round. All charge around $35/24 per adult/child for a half-day trip. Prices for full-day trips depend on how far off the coast you go; prices cost $50 to $100 for children and $75 to $150 for adults. A license costs an extra $11 per person. Most also offer overnight and three-day trips, plus special charters for large groups. The most reputable include:

**H&M Landing** (Map p239; ☎ 619-222-1144; www .hmlanding.com; 2803 Emerson St) On Shelter Island.
**Islandia Sportfishing** (Map pp244-5; ☎ 619-222-1164; www.islandiasport.com; 1551 West Mission Bay Dr)
**Point Loma Sport Fishing** (Map p239; ☎ 619-223-1627; www.pointlomasportfishing.com; 1403 Scott St)
**Seaforth Sportfishing** (Map pp244-5; ☎ 619-224-3383; www.seaforthlanding.com; 1717 Quivira Rd) In Quivira Basin on Mission Bay.

Look for discount coupons in the *Reader* (p235).

## Boating

Rent power and sailboats, rowboats, kayaks and canoes on Mission Bay. Try either of the following:
**Mission Bay Sportcenter** (Map pp244-5; ☎ 858-488-1004; www.missionbaysportcenter.com; 1010 Santa Clara Pl)
**Resort Watersports** (www.resortwatersport.com) Catamaran Resort Hotel (Map pp244-5; ☎ 858-539-8696; 3981 Mission Blvd); Bahia Resort Hotel (Map pp244-5; ☎ 858-539-7696; 998 West Mission Bay Dr)

Ocean kayaking is a good way to see sea life, and explore cliffs and caves inaccessible from land. **Family Kayak** ( ☎ 619-282-3520; www .familykayak.com) has guided single- and multi-day trips and classes, both from $55 for three hours. It's easy to explore the caves and cliffs around La Jolla from the put-in of **OE Express** (Map p247; ☎ 858-454-6195; www .oeexpress.com; 2158 Avenida de la Playa) in La Jolla Shores; a two-hour rental costs $28 for a single kayak, $40 for a double. It also guides tours. If you want to rent a kayak in Mission

Bay, call **Windsport** (Map pp244-5; ☎ 858-488-4642, 888-488-7656; www.windsport.net; 844 W Mission Bay Dr), across from the roller coaster; a single/double costs $15/20 per hour.

Experienced sailors can charter yachts and sailboats for trips on San Diego Bay and out into the Pacific. Quite a few charter companies are based around Shelter and Harbor Islands (on the west side of San Diego Bay near the airport), including the following:
**Harbor Sailboats** (Map p239; ☎ 619-291-9568, 800-854-6625; www.harborsailboats.com; 2040 Harbor Island Dr, Suite 104)
**San Diego Yacht Charters** (Map p239; ☎ 619-297-4555, 800-456-0222; www.sdyc.com; 1880 Harbor Island Dr)
**Shelter Island Sailing** (Map p239; ☎ 619-222-0351; www.shelterislandsailing.com; 2240 Shelter Island Dr)

## Whale Watching

Gray whales pass San Diego from mid-December to late February on their way south to Baja California and again in mid-March on their way back up to Alaskan waters. Their 12,000 mile round-trip journey is the longest migration of any mammal on earth.

Cabrillo National Monument (p279) is the best place to see the whales from land, where you'll also find exhibits, whale-related ranger programs and a shelter from which to watch the whales breach (bring binoculars). If you find yourself further north, Torrey Pines State Reserve and La Jolla Cove are also good spots for whale-watching.

Half-day whale-watching boat trips are offered by all of the companies that run daily fishing trips (p281). The trips generally cost $20/15 per adult/child for a three-hour excursion, and the companies will even give you a free pass to return again if you don't spot any whales. Look for coupons and special offers in the *Reader* (p235).

## Hang-Gliding

Glider riders hang at **Torrey Pines Gliderport** (Map p247; ☎ 858-452-9858; www.flytorrey.com; 2800 Torrey Pines Scenic Dr), in La Jolla, a world-famous gliding location. Tandem flights in a hang-glider cost $150 per person for 20 minutes. This is also one of the best gliding schools in the country; if you've ever wanted to learn to glide, here's your chance.

Experienced pilots can join in if they have a USHGA Hang 4 rating and take out an associate membership of the Torrey Pines Hang Glider Association.

## SLEEPING

High-season summer rates for double-occupancy rooms are listed here; suites cost more. Prices drop significantly between September and June. For more San Diego lodgings, see p260.

### La Jolla                    Map p247

It's hard to find a room in La Jolla for under $100. The least expensive places are on La Jolla Blvd, south of town. Longer stays yield lower rates. If you're room hunting on a busy night, there are several large chain hotels, such as Embassy Suites and Marriott, inland on La Jolla Village Dr.

**La Jolla Village Lodge** ( ☎ 858-454-0791, 800-454-4361; www.lajollavillagelodge.com; 1141 Silverado St; r $120-210) Right at the edge of downtown La Jolla, this cookie-cutter Travelodge motel charges higher prices than it could in any other location, but you can walk everywhere.

**La Jolla Beach Travelodge** ( ☎ 858-454-0716, 800-454-4361; www.lajollatravelodge.com; 6750 La Jolla Blvd; r $120-200; P ☎ ) Near Windansea beach, this nothing-special motel has fridges and microwaves.

**Holiday Inn Express** ( ☎ 858-454-7101, 800-451-0358; www.hiexlajolla.com; 6763 La Jolla Blvd; r $110-200; P ☎ ) Across from the Travelodge, you'll find comparable rooms, some with full kitchens and pull-out sofas.

**Scripps Inn** ( ☎ 858-454-3391; 555 Coast Blvd; r $190-260; P ) Tucked behind the San Diego Museum of Contemporary Art, across from the water, this cozy inn has immaculate rooms that feel like a well-loved beach cottage. Its 13 units sell out quickly – book early.

**Shell Beach Apartment Motel** ( ☎ 858-459-4306; www.lajollacove.com; 981 Coast Blvd; apt from $180; P ) An assemblage of different buildings from single-story cedar-shingled condos to three-story brick apartment houses; the beachside lodgings include units with kitchens.

La Jolla's top hotels often run specials and packages, especially in the off-season. Rates given are for high season.

**La Valencia** ( ☎ 858-454-0771, 800-451-0772; www.lavalencia.com; 1132 Prospect St; r $275-550; P ☎ ☎ ) La Jolla's iconic hotel, the 1926 pink-walled, Mediterranean-style, William Templeton

Johnson–designed La Valencia exemplifies classic Southern California style. Some rooms could use updating and you'll find more modern amenities across the street at the Parisi, but for romance and the ghosts of Depression-era Hollywood stars, it takes the cake.

**Grande Colonial** ( ☎ 858-454-2181, 800-826-1278; www.thegrandecolonial.com; 901 Prospect St; r $260-380; ☎ P ) Demure stepsister to La Valencia, the smartly decorated 1927 Grande Colonial exudes conservative sophistication. Great beds, odd-shaped rooms, and sunny yellow-painted walls with white trim add to the charm. If you like historic hotels, this one's terrific.

**Hotel Parisi** ( ☎ 858-454-1511, 877-472-7474; www.hotelparisi.com; 1111 Prospect St; r $295-495; P ☐ ) Despite its self-conscious beauty, the Parisi is one of San Diego's top boutique hotels for sumptuous rooms and contemporary style. Dress in Armani and blend right in.

**Estancia La Jolla Hotel & Spa** ( ☎ 858-550-1000, 877-437-8262; www.estancialajolla.com; 9700 N Torrey Pines Rd; r $240-390; P ☐ ☎ ) Opened in 2003, this rambling rancho-style resort with its pathways, patios and lush gardens is down-to-earth, romantic and cushy all at once. Unwind by the huge pool, during an expert massage at the spa, or while sipping killer margaritas by the outdoor fireplace. Rooms feature custom furniture, luxurious linens and big bathrooms. Two restaurants.

**Lodge at Torrey Pines** ( ☎ 858-453-4420, 800-995-4507; www.lodgetorreypines.com; 11480 N Torrey Pines Rd; r $325-625; P ☐ ☎ ) San Diego's top-rated hotel was inspired by the architecture of Greene & Greene, the turn-of-the-20th-century Arts and Crafts masters who designed the Gamble House in Pasadena (p123). The entire lodge is built in perfect Craftsman style, right down to the lap joints in the cherry-wood wainscoting and the column footings of random-set stone. Discretely luxurious rooms have Mission oak-and-leather furniture a la Stickley, Tiffany-style lamps, plein air paintings and basket-weave bathroom-floor tiling of marble. There's a stellar full-service spa and even a croquet lawn.

### Mission Beach & Pacific Beach                 Map pp244–5

Pacific Beach (PB) has most of the beachside accommodations. Motels provide better value in winter than summer, when rates are high and availability scarce (summer rates are listed here).

### BUDGET
None of the following budget properties is appropriate for finicky travelers, or those who demand good housekeeping and firm mattresses.

**Banana Bungalow** ( ☎ 858-273-3060; www.banana bungalow.com; 707 Reed Ave; dm $20, r from $49; ⬛ ) Right on Mission Beach, the Bungalow has a top location, a beach-party atmosphere and is reasonably clean, but it's very basic and gets crowded. The communal area is a patio, which fronts right on the boardwalk; it's a great place for people-watching and beer drinking. Breakfast included. No air-con.

**Mission Bay Motel** ( ☎ 858-483-6440; www.mission baymotel.com; 4221 Mission Blvd; r $100-120; P ⬛ ) Somewhat dumpy motel overlooking a parking lot and a busy street. It has no air-con, but the beach and Garnet Ave are both nearby.

**Pacific View Motel** ( ☎ 858-483-6117; www.pacific viewmotel.com; 610 Emerald St; r $80-110; P ) This divey '60s-era motel sits right on the beach, but doesn't face the water. Terrible mattresses, cheap rates. No air-con.

**Santa Clara Motel** ( ☎ 858-488-1193; 839 Santa Clara Pl; r $75-110; P ) This bare-bones motel in Mission Beach has brusque service, and you can't reserve in advance, but rates are the cheapest you'll find.

### MID-RANGE & TOP END
All of the following provide clean rooms and good service.

**Beach Cottages** ( ☎ 858-483-7440; 4255 Ocean Blvd; r $120-180, cottages from $230; P ) Family owned and operated, the Beach Cottages bears the standard for service in PB and has everything from plain motel rooms to cozy 1940s beachfront cottages. Compared with area motels, this place is a bargain, especially if you're traveling in a group and manage to secure one of the cottages. Book long in advance. No air-con.

**Beach Haven Inn** ( ☎ 858-272-3812, 800-831-6323; www.beachhaveninn.com; 4740 Mission Blvd; r $140-150, with full kitchen $160; P ⬛ ) You get more for your money than at most places in PB by staying a block from the beach at this friendly, well-run two-story motel – though the mattresses could be firmer.

**Best Western Blue Sea Lodge** ( ☎ 858-488-4700, 800-258-3732; www.bestwestern-bluesea.com; 707 Pacific Beach Dr; r $170-280; P ⬛ ) Although every up-to-date room at this well-run motel is decorated with attractively upholstered furniture and granite bathroom counters, and has fridges and microwaves, you're mostly paying for the beachside location. Still, the rooms are some of the best you'll find in a PB motel.

**Crystal Pier Hotel** ( ☎ 858-483-6983, 800-748-5894; www.crystalpier.com; 4500 Ocean Blvd; cottages $270-420 summer, $225-355 winter; P ) Charming, wonderful, and unlike anyplace else in San Diego, Crystal Pier has cottages built right on the pier above the water. All have full ocean views and kitchens, but the original 1936 clapboard units are the best – though the newer, larger cottages sleep more people. For stays between July and December, book on the morning of January 1; for January and June, book on November 15 (keep hitting redial on the phone; it's worth the hours of aggravation). Minimum-stay requirements vary by season. No air-con.

**Pacific Terrace Hotel** ( ☎ 858-581-3500, 800-344-3370; www.pacificterrace.com; 610 Diamond St; r $260-445; ⬛ P ⬛ ) The only full-service hotel in PB has rooms with great views, but rates are ridiculously high considering you can see nearly the same thing from the boardwalk. You get much more for your money at the hotels on Mission Bay.

## Mission Bay Map pp244–5
If you want to stay by the water, check out Mission Bay, where you'll get more bang for your buck than you will on the ocean. Rates fluctuate wildly depending on occupancy, but you can sometimes score a fantastic deal. Many rooms sleep four; some suites can accommodate as many as seven.

**Catamaran Resort Hotel** ( ☎ 858-488-1081, 800-422-8386; www.catamaranresort.com; 3999 Mission Blvd; r $159-285; P ⬛ ) Tropical landscaping surrounds this bayside destination resort, perfect for families. Sail, kayak, play tennis, and rent a bike or skates and ride around Mission Bay. Rooms are in low-rise buildings or in a 14-story tower; some have views and full kitchens. The resort hosts a luau on summer evenings.

**Paradise Point Resort** ( ☎ 858-274-4630, 800-344-2626; www.paradisepoint.com; 1404 Vacation Rd; r $229-329; P ⬛ ) The grounds are so lush and dotted with so many palms that you'll feel like you're in Hawaii at this upper-end full-service resort, whose rooms are in small low-rise buildings and bungalows. Five swimming pools. Full-service spa.

Other great resorts include:

**Bahia Resort Hotel** ( ☎ 858-488-0551, 800-576-4229; www.bahiahotel.com; 998 W Mission Bay Dr; r $140-260; ☻ P )

**Hyatt Regency Islandia** ( ☎ 619-224-1234, 800-223-1234; www.hyatt.com; 1440 Quivira Rd; r $160-270; ☻ P )

For super budget, **Campland on the Bay** ( ☎ 858-581-4260, 800-422-9386; www.campland.com; 2211 Pacific Beach Dr; sites $35-145; P ☻ ) has more than 40 acres fronting Mission Bay. There's a restaurant, pool, boating facilities and full RV hookups. Site costs vary depending on their proximity to the water. The location is great, but the tent area is not very attractive – too many RVs, not enough trees – and it gets crowded. Reservations are a good idea in the warmer months. The RV-only section of Campland is **De Anza Harbor Resort** (Map pp244–5; ☎ 858-273-3211, 800-924-7529; sites $35-190).

## Ocean Beach    Map pp244–5

Note that Ocean Beach (OB) is under the outbound flight path of jets departing San Diego airport, which won't be a problem if you rise at 6am. Otherwise, if you're a light sleeper who lingers in bed, stay somewhere else or bring earplugs.

**Ocean Beach International Hostel** ( ☎ 619-223-7873, 800-339-7263; www.californiahostels.com; 4961 Newport Ave; dm $16-20, r $20-25; ☐ ) The cheapest option is only a couple of blocks from the ocean; it's a friendly, fun place that's popular with Europeans. Bus No 35 from downtown passes Newport Ave a block east of the hostel. No air-con.

**Inn at Sunset Cliffs** ( ☎ 619-222-7901, 866-786-2543; www.innatsunsetcliffs.com; 1370 Sunset Cliffs Blvd; r from $150; P ☻ ) Smack dab on the ocean at the north end of Sunset Cliffs, you could throw a rock from your door and hit the water at this seaside vacation motel that bursts with blooming roses. Some rooms have full kitchens. Ask about discounts. The top choice in OB.

**Ocean Beach Hotel** ( ☎ 619-223-7191; www.obhotel.com; 5080 Newport Ave; r without ocean-view $110-130, with ocean-view $130-175; P ) Walk everywhere

in OB from this three-story motel on the beach. Rooms are small, but have fridges and microwaves.

**Ocean Villa Motel** ( ☎ 619-224-3481, 800-759-0012; www.oceanvillainn.com; 5142 W Point Loma Blvd; r $130-190; P ☻ ) Further north than Ocean Beach Hotel but also close to the sea, this straightforward motel is clean and well run, and allows some pets. Add $10 for a kitchen.

### Point Loma Area

**HI San Diego Point Loma Hostel** (Map pp244-5; ☎ 619-223-4778; www.sandiegohostels.org; 3790 Udall St; dm members/nonmembers $17/20; ☐ ) It's a 20-minute walk from the heart of Ocean Beach to this HI hostel in Loma Portal, which is near a market and Laundromat. Bus Nos 23 (from downtown, weekdays only) and 35 (from Old Town, daily) run along nearby Voltaire St. Includes breakfast. No lock-out times. No air-con.

If you like yachts and harbor views, consider these landscaped breakwaters at Shelter Island and Harbor Island.

**Best Western Island Palms Hotel** (Map p239; ☎ 619-222-0561; www.islandpalms.com; 2051 Shelter Island Dr; r $140-180; P ☐ ☻ ) The Island Palms, a small Polynesian-themed resort hotel fronting the yacht harbor, has comfortable, well-maintained upper-end-chain-motel-style rooms; those with a marina view cost $180, a bargain in these parts. Free bike rentals, too.

**Humphrey's Half Moon Inn** (Map p239; ☎ 619-224-3411, 800-542-7400; www.halfmooninn.com; 2303 Shelter Island Dr; non-water-view r $165-185; P ☐ ☻ ) This 182-room resort hotel has a tropical-island atmosphere and rooms in two-story satellite buildings; those facing the water cost an extra $150. There's a good jazz club on-site.

**Sheraton Harbor Island** (Map p239; ☎ 619-291-2900, 800-325-3535; www.sheraton.com/sandiegomarina; 1380 Harbor Island Dr; r $180-290; P ☐ ☻ ) Designed for businesspeople traveling with spouses on leisure vacations, the Sheraton is near the airport, and has spacious rooms with super-comfy beds, feather pillows, and crisp linens. Request a room overlooking the yacht harbor rather than the airport.

## Coronado    Map p239

Rates are highest at the southern end of Coronado (near the Hotel del Coronado) because you can walk to the beach and shops. At the quiet, residential northern end, the naval base blocks beach access and there are fewer shops and restaurants, but you can walk to the ferry to downtown San Diego.

In winter the following rates drop substantially.

### BUDGET

**Coronado Village Inn** ( ☎ 619-435-9318; www.coronadovillageinn.com; 1017 Park Pl; r $85-95) The top budget choice in pricey Coronado, this 15-room 1928 hotel has no amenities, such as air-conditioning or oversized bathrooms, but its tidy rooms and location – two blocks from the beach, half a block to shops and restaurants – more than compensate.

**Coronado Island Inn** ( ☎ 619-435-0935, 888-436-0935; www.coronadoinn.com; 301 Orange Ave; r $100-125; P ⚓ ) Some of the standard-issue rooms have kitchens; all have access to the pool at the motel's sister property, the Coronado Inn, across the street (below).

**El Rancho Motel** ( ☎ 619-435-2251; www.elranchocoronado.com; 370 Orange Ave; r $100-120; P ) Snagging one of the eight rooms at this clean and simple motel requires either luck or reservations.

### MID-RANGE

**Crown City Inn** ( ☎ 619-435-3116, 800-422-1173; www.crowncityinn.com; 520 Orange Ave; r $119-159; P ⚓ ⚓ ) This two-story motel with exterior corridors encircles a small parking area with a little pool. If its well-kept rooms were nearer the beach, they would cost $200 per night.

**Coronado Inn** ( ☎ 619-435-4121, 800-598-6624; www.coronadoinn.com; 266 Orange Ave; r $125-175, with kitchen $185-195; P ⚓ ⚓ ) The owner keeps this handsome motel near the ferry in tip-top shape. Rooms are large; some have full kitchens.

Also consider:

**El Cordova Hotel** ( ☎ 619-435-4131, 800-229-2032; www.elcordovahotel.com; 1351 Orange Ave; r $129-209; ⚓ ) Mediterranean-style 1930s tourist-class hotel built around an outdoor courtyard of shops and restaurants.

**La Avenida** ( ☎ 619-435-3191, 800-437-0162; www.laavenidainn.com; 1315 Orange Ave; r $150-180; P ⚓ ⚓ ) Motel-style rooms.

### TOP END

**Hotel del Coronado** ( ☎ 619-435-6611, 800-468-3533; www.hoteldel.com; 1500 Orange Ave; r $280-505; P ⚓ ⚓ )

San Diego's iconic hotel, the Del provides the true Coronado experience. Aside from over a century of history, there are tennis courts, a pool, full-service spa, shops, restaurants, manicured grounds and a white-sand beach at the edge of the Pacific. However, half the accommodations are not in the main Victorian-era hotel, but in an adjacent seven-story building constructed in the 1970s. For a sense of place, book a room in the original hotel.

**Glorietta Bay Inn** ( ☎ 619-435-3101, 800-283-9383; www.gloriettabayinn.com; 1630 Glorietta Blvd; rooms $150-265; P ⚓ ⚓ ) Overshadowed by the neighboring Hotel Del, the Glorietta is built around the 1908 Spreckels Mansion. Guestrooms are in both the mansion and modern two-story buildings. New rooms have handsome furnishings and extras, such as triple-sheeted beds and high-end bath products. Mansion rooms start at $250 and have extra amenities, including 600-thread-count sheets. Stop in and see the gorgeous music room, even if you're not staying here.

Also consider the following:

**Loews Coronado Bay Resort** ( ☎ 619-424-4000, 800-235-6397; www.loewshotels.com; 4000 Coronado Bay Rd; r $240-285; P ⚓ ⚓ ) Cushy full-service resort.

## EATING

In coastal San Diego, you're never very far from downtown (La Jolla is furthest, only 20 minutes by car), so remember to also check out the restaurant listings for downtown (p262).

### La Jolla                                    Map p247

There's lots to choose from in La Jolla, one of San Diego's major dining outposts.

### BUDGET

**Wahoo's Fish Tacos** ( ☎ 858-459-0027; 637 Pearl St; dishes $2-6; ⚓ 10:30am-10pm Mon-Sat, 10:30am-9pm Sun) Inexpensive and popular with the surf culture, Wahoo's does wonderful things with rice, beans, grilled veggies, meats and fish. There's cold beer and reggae, too.

**Porkyland** ( ☎ 858-459-1708; 1030 Torrey Pines Rd; dishes $3-5; ⚓ 8am-8pm) Here you can pork out on cheap Mexican and still have money left for beer.

**Girard Gourmet** ( ☎ 858-454-3321; 7837 Girard Ave; dishes under $8; ⚓ 7am-9pm Mon-Sat, 7am-7pm Sun) There's everything from chicken salad to chocolate cake at this Belgian delicatessen, which makes its own pastries and serves pre-plated hot foods you select from the glass case. La Jolla's best bargain.

**Coffee Cup Café** ( ☎ 858-454-2819; 1109 Wall St; dishes $6-9; 🕑 8am-3pm) Why wait until dinner for eclectic fusion cooking when you can have it for breakfast and lunch at the Coffee Cup? Good spot for innovative eating at sensible prices, from American standards to inventive Chino-Latino dishes.

**Harry's Coffee Shop** ( ☎ 858-454-7381; 7545 Girard Ave; dishes $5-10; 🕑 6am-3pm) Classic coffee shop has tufted brown-and-gold vinyl booths and a posse of regulars from blue-haired socialites to sports celebs. The cooking is standard-issue American – pancakes, tuna melts and iceberg-lettuce salads – but it's the aura of the place that makes it special.

Also recommended:

**Royal Thai** (Map p247; ☎ 858-551-8424; 757 Pearl St) A branch of the Royal Thai restaurant in San Diego's Gaslamp Quarter (p263).

### MID-RANGE

**Barolo** ( ☎ 858-622-1202; 8935 Towne Center Dr; mains $10-18; 🕑 lunch Mon-Fri, dinner daily) Don't let its shopping-center location fool you: Barolo serves authentic Italian cooking prepared by an off-the-boat chef who makes his own pasta and seven different nightly specials. Reasonable prices, beautiful food. *Meraviglioso!*

**My Place** ( ☎ 858-454-3535; 7777 Girard Ave; mains lunch $8-20, dinner $13-25; 🕑 lunch daily, dinner Tue-Sat) Francophiles loves this casual sidewalk eatery that serves Cal-French café cuisine, including *moules mariniére* (mussels in white wine) with hand-cut fries, grilled sardines with lemon-pesto, steak frites, and blue-corn-battered calamari.

**George's Ocean Terrace Bistro** ( ☎ 858-454-4244; 1250 Prospect St; mains $15-20) Upstairs from George's at the Cove (p287), this 2nd-floor outdoor bistro has drop-dead views and serves main-sized salads, steaks and seafood. Make reservations for peak hours.

Also recommended:

**Trattoria Acqua** ( ☎ 858-454-0709; 1298 Prospect St; mains lunch $9-15, dinner $15-28) Scrumptious Northern Italian downtown.

**Come on In** ( ☎ 858-551-1063; 1030-B Torrey Pines Rd; mains breakfast & lunch $6-9, dinner $12-19; 🕑 breakfast, lunch & dinner) Wholesome homemade soups and basic meat-and-mashed-potatoes mains.

### TOP END

**George's at the Cove** ( ☎ 858-454-4244; 1250 Prospect St; mains $29-42; 🕑 dinner) Sweeping ocean vistas complement the artistry on the plate at La Jolla's top special-occasion restaurant. Even if its swank dining room had no view, chef Trey Fochee's superbly crafted Euro-Cal cuisine would still rank among the best in San Diego. Make reservations and polish your shoes.

**Tapénade** ( ☎ 858-551-7500; 7612 Fay Ave; mains lunch $13-18, dinner $25-36) Foodies thrill for the brilliant, sunny flavors of Tapénade, San Diego's finest for Provençal French (think ratatouille and wine reductions, not potatoes and cream-based sauces). At lunch there's an $18 two-course meal. On Thursday it serves up half-price food specials in the bar.

**Nine-Ten** ( ☎ 858-964-5400; 910 Prospect St; mains lunch $9-14, dinner $26-35; 🕑 6:30am-10pm) Modern art adorns the walls at this sleek, understated downtowner that serves up-to-the-minute contemporary cuisine. It's also the only morning-til-night restaurant in La Jolla. If you can't swing dinner, come for the $23 three-course lunch. Great burgers, too.

**Marine Room** ( ☎ 858-459-7222; 2000 Spindrift Dr; mains lunch $15-25, dinner $26-38; 🕑 lunch Tue-Sun, dinner nightly) When money is no object and you want high-drama cooking and views, book a sunset table at the Marine Room, which sits smack dab on the sand and presents highly stylized contemporary-French cuisine to the country-club set. Come at high tide on a full moon, when waves splash against the windows.

## Mission Beach & Pacific Beach
Map pp244–5

You can eat well for not a lot of money at these two beach communities. Both have a young, mostly local scene; PB has the bulk of the restaurants, however, especially along Garnet Ave.

**Eggery** ( ☎ 858-274-3122; 4150 Mission Blvd; mains $6-8; 🕑 breakfast & lunch) Head to the Eggery for breakfast. It has no view, but makes one of the best breakfasts at the beach; try the French toast.

**Kono's** ( ☎ 858-483-1669; 704 Garnet Ave; 🕑 breakfast & lunch) This place makes $5 breakfast burritos that you eat out of a basket in view of Crystal Pier.

**Broken Yolk** ( ☎ 858-270-9655; 1851 Garnet Ave; mains $5-9; ☺ breakfast & lunch) If you're shopping on Garnet, the Broken Yolk cooks up 47 omelette specials.

**Green Flash** ( ☎ 619-270-7715; 701 Thomas Ave; mains breakfast & lunch $5-10, dinner $10-24; ☺ 8am-10pm) A terrific breakfast or lunch spot for eggs, meaty burgers, big salads and triple-decker clubs, the Flash also has a weekday Happy Hour from 3pm to 7pm. Score a table outside on the patio. Dinners are OK, but you'll get more for your money inland.

**World Famous** ( ☎ 858-272-3100; 711 Pacific Beach Dr; mains breakfast & lunch $7-12, dinner $18-27; ☺ 7am-11pm) The same goes for this inappropriately named eatery, where you can watch the surf while eating sandwiches and burgers; popular at breakfast, too.

**Mission Café** ( ☎ 858-488-9060; 3795 Mission Blvd; dishes $6-9; ☺ breakfast & lunch) Down in Mission Beach, you can have French toast of homemade cinnamon bread at breakfast or Chino-Latino specialties at lunch, such as rosemary potatoes with black beans, salsa and eggs, or braised teriyaki tofu. Famously good coffee, too.

**Zen 5** ( ☎ 858-490-0121; 1130 Garnet Ave; mains $8-16; ☺ lunch Sat & Sun, dinner daily) Sushi is the star of the show at this young, energetic restaurant with fast, friendly servers in Pacific Beach. At Happy Hour, 5pm to 7pm nightly, appetizers are half-price.

## Ocean Beach                    Map pp244–5

Dining on a shoestring? You'll do great in OB. Most places are concentrated on Newport Ave.

**OB People's Market** ( ☎ 619-224-1387; cnr Voltaire & Sunset Cliffs Blvd; ☺ 8am-9pm) For vegetarian groceries, check out this organic cooperative with bulk foods, fresh soups, and excellent pre-made sandwiches, salads and wraps, most under $5. No meat.

**Hodad's** ( ☎ 619-224-4623; 5010 Newport Ave; burgers $5) OB's legendary burger joint serves great shakes and succulent hamburgers wrapped in paper. No shirt, no shoes, no problem.

**Ortega's Cocina** ( ☎ 619-222-4205; 4888 Newport Ave; mains $5-9; ☺ breakfast, lunch & dinner Wed-Mon) Ortega's is so popular that people queue up for a spot at the counter. Seafood is the specialty, but all its soulful, classic Mexican dishes are delicious.

**Rancho's Cocina** ( ☎ 619-226-7619; 1830 Sunset Cliffs Blvd; mains $4-12; ☺ 8am-10pm) Two blocks south of Newport Ave, Rancho's makes its own mole – a spicy sauce made with chilies and chocolate. In addition to Mexican standards, it also serves healthy and flavorful vegetarian and vegan dishes.

## Point Loma Area                Map p239

**Point Loma Seafoods** ( ☎ 619-223-1109; 2805 Emerson St; dishes $5-11; ☺ 9am-6:30pm Mon-Sat, 11am-6:30pm Sun) Order at the counter at this fish market-cum deli and grab a seat at a picnic table for off-the-boat-fresh seafood and icy cold beer. Located in the Shelter Island Marina, it's a San Diego institution. Great sushi, too.

## Coronado                        Map p239
### BUDGET & MID-RANGE

**1134 Cafe** ( ☎ 619-437-1134; 1134 Orange Ave; dishes under $7; ☺ 6am-9pm) Bright, airy café serves good scrambles, muffins and strong coffee at breakfast; at lunch and dinner there are soups, quiches and salads.

**Nite & Day** ( ☎ 619-435-9776; 847 Orange Ave; ☺ 24hr) For a refreshing change of pace in squeaky-clean Coronado, try this eat-at-the-counter greasy spoon for breakfast 'round the clock.

**Coronado Brewing Company** ( ☎ 619-437-4452; 170 Orange Ave; most mains $8-12) The delicious house brew goes well with the tasty pizza, pasta, sandwiches and fries at this good-for-your-soul, bad-for-your-diet bar and grill near the ferry.

**Mc P's** ( ☎ 619-435-5280; 1107 Orange Ave; dishes $8-18) Homey Irish fare – corned beef, stew, meatloaf – won't win any awards for innovation, but it's consistently good and goes down well with pints o' Guinness. Live music on weekends. Patio seating.

**Rhinoceros Cafe & Grill** ( ☎ 619-435-2121; 1166 Orange Ave; mains lunch $5-12, dinner $13-22) For pasta, salads, sandwiches and dinner specials.

### TOP END

**Chez Loma** ( ☎ 619-435-0661; 1132 Loma Ave; mains $20-29; ☺ brunch Sunday, dinner daily) Inside an 1899 cottage, this cozy French bistro serves updated classics, such as beef bourguignon, roast duckling and seafood cassoulet. For a bargain, come before 6pm for the $25 three-course prix-fixe menu.

**Prince of Wales** ( ☎ 619-435-6611; Hotel del Coronado, 1500 Orange Ave; mains $27-40; ☺ dinner Tue-Sun) It's hard to beat the romance of supping at the Hotel del Coronado, especially at a table overlooking the sea from the veranda of its 1st-class dining room, where silver service and French-inspired cuisine set the perfect tone for popping the question or fêting an important anniversary.

**Point Azura** ( ☎ 619-424-4477; Loews Coronado Bay Resort, 4000 Coronado Bay Rd; mains $27-33; ☽ dinner Tue-Sat) Grand for romantic, white-tablecloth Euro-Cal dining with views, and its to-die-for lobster risotto and superb five-course vegetarian tasting menu ($45).

## DRINKING & ENTERTAINMENT

For information about cinema, classical music, live theater, spectator sports and acquiring tickets to events, see p267.

### Coffeehouses

**Pannikin** (Map p247; ☎ 858-454-5453; 7467 Girard Ave, La Jolla; ☽ 7am-8pm) Popular for its traditional Italian espresso and Mexican chocolate, the Pannikin sometimes has live music on Friday evening.

**Living Room Coffeehouse** (Map p247; ☎ 858-459-1187; 1010 Prospect St, La Jolla; ☽ 6am-midnight) Check your email and munch on sandwiches and pastries at the La Jolla branch of the popular Hillcrest café (p266).

**Zanzibar** (Map pp244-5; ☎ 858-272-4762; 976 Garnet Ave, Pacific Beach; ☽ 7am-11pm) Popular for its focaccia-bread pizza and homemade soups, Zanzibar also has Wi-Fi.

**Café 976** (Map pp244-5; ☎ 858-272-0976; 976 Felspar, Pacific Beach; ☽ 7am-11pm) Not everyone in PB spends the days surfing; some drink coffee and reads books at this side-street café.

**Newbreak Coffee Co & Café** (Map pp244-5; ☎ 619-224-6666; 1959 Abbot St, Ocean Beach; ☽ 7am-6pm) A popular hangout for teetotalers and caffeine junkies in bar-crazy OB, the Newbreak also has Internet kiosks and Wi-Fi.

### Bars & Clubs
**LA JOLLA**                                            **Map p247**
The bulk of the bars in La Jolla are clustered around Prospect St and Girard Ave downtown.

**Beach House Brewery** ( ☎ 858-456-6279; 7536 Fay Ave) Escape from the madding crowds of downtown, and watch the game, down a pint and shoot some pool at this off-the-beaten-path locals' hangout that has indoor-outdoor seating.

**Karl Strauss Brewery** ( ☎ 858-551-2739; cnr Wall St & Herschel Ave) A branch of the downtown

microbrewery, Karl Strauss makes darn good beer. Pitchers cost $10 from 4pm to 6:30pm weekdays.

**Comedy Store** ( ☎ 858-454-9176; 916 Pearl St) One of the area's most established comedy venues, the Comedy Store also serves meals, drinks and barrels of laughs. Expect a cover charge ($15 to $20 on weekends with a two-drink minimum).

**Moondoggies** ( ☎ 858-454-9722; 909 Prospect St, 2nd fl) Frat boys do shots at this La Jolla bar, where there's dancing to hip-hop and Top 40 after 10pm Thursday to Saturday.

**Elario's** ( ☎ 858-551-3620; 7955 La Jolla Shores Dr, 11th fl) Sip cocktails while tapping your toe to jazz-piano standards on Thursday to Saturday evenings atop the Hotel La Jolla, about 10 minutes from downtown.

**La Sala** ( ☎ 858-454-0771; La Valencia Hotel, 1132 Prospect St) For civilized cocktails or Sunday afternoon Bloody Marys, visit the romantic, ocean-view lobby bar of La Valencia Hotel, which becomes a piano lounge on Friday and Saturday evenings.

**PACIFIC BEACH**                                       **Map pp244-5**
In PB look for bars and clubs on and around Garnet Ave, as well as near the beach. Most open at 4pm Monday to Thursday, noon on Friday and Saturday.

**Blind Melons** ( ☎ 858-483-7844; 710 Garnet Ave) The club books a solid line up of blues musicians with the occasional rock act thrown in for good measure at PB's main venue for live music.

**Club Tremors** ( ☎ 858-272-7278; 860 Garnet Ave) A dance club popular with a young crowd, Tremors has a low cover charge and cheap snacks.

**Moondoggies** ( ☎ 858-483-6550; 832 Garnet Ave) Next door to Club Tremors, Moondoggies has a large patio, big-screen TVs, pool tables, good food and an extensive tap selection; there's a second location in La Jolla.

**Society Billiard Cafe** ( ☎ 858-272-7665; 1051 Garnet Ave; ☽ 11am-2pm) Why settle for a beat-up pool table in the back of a dark bar when you can visit San Diego's plushest pool hall? The billiard room has 15 full-sized tables, snacks and a **bar** ( ☽ 11am-2am).

**Coaster Saloon** ( ☎ 858-488-4438; 744 Ventura Pl, Mission Beach) Old-fashioned neighborhood bar has front-row views of the Belmont Park roller coaster and draws an unpretentious crowd. Good margaritas.

**OCEAN BEACH**      **Map pp244–5**

In OB there are fewer choices than PB; most of them lie around Newport Ave.

**Winston's** ( ☎ 619-222-6822; 1921 Bacon St) Bands play most nights, often featuring live reggae. On Sunday there's a football party. On Monday night a Grateful Dead cover band draws stoners and Jerryophilics.

## Classical Music

**La Jolla Symphony & Chorus** ( ☎ 619-534-4637; www.lajollasymphony.com) holds quality concerts at UCSD's Mandeville Auditorium from October to June.

## Cinemas

**Cove** (Map p247; ☎ 619-819-0236; 7730 Girard Ave), in La Jolla, shows new independent films and European releases.

## SHOPPING

Most of coastal San Diego's shopping is limited to surf shops and bikini boutiques. A notable exception: Newport Ave in Ocean Beach, where a dozen antiques consignment shops line either side of the main drag. In La Jolla, the skirt-and-sweater crowd pays retail for cashmere sweaters and expensive tchotchkes (trinkets) downtown. Thrift shoppers head to Garnet Ave in Pacific Beach for vintage and recycled drag. Most stores buy, sell and trade.

If you like malls, make a bee line for the **University Towne Centre** (Map p239; ☎ 858-546-8858; 4545 La Jolla Village Dr), east of I-5 in La Jolla; anchor stores include Nordstrom, Macy's, Robinsons May, and Sears.

**South Coast Wahines** (Map pp244-5; ☎ 858-273-7600; 4500 Ocean Front Blvd, Pacific Beach) At the foot of Garnet Ave at the Crystal Pier in Pacific Beach, South Coast carries spiffy surf apparel for women.

**Pilar's Beachwear** (Map pp244-5; ☎ 858-488-3056; 3745 Mission Blvd, Mission Beach) For swimwear, women should head to Pilar's, which has all the latest styles in all sizes.

**Gone Bananas** (Map pp244-5; ☎ 858-488-4900; 3785 Mission Blvd, Mission Beach) If you don't find anything at Pilar's, head up the street for a large selection of mix-and-match bikinis and one-pieces, including Body Glove, Mossimo, Sauvage and three dozen other brands.

**South Coast Surf Shops** (Map pp244-5; ☎ 619-223-7017; 5023 Newport Ave, Ocean Beach) Apathetic surfer dudes man the counter at this beach-apparel

and surf-gear shop that carries a good selection of Quiksilver, Hurley, Billabong and O'Neill for men and women.

**Buff** (Map pp244-5; ☎ 858-581-2833; 1059 Garnet Ave) You'll find a wide range of outrageous clothes, many of them suitable for Halloween costumes, at this super-fun shop. Hot accessories, too.

**Buffalo Exchange** (Map pp244-5; ☎ 858-273-6227; 1007 Garnet Ave) If you need something to wear to dinner, Buffalo carries a good selection of contemporary and vintage fashions, including designer labels.

## GETTING THERE & AROUND

For details on getting to/from the San Diego metropolitan area, as well as getting to and from the airport, riding MTS buses, and traveling by train, taxi and rental car, see p272.

### Bicycle

Pacific Beach, Mission Beach, Mission Bay and Coronado are all great places to ride a bike. The **San Diego Bicycle Coalition** ( ☎ 858-487-6063; www.sdcbc.org) has maps and a wealth of information about biking in and around the city.

All public buses are equipped with bike racks and will transport two-wheelers for free. Inform the driver before boarding, then stow your bike on the rack on the tail end of the bus. Useful routes include:

**No 34** Between downtown and La Jolla (via Ocean Beach, Mission Bay, Mission Beach and Pacific Beach).
**No 41** Between Fashion Valley Center and UCSD.
**No 150** Between downtown and University Towne Centre.
**No 301** Between University Towne Centre and Oceanside.
**No 902** Between downtown and Coronado.

For more information, call the MTS (p272).

The following outfits all rent bicycles, from mountain and road bikes to kids' bikes and cruisers. In general, expect to pay about $7 per hour, $10 to $20 per half-day (four hours) and $20 to $25 per day.

**Bikes & Beyond** (Map p239; ☎ 619-435-7180; Coronado Ferry Landing, foot of Orange Ave)
**Cheap Rentals** (Map pp244-5; ☎ 858-488-9070, 800-941-7761; www.cheap-rentals.com; 3685 Mission Blvd, Mission Beach)
**Hamel's Beach Rentals** (Map pp244-5; ☎ 858-488-5050; 704 Ventura Pl, Mission Beach)
**Holland's Bicycles** (Map p239; ☎ 619-435-3153; www.hollandsbicycles.com; 977 Orange Ave, Coronado)

## Boat

San Diego Harbor Excursion operates the **Coronado Ferry** ( ☎ 619-234-4111, 800-442-7847; www .sdhe.com) from the foot of Orange Ave. Ferries make the 15-minute trip from San Diego's Broadway Pier at 1050 N Harbor Dr every hour on the hour, and leave Coronado on the half hour. A one way trip costs $2.25, and the ferry operates from 9:30am to 9:30pm Sunday to Thursday, and to 10:30pm Friday and Saturday. Take your bike on the ferry for an additional $0.50. **San Diego Water Taxi** ( ☎ 619-235-8294; www.sdhe.com) provides on-call transportation between Coronado, Shelter Island and San Diego from 2pm to 10pm Monday to Friday, and 11am to 11pm Saturday and Sunday ($6).

# SAN DIEGO NORTH COAST

Strung together like pearls on a strand, a handful of small beach towns extend northward from La Jolla to the Camp Pendleton Marine Base in northern San Diego County, which locals simply call 'North County.' Beginning with the pretty little seaside community of Del Mar, this stretch of land resembles the San Diego of 40 years ago, though more and more development, especially east of I-5, has turned North County into a giant bedroom community for San Diego and Orange County. Still, the beaches here are terrific, and the small seaside settlements are good places to stay for a few days if you want to soak up the laid-back SoCal scene. There's not a lot of sightseeing to do, but you can work on your tan and catch up on your reading while watching the sun glisten on the Pacific. A note on eating: Unless you're planning to drink a lot, it's not unreasonable to drive to San Diego for dinner. Via I-5 in non-rush-hour traffic, Del Mar is only 20 to 30 minutes away, Oceanside 45 to 60 minutes.

## Getting There & Around

From the south, take N Torrey Pines Rd to Del Mar for the most scenic approach to North County. Continue along the coast on S21 (which changes its name from Camino del Mar to Pacific Coast Hwy to Old Hwy 101, going north). The I-5 is quicker and

continues to LA. Avoid driving during rush hour (7am to 10am and 3pm to 7pm Monday to Friday).

Bus No 101 departs from University Towne Centre and follows the coastal road to Oceanside, while bus No 310 operates express service up I-5; for information call the **North County Transit District** (NCTD; ☎ 760-966-6500; www.gonctd .com). The NCTD also operates the *Coaster* commuter train, which originates in San Diego, and makes stops in Solana Beach, Encinitas, Carlsbad and Oceanside. All NCTD buses and trains have bike racks. Greyhound buses stop at Oceanside and San Diego, but nowhere in between.

The **San Diego North County Convention & Visitors Bureau** ( ☎ 760-745-4741, 800-848-3336; www .sandiegonorth.com; 360 N Escondido Blvd), in Escondido, is an excellent source for information on all of North County, including inland locations. Request a free visitors guide.

## DEL MAR

### pop 4400

The ritziest of North County's seaside suburbs, Del Mar has good (if pricey) restaurants, unique galleries, high-end boutiques and a horse-racing track, which is the site of the annual county fair. Downtown Del Mar (sometimes called 'the village') extends for about a mile along Camino del Mar. At its hub, where 15th St crosses Camino del Mar, the tastefully designed shopping center Del Mar Plaza has restaurants, boutiques and upper-level terraces that look out to sea.

### Sights & Activities

At the beach end of 15th St, **Seagrove Park** abuts the beach and overlooks the ocean. This little stretch of well-groomed beachfront lawn is a community hub frequented by locals. It's perfect for a picnic.

The **Del Mar Racetrack & Fairgrounds** (Map p246; ☎ 858-755-1141; www.dmtc.com; admission $5) was founded in 1937 by a prestigious group, including Bing Crosby and Jimmy Durante. The lush gardens and pink, Mediterranean-style architecture are a visual delight. Get gussied up. The thoroughbred racing season runs from mid-July to mid-September.

Brightly colored hot-air balloons are a trademark of the skies above Del Mar, on the northern fringe of the metropolitan area. For flights, contact **California Dreamin'** ( ☎ 951-699-0601, 800-373-3359; www.californiadreamin.com).

The *Reader* (p235) carries other balloon company listings and frequently contains hot-air excursion discount coupons. Flights are usually at sunrise or sunset. They last an hour (though up to three hours may be required for instruction and transportation) and cost around $160 on weekdays.

## Sleeping

Rooms in Del Mar in summer aren't cheap. For the best rates stay 0.5 miles south of town at one of the first two properties listed here.

**Best Western Stratford Inn** (Map p246; ☎ 858-755-1501, 800-446-7229; www.pacificahost.com; 710 Camino Del Mar; r $150-220; P ☒ ) A motel complex with well-kept rooms, the Stratford also has laundry facilities and two pools. Some units have kitchenettes and distant ocean views.

**Carriage House Inn** (Map p246; ☎ 858-755-9765, 800-453-4411; www.delmarinn.com; 720 Camino Del Mar; r $135-190; P ☒ ) Faux Tudor-style hotel tries hard to please its guests, though it could use a few upgrades. Continental breakfast delivered to every room. Afternoon tea service, too.

**Del Mar Motel** (Map p246; ☎ 858-755-1534, 800-223-8449; www.delmarmotelonthebeach.com; 1702 Coast Blvd; r $200-225, ocean view $265; P ) There's nothing memorable about the only beachside motel in Del Mar, except for the price of its rooms. You're paying for the location on the sand, not the amenities. Some units sleep five.

**L'Auberge Del Mar Resort & Spa** (Map p246; ☎ 858-259-1515, 800-553-1336; www.laubergedelmar.com; 1540 Camino Del Mar; r $265-490; P ☐ ☒ ) Rebuilt in the 1990s on the grounds of the historic Hotel del Mar, where 1920s Hollywood celebrities once frolicked, L'Auberge continues its long tradition of European-style elegance and service with luxurious linens, a full-service spa and lovely gardens.

## Eating

Head to **Del Mar Plaza** (Map p246; 1555 Camino Del Mar) to pick up groceries and sandwiches for the beach at **Harvest Ranch Market** (Map p246; ☎ 858-847-0555; ☼ 8am-9pm). Or check out the patio and restaurants atop the plaza for North County's best vantage points. Come before sunset. Try the following:

**Il Fornaio** (Map p246; ☎ 858-755-8876; mains $10-21) Although it's a chain restaurant, Il Fornaio and its adjacent wine bar Enoteca have great rooftop views. Stick to pizza, salad and vino; there's a smoking area, too.

**Epazote** (Map p246; ☎ 858-259-9966; mains lunch $10-14, dinner $16-24) The Southwestern-Asian cuisine is well spiced and flavorful; the view is even better.
**Pacifica Del Mar** (Map p246; ☎ 858-792-0476; mains lunch $11-16, dinner $22-32) The seafood is fresh and the preparations inventive, but it's expensive at dinner.

Other eating options in Del Mar include the following.

**Jake's Del Mar** (Map p246; ☎ 858-755-2002; 1660 Coast Blvd; mains lunch $9-14, dinner $18-27; ☼ lunch Tue-Sun, dinner daily) For beachside drinks and half-price appetizers from 4pm to 6pm weekdays and 2:30pm to 4:30pm on Saturday, head to Jake's. The view's great, the food nothing special.

**Café Del Mar** (Map p246; ☎ 858-481-1133; 1247 Camino Del Mar; mains lunch $8-13, dinner $9-19) Dine in the courtyard, beneath the canopy of a coral tree, on entree-sized salads (try the warm chicken salad), pizza from the wood-fired oven, and simple grilled and roasted meats. Lots of veggie choices, too. Smoking section.

**Sbicca** (Map p246; ☎ 858-481-1001; 215 15th St; mains lunch $7-12, dinner $16-28) Family-owned contemporary California bistro cooks up flavorful combinations, such as tomato-saffron seafood paella or maple-roasted pork prime rib. Prices are good at lunch when inventive salads and sandwiches take center stage. Sit upstairs. Make reservations.

**Americana Restaurant** (Map p246; ☎ 858-794-6838; 1454 Camino del Mar; mains breakfast & lunch $7-12, dinner $19-25; ☼ breakfast & lunch daily, dinner Tue-Sat) Consider the Americana Restaurant for regional American cooking, from cheese grits to chicken Reubens.

**Osteria del Pescatore** (Map p246; ☎ 858-509-9293; 1201 Camino Del Mar; mains $14-25; ☼ lunch Tue-Sat, dinner daily) For Italian pasta, meats and seafood, check out this place.

**Arterra** (Map p246; ☎ 858-369-6032; Marriott Hotel, 11966 El Camino Real; mains lunch $13-19, dinner $27-33; ☼ breakfast, lunch & dinner) If you're a food fetishist you'll enjoy this big player on the celebrity-chef circuit. Its high-style farm-fresh California cuisine garners accolades, but prices are high and the vibe corporate.

## SOLANA BEACH
pop 13,500

Solana Beach is the next town north from Del Mar – it's not quite as posh, but it has good beaches and the **Cedros Design District** (Map p246; Cedros Ave), which has unique home-furnishings stores, art and architecture studios, antiques shops and handcrafted-clothing boutiques. If you're remodeling your house, you'll love Cedros Ave. For camping and travel gear, stop by **Adventure 16** (Map p246; ☎ 858-755-7662; 143 S Cedros Ave, Suite M).

Music lovers flock to the **Belly Up Tavern** (Map p246; ☎ 858-481-2282, 858-481-8140; 143 S Cedros Ave), a converted warehouse and bar that consistently books good bands that run the gamut from jazz to funk. Cover charges range from $5 to $40; call ahead.

Some of the better food options include:

**Wild Note Café** (Map p246; ☎ 858-259-7310; 143 S Cedros Ave; mains lunch $6-12, dinner $12-20; ☼ lunch daily, dinner Tue-Sun) The jazzy café at the Belly Up has concrete floors and open-truss ceilings, and serves some of the best burgers around. Great salads, grilled fish and steak round out the menu. Make reservations for dinner.

**Zinc Café** (Map p246; ☎ 858-793-5436; mains $5-7; ☼ 7am-5pm) Order at the counter and sit outside at this all-veg café, which serves salads, vegetarian chili and pizza good enough to satisfy all but the most hardcore carnivores.

**Tony's Jacal** (Map p246; ☎ 858-755-2274; 621 Valley Ave; mains lunch $6-11, dinner $8-16; ☼ lunch Mon-Sat, dinner daily) Open since 1946, Tony's is a Spanish-style roadhouse with rough-hewn wood beams, dark wood paneling, icy-delicious margaritas and some of North County's best traditional Mexican. Make reservations for dinner. (Valley Ave goes north of Via de la Valle, just west of I-5.)

## CARDIFF-BY-THE-SEA
pop 12,000

Shortened to 'Cardiff' by most, this stretch of restaurants, surf shops and New Age–style businesses along the Pacific Coast Hwy is good for surfing and is popular with a laid-back crowd, though it's losing ground to ever-growing shopping centers along the main drag, San Elijo Ave, one block east of the coast highway. The nearby **San Elijo Lagoon** (Map p246; ☎ 760-436-3944; www.sanelijo.org) is a 1000-acre ecological preserve popular with bird-watchers for its herons, coots, terns, ducks, egrets and more than 250 other species. A seven-mile network of trails leads through the area. At **Cardiff State Beach** ( ☎ 760-753-5091; www.parks.ca.gov; ☼ 7am-sunset; **P** $6), just south of Cardiff-by-the-Sea, the surf break on the reef is mostly popular with long boarders,

but it gets very good at low tide with a big north swell. A little further north, **San Elijo State Beach** has good winter waves.

### Sleeping & Eating

**San Elijo State Beach Campground** ( ☎ 760-753-5091, reservations 800-444-7275; tent/RV sites in summer $26/39) Overlooks the surf at the end of Birmingham Dr.

**Pipes Café** (Map p246; ☎ 760-632-0056; 121 Liverpool Ave; mains $4-6; ☼ 7am-3pm) Barefoot surfers chow down egg burritos and scrambles here before hitting the water. At lunch there are sandwiches, too.

**Ki's Restaurant** (Map p246; ☎ 760-436-5236; 2591 S Coast Hwy 101; mains lunch $6-9, dinner $11-17; ☼ 8am-9pm) A great indie café and a hub of activity, Ki's makes awesome smoothies, health-burgers and salads; there's also a great 2nd-floor ocean view. Live music Friday nights.

**Trattoria Positano** (Map p246; ☎ 760-632-0111; 2171 San Elijo Ave; mains $10-14) For white-tablecloth Italian food book a table at this homey mom-and-pop trattoria, one block inland from the highway.

## ENCINITAS
pop 58,500

Peaceful Encinitas has a decidedly down-to-earth vibe, perfect for a day trip or a weekend escape. Yogi Paramahansa Yoganada founded his **Self-Realization Fellowship Retreat & Hermitage** (Map p246) here in 1937, and the town has been a magnet for holistic healers and natural-lifestyle seekers ever since. The gold lotus domes of the hermitage – conspicuous on Old Hwy 101 (S21) – mark the southern end of Encinitas and the turn-out for **Swami's**, a powerful reef break surfed by territorial locals. There's a parking lot just south of the hermitage, on the western side of Old Hwy 101, which gives a good view of the surf. If you practice yoga or meditation, you must visit the hermitage's **Meditation Garden** (entrance 215 K St; ☼ 9am-5pm Tue-Sat, 11am-5pm Sun), which has wonderful ocean vistas; the entrance is west of Old Hwy 101.

The heart of Encinitas lies north of the hermitage between E and D Sts. Apart from outdoor cafés, bars, restaurants and surf shops, the town's main attraction is **La Paloma Theater** (Map p246; ☎ 760-436-7469; 471 S Coast Hwy 101), built in 1928. La Paloma shows current movies nightly.

SAN DIEGO

Approximately 80% of all the poinsettias sold worldwide originated in the inland hills that are used for commercial flower farms, most notably the **Paul Ecke Poinsettia Ranch** (Map p246; ☎ 760-753-1134; www.ecke.com), which was established in 1923. In December there's an enormous poinsettia display at the ranch, and in spring, once poinsettia season has passed, the ranch's 50 acres burst into bloom with an array of flowers, which look spectacular from I-5. Try to visit in early spring (March to early May), when ranunculus, another flower variety, explode in a rainbow of color (it's a great place to photograph kids). Call for directions.

The 30-acre **Quail Botanical Gardens** (Map p246; ☎ 760-436-3036; www.qbgardens.com; adult/child $8/3; 9am-5pm) has a large collection of California native plants and sections planted with flora of various regions of the world, including Australia and Central America. At the children's garden, there are special activities for little ones; call for details. From I-5, go east on Encinitas Blvd to Quail Gardens Dr.

## Sleeping & Eating

**Moonlight Beach Motel** (Map p246; ☎ 760-753-0623; 800-323-1259; www.moonlightbeachmotel.com; 233 2nd St; r $105-125; P ) Upstairs rooms have private decks and partial ocean views at this mom-and-pop motel, one-and-a-half blocks from the sea. Not all rooms have air-con; some could use upgrading, but they're clean and quiet.

**Best Western Encinitas Inn & Suites** (Map p246; ☎ 760-942-7455, 866-326-4648; www.bwencinitas.com; 85 Encinitas Blvd; r $140-160; P ) If you wear nail polish and white pants, you'll be better off at this hotel, which has all modern conveniences and up-to-date furnishings.

**Swami's Café** (Map p246; ☎ 760-944-0612; 1163 S Coast Hwy; mains $5-7; breakfast & lunch) For breakfast burritos, stir frys, salads and smoothies, you can't beat Swami's. There's lots for vegetarians, too.

**El Callejon** (Map p246; ☎ 760-634-2793; 345 Pacific Coast Hwy; mains $6-13) Raucous fun Mexican joint at the north end of town. Full bar.

**Trattoria I Trulli** (Map p246; ☎ 760-943-6800; 830 S Coast Hwy; mains $11-20) Just one taste of the homemade gnocchi, ravioli or lasagna, and you'll know why this mom-and-pop Italian trattoria is always packed. Reservations recommended.

**Siamese Basil** (Map p246; ☎ 760-634-2793; 527 S Coast Hwy; mains $8-14; 11am-10pm) Check out this eatery for Thai food.

**Chuao Chocolatier** (Map p246; ☎ 760-635-1444; 937 S Coast Hwy) If you like chocolate, this is a must-visit; it's in the Lumber Yard shopping center.

## CARLSBAD

pop 78,500

Carlsbad's most famous attraction is Legoland. After Encinitas, Carlsbad is the best place to stay if you want to be within walking distance of shopping, restaurants and the beach. Rather than being stretched out along the highway like many North County towns, it has a solid downtown of four square blocks between I-5 and Carlsbad Blvd (which run north–south and are connected by Carlsbad Village Dr running east–west). The **Visitor Information Center** (Map p246; ☎ 760-434-6093; www.carlsbadca.org; 400 Carlsbad Village Dr) is housed in the original 1887 Santa Fe train depot.

The town came into being when the railroad came through in the 1880s. John Frazier, an early homesteader, former sailor and ship's captain, sank a well and found water that had a high mineral content, supposedly the identical mineral content of spa water in Karlsbad (hence the town's name), in Bohemia (now the Czech Republic). He capitalized on it and built a grand spa hotel, which prospered until the 1930s. The Queen Anne–style building that was the hotel is now **Neiman's Restaurant & Bar** (Map p246; ☎ 760-729-4131; 2978 Carlsbad Blvd), where the atmosphere is appreciably better than the parsley sprig and orange slice garnished food.

## Sights & Activities
### LEGOLAND CALIFORNIA

Modeled loosely after the original Legoland, in Denmark, **Legoland California** (Map p246; ☎ 760-918-5346; www.lego.com/legoland/california; 10am-8pm daily mid-Jun–late-Aug, 10am-5pm otherwise, closed Tue & Wed fall-spring; adult/child 3-12 $44/37, two-day tickets $52/45) is an enchanting fantasy environment built entirely of those little colored plastic building blocks that many of us grew up with. Highlights include **Miniland**, in which the skylines of major metropolitan cities have been spectacularly recreated entirely of Lego. At **Water Works**, kids play with water and music. There's also face-painting, boat rides and several roller coasters scaled down for kids. Compared with some of the bigger, flashier parks, such as Disneyland and SeaWorld, it's all rather low-key and far less commercial – though there are plenty of opportunities to buy Lego. At least it sparks creativity. The park is best for pre-adolescent kids. If you have toddlers, pick up the brochure 'What to do When You're Two' for age-appropriate activities.

To get to Legoland, take the Legoland/Cannon Rd exit off I-5 and follow the signs. From downtown Carlsbad or downtown San Diego, take the *Coaster* to the Carlsbad Village Station, from where bus No 344 goes straight to the park. Call to inquire about discounts.

### CARLSBAD RANCH

From March to May, the 50-acre flower fields of **Carlsbad Ranch** (Map p246; ☎ 760-431-0352; http://visit.theflowerfields.com; adult/child $8/5; 9am-5pm) are ablaze in a sea of carmine, saffron and the snow-white blossom of ranunculus. The fields are two blocks east of I-5; take the Palomar Airport Rd exit, go east, then left on Paseo del Norte Rd – look for the windmill. Call for an events schedule.

### BATIQUITOS LAGOON

One of the last remaining tidal wetlands in California, Batiquitos Lagoon separates Carlsbad from Encinitas. A self-guided tour lets you explore area plants, including the prickly pear cactus, coastal sage scrub and eucalyptus trees, as well as lagoon birds, such as the great heron and the snowy egret. One of the artificial islands in the lagoon is a nesting site for the California least tern and the western snowy plover, both endangered species. You can hike the reserve anytime, but stop by the **Nature Center** ( ☎ 931-0800; www.batiquitosfoundation.org; noon-4pm Wed-Fri, 10am-2pm Sat & Sun) if it's open. The Four Seasons Aviara resort and golf course hug the lagoon's northern edge, while its eastern side is bordered by La Costa Resort & Spa (p296).

### OTHER ATTRACTIONS

One of the best ways to appreciate the coast is from the air. You can take a thrilling open-cockpit ride in a 1920s biplane with **Barnstorming Adventures** ( ☎ 760-438-7680, 800-759-5667; www.barnstorming.com; flights from $120 for 2 people).

Alternative health guru Deepak Chopra leads seminars on mind-body medicine, complemented by specialized spa treatments, at the **Chopra Center** (Map p246; ☎ 760-494-1600, 888-424-6772; www.chopra.com) at the La Costa Resort & Spa (p296). If you're a musician, you'll love the **Museum of Making Music** (Map p246; ☎ 760-438-5996, 877-551-9776; www.museumofmakingmusic.com; 5790 Armada Dr; adult/child $5/3; 10am-5pm Tue-Sun), which has historical exhibits and listening stations; call for directions. If you wonder what the hills looked like before they got subdivided, visit the 27-acre hilltop **Leo Carrillo Ranch Historic Park** (Map p246; ☎ 760-476-1042; www.carrillo-ranch.org; admission free; 9am-6pm Tue-Sat, 11am-6pm Sun). Several farm buildings and exhibits provide insight into local history, but the small park is surrounded by a maze of tract housing.

The long, sandy **beaches** of Carlsbad are great for walking and searching for seashells. Good access is from Carlsbad Blvd, two blocks south of Carlsbad Village Dr, where there's a boardwalk, rest rooms and free parking.

## Sleeping

Three miles south of downtown you can camp at **South Carlsbad State Park Campground** (Map p246; ☎ 760-438-3143, reservations 800-444-7275; tent sites $16-21, RV sites $26-31; P ), which has 222 tent and RV sites.

**Motel 6** (Map p246; ☎ 760-434-7135; www.motel6.com; 1006 Carlsbad Village Dr; s $50-64, d $56-70) For no-frills lodging, you won't find cheaper.

**Surf Motel** (Map p246; ☎ 760-729-7961, 800-523-9170; www.surfmotelcarlsbad.com; 3135 Carlsbad Blvd; r $100-130) The second-cheapest place in town has thin pillows and more-or-less clean rooms.

**Best Western Beach Terrace Inn** (Map p246; ☎ 760-729-5951, 800-433-5415; www.beachterraceinn.com; 2775 Ocean St; r $170-250; P ) Great location and well-kept rooms, but it's pricey. This 1970s white-stucco motel with cookie-cutter furnishings has some rooms fronting the beach.

**Carlsbad Inn Beach Resort** (Map p246; ☎ 760-434-7020, 800-235-393; 3075 Carlsbad Blvd; r $205-290; P ) A faux-Tudor upper-end-tourist-class hotel cum time-share property on the beachfront, this inn has oodles of activities, from ceramics to Ping Pong tourneys.

Carlsbad has two splurge-worthy luxury resorts; both offer discounted packages.

**Four Seasons Aviara** (Map p246; ☎ 760-603-6800, 800-332-3442; www.fourseasons.com/aviara; 7100 Four Seasons Point; r from $375; P 🖳 🏊) Offers superb service and top-flight amenities, but feels a touch suburban, like a gated-community on steroids.

**La Costa Resort & Spa** (Map p246; ☎ 760-438-9111, 800-729-4772; www.lacosta.com; Costa Del Mar Rd; r from $300; P 🖳 🏊) The spectacular grounds, beautiful architecture and stunning spa are offset by so-so service.

## Eating

**Armenian Cafe** (Map p246; ☎ 760-720-2233; 3126 Carlsbad Blvd; mains $8-15; 🕙 8am-9pm) In addition to omelettes, salads and sandwiches, the café also serves delicious dolmas, kebabs and Middle Eastern specialties.

**Pizza Port** (Map p246; ☎ 760-720-7007; 571 Carlsbad Village Dr; pizzas $7-16; 🕙 11am-11pm) Head to Pizza Port for the best pizza pies and locally brewed beer.

**Pelly's Fish Market & Café** (Map p246; ☎ 760-431-8454; 7110 Avenida Encinas; dishes $5-12; 🕙 10am-7pm Mon-Sat, 10am-6pm Sun) Order at the counter at this shopping center fish market that grills fresh-caught seafood and serves mm-mm-good chowder in paper bowls. Next to Ralph's supermarket, off Poinsettia Ave Exit from I-5.

## Shopping

Big-name retailers, such as Donna Karan and Kenneth Cole, have outlets at the **Carlsbad Company Stores** (Map p246; ☎ 760-804-9000, 888-790-7467; Paseo del Norte; 🕙 10am-8pm). Take I-5 to Palomar Airport Rd; go east to Paseo del Norte and turn north.

## OCEANSIDE

pop 167,000

Home for many of the employees who work at giant Camp Pendleton Marine Base on the town's northern border, Oceanside has a huge military presence, ensuring little cultural subtlety or diversity. Oceanside lacks the charm of Encinitas and Carlsbad – too much bass, not enough treble. Most points of interest lie along the coast, unless you're in the market for automotive parts or a military-style jacket. Amtrak, Greyhound, the *Coaster* and MTS buses all stop at the **Oceanside Transit Center** (235 S Tremont St).

Stop in at the **California Welcome Center** (Map p246; ☎ 760-721-1101, 800-350-7873; www.oceanside

chamber.com, www.californiawelcomecenter.org; 928 N Coast Hwy; 🕙 9am-5pm), which has helpful staff, for coupons for local attractions, as well as maps and information for the San Diego area and the entire state.

## Sights & Activities

The wooden **Oceanside Pier**, which extends more than 1900ft out to sea, is so long that there's an **electric shuttle** ( ☎ 760-433-7829; 🕙 10-8pm) that transports people to the end (50c). You'll also find bait-and-tackle shops, with poles to rent and lights for night fishing. Two major surf competitions – the West Coast Pro-Am and the National Scholastic Surf Association (NSSA) – take place near the pier in June.

See a history of surf contests at the wonderful **California Surf Museum** (Map p246; ☎ 760-721-6876; www.surfmuseum.org; 223 N Coast Hwy; admission free; 🕙 10am-4pm; closed Tue-Wed in winter). Displays include the whopping 8ft-long, 85lb redwood board that once belonged to Baird Fraser, plus photos and surf memorabilia of Duke Kahanamoku, the Olympic gold-medal swimmer and surfer who died in 1968.

Little remains from the 1880s, when the new Santa Fe coastal railway came through Oceanside, but a few buildings designed by Irving Gill and Julia Morgan still stand. The Welcome Center has a pamphlet describing a self-guided history walk.

At the northern end of the waterfront, the extensive Oceanside Harbor provides slips for hundreds of boats. **Helgren's** (Map p246; ☎ 760-722-2133; www.helgrensportfishing.com; 315 Harbor Dr S) leads a variety of charter trips for sportfishing ($34/60 half/full day) and whale-watching ($18 full day).

Founded in 1798, **Mission San Luis Rey de Francia** (Map p246; ☎ 760-757-3651; www.sanluisrey.org; 4050 Mission Ave, Hwy 76; admission $5; 🕙 10am-4pm) was the largest California mission and the most successful in recruiting Native American converts. It was known as the 'king of the missions,' and at one point some 3000 neophytes lived and worked here. After the Mexican government secularized the missions, San Luis fell into ruin; the adobe walls of the church, from 1811, are the only original parts left. Inside there are displays on work and life in the mission, with some original religious art and artifacts. The mission is four miles inland.

Behind the mission, tranquil **Heritage Park Village & Museum** (Map p246; ☎ 760-966-4545; grounds ⊙ 9am-4pm, buildings 1-3pm Sun only) preserves historic structures from the early 20th century, including a doctor's office, a jail and a blacksmith shop.

If you want to surf, visit **Action Beach Board Shop** (Map p246; ☎ 760-722-7101; www.actionbeach .com; 310 Mission Ave) to rent surfboards ($10/20 two hours/full day), wet suits ($5/10 two hours/full day) and other items. **Team Wahine Surfing School** ( ☎ 760-439-5679; www.teamwahine .com) gives year-round lessons ($55 first hour, including gear) and has surf camps for kids.

## Sleeping & Eating

Budget motels aren't hard to find, but they fill up on weekends in summer.

**Oceanside Days Inn** (Map p246; ☎ 760-722-7661; www.daysinn.com; r $85-120; ⓟ ) For a basic motel, the mattresses are surprisingly good. Near the Oceanside Harbor Dr exit.

**Ruby's Diner** (Map p246; ☎ 760-433-7829) This mid-priced '50s-style diner on the pier has good burgers and milkshakes, and a full bar.

**Beach Break Café** (Map p246; ☎ 760-439-6355; 1902 S Coast Hwy; mains under $8; ⊙ breakfast & lunch) Fuel up on eggs, sandwiches and salads at this surfers' diner on the east side of the road in a small shopping center.

**Kealani's** (Map p246; ☎ 760-722-5642; 207 N Coast Hwy at Mission; mains $4-6; ⊙ 11am-8pm Mon & Tue, 11am-6pm Wed, 11am-8pm Thu-Sat) If you like traditional Hawaiian plate lunches, such as teriyaki chicken and grilled Mahi Mahi, Kealani's makes them right: all come with rice and macaroni salad.

SAN DIEGO

# Palm Springs & the Deserts

Forget about green. At first the deserts seem barren and desolate, but after the initial shock of the heat and aridity wears off, the stark landscape, brilliantly clear light and sweeping expanses captivate the imagination, taking on a special beauty all their own.

Palm Springs sits atop a giant aquifer and gets its name from the hot springs around which the city was built. The first hotels opened for those seeking the health benefits of the springs and the dry desert climate. From the late 1920s it became known as a resort area and as a winter getaway for Hollywood stars, many of whom built single-story modernist homes in the 1940s and '50s. (If you love mid-century modern, you'll go nuts in Palm Springs.) The city's popularity faded in the late '60s, but today Palm Springs is back on the map. A huge gay and lesbian community has sprung up over the last two decades, and many people now live in the city year-round.

Once you leave the subdivisions that surround Palm Springs, the desert stretches out as far the eye can see, interrupted only by chocolate-colored hills and towering mountain peaks. Joshua Tree National Park, a favorite of rock climbers, supports wacky-looking trees and marks the line between the Colorado and Mojave Deserts. And beyond the nearly two-mile-high San Jacinto Mountains, the gigantic Anza-Borrego Desert State Park thrills with its wide open spaces and desolate hills. Spend a few days in this vast, wild land, and your new favorite colors may be tan, chestnut and gold.

## HIGHLIGHTS

- Whisking 6000ft up the San Jacinto Mountains aboard the **Palm Springs Aerial Tramway** (p301)
- Lazing poolside, vodka-tonic in hand, at one of Palm Springs' mid-century modern **hotels** (p308)
- Ogling the funny-looking trees and zipping up and down giant rocks at **Joshua Tree National Park** (p314)
- Watching for wildlife – and maybe even spotting a rare bighorn sheep – on a hike at the **Indian Canyons** (p303)
- Oohing and aahing at the vast expanse of desert that unfurls below you from Font's Point at **Anza-Borrego Desert State Park** (p319)

PALM SPRINGS & THE DESERTS

| Palm Springs Aerial Tramway |
| Joshua Tree National Park |
| ★★ Palm Springs |
| ★ Indian Canyons |
| ★ Anza-Borrego Desert State Park |

- PALM SPRINGS POP: 44,800
- AVERAGE TEMPS: JAN 40/69°F, JUL 64/102°F

## PALM SPRINGS & THE DESERTS

**INFORMATION**
Anza-Borrego Desert State
Park Visitor Center..........**1** B3

**SIGHTS & ACTIVITIES** (pp320–1)
Borrego Palm Canyon Nature
Trail......................(see 10)
Cactus Loop Nature Trail.....**2** B3
Elephant Trees Discovery Trail.**3** B3
Indian Morteros..................**4** B4
Indian Pictographs...............**5** B4
Narrows Earth Trail..............**6** B3
Peg Leg Smith Monument......**7** B3
Yaqui Well Nature Trail.........**8** B3

**SLEEPING**          (pp321–2)
Arroyo Salado Campground....**9** B3
Borrego Palm Canyon
Campground.................**10** B3
Bow Willow Campground......**11** B4
Culp Valley Campground......**12** B3
Fish Creek Primitive Camp...**13** B4
Mountain Palm Springs
Campground.................**14** B4
Tamarisk Grove Campground.**15** B3
Yaqui Pass Campground......**16** B3
Yaqui Well Campground......(see 8)

# PALM SPRINGS

**pop 44,500**

Resort hounds love Palm Springs. About 3.5 million visitors come here in the cooler months, generally October through April, to play golf and tennis and enjoy the desert climate of the Coachella Valley, the 300-sq-mile valley that stretches eastward from Palm Springs. From young newlyweds meandering the streets of downtown, to circuit-party gay boys lounging by swimming pools, to LA matrons recovering from face-lifts behind the bougainvillea-covered walls of gated compounds, people are here to relax.

## ORIENTATION

Palm Springs has a compact downtown area, centered on four blocks of Palm Canyon Dr, with shops, banks, restaurants and a few sights. In this part of town, traffic goes south on Palm Canyon Dr and north on Indian Canyon Dr. Tahquitz Canyon Way divides these streets into north and south (eg N Palm Canyon Dr and S Palm Canyon Dr). At the south end of town, Palm Canyon Dr abruptly turns eastward and becomes E Palm Canyon Dr. When winter drivers crowd the main drag, Sunrise Way is the fastest north–south route through town.

South of downtown, restaurants and chain motels extend along E Palm Canyon Dr and Hwy 111 from Palm Springs to Cathedral

ity, the first in a string of towns sprawling outward through the Coachella Valley. The towns bleed together and have little individual identity in the way Palm Springs does.

## INFORMATION
### Bookstores
Look for large chain bookstores in the area's malls and shopping centers, southeast of town (see p312).

**Peppertree Bookstore** (Map p305; ☎ 760-325-4821; www.peppertreebookstore.com; 622 N Palm Canyon Dr) Palm Springs' only in-town bookstore often hosts readings. Small store, good selection.

### Internet Access
**Malajava** (Map p305; ☎ 760-325-3494; 300 N Palm Canyon Dr; per 30min $4; 🕙 6am-6pm, shorter in summer)

**Palm Springs Public Library** (Map p305; ☎ 760-322-7323; www.palmspringslibrary.org; 300 Sunrise Way; 🕙 9am-8pm Mon-Tue, 9am-5:30pm Wed-Thu, 10am-5:30pm Fri, 9am-5:30pm Sat) Has 20 terminals with word-processing programs and free Internet access.

### Media
**Desert Sun** Palm Springs' daily newspaper has mostly local news.

**KWXY 1340AM, 98.5FM** Campy Rat Pack cocktail music that matches Palm Springs' mid-century architecture.

**Los Angeles Times** The West Coast's most important newspaper gets delivered to Palm Springs daily.

### Medical Services
**Desert Regional Medical Center** (Map p305; ☎ 760-323-6511; 1150 N Indian Canyon Dr) Has 24-hour emergency care. Contact the hospital during business hours for nonemergency medical assistance.

### Money
Look for ATMs all over downtown, as well as in supermarkets.

**Anderson Travel** (Map p305; ☎ 760-325-5556; 100 E Tahquitz Canyon Way; 🕙 9am-4:30pm Mon-Fri) Exchanges foreign currency and provides foreign-currency traveler's checks; call ahead for large sums.

### Post
**Palm Springs Post Office** (Map p305; ☎ 760-322-4111, 800-275-8777; 333 E Amado Rd; 🕙 9am-5pm Mon-Fri, 9am-5pm Sat) The city's main office provides all postal services.

### Tourist Information
**Uptown Visitors Center** (Map p305; ☎ 760-327-2828; 477 N Palm Canyon Dr, Suite 101; 🕙 10am-4pm) The secondary office of the Visitor Information & Reservation

Center provides all the same services as the main office, but you can walk to this one from downtown.

**Visitor Information & Reservation Center** (Map p302; ☎ 760-778-8418, 800-347-7746; www.palm-springs.org; 2901 N Palm Canyon Dr; 🕙 9am-5pm) North of town, at the tramway turnoff, the center provides free hotel bookings, special interest guides, maps, and many tourist publications, including *Palm Springs Official Visitors Guide* and *Gay Palm Springs Visitors Guide* (both free). Fans of modernism can pick up a map, *Palm Springs Modern* ($5), which will guide them to homes – many of them private – designed by Albert Frey, Richard Neutra, Donald Wexler, and George and Bob Alexander.

## SIGHTS
In summertime, many sights have reduced hours; call ahead.

### Palm Springs Aerial Tramway
The highlight of a visit to Palm Springs is a trip in this revolving **cable car** (Map p302; ☎ 760-325-1391, 760-325-1449, 888-515-8726; www.pstramway.com; adult/child $21/14; 🕙 10am-8pm Mon-Fri, 8am-8pm Sat & Sun), which climbs nearly 6000 vertical feet, from the desert floor up the San Jacinto Mountains, in about 14 minutes. You ascend through visibly different vegetation zones from the Valley Station (2643ft) to the Mountain Station (8516ft). It's 30°F to 40°F cooler as you step out into pine forest at the top, so bring some warm clothing – the trip up is said to be the equivalent (in temperature) of driving from Mexico to Canada.

The **Mountain Station** at the top of the tramway has a bar, a sit-down restaurant, a cafeteria, an observation area and a theater showing films on the tramway and the park. The restaurant, **Elevations** ( ☎ 760-327-1590; mains $23-29; 🕙 lunch & dinner), has a meat-and-seafood menu. Reservations are recommended; last seating is at 7:30pm. The views over the valley are brilliant.

Allow time (a day or two if you're a back-country enthusiast) at the top to enjoy the **Mt San Jacinto Wilderness State Park**. There are miles of trails, including a nontechnical route up to the San Jacinto peak (10,804ft), which are used for hiking in summer, and snowshoeing and cross-country skiing in winter. There are also several primitive campgrounds (free). Anyone heading into the backcountry (even for a few hours) must register for a wilderness permit at the ranger station just outside the Mountain Station;

for information and advance permits, contact the **state park rangers** ( ☎ 909-659-2607, 909-659-2117). Pick up maps ($1 to $7), books and gifts at the **State Park Visitor Information Center** on the lower level of the Mountain Station. Outside the Mountain Station, look for the **Adventure Center**, where you can rent snowshoes ($15 per day) and cross-country skis (adult/child $18/10 per day) when there's ample snow. Staff members are knowledgeable about snow conditions and backcountry routes.

The last car comes down at 9:45pm. A Ride 'n' Dine combination ticket (adult/child $30/19) includes a so-so buffet dinner at the cafeteria at the top. The ticket can be purchased after 3pm and dinner is served from 4pm. It's not bad for $9/5 extra, bu if you arrive late you may not have enoug time for a leisurely look around at the top

You can also hike to the top of the tram way via the Skyline Trail, which starts nea the Palm Springs Desert Museum. This is a extremely challenging hike, recommende only for the very fit who have a whole day t spend; leave no later than 7am. The rewar besides stellar views and multiple climati zones, is a free tram ride down.

Allow three hours to park, ride the tran and take a leisurely stroll once at the top. T reach the tramway, head north from tow on Palm Canyon Dr to Tramway Rd, tur left (toward the mountains) and continu 3½ miles to the base station.

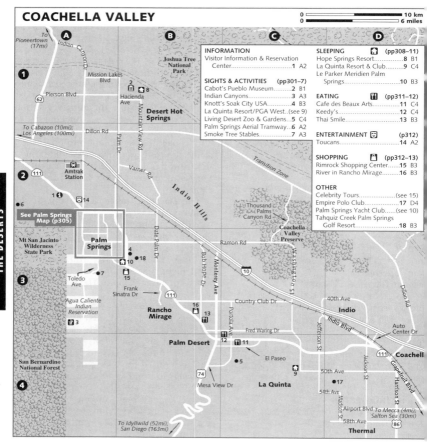

**COACHELLA VALLEY**

0 — 10 km
0 — 6 miles

**INFORMATION**
Visitor Information & Reservation
Center...................................1 A2

**SIGHTS & ACTIVITIES** (pp301–7)
Cabot's Pueblo Museum............2 B1
Indian Canyons.........................3 A3
Knott's Soak City USA...............4 B3
La Quinta Resort/PGA West..(see 9)
Living Desert Zoo & Gardens....5 C4
Palm Springs Aerial Tramway....6 A2
Smoke Tree Stables...................7 A3

**SLEEPING** (pp308–11)
Hope Springs Resort.................8 B1
La Quinta Resort & Club...........9 C4
Le Parker Meridien Palm
Springs...............................10 B3

**EATING** (pp311–12)
Cafe des Beaux Arts................11 C4
Keedy's..................................12 C4
Thai Smile..............................13 B3

**ENTERTAINMENT** (p312)
Toucans..................................14 A2

**SHOPPING** (pp312–13)
Rimrock Shopping Center........15 B3
River in Rancho Mirage...........16 B3

**OTHER**
Celebrity Tours......................(see 15)
Empire Polo Club....................17 D4
Palm Springs Yacht Club......(see 10)
Tahquiz Creek Palm Springs
Golf Resort..........................18 B3

**DESERT SURVIVAL 101**

The desert is an unforgiving place, but if you take precautions you'll have nothing to fear. Prepare for the worst, and expect the best.

The biggest concern? Water. Don't risk being stranded without it. Plan on carrying and drinking at least a gallon of water per day, double if you're hiking or boozing it up. To determine if you're getting dehydrated, check your urine's color; it should be clear or pale yellow, but never darker (unless you take a lot of vitamins).

Summertime temperatures can reach 120°F, but you won't feel yourself sweat so be sure to increase your electrolyte (sodium and potassium) intake. Eat salty foods and consume sports drinks high in sodium and potassium. However, avoid salt tablets unless a physician recommends them, as they can sometimes do more harm than good. See p372 for more information on heatstroke. You should also wear a hat and use lip balm. To minimize water loss through the skin, wear loose-fitting, light-colored, long-sleeved clothing. Bring warmer clothing for the nighttime, especially if you're camping; the desert can get surprisingly chilly after dark.

Not to scare you, but a simple back-road drive can turn disastrous if the car breaks down or gets stuck in sand. And a short walk can turn fatal if you get lost or injured. Take precautions. Be sure your vehicle is in good condition, and don't push it beyond its limits. Never venture alone into remote areas. Always tell someone where you're going and when you'll be back. Carry extra water. If you get stuck, stay with your vehicle and wait for rescue; a car is easier to spot than a hiker. If you become hopelessly lost on foot, seek the closest shady spot and stay put. You'll only get dehydrated and exhausted by walking around.

Harsh light and wide open spaces can play tricks on your vision, making it hard to judge distance or find appropriate landmarks. Always carry a compass and map, and know how to use them; GPS units can be helpful, but batteries fail and units malfunction.

Cell phones don't work everywhere. Carry a small mirror, matches and perhaps even flares so you can signal for help. A tent or groundsheet can provide vital sun protection as well as increase your visibility. Also useful: a flashlight, a pocketknife, a first-aid kit and extra food.

## ndian Canyons

treams flowing from the San Jacinto Mountains sustain a rich variety of plants n the canyons around Palm Springs. The **anyons** (Map p302; ☎ 760-325-3400, 800-790-3398; www.indian-canyons.com; adult/child $6/2; �९ 8am-5pm) vere home to Native-American communities for hundreds of years and are now part f the Agua Caliente Indian Reservation. It's delight to hike these canyon oases, shaded y fan palms and surrounded by towering cliffs. From downtown, head south on Palm Canyon Dr (continue straight when he main road turns east) for about 2 miles o the reservation entrance. From here, it's miles up to the Trading Post, which sells ats, maps, water and knick-knacks. At the ntrance to each canyon there's a trail post vith a map and information about that particular hike.

Closest to the entrance gate of the reservation is **Andreas Canyon**, where there's a pleasant picnic area. Nearby are imposing ock formations where you can find Native-American mortar holes, used for grinding seeds, and some rock art. The trail up the canyon is an easy walk.

About a 20-minute walk south from Andreas Canyon is **Murray Canyon**, which can't be reached by road and is therefore less visited. It's a good place for bird-watching, and bighorn sheep might be seen on the slopes above the canyon.

Following the winding access road to the end brings you to the 15-mile-long **Palm Canyon**, the most extensive of the canyons, with good trails and a store selling snacks and souvenirs. In the morning, look for animal tracks in the sandy patches.

## Tahquitz Canyon

Opened in 1999 after having been closed for 30 years, **Tahquitz Canyon** (Map p305; ☎ 760-416-7044; www.tahquitzcanyon.com; admission $12.50; �९ 7:30am-5pm, closed summer) is a historic and sacred centerpiece for the Agua Caliente people. It was traditionally home to Agua Caliente ancestors, but was taken over by teenage squatters in the 1960s. Eventually the canyon became a point of contention between the

PALM SPRINGS &
THE DESERTS

---

**WATER, WATER EVERYWHERE?**

Spend the day splashing in a giant swimming pool or golfing on a lush green fairway, and you might forget you're in the desert. Just where exactly does Palm Springs get all this water? For the most part, it comes from underground. The city sits atop a giant aquifer. If you read the press releases from real-estate developers and golf-course operators, they'll all tell you that the water they pump out makes its way right back into the ground, ensuring a big supply for years to come. Not exactly.

A significant portion of the water evaporates, and some of it that does reach the aquifer carries increased levels of salt that it picks up as it percolates down through the ground. In fact, so much water is being taken out of the ground in the Coachella Valley (the 300-sq-mile valley that extends eastward from Palm Springs) that the valley is sinking about an inch per year. Locals are finally realizing that they can't turn the desert into another Hawaii, and water conservation has begun – but not in earnest. Don't expect to see the golf courses turn brown anytime soon; they attract too much money.

Even if the aquifer does dry up, the city and surrounding communities have already begun importing water from Northern California to ensure a steady supply. But even that won't last forever, not with global warming threatening, in the not-so-distant future, to decimate the annual Sierra Nevada snow pack, the ultimate source of all California's water. Only time will tell how long the valley will remain an oasis. For now, though, slather on the suntan oil and pass the margaritas; it's gonna be a lovely day poolside.

---

Agua Caliente, local law enforcement agencies and squatters who claimed the right to live in its alcoves and caves. A major clean-up raid rid the canyon of inhabitants, but it took years to haul trash, erase graffiti and get the area back to its natural state.

It's still off-limits to independent hikers, but you can visit its 60ft waterfall, rock art and ancient irrigation system on a guided 2-mile, two-hour hike. Tribal rangers lead the hikes; call for reservations (last tour leaves at 3pm). The visitors center at the canyon entrance shows a video about the legend of Tahquitz, has exhibits about the canyon and offers a great view over Coachella Valley.

## Palm Springs Desert Museum

At the end of Tahquitz Canyon Way, west of N Palm Canyon Dr, this **museum** (Map p305; ☎ 760-325-0189; www.psmuseum.org; 101 Museum Dr; adult/child $7.50/3.50; ☼ 10am-5pm Tue & Wed, noon-8pm Thu, 10am-5pm Fri & Sat, noon-5pm Sun) has a small but good modern art collection, including an impressive piece by Seattle glass artist Dale Chihuly. There are also some excellent Cahuilla baskets. Outside there's a sculpture garden with desert plants. The museum also has a 400-seat theater.

## Village Green Heritage Center

This grassy little **square** (Map p305; ☎ 760-323-8297; 221 S Palm Canyon Dr) in the heart of downtown has some 'heritage' attractions, thoug most people use it as a place to sit and ea ice cream and fudge, which you can buy a the nearby sweets store. The true histori sites surrounding the square include th **Agua Caliente Cultural Museum** (Map p305; ☎ 76 323-0151; www.accmuseum.org; admission free; ☼ 10am 5pm Wed-Sat, noon-5pm Sun), which has picture and artifacts on the tribe's history; **Ruddy General Store**, a reproduction of a 1930s gen eral store; and the 1884 **McCallum Adobe**, sai to be the oldest building in Palm Spring The buildings are open from 10am to 4pm Thursday to Saturday, noon to 3pm Sunda and Wednesday; adult admission costs $ to each building (pay as you enter), kid are free.

## Living Desert Zoo & Gardens

Though the desert looks barren, its home to numerous species of plants and animals tha live nowhere else. At this desert-species **zo and botanical gardens** (Map p302; ☎ 760-346-5694 www.livingdesert.org; 47-900 Portola Ave; adult/child $11 6.50; ☼ 8am-1:30pm mid-Jun–Aug, 9am-5pm Sep–mid Jun), south of Hwy 111 in Palm Desert, you' see a wide variety of desert plants and ani mals, plus terrific exhibits on desert geol ogy and Native-American culture. Between Thanksgiving and January 1, the museum also presents its Wildlights show, an evening light festival featuring lights on the trees and

PALM SPRINGS & THE DESERTS

# PALM SPRINGS

0 — 1 km
0 — 0.5 miles

**INFORMATION**
Anderson Travel..........................**1** B5
Desert Regional Medical Center..**2** B4
Lalajava.................................(see 6)
Palm Springs Post Office............**3** B4
Palm Springs Public Library........**4** C5
Peppertree Bookstore.............(see 28)
Uptown Visitors Center .............**5** A4

**SIGHTS & ACTIVITIES**       (pp301–7)
Agua Caliente Cultural
    Museum..............................(see 12)
Big Horn Bike Adventures...........**6** A4
McCallum Adobe.....................(see 12)
Palm Springs Air Museum...........**7** D3
Palm Springs Desert Museum......**8** A4
Ruddy's General Store...............(see 12)
Skyline Trail...............................**9** A4
Tahquitz Canyon.......................**10** A6
Urban Yoga Center...................**11** B4
Village Green Heritage Center...**12** A5

**SLEEPING**            (pp308–11)
Alpine Gardens Hotel.............**13** B6
Best Western Las Brisas Hotel.**14** B5
Caliente Tropics Resort..........**15** B6
Casa Cody Inn......................**16** A5
Casitas Laquita.....................**17** B6
Chase Hotel at Palm
    Springs..........................(see 16)
Desert Hills Hotel..................**18** A5
Hacienda at Warm Sands.......**19** B5
Inn Exile..............................**20** B6
Inndulge..............................**21** B5
Korakia Pensione..................**22** A5
La Posada............................**23** A3
Las Palmas Hotel...................**24** A3
Orbit In...............................**25** A5
Orchid Tree Inn.....................**26** A5
Palm Court Inn......................**27** A3
Pepper Tree Inn....................**28** A4
Queen of Hearts Resort..........**29** B6
Super 8 Motel.......................**30** A3

Viceroy...............................**31** A5
Villa Rosa Inn.......................**32** B6
Villa Royale Inn.....................**33** B6
Village Inn...........................**34** A5
Vista Grande.......................(see 19)

**EATING**            (pp311–12)
Aspen Mills..........................**35** C5
Bit of Country.......................**36** A5
Blue Coyote Grill...................**37** A4
Churchill's Fish & Chips..........**38** A6
Davey's...............................**39** B6
Delhi Palace........................(see 24)
El Mirasol............................**40** B6
Johannes.............................**41** B5
Le Vallauris..........................**42** A5
Native Foods........................**43** C6
Peeraya Thai.........................**44** A3
Tyler's Burgers......................**45** A5
Wang's in the Desert..............**46** B5
Zin....................................(see 53)

**DRINKING**              (p312)
Deck...................................**47** A4
Hunter's Video Bar..................**48** B5
Palm Springs Koffi..................**49** A4
Rainbow Cactus Café..............**50** B5

**ENTERTAINMENT**          (p312)
Blue Guitar..........................(see 53)
Heaven................................**51** B6
Melvyn's...............................**52** A5
Palm Springs Follies.............(see 53)
Plaza Theater.......................**53** A5
Spa Resort Casino..................**54** B4

**SHOPPING**          (pp312–13)
Modern Way..........................**55** A2
Trina Turk.............................**56** A4

**OTHER**
East Canyon Hotel & Spa..........**57** B3
Marlene Institut de Beauté........**58** A3
Rosanna's Salon & Day Spa.......**59** A5
Salon 119 – A Day Spa.............**60** A4
Spa at Viceroy......................(see 31)

**PALM SPRINGS & THE DESERTS**

**ALTERNATIVE ENERGY**

California is a massive consumer of fossil fuels, but the state has also established some full-scale projects such as windmill farms to exploit alternative sources of energy. The desert regions offer not only abundant sunshine, but lots of wind and tremendous geothermal heat. The windmills are a wonderful sight, their blades the size of airplane wings, rotating on top of 80ft towers. There are thousands of them lined up at locations such as the San Gorgonio Pass near the north end of Palm Springs, and the Tehachapi Pass west of Mojave, where geographical conditions reliably produce strong winds. As air in the desert heats and rises during the day, cooler air is drawn in from the coastal areas, accelerating as it goes through the narrow passes (the average wind speed in the San Gorgonio Pass is 15mph to 20mph). The older generators (many imported from Denmark) have a capacity of around 40kW to 50kW. But with technology rapidly developing, the newer turbines are much larger and have a capacity of around 500kW. For more information, call the **Desert Wind Energy Association** ( ☎ 760-329-1799) or go see the windmills up close with Palm Springs Windmill Tours (p308).

The earth itself is another potential source of power. The Salton Trough, extending from the Gulf of California through the Imperial and Coachella Valleys, was created by massive sections of the earth's crust moving apart. This movement creates fractures and stress points. These not only cause earthquakes but also allow molten magma to work its way close to the earth's surface, heating the groundwater. In some places, this creates natural hot springs, but the heat can also be tapped to provide steam to power generators. Geothermal power plants operate at a number of sites near the Salton Sea, which is the deepest part of the trough, and the thinnest part of the earth's crust.

special animal shapes, for an additional $7; call for exact hours and dates. Plan for 1½ to 3½ hours to explore the Living Desert, plus a 30-minute drive each way. Last admission is one hour before closing.

### Palm Springs Air Museum

Adjacent to the Palm Springs International Airport, the **Air Museum** (Map p305; ☎ 760-778-6262; www.air-museum.org; 745 N Gene Autry Trail; adult/child $10/5; � 10am-5pm) has an exceptionally good collection of WWII aircraft, photos and flight memorabilia, as well as a large theater where movies are shown regularly for no additional charge. Hours are shorter in summer; call ahead to confirm.

### Cabot's Pueblo Museum

Inside a rambling 1913 adobe house built by a wealthy East Coaster (of the legendary Cabot clan) who traded high society for the solitude of the desert, this quirky **museum** (Map p302; ☎ 760-329-7610; www.cabotsmuseum.org; 67-616 E Desert Ave; Desert Hot Springs; adult/child $6/4; ☺ 10am-3pm Fri & Sat Oct-May) displays Native-American basketry and pottery, as well as a photo collection from Cabot's turn-of-the-20th-century travels to Alaska. It's a good stopover if you've got extra time and appreciate the idiosyncratic.

### Knott's Soak City USA

On a hot day, the kids will go nuts for this **water park** (Map p302; ☎ 760-327-0499; www.knotts.com/soakcity; 1500 S Gene Autry Trail; adult/child $25/13; ☺ daily Mar-Sep, Sat & Sun Oct) where there's a wave pool, water slides and mister beaches.

## ACTIVITIES

At noon there's not much to do except hang around a pool, head to the mountains via the aerial tramway or take refuge somewhere air-conditioned such as a museum or shopping center (there are plenty to choose from). Plan to hike and sightsee in the morning before the midday heat sets in. In the afternoon lie by the pool, catch up on your reading and take a long nap before an extended cocktail hour.

### Golf

Golf is huge here, with more than 100 public, semiprivate, private and resort golf courses in and around Palm Springs. It takes one million gallons of water per day to irrigate the golf courses. The local College of the Desert even has a School of Golf Management. There are several big tournaments annually; check with the visitors center for dates. Greens fees run from $26 to $215 epending on the course, season and day f the week. Most hotels can make arrangements for their guests to play on at least one cal course. You can receive substantial vings through **Stand-by Golf** ( ☎ 760-321-2665; ww.standbygolf.com; ⏰ 6:30am-9pm), which can rovide guaranteed tee times, at a discount, r same-day or next-day play at 40 courses. ee p46 for more information.

## iking

he best way to appreciate the subtlety of he desert is on foot. Take all necessary precautions to protect yourself from the heat see p303).

For hiking in the immediate Palm Springs rea check out the Indian Canyons (p303) nd the San Jacinto Mountains at the top of he aerial tramway (p301). Also consider a isit to Joshua Tree National Park (p314). **Trail Discovery Outdoor Guide Service** ( ☎ 760-25-4453, 888-867-2327; www.palmspringshiking.com) ffers excellent and educational guided hiking trips locally and in Joshua Tree National ark. It operates fewer trips during summer. Call for availability and prices.

## ycling

alm Springs and the valley have an excellent network of bike paths that are great or getting around. **Big Horn Bike Adventures** Map p305; ☎ 760-325-3367; cnr N Palm Canyon Dr & mado Rd; ⏰ 8am-4pm Thu-Tue), in downtown Palm Springs, rents a wide range of bikes ($6 to $12 per hour, $20 to $39 per day, $85 to $90 per week) and sometimes leads tours of the Indian Canyons by advance notice. It's also a good general resource for biking information. There are no reservations for bike hire: first-come, first-serve only.

## Horseback Riding

**Smoke Tree Stables** (Map p302; ☎ 760-327-1372; www.smoketreeranch.net; 2500 Toledo Ave) arranges trail rides, from one-hour outings to all-day treks. The cost is about $35 per hour for both novice and experienced riders. Rides leave on the hour from 8am to 5pm in winter and from 8am to noon in summer, but call ahead to secure a spot.

## Yoga

You can take yoga classes every day at **Urban Yoga Center** (Map p305; ☎ 760-320-7702; www.urban yoga.org; 750 N Palm Canyon Dr; drop-in classes $12), which offers specialized classes including beginning-to-intermediate Hatha, improvisational Ashtanga and belly-dancing basics.

## TOURS
### Guided Tours

Catch up on the gossip and glamour of Palm Springs with **Celebrity Tours** (Map p302; ☎ 760-770-2700; www.celebrity-tours.com; 4751 E Palm Canyon Dr; adult/child 1hr tour $20/10, 2hr tour $25/12), based at

---

### SOAK AWAY YOUR TROUBLES

If too much traveling has left you frazzled and achy, and you're having trouble getting into the hedonistic Palm Springs groove, then a spa might be just the thing to cure what ails you. Palm Springs has 21 to choose from, ranging from simple to sumptuous. Here are a few favorites. Make reservations.

**East Canyon Hotel & Spa** (Map p305; ☎ 760-320-1928; 288 E Camino Monte Vista) Palm Springs' only exclusively gay spa has facials, wraps, massages and reflexology.

**Marlene Institut de Beauté** (Map p305; ☎ 760-318-6718; 1492 N Palm Canyon) Deep-cleaning French facials, and body and makeup treatments in a small, indie spa.

**Rosanna's Salon & Day Spa** ( ☎ 760-325-4800; 353 S Palm Canyon Dr) Massage and body treatments, tanning and a full-service salon that also does hair extensions.

**Palm Springs Yacht Club** (Map p302; ☎ 760-770-5000; 4200 E Palm Canyon Dr) Ritzy, glitzy and fabulous, the spa at Le Parker Meridien Palm Springs (p311) is a fave of society ladies and the occasional celeb.

**Salon 119 – A Day Spa** (Map p305; ☎ 760-327-4800; 119 N Indian Canyon Dr) Get a topflight manicure and cut-and-color, followed by a relaxing massage.

**Spa at Viceroy** (Map p305; ☎ 760-320-4117; 415 S Belardo Rd) Swanky full-service spa with salt scrubs, wraps, facials, botanical baths and a high-end salon. Custom treatments even include yoga for the face.

**Spa Resort Casino** (Map p305; ☎ 760-325-1461; 100 N Indian Canyon Dr) The valley's original hot springs are part of the Native-American casino complex (p312); day visitors pay $35 to soak in the waters.

**THE PS CELEBRITY CIRCUIT**

Everyone knows about the dead celebs who used to spend time in Palm Springs, but just who comes here today? Here's a short list of the town's big-name homeowners:

- Brad Pitt and Jennifer Aniston
- Barbra Streisand
- Nancy Sinatra
- Barry Manilow
- Sidney Sheldon
- Natalie Cole
- Arnold Schwarzenegger and Maria Shriver
- Henry Kissinger
- Lily Tomlin

Vons Rimrock Plaza Shopping Center. You can do it yourself with a map from the visitors center (see Self-Guided Tours, right), but you won't get the amusing commentary and juicy dish. The bus tours run all year by reservation.

**Desert Adventures** ( ☎ 760-324-5337, 888-440-5337; www.red-jeep.com; 2/4hr tour $69/99) runs excellent guided jeep tours of the Indian Canyons, the Santa Rosa Mountains, around the Bighorn Sheep Preserve, along the San Andreas Fault and to other hard-to-reach areas. The driver-guides are full of information on the natural environment and Native-American lore.

Palm Springs' modern and international-style buildings are becoming increasingly recognized as these two movements take their place *en vogue*. **Palm Springs Modern Tours** ( ☎ 760-318-6118; psmoderntours@aol.com; $55). This tour covers the 1920s to the '70s but pays special attention to the '50s and '60s, when architects such as Albert Frey, Richard Neutra and John Lautner were major players on the Palm Springs scene. The 2½-hour van tour provides an extensive overview. Make reservations.

If the gigantic windmills on Palm Springs' windy north side have captivated your imagination, call **Palm Springs Windmill Tours** ( ☎ 760-251-1997, 760-320-1365; www.windmilltours.com; adult/child $23/10; ⏰ Wed-Sat) and learn all about the groves of whirring turbines. Call for tour times; reservations are required at least 24 hours in advance.

## Self-Guided Tours

The Visitor Information & Reservation Center has brochures for two good self-guided tours. The *Public Art and Historic Site Tour Map* (free) covers 37 sites throughout Palm Springs; most you can see on foot around downtown, but you'll need to drive to a few. *Palm Springs Map of the Stars' Homes* ($5) takes you to the abodes of the city's rich and famous, but you'll need a car and sometimes you'll only see the bougainvillea-covered wall of a compound.

## FESTIVALS & EVENTS

There are large-purse, celebrity golf tournaments each month here. Contact the **Visitor Information & Reservation Center** (Map p302; ☎ 760-778-8418, 800-347-7746; www.palm-springs.org; 2901 N Palm Canyon Dr; ⏰ 9am-5pm) for a complete calendar of events.

**Villagefest** ( ☎ 760-320-3781; ⏰ 6-10pm Thu Oct-May, 7-10pm Thu Jun-Sep) Every Thursday evening the downtown blocks of N Palm Canyon Dr, from Baristo Rd to Amado Rd, are closed to traffic for this certified farmers market that is joined by musicians, food vendors and purveyors of art and handicrafts.

**Palm Springs International Film Festival** ( ☎ 760-322-2930; www.psfilmfest.org) Early January brings a film festival with over 200 films from more than 60 countries.

**Desert Swing'N Dixie Jazz Festival** ( ☎ 760-333-7932; www.desertjazz.org) In late March or early April this festival features three days of dancing and music, with a special jazz-gospel session on Sunday. The event is organized by the Dixieland Jazz Society of the Desert, which holds monthly jazz dances around Palm Springs; call for details.

**White Party** ( ☎ 888-777-8886; www.jeffreysanker.com) On Easter weekend, this four-day-long party is one of the biggest gay dance events in the entire US.

**Coachella Valley Music & Arts Festival** ( ☎ 310-788-7060; www.coachella.com; day tickets around $75) In late April or early May, 25 miles east of Palm Springs, Indio's Empire Polo Club (Map p302) hosts one of the hottest two-day music festivals of its kind. Artists range from hip indie no-names such as the Cubby Creatures to DJs Sasha & Digweed to pop idols such as Björk and Radiohead.

## SLEEPING

Rates quoted here are for midwinter, when prices are highest. Come summer, rates drop significantly, sometimes by more than 50%. Almost everyplace serves a continental breakfast in the morning; some are better than others. If it matters, ask exactly what is served before you reserve. Many properties have rooms with full or partial kitchens, which can help you cut your food bills and allow you to spend more on lodging.

The Visitor Information & Reservation Center operates a free **lodging-reservation service** ( ☎ 760-778-8418, 800-347-7746; www.palm-springs.org) that includes all hotels and inns in town.

## Budget

**Alpine Gardens Hotel** (Map p305; ☎ 760-323-2231, 888-299-7455; www.alpinegardens.com; 1586 E Palm Canyon Dr; r $60-85, with kitchen $115; P ▣ ) All 10 rooms at this beautifully landscaped, impeccably kept motel, c 1954, have redwood-beamed ceilings, refrigerators, and slightly kitsch but extra-charming furnishings. Tops in its class.

**Village Inn** (Map p305; ☎ 760-320-8622, 866-320-8622; www.palmspringsvillageinn.com; 855 N Indian Canyon Dr; r $60-70; P ▣ ) All rooms have VCRs and refrigerators at this clean, well-maintained 16-unit motel north of town – but the mattresses are soft. Still, it's a great bargain.

Other options include the standard-issue **Palm Court Inn** (Map p305; ☎ 760-416-2333, 800-667-7918; www.palmsprings.com/hotels/palmcourtinn; 1983 N Palm Canyon Dr; r $59-109; ▣ ) and the nothing-special **Super 8 Motel** (Map p305; ☎ 760-22-3757, 800-800-8000; www.super8.com; 1900 N Palm Canyon Dr; P ▣ ).

If you want to camp in the area, head to Joshua Tree National Park (p318) or Mount San Jacinto Wilderness State Park (p301).

## Mid-Range

Shelling out a little more will put you within walking distance of downtown's major sights and nightlife.

**Casa Cody Inn** (Map p305; ☎ 760-320-9346, 800-231-2639; www.casacody.com; 175 S Cahuilla Rd; r $100-160; P ▣ ) One of the best values in the area, the charming Casa Cody has individual Spanish-style bungalows tucked beneath towering palms amid lush greenery. Some units have kitchens. It's a quiet place, though, so families with loud kids might not be happy here.

**Chase Hotel at Palm Springs** (Map p305; ☎ 760-320-8866, 877-532-4273; www.chasehotelpalmsprings.com; 200 W Arenas Rd; r $100-130; P ) A classic mid-century motel complex with large open spaces, the Chase has immaculately kept oversized rooms decorated with contemporary furnishings. It's great value. Friendly service.

**Orchid Tree Inn** (Map p305; ☎ 760-325-2791; 800-733-3435; www.orchidtree.com; 261 S Belardo Rd; r $110-185; P ▣ ) There's a separate pool for kids at this 1930s Spanish-style compound, which has comfortable, unpretentious rooms. No two rooms are alike and many have kitchens. Its convenient location means that you can walk almost everywhere downtown.

**Villa Rosa Inn** (Map p305; ☎ 760-327-5915, 800-457-7605; www.villarosainn.com; 1577 S Indian Trail; r $110-140; P ▣ ) Six rooms surround a Mexican-tile pool deck at this 1948 inn, which is south of town in a residential neighborhood.

**Best Western Las Brisas Hotel** (Map p305; ☎ 760-325-4372, 800-346-5714; www.bestwestern.com; 222 S Indian Canyon; r $90-190; P ▣ ) Flourishing gardens surround a central courtyard and pool at this beautifully kept motel-resort within walking distance of downtown; rates include full hot breakfast. On-site bar.

Also check out the following:

**Desert Hills Hotel** (Map p305; ☎ 760-325-2777; www.deserthillspalmsprings.com; 601 W Arenas Rd; r $110-150; ▣ ) A '50s-modern, 14-room, single-story hotel.

**Pepper Tree Inn** (Map p305; ☎ 760-318-9850, 866-887-8733; www.peppertreepalmsprings.com; 622 N Palm Canyon Dr; r $130-170; P ▣ ) Medium-size hotel with big, modern rooms. Decorated in Spanish style.

**Caliente Tropics Resort** (Map p305; ☎ 760-327-1391, 866-468-9595; www.calientetropics.com; 411 E Palm Canyon Dr; r $125-240; P ▣ ) Impeccably kept Tiki-style motor lodge.

## Top End

**Korakia Pensione** (Map p305; ☎ 760-864-6411; www.korakia.com; 257 S Patencio Rd; r $130-290; ▣ ) A Moroccan-style compound built in the 1920s, Korakia is one of Palm Springs' romantic gems. It's so authentically decked out that you might mistakenly detect jasmine in the air. The antique-filled rooms have sumptuous beds with luxurious linens, and bathrooms with custom stone tile that echoes the masonry work of the inn's fountain courtyards and outdoor fire pits. Bring groceries – many units have kitchenettes – and you'll never have to leave.

**Villa Royale Inn** (Map p305; ☎ 760-327-2314, 800-245-2314; www.villaroyale.com; 1620 S Indian Trail; r $150-220; ▣ ) A top hideaway for a honeymoon or a kiss-and-make-up weekend, the 1947 Villa Royale has 31 cozy rooms and suites in a charming Spanish-style compound bursting with bougainvillea. Hold hands by candlelight in Europa, the inn's intimate dining room, which serves Franco-Italian cuisine. The best meal may be the Sunday $20 all-you-can-drink champagne brunch.

**Viceroy** (Map p305; ☎ 760-320-4117, 800-237-3687; www.viceroypalmsprings.com; 415 S Belardo Rd; r $210-320; ☒ ) Wear a Pucci dress and blend right in at this '60s-chic mini-resort done up in black, white and lemon-yellow (think Austin Powers meets Givenchy). There's also a full-service spa (p307), as well as a fab but pricey restaurant for a white-linen luncheon or swanky supper.

**Orbit In** (Map p305; ☎ 760-323-3585, 877-996-7248, www.orbitin.com; 562 W Arenas Rd; r $160-270; ☒ ) Hip, stylish and retro, the Orbit's rooms are outfitted with high-end original pieces of mid-century-modern furniture.

**Hope Springs Resort** (Map p302; ☎ 760-329-4003; www.hopespringsresort.com; 68075 Club Circle Dr; r from $150; ☒ ) This modernist's mecca north of Palm Springs offers 10 impeccably stylish rooms and fantastic views. It also boasts a natural hot spring that flows through three pools.

---

### GAY & LESBIAN LODGING

There's a lot of gay lodging in Palm Springs, approximately 40 resorts in all, ranging from sleazy to sumptuous. Some of the better ones are listed below. Those that cater to men are necessarily broken down on a 'sexual temperature' of one to ten, one meaning that the place has no perceptible sex vibe, and ten meaning that the joint may as well be a bathhouse.

#### Men's Resorts

**Las Palmas Hotel** (Map p305; ☎ 760-327-6883, 866-522-7272; www.laspalmas-hotel.com; 1404 N Palm Canyon Dr; r $130-190; P ☒ ) Palm trees surround the pool deck at this smartly appointed, clothing-optional, compact resort for men, with colorful rooms sporting Moroccan-style furnishings and sumptuous mattresses (the same type used at five-star hotels). Great value. Clothing optional. Sexual temperature: 3

**Hacienda at Warm Sands** (Map p305; ☎ 760-327-8111, 800-359-2007; www.thehacienda.com; 586 Warm Sands Dr; r $150-310; P ☐ ☒ ) The Hacienda raises the bar for service and luxury in gay lodging. Choose from nine different pillow types, or request a tenth: the affable innkeepers – never intrusive, always available – will make sure you have just the pillow you want. (Now that's service.) Lunch is included in the rate. Flawless landscaping. Clothing optional. Bring your own lover. Sexual temperature: 2

**Inndulge** (Map p305; ☎ 760-327-1408, 800-833-5675; www.inndulge.com; 601 Greenfall Rd; r $115-140; P ☐ ☒ ) Rooms at this well-maintained mid-century property have extra amenities such as good bedding and refrigerators; some have full kitchens. Well-landscaped. Clothing optional. Sexual temperature: 7

Of the sexier men's resorts (sexual temperature: 7+), you'll find the best facilities and landscaping at the following:

**Vista Grande** (Map p305; ☎ 760-320-1667, 800-669-1069; www.mirage4men.com; 574 Warm Sands Dr; r $80-120; P ☒ ) Lush tropical landscaping.

**Inn Exile** (Map p305; ☎ 760-327-6413, 800-962-0186; www.innexile.com; 545 Warm Sands Dr; r $90-120; P ☒ ) Stark, postmodern architecture.

**La Posada** (Map p305; ☎ 760-323-1402, 888-411-4949; www.laposada.com; 120 W Vereda Sur; r $130-190; P ☒ ) Just west of Palm Canyon Dr. Beautiful grounds.

#### Women's Resorts

**Casitas Laquita** (Map p305; ☎ 760-416-9999; www.casitaslaquita.com; 450 E Palm Canyon Dr; r $135-145, ste from $170; P ☒ ) All the rooms are individually decorated and have kitchens at this Spanish-style compound, which has a great pool and manicured grounds. If you can swing it, request the romantic cottage with its private backyard and barbecue.

**Queen of Hearts Resort** (Map p305; ☎ 760-322-5793, 888-275-9903; www.queenofheartsps.com; 435 Avenida Olancha; r $105-150; P ☒ ) This was Palm Springs' first gay-only resort, which opened as the Desert Knight in 1960. Now it's exclusively for women, with lovely rooms (most with kitchens) and robes, a sparkling pool and complimentary breakfast. Call for directions.

**Le Parker Meridien Palm Springs** (Map p302; ☎ 760-770-5000, 800-543-4300; www.theparkerpalmsprings.com; 4200 E Palm Canyon Dr; r from $395; 🖥 🏊 ) If you're a resort hound looking for the top pick for a no-holds-barred splurge in Palm Springs, the Parker is the pinnacle of luxury.

**La Quinta Resort & Club** (Map p302; ☎ 760-564-4111, 800-598-3828; www.laquintaresort.com; 49499 Eisenhower Dr, La Quinta; r from $415; 🅿 🖥 🏊 ) Opened in 1926, the sprawling La Quinta has cushy ultraprivate bungalows, spectacular grounds, 41 pools, 53 hot tubs and 90 holes of golf (p46).

## EATING

Palm Springs isn't what you'd call a 'food town.' It's better known for cocktails than dining. Still, you can find pretty good food, but few places are on par with big-city restaurants.

### Budget

**El Mirasol** (Map p305; ☎ 760-323-0721; 140 E Palm Canyon Dr; mains $7-15) The menu is small but the food excellent at everybody's favorite Mexican place. There's great margaritas, too.

**Tyler's Burgers** (Map p305; ☎ 760-325-2990; 149 S Indian Canyon Dr; burgers $5-9) If you're hungry for a burger, this is the place. Expect a wait at lunchtime, but it's worth it.

**Aspen Mills** (Map p305; ☎ 760-323-3123; 555 S Sunrise Way; sandwiches $5-7; 🕒 Mon-Sat 7am-6:30pm; 🅿 ) Though this bakery (located next to Blockbuster Video) makes some of the best to-go sandwiches in town, you can also eat them here. Great homemade bread, muffins and brownies.

**Churchill's Fish & Chips** (Map p305; ☎ 760-325-3716; 665 S Palm Canyon Dr; mains $5-11; 🅿 ) With a British-pub atmosphere and jolly good fish and chips, Churchill's also serves shrimp, scallops and clams. Guinness on tap.

**Delhi Palace** (Map p305; ☎ 760-325-3411; 1422 N Palm Canyon Dr; mains $8-15; 🕒 closed Tue in summer) Satisfy a craving for curry at this Indian spot just north of downtown. At lunch there's an $8 all-you-can-eat buffet.

**Keedy's** (Map p302; ☎ 760-346-6492; 73-633 Hwy 111; mains under $8; 🕒 breakfast & lunch) In fancy and expensive Palm Desert, Keedy's serves straightforward and cheap eggs, pancakes, hamburgers and milkshakes.

**Thai Smile** (Map p302; ☎ 760-341-6565; 42-467 Bob Hope Dr; mains lunch $6, dinner $6-14; 🅿 ) Also in Palm Desert, Thai Smile is in a shopping plaza next to the River shopping mall. It serves standards such as pad Thai and unusual dishes such as grilled-eggplant salad.

Also recommended:
**Bit of Country** (Map p305; ☎ 760-325-5154; 418 S Indian Canyon Dr; breakfast $4-9) For fans of big, hearty breakfasts.
**Native Foods** (Map p305; ☎ 760-416-0070; 1775 E Palm Canyon Dr; mains $9-13) Great vegan fare.

### Mid-Range

**Peeraya Thai** (Map p305; ☎ 760-320-8385; 2249 N Palm Canyon; mains $8-12; 🕒 lunch Mon-Sat, dinner daily, closed mid-Jul–mid-Aug) Palm Springs' best Thai restaurant is an off-the-beaten-path hole-in-the-wall in the north end of town.

**Wang's in the Desert** (Map p305; ☎ 760-325-9264; 424 S Indian Canyon Dr; mains $9-15; 🕒 dinner; 🅿 ) A stream runs through this Cal-Chinese restaurant, where the minimalist decor, giant cocktails and family-style service draw big crowds for the always-delicious cooking. Come early or make reservations.

**Blue Coyote Grill** (Map p305; ☎ 760-327-1196; 445 N Palm Canyon Dr; mains $14-25) The courtyard tables are the most coveted at this lively cantina serving Mexican and Southwestern standards, but the real standout is the legendary Wild Coyote margarita.

**Cafe des Beaux Arts** (Map p302; ☎ 760-346-0669; 73-640 El Paseo; mains $14-24) For a civilized lunch in Palm Desert after shopping on chichi El Paseo Dr, dine on simple and satisfying French café cuisine, from niçoise salad to steak au poivre.

### Top End

**Le Vallauris** (Map p305; ☎ 760-325-5059; 385 W Tahquitz Canyon Way; mains lunch $15-26, dinner $23-38; 🕒 closed summer; 🅿 ) The premier choice for special-occasion dining, Le Vallauris serves up perfectly crafted contemporary-French haute cuisine. Though lovely, the stately dining room is a bit stiff; for maximum romance dine al fresco beneath giant ficus trees. Wear high heels, and bring your credit card.

**Zin** (Map p305; ☎ 760-322-6300; 198 S Palm Canyon Dr; mains $13-27; 🕒 dinner) This casual white-tablecloth bistro serves surprisingly good food, especially considering its location on the tourist strip. Its American-Belgian menu features *moules-frites* (mussels and French fries), steaks, ribs and fish. Big portions, friendly service.

**Davey's** (Map p305; ☎ 760-320-4480; 292 E Palm Canyon Dr; mains $16-27; Ⓧ dinner, closed Mon in summer; Ⓟ ) A throwback to 1970s-modern dining, Davey's serves dependably good continental cuisine (read: prime rib, shrimp scampi, veal piccata) in a retro-chic dining room with red vinyl banquettes. Great steaks.

**Johannes** (Map p305; ☎ 760-778-0017; 196 S Indian Canyon Dr; mains $22-34; Ⓧ dinner Tue-Sun) The chef-owner's Austrian roots shine through the contemporary Euro-Cal cuisine at this spartan, special occasion (read: pricey) spot for diners who like imaginative cooking without a lot of fuss. The escargots are delish.

## DRINKING

Meandering on foot along Palm Canyon Dr in downtown Palm Springs is quite entertaining on almost any night; the warm air and minimal need for clothing make people uncommonly jovial.

### Bars

**Deck** (Map p305; ☎ 760-325-5200; 262 S Palm Canyon Dr) Overlook the mountains from the deck at this second-floor lounge with two fire pits; the Deck serves tapas too.

**Village Pub** (Map p305; ☎ 760-323-3265; 262 S Palm Canyon Dr) A casual place for kicking back with your buds, the pub has live music, darts and beer on tap.

### Cafés

**Palm Springs Koffi** (Map p305; ☎ 760-416-2244; 515 N Palm Canyon Dr; Ⓧ 6am-7pm) Palm Springs' best café for strong organic coffee.

## ENTERTAINMENT
### Live Music

**Blue Guitar** (Map p305; ☎ 760-327-1549; 120 S Palm Canyon Dr) Hear live jazz and blues upstairs Friday to Sunday nights, at this venue next door to the Plaza Theater; call for the current schedule. It's owned by Kal David, the celebrity guitarist.

**Melvyn's** (Map p305; ☎ 760-325-0046; 200 W Ramon Rd) There's music every night, from piano and vocals to jazz combos, at this old-guard standby in the Ingleside Inn. It's popular with retired celebs. Sunday afternoon jazz is a long-standing tradition. Shine your shoes.

### Gay & Lesbian Venues

**Toucans** (Map p302; ☎ 760-416-7584; 2100 N Palm Canyon Dr) A swinging gay and lesbian venue with tropical froufrou and a dance floor, Toucans gets packed on weekends. Drinks are two-for-one on Tuesdays.

**Heaven** (Map p305; ☎ 760-416-0950; 611 S Palm Canyon Dr; cover after midnight $5-10; Ⓧ to 4am Fri & Sat) Heaven bills itself as mixed but it's a predominantly gay dance club with flashing lights and disco balls. It has two bars and a dance floor, lounge and smoking room.

Arenas Rd runs perpendicular to Palm Canyon Dr; there's a concentration of gay and lesbian hangouts two blocks east. Among them are the following:

**Hunter's Video Bar** (Map p305; ☎ 760-323-0700; 302 E Arenas Rd) Mostly male clientele, lots of TV screens, a fun dance scene and two pool tables.

**Rainbow Cactus Café** (Map p305; ☎ 760-325-3868; cnr Arenas Rd & S Indian Canyon Dr) A nice restaurant for lunch or dinner, with a lively piano bar. The piano bar is very popular for the brunch it serves Saturday and Sunday.

### Casinos

Legal gambling is possible just a few blocks from Palm Canyon Dr.

**Spa Resort Casino** (Map p305; ☎ 760-883-2000, 800-258-2946; 401 E Amado Rd; Ⓧ 24hr) Empty your pockets at Palm Springs' Native-American casino.

### Theater

**Palm Springs Follies** (Map p305; ☎ 760-327-0225; www .psfollies.com; 128 S Palm Canyon Dr; tickets $39-89) The historic Plaza Theater, dating from 1936, hosts this Ziegfeld Follies–style revue that includes music, dancing, showgirls and comedy. The twist? Many of the performers are as old as the theater – all are over 50, some as old as 80. But this is by no means the amateur hour. Palm Springs can pull some big names out of its celebrity closet, and the show has featured such stars as Bing Crosby, Doris Day and Jack Benny. Tickets aren't cheap, but the cast-from-the-past turns out a great performance with flash and splash. There are evening shows and matinees from November to May; reservations recommended.

## SHOPPING

Browse the shops and galleries along Palm Canyon Dr downtown, but don't expect to find much more than expensive shops and galleries geared for tourists – still, it's worth a look. The major retailers that once had stores in Palm Springs (eg Saks Fifth Avenue) have

**DETOUR: SALTON SEA**

In 1905 the Colorado River flooded and overflowed into irrigation channels, nearly inundating the entire Imperial Valley. It took 18 months, 1500 workers, $12 million and half a million tons of rock to put the Colorado River back on its course to the Gulf of Mexico. As a result the previously dry Salton Sink became a lake, 45 miles long and 17 miles wide. It had no natural outlet and, as evaporation reduced its size, the natural salt levels became more concentrated. The Salton became an inland sea, with its surface actually 228ft below the level of the sea in the Gulf of California and its water over 1½ times as salty.

The largest lake in California, the Salton Sea is surprisingly unattractive. The only real reason to visit is for bird-watching: migratory and endangered birds that stop here include snow geese, mallard, brown pelicans, bald eagles and peregrine falcons. The **Sonny Bono Salton Sea National Wildlife Refuge** ( ☎ 760-348-5278; 906 W Sinclair Rd; ☒ 7am-3:30pm Mon-Fri year-round, 8am-4:30pm Sat & Sun Nov-Mar) is off Hwy 111 between Niland and Calipatria.

Fishing is popular, though not recommended because of the high concentration of selenium in the fish. There are three boat-launching ramps, and small boats may be launched anywhere round the shoreline.

Swimming is unpleasant – the water is murky with plankton and the salt stings the eyes – and not recommended at the southern end of the sea because of pollution.

Due to its warm climate, 'snowbirds' – people from cold climates who migrate to warm environments for the winter – tend to like the area. Most of them congregate in Slab City, south of I-10 (Santa Monica Fwy) and east of Niland, which becomes a veritable urban RV-scape from November to May. One eccentric site worth turning off Hwy 111 to see is **Salvation Mountain**, a 100ft-high hill constructed of concrete and hand-mixed adobe and covered with brightly colored Christian declarations. It's the continual life work of Leonard Knight, who has been living behind his mountain and refreshing its acrylic cloak daily since 1985. Turn east off the highway at Niland and you can't miss it.

If you want to stay overnight, the **Salton Sea State Recreation Area** ( ☎ 760-393-3052; www .parks.ca.gov; Hwy 111), 25 miles south of Indio, has several undeveloped **campgrounds** (tent/RV sites $18/23). Bombay Beach Campground, south of the visitors center on the eastern shore, is the best of these. Sites are distributed on a first-come first-served basis. The 'beach' here was formed by sinking old vehicles – including buses – into the mud of the Salton Sea. The idea was to create cavernous formations that would grow marsh plant life and help support the birdlife here. If it's going to work at all, it's got a long way to go.

all moved to the malls in and around Palm Desert. Dates, as in the fruit, are the most common gift to take home from the Palm Springs area; 90% of the US supply comes from the surrounding Coachella Valley.

**Trina Turk** (Map p305; ☎ 760-416-2856; 891 N Palm Canyon Dr) Find shagadelic resort-chic drag at Palm Springs' best – some say only – clothingboutique. If you love hip clothes, don't miss this place.

**Modern Way** (Map p305; ☎ 760-320-5455; 2755 N Palm Canyon Dr) Stylin' consignment shop for collectors of modern furniture.

**El Paseo** (Map p302; ☎ 760-568-1441, 760-341-4888; www.elpaseo.com) For serious shopping at mid-range and high-end retailers, head to El Paseo, the main shopping street in Palm Desert, dubbed the Rodeo Dr of the desert. To get there, head 14 miles southeast of Palm

Springs via Hwy 111. El Paseo runs parallel to Hwy 111, one block south of the highway.

**River in Rancho Mirage** (Map p302; ☎ 760-341-2711; 71-800 Hwy 111 at Bob Hope Dr) En route to El Paseo you'll pass several shopping centers, the River in Rancho Mirage among them. It has about 20 upscale stores, restaurants and a big movie complex.

**Desert Hills Premium Outlets** ( ☎ 951-849-6641; 48400 Seminole Dr) Twenty minutes northwest of Palm Springs, off I-10 (Santa Monica Fwy) in Cabazon, this place has retail outlets from Gap to Gucci.

## GETTING THERE & AWAY
### Air
**Palm Springs International Airport** (Map p305; ☎ 760-318-3800; www.palmspringsairport.com; 3400 E Tahquitz Canyon Way) is served by Alaska, America

West, American, Continental, Delta, Horizon Air, Northwest (seasonally), Sun Country and United. The airport sits at the east end of Tahquitz Canyon Way, convenient to downtown.

### Bus & Train

**Greyhound** (760-325-2053, 800-231-2222; www.greyhound.com; 311 N Indian Canyon Dr) has eight buses to LA ($22, around three hours) between 8am and 10:30pm daily (buy your ticket on the bus when the station is closed).

**Amtrak** ( ☎ 800-872-7245; www.amtrak.com) operates a train service to and from LA on Wednesdays, Fridays and Sundays via the *Sunset Limited,* which continues to Orlando, Florida. Amtrak buses provide service the rest of the week, but you must make advance reservations. Buses pick up at the Sunline bus stop at the airport. Trains pick up at Indian Canyon Dr and I-10. The fare to LA ranges from $15 to $30, depending on demand. Bear in mind that schedules are inconvenient (read: the middle of the night), and the train usually runs late.

### Car & Motorcycle

From LA take I-10, the main route into and through the Coachella Valley; the trip to Palm Springs takes about two hours. Hwys 243 and 74, the 'Palms to Pines Hwy,' is the more scenic route and worth the detour if you have extra time. Major rental car companies all have desks at the airport in Palm Springs.

You can rent a current-model Harley Davidson motorcycle from **Eaglerider** ( ☎ 760-251-5990, 877-736-8243; www.eaglerider.com; Palm Springs International Airport) for $75 to $130 per day; specials are usually available, and you can return the bike in a different city. When you ride a motorcycle in the desert, pay extra attention to remaining well hydrated. The hot, dry wind against your body causes rapid dehydration. Avoid riding with your skin exposed for any longer than a few minutes.

### GETTING AROUND
### To/From the Airport

Unless your hotel provides airport transfers, plan to take a taxi (see right); figure about $12 to downtown hotels.

If you're going to one of the communities outside Palm Springs (such as Palm

Desert), call for advance reservations with one of these reputable shuttle companies:
**At Your Service** ( ☎ 760-343-0666, 888-700-7888)
**Good Life Transportation** ( ☎ 760-341-2221)

### Car

Though you can walk to most sights in downtown Palm Springs, you'll need a car to get to most places around town. Rent one at the airport, where all major agencies have counters. For contact information, see p367.

### Public Transportation

**SunBus** ( ☎ 760-343-3451; www.sunline.org), the local bus service, is described by a reader as 'lethargic and unpredictable,' which is basically true. It does, however, service most of the valley from about 6am to 10pm, and the air-conditioned buses are clean and comfortable. Line 111 follows Hwy 111 between Palm Springs and Palm Desert (one hour) and Indio (about 1½ hours). You can transfer to other lines that loop through the various communities. The standard fare is $1 (exact change required), plus 25¢ for a transfer. All buses have wheelchair lifts and a bicycle rack.

### Taxi

Palm Springs taxis operate on meters. The starting fee is $2.35; each mile costs $2.30. On weekends downtown you can often flag a taxi. At other times, you'll need to call. If you know you're going to need a car at a certain time, say, to go to the airport in the morning, book in advance.
**Ace Taxi** ( ☎ 760-835-2445; ☾ 6am-2am)
**American Cab** ( ☎ 760-775-1477; ☾ 24hr)
**Palm Springs Taxi** ( ☎ 760-323-5100; ☾ 6am-10pm)

# JOSHUA TREE NATIONAL PARK

Joshua Tree National Park straddles the transition zone between the Colorado Desert and the higher, cooler Mojave Desert. The latter supports the distinctive Joshua trees, which look like something out of a Dr Seuss book, especially in spring when some trees dramatically send up a huge clusters of creamy-white blossoms. Wonderfully shaped rocky outcroppings (mostly of quartz monzonite) draw rock climbers, who consider 'J-Tree' the best place to climb in California.

Backpackers are less enthusiastic, since there is no natural water flow, but day hikers and campers enjoy the array of subtle desert hues and the chance to scramble up, down and around giant boulders. Vehicle entry, good for seven days, costs $10; walkers and cyclists pay $5 (also for seven days).

## ORIENTATION
The most whimsically dramatic conglomeration of rocks is in the area known locally as Wonderland of Rocks' area, while the biggest trees are near Covington Flats. To see the transition from the high Colorado Desert/Sonoran Desert to the low Mojave, drive along the Pinto Basin Rd, which drops from the Twentynine Palms area into the Pinto Basin, connecting the high and low desert and the northern and southern entrances of the park. Twentynine Palms Hwy (Hwy 62) borders the north side of the park, I-10 the south side. At the entrance gate, rangers provide a foldout brochure and map, as well as a park newspaper that includes information about hiking trails and ranger-led programs.

The town of Joshua Tree where the access road to the western entrance of the national park branches off Twentynine Palms Hwy, has the most soul of any town near the park and is a favorite of artists and writers. By the northern entrance to the national park, the town of Twentynine Palms (named after the original 29 palm trees behind the visitor center) serves the park and the nearby Marine Corps Combat Training Center (don't freak out if you hear a kaboom every once in awhile). Most of the Twentynine Palms sprawls along Twentynine Palms Hwy; where the highway crosses Adobe Rd there's a sort of downtown.

## INFORMATION
Pick up food and gasoline in Joshua Tree or Twentynine Palms. In the town of Joshua Tree, you'll find camping supplies, maps, books and helpful information at **Coyote Corner** (Map pp316-17; ☎ 760-366-9683; cnr Twentynine Palms Hwy & Park Blvd; 🕓 9am-6pm).

### Emergency
For emergency assistance, call either ☎ 911 or ☎ 909-383-5651 from any telephone in the park. You'll find emergency telephones at Hidden Valley Campground and the Indian Cove ranger station. For first-aid contact a ranger.

---

### DETOUR: PIONEERTOWN

From Hwy 62 (Twentynine Palms Hwy) in the town of Yucca Valley, head 5 miles north up Pioneer Town Rd, and you'll drive straight up a hill and into the past. **Pioneertown** (www .pioneertown.com) was built as a movie backdrop by Roy Rogers, Dale Evans, Gene Autry and a few other of Hollywood's big time Western folk in 1946 and has hardly changed since. The idea was that actors would have homes here, become part of the set and really live the Wild West life they acted out. The main street (Mane St) is lined with buildings that were used in countless Western movies and TV shows, including *Gunfight at the OK Corral*. You can witness a 'real' gunfight in the street here from April to November at 2:30pm on Saturdays and Sundays; it's a little cheesy but has high kitsch value, and kids love it.

If it's open, definitely check out **Pioneer Bowl** ( ☎ 760-365-3615; 🕓 10am-7pm Fri-Sun), an old-fashioned bowling alley built for Roy Rogers in 1947. It's still in use, with original equipment and an amazing collection of vintage arcade games for which any good antique hound would pay big bucks. Its saloon sells beer, buffalo burgers and ice-cream concoctions.

If you like music, make it a point to visit **Pappy & Harriet's Pioneertown Palace** ( ☎ 760-365-5956; www.pappyandharriets.com; mains lunch $6-9, dinner $8-25; 🕓 11am-late Thu-Sun, from 5pm Mon), an Old West honky-tonk bar that defines nightlife in the Joshua Tree area. Expect plenty of cowboy hats, cheap beer, real Tex-Mex food (pinto beans and mesquite-fired beef and chicken slathered with barbecue sauce), burgers and cheese fries – portions are huge. Make reservations. Best of all, there's free live music every night it's open. But call ahead for the show calendar: sometimes it has big names, from Leon Russel to Shelby Lynne, and you'll need tickets.

If all this fun leaves you too tipsy to drive home, you can stay at **Pioneertown Motel** ( ☎ 760-365-4879; www.brainprod.com/ptmotel; r $55-65) or Rimrock Ranch Cabins (p319).

**PALM SPRINGS & THE DESERTS**

# JOSHUA TREE NATIONAL PARK

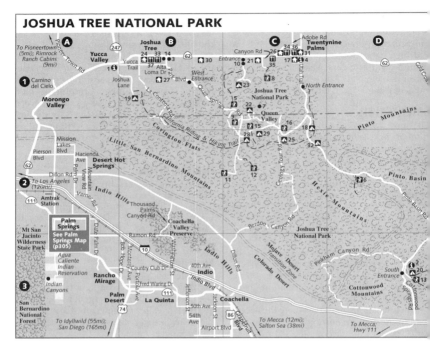

## Internet Access

**Tommy Paul's Beatnik Cafe** (Map pp316-17; ☎ 760-366-2090; 61597 Twentynine Palms Hwy; per 15min $2; ⊗ 11am-midnight Sun-Thu, to 2am Fri & Sat)

## Internet Resources

**National Parks Service** (www.nps.gov/jotr) The NPS website has extensive information on the park, from activities and accessibility to weather and wildflowers.

## Tourist Information

The NPS operates three visitor centers. The Oasis Visitor Center, the park's main information center, also serves as park headquarters. You can find lots of information online at www.nps.gov/jotr.

**Black Rock Nature Center** (Map pp316-17; ☎ 760-367-3001; ⊗ 8am-4pm Sat-Thu, noon-8pm Fri, closed Jun-Sep) In the northwest corner of the park.

**Cottonwood Visitor Center** (Map pp316-17; Pinto Basin Rd; ⊗ 8am-4pm) A few miles inside the park's southern entrance.

**Oasis Visitor Center** (Map pp316-17; ☎ 760-367-5500; National Monument Dr; ⊗ 8am-5pm) Stock up on books and maps, and talk to a ranger at park headquarters, just outside the park's northern boundary in Twentynine Palms.

Though the primary function is to promote their member businesses, the chambers can be a good resource for general information about the area.

**Joshua Tree Chamber of Commerce** (Map pp316-17; ☎ 760-366-3723; www.joshuatreechamber.org; 61325 Twentynine Palms Hwy; ⊗ 10am-3pm Mon-Fri)

**Twentynine Palms Chamber of Commerce** (Map pp316-17; ☎ 760-367-3445; www.29chamber.com; 6455a Mesquite Ave; ⊗ 9am-5pm Mon-Fri)

## SIGHTS

Those who enjoy history and local lore must tour the **Desert Queen Ranch** (Map pp316-17; reservations ☎ 760-367-5555; adult/child $5/2.50; ⊗ tours 10am & 1pm daily Oct-May, 5:30pm Wed & Fri Jun-Sep), around 2 miles northeast of Hidden Valley Campground up a dirt road. Russian immigrant William Keys built a homestead on 160 acres here in 1917 and over the next 60 years set up a full working ranch, school, store and workshop, which still stand pretty much as they did when Keys died in 1969. The half-mile walking tour lasts 90 minutes. Reservation recommended; book on the phone or in person at the Oasis Visitor Center.

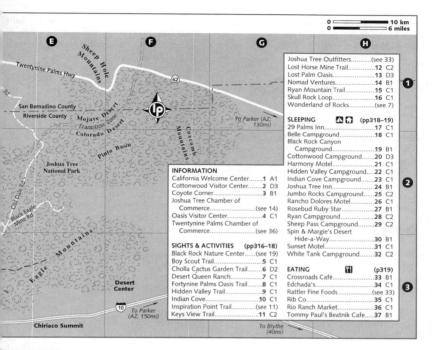

## ACTIVITIES

### Hiking

You really have to get away from your car to appreciate Joshua Tree's trippy lunar landscapes. The visitor centers provide maps and advice about the 12 short nature walks (which range from 0.25 miles to 1.3 miles) and six hiking trails that focus on different features of the park. Trails include Fortynine Palms Oasis, Hidden Valley, Lost Horse Mine, Inspiration Point, Ryan Mountain, Cholla Cactus Garden and Lost Palm Oasis. If you don't have a lot of time, the 0.25mi **Skull Rock Loop** is an easy loop, as is **Keys View Trail**, which provides views of the entire Coachella Valley.

Ask at the visitor center which nature trails are best suited for children. To encourage kids' imagination, pick up a Junior Ranger booklet at the visitor center. After completing several activities, kids get awarded a badge by rangers.

Longer hikes present a challenge because of the need to carry water: at least two gallons per person per day. Overnight backcountry hikers must register (to aid in census-taking,

fire safety and rescue efforts) and deposit the stub at one of 12 backcountry boards in parking lots throughout the park. Cars left overnight not identified on a registration card may be cited or towed away.

The well-traveled, 16-mile **Boy Scout Trail**, on the western side of the park, starts from either the Indian Cove or Keys West backcountry board.

A 35-mile-long stretch of the **California Riding & Hiking Trail**, a trail system administered by California State Parks, passes through Joshua Tree; plan two to three days to hike the trail through the park.

To protect fragile soil crusts (cryptobiotic soil), which allow plant life to grow and keep the desert from blowing away, stay on established trails. For more information, check with rangers.

### Rock Climbing

From boulders to cracks to multipitch faces, there may be more routes here than anywhere else in the US. The longest climbs are not much more than 100ft or so, but there are many challenging technical routes, and most can be easily top-roped for training. Some of the most popular climbs are in the **Hidden Valley** area.

A specialized climbing book, such as *Joshua Tree Rock Climbing Guide* by Randy Vogel, is a must. The kind folks at Coyote Corner (p315), in the town of Joshua Tree, carry climbing books and route diaries that you can thumb through or buy.

For a day of instruction or for a guided climb, contact **Uprising Outdoor Adventure Guides** ( ☎ 760-366-3799, 888-254-6266; www.uprising.com). **Nomad Ventures** (Map pp316-17; ☎ 760-366-4684; www .nomadventures.com; cnr Twentynine Palms Hwy & Park Blvd; ☻ 8am-6pm, later Sat & Sun), in the town of Joshua Tree, is the best place to buy the latest and greatest gear.

### Cycling

Joshua Tree National Park is popular for biking, though bicycles must stay on the roads and trails. A mountain bike or, at minimum, a hybrid bike is necessary for the many unpaved roads.

Two favorite bicycle routes are the challenging **Pinkham Canyon Rd**, which begins at the Cottonwood Visitor Center, and the **Old Dale Rd**, which starts 6½ miles north of there. The **Queen Valley** road network is a more gentle set of trails and has bike racks along the way so people can lock up their bikes and go hiking.

Bikes are a great means of transportation here: hop on your two-wheel steed to get from your campground to any destination and you'll have gorgeous scenery along the way.

## SLEEPING

There are no lodges in the park, only campgrounds. You can find motels, inns and B&Bs in the surrounding communities of Joshua Tree and Twentynine Palms.

### Camping

There are nine campgrounds in the park; see Map pp316–17 for locations. Rent gear – from tents and bags to stoves and water jugs – from **Joshua Tree Outfitters** (Map pp316-17; ☎ 760-366-1848; 61707 Twentynine Palms Hwy, Joshua Tree; **P** ).

**Black Rock Canyon** ( ☎ 800-365-2267; http://reserva tions.nps.gov; sites $10; **P** ) and **Indian Cove** ( ☎ 800-365-2267; http://reservations.nps.gov; sites $10) have sites by reservation only; campsites at **Hidden**

**Valley**, **Ryan**, **Sheep Pass**, **Jumbo Rocks**, **Belle**, **White Tank**, and **Cottonwood** (sites $10) are available on a first-come, first-served basis only. At busy times, during spring and fall, find a site before noon and stake your claim.

Water is available at Black Rock Canyon and Cottonwood campgrounds, and close to Indian Cove; there are no showers anywhere.

Only the three campgrounds with water cost money; of these, only Black Rock and Cottonwood have flush toilets. All other campgrounds are free and have pit toilets, picnic tables and fireplaces, but no water. Jumbo Rocks is especially attractive for its sheltered rock alcoves that act as perfect sunset/sunrise-viewing platforms.

Backcountry camping is permitted, but not less than a mile from the nearest road, or 500ft from the nearest trail, and not in any wash or day-use area. Fires are strictly forbidden.

### Motels, Inns & Cabins

Twentynine Palms has the biggest selection of accommodations near the national park, but some are no-tell motels (geared more toward hourly than nightly rentals). Joshua Tree has fewer places, but more diversity.

**Harmony Motel** (Map pp316-17; ☎ 760-367-3351; www.harmonymotel.com; 71161 Twentynine Palms Hwy; r $60-70; **P** ▯ ▧ ) A peaceful spot on the western edge of Twentynine Palms, the area's best motel has a small pool, large rooms (several with kitchens), gorgeous views and nooks for reading or meditating, a favorite pastime of the owner. U2 wrote and recorded the *Joshua Tree* album here. Top pick for its class.

**29 Palms Inn** (Map pp316-17; ☎ 760-367-3505; www .29palmsinn.com; 73950 Inn Ave; cabins $75-135; **P** ▯ ▧ ) Built on and around the Oasis of Mara, this charming collection of old adobe-and-wood cabins is the best place to stay in Twentynine Palms. Some cabins have decks and fireplaces, perfect on a cool desert evening. The continental breakfast includes scratch muffins. There's also a great restaurant (p319) in the premises.

**Joshua Tree Inn** (Map pp316-17; ☎ 760-366-1188; www.joshuatreeinn.com; 61259 Twentynine Palms Hwy; r $75-95; **P** ▧ ) Gram Parsons overdosed at this large U-shaped motel (and his fans still flock here to stay in Room 8) in Joshua Tree. It could use a fluff job, but it's an OK place to stay and has a nice pool.

**Spin & Margie's Desert Hide-a-Way** (Map pp316-17; ☎ 760-366-9124; www.deserthideaway.com; 64491 Twentynine Palms Hwy; ste $105-140; **P** ) Every boldly colorful, snappy-looking suite has its own kitchen at this delightful and homey four-room inn, situated on three fenced-in acres in Joshua Tree. Charming, knowledgeable and gregarious owners ensure a relaxed and wonderful visit.

**Rosebud Ruby Star** (Map pp316-17; ☎ 760-366-4676, 877-887-7370; www.rosebudrubystar.com; s/d $140/155, cabins from $155, houses from $235; **P** 🖵 ) Just south of Joshua Tree near the western entrance of the park, this out-of-the-way Western-style charmer has two guest rooms, a cabin that sleeps up to five people, and two houses that sleep from four to six people. There's a two-night minimum stay at peak times.

**Rimrock Ranch Cabins** ( ☎ 760-228-1297; www.rimrockranchcabins.com; 50857 Burns Canyon Rd; cabins $100-150; **P** 🖳 ) For an off-the-beaten-path hideaway where time slows down and tensions melt away, book a cabin at Rimrock Ranch, 9 miles northwest of Yucca Valley, or about 20 minutes from Joshua Tree. Built in the '40s as the area's first homestead, its four lovingly decorated cabins each come with a kitchen and a private patio, perfect for stargazing. Two-night minimum stay on weekends.

There are two down-market (read: plain and dumpy) roadside desert motels in Twentynine Palms that have cheap rates: **Sunset Motel** (Map pp316-17; ☎ 760-367-3484; www.sunsetmotel29.com; 73842 Twentynine Palms Hwy; r $42-52; **P** 🖵 🖳 ) Clean and friendly. **El Rancho Dolores Motel** (Map pp316-17; ☎ 760-367-3528; www.virtual29.com/a-z/dolores; 73352 Twentynine Palms Hwy; r from $35-80; **P** 🖵 🖳 ) Large pool, cable TV.

## EATING
Twentynine Palms has OK food, but – other than the 29 Palms Inn – not much character to its restaurants. Joshua Tree is more fun; its places have microbrew beers, live music and vegan food.

### Twentynine Palms
**Rio Ranch Market** (Map pp316-17; ☎ 760-367-7216; cnr Twentynine Palms Hwy & Adobe Rd; 🕑 7am-10pm; **P** ) Shop here for groceries and produce.

**Edchada's** (Map pp316-17; ☎ 760-367-2131; 73502 Twentynine Palms Hwy; meals $6-11; 🕑 11am-9pm; **P** ) There's nothing to write home about at this standard-issue Mexican eatery, but the margaritas are huge and you won't leave hungry.

**Rib Co** (Map pp316-17; ☎ 760-367-1663; 72183 Twentynine Palms Hwy; mains $7-15; 🕑 dinner; **P** ) The fun atmosphere and good barbecue make this worth a look. Expect sandwiches, burgers, chicken and ribs, plus salads and a few veggie items.

**29 Palms Inn** (Map pp316-17; ☎ 760-367-3505; mains lunch $6-9, dinner $12-23; **P** ) One of the best places to eat in the area, the inn makes its own bread, grills great steaks and serves a variety of nightly specials. Well worth a detour. Make reservations.

### Joshua Tree
**Tommy Paul's Beatnik Cafe** (Map pp316-17; ☎ 760-366-2090; 61597 Twentynine Palms Hwy; 🕑 11am-midnight Sun-Thu, to 2am Fri & Sat; **P** ) Joshua Tree's primary coffeehouse serves sandwiches and light meals, and has something doing almost every night. Monday and Thursday are karaoke night; Saturday a band plays. There's a young crowd and Internet access, too (p316).

**Crossroads Café** (Map pp316-17; ☎ 760-366-5414; 61715 Twentynine Palms Hwy; dishes under $8; 🕑 6:30am-8pm Sun-Tue & Thu, 6:30am-9pm Fri & Sat, closed Wed; **P** ) One of the few places for consistently good food around Joshua Tree, Crossroads serves healthy breakfasts, huge sandwiches, big salads and tasty dinner specials.

**Rattler Fine Foods** (Map pp316-17; ☎ 760-366-1898; 61705 Twentynine Palms Hwy; dishes under $8; 🕑 9am-5:30pm, closed Tue & Jul-Aug; **P** ) This tiny gourmet specialty-food store makes terrific take-out foods and boxed lunches. Superb artisanal cheeses, prosciutto, delicious salads and killer brownies.

## GETTING THERE & AROUND
The only way to reach Joshua Tree is by car. Rent one in Palm Springs or Los Angeles (see p367). From LA the trip takes two to three hours via I-10; from Palm Springs it takes an hour.

# ANZA-BORREGO DESERT STATE PARK

Encompassing some of the most spectacular and accessible desert scenery anywhere, the little-developed Anza-Borrego is enormous. Occupying almost a fifth of San Diego County, it's the largest state park in the USA outside Alaska. Its human history goes back

10,000 years, evidenced by the site's Native-American pictographs. In spring, wildflowers bloom in brilliant displays of bright color, a striking contrast to the subtle earth tones you'll see here all year long.

Summers here are extremely hot, more so than in Joshua Tree. The average daily maximum temperature in July is 107°F, but it can reach 125°F.

## ORIENTATION
If you're short on time or if it's your first visit, head for **Borrego Springs** (Map p300; population 2989, elevation 590ft), a two-street township with a market and a handful of restaurants and motels. Its excellent visitor center and its easy-to-reach sights – including Font's Point and Borrego Palm Canyon – are fairly representative of the park as a whole.

The desert's southernmost region, south of and including Blair Valley, is the least visited and – aside from those in Blair Valley – has few developed trails and facilities. Attractions here, besides the solitude, include Goat Trestle and the Carrizo Badlands, which has an overlook affording great views. The Split Mountain area, in the desert's southeast, is popular with 4WD vehicles, but also contains interesting geology and spectacular wind caves.

## INFORMATION
The **Anza-Borrego Desert State Park Visitor Center** (Map p300; visitor center ☎ 760-767-4205, administration ☎ 760-767-5311; www.anzaborrego.statepark.org; 200 Palm Canyon Dr; ☼ 9am-5pm Nov-May, 9am-5pm Sat & Sun Jun-Oct), 2 miles west of Borrego Springs township, is built partly underground and, from the parking lot, it looks just like a low scrubby hill. The walls are faced with local stone and blend beautifully with the mountain backdrop. Around the center is a selection of plants that you'll encounter in the park, all clearly labeled. Inside, a small theater shows a short slide show on the natural history of the park, and there are exhibits on desert flora and fauna as well as a good selection of publications. Staff are helpful and well informed. Be sure to pick up the park newspaper, which has a handy trail guide and map.

Depending on winter rains, spring wildflowers in Anza-Borrego can be absolutely stunning. The flowers blossom in late February at lower elevations and reach their best over subsequent months at successively higher levels. Call the **Wildflower Hotline** (☎ 760-767-4684) to find out what wildflowers are blooming.

A free park-use permit is required for any car leaving the highway to access the park and is good for overnight camping. Fires are permitted in metal containers only; wood gathering is prohibited.

In an emergency, dial ☎ 911. Cell phones don't work everywhere in the park; if necessary, climb to the highest peak for service.

## SIGHTS
Northeast of Borrego Springs, where S22 takes a 90-degree turn to the east, there's a pile of rocks just north of the road. This the **Peg Leg Smith Monument** (Map p300), is a monument to Thomas Long 'Peg Leg' Smith – mountain man, fur trapper, Native-American fighter, horse thief, liar and Wild West legend. Around 1829, Peg Leg passed through Borrego Springs on his way to LA and supposedly picked up some rocks that were later found to be pure gold. Strangely he didn't return to the area until the 1850s when he was unable to find the lode. Nevertheless, he told lots of people about it (often in exchange for a few drinks), and many came to search for the gold and add to the myths.

On the first Saturday of April, the **Peg Leg Liars Contest** is a hilarious event in which amateur liars compete in the Western tradition of telling tall tales. Anyone can enter so long as the story is about gold and mining in the Southwest, is less than five minutes long and is anything but the truth.

A 4-mile dirt road, usually passable without 4WD (check with the visitor center) goes south of S22 to **Font's Point** (Map p300 1249ft), which offers a spectacular panorama over the Borrego Valley to the west and the Borrego Badlands to the south. Walking the 4 miles to the point is a good way to *really* be amazed when the desert seemingly drops from beneath your feet.

South of Hwy 78 at Ocotillo Wells there's a **ranger station** (☎ 760-767-5391). From here paved Split Mountain Rd takes you pas the **Elephant Trees Discovery Trail** (Map p300) one of the few places to see a 'herd' of the unusual elephant trees whose name comes from their resemblance to an elephant's leg Related to frankincense and myrrh, the trees have a wonderful fragrance not unlike department stores around the holidays. The trees were thought not to exist in the Colorado Desert until a full-fledged hunt was launched in 1937, during which 75 were discovered in the Fish Creek area. Expect to see (and hear) 4WD off-road vehicles around Ocotillo Wells.

About 4 miles south along Split Mountain Rd is a dirt-road turnoff for Fish Creek primitive campground (p322); another 4 miles brings you to **Split Mountain** (Map p300). The road – popular with 4WD enthusiasts – goes right through Split Mountain between 600ft-high walls created by earthquakes and erosion. The gorge is about 2 miles long from north to south. At the southern end, several steep trails lead up to delicate caves carved into the sandstone outcroppings by the wind.

In the west of the park, around 5 miles south of Scissors Crossing (where S2 crosses Hwy 78) is **Blair Valley** (Map p300), known for its Native-American pictographs and *morteros* (hollows in rocks used for grinding seeds). The area also offers nice campgrounds and hiking trails.

A monument at Foot and Walker Pass marks a difficult spot on the Butterfield Overland Stage Route, and in **Box Canyon** you can still see the marks of wagons on the Emigrant Trail. A steep 1-mile climb leads to **Ghost Mountain** and the remains of a house occupied by the family of desert recluse Marshall South.

## ACTIVITIES
### Hiking

The **Borrego Palm Canyon Nature Trail**, a popular self-guided loop trail that goes northeast from the Borrego Palm Canyon Campground, climbs 350ft in 3 miles past a palm grove and waterfall, a delightful oasis in the dry, rocky countryside. However, the trail got washed away in a flash flood in 2003, and the park may or may not re-open it. Check at the visitor center.

The **Hellhole Canyon/Maidenhair Falls Trail** starts from the Hellhole Canyon Trailhead, miles west of the visitor center on S22, and climbs past several palm oases to a seasonal waterfall that supports bird life and a variety of plants.

In a 3-mile round-trip you can see pictographs and a nice view of the Vallecito Valley from the **Pictograph/Smuggler's Canyon Trail**, which starts 3½ miles from S2 in Blair Valley.

A variety of other short trails have been laid out, many of them with interpretive signs or self-guiding brochures – different trails highlight different features. The 1-mile **Cactus Loop Nature Trail** is a good place to see a variety of cacti. Nearby, the 2-mile **Yaqui Well Nature Trail** has many labeled desert plants and passes a natural water hole that attracts a rich variety of birdlife as well as the occasional bighorn sheep in winter. The short **Narrows Earth Trail**, 2 miles east of Tamarisk Grove, highlights the local geology; look for the unusual chuparosa shrubs, which attract hummingbirds.

For trailhead locations see Map p300.

### Mountain Biking
Both primitive roads and paved roads are open to bikes. Popular routes are Grapevine Canyon, Oriflamme Canyon and Canyon Sin Nombre. The visitor center has a free mountain-bike guide. **Carrizo Bikes** (☎ 760-767-3872; 648 Palm Canyon Dr; bike hire per hour/24hr $10/32), in Borrego Springs, rents bikes and also leads guided rides.

## SLEEPING
### Camping
Camping is permitted anywhere in the park as long as you're not within 200 yards of any road or water source. You can't light a fire on the ground, and gathering vegetation (dead or alive) is prohibited.

**Borrego Palm Canyon Campground** (Map p300; reservations ☎ 800-444-7275; tent/RV sites $13/19; P) In summer 2003, the campground was devastated by a flash flood and closed indefinitely pending reconstruction. At press time, no date had yet been set, but park administration planned to rebuild everything, including RV hookups and bathrooms with flush toilets and showers.

**Tamarisk Grove Campground** (Map p300; reservations ☎ 800-444-7275; sites $17; ☺ Nov-May; P) Twelve miles south of Borrego Springs near Hwy 78, Tamarisk is smaller than Borrego Palm Canyon but has more shelter. It also has flush toilets.

**Bow Willow Campground** (Map p300; sites $9; P) Off S2 in the southern part of the park, Bow Willow has only 16 sites, with water, pit toilets, tables and fire pits. No reservations.

There are several other primitive camp-grounds in the park – **Culp Valley**, **Arroyo Salado**, **Yaqui Well**, **Yaqui Pass**, **Fish Creek** and **Mountain Palm Springs** – which are free and have pit toilets but no water and only minimal facilities. Information about all camp-grounds can be obtained from any ranger station or visitor center in the park, or on-line at www.anzaborregostatepark.org.

## Motels & Resorts
The following are in Borrego Springs, 2 miles from the park. In summer temperatures soar and rates drop; prices following are for winter.

**Oasis Motel & RV Park** ( ☎ 760-767-5409; www.oasis motelborrego.com; 366 Palm Canyon Dr; r $75, with kitchenette $95; P 🐾 ) The cheapest place in town has rooms that are a bit run-down, but they have all standard amenities.

**Hacienda del Sol** ( ☎ 760-767-5442; www.hacienda delsol-borrego.com; 610 Palm Canyon Dr; r $70, kitchen units $100-130; P 🐾 ) A step up from the Oasis, this place has fresher rooms with cable TV and in-room coffeemakers.

**Palm Canyon Resort** ( ☎ 760-767-5341, 800-242-0044; www.pcresort.com; 221 Palm Canyon Dr; r $95-130; P 🐾 ) Spend a little more than at the area motels and you'll get a comfy room and two pools to choose from at this large resort, 0.25 miles from the park's visitor center. There's also an on-site restaurant, laundry, store and RV parking too.

**Palms at Indian Head** ( ☎ 760-767-7788, 800-519-2624; www.thepalmsatindianhead.com; 2220 Hoberg Rd; r incl breakfast $100-190; P 🖥 🐾 ) One mile north from Palm Canyon Dr, the Palms is a mid-century resort hotel on 240 acres abutting the state park. Aside from having a 25-yard-long pool – the biggest in town – it also has direct access to the park. Suites have wood-burning fireplaces. The Palms also has a great Krazy Koyote grill (right).

Luxury has two faces here:

**Borrego Valley Inn** ( ☎ 760-767-0311, 800-333-5810; www.borregovalleyinn.com; 405 Palm Canyon Dr; r $110-170; P 🐾 ) This small inn, with its contemporary architecture and Spanish-style details, has the feel of an intimate spa-resort, perfect for adults. One pool is clothing-optional. Rates include a healthy breakfast and evening cocktails.

**La Casa del Zorro** ( ☎ 760-767-5323, 800-824-1884; www.lacasadelzorro.com; 3845 Yaqui Pass Rd; r $195-410,

casitas from $210; P 🖥 🐾 ) The area's top luxury resort has manicured grounds, Southwestern architecture, spacious rooms and a formal lobby and dining room (jackets required at dinner). If you want to spend some serious cash, this is the place to do it. Most rooms have wood-burning fireplaces; some casitas have private pools.

## EATING
There aren't a lot of places to eat. The following are located in Borrego Springs 2 miles east of the park. In summer many places keep shorter hours; call ahead.

**Center Market** ( ☎ 760-767-3311; 590 Palm Canyon Dr; 🕒 8:30am-6:30pm Mon-Sat, 8:30am-5pm Sun; P ) Ignore the market on Christmas Circle and go to this market for a wide selection of good produce. It's in the Center, the shopping center across from the mall, where you'll also find a liquor store.

**Jilberto's Taco Shop** ( ☎ 760-767-1008; 659 Palm Canyon Dr; most dishes under $5; P ) Jilberto's serves excellent Mexican food, but the atmosphere lacks charm. Most folks eat at the outdoor tables.

**Carlee's Place** ( ☎ 760-767-3262; 660 W Palm Canyon Dr; mains lunch $6-12, dinner $12-23; P ) Local pick Carlee's, near Christmas Circle, for its burgers, salads, pasta, steak dinners and atmosphere – though the pool table is a big draw too. There's live music on Friday karaoke on Saturday.

**Krazy Koyote Saloon & Grill** ( ☎ 760-767-7788 2220 Hoberg Rd; mains $9-24; 🕒 dinner Wed-Sat; P ) The bar and grill at the Palms at India Head resort has good Southwestern- and American-style cooking, including prim steaks. The atmosphere is fun and the view terrific.

## GETTING THERE & AWAY
You'll need a car to get to Anza-Borrego Desert State Park. From San Diego, I-8 to S2 takes longest, but it's easiest because it mostly follows freeway. Alternatively take the scenic and twisty Hwy 79 from I-8 north through Cuyamaca Rancho State Park and into Julian, then head east on Hwy 78. Plan on 2½ hours of driving, whichever route you take.

From Palm Springs, take I-10 to Indio to Hwy 86 south along the Salton Sea. Turn west on S22. Plan 1½ to two hours.

# Santa Barbara

Majestic mountains tower 3000ft above the oh-so-civilized seaside city of Santa Barbara (SB), where the low-slung red-tile roofs, white-stucco buildings and let's-take-a-siesta vibe make it feel more like the Mediterranean than go-go SoCal. The handsome city has even 'branded' itself with the registered-trademark name of the 'American Riviera.' That might be an overstatement – one look at an approaching fog bank off the Pacific and the empty cafés at midnight, and you'll know you're in California, not the south of France. Still, downtown Santa Barbara has outstanding architectural integrity, a masterpiece of a courthouse, and noteworthy art and natural history museums. Five colleges, including the University of California at Santa Barbara (UCSB), give the town a youthful vivacity, and balance its more staid yachting and retirement communities.

Santa Barbara is one of only a handful of California cities where you can arrive by train, walk almost anywhere and never need a car. The city even has a website called **Santa Barbara Car Free, Carefree** (www.santabarbaracarfree.com) to help visitors plan a trip without having to drive. If your Southern California jaunt leaves you road weary, a couple of days spent in Santa Barbara by the glittering blue Pacific might be just what the doctor ordered.

Outside Santa Barbara, the surrounding Santa Ynez mountains have terrific hiking and camping, and the nearby grape-growing regions produce some of California's great wines.

## HIGHLIGHTS

- Ascending the 85ft tower of the **Santa Barbara County Courthouse** (p326) in downtown Santa Barbara for jaw-dropping views

- Taking to the sea on a whale-watching sailboat **cruise** (p330)

- Hiking the foothills of the **Santa Ynez Mountains** (p331), thousands of feet above the coastal fog

- Brushing up on your California history at downtown Santa Barbara's **El Presidio de Santa Barbara State Historic Park** (p329)

- Pedaling along the beach on the **Cabrillo Blvd bike path** (p330)

- Exploring the Santa Barbara Wine Country and tasting California's best pinot noir in the **Santa Ynez Valley** (p338)

- Escaping civilization at **Channel Islands National Park** (p346)

Santa Ynez Valley
★
Santa Ynez ★
Mountains

Santa Barbara
★★ Cabrillo Blvd

Channel Islands
National Park
★

| SANTA BARBARA POP: 92,300 | AVERAGE TEMPS: JAN 45/64°F, JUL 59/75°F |
| --- | --- |

# ORIENTATION

Santa Barbara's coast faces south, not west, an important fact to remember when navigating town. Downtown Santa Barbara is laid out in a square grid – its main artery is State St, which runs north–south. State St divides the east side from the west side. Lower State St (south of Ortega St) has a large concentration of bars, while Upper State St (north of Ortega St) has most of the pretty shops and museums. Cabrillo Blvd hugs the coastline and turns into Coast Village Rd as it enters the eastern suburb of Montecito.

Santa Barbara is surrounded by small affluent communities: Hope Ranch to the west, Montecito and Summerland to the east. UCSB is just west of Hope Ranch in Isla Vista, and most of Santa Barbara's college crowd lives around the campus or in neighboring Goleta.

The Santa Barbara Visitor Center (right) has free maps. You can also buy maps in bookstores or at Pacific Travelers Supply (below).

# INFORMATION

## Bookstores

Unlike most other Southern California communities, Santa Barbara is a great place to buy books.

**Book Den** (Map pp328-9; ☎ 805-926-3321; 11 E Anapamu St) The oldest used bookstore in California specializes in history, art, architecture and academic-press titles. It has an excellent tracking system for locating used books. Bibliophiles and perpetual students, beware: you may never get out of here.

**Chaucer's Books** (Map pp326-7; ☎ 805-682-6782; 3321 State St) Best selection in town for any new book you could ever want.

**Lost Horizon** (Map pp328-9; ☎ 805-962-4606; 703 Anacapa St) Impeccably kept shop for hard-to-find, high-end hardcover books and multivolume sets.

**Pacific Travelers Supply** (Map pp328-9; ☎ 805-963-4438, 800-546-8060; 12 W Anapamu St) The best spot in town to buy guidebooks and maps, as well as miscellaneous travelers' accessories.

## Internet Access

**Hot Spots Visitor Centre** (Map pp328-9; ☎ 805-963-4233; 36 State St; ☽ 24hr) High-speed access costs 20¢ per minute; wireless is free (bring your own computer).

## Laundry

**Laundromat** (Map pp328-9; cnr Arrelaga & State Sts) A self-service laundry behind Cantwell's Deli.

## Library

**Santa Barbara Public Library** (Map pp328-9; ☎ 805-962-7653; www.sbplibrary.org; 40 E Anapamu St; ☽ 10am-9pm Mon-Thu, 10am-5:30pm Fri & Sat, 1-5pm Sun) The main branch of the public library also has computers for public use.

## Media

**Independent** (www.independent.com) Published on Thursday; has thorough events listings and reviews.
**Santa Barbara News-Press** (www.newspress.com) Santa Barbara's daily newspaper also has an events calendar and a special Friday supplement called 'Scene.'

## Medical Services

**Santa Barbara Cottage Hospital** (Map pp326-7; ☎ 805-682-7111; cnr Pueblo & Bath Sts; ☽ 24hr) Emergency room operating 24/7.

## Money

Looks for banks and ATMs along State St.
**Paul A Brombal Coin & Jewelry** (Map pp326-7; ☎ 805-687-3641; 3601-A State St; ☽ 9:30am-5pm Mon-Fri, 10am-2pm Sat) Exchanges currency; call ahead. It's on the corner of Ontare.

## Post

**Post office** (Map pp328-9; ☎ 805-564-2226; 836 Anacapa St; ☽ 8am-6pm Mon-Fri, 9am-5pm Sat) Full-service post office

## Tourist Information

**Hot Spots Visitor Center** (Map pp328-9; ☎ 805-564-1637, 800-793-7666; 36 State St; ☽ 9am-9pm Mon-Sat, 9am-4pm Sun Apr-Nov, shorter hours Dec-Mar) Helps book lodgings, particularly useful if you show up in town without a reservation and want to stay the night. It's inside a 24-hour café with Internet access.
**Santa Barbara Visitor Center** Beachfront (Map pp328-9; ☎ 805-965-3021, 800-676-1266; www.santabarbaraca .com; 1 Garden St; ☽ 9am-5pm Mon-Sat, 10am-5pm Sun Sep-Jun, 9am-6pm Jul & Aug); Harborside (Map pp328-9; ☎ 805-884-1475; 113 Harbor Way, 4th fl, Santa Barbara Maritime Museum; ☽ 11am-5pm, to 6pm summer) Pick up maps and brochures, and consult with the busy but helpful staff. The harborside branch has information on Channel Islands National Park, Los Padres National Forest and outdoor activities.

# SIGHTS

Pick up a free map from the visitors centers for the self-guided 12-block **Red Tile walking tour**. It's an excellent way to take in all of the major downtown sights and historic landmarks.

# SANTA BARBARA

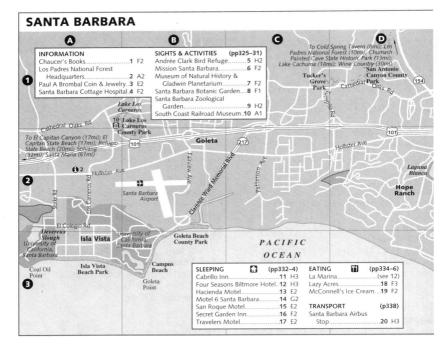

**INFORMATION**
Chaucer's Books.........................1  F2
Los Padres National Forest
Headquarters..........................2  A2
Paul A Brombal Coin & Jewelry..3  E2
Santa Barbara Cottage Hospital..4  F2

**SIGHTS & ACTIVITIES   (pp325–31)**
Andrée Clark Bird Refuge.........5  H2
Mission Santa Barbara.............6  F2
Museum of Natural History &
Gladwin Planetarium..............7  F2
Santa Barbara Botanic Garden...8  F1
Santa Barbara Zoological
Garden.................................9  H2
South Coast Railroad Museum..10  A1

**SLEEPING**                          (pp332–4)
Cabrillo Inn.............................11  H3
Four Seasons Biltmore Hotel..12  H3
Hacienda Motel......................13  E2
Motel 6 Santa Barbara............14  G2
San Roque Motel....................15  E2
Secret Garden Inn..................16  F2
Travelers Motel......................17  E2

**EATING**                            (pp334–6)
La Marina...............................(see 12)
Lazy Acres............................18  F3
McConnell's Ice Cream...........19  F2

**TRANSPORT**                         (p338)
Santa Barbara Airbus
Stop...................................20  H3

## Santa Barbara County Courthouse

The 1929 **courthouse** (Map pp328-9; ☎ 805-962-6464; 1100 Anacapa St; admission free; ☽ 8am-5pm Mon-Fri, 10am-5pm Sat & Sun) is one sight not to be missed. Built in Spanish-Moorish Revival style, it features hand-painted ceilings, wrought-iron chandeliers, and tiles from Tunisia and Spain. You're free to explore it on your own, but you'll get a lot more out of the free docent-led tour offered at 2pm Monday through Saturday, and at 10:30am Monday, Tuesday and Friday. Be sure to have a look at the mural room, and go up the 80ft clock tower for your panoramic shots of the city.

## Santa Barbara Museum of Art

This well-regarded art **museum** (Map pp328-9; ☎ 805-963-4364; www.sbma.net; 1130 State St; adult/student/senior $7/4/5, Sun free; ☽ 11am-5pm Tue-Sun) displays European and American celebs – Monet, Matisse, Hopper and O'Keeffe – as well as Asian art, photography and classical sculpture. There's also an interactive children's gallery, a café that makes good sandwiches, and a museum shop.

## Santa Barbara Historical Museum

Located in an adobe complex, this educational **museum** (Map pp328-9; ☎ 805-966-1601; www.santabarbaramuseum.com; 136 E De La Guerra St; admission by donation; ☽ 10am-5pm Tue-Sat, noon-5pm Sun) has an exhaustive collection of local memorabilia that ranges from the mundane, such as antique furniture, to the intriguing, such as the intricately carved coffer that belonged to Padre Serra. You can also learn about Santa Barbara's involvement in toppling the last Chinese monarchy, a rather obscure chapter in history. Free guided tours are given at 1:30pm Wednesday, Saturday and Sunday.

## Mission Santa Barbara

Called the 'Queen of the Missions,' **Mission Santa Barbara** (Map pp326-7; ☎ 805-682-4713, tour info 805-682-4149; www.sbmission.org; 2201 Laguna St; adult/child $4/free; ☽ 9am-5pm) sits on a majestic perch 0.5 miles north of downtown. It was established on December 4 (the feast day of St Barbara) in 1786, as the 10th California mission. Three adobe structures preceded the current stone version from 1820; its main facade integrates neoclassical-style

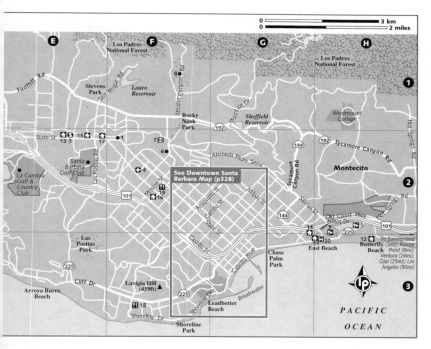

columns. Today the mission still functions as a Franciscan friary, as well as a parish church and museum. The church features Chumash wall decorations, and the gardens in the courtyard evoke tranquility. Behind it is an extensive cemetery with 4000 Chumash graves and the elaborate mausoleums of early California settlers.

## Waterfront

The southern end of State St gives way to **Stearns Wharf** (Map pp328–9), a rough, wooden pier with a few snack and souvenir shops.Built in 1872 by John Peck Stearn, it's the oldest continuously operating wharf on the West Coast. During the 1940s it was owned by Jimmy Cagney and his two brothers. Partly destroyed by a 1998 fire, it has now been restored. Also on the wharf, slated to open in fall 2005, look for the new **Sea Center** (Map pp328-9; ☎ 805-682-4711; www.sbnature.org), which has hands-on exhibits and touch pools especially for kids. Southwest of the wharf, right in the harbor, the small **Santa Barbara Maritime Museum** (Map pp328-9; ☎ 805-962-8404; www.sbmm.org; 113 Harbor Way; adult/

child/senior $6/3/3; ☺ 10am-6pm summer, 10am-5pm winter) celebrates the town's briny history with memorabilia and hands-on exhibits, including a big-game fishing chair from which you can 'reel in' a trophy marlin. Elsewhere you can take a virtual trip through the Santa Barbara Channel and peek through a 45ft-tall US Navy periscope. Admission is free on the third Thursday of the month.

## Santa Barbara Botanic Garden

A mile north of the Museum of Natural History, this 65-acre **botanic garden** (Map pp326-7; ☎ 805-682-4726; www.sbbg.org; 1212 Mission Canyon Rd; adult/child/teen/senior $6/1/3/4; ☺ 9am-5pm summer, 9am-4pm winter) is devoted to California's native flora. Around 5.5 miles of trails meander through cacti, redwoods, wildflowers and past the old mission dam, built by the Chumash to irrigate the mission's fields. If you like gardens, this is a must-visit.

## Museum of Natural History & Gladwin Planetarium

If only for its beautiful architecture and landscaping, visit this **museum** (Map pp326-7;

# DOWNTOWN SANTA BARBARA

0 — 500 m
0 — 0.3 miles

**A** **B** **C** **D**

To Mission
Santa Barbara
Laguna St

6 ✚

To Loreto Plaza;
Chaucer's Books

Santa Barbara St
E Islay St
Garden St
E Valerio St
E Anacapa St

To Daily
Grind

22 🏠

3

Alameda
Park

39 🍴

Milpas St

Quarantina St
Salsipuedes St

W Micheltorena St
State St
W Sola St
E Victoria St
E Anapamu St

59
65
54
45
33
49
55
31
4
53 🍴
13
28 🏠
Ortega
Park

Olive St
Vine Ave
Laguna St

32 🍴

Garden St

9

1
16
60
5
44 🍴

51 📧

Bath St
De La Vina St

Spencer
Adams
Park

W Anapamu St

67
66
63
42
56
57
37 🍴
Historic
Paseo
14
41
Ortega St
Cota St

To Goleta; UCSB;
Santa Barbara
Airport

101

W Figueroa St
W Carrillo St
W Cañon Perdido St

De La Guerra St

Chapala St

58
62
61
38
40 🍴
Vera
Cruz
Park

Haley St

To Santa Barbara Zoological
Garden; Andrée Clark Bird
Refuge; Ventura; Los Angeles

101

Gutierrez St
Yanonali St
Garden St

64
25
46
48 🍴
50

Castillo St

Mission Creek

36 🍴
35 🍴

Chase Palm
Park

San Andres St
Cañon
Perdido St
De La
Guerra St
Loma Alta Dr

Ortega St
San Pascual St
Cota St
Coronel Pl
Ranchera St

Gray Ave
Anacapa St
Helena Ave
State St

7 ℹ️

Amtrak
Station

Miramonte Dr

Montecito St
Bath St
Natoma Ave
Mason St

21
11
26
29
47
2
8
68
30
Cabrillo Blvd
East Beach
Stearns
Wharf

West Beach

Honda
Valley
Park

Arroyo Ave
Coronel St
Weldon Rd
Ladera St
Loma Alta Dr

20
27
23
19
24
Ambassador
Park

17

43 🍴

Pershing
Park

18

Plaza del
Mar Park

Santa
Barbara
City College

Sand
Bar

10

PACIFIC
OCEAN

Santa
Barbara
Harbor

To Lazy Acres
(0.7miles)

Cliff Dr
Barranca Ave
Oceano Ave

225

15
Harbor
Way
12
34

Breakwater

Leadbetter
Beach

Point
Castillo

San Onofre St
Las Ondas St
San Clemente St
La Plata

Shoreline Dr

Shoreline
Park

LP

| INFORMATION | | |
|---|---|---|
| Book Den | 1 | B2 |
| Hot Spots Visitor Center | 2 | D4 |
| Laundromat | 3 | A2 |
| Lost Horizon | (see 40) | |
| Pacific Travellers Supply | 4 | B2 |
| Post Office | 5 | B3 |
| St Francis Medical Center | 6 | B1 |
| Santa Barbara Public Library | (see 55) | |
| Santa Barbara Visitor Center | 7 | D4 |
| Santa Barbara Visitor Center | (see 15) | |

| SIGHTS & ACTIVITIES | (pp325–31) | |
|---|---|---|
| Beach House | 8 | D4 |
| El Presidio State Historic Park | 9 | C2 |
| Los Baños del Mar | 10 | C5 |
| Moreton Bay Fig Tree | 11 | C4 |
| Paddle Sports | 12 | C6 |
| Santa Barbara County Courthouse | 13 | B2 |
| Santa Barbara Historical Museum | 14 | C3 |
| Santa Barbara Maritime Museum | 15 | C5 |
| Santa Barbara Museum of Art | 16 | B2 |
| Sea Center | 17 | D4 |
| Sea Landing | (see 18) | |
| Sunset Kidd's Sailing Cruises | (see 12) | |
| Truth Aquatics | 18 | C5 |
| Wheel Fun | (see 8) | |

| SLEEPING | (pp332–4) | |
|---|---|---|
| Brisas del Mar | 19 | C5 |
| Colonial Beach Inn | 20 | B3 |
| Eagle Inn | 21 | C4 |
| El Prado | 22 | A2 |
| Franciscan Inn | 23 | C5 |

| Hotel Oceana | 24 | C5 |
|---|---|---|
| Hotel Santa Barbara | 25 | C3 |
| Hotel State Street | 26 | C4 |
| Inn by the Harbor | 27 | C5 |
| Inn of the Spanish Garden | 28 | C2 |
| Santa Barbara Tourist Hostel | 29 | C4 |
| Villa Rosa | 30 | C5 |

| EATING | (pp334–6) | |
|---|---|---|
| Arigato | 31 | A2 |
| Arnoldi's | 32 | C2 |
| Bouchon | 33 | A2 |
| Brophy Brothers | 34 | C6 |
| D'Angelo Pastry & Bread | 35 | C4 |
| Esau's Coffee Shop | 36 | C4 |
| Intermezzo | 37 | B3 |
| Italian & Greek Delicatessen | 38 | C3 |
| La Super Rica | 39 | D2 |
| Olio e Limone | (see 33) | |
| Pacific Crepes | 40 | C4 |
| Paradise Café | 41 | C3 |
| Roy | 42 | B3 |
| Santa Barbara Shellfish Company | 43 | D5 |
| Sojourner Café | 44 | B2 |
| Tupelo Junction | 45 | B2 |
| Waterfront Grill & Endless Summer | (see 34) | |
| Wine Cask | (see 37) | |

| DRINKING | (pp336–7) | |
|---|---|---|
| Blue Agave | 46 | C4 |
| Brew House | 47 | C4 |
| Chad's | 48 | B3 |
| Epiphany | 49 | A2 |
| Firebird | (see 46) | |

| Hades | (see 47) | |
|---|---|---|
| Hot Spots Espresso Co | (see 2) | |
| James Joyce | 50 | C3 |
| Muddy Waters | 51 | D3 |
| Red's Espresso Bar and Gallery | 52 | C4 |
| SB Roasting Co | (see 35) | |
| Sportsman Lounge | 53 | B2 |

| ENTERTAINMENT | (p337) | |
|---|---|---|
| Arlington Center for the Performing Arts | 54 | A2 |
| Center Stage Theater | (see 62) | |
| Granada Theatre | 55 | B2 |
| Lobero Theatre | 56 | B3 |
| Soho | (see 31) | |

| SHOPPING | (pp337–8) | |
|---|---|---|
| Blue Bee & Blue Beetle | 57 | B3 |
| Bryan Lee | 58 | B3 |
| Diani | 59 | A2 |
| La Arcada | 60 | B2 |
| Particle | 61 | B3 |
| Paseo Nuevo | 62 | B3 |
| Tom's Toys | 63 | B3 |
| True Grit | 64 | C3 |
| Victorian Vogue & the Costume Shop | 65 | B2 |

| TRANSPORT | (p338) | |
|---|---|---|
| Greyhound | 66 | B3 |
| MTD Transit Center | 67 | B3 |

| OTHER | | |
|---|---|---|
| Santa Barbara Trolley Main Stop | 68 | D4 |

☎ 805-682-4711; www.sbnature.org; 2559 Puesta del Sol Rd; adult/child/senior & teen $7/4/6; ☼ 10am-5pm) two blocks north of the mission and 1 mile south of the botanic garden. The Chumash exhibit is worth a look, as is the complete skeleton of a blue whale; other exhibits lack sparkle. It's free on the third Sunday of the month. Kids especially like the **planetarium** (admission $3), which has intro-to-astronomy shows for children, called 'Twinkle, Twinkle Little Stars,' as well as adult programs that explore current scientific theory; call for show times.

## Santa Barbara Zoological Garden

The **zoo** (Map pp326-7; ☎ 805-962-5339; 500 Niños Dr; adult/child under 12/senior $9/7/7; ☼ 10am-5pm; P $3) has gorgeous gardens as well as 700 animals from around the world, including big cats, monkeys, elephants and giraffes. The 100-year-old vegetation was once part of a palatial estate.

Just east of the zoo, the **Andrée Clark Bird Refuge** (Map pp326-7; 1400 E Cabrillo Blvd; admission free) consists of a lagoon, gardens and a path from where you can observe nesting freshwater birds.

## El Presidio de Santa Barbara State Historic Park

One of four in California, this 18th-century former Spanish **fort** (Map pp328-9; ☎ 805-966-9719; www.sbthp.org; E Cañon Perdido St; admission by donation; ☼ 10:30am-4:30pm), between Anacapa and Santa Barbara Sts, harbors some of the city's oldest structures, which seem to be in constant need of propping up and restoring.

Founded in 1782 to protect the missions between Monterey and San Diego, the presidio also served as a social and political hub, and as a stopping point for traveling Spanish military.

Be sure to visit the chapel, with an interior that explodes in kaleidoscopic color and features some interesting trompe l'oeil effects.

---

### MORETON BAY FIG TREE

Near the corner of Montecito and Chapala Sts, look out for the Moreton Bay fig tree (Map pp328-9). Imported from Brisbane, Australia, and planted in 1877, the tree is believed to be the largest of its kind in North America. Not only is it a whopping 78ft tall (almost eight stories!), but it has a 171ft canopy, reputedly enough to provide shade to 1000 people at a time. The tree used to provide shelter to Santa Barbara's homeless population, who were dubbed 'tree people'; some of them even tried to use the tree as a mailing address.

---

**TOP FIVE FREEBIES**

- Climb to the top of the courthouse tower (p326) for panoramic views

- Smell the brilliant roses blooming in front of the Mission Santa Barbara (p326)

- Wander back in time at the Santa Barbara Historical Museum (p326)

- Window shop along State St (p337), ending up at the beach and Stearns Wharf

- Stand on the bluffs with binoculars and spot whales (February to May) from Shoreline Park (p332)

---

## South Coast Railroad Museum

If you go gaga for trains, don't miss this **museum** (Map pp326-7; ☎ 805-964-3540; www.goleta depot.org; 300 N Los Carneros Rd; admission by donation; ☒ 1-4pm Wed-Sun). It houses a sizable collection of railroad artifacts, old photographs and a 300-sq-ft model railroad. Children get a kick out of riding the miniature train ($1). The museum is 0.3 miles from the Los Carneros exit off Hwy 101 in a 1901 Southern Pacific Railroad depot in Goleta, 8 miles northwest of downtown Santa Barbara.

## Beaches

The long sandy stretch between Stearns Wharf and Montecito is **East Beach** (Map pp328-9); it's Santa Barbara's largest and most popular beach, and has a dozen volleyball nets for pick-up games. At its eastern end Armani swimsuits and Gucci sunglasses abound at the narrow but chic **Butterfly Beach** (Map pp326-7), in front of the Biltmore Hotel.

Between Stearns Wharf and the harbor, **West Beach** (Map pp328-9) has calm water, and is popular with families and tourists staying in nearby motels. On the other side of the harbor, **Leadbetter Beach** (Map pp328-9) is a good spot for surfing and windsurfing, with access to a grassy picnic area atop the cliffs.

West of Santa Barbara near the junction of Cliff Dr and Las Positas Rd, **Arroyo Burro Beach** (Map pp326-7; also called Hendry's) has a parking lot, picnic area and restaurant. It's flat, wide, away from tourists and great for families with kids.

## ACTIVITIES
### Cycling & Skating

For info on biking in Santa Barbara, contact the **Santa Barbara Bicycle Coalition** ( ☎ 805-568-3046; www.sbbike.org), which also has on-line printable bike tours.

The Cabrillo Blvd **beachfront bike path** runs for 3 miles along the water, between the Andrée Clark Bird Refuge and Leadbetter Beach. The **Goleta Bikeway** continues west to UCSB. **Wheel Fun** (Map pp328-9; ☎ 805-966-2282; www.wheelfunrentals.com; 22 State St) rents bikes near the beach at the foot of State St. Bikes cost about $8/24 per hour/day; in-line skates are $5/12.

### Boating

The whale-watching season runs from February 15 to May 15. The following companies offer trips to see them, but this list is not comprehensive; you can also wander the harbor, talk to captains and pick a boat based on whom you like best. Always make sure the vessel is Coast Guard certified – and that you dig the captain.

**Sea Landing** (Map pp328-9; ☎ 805-882-0088, 888-779-4425; www.condorcruises.com; 310 Cabrillo Blvd), on the beach at the foot of Bath St, rents kayaks, jet skis and jet boats and also operates whale-watching excursions to the Channel Islands aboard the *Condor Express*, a state-of-the-art high-speed catamaran that is stable enough for most stomachs. Trips last about 4½ hours and cost $77/40 per adult/child. Whale sightings are guaranteed, so if you miss out you can come back for a free trip. It also runs half-day fishing excursions for $37/30.

**Santa Barbara Sailing Center** (Map pp328-9; ☎ 805-962-2826; www.sbsail.com; 133 Harbor Way), next to Sea Landing in the harbor, will take you sailing on the *Double Dolphin*, a 50ft sailing catamaran (adult/child $32/20). If you want to pilot your own craft, it also rents paddle boats, motor boats, fishing boats and sailboats. In season there's whale-watching, too.

**Sunset Kidd's Sailing Cruises** (Map pp328-9; ☎ 805-962-8222; www.sunsetkidd.com; 125 Harbor Way) will take you on a two-hour whale-watching trip in an 18-passenger sailboat for $35 for adults and kids. In summer it also operates pleasure trips for the same price.

**Truth Aquatics** (Map pp328-9; ☎ 805-962-1127, 888-779-4425; www.truthaquatics.com; 301 Cabrillo Blvd) runs scuba diving trips, kayaking excursions and an occasional hiker's shuttle to the Channel Islands (p346).

**Santa Barbara Adventure Co** ( ☎ 805-452-1942, 888-773-3239; www.sbadventureco.com) leads guided kayaking trips that focus on marine ecology; ask about stargazing floats.

**Paddle Sports** (Map pp328-9; ☎ 805-899-4925, 888-254-2094; www.kayaksb.com; 117-B Harbor Way) leads kayaking trips and offers instruction.

## Surfing

Santa Barbara's south-facing coast and proximity to the wind-breaking Channel Islands make it a good spot for plying the waves on a surfboard. **Rincon Point** has long, glassy, point-break waves; **Leadbetter Point** and **Goleta Beach** are best for beginners. Unless you're a novice, conditions are too mellow in summer; head to Orange County's beaches (p214), then come back in winter when the swells kick back up.

**Santa Barbara Adventure Co** ( ☎ 805-452-1942, 888-773-3239; www.sbadventureco.com) teaches surfing and includes all the necessary accoutrements; classes cost $95 per person. You can rent soft (foam) boards from the **Beach House** (Map pp328-9; ☎ 805-963-1281; 10 State St) for $7/21 per hour/half-day; wet suits cost $3 to $4 per hour, $8 to $10 per half-day. It also has boogie boards for $4/10 per hour/half-day.

## Hiking

The Santa Ynez foothills (part of Los Padres National Forest, p343) are part of the mountain chain that towers over the city. By car it takes 20 minutes to reach them from downtown. The hills are full of hiking trails, most of which cut through rugged chaparral and steep canyons, from where you'll have jaw-dropping coastal views. The

hike through **Rattlesnake Canyon** is popular with locals, as is the one along the Tunnel Trail to **Inspiration Point**.

The best place for gathering information and maps is **Pacific Travelers Supply** (Map pp328-9; ☎ 805-963-4438, 800-546-8060; 12 W Anapamu St). Also check the Maritime Museum branch of the SB **visitors center** (Map pp328-9; ☎ 805-884-1475; 113 Harbor Way, 4th fl, Santa Barbara Maritime Museum; ⏰ 11am-6pm summer, 11am-5pm winter) for info on the entire Los Padres National Forest. If you're here in winter, inquire about the best places to see the monarch butterflies roosting in the trees, an extraordinary sight.

In summer, when the city is shrouded in cool coastal fog, the inland hills will likely be sunny and hot; wear layers and carry plenty of water, sunscreen and a hat. Likewise in winter the coast may be only slightly chilly, while the hills are downright cold; after a January rainstorm in town, you may even see a dusting of snow on the peaks.

## Swimming

Other than in the sea, you can also swim in **Los Baños del Mar** (Map pp328-9; ☎ 805-966-6110; 401 Shoreline Dr; adult/child $4/2), a municipal outdoor pool near West Beach that's good for recreational and lap swimming. For little ones under eight years old, there's a wonderful wading pool.

## TOURS

For tours exclusively on the water, see Boating (opposite).

**Santa Barbara Old Town Trolley** (Map pp328-9; ☎ 805-965-0353; www.sbtrolley.com; adult/child $16/8; ⏰ 10am-5pm) operates 90-minute guided tours in an open-sided San Francisco–style, motorized cable car. It gives a great overview of the city's sights and attractions, and allows you

---

### SANTA BARBARA'S OIL SPILL

On January 29, 1969, Platform A, an oil-drilling rig off the Santa Barbara coast, triggered a massive oil spill. A well, drilled 3500ft into the earth by Union Oil Co, burst and over the next 11 days, 200,000 gallons of crude oil spewed out of the earth and into the sea, creating an 800-sq-mile oil slick and devastating nearly 40 miles of coastline. Thousands of birds and immeasurable numbers of marine creatures perished. Santa Barbara's citizens mobilized and successfully changed legislation governing off-shore drilling, in what many believe sparked the modern-day environmental movement.

Coincidentally, 1969 was also the year that the Cuyahoga River in Ohio burst into flames. The following year President Richard Nixon established the Environmental Protection Agency, and on April 22 the world celebrated the first Earth Day.

---

**KEEPING THE KIDS ENTERTAINED**

Santa Barbara is ready-made for kids:

■ Museum of Natural History (p327) – Giant skeletons and a pitch-dark planetarium captivate kids' imaginations.

■ Shoreline Park (Map pp328-9) – Long, open, flat and grassy; kids can run around here while you keep an eye on them; terrific playground and nifty lookouts over the harbor from the west end of town.

■ Arroyo Burro Beach (aka Hendry's, p330) – Wide sandy beach, away from the tourists, popular with local families.

■ Santa Barbara Zoological Garden (p329) – The giraffes, lions, gorillas and elephants are well cared for; lush gardens overlook the ocean.

■ Sea Center (p327) – See a 70ft whale, fidget with hands-on exhibits and finger the sea critters that live in the touch pool.

■ Santa Barbara Museum of Art (p326) – Little ones can get crafty with paper and art supplies in their own dedicated area of the museum, downstairs by the café.

■ Kids' World – Climb on the giant wooden play structure in Alameda Park at the corner of Garden St and Micheltorena St downtown.

■ Los Baños del Mar (p331) – Children under eight love to splash around in their own special wading pool near West Beach.

■ Maritime Museum (p327) – Kids can color and draw in a play area just for them; the gorgeous model ships hold their attention, too.

■ South Coast Railroad Museum (p330) – Ride the miniature train and check out the model railroad; then come back to town and head to the depot at the foot of State St for an up-close sighting of the passenger trains that run through town every day.

---

to get on and off at 16 different stops. Start the tour at Stearns Wharf, or call for other pick-up points. Pay the driver directly.

Take a guided tour of the city with **Land and Sea Tours** ( ☎ 805-683-7600; www.out2seesb.com; adult/child $20/10), then drive right into the water for a tour in an amphibious vehicle.

**Cloud Climbers Jeep Tours** ( ☎ 805-965-6654; www.ccjeeps.com) runs guided jeep tours of the mountains and forest above town, including hiking/driving tours, horseback riding/driving tours, family outings, wine-country jaunts, and sunset-chasing journeys for adults. For three- to six-hour tours they cost $69 to $125 per adult and $50 per child.

## FESTIVALS & EVENTS

Santa Barbara throws a good party. For the current calendar of events, contact the Santa Barbara Visitor Center (p325).

**Santa Barbara International Film Festival**
( ☎ 805-963-0023; www.sbfilmfestival.org) Film buffs arrive in droves for this always-wonderful fest, which takes place in mid-January to early February and presents new independent US and foreign films.

**Summer Solstice Parade** ( ☎ 805-965-3396; www.solsticeparade.com) Kicking off the summer, this wacky parade in late June feels like something out of Marin County in Northern California or a Burning Man processional, not a staid Santa Barbara event.

**Santa Barbara County Fair** ( ☎ 805-925-8824; www.santamariafairpark.com) In mid-July, this old-fashioned county fair has agriculture booths, rides, and lots of food and wine. The fairgrounds are in Santa Maria, about an hour north of SB.

**Old Spanish Fiesta Days** ( ☎ 805-962-8101; www.oldspanishdays-fiesta.org) The town gets packed in early August for this slightly overrated festival.

**Gay Pride Festival** ( ☎ 805-962-1403; www.gaysantabarbara.org) In September, look for this fun fest.

## SLEEPING

Don't show up in Santa Barbara and expect to find a cheap room at the last minute, especially on weekends. A bottom-of-the-heap dive motel that's $50 on weekdays can triple in price on a Saturday night. Tariffs quoted here are high-season published rates. Book in advance, and you can almost always do better. Because nights are generally cool, most places don't have air-conditioning. Unless otherwise noted, the lodgings listed here are without air-con. Although the midrange listings might seem high, you can save money by booking the ones that have kitchens (it's pricey to eat in SB, but not if you cook for yourself).

## Budget
### HOSTELS
**Santa Barbara Tourist Hostel** (Map pp328-9; ☎ 805-963-0154; www.sbhostel.com; 134 Chapala St; dm r $22, private r $59-79; **P** 🖳 ) Right next to the train station (bring earplugs), this raucous little hostel feels like a college dorm (average age of guests is 18 to 25). In addition to having use of a kitchen, pool table, lockers, laundry and book exchange, you can rent in-line skates, bikes and boogie boards. You must have proof that you're a traveler to stay here.

### MOTELS & HOTELS
For a cheap room on a busy weekend, you may have to drive north on Hwy 101 toward Santa Maria, where you'll find properly low rates for plain motel rooms.

   **Hotel State Street** (Map pp328-9; ☎ 805-966-6586; www.hotelstatestreet.com; 121 State St; r $55-95) One of the best deals in town for those willing to share a bathroom, this hotel's good-sized rooms are spotless, and many have big windows, a sink and TV, but no phone. It's only two blocks to the beach and right next to the train station, so bring earplugs and ask for the quietest room.

   **Motel 6 Santa Barbara** (Map pp326-7; ☎ 805-564-1392, 800-466-8356; www.motel6.com; 443 Corona del Mar; s $86-100, d $92-106; **P** 🖳 ) The original property in the now-giant chain, this Motel 6 has no six-dollar rooms anymore, but considering its location right near the beach, it remains a bargain. Book as far in advance as possible; it fills up every night.

   **San Roque Motel** (Map pp326-7; ☎ 805-687-6611; www.sanroque.com; 3344 State St; s $70-90, d $80-100; **P** 🖳 🖳 ) This two-story, mid-century motel has some pretty landscaping and standard-issue rooms, with extras such as refrigerator and microwave (request when you book), and an on-site laundry. You'll need a car to sightsee.

   The two cheapest places follow. Avoid them both on weekends, when they gouge guests:

**Hacienda Motel** (Map pp326-7; ☎ 805-687-6461; www.haciendamotel.com; 3643 State St; r $60-140; **P** 🖳 ) Standard-issue rooms.
**Travelers Motel** (Map pp326-7; ☎ 805-687-6009; www.travelersmotelsb.com; 3222 State St; r $50-80; **P** ) The bedding is clean, but you may see cigarette burns on the furniture or peeling paint under the sink.

### CAMPING
There is no campground anywhere near downtown, but about 17 miles and 20 miles west of town, respectively, right on the beach off Hwy 101, are **El Capitan State Beach** and **Refugio State Beach** (both ☎ 805-968-1033, reservations ☎ 800-444-7275; info www.parks.ca.gov, reservations www.reserveamerica.com; sites $16-21; **P** ). Refugio is a popular surf spot and student hangout, while El Capitan, perched on low bluffs, is more popular with families. Amenities include flush toilets, hot showers, picnic tables and barbecues. There's also camping in the Los Padres National Forest and at Lake Cachuma (p343).

## Mid-Range
**Cabrillo Inn** (Map pp326-7; ☎ 805-966-1641, 800-648-6708; www.cabrillo-inn.com; 931 E Cabrillo Blvd; r $129-189; **P** 🖳 ) Right across from the beach at the east end of town, this motel is a great bet, especially for families with kids, who will love the two sundecks and two pools (one heated). Most rooms have partial ocean views; for a full ocean view, add another $30 to $60. Score a good rate, and this place is excellent for value and location.

   **El Prado** (Map pp328-9; ☎ 805-966-0807, 800-669-8979; www.elprado.com; 1601 State St; r $85-145; **P** 🖳 ) Just north of downtown, about a mile from the beach, El Prado has better-than-average clean motel rooms with attractive furnishings, and landscaping surrounding the large heated pool. Good value. Ask about specials.

   **Franciscan Inn** (Map pp328-9; ☎ 805-963-8845; www.franciscaninn.com; 109 Bath St; r $115-170, with kitchen $150-195; **P** 🖳 ) Country furnishings and comfy quilts lend charm to this well-kept near-the-beach motel. It has a nice pool, big TV sets, a Jacuzzi and guest laundry, and its rates include breakfast and afternoon drinks.

   **Brisas del Mar** (Map pp328-9; ☎ 805-966-2219, 800-468-1988; www.sbhotels.com; 223 Castillo St; r with full kitchen $166-226; **P** 🖳 ) It may seem pricey at first, but when you factor in the full kitchen, space to sleep four comfortably, and the short walk to the beach, this impeccably kept, mid-century, high-end motel suddenly seems like a bargain. If you can't quite swing it, though, the adjacent and affiliated **Inn by the Harbor** (Map pp328-9; ☎ 805-963-7851, 800-626-1986; www.sbhotels.com; 433 W Montecito St; r $124-154, with full kitchen $144-174; P ⚲ ) is kept just as nicely – but its rooms are smaller, however thoughtfully decorated in hunter green tones. Both properties have the spirit of a beach-vacation rental, and each includes evening wine and cheese.

**Secret Garden Inn** (Map pp326-7; ☎ 805-687-2300, 800-676-1622; www.secretgarden.com; 1908 Bath St; r $135-235) Tucked behind a high hedgerow in a residential neighborhood, the Secret Garden Inn has cottage rooms decorated with a down-to-earth mishmash of folksy, country-style furnishings. The cheapest rooms are in the main house; all others have private entrances. Look out for the commemorative Charles-and-Diana tea tin in the dining room. One of a few B&Bs good for kids and dogs. Full breakfast.

Also well worth a visit:

**Eagle Inn** (Map pp328-9; ☎ 805-965-3586, 800-767-0030; www.theeagleinn.com; 232 Natoma Ave; r $99-195; P ) Small Spanish-style hotel with king beds.

**Colonial Beach Inn** (Map pp328-9; ☎ 805-963-4317, 800-649-2669; www.sbhotels.com; 223 Castillo St; r $134-184, with kitchen $174-204; P ⚲ ) Decor inspired by the American South; two rooms have kitchens.

**Villa Rosa** (Map pp328-9; ☎ 805-966-0851; www.villa rosainnsb.com; 15 Chapala St; r $199-285; ⚲ ) Charming inn with flower-festooned courtyard, pool, Jacuzzi, and evening wine and cheese.

## Top End

**Hotel Santa Barbara** (Map pp328-9; ☎ 805-957-9300, 888-259-7770; www.hotelsantabarbara.com; 533 State St; r $159-259; P ) As unpretentiously sophisticated as its namesake city, the 1925 Hotel SB has rooms done up in Provence-meets-the-beach style, with rattan and blonde-wood furnishings, and sunny Mediterranean colors. Best of all, you can walk everywhere. It serves continental breakfast, too. Top choice downtown for upper-middle budgets.

**Hotel Oceana** (Map pp328-9; ☎ 805-965-4577, 800-965-9776; www.hoteloceana.com; 202 W Cabrillo Blvd; r $229-400; P ) An assemblage of four once-independent motels across the street from West Beach, the Oceana has been entirely restyled and updated from 1950s kitsch to new-millennium chic, with aggressive color schemes, crisp cotton sheets, down comforters and aromatherapy bath products.

**Inn of the Spanish Garden** (Map pp328-9; 805-564-4700, 866-564-4700; www.spanishgardeninn.com; 915 Garden St; r $235-345; P ⚌ ⚲ ) An enclave of red-tile-roofed, Spanish-style adobes surround a central courtyard at one of Santa Barbara's off-the-beaten-path gems. Beds have luxurious linens; bathrooms have oversize soaking tubs. Lush palms surround the pool, and the outdoor courtyard gets lit with candles every evening. Breakfast included.

**El Capitan Canyon** ( ☎ 805-685-3887, 866-352-2729; www.elcapitancanyon.com; 11560 Calle Real; safari tents $135, cabins $185-305; P ⚲ ) If you love to camp but hate to wake up on the ground with dirt under your nails, book a stay at El Capitan Canyon, where you can sleep in a tent or cabin on a top-quality mattress with high-thread-count sheets. Each site has its own picnic table and fire pit. No cars are allowed tentside, so it feels like a walk-in campground – but oh! that bed. It's sandwiched between the Santa Ynez mountains and a state beach, 17 miles west of Santa Barbara, off Hwy 101 northbound (30 minutes). There's on-site massage, a café and a yurt for yoga. Ask about family cabins if you're with kids.

**Four Seasons Biltmore Hotel** (Map pp326-7; ☎ 805-969-2261, 800-332-3442; www.fourseasons.com; 1260 Channel Dr; r $500-700; P ⚌ ⚲ ) Don white linen and live like the Great Gatsby at the oh-so-cush 1927 Biltmore, Santa Barbara's iconic beachfront resort, where rooms are decorated in retro-'20s chic and every detail is perfect. Bathrooms have Mediterranean-style custom tiles, huge soaking tubs, French-milled soaps and 300-jet waterfall showers; bedrooms are decked out with ultra-high-thread-count sheets and 40-inch flat-screen TVs. Air-con and state-of-the-art spa, too. Perfect for a honeymoon or a great big splurge.

# EATING
## Budget

**La Super Rica** (Map pp328-9; ☎ 805-963-4940; 622 N Milpas St; dishes under $6; ☻ 11am-9pm) Culinary guru Julia Child called this unmarked roadside shack her favorite Mexican restaurant. Who are we to argue? Order from the window, then join local families at the picnic-style tables for authentic south-of-the-border cooking. Avoid peak meal times, when the place gets packed.

**Santa Barbara Shellfish Company** (Map pp328-9; ☎ 805-966-6676; 230 Stearns Wharf; dishes $5-9; ☺ 11am-9pm) If it has a shell and it lives in the ocean, it's served at this end-of-the-wharf crab shack that's more of a counter joint than a sit-down restaurant – the food and atmosphere go best with beer, not chardonnay. Decent prices; great water views; same owners for 25 years. Top budget pick.

**D'Angelo Pastry & Bread** (Map pp328-9; ☎ 805-962-5466; 25 W Gutierrez St; dishes under $7; ☺ 7am-2pm) Come in the morning for fresh-from-the-oven flaky croissants, poached eggs and big cups of strong coffee at this sidewalk café-cum-bakery, off Lower State St.

**Italian & Greek Delicatessen** (Map pp328-9; ☎ 805-962-6815; 636 State St; dishes $5-9; ☺ 10am-6pm Mon-Sat, 11am-5pm Sun) There's nothing fancy here, just scrumptious gyros and torpedo sandwiches that you order at the counter and eat at a table covered in a red-and-white-checked, vinyl tablecloth. You can also fill your picnic basket with cold cuts, stuffed grape leaves, potato salad and other tasty to-go foods.

**Esau's Coffee Shop** (Map pp328-9; ☎ 805-965-4416; 403 State St; dishes under $8; ☺ 6am-1pm Sun-Thu, 6am-1pm & 9pm-3am Fri & Sat) Cozy up in one of the orange-plastic booths at this no-frills coffee shop for straight-shooting diner food, from bacon and eggs to burgers and fries.

**Sojourner Café** (Map pp328-9; ☎ 805-965-7922; 134 E Cañon Perdido; dishes $4-12; ☺ 11am-11pm) If you're a vegetarian, you may wind up eating all your meals here – the food is just that good at this friendly, upbeat, mostly veg café, which gets creative with vegetables, tofu, tempeh, chicken, fish, rice, seeds, and other healthy ingredients. Outdoor seating too.

Stock up on fresh produce, nuts and honey at the **farmers market** ( ☎ 805-962-5354) held late afternoon Tuesday on the 500 block of State St between E Haley and E Cota Sts, and Saturday morning at the corner of Santa Barbara and Cota Sts. For the best groceries, head to **Lazy Acres** (Map pp328-9; ☎ 805-564-4410; 302 Meigs Rd; ☺ 7am-10pm), which is reached most easily by car. The best place for homemade ice cream is **McConnell's Ice Cream** (Map pp326-7; ☎ 805-569-2323; 201 W Mission St; ☺ 11am-10:30pm Sun-Thu, 11am-11pm Fri & Sat summer, shorter winter hours).

## Mid-Range

**Intermezzo** (Map pp328-9; ☎ 805-966-9463; 813 Anacapa St; mains $12-17; ☺ 11am-11pm) Foodies take note: the swank and stylin' little sister of the Wine

Cask (p336) serves a less formal menu that's every bit as gratifying. Same chef, same kitchen, *way lower* prices. Great for cocktails, too.

**Tupelo Junction** (Map pp328-9; ☎ 805-899-3100; 1212 State St; mains breakfast $7-14, lunch $11-14, dinner $11-21) Southern-style comfort food is the specialty at this always-bustling State St café, which is especially good for breakfast and lunch. Try the crabmeat eggs Benedict or the fried-chicken salad.

**Arnoldi's** (Map pp328-9; ☎ 805-962-5394; 600 Olive St; dinner $12-19; ☺ dinner) There's not a tourist in sight at this down-to-earth, locals-only, mom-and-pop Italian favorite that serves big portions. Dinners come with soup and salad. Stick your head out back to watch the paisanos shoot bocce ball.

**Roy** (Map pp328-9; ☎ 805-966-5636; 7 W Carillo St; dinner $20; ☺ 6pm-midnight) Roy serves later than anyplace else in town, and 20 bucks buys you a damn good three-course meal with soup, salad and choice of entree, from linguini to lamb chops. It's hip and happening, and popular with scenesters on weeknights; on weekends it gets packed with 20- and 30-something Bacchanalian revelers. Call ahead or wait. Major bar scene.

**Arigato** (Map pp328-9; ☎ 805-965-6074; 1225 State St; maki $5-12, mains $14-18; ☺ dinner) You'll find no better sushi in town than at this State St storefront that packs them in every night. Hot food, too. Expect a wait.

**Paradise Cafe** (Map pp328-9; ☎ 805-962-4416; 702 Anacapa St; dishes $9-21; ☺ 11am-11pm) In addition to serving fantastic oak-grilled burgers (the best in SB), it also whips up great salads, pretty good grilled meats and seafood, and a respectable brunch. Sit outside on the big patio (no smoking). Great wine list that's reasonably priced.

**Pacific Crepes** (Map pp328-9; ☎ 805-882-1123; 705 Anacapa St; mains $7-13; ☺ lunch & dinner Tue-Sat, brunch Sun) Francophiles escape the State St lunch crowd and steal away to this modest café for buckwheat crepes, Niçoise salad and homemade soups. It's open for dinner, too

There are two spots for seafood by the harbor (as opposed to the wharf); both are exclusively tourist restaurants and serve pretty good, but pricey meals:

**Brophy Brothers** (Map pp328-9; ☎ 805-966-4418; 119 Harbor Way; mains $17-19; ☺ 11am-10pm) The long-time favorite for its fresh-off-the-dock fish and seafood, its party atmosphere and its salty harborside setting. People love the clam chowder and *cioppino* (seafood stew), served with chewy sourdough. Tables on the upstairs deck are worth the long wait; they're quieter and have the best views.

**Waterfront Grill & Endless Summer** (Map pp328-9; ☎ 805-564-1200; 113 Harbor Way; mains $13-28) Waterfront (☺ dinner); Endless Summer (☺ 11:30am-9pm) For someplace dressier than Brophy Brothers that takes reservations, book a table in the nautical-theme dining room, or outside overlooking the sailboats. Come between 5pm and 6:30pm for $10 to $12 dinner specials such as an 8oz steak or grilled salmon. Upstairs at the publike Endless Summer, the scene is casual (and cheaper), with fish and chips, burgers, billiards and beer.

## Top End

**Bouchon** (Map pp328-9; ☎ 805-730-1160; 9 W Victoria St; mains $23-29; ☺ dinner) The perfect, unhurried, follow-up dinner to a day in Wine Country, convivial Bouchon's bright, flavorful California cooking uses only locally grown small-scale-farm produce and meats, which marry beautifully with the more than 50 local wines by the glass. For romance, book a table on the cozy candlelit patio.

**Olio e Limone** (Map pp328-9; ☎ 805-899-2699; 11 W Victoria St; mains $15-28; ☺ dinner) Go next door to Bouchon for *perfetto* modern Tuscan.

**Wine Cask** (Map pp328-9; ☎ 805-966-9463; 813 Anacapa St; mains lunch $13-22, dinner $26-36; ☺ lunch Mon-Fri, dinner daily) The Wine Cask, inside a 19th-century Spanish-style adobe with two-story-high gold-leaf-stenciled ceilings, is Santa Barbara's sexiest table for serious eating. On balmy evenings (or at lunch), feast on the invigorating New California menu outdoors in the romantic garden courtyard. The wine list brags 2500 labels, with vintages dating back to 1900. One detail: verify the price of the bottle before you let the sommelier pick a wine for you.

**La Marina** (Map pp326-7; ☎ 805-969-2261; Four Seasons Biltmore, 1260 Channel Dr; mains $25-40, 4-course menu $57, with wine $87; ☺ dinner) Settle into an overstuffed chair beneath the vaulted wooden ceiling in the formal 1920s dining room at the Four Seasons Biltmore for French-inspired contemporary California cuisine, expertly prepared and artfully presented. Try the four-course prix-fixe menu, each paired with a separate wine. Make reservations and request an ocean-view table.

# DRINKING
## Cafés

**Muddy Waters** (Map pp328-9; ☎ 805-966-6328; 508 E Haley St; ☺ 6am-10pm) SB's coolest café, on the corner of Olive St, has quiet corners, a good bulletin board, Internet access, a pool table and an outdoor back patio.

**Red's Espresso Bar and Gallery** (Map pp328-9; ☎ 805-966-5906; 211 Helena Ave; ☺ 6:30am-8pm Mon-Fri, 7am-10pm Sat) Local artists display their work at this funky little café that sometimes has a barbecue (Wednesday and Saturday) and live music; call ahead.

**Hot Spots Espresso Co** (Map pp328-9; ☎ 805-963-4233; 36 State St; ☺ 24hr) All-night owls, 12-steppers and anyone else looking for an alternative to a bar wind up at Hot Spots sooner or later, sipping on espresso and surfing the Net.

**SB Roasting Co** (Map pp328-9; ☎ 805-966-0320; 321 Motor Way; ☺ 6am-9pm) This place roasts its own coffee, one block off State St, in an industrial space.

## Bars

**Sportsman Lounge** (Map pp328-9; ☎ 805-564-4411; 20 W Figueroa; ☺ 7am-2am) There's no glitz or glamour here, just a plain-old dive bar with a great jukebox.

**Blue Agave** (Map pp328-9; ☎ 805-899-4694; 20 E Cota St; ☺ 5pm-2am Wed-Sat) Head upstairs (downstairs it serves food) to one of the cush velvet-line booths or grab a seat by the fire at this boho-chic lounge for the over-30 set. The music is up enough to groove, but not so loud you can't talk. Weekends it's another story.

**Firebird** (Map pp328-9; 14 E Cota St) If Blue Agave is too packed – or even if it's not – head next door to this candle-lit lounge, where you can talk philosophy with an arty crowd or smooch in the dark with your sweetheart. Thirty wines available by the glass. Serves cheese and dessert.

**Brew House** (Map pp328-9; ☎ 805-884-4664; 229 W Montecito St) Crafts its own beer, serves wines by the glass, and has cool art and awesome fries. It's raucous good fun, and has live music Wednesday to Saturday from 9pm to close. On Wednesday it serves all-you-can-eat ribs; arrive early.

**Chad's** (Map pp328-9; ☎ 805-568-1876; 625 Chapala St) Great for happy hour, Chad's brims with recent college grads swilling martinis. There's also an earnest menu of grown-up-frat-boy food for unfussy eaters.

**James Joyce** (Map pp328-9; ☎ 805-962-2688; 513 State St) Brings the ambience of a Dublin pub to California, with a neat carved ceiling, dart boards and a crackling fireplace. On Saturday night the house band heats up the crowd with Dixieland jazz.

**Epiphany** (Map pp328-9; ☎ 805-564-7100; 21 W Victoria St) Ideal for a glass of bubbly if you're wearing heels and a dress (or if you want to impress someone who is); it's also a chic little restaurant.

**Hades** (Map pp328-9; ☎ 805-962-2754; 235 W Montecito St) SB's only gay bar has a dance floor and outdoor smoking section. It's hit or miss, but can be great fun sometimes.

## ENTERTAINMENT

Santa Barbara's after-dark scene centers around lower State and Ortega Sts. Most places have happy hour and college nights, when the booze is cheap and the atmosphere rowdy. Check the *Independent* and the *Santa Barbara News-Press* (see p325) for up-to-date listings on what's doing in town.

**Soho** (Map pp328-9; ☎ 805-962-7776; www.sohosb .com; 1221 State St) There's jazz on Monday night, blues several times per month, rock, bluegrass, funk, soul, salsa and folk on other nights at this 2nd-floor club (above McDonald's) with exposed brick walls and an open-truss ceiling. Cover charge costs $5 to $15.

Santa Barbara supports a variety of theatre companies and beautiful historic venues. For a current list of performing-arts events, pick up the *Santa Barbara Performing Arts Guide*, a fold-out brochure available at the Santa Barbara Visitor Center (p325); or you can check directly with the **Santa Barbara Performing Arts League** ( ☎ 805-563-8068; www.sb performingartsleague.org), a consortium of all the companies, which has ticket and show information for everything playing that season.

**Arlington Center for the Performing Arts** (Map pp328-9; ☎ 805-963-4408; 1317 State St) Aside from being home to the Santa Barbara Symphony, this is a drop-dead-gorgeous, old-fashioned movie palace when the orchestra isn't playing; see a film here if you can.

**Lobero Theatre** (Map pp328-9; ☎ 805-963-0761; 33 E Cañon Perdido St) One of California's oldest theaters (1873), presents ballet, modern dance, chamber music and special events, often featuring internationally renowned top talent.

**Granada Theatre** (Map pp328-9; ☎ 805-966-2324; 1216 State St) This 1930s Spanish-Moorish–style theater will become the new home of several arts institutions – including the ballet, the opera and the symphony – once it reopens in 2006, following a complete restoration.

**Center Stage Theater** (Map pp328-9; ☎ 805-963-0408; www.centerstagetheater.org; 751 Paseo Nuevo) For live theater, check out this space in the Paseo Nuevo mall.

## SHOPPING

Shops along State St carry clothing, knick-knacks, antiques and books.

**Paseo Nuevo** (Map pp328-9; btwn Cañon Perdido & Ortega Sts) This is a good-looking outdoor mall anchored by Nordstrom and Robinsons-May department stores, with various retail chains, such as Gap and Victoria's Secret.

**La Arcada** (Map pp328-9; 1114 State St) Near Figueroa St, this is a historical red-tile passageway designed by Myron Hunt (builder of the Rose Bowl in LA) filled with boutiques, restaurants and whimsical public art.

**Historic Paseo** (Map pp328-9; State St) Another lovely, flower-festooned courtyard, opposite Paseo Nuevo.

You will find some terrific boutiques in Santa Barbara, but very few used-clothing stores. For killer thrift shopping, drive to Ventura (p344).

**Blue Bee & Blue Beetle** (Map pp328-9; ☎ 805-897-1137; 923-925 State St) Find eclectic, stylin' clothes at one of the best indie boutiques in town; there's also a denim shop and a men's section tucked in back.

**Diani** (Map pp328-9; ☎ 805-966-3114; 1324 State St, Arlington Plaza) Carries more high-fashion–oriented, Euro-inspired designs, with a touch of funky soul thrown in for good measure.

**Bryan Lee** (Map pp328-9; ☎ 805-963-0206; 802 State St) The men's clothes are best here, and have a European feel about them.

**Particle** (Map pp328-9; ☎ 805-899-4245; 1 W Ortega St) Men should also check out this place for hip and trendy styles.

**True Grit** (Map pp328-9; ☎ 805-564-1355; 625 State St) Appeals primarily to the younger, trendy club-going set.

**Victorian Vogue & the Costume Shop** (Map pp328-9; ☎ 805-962-8824; 1224 State St) For vintage and drag, from fabulous to outrageous, stop by this shop, which also rents costumes and has fun kids' stuff, too.

SANTA BARBARA

**Tom's Toys** (Map pp328-9; ☎ 805-564-6622; 1035 State St) If you have kids with you, they'll have a blast at this great indie shop that sells lots of neat stuff for little ones, from Teddy bears to old-school wooden toys.

### GETTING THERE & AWAY

The small **Santa Barbara Airport** (Map pp326-7; ☎ 805-967-7111; www.flysba.com; 500 Fowler Rd), in Goleta about 8 miles west of downtown via Hwy 101, has scheduled flights to/from LA, San Francisco, Denver, Phoenix and other western US cities. The following agencies have car-rental desks at the airport:

**Avis** ( ☎ 800-331-1212; www.avis.com)
**Budget** ( ☎ 800-527-0700; www.budget.com)
**Enterprise** ( ☎ 800-261-7331; www.enterprise.com)
**Hertz** ( ☎ 800-654-3131; www.hertz.com)
**National** ( ☎ 800-227-7368; www.nationalcar.com)
**Thrifty** ( ☎ 800-847-4389; www.thrifty.com)

**Santa Barbara Airbus** ( ☎ 805-964-7759, 800-423-1618; www.santabarbaraairbus.com) shuttles between LA International Airport (LAX) and Santa Barbara ($40/75 one way/round-trip, 14 departures per day). The more people in your party, the cheaper the fare. Also consider buying discounted tickets online.

**Greyhound** (Map pp328-9; ☎ 805-965-7551; www.greyhound.com; 34 W Carrillo St) operates nine buses daily to LA ($12, 2¼ to three hours) and up to seven to San Francisco ($26, 5½ to 7½ hours).

**Amtrak** (Map pp328-9; ☎ 800-872-7245; www.amtrak.com; 209 State St) has direct train services to LA ($17, 2½ hours) and San Diego ($26, 5½ hours) via the *Pacific Surfliner* and *Coast Starlight*.

Santa Barbara is bisected by Hwy 101. For downtown, take the Garden St or Cabrillo Blvd exits. Parking on the street and in any of the 10 municipal lots is free for the first 90 minutes (and all day Sunday).

### GETTING AROUND

A taxi from the airport costs about $25 plus tip. **Super Ride** ( ☎ 800-977-1123; www.superride.net) provides a door-to-door shuttle service from the airport to downtown for about $20 for one person, $25 for two.

Buses operated by **Santa Barbara Metropolitan Transit District** (MTD; ☎ 805-683-3702; www.sbmtd.gov) cost $1.25 (exact change) per ride and travel all over town and to adjacent communities, including Goleta and Mon-

tecito; request a free transfer when you pay your fare. The **MTD Transit Center** (1020 Chapala St) has details on routes and schedules.

The Downtown-Waterfront Shuttle bus (operated by MTD) runs every 10 minutes from 10:15am to 6pm along State St to Stearns Wharf. A second route travels from the zoo to the yacht harbor at 13-to-30-minute intervals. The fare is 25¢ per ride; transfers between routes are free.

Taxis are metered and cost $1.90 for the drop rate (initial fare), plus $2.70 per mile. Try one of the following companies:

**Blue Dolphin** ( ☎ 805-962-6886)
**Gold Cab** ( ☎ 805-685-9797)
**Rose Cabin** ( ☎ 805-564-2600, 866-767-3222)
**Yellow Cab** ( ☎ 805-965-5111, 800-549-8294)

# AROUND SANTA BARBARA

Santa Barbara marks the dividing line between Northern and Southern California, and there are echoes of each region's distinctive qualities in the communities surrounding the city. To the north, the Santa Maria and Santa Ynez Valleys produce wines on par with the better-known Napa and Sonoma Valleys. Inland communities, such as Ojai, capture the look of California before the once-ubiquitous rolling hills got bulldozed to make way for tract homes. Ventura has the ungentrified look of a small California city before the days of chain stores.

But there's one place that's special entirely unto itself: Channel Islands National Park. When you need a complete break from civilization, hop on a boat for the park, where you can meditate on fields of sunny-yellow coreopsis flowers in spring, watch whales breach in winter, and giggle at the sea lions lazing on the rocks all year long.

## SANTA BARBARA WINE COUNTRY

Santa Barbara's Wine Country unfurls along winding country lanes amid oak-dotted rolling hills that stretch for miles. In the spring, when the grass is still green, wildflowers bloom a rainbow of colors; later in summer the grasses turn gold and brown, and make a shimmering sound when the wind blows through them. This is the California of old. Take your time.

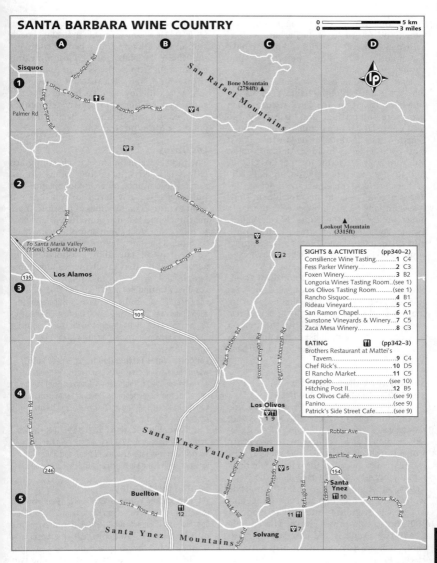

# SANTA BARBARA WINE COUNTRY

| SIGHTS & ACTIVITIES | (pp340–2) |
| --- | --- |
| Consilience Wine Tasting | 1 C4 |
| Fess Parker Winery | 2 C3 |
| Foxen Winery | 3 B2 |
| Longoria Wines Tasting Room | (see 1) |
| Los Olivos Tasting Room | (see 1) |
| Rancho Sisquoc | 4 B1 |
| Rideau Vineyard | 5 C5 |
| San Ramon Chapel | 6 A1 |
| Sunstone Vineyards & Winery | 7 C5 |
| Zaca Mesa Winery | 8 C3 |

| EATING | (pp342–3) |
| --- | --- |
| Brothers Restaurant at Mattei's Tavern | 9 C4 |
| Chef Rick's | 10 D5 |
| El Rancho Market | 11 C5 |
| Grappolo | (see 10) |
| Hitching Post II | 12 B5 |
| Los Olivos Café | (see 9) |
| Panino | (see 9) |
| Patrick's Side Street Cafe | (see 9) |

To get acquainted with the Wine Country you should watch the film *Sideways* before you go; you'll recognize many of the locations mentioned here.

## Orientation & Information

The Wine Country is north of Santa Barbara; you can get there in just under an hour, via Hwys 154 (San Marcos Pass Rd) and 101. The Santa Ynez Valley, where you'll find most of the wineries, lies south of the Santa Maria Valley. If you're tight on time, plan to see only the Santa Ynez Valley; if you've got the whole day, see both.

For a half-day trip, expect to spend no less than four hours, which will allow you to see one winery or tasting room, have lunch and return to Santa Barbara. Otherwise make it a full-day trip, and plan to have lunch and possibly dinner before returning to the city.

Hwy 246 runs east–west, via Solvang, across the bottom of the Santa Ynez Valley, but it's busier than the back roads, which are more interesting; thus, use Hwy 246 as a connector, not as your primary route. North–south secondary roads where you'll find good wineries include Alamo Pintado Rd from Hwy 246 to the town of Los Olivos, and Refugio Rd into neighboring Ballard.

The cute little one-street town of Los Olivos is a good place to stop for lunch, since it's essentially on the line between the Santa Ynez Valley and the Santa Maria Valley. Grand Ave, the main street, heads south and turns into Alamo Pintado Rd. A great route to take from here is the beautiful Foxen Canyon Wine Trail (opposite).

The **Santa Barbara Vintners' Association** ( ☎ 805-668-0881, 800-218-0881; www.sbcountywines.com; PO Box 1558, Santa Ynez, CA 93460-1558) publishes a touring map of all the wineries in the area and has some useful information about the area on its website, including a list of lodgings. You can pick up its map in the Santa Barbara Visitor Center (p325).

## Santa Ynez Valley Wineries
### SUNSTONE VINEYARDS & WINERY
You'd swear you were in Provence at this destination **winery** ( ☎ 805-688-9463, 800-313-9463; www.sunstonewinery.com; 125 Refugio Rd; tastings $5; ☾ 10am-4pm) that looks like an 18th-century stone farmhouse. If you like merlot, this is the place. Because the climate here is remarkably similar to St Helena in the Napa Valley, Sunstone crafts great Bordeaux-style wines and blends of cabernet franc and cabernet sauvignon – and they're made of 100% organically grown grapes. This entirely family-run estate is the closest winery to Santa Barbara (45 minutes), just south of Hwy 246, but no buses are allowed here, so you're guaranteed great, personalized service. Bring a picnic to eat in the courtyard beneath the gnarled oaks.

### RIDEAU VINEYARD
Inside a restored 1884 adobe house with a wraparound veranda and mature oaks out back, this **winery** ( ☎ 805-688-0717; www

.rideauvineyard.com; 1562 Alamo Pintado Rd; tastings $7-10; ☾ 11am-5pm) was the first stagecoach stop in Los Olivos. Today people come for the Rhône varietals, good chardonnay and great syrah. Stop by the kitchen to taste the cheeses and New Orleans–style specialties that you can buy to take home. The gift shop also carries shiny, girly tchotchkes (jeweled picture frames, jewelry boxes), good for Mom or Grandma.

## Los Olivos
The four-block main street in charming Los Olivos is lined with tasting rooms, shops, several restaurants, and a luxurious inn and full-service spa. If you're short on time but want to taste as many wines as possible, there are three good tasting rooms here, right next to each other. Ask about shipping wine back to other US states before you assume that you can; not all states allow alcohol to be sent across their borders (ask wineries how some people have gotten around this).

**Los Olivos Tasting Room** ( ☎ 805-688-7406, 805-688-6632, 800-209-8103; www.losolivostastingroom.com; 2905 Grand Ave; ☾ 11am-5:30pm) The first independent tasting room in California sits right on the main drag and specializes in high-end pinot noir that you can't taste anywhere else.

**Longoria Wines Tasting Room** ( ☎ 805-688-0305; www.longoriawine.com; 2935 Grand Ave; ☾ noon-4:30pm Mon, Wed & Thu, 11am-4:30pm Fri-Sun) Run by one of the most experienced vintners in Santa Barbara County, Longoria's tasting room specializes in pinot, cabernet franc and syrah.

**Consilience Wine Tasting** ( ☎ 805-691-1020; www.consiliencewines.com; 2933 Grand Ave; ☾ 11am-5pm) Specializes in vineyard-designated syrah and Rhône varietals, with some pinot noir and zinfandels as well.

## Santa Maria Valley
At **Fess Parker Winery** ( ☎ 805-688-1545; www.fessparker.com; 6200 Foxen Canyon Rd; tastings $7; ☾ 11am-5pm Mon-Fri, 10am-5pm Sat & Sun) you can sip wine outside on the veranda by the lush green lawn or inside by the fireplace at this beautiful estate with 120 acres of vineyards. The two biggest wines here are Burgundy (pinot and chardonnay) and Rhône (syrah and viognier). Enjoy a bottle with a picnic (self-catered) under the oaks. Afternoons and weekends get packed, when busloads come to see the winery featured as Frass Canyon in the film *Sideways* and owned by the actor who played Davey Crockett on TV.

## A WINE COUNTRY PRIMER

Though large-scale winemaking has only been happening here since the 1980s, Santa Barbara's climate has always been perfect for growing grapes. Two parallel, east–west-trending mountain ranges (the Santa Ynez and the San Rafael) cradle the region and funnel coastal fog eastward off the Pacific into the valleys between. The further inland you go, the warmer it gets. At the shore, fog and low clouds can hover all day, keeping the weather downright chilly, even in July, while only a few miles inland, temperatures can soar a full 30°F hotter, sometimes approaching 100°F in mid-July. These delicately balanced microclimates support two major varieties of grape.

Near the coast in the Santa Maria Valley, pinot noir – a particularly fragile grape – and other Burgundian varieties thrive in the fog. Inland in the warmer Santa Ynez Valley, where there can be as much as a 50°F variance in temperatures from day to night, Rhône-style grapes do best; these include syrah, morvedre and viognier. (Bordeaux-style wines, such as cabernet franc and cabernet sauvignon, get a bad rap in Santa Barbara County, and are usually associated only with Napa, Sonoma and Alexander Counties in Northern California. Nonetheless, there are a few pockets in the Santa Ynez Valley where you'll find some fine cabernet franc, often at good prices too.)

As you work your way through Wine Country you'll see vineyards and you'll see wineries. They are not the same thing. The term vineyard refers only to the place where grapes are grown. A winery, on the other hand, is the place where the grapes are actually fermented into wine. Wineries buy grapes from vineyards. However, if a winery makes wine using grapes from its own vineyards, it's properly called an estate, as in 'estate grown' or 'estate bottled.' But estates, too, ferment grapes from other vineyards as well as their own. When you see 'vineyard-designated' wines, that means that a winery buys grapes from a particular vineyard known for its superior quality, say, Bien Nacito Vineyard. Thus you may come across two different wines both made with grapes from Bien Nacito Vineyard (an exceptionally fine vineyard in the Santa Maria Valley).

But it all comes down to personal taste. If you don't like pinot noir, who cares how well it grows here? And if you're a neophyte, completely uncertain of what to try, don't be afraid to ask questions. Vintners are always happy to share their knowledge with people who are interested. And if you don't know how to taste wine or what to look for, ask the person behind the counter in the tasting room to help you discover what you like. Just remember to spit out the wine when you're done tasting it. Even the slightest buzz will diminish your capacity to distinguish one from another.

Just north, stop by the smaller **Zaca Mesa Winery** ( ☎ 805-688-9339; www.zacamesa.com; 6905 Foxen Canyon Rd; ☉ 10am-4pm) for Rhône-style wines. It's well worth a visit if you have extra time or if Fess Parker Winery is too busy. There's a picnic area.

Once a working cattle ranch, **Foxen Winery** ( ☎ 805-937-4251; www.foxenvineyard.com; 7200 Foxen Canyon Rd, Santa Maria; tastings per 5 wines $3-7; ☉ noon-4pm Mon-Fri, 11am-4pm Sat & Sun) is known for its diverse varietals – warm-climate cabernets, cool-climate pinot noirs and great Rhône-style wines – that it sources from the best vineyards in the area. This is one of the finest, most diverse wineries in the county. Its tiny, dressed-down tasting room, with concrete floor and corrugated-metal roof, sits in one of the prettiest stretches of the Santa Maria

Valley, near the north end of Wine Country at mileage marker 16, about half an hour north of Los Olivos. Only those-in-the-know make the journey to this special place.

Just north of Foxen, **Rancho Sisquoc** ( ☎ 805-934-4332; www.ranchosisquoc.com; ☉ 10am-4pm) crafts a terrific malbec and surprisingly good cabernet. It also has a good picnic area. Turn off Foxen Canyon Rd when you spot the **San Ramon Chapel**, the drafty little church built in 1875, where you can attend Mass at 10:30am on Sunday; it's on the east side of the road.

## Foxen Canyon Wine Trail

The very beautiful Foxen Canyon Wine Trail runs north from Hwy 154, just west of Los Olivos' main drag, and into the Santa Maria Valley, a more rural area with fewer visitors. It's a must-see for oenophiles or those wanting to get off the beaten path.

The Foxen Canyon Wine Trail follows Foxen Canyon Rd; most wineries are within 15 miles of Los Olivos. For the simplest loop, go up Foxen Canyon Rd to Sisquoc, a blink-and-miss-it community where several roads intersect. Turn left onto Palmer Rd, which will take you to Hwy 101 and south to Santa Barbara. Every time you stop at a winery, ask for directions.

If you continue further north for a scenic drive, Foxen Canyon Rd ultimately brings you to the small city of Santa Maria, where there's nothing terribly interesting to see. The road eventually reaches Hwy 101, but pay attention: read signs every time another road intersects with the road you're on, even if there's no stop sign. In brief, Foxen Canyon Rd makes stair steps, at right angles, before it suddenly becomes Betteravia Rd – way up the valley – and intersects with Hwy 101, just south of Santa Maria.

## Eating

Many of the wineries have picnic areas; ask at the tasting room. It's polite to buy a bottle of wine before you spread out your blanket on the lawn.

**El Rancho Market** ( ☎ 805-688-4300; 2886 Old Mission Dr) Known for its fantastic delicatessen, local meats, wine selection and boxed lunches, this is the place to stop if you want to fill a picnic basket. It's just off Hwy 246, 0.3 miles west of Refugio Rd.

**Panino** ( ☎ 805-688-9304; 2900 Grand Ave, downtown Los Olivos; sandwiches under $8; ☺ 9am-5pm) There are 10 different kinds of veggie sandwiches as well as special sandwiches, such as curried chicken, that you order at the counter and eat outside at an umbrella table. Good salads, too

**Grappolo** ( ☎ 805-688-6899; 3678 Sagunto St, Santa Ynez; mains lunch $7-15, dinner $11-22; ☺ lunch Tue-Sun, dinner daily) The chef-owner is from Tuscany at the local Italian favorite for, which serves up crispy pizza, pasta, wonderful salads, rotisserie chicken and grilled meats in a lively dining room to a convivial crowd. It's near Hwy 246.

**Chef Rick's** ( ☎ 805-693-5100; 1095 Edison St, Santa Ynez; mains lunch $10-17, dinner $19-29; ☺ 11am-9pm Mon-Sat) Down-home Southern cookin' meets contemporary-California style at Chef Rick's. If you're not up for a plate of Louisiana crispy catfish or skillet-grilled steak, opt for a barbecue shrimp sandwich or a Georgia-fried-chicken salad. Huge portions.

**Hitching Post II** ( ☎ 805-688-06776; 406 E Hwy 246, Buellton; dinner $19-34; ☺ 5-9:30pm) You'll be hard-pressed to find better steaks and chops *anywhere* than at this legendary, old-guard, dressed-down country steakhouse that serves locally raised meats and makes its

---

### DETOUR: SOLVANG

Perhaps the Wine Country towns seem too civilized and orderly – too *beige*. If you're feeling more like chasing windmills than tasting wine, you're in luck, especially if you go nuts for handmade fudge and home-spun kitsch.

From Hwy 154, heading north from Santa Barbara or south from Los Olivos, turn onto Hwy 246 eastbound. Then just look for the windmills on the horizon. Seriously.

Compulsively cute and insistently charming Solvang (population 5000), aka 'Little Denmark,' was founded in 1911 by bona fide Danes – although the cute-as-a-button design ethic and the knick knack–packed shops didn't come 'til later. Note: Folks who insist on calling themselves 'travelers' instead of 'tourists' should stay away.

But Solvang has culture! The **Elverhøj Museum of History and Art** ( ☎ 805-686-1211; 1624 Elverhoy Way; admission free; ☺ 1-4pm Wed-Sun) has displays on Danes in America. And Solvang has B&Bs! Reserve through the **Visitors Bureau** ( ☎ 800-468-6765; www.solvangusa.com; 1639 Copenhagen Dr btwn 1st & 2nd Sts; ☺ 10am-4pm). Heck, Solvang even has an old mission church.

But the best reason to come? Solvang has pastries: **Solvang Restaurant** ( ☎ 805-688-4645; 1672 Copenhagen Dr; sweets $1-5; ☺ 6am-3pm Mon-Fri, 6am-5pm Sat & Sun) makes finger-lickin' *aebleskivers* (pastries with jam), as well as strudels and *kringles* (thin oval pastries) galore.

In fact, pick up some extra *aebleskivers* (handmade fudge) for your 'traveler' friends who insisted on getting out of bed at 6am to brave the freezing-cold wind and fog on a day trip to the Channel Islands. They'll need 'em.

own pinot noir (which is damn good, by the way). Every meal comes with salad and soup or shrimp cocktail. Make reservations; it's casual.

**Brothers Restaurant at Mattei's Tavern** ( ☎ 805-688-4820; 2350 Railway Ave, Los Olivos; mains $19-36; ⏱ 5-9pm) The Old West lives on at Mattei's (pronounced 'Matty's'), which was originally a stagecoach stop and tavern when it opened in 1886, and it still looks like one. The menu lists American-country comfort food, such as prime rib with garlic mashers and lemon-chive pork chops with apple sauce. Make reservations and get gussied up.

Also check out the following:

**Los Olivos Café** ( ☎ 805-688-7265; 2879 Grand Ave, Los Olivos; mains lunch $9-13, dinner $12-24) Eclectic menu, from pizzas and steak to seafood and homemade meatballs.

**Patrick's Side Street Cafe** ( ☎ 805-686-4004; 2375 Alamo Pintado Rd, Los Olivos; mains lunch $10-18, dinner $16-25; ⏱ lunch Tue-Sun, dinner Wed-Sun) Consistently good California cuisine in downtown Los Olivos.

## ALONG HIGHWAY 154

Highway 154 (San Marcos Pass Rd) heads north of Santa Barbara through the Los Padres National Forest. It bisects the Santa Barbara Wine Country and the Santa Ynez Valley before joining up with Hwy 101 north of Los Olivos.

### Chumash Painted Cave State Historic Park

This tiny **historic site** ( ☎ 805-733-3713; www.parks .ca.gov; ⏱ dawn-dusk) shelters vivid pictographs painted by the Chumash over 400 years ago. The cave is protected by a metal screen, so a flashlight is helpful for getting a good view. Look for the turnoff to Painted Cave Rd, about 8 miles north of Santa Barbara; the last stretch of the road is narrow and steep and not suited for RVs.

### Los Padres National Forest

Los Padres National Forest covers about two million acres of coastal mountains in various pockets stretching from the Carmel Valley to the western edge of Los Angeles County. It's great for hiking, camping, horseback riding, mountain biking and other outdoor pursuits. For information, check with the Maritime Museum branch of the **Santa Barbara Visitor Center** (Map pp328-9; ☎ 805-884-1475; Santa Barbara Maritime Museum, 113 Harbor Way, 4th fl; ⏱ 11am-6pm

summer, 11am-5pm winter) or with the **Los Padres National Forest Headquarters** (Map pp326-7; ☎ 805-968-6640; www.r5.fs.fed.us/lospadres; 6755 Hollister Ave, Suite 150; ⏱ 8am-4:30pm Mon-Fri) in Goleta. If you're traveling by car, you must display a National Forest Adventure Pass in order to park in the forest. Passes cost $5 per day, and you can purchase them at the Forest Headquarters and Maritime Museum; for more on the pass system, log on to **Forest Service Adventure Pass** (www.fsadventurepass.org) or call headquarters.

Paradise Rd, which crosses Hwy 154 north of San Marcos Pass, provides the best access to developed facilities in the forest. About 4 miles up the road there's a ranger station with posted maps and information. There are three **campgrounds** (sites $12) before the ranger station and one just past it. At Red Rocks (clearly marked from the ranger station), the Santa Ynez River deeply pools among rocks and waterfalls, creating a great swimming and sunning spot. Many hiking trails radiate out from here.

Paradise Rd also gives access to a great slice of Americana: **Cold Spring Tavern** ( ☎ 805-967-0066; 5595 Stagecoach Rd), a legendary stagecoach stop that's still a popular watering hole and restaurant. A rough-hewn plank floor connects a warren of dimly lit rooms decorated with an odd assortment of Western memorabilia, and framed photographs and newspaper articles. The food, alas, is mediocre and overpriced. The turnoff to Stagecoach Rd is about 0.3 miles north of the junction of Paradise Rd and Hwy 154. Follow it for about 3 miles to the tavern, passing underneath the fabulous San Marcos Bridge.

### Lake Cachuma County Park

Lake Cachuma is a haven for anglers and boaters and also has a large **campground** ( ☎ 805-686-5054; tent/RV sites $18/25), with picnic tables, barbecues, flush toilets and hot showers. Sites are on a first-come, first-serve basis and fill quickly on weekends. You can also rent a **yurt** ( ☎ reservations 805-686-5050; per night $45-65), essentially a tent cabin on a redwood deck. Park admission is $6 per vehicle.

## VENTURA
### pop 101,000

Ventura, an agricultural and manufacturing center, may not be the most enchanting coastal city, but it has its charms, especially in its ungentrified historic downtown along Main St, north of Hwy 101 via Seaward Ave. Here, you'll find a terrific assortment of antique and thrift shops, as well as the town's **Visitor Center** ( ☎ 805-648-2075, 800-333-2989; www.ventura-usa.com; 89 S California St, Suite C; 🕑 8:30am-5pm Mon-Fri, 9am-5pm Sat, 10am-4pm Sun).

## Sights

Ventura's roots go back to the 1782 **Mission San Buenaventura** ( ☎ 805-643-4318; 211 E Main St; admission $1; 🕑 10am-5pm Mon-Sat, 10am-4pm Sun), the last mission founded by Padre Junípero Serra. The restored church is still home to an active congregation. A stroll around the complex is a meditative experience, and leads you through a courtyard and a small museum, past statues of saints and 250-year-old paintings of the stations of the cross.

The mission's original foundations and related artifacts are among items on display in the nearby **Albinger Archaeological Museum** ( ☎ 805-648-5823; 113 E Main St; 🕑 10am-4pm Wed-Sun, shorter winter hours).

Across the street, the **Ventura County Museum of History & Art** ( ☎ 805-653-0323; www.vcmha.org; 100 E Main St; adult/child/senior $4/1/3; 🕑 10am-5pm Tue-Sun) has an eclectic mix of exhibits. Highlights include some 300 quarter-life-sized historical figures, dressed in period costumes (by George Stuart), and an exhibit tracing Ventura's history from the Chumash period to the present.

Ventura Harbor (southwest of Hwy 101 via Harbor Blvd) is the departure point for boats to the Channel Islands (p346). Even if you don't embark on an island adventure, the **Channel Islands National Park Visitor Center** ( ☎ 805-658-5730; 1901 Spinnaker Dr; 🕑 8:30am-5pm) has a small natural history display and a three-story lookout from where you can view the islands – on a clear day, at least. On Saturday and Sunday, at 11am and 3pm, rangers lead interpretive programs on tide pools, a terrific primer on California marine ecology.

## Sleeping

**Bella Magiore Inn** ( ☎ 805-652-0277, 800-523-8479; 67 S California St; r $75-175; ⓟ ) If you want to stay the night, the location is great at this 1921 hotel, just off Main St, within walking distance of the harbor. The simple rooms aren't fancy but have good character; quieter rooms are in the back.

**Clocktower Inn** ( ☎ 805-652-0141, 800-727-1027; www.clocktowerinn.com; 181 E Santa Clara St; r $90-129; ⓟ ) For more amenities consider this small modern (c 1985) hotel.

## Eating

Despite its dowdy appearance, Ventura has some good restaurants. It's feasible to walk to each of the following before deciding where you want to eat.

**Nature's Grill** ( ☎ 805-643-7855; 566 E Main St; mains $5-8; 🕑 11am-9pm) The mostly vegetarian menu has 11 different salads, chicken and fish dishes, and a dozen hot veggie entrees. Great for vegans, too. Order at the counter.

**Anacapa Brew Pub** ( ☎ 805-643-2337; 472 E Main St; mains $8-18; 🕑 closed lunch Mon) Crafts its own microbrews and makes a mean pulled-pork sandwich.

**Cafe Fiore** ( ☎ 805-653-1266; 66 S California St; mains lunch $9-13, dinner $9-24) The most stylish place in town packs in Ventura's bon vivants, who sip cold gin while savoring contemporary Italian cooking, from pizza to osso bucco; make reservations.

**Jonathan's at Peirano's** ( ☎ 805-648-4853; 204 E Main St; mains $17-26; 🕑 dinner Tue-Sun) Jonathan's serves Euro-Mediterranean cooking, from *puttanesca* to paella; make reservations. The attached bar, **J's Tapas** (dishes $6-13) serves smaller plates from the same kitchen and has many wines by the glass.

## Shopping

There's kick-ass thrift shopping in Ventura, especially at the **Retarded Children's Thrift Shop** ( ☎ 805-485-6690, 800-228-1413; 265 E Main St). For used books head to **Bank of Books** ( ☎ 805-643-3154; 391 E Main St) and the much larger **Abednego Book Shoppe** ( ☎ 805-643-9350; 2160 E Thompson Blvd).

## Getting There & Away

**Greyhound** ( ☎ 805-653-0164; 291 E Thompson Blvd) runs up to five buses daily from LA ($12, 2½ hours) en route to Santa Barbara ($8.50, 40 minutes). **Amtrak** ( ☎ 800-872-7245; www.amtrak.com; cnr Harbor Blvd & Figueroa) operates four daily trains to Santa Barbara ($8.50, 40 minutes) and four to LA ($14, two hours).

# OJAI

pop 8000

Ojai (pronounced *oh*-hi, meaning 'moon' to the Chumash) has long drawn artists and spiritual seekers. Several metamind institutes, including the Krishnamurti Foundation and the Krotona Institute of Theosophy, have set up residence here. Ojai is famous for the rosy glow that emanates both from its mountains at sunset – the Pink Moment – and from the faces emerging from spa treatments. In fact, the scenery here is so stunning that Frank Capra felt the Ojai Valley worthy of representing the mythical Shangri-La in his 1937 movie *Lost Horizon*. Bring shorts: it gets hot here in summer. For information, head to the **Ojai Chamber of Commerce** ( ☎ 805-646-8126; www.the-ojai.org; 150 W Ojai Ave; 9:30am-4:30pm Mon & Wed-Fri, 10am-4pm Sat & Sun).

The 9-mile **Ojai Valley Trail**, converted from old railway tracks, is popular with walkers, joggers, cyclists and equestrians. It links with Ventura's Foster Park.

Ojai is famous for its annual **Ojai Music Festival** ( ☎ 805-646-2053; www.ojaifestival.org), a longstanding classical music fest.

Shoppers enjoy nosing around **Arcade Plaza**, a maze of mission revival-style buildings on Ojai Ave (the main thoroughfare), which contains cutesy boutiques and galleries. The indoor-outoor **Bart's Books** ( ☎ 805-646-3755; 302 W Matilija St), one block north of Ojai Ave, is worth at least a half-hour browse. **Firehouse Pottery & Gallery** ( ☎ 805-646-9453; www.firehouse -pottery.com; 109 S Montgomery St) carries nifty ceramics and hand-blown glassware. Mingle with residents at the **farmers market** (301 E Matilija St; 9am-1pm Sun).

## Sleeping

**Farm Hostel** ( ☎ 805-646-0311; www.hostelhandbook .com/farmhostel; PO Box 723, Ojai, CA 93024; dm $15; P ) Connect with the land at this working family farm set in a large organic orchard, which reflects the serene and spiritual aura of Ojai. Guests stay in gender-segregated dorms and there's a communal veggie kitchen. It's 10 minutes from town; reservations are mandatory. Proof of international travel is also required. Free pickups from downtown Ventura.

**Ojai Valley Inn & Spa** ( ☎ 805-646-5511, 800-422-6524; www.ojairesort.com; r from $400; P ) At the extreme other end of the spectrum, this luxury resort on the western end of town has manicured gardens, golf courses and a fabulous spa.

The knotty pine–paneled rooms and cottages at the **Rose Garden Inn** ( ☎ 805-646-1434, 800-799-1881; www.rosegardeninnofojai.com; 615 West

Ojai Ave; r $80-125, cottages $90-175; ) have good character, while the **Best Western Casa Ojai** ( ☎ 805-646-8175, 800-255-8175; www.ojaiinn.com; 1302 Ojai Ave, r $90-150; ) has better-than-average motel rooms.

## Eating

**Boccali's** ( ☎ 805-646-6116; 3277 Ojai-Santa Paula Rd; mains $8-16; lunch Wed-Sun, dinner daily) Only locals know about this mom-and-pop, homestyle-Italian, roadside café, 2 miles east of town, where hand-thrown pizza and pasta are the specialties year-round. But summer is the best time to come, when the restaurant's extensive gardens (right outside) yield giant tomatoes, peppers and eggplant. The warm-off-the-vine tomato salad is fantastic; pair it with hot garlic bread for a great meal. There's homemade lemonade, too.

**Ranch House** ( ☎ 805-646-2360; S Lomita Ave; dinner mains $23-30, brunch $21; dinner Wed-Sun, brunch Sun only) Hold hands by candlelight in the lush gardens of Ojai's top choice for white-tablecloth contemporary Euro-Cal cooking. There's Sunday brunch, too.

**Seafresh Seafood** ( ☎ 805-646-7747; 533 E Ojai Ave; mains $8-19; 11am-9pm) If you're craving seafood, head here.

## Getting There & Around

Ojai is 35 miles east of Santa Barbara via Hwy 150, and 14 miles inland from Ventura off Hwy 33. Hwy 150 is the prettier route. The only direct bus service is from the city of Ventura. Take the Greyhound bus or Amtrak train to Ventura (opposite), then board bus

---

**DETOUR: SUMMERLAND**

Antique hounds love Summerland (population 1545), where you won't find any bargains, but you will get to ooh and ahh over beautiful furniture from centuries gone by. Head south on Hwy 101 to exit 91. Park on Lillie Ave and walk around town. There are some hidden shops on the hill just up from the main drag. Stop for lunch at **Stacky's** ( ☎ 805-969-9908; 2315 Lillie Ave; 7am-7:30pm), a knotty pine–paneled, old-school, eat-out-of-a-basket diner. If you want a plate and a waiter, walk across the street to **Summerland Beach Café** ( ☎ 805-969-1019; 2294 Lillie Ave; 7am-3pm), which is known for its fluffy omelettes.

No 16 ($1.25, one hour, once hourly) at Main and Figueroa Sts, which goes straight to downtown Ojai. The bus company is **SCAT** ( ☎ 805-487-4222; www.scat.org).

## CHANNEL ISLANDS NATIONAL PARK

If you're on the Santa Barbara coast on a clear day, when there's no looming fog bank off the coast, you'll spot several islands looming before the horizon. These are the Channel Islands, an eight-island chain off the Southern California coast, stretching from Santa Barbara to San Diego. Five of them – San Miguel, Santa Rosa, Santa Cruz, Anacapa and tiny Santa Barbara – comprise Channel Islands National Park. Rich with unique species of flora and fauna, extensive tide pools and kelp forests, the islands are home to over 100 plant and animal species found nowhere else in the entire world, earning them the nickname 'California's Galapagos.' Most of these species are plants – don't expect to disembark and see a menagerie of whacked-out-looking wildlife (bless their hearts – the folks at the National Park Service get a tiny bit over-enthusiastic in their brochure writing).

Originally inhabited by the Chumash and Gabrieleño Indians (who were taken to the mainland missions in the early 1800s), the islands were subsequently taken over by sheep ranchers and the US Navy until the mid-1970s, when conservation efforts began. San Miguel, Santa Rosa, Anacapa and Santa Barbara Islands are now owned by the **National Park Service** (NPS; ☎ 805-658-5700; www .nps.gov/chis), which also owns about 20% of Santa Cruz Island. The NPS has its work cut out for it. Human beings have left a heavy footprint. Livestock overgrazed, causing erosion, and rabbits fed on native plants. The US military even practiced bombing techniques on San Miguel. Threats still remain: feral pigs dig deep trenches rooting out bulbs (you may encounter these pigs – or signs of their hooved handiwork), and invasive plant species, such as mustard, ice plant and range grasses, squeeze out native plants.

Park information is available at the Channel Islands National Park Visitors Center (p344).

## Sights & Activities

**Anacapa**, which is actually three separate islets, gives a memorable introduction to the islands' ecology. Besides checking out the small museum, be sure to ask about rangerled programs; occasionally park rangers scuba dive while carrying a video camera, broadcasting the images on a monitor that you can watch on the dock.

Thousands of brown pelicans nest and raise chicks here. It's a conservation success story: in 1970 only one chick survived, on West Anacapa. Scientists determined that DDT (a pesticide) flowing from sewage systems into the ocean made its way into the kelp that fish ate. When pelicans feasted on contaminated fish, the DDT caused the shells of their eggs to become so fragile the eggs broke under the parent bird's weight, leading to a 1972 federal ban on DDT.

**Santa Cruz**, the largest island, has two mountain ranges with peaks reaching 2450ft (Mt Diablo). You can swim, snorkel, scuba dive and kayak. There are excellent hikes, too, including the **Scorpion Canyon–Island Jay hike**. Starting in the upper campground, scramble across the old stream bed, then head steeply uphill to the old oil well for fantastic views. Connect with Smugglers Rd atop the hill and loop back to Scorpion Anchorage.

The Chumash called **Santa Rosa** 'Wima' (Driftwood) because of the logs that often came ashore here. They built plank canoes called *tomols* from the logs. This island has rare Torrey pines, sandy beaches and nearly 200 bird species.

In 1959 an archaeologist hiking in **Arlington Canyon** discovered a human femur 30ft below the surface of the ground, exposed by stream bank erosion. 'Arlington Woman' dates from the end of the last Ice Age, about 13,000 years ago.

**San Miguel**, the most remote of the four northern islands, guarantees solitude and a wilderness experience, but it's often windy and shrouded in fog. Some sections are off-limits to prevent disruption of the fragile ecosystem.

**Santa Barbara** is home to the humongous northern elephant seal and Xantus' murrelets, a bird that nests in cliff crevices. There's also a visitors center.

Most visitors come between June and September; however, the prettiest times to visit are during the spring wildflower season (April and May) and in September and October, when the fog clears.

## Tours

**Island Packers** ( ☎ 805-642-1393, recorded information ☎ 805-642-7688; www.islandpackers.com; 1867 Spinnaker Dr), near the Ventura Visitor Center, leads trips year-round and offers packages to all the islands; from December to March it operates terrific one-day whale-watching excursions. Rates cost $20 to $60; call for details. Overnight campers pay more. Staff provide excellent interpretation of the history and ecology of the islands. Ask about guided hikes.

Truth Aquatics (p330), the park's Santa Barbara–based concessionaire, leads comparable excursions, also with excellent interpretation.

Most trips require a minimum number of participants, and may be canceled due to surf and weather conditions. If you camp overnight and the seas are rough the next day, you could get stuck. In short, landing is never guaranteed. Reservations are recommended for weekend, holiday and summer trips, and credit card or advance payment is required.

## Sleeping

All of the islands have primitive **campgrounds** ( ☎ reservations 800-365-2267; www.nps.gov; sites $12), which are open year-round. Each ground has pit toilets and picnic tables, but you must pack everything in and out, including trash. Water is only available on Santa Rosa and Santa Cruz Islands. Due to fire danger, campfires aren't allowed, but you can use a camp stove. Be prepared to trek up to 1.5 miles to the campground from the landing areas.

The campground on Santa Barbara is large, grassy and surrounded by hiking trails; the one on Anacapa is high, rocky and isolated. Camping on San Miguel, with its unceasing wind, fog and volatile weather, is not for the faint of heart. Santa Rosa's campground has wonderful views of Santa Cruz. It's sited in a eucalyptus grove in a canyon (it can get very windy). Del Norte, a backcountry campground on Santa Cruz, lies in a shaded oak grove, 3.5 miles from the landing.

## Getting There & Away

Access to the Channel Islands is via Ventura (p343). See opposite for information on boat travel to the islands and tour options; see p330 for excursions.

To get to the Channel Islands National Park Visitors Center and the boat docks in Ventura, from Hwy 101 northbound, exit at Victoria Ave, turn left on Victoria and right on Olivas Park Dr to Harbor Blvd; Olivas Park Dr runs straight into Spinnaker Dr. From Hwy 101 southbound, exit at Seaward Ave onto Harbor Blvd, then turn right on Spinnaker Dr.

Boating to the islands can be rough; those prone to seasickness should consider taking a 25-minute flight to Santa Rosa Island, from either Santa Barbara or Camarillo, with **Channel Islands Aviation** ( ☎ 805-987-1301; www .flycia.com; 305 Durley Ave, Camarillo; day trips adult/child $130/103; campers round-trip $200).

# Directory

## CONTENTS

## ACCOMMODATIONS

Southern California offers all types of places to unpack your suitcase, from hostels, campgrounds and B&Bs to chain motels, hotels and luxury resorts. If you're traveling in the busy summer season (June to September), we recommend you make reservations as early as possible. Rooms can also be scarce and prices high around major holidays (see p356).

Prices listed in this book are for peak-season travel (usually summer) and, unless stated otherwise, do not include taxes.

The budget category comprises campgrounds, hostels and simple hotels where rates rarely exceed $100 for a double. Most of our listings fall into the mid-range category, which generally offers the best value for money. Expect to pay between $100 and $200 for a clean, comfortable and decent-sized double room with at least a modicum of style, a private bathroom and a slew of amenities, including cable TV, direct-dial telephone, a coffeemaker, perhaps a microwave and a small refrigerator. Many mid-range properties have swimming pools.

Accommodations at the top end (costing over $200 per double) offer an international standard of amenities and perhaps a scenic location, special decor or historical ambience. Swimming pools are pretty standard and facilities such as saunas, fitness rooms and business centers are commswon. Unless you're going to use these facilities, though, it's rarely worth the extra cost over mid-range hotels.

By law, all hotels must have at least one room compliant with the American Disabilities Act. If you're a smoker be sure to ask about the availability of smoking rooms as many lodgings in California are exclusively nonsmoking. Rooms reserved for smokers are often in less desirable locations. Air-conditioning is a standard amenity except in beachfront properties. Accommodations offering their guests Internet access are identified in this book with the Internet icon ( 🖳 ).

Prices listed in this book do not – and in fact cannot – take into account seasonal or promotional discounts. Many establishments offer significantly lower rates during the off-season, especially in winter (except in the desert and the ski areas). In the cities, hotels geared primarily toward business travelers often have severely discounted weekend specials. Membership in the **American Automobile Association** (AAA; ☎ 800-874-7532; www.aaa.com) or another automobile club, the **American Association of Retired Persons** (AARP; ☎ 800-687-2277; www.aarp.org) and other organizations may yield modest savings (usually around 10%) at any time of the year.

Online agencies such as www.orbitz.com, www.expedia.com, www.travelocity.com and www.hotel.com may offer you a better rate than what you'd get if you booked directly with the hotel. A handy Web resource is **TripAdvisor** (www.tripadvisor.com), which features both reader and published reviews, and also simultaneously searches for rates offered by the aforementioned agencies for some of the properties. For an even more exhaustive rate comparison, try **Travelaxe** (www.travelaxe

.com), which has several filters to help you narrow down your search (eg distance from the town center or airport, price, comfort level). It requires a free software download (spyware-free, so they say). You should also check out hotel websites for special online rates or packages.

## B&Bs

Bed-and-breakfast lodging usually offers high-end accommodations in converted private homes, typically lovely old Victorians or other heritage buildings. Owners usually take great pride in decorating the guest rooms and common areas and a personal interest in ensuring that you enjoy your stay. People in need of lots of privacy may find B&Bs a bit too intimate. Rates often include a lavish, usually homecooked, breakfast. Amenities vary widely, but rooms with TV and telephone are the exception; the cheapest units share bathroom facilities. Most B&Bs require advance reservations, though some will accommodate the occasional drop-in guest. Smoking is generally prohibited and minimum stays are common in peak season and on weekends.

Many places belong to the **California Association of Bed & Breakfast Inns** ( ☎ 831-462-9191; www.cabbi.com).

## Camping

Camping in Southern California can be so much more than a cheap way to spend the night. Some of the nicest sites have you waking up to ocean views, splendid rock formations or a canopy of pines. Nearly all are open year-round, although if you camp in the desert in summer you might bake alive in your tent.

Basic campsites usually have fire pits and picnic benches and access to drinking water and pit toilets. These are most common in national forests and on Bureau of Land Management (BLM) land. Campgrounds in state and national parks tend to have more amenities, including flush toilets, sometimes hot showers and RV (recreational vehicle) hookups. Private campgrounds are usually located close to cities and cater more to the RV crowd.

Most campgrounds accept reservations for all or some of their sites. The following websites let you search for locations, check availability, book a site, view maps and get driving directions.

**National Recreation Reservation Service** (NRRS; ☎ 877-444-6777, outside the US ☎ 518-885-3639; www.reserveusa.com; per reservation $9) Reservations for campgrounds in national forests, national parks and BLM land; up to 240 days in advance.

**Reserve America** ( ☎ 800-444-7275, outside the US ☎ 916-638-5883; www.reserveamerica.com; per reservation $7.50) Reservations for camping in national forests, California State Parks and private sites; up to seven months in advance.

## Hostels

Southern California has five hostels affiliated with **Hostelling International USA** (HI-USA; ☎ 800-909-4776; www.hiusa.org). Two are in San Diego, two in LA and one in Fullerton, near Disneyland; see those chapters for details. Dorms in HI hostels are gender-segregated and alcohol and smoking are prohibited.

Independent hostels tend to be more convivial places with regular guest parties and other events. Some include a light breakfast in their rates, arrange local tours or pick up guests at transportation hubs. Some hostels say they accept only international visitors (basically to keep out destitute locals), but Americans who look like they are travelers are usually admitted, especially during the slower months.

Besides dorms sleeping three to 10 people, many hostels increasingly offer private rooms for couples and families, although bathrooms are still often shared. Other typical features include a kitchen, lockers, Internet access, a laundry room and a common room with TV, games and books.

Reservations are always a good idea, especially in summer. Most hostels take bookings online and by phone, fax, mail or email. Many independent hostels belong to reservation services such as www.hostels.com or www.backpackers.com, which sometimes offer lower rates.

## Hotels & Motels

Hotels differ from motels in that they don't surround a parking lot and usually have some sort of a lobby. Hotels may provide extra services such as laundry, but such conveniences usually come at a price. If you walk in without reservations, always ask to see a room before paying for it, especially at motels.

### THE CHAIN GANG

For additional chain hotels not included in this guide, call these numbers:

#### Budget
**Days Inn** ( ☎ 800-329-7466; www.daysinn.com)
**Econo Lodge** ( ☎ 877-424-6423; www.econo lodge.com)
**Super 8** ( ☎ 800-800-8000; www.super8.com)

#### Mid-Range
**Best Western** ( ☎ 800-780-7234; www.best western.com)
**Clarion Hotel** ( ☎ 877-424-6423; www.clarion hotel.com)
**Comfort Inn** ( ☎ 877-424-6423; www.comfort inn.com)
**Fairfield Inn** ( ☎ 800-228-2800; wwwfairfieldinn .com)
**Hampton Inn** ( ☎ 800-426-7866; www.hampton inn.com)
**Holiday Inn** ( ☎ 800-465-4329; www.holiday -inn.com)
**Howard Johnson** ( ☎ 800-446-4656; www .hojo.com)
**Quality Inn & Suites** ( ☎ 877-424-6423; www.qualityinn.com)
**Travelodge** ( ☎ 800-578-7878; www.travelodge .com)

#### Top End
**Hilton** ( ☎ 800-445-8667; www.hilton.com)
**Hyatt** ( ☎ 888-591-1234; www.hyatt.com)
**Marriott** ( ☎ 888-236-2427; www.marriott.com)
**Radisson** ( ☎ 888-201-1718; www.radisson .com)
**Ramada** ( ☎ 800-272-6232; www.ramada.com)
**Sheraton** ( ☎ 888-625-5144; www.sheraton .com)
**Westin** ( ☎ 800-228-3000; www.westin.com)

Rooms are often priced by the size and number of beds in a room, rather than the number of occupants. A room with one double or queen-size bed usually costs the same for one or two people, while a room with a king-size bed or two double beds costs more. Rooms with two doubles can accommodate up to four people, making them a cost-saving choice for families and small groups. A small surcharge often applies to the third and fourth person, but children under a certain age (this varies) often stay free. Cribs or rollaway beds usually incur an extra charge.

Room location may also affect the price; recently renovated or larger rooms, or those with a view, are likely to cost more. Hotels facing a noisy street may charge more for quieter rooms.

Many hotels offer suites for people in need of more elbow room. While this should technically get you at least two rooms, one of them a bedroom, this is not always the case as some properties simply call their larger rooms 'suites' or 'junior suites.' Always ask about a suite's size and layout before booking.

Make reservations at chain hotels by calling their central reservation lines, but to learn about specific amenities and possible local promotions, call the property directly. Every listing in this book includes local direct numbers.

### Resorts
One type of accommodation Southern California has plenty of is full-service luxury resorts, usually with integrated spas offering the latest in pampering techniques. For busy urbanites they serve as quick getaways, places that offer a respite from the rat race and restore balance to body and soul. Luxury resorts are normally so attractive that they're often destinations in themselves.

Expect very comfortable, attractively designed rooms with quality furnishings and outfitted with pillow-top mattresses, fancy linens, down comforters and fluffy terry-cloth robes. Services include in-room massages, shoeshine, and evening turndown; some require an extra fee. On the premises expect a restaurant of excellent caliber serving three meals a day.

### BUSINESS HOURS
Standard business hours, including for most government offices, are 9am to 5pm Monday to Friday. Bank hours are usually from 9am or 10am to 5pm or 6pm weekdays; many branches are now also open on Saturday, usually from 9am to 1pm or 2pm but sometimes until 5pm. Post offices are open from 8am to 4pm or 5:30pm weekdays, and many are open from 8am to 2pm on Saturday.

Most shops open doors around 10am, although noon is common for boutiques and art galleries. Closing time is anywhere from 6pm to 9pm or 10pm in shopping malls. Typical Sunday hours are noon to 5pm (until 6pm in malls).

Convenience stores and supermarkets have longer hours, often not closing until 10pm or midnight; in cities, some stay open around the clock.

Restaurants, bars and pubs don't follow standard hours. In general, kitchens close around 9:30pm or 10pm, and bars anywhere between midnight and 2am. Always call ahead to confirm the hours if you've got your eye on a particular place.

## CHILDREN

Southern California is a tailor-made destination for traveling with kids. Just be sure you don't make the schedule overly packed and involve the kids in the day-to-day trip planning. Lonely Planet's *Travel with Children* offers a wealth of tips and tricks on the subject. The website www .travelwithyourkids.com is another good general resource.

### Practicalities

Children enjoy a wide range of discounts for everything from museum admissions to bus fares and motel stays. The definition of a 'child' varies – in some places anyone under 18 is eligible, while others put the cut-off at age six. Airlines usually allow infants (up to the age of two) to fly for free, while older children requiring a seat of their own qualify for reduced fares. Many also offer special kids' meals, although you need to pre-order them.

Hotels and motels commonly have rooms with two double beds or a double and a sofa bed, which are ideal for families. Even those that don't can bring in rollaway beds, usually for a small extra charge. Some properties offer 'kids stay free' promotions, although this may apply only if no extra bedding is required. Some B&Bs don't welcome children.

Larger hotels often have a babysitting service, and other hotels may be able to help you make arrangements. Alternatively, look in the Yellow Pages for local agencies. Be sure to ask whether sitters are licensed, what they charge per hour, whether there's a minimum fee and whether they charge extra for meals and transportation.

It's perfectly fine to bring your kids, even toddlers, along to casual restaurants (though not to upscale ones at dinnertime) and daytime events. Most eateries have high chairs, and if they don't have a specific children's menu, they can usually make a kid-tailored meal. For more details, see p51.

In vehicles, children under the age of six or weighing less than 60 pounds must be restrained in a child safety or booster seat. Most car-rental firms rent these for about $5 per day, but it is essential that you book them in advance.

Baby food, infant formulas, soy and cow's milk, disposable diapers (nappies) and other necessities are all widely available in drugstores and supermarkets. Breastfeeding in public is legal, although most women are discreet about it. Public toilets – in airports, stores, shopping malls, cinemas etc – usually have nappy-changing tables.

### Sights & Activities

It's easy to keep kids entertained no matter where you travel in Southern California. The major attractions are, of course, the big theme parks such as Disneyland (p199) in Anaheim, SeaWorld (p278) in San Diego and Universal Studios Hollywood (p121) in Los Angeles.

Thanks to mostly sunny skies and warm temperatures, Southern California's great outdoors yield lots of possibilities as well. A day spent swimming, bodysurfing, snorkeling, bicycling, kayaking, horseback riding, walking or otherwise engaging in physical activity is sure to leave the little ones ready for sleep by the day's end. Many outfitters and tour operators also have dedicated kids' tours.

Even in the cities there's usually no shortage of entertaining options. You can take the kids to parks, playgrounds, public swimming pools, zoos or child-friendly museums.

For some specific suggestions, check out the City for Children sections in the destination chapters. In addition, most tourist offices can lead you to local resources for children's programs, childcare facilities and pediatricians.

# CLIMATE CHARTS

For general advice on climate and the best times to travel in Southern California, see p9.

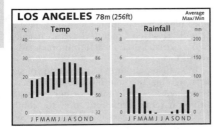

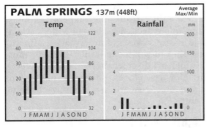

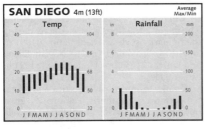

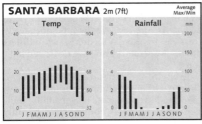

# COURSES

The *LA Weekly* advertises courses, including the occasional weekend acting course. **Robert McKee's Story Seminar** (www.mckeestory .com/homepage.htm) is a three-day screenwriting course, shown in the film *Adaptation,* offered several times a year.

For information about cooking courses, see p52.

# DANGERS & ANNOYANCES

By and large, Southern California is not a dangerous place. The most publicized problem is violent crime, but incidents are mostly confined to areas that few travelers would visit. Wildlife may pose some danger, and of course there is the dramatic, albeit unlikely, possibility of a natural disaster, such as an earthquake. Prepare for the worst, but expect the best.

## Crime

Despite the high crime statistics in the US, travelers will rarely get tricked, cheated or conned simply because they're tourists. Potential violence is a problem for all but there's no need to be overly worried. Most cities have some areas that are known as 'bad neighborhoods' and these should be avoided, particularly after dark. See the Dangers & Annoyances sections in the destination chapters for details on which areas to avoid or ask hotel staff or police officers for further details. Outside the cities, crime of all kinds drops dramatically.

Always maintain your street smarts and an awareness of your surroundings. Exercise particular caution in parking areas at night. Try to use ATMs in well-lit and well-trafficked areas. Don't carry lots of cash; keep the bulk of your money and your passport in a money belt inside your clothes; and don't leave valuables in the open in your hotel room (lock them in the room safe or hotel safe). If your car is bumped from behind by another vehicle in a remote area, try to keep going to a well-lit area, gas station or even a police station.

If a mugger accosts you, there's no failsafe policy. Handing over whatever the mugger wants may prevent serious injury, and having a separate amount of money in a front pocket, which can be handed over quickly, is often recommended. Muggers are not too happy to find their victims penniless.

That said – don't meditate on crime. The American media tend to blow crime out of proportion, giving the impression that you're going to get shot if you set foot on the wrong street. Don't panic. Protect yourself as best you can, then focus your awareness on having a great trip. You'll save yourself a lot of unnecessary mental anguish.

## Earthquakes

Earthquakes happen all the time but most are so tiny they are detectable only by sensitive seismological instruments. If you're caught in a serious earthquake, get under a desk, table or doorway. Protect your head and stay clear of windows, mirrors or anything that might fall. Don't head for elevators or go running into the street. If you're in a shopping mall or large public building, expect the alarm and/or sprinkler systems to come on.

If outdoors, get away from buildings, trees and power lines. If you are driving, pull over to the side of the road away from bridges, overpasses and power lines. Stay inside the car until the shaking stops. If you are on a sidewalk near buildings, duck into a doorway to protect yourself from falling bricks, glass and debris. Prepare for aftershocks. Use the telephone only if absolutely necessary. Turn on the radio and listen for bulletins.

## Scams

There are no scams unique to Southern California. A healthy skepticism is your best defense. In restaurants it pays to study your final bill as some servers have been observed slipping in an extra drink or adding their tip to the final tally without telling you (thereby hoping for a double tip). European visitors, who are perceived as cheap tippers, are especially prone to falling victim to this annoying practice.

## Wildlife

Mountain lions – also called cougars or pumas – inhabit forests and mountains throughout Southern California, especially in areas teeming with deer, which includes some areas near the coast. In January 2004, one mountain biker was killed and another injured in Whiting Ranch Wilderness Park in Orange County, but generally attacks on humans are rare. If you encounter a cougar, face the animal and retreat slowly, trying to appear large by raising your arms or grabbing a stick. If attacked, you'll need to fight back, shouting and throwing objects at it.

Although an estimated 16,000 to 24,000 black bears roam around California, chances of bear encounters in the southern part of the state are exceedingly unlikely and limited to the San Gabriel Mountains and the San Bernardino Mountains east of LA. Look for instructions posted at trailheads and campgrounds.

Watch your step when hiking, especially on hot summer afternoons when rattlesnakes like to bask in the middle of the trail. Also beware of scorpions and black widow spiders, which hide under rocks and wood piles (see p372 for more information).

## DISABLED TRAVELERS

If you have a physical disability, there's no better place for travel within the US than California. The Americans with Disabilities Act (ADA) requires that all public buildings (including hotels, restaurants, theaters and museums) be wheelchair accessible. Buses and trains must have wheelchair lifts and telephone companies are required to provide relay operators (available via TTY numbers) for the hearing impaired. Many banks provide ATM instructions in braille, and you'll find dropped curbs at most intersections and sometimes audible crossing signals as well.

If you're worried about stairs, be sure to ask about the availability of an elevator. Major car-rental agencies offer hand-controlled vehicles and vans with wheelchair lifts at no extra charge, but you *must* reserve them well in advance.

All major airlines, Greyhound buses and Amtrak trains can accommodate people with disabilities, although they usually need at least a day or two advance notice. Just describe your specific needs when making reservations. Seeing-eye dogs are permitted to accompany passengers.

Most national and state parks and recreation areas have paved or boardwalk-style nature trails. For free admission to national parks, blind or permanently disabled US citizens and permanent residents can get a Golden Access Passport (see www.nps.gov/fees_passes.htm for more information).

*Barrier-Free Travel: A Nuts and Bolts Guide for Wheelers and Slow Walkers* by Candy B Harrington is an excellent resource for planning your trip. It was written by the editor of **Emerging Horizons** (www.emerginghorizons.com), a quarterly magazine for mobility-impaired travelers available both in print and online.

*A Wheelchair Rider's Guide: Los Angeles and Orange County Coast*, by Erick and Elisa Mikiten, is available for free in print and can also be downloaded from the website of the **California Coastal Conservancy** ( ☎ 510-286-0933; www.coastalconservancy.ca.gov).

*Access Guide: In San Diego* is published by **Accessible San Diego** ( ☎ 858-279-0704; www.accesssan diego.org). It costs $5 and contains details about hotels, restaurants, sights and transportation in San Diego.

For an insider's view of Disneyland 'on wheels,' see the **Theme Park Access Guide** (www .mouseplanet.com/tag/dlintro.htm) by Tony Phoenix and Adrienne Vincent-Phoenix.

There are a number of organizations and tour providers that specialize in serving disabled travelers:

**Access-Able Travel Source** ( ☎ 303-232-2979; www .access-able.com) This excellent website has many useful links.

**Mobility International** (www.miusa.org) UK ( ☎ 020-7403-5688); US ( ☎ 541-343-1284) Advises disabled travelers on mobility issues and runs an educational exchange program.

**Moss Rehabilitation Hospital's Travel Information Service** (www.mossresourcenet.org/travel.htm) Lists extensive useful contacts.

**New Directions** ( ☎ 805-967-2841, 888-967-2841; www.newdirectionstravel.com) Specializes in developmentally disabled travelers.

**Society for Accessible Travel & Hospitality** (SATH; ☎ 212-447-7284; www.sath.org) Lots of useful links and information for disabled travelers.

## DISCOUNT CARDS

If Southern California's theme parks are the focus of your trip, a **Southern California CityPass** (www.citypass.com) may be a wise investment. Passes cost $179 for adults and $129 for children ages three to nine, and buy three-day admission to Disneyland and Disney's California Adventure, one-day admission each to Knott's Berry Farm and SeaWorld and another day at either the San Diego Zoo or the San Diego Wild Animal Park. Passes are valid for 14 days from the day of the first use and may be purchased online or at any of the attractions. The total savings are $75 for adults and $58 for children.

The Hollywood CityPass (p78) is a similar deal but is limited to attractions within Los Angeles.

If you're a full-time student, never leave home without an **International Student Identity Card** (ISIC; www.isiccard.com), which entitles you to discounts on movie and theater tickets, travel insurance and admission to museums and other attractions. For non-students under 26, the same organization also issues the International Youth Travel Card (IYTC), which offers many of the same savings and benefits. You can apply for either on the website or through student unions, hosteling organizations and youth-oriented travel agencies such as STA Travel.

International and US students can also buy the **Student Advantage Card** ( ☎ 877-256-4672; www.studentadvantage.com) for $20 per year for 15% savings on Amtrak and Greyhound plus discounts up to 50% at participating hotels, shops and airlines.

People over the age of 65 (sometimes 55, 60 or 62) often qualify for the same discounts as students; any identification showing your birth date should suffice as proof of age. Members of the **American Association of Retired Persons** (AARP; ☎ 800-687-2277; www.aarp.org; annual membership fee $12.50), an advocacy group for Americans 50 years and older, and of the **American Automobile Association** (AAA; ☎ 800-874-7532; www.aaa.com) or its foreign affiliates qualify for small discounts (usually 10%) in many places. Just make it a habit to ask every time you book a room, reserve a car, order a meal or pay an entrance fee, especially since these discounts are not usually advertised.

Also look for discount coupons in tourist offices, hotels, gas stations and newspapers. Be aware that discounts may have restrictions and conditions or may not be valid at peak times, so always read the fine print. Online hotel discount coupons are available through **Roomsaver** (www.roomsaver.com).

## FESTIVALS & EVENTS

Southern California has a wonderful and packed schedule of festivals and special events taking place throughout the year. The following list is an overview of some of the major festivities, each of which is detailed in the relevant destination chapter.

### January & February
**Rose Parade** (Los Angeles, p137) January 1
**Chinese New Year** (Los Angeles, p137) Late January/ early February

**March**
**LA Marathon** (Los Angeles, p137) First Sunday in March

**April & May**
**Los Angeles Times Festival of Books** (Los Angeles, p137) Third weekend in April
**Fiesta Broadway** (Los Angeles, p137) Last Sunday in April
**Coachella Valley Music Festival** (Indio, Palm Springs, p308) Late April/early May
**Cinco de Mayo** (most cities, especially Los Angeles, p137) Early May

**June**
**LA Pride** (Los Angeles, p84) Mid-June
**Summer Solstice Parade** (Santa Barbara, p332) Late June

**July**
**Central Avenue Jazz Festival** (Los Angeles, p137) Late July
**Festival of the Arts & Pageant of the Masters** (Laguna Beach, p228) July to August
**US Open Sandcastle Competition** (San Diego, p259) Mid-July
**San Diego Gay Pride** (San Diego, p259) Late July

**August**
**Nisei Week Japanese Festival** (Los Angeles, p137) Early to mid-August
**Sunset Junction Street Fair** (Los Angeles, p137) Mid-August
**African Marketplace & Cultural Faire** (Los Angeles, p137) Late August/early September
**San Diego Street Scene** (San Diego, p259) Late August

**September**
**Fleet Week** (San Diego, p259) Mid- to late September
**Los Angeles County Fair** (Los Angeles, p138) Mid- to late September
**Abbot Kinney Street Festival** (Los Angeles, p138) Late September

**October**
**West Hollywood Halloween Carnival** (Los Angeles, p138) October 31

**November**
**Mariachi Festival** (Los Angeles, p138) Mid-November
**Doo Dah Parade** (Los Angeles, p138) Sunday before Thanksgiving
**Hollywood Christmas Parade** (Los Angeles, p138) Sunday after Thanksgiving

**December**
**Christmas Boat Parade** (Newport Beach, p223) Week before Christmas
**Las Posadas** (Los Angeles, p138; San Diego, p260) Late December

## FOOD

This guide includes eating options to match all tastes and travel budgets. Budget eateries include takeouts, delis, cafés, snack bars, markets and basic restaurants where you can fill up for $10 or less. At mid-range establishments, you usually get tablecloths, full menus, beer and wine lists and main courses from $10 to $20. Top-end places tend to be full gourmet affairs with fussy service, creative and freshly prepared food and matching wine lists; expect mains to start at $20. Remember that your final tally will be swelled by the 8.25% sales tax and a tip of 15% to 20%.

Since most restaurants serve lunch and dinner daily, we've spelled out only deviations from this basic rule in our reviews.

There is no smoking inside restaurants, although some have patios or sidewalk tables where lighting up may still be tolerated.

For the full run-down of cuisine, customs and table manners in Southern California, see p48.

## GAY & LESBIAN TRAVELERS

Southern California is a magnet for gay travelers with major hot spots being West Hollywood (WeHo) and Silver Lake in LA, the Hillcrest area of San Diego and the desert resort of Palm Springs. LA's Long Beach and Orange County's Laguna Beach also have small gay communities. All of these hubs have humming nightlife scenes, magazines, associations and support groups, and major Gay Pride celebrations. As elsewhere, the scene is predominantly male-oriented, although lesbians won't feel left out. For an overview of the LA scene, see p84. For details about gay resorts in Palm Springs, see p310.

**Damron** (www.damron.com) publishes the classic gay travel guides, including *Men's Travel Guide* and *Women's Traveler*. Damron's *Accommodations* lists gay-owned and gay-friendly hotels, B&Bs and guesthouses nationwide. **Out & About** (www.outandabout.com) publishes a monthly newsletter for gay and lesbian travelers as well as downloadable travel guides with lots of juicy information about numerous destinations, including all the relevant ones in Southern California.

If you find yourself in need of counseling or referrals of any kind, contact the **Gay & Lesbian National Hotline** ( ☎ 888-843-4564; www .glnh.org).

## HOLIDAYS

On the following national holidays banks, schools and government offices (including post offices) all close, and transportation, museums and other services operate on a Sunday schedule. Holidays falling on a weekend are usually observed the following Monday.

**New Year's Day** January 1
**Martin Luther King Jr Day** Third Monday in January
**Presidents' Day** Third Monday in February
**Memorial Day** Last Monday in May
**Independence Day** July 4 (aka the Fourth of July)
**Labor Day** First Monday in September
**Columbus Day** Second Monday in October
**Veterans' Day** November 11
**Thanksgiving Day** Fourth Thursday in November
**Christmas Day** December 25

## INSURANCE

No matter how long or short your trip, make sure you have adequate travel insurance. At a minimum you need coverage for medical emergencies and treatment, including hospital stays and an emergency flight home. Medical treatment in the USA is of the highest caliber, but the expense could kill you.

While you may find a policy that pays doctors or hospitals directly, many healthcare professionals still demand payment at the time of service, especially from out-of-towners. Except in emergencies, call around for a doctor willing to accept your insurance. Be sure to keep all receipts and documentation. Some policies ask you to call (reverse charges) a center in your home country for an immediate assessment of your problem. For further details, see p370.

You should also consider coverage for luggage theft or loss. If you already have health insurance or a homeowners or renters policy, check what they will cover and only get supplemental insurance to protect against the rest. If you have prepaid a large portion of your vacation, trip cancellation insurance is a worthwhile expense.

For information about what insurance you need while driving in Southern California,

see p368. Agencies offering comprehensive travel insurance include the following:

**Insure.com** ( ☎ 800-556-9393; www.insure.com) An independent website that compares quotes from 200 US-based insurance companies.
**Quoteline Direct** ( ☎ 0870-444-0870; www.quoteline direct.co.uk) Compares quotes from 30 UK-based insurance companies.
**Travel Guard** ( ☎ 877-370-4742; www.travelguard .com) A major insurer with offices worldwide.
**Travelex** ( ☎ 800-228-9792; www.travelex.com) Another big company.

## INTERNATIONAL VISITORS
### Entering the USA

Getting into the USA can be a bureaucratic nightmare, especially as the rules keep changing. For up-to-date information about entry requirements and eligibility, we highly recommend checking with a US consulate in your home country. For background information, also check the visa website of the **US Department of State** (www.unitedstates visas.gov).

Under the US Visa Waiver Program, visas are currently not required for citizens of 27 countries for stays up to 90 days (no extensions allowed) as long as they have a machine-readable passport (MRP). If you don't have an MRP, you will need a visa to enter the US. Starting on October 26, 2005, this requirement will tighten as passports must not only be machine-readable but also contain biometric information (eg fingerprints or an iris scan). If you're from a visa-waiver country, don't have such a passport and want to come to the US after October 26, 2005, you will need to apply for a visa.

Canadian citizens are exempt from both visa and passport requirements but must show proof of citizenship.

Citizens from all other countries need to apply for a visa in their home country. The process costs a nonrefundable $100, involves a personal interview and can take several weeks, so you should apply as early as possible.

In 2004, the US Department of Homeland Security introduced a new set of security measures called US-VISIT. Upon arrival in the US, all visitors will be photographed and have their index fingers scanned. Eventually, this biometric data will be matched when you leave the US. The goal is to ensure that the person who entered the US is the same as the one leaving it and to catch people who've overstayed the terms of their admission. For full details about US-VISIT, check with a US consulate or www .dhs.gov/us-visit.

## Customs

US customs allows non-US citizens or residents over the age of 21 to bring 1L of alcohol, 200 cigarettes or 50 cigars or 2kg of smoking tobacco, and $100 worth of gifts into the US. An additional 100 cigars may be brought in under your gift exemption.

Importing or exporting money in any form up to a value of $10,000 can be done without formality, but larger amounts must be reported to customs. Unless you're curious about US jails, don't even think about bringing in illegal drugs.

California is an important agricultural state. To prevent the spread of pests and diseases there are certain food items (including meats, fresh fruit and vegetables) that may not be brought into the state. Bakery items, chocolates and hard-cured cheeses are admissible.

If you drive into California across the border from Mexico or the neighboring states of Oregon, Nevada and Arizona, you may have to stop for a quick inspection and questioning by officials of the California Department of Food and Agriculture.

For complete information, visit the US Customs and Border Protection website at www.cbp.gov.

## Embassies & Consulates
### US EMBASSIES & CONSULATES

Visas and other travel-related documents are handled by consulates, not embassies. While embassies are located in capital cities, the US maintains consulates in many other major cities. To find the US consulate nearest to you, contact the US embassy in your country. If your country isn't listed here, see www.travel .state.gov/visa/questions_embassy.html.

**Australia** ( ☎ 02-6214-5600; Moonah Pl, Yarralumla, ACT 2600)

**Canada** ( ☎ 613-238-5335; 490 Sussex Dr, Ottawa, Ontario K1N 1G8)

**France** ( ☎ 01-43-12-22-22; 2 Ave Gabriel, 75008 Paris)

**Germany** ( ☎ 030-830-50; Neustädtische Kirchstrasse 4-5, 10117 Berlin)

**Ireland** ( ☎ 01-668-8777; 42 Elgin Rd, Dublin 4)

**Israel** ( ☎ 03-519-7575; 71 Hayarkon St, Tel Aviv 63903)

**Italy** ( ☎ 06-467-41; Via Veneto 119/A, 00187 Rome)

**Japan** ( ☎ 03-3224-5000; 1-10-5 Akasaka, Minato-ku, Tokyo 107-8420)

**The Netherlands** ( ☎ 070-310-9209; Lange Voorhout 102, 2514 EJ The Hague)

**New Zealand** ( ☎ 04-462-6000; 29 Fitzherbert Tce, Thorndon, Wellington)

**UK** ( ☎ 020-7499-9000; 24 Grosvenor Sq, London W1A 1AE)

### CONSULATES IN LOS ANGELES

Most foreign embassies are in Washington, DC, but many countries, including the following, have consular offices in LA. For additional countries, visit www.ss.ca.gov /business/ibrp/fgncons.htm.

**Australia** (Map pp70-1; ☎ 310-229-4800; 2049 Century Park E, 19th fl) Near Beverly Hills.

**Canada** (Map pp64-5; ☎ 213-346-2700; 550 S Hope St, 9th fl) Downtown.

**France** (Map pp70-1; ☎ 310-235-3200; 10990 Wilshire Blvd, Suite 300) Westwood.

**Germany** (Map pp68-9; ☎ 323-930-2703; 6222 Wilshire Blvd, Suite 500) Mid-City.

**Italy** (off Map pp70-1; ☎ 310-826-5998; 12400 Wilshire Blvd, Suite 300) Near Santa Monica.

**Japan** (Map pp64-5; ☎ 213-617-6700; 350 S Grand Ave, Suite 1700) Downtown.

**The Netherlands** (off Map pp70-1; ☎ 310-268-1598; 11766 Wilshire Blvd, Suite 1150) Near Westwood.

**New Zealand** (off Map pp70-1; ☎ 310-207-1605; 12400 Wilshire Blvd, Suite 1150) Near Santa Monica.

**South Africa** (Map pp68-9; ☎ 310-651-0902; 6300 Wilshire Blvd, Suite 600) Mid-City.

**UK** (off Map pp70-1; ☎ 310-481-0031; 11766 Wilshire Blvd, Suite 400) Near Westwood.

## Money

For exchange rates, see the inside cover of this book. For an overview of how much things cost in Southern California, see p9.

When changing money, compare rates and fees. In the larger cities, currency exchange offices may offer better conditions than banks. In rural areas, exchanging money can be a problem, so make sure you have plenty of cash, a credit card or US dollar traveler's checks on hand.

Usually the best and quickest way to obtain cash is by making a withdrawal from your bank account back home by using an ATM. Most are linked to international networks such as Cirrus, Plus, Star and Maestro. They're ubiquitous and accessible around the clock.

**DIRECTORY**

Credit cards are almost universally accepted and, in fact, you'll find it hard or impossible to rent a car, book a room or order tickets over the phone without one. A credit card may also be vital in emergencies. Most ATMs also spit out cash if you use your credit card. This method tends to be more expensive because, in addition to a service fee, you'll be charged interest immediately (ie there's no grace period as with purchases).

For exact fees, check with your bank or credit-card company.

## Post

The **US Postal Service** (USPS; www.usps.com) is inexpensive and reliable. Standard letters up to 1oz (about 30g) cost 37¢ within the US, 60¢ to Canada and Mexico and 80¢ to all other countries. Rates for postcards are 23¢, 50¢ and 70¢, respectively. Postal rates increase by a penny or more every few years. For other rates, zip (postal) codes and general information, stop by any post office, call the USPS toll-free helpline ( ☎ 800-275-8777) or visit the website.

Mail can be sent general delivery (poste restante) to any post office that has its own zip code. There is no charge, but you must show photo identification when picking up mail. Post offices will hold mail for 10 days.

## Practicalities

- The dominant newspaper, the *Los Angeles Times*, is read throughout Southern California. The *San Diego Union Tribune* is read primarily in San Diego County.
- The NTSC system (not compatible with PAL or SECAM) is used for videos.
- Electrical supply is 110V AC, 50/60Hz. Some electrical appliances have adjustable current-selector switches.
- The US uses the imperial system, but you'll sometimes see roadside mileage signs written in both kilometers and miles. To convert between metric and imperial, see the chart on the inside front cover.

## Telephone
### PAY PHONES

In the age of cell phones, public pay phones are becoming a dying breed. Those still around are usually coin-operated, although some accept credit cards. Really fancy ones (such as those at airports) have data ports so you can access the Internet using your lap-

top. Local calls usually cost 35¢ minimum and increase with the distance and length of call. In most cases you'll be better off using a prepaid phonecard available in convenience stores, supermarkets, newsstands and electronics stores. Be sure to read the fine print before buying such a card as many contain hidden charges such as 'activation fees' or a per-call 'connection fee.' However, a surcharge of about 30¢ for calls made from pay phones is normal.

### PHONE CODES

US phone numbers consist of a three-letter area code followed by a seven-digit local number. When dialing a number within the same area code, just punch in the seven-digit number. Long-distance calls must be preceded by ☎ 1. For direct international calls, dial ☎ 011 plus the country code plus the area code plus the local phone number. If you're calling from abroad the country code for the US is ☎ 1.

For local directory assistance, dial ☎ 411. For directory assistance outside your area code, dial ☎ 1 plus the area code plus ☎ 555-1212; this is charged as a long-distance call. For international assistance, dial ☎ 00.

Toll-free numbers begin with ☎ 800, ☎ 866, ☎ 877 or ☎ 888 and must be preceded by ☎ 1. Most can only be used within the USA, some only within the state, and some only outside the state. To find any toll-free number, call ☎ 800-555-1212 (no charge).

### MOBILE PHONES

Mobile (cell) phones are ubiquitous in Southern California. The only foreign phones that work in North America are tri-band models, operating on GSM 1900 as well as other frequencies. If you don't have such a phone, you can rent one from **TripTel** ( ☎ 310-645-3500; www .triptel.com), at the Los Angeles International Airport (outside the customs gate in the Tom Bradley International terminal). Rentals cost $3 per day ($15 per week) plus $1.25 per minute for incoming and outgoing calls within the US ($2.50 for international calls), including taxes.

## Time

California is in the Pacific time zone, which is Greenwich mean time minus eight hours. When it's noon in LA, it's 3pm in New

York, 8pm in London and 6am (the next day) in Sydney or Auckland. Daylight saving time comes into effect on the first Sunday in April, when clocks are put forward one hour, and ends on the last Sunday in October.

See p373 for a map of time zones.

## INTERNET ACCESS

Surfing the Web and checking email is rarely a problem while traveling in Southern California. Web access is usually free at public libraries but downsides may include registration requirements, time limits, long lines and slow connections. Otherwise, Internet cafés are plentiful and are listed in the Information sections of the destination chapters; the cost of online time ranges from $4 to $8 per hour. Hostels and hotels offering guest terminals with Internet access are identified in this book with an Internet icon ( 🖳 ).

If you're traveling with your own laptop, you'll find that most hotels have the technology that lets you plug in from the comfort of your own room. High-speed access is especially common in hotels courting a business clientele and many properties now also offer wireless access. To find wireless hot spots anywhere, try the directories at www.wi-fihotspotlist.com/browse/ca and www.hotspot-locations.com.

Beware of digital phones without built-in data ports, which may fry your modem unless you're using a digital-to-analog converter. Depending on where you bought your laptop, you also need adapters for US electrical outlets and telephone sockets. Both are available in larger electronics stores.

For more information on traveling with a portable computer and the gadgets you might need to help you get online, see www.igo.com or www.teleadapt.com.

See p11 for websites that might be useful when traveling in Southern California.

## LEGAL MATTERS

If you are stopped by the police, remain courteous at all times and, if driving, keep your hands where the cop can see them, ie atop the steering wheel. Don't get out of the car unless asked. There is no system of paying fines on the spot. Attempting to pay the fine to the officer is frowned upon at best and may lead to a charge of attempted bribery. For traffic offenses, the police of-

---

**MEET 'NO-SMO KING'**

There are few places on earth more friendly toward nonsmokers – and more hostile to those who do light up – than Southern California. By law, smoking is *forbidden* inside or within 20ft of any public building as well as in restaurants and bars, although some still allow it on their patios. As of summer 2004 cigarettes also became a no-no on nearly all of LA's beaches (except in the South Bay) as well as those in San Clemente (Orange County) and Solana Beach (San Diego), with more likely to be added to the list. Even Governor Schwarzenegger, who set up a tent outside his office building so he could puff on his beloved cigars, jumped on the bandwagon when proposing a ban on smoking in state prisons. SoCal smokers are definitely a dying breed.

---

ficer will explain the options to you. There is usually a 30-day period to pay a fine. Most matters can be handled by mail.

If you are arrested for more serious offenses, you have the right to remain silent and are presumed innocent until proven guilty. There is no legal reason to speak to a police officer if you don't wish, but never walk away from one until given permission. Everyone arrested has the right to make one phone call. If you don't have a lawyer, friend or family member to help you, call your embassy. The police will give you the number upon request.

If driving in California, you need to carry your driver's license (p367) and obey road rules carefully (p368). The highest permissible blood-alcohol limit is 0.08%. Driving under the influence (DUI) is a serious offense that entails stiff fines, a suspended license, higher insurance premiums and other nasty consequences. Consuming alcohol anywhere other than at a residence or licensed premises is also a no-no, which puts parks, beaches and the rest of the great outdoors off limits. It is also illegal to carry open containers of alcohol inside a vehicle, even in the passenger section, even if they are empty. Containers that are full and sealed may be carried, but if they have ever been opened they must be stored in the trunk.

**THE LEGAL AGE FOR...**

- Drinking alcohol: 21
- Driving a car: 16
- Military service: 17
- Sexual consent: 18
- Smoking tobacco: 18
- Voting in an election: 18

Possession of under 1oz of marijuana is a misdemeanor in California, and though it is punishable by up to one year in jail, a fine is more likely for first-time offenders. Possession of any other drug, including cocaine, ecstasy, LSD, heroin, hashish or more than an ounce of weed, is a felony punishable by lengthy jail sentences, depending on the circumstances. For foreigners, conviction of any drug offense is grounds for deportation.

## MAPS

Most visitors centers distribute free (but often very basic) maps, but if you're doing a lot of driving, a detailed road map or atlas, such as those published by Rand McNally, may be indispensable. Members of the **American Automobile Association** (AAA; ☎ 800-874-7532; www.aaa.com) or one of its international affiliates, can get AAA's high-quality maps for free from any local office. Bookshops and tourist offices usually stock a good assortment of maps, while newsagents and gas stations have a more limited selection. For downloadable maps and driving directions try, **Mapquest** (www.mapquest.com) or **Yahoo! Maps** (http://maps.yahoo.com).

## SHOPPING

Southern Californians spend a lot of time spending their money and there's certainly no shortage of big malls, department stores, outlet centers, boutiques and markets to help them do it. To many visitors the sheer variety and quantity of consumer goods can be as staggering as it is tempting. There's really nothing you can't buy here, be it computers or couture, flip-flops or funky designer outfits, anime DVDs or sex toys, surf gear or antiques. Orange County has the biggest concentration of malls, while LA is best for boutique- and gallery-hopping and also has unique items such as clothing worn by the stars.

## SOLO TRAVELERS

There are no particular problems or difficulties traveling alone in Southern California. Although it is not for everybody, a major advantage is the freedom to do anything and to go anywhere you want whenever you want.

Americans are generally friendly and easy to talk to. Women don't need to be afraid of initiating conversation, even with men. Unless you're overtly coquettish, it most likely won't be interpreted as a sexual advance. Hostels are great places for hooking up with other people, as are guided tours, major tourist attractions and Internet cafés.

Issues of safety are slightly different for women than they are for men – see p361 for more specific information. In general, don't advertise where you're staying or that you're traveling alone. If you're going for a long hike, be sure to let someone – anyone – know about your intended whereabouts in case something should happen to you. Carrying a cell phone can be a lifesaver in this situation and other emergencies.

## TOURIST INFORMATION

California has no tourist offices in other countries, but the state-funded **California Tourism** ( ☎ 800-462-2543; www.visitcalifornia.com) operates an excellent website packed with useful pre-trip planning information. The office will also mail out a free information package, including a magazine-sized visitors' guide, although the website has just about all the same information, without all the paper.

The state government also operates several California Welcome Centers, including the following Southern California branches, where staff dispense maps and brochures and help find accommodations.
**Los Angeles** (Map pp68-9; ☎ 310-854-7616; 8500 Beverly Blvd, Suite 150)
**Oceanside** (Map p246; ☎ 760-721-1101; 928 N Coast Hwy) In northern San Diego County.
**Santa Ana** ( ☎ 714-667-0400; 2800 N Main St, Suite 112) In the Westfield Shoppingtown mall in Orange County.
**Yucca Valley** (Map pp316-17; ☎ 760-365-5464; 56711 Twentynine Palms Hwy) Near Joshua Tree National Park.

## TOURS

**Backpacker Bus** ( ☎ 888-464-6460; www.backpackerbus.com) A hop-on hop-off service operating various loops, including one between LA, San Diego and Big Bear Lake ($55, all three legs).

**Backroads** ( ☎ 510-527-1555, 800-462-2848; www.back roads.com) Active guided and self-guided tours throughout the world, including a five-day tour of Santa Barbara and the Wine Country by bike, kayak and on foot ($2000).

**California Motorcycle Tours** ( ☎ 858-677-9892, 888-408-7631; www.ca-motorcycletours.com) San Diego–based outfit offering various trips, including a seven-day 'Beach & Mountain Tour' that takes in all of Southern California's hot spots ($2850, including Harley Sportster rental, lodging and food).

**Elderhostel** ( ☎ 877-426-8056; www.elderhostel.org) This nonprofit organization offers guided tours throughout the world, including Southern California, for active people over 55. Includes bus and walking tours.

## WOMEN TRAVELERS

Southern California is generally a safe place to travel for women, even alone and even in the cities. Of course, this doesn't mean you can let your guard down and blindly entrust your life to every stranger. Simply use the same common sense you would at home.

Going alone to cafés and restaurants is perfectly acceptable, although how comfortable you feel depends entirely on you. In bars and nightclubs, solo women are likely to attract attention from men, but if you don't want company, most will respect a firm 'no thank you.' If you feel threatened, protesting loudly will often make the offender slink away with embarrassment – or will at least spur other people to come to your defense.

Good online resources for women travelers include **Journeywoman** (www.journeywoman .com) and **Her Own Way** (www.voyage.gc.ca/main/pubs /PDF/her_own_way-en.pdf). The latter, published by the Canadian government, contains lots of good general advice.

Although physical attack is unlikely it does, of course, happen. If you are assaulted, call the **police** ( ☎ 911) immediately and/or contact a women's or rape crisis center. The latter can also help in dealing with all kinds of emotional and physical issues surrounding an assault and make referrals to useful organizations and support groups. To find one near you, call the 24-hour **National Sexual Assault Hotline** ( ☎ 800-656-4673; www.rainn.org).

# Transportation

## CONTENTS

---

### THINGS CHANGE...

The information in this chapter is particularly vulnerable to change. Check directly with the airline or a travel agent to make sure you understand how a fare (and ticket you may buy) works and be aware of the security requirements for international travel. Shop carefully. The details given in this chapter should be regarded as pointers and are not a substitute for your own careful, up-to-date research.

---

# GETTING THERE & AWAY

## AIR
### Airports & Airlines

If you're traveling to Southern California from overseas, you'll most likely first touch down on US soil at **Los Angeles International Airport** (LAX; ☎ 310-646-5252; www.lawa.org), one of the world's busiest. This giant hub also handles most domestic arrivals, although in some instances flying into one of the following regional airports may be cheaper and more convenient to your final destination. Also see the regional chapters for details.

**Bob Hope Airport** (code BUR; ☎ 818-840-8840, 800-835-9287; www.burbankairport.com) In Burbank, LA County.
**John Wayne Airport** (code SNA; ☎ 949-252-5200; www.ocair.com) In Santa Ana, Orange County.

**Long Beach Airport** (code LGB; ☎ 562-570-2600; www.longbeach.gov/airport) In southern LA County.
**Ontario International Airport** (code ONT; ☎ 909-937-2700, 866-456-3900; www.lawa.org/ont) In Riverside County, east of LA.
**Palm Springs International Airport** (code PSP; ☎ 760-318-3800; www.palmspringsairport.com)
**San Diego International Airport** (code SAN; ☎ 619-231-2100; www.san.org)
**Santa Barbara Airport** (code SBA; ☎ 805-967-7111; www.flysba.com)

Major domestic and international carriers serving Southern California include the following:

### Domestic Airlines
**AirTran** (code FL; ☎ 800-247-8726; www.airtran.com)
**Alaska Air** (code AS; ☎ 800-426-0333; www.alaska air.com)
**America West** (code HP; ☎ 800-235-9292; www.america west.com)
**American Airlines** (code AA; ☎ 800-433-7300; www.aa.com)
**Continental** (code CO; ☎ 800-525-0280; www.continental.com)
**Delta** (code DL; ☎ 800-221-1212; www.delta.com)
**Frontier Air** (code F9; ☎ 800-432-1359; www.frontier airlines.com)
**Jet Blue** (code B6; ☎ 800-538-2583; www.jetblue.com)
**Northwest Airlines** (code NW; ☎ 800-225-2525; www.nwa.com)
**Southwest** (code WN; ☎ 800-435-9792; www.south west.com)
**United Airlines** (code UA; ☎ 800-241-6522, 800-538-2929; www.united.com)
**US Airways** (code US; ☎ 800-428-4322; www.usair ways.com)

### International Airlines
**Aer Lingus** (code EI; ☎ 800-474-7424; www.aer lingus.com)
**Aeromexico** (code AM; ☎ 800-237-6639; www.aero mexico.com)
**Air Canada** (code AC; ☎ 888-247-2262; www.air canada.com)
**Air France** (code AF; ☎ 800-237-2747; www.airfrance.com)
**Air New Zealand** (code NZ; ☎ 800-262-1234; www.air newzealand.com)
**Alitalia** (code AZ; ☎ 800-223-5730; www.alitalia.com)

**British Airways** (code BA; ☎ 800-247-9297; www.british airways.com)
**Cathay Pacific** (code CX; ☎ 800-228-4297; www.cathay pacific.com)
**Iberia** (code IB; ☎ 800-772-4642; www.iberia.com)
**Japan Airlines** (code JL; ☎ 800-525-3663; www.japan air.com)
**JetsGo** (code SG; ☎ 866-440-0441; www.jetsgo.com)
**KLM** (code KL; ☎ 800-374-7747; www.klm.com)
**Lufthansa** (code LH; ☎ 800-645-3880; www.lufthansa .com)
**Mexicana** (code MX; ☎ 800-531-7921; www.mexicana .com)
**Qantas** (code QF; ☎ 800-227-4500; www.qantas.com)
**Singapore Airlines** (code SQ; ☎ 800-742-3333; www.singaporeair.com)
**Virgin Atlantic** (code VS; ☎ 800-862-8621; www.virgin-atlantic.com)
**WestJet** (code WS; ☎ 888-937-8538; www.westjet.com)

## Tickets

Everybody loves a bargain and timing is key when it comes to snapping up cheap airfares. You can generally save a bundle by booking early, traveling midweek (Tuesday to Thursday) or flying in the late evening or early morning. Some airlines offer lower fares if you stay over a Saturday.

Your best friend in ferreting out deals is the Internet. Online agencies are good places to start, but they are best when used in conjunction with other search engines, such as **ITA Software** (www.itasoftware.com). This search matrix finds the cheapest fare on a particular day or within a 30-day period, sorts results by price and alerts you to potential downsides such as long layovers, tight connections or overnight travel. It may also pay to check out the airlines' own websites for promotional fares or to sign up for free weekly email newsletters that list late-breaking special fares. Even the old-fashioned newspaper can yield deals, especially in times of fare wars. And don't forget about travel agents, who can be especially helpful when planning extensive trips or complicated routes.

## Asia

Tokyo, Seoul, Bangkok and Hong Kong are among the Asian cities that have good flight connections to LA. Many flights go via Honolulu, but stopovers usually cost extra. Reliable travel agencies include:
**Four Seas Tours** Hong Kong ( ☎ 2200-7760; www.four seastravel.com/english)

**No 1 Travel** Tokyo ( ☎ 03-3205-6073; www.no1-travel .com)
**STA Travel** Bangkok ( ☎ 02-236-0262; www.statravel .co.th); Hong Kong ( ☎ 2736-1618; www.statravel.com .hk); Singapore ( ☎ 6737-7188; www.statravel.com.sg); Tokyo ( ☎ 03-5391-2922; www.statravel.co.jp)

### Australia & New Zealand

The dominant carriers from Down Under are Air New Zealand and Qantas, although United Airlines and American Airlines also fly across the Pacific Ocean. Prices are higher if you stop over in Honolulu. Try the following agents:

**Australia**
**Flight Centre** ( ☎ 133-133; www.flightcentre.com.au)
**STA Travel** ( ☎ 1300-733-035; www.statravel.com.au)
**Travel.com.au** ( ☎ 1300-130-482; www.travel.com.au)

**New Zealand**
**Flight Centre** ( ☎ 0800-243-544; www.flightcentre.co.nz)
**STA Travel** ( ☎ 0508-782-872; www.statravel.co.nz)
**Travel.co.nz** ( ☎ 0800-468-332; www.travel.co.nz)

### Canada

Air Canada, American Airlines, United Airlines, America West and Canadian discount carriers WestJet and JetsGo all offer regular nonstop service to LAX from most major Canadian cities. WestJet also flies to Palm Springs from Calgary. **Travel Cuts** ( ☎ 800-667-2887; www.travelcuts.com) is Canada's national student travel agency. For online bookings, check out www.expedia.ca and www.travel ocity.ca.

### Continental Europe

Many airlines, including Air France, Lufthansa, Alitalia and Iberia, have direct flights to LA from major European cities. Many other international and US airlines arrive via a stop in a gateway city (usually Chicago or Miami) and continue on domestic flights. Recommended travel agents:

**France**
**Anyway** ( ☎ 0892-893-892; www.anyway.fr)
**Lastminute** ( ☎ 0892-705-000; www.lastminute.fr)

TRANSPORTATION

**Nouvelles Frontières** ( ☎ 0825-000-747; www.nouvelles
-frontieres.fr)
**OTU Voyages** ( ☎ 01-49-72-57-16; www.otu.fr) Specializes in student and youth travelers.
**Voyageurs du Monde** ( ☎ 01-40-15-11-15; www.vdm
.com)

### Germany
**Expedia** (www.expedia.de)
**Just Travel** ( ☎ 089-747-3330; www.justtravel.de)
**Lastminute** ( ☎ 01805-284-366; www.lastminute.de)
**STA Travel** ( ☎ 01805-456-422; www.statravel.de)

### Italy
**CTS Viaggi** ( ☎ 06-462-0431; www.cts.it)

### Netherlands
**Airfair** ( ☎ 020-620-5121; www.airfair.nl)

### Spain
**Barcelo Viajes** ( ☎ 902-116-226; www.barcelo
viajes.com)

## Mexico
Aeromexico and Mexicana are among the
airlines with frequent flights to LA from
most major Mexican cities. Aeromexico has
flights to Ontario and San Diego as well.
Also look into flights to Tijuana, just across
the border from San Diego, which may actually be cheaper.

## UK & Ireland
One of the busiest and most competitive air
sectors in the world is from the UK to the
USA. American Airlines, British Airways,
Continental, United Airlines and Virgin Atlantic all operate several direct flights daily
from London to LA. Aer Lingus and American Airlines fly nonstop from Dublin to LA,
although you'll find more choices and probably cheaper fares by going via London.

Besides the travel agencies listed here,
also look for special deals in the travel pages
of the weekend broadsheet newspapers or in
*Time Out,* the *Evening Standard* and the free
magazine *TNT.* Whatever agency you book
with, make sure it's registered with the Association of British Travel Agents (ABTA),
which will guarantee a refund or alternative
ticket if you've paid money to an agent who
ends up going out of business.
**Bridge the World** ( ☎ 0870-444-7474; www.b-t-w.co.uk)
**Flight Centre** ( ☎ 0870-890-8099; www.flightcentre.co.uk)
**Flightbookers** ( ☎ 0870-010-7000; www.ebookers.com)

**North South Travel** ( ☎ 01245-608-291; www.north
southtravel.co.uk) Donates part of its profit to projects in
the developing world.
**Quest Travel** ( ☎ 0870-442-3542; www.questtravel.com)
**STA Travel** ( ☎ 0870-160-0599; www.statravel.co.uk)
**Trailfinders** ( ☎ 0845-058-5858; www.trailfinders.co.uk)
**Travel Bag** ( ☎ 0870-890-1456; www.travelbag.co.uk)

## USA
Domestic airfares fluctuate hugely depending on the season, day of the week, length of
stay and flexibility of the tickets for changes
and refunds. Still, nothing determines fares
more than demand, and when business is
slow, airlines lower fares to fill seats. Discount carriers such as AirTran, America
West, Frontier Air, Jet Blue and Southwest
have been giving the big guys, including
United Airlines, American Airlines and US
Airways, a run for their money.

The following agencies are recommended
for online bookings:
**Cheap Tickets** (www.cheaptickets.com)
**Expedia** (www.expedia.com)
**ITN** (www.itn.net)
**Lowest Fare** (www.lowestfare.com)
**Orbitz** (www.orbitz.com)
**STA Travel** (www.sta.com)
**Travelocity** (www.travelocity.com)

## LAND
### Border Crossings
San Ysidro on the US–Mexican border between San Diego and Tijuana is the world's
busiest border crossing. Traveling into
Mexico is usually not a problem but coming back into the US almost always entails
a long wait, especially if you're driving.
The US Department of Homeland Security
maintains a handy website at http://apps
.cbp.gov/bwt showing the current border
wait times. If you're not a US citizen or permanent resident, be sure to bring all of the
necessary documents (p356). For details on
traveling between San Diego and Tijuana,
see p270.

### Bus
**Greyhound** ( ☎ 800-231-2222, passes ☎ 888-454-7277,
402-330-8552; www.greyhound.com) is the king of
the bus world in the US, plowing along a
nationwide route system serving some 2200
destinations, including dozens in Southern
California. See the boxed text opposite for
some sample fares.

**SAMPLE BUS FARES**

| Route | Adult Fare | Duration | Frequency |
| --- | --- | --- | --- |
| Las Vegas-San Diego | $51 | 8½hr | 2 direct buses daily |
| Phoenix-LA | $39 | 6½-10hr | up to 8 daily |
| San Francisco-LA | $45 | 7-13hr | up to 14 daily |

For those planning on making the bus their main method of travel to, from and around Southern California, Greyhound offers a variety of unlimited travel passes (called Discovery Pass or Domestic Ameripass). These are available for periods ranging from seven to 60 consecutive days and cost from $229 to $642. Seniors over 62 and students with a Student Advantage Card (see p354) qualify for a 10% discount, while children under 12 pay half price. Also check the website for special promotions.

Passes may be bought at Greyhound terminals up to the departure date and online at least two weeks prior to the first day of travel.

Overseas travelers qualify for the slightly cheaper international versions of these passes, which are sold worldwide through select ticket agents and online at least 21 days before your first Greyhound trip. You can look up the nearest agent in your home country right on the website. If you're already in the US, you can still buy the Domestic Ameripass.

### Car & Motorcycle

If you're driving into the USA from Canada or Mexico, bring your vehicle's registration papers, liability insurance and driver's license. With rare exceptions, cars rented in the US may not be taken into Mexico. For road rules and other general driving information, see p366.

### Train

**Amtrak** ( ☎ 800-872-7245; www.amtrak.com) operates a fairly extensive rail system throughout the US. The trains are comfortable, if a bit slow, and are equipped with dining and lounge cars on long-distance routes. Southern California is served by three interstate Amtrak trains:

**Coast Starlight** Travels along the West Coast daily from Seattle to LA (from $126, 35 hours) via Portland, Sacramento and Oakland.

**Southwest Chief** Daily departures between Chicago and LA (from $191, 43 hours) via Kansas City, Albuquerque and Flagstaff.

**Sunset Limited** Thrice-weekly service between Orlando and LA (from $128, 68 hours) via Tucson, El Paso and New Orleans.

See p369 for details about Amtrak service within Southern California, how to buy tickets and the California Rail Pass.

For overseas visitors making Southern California part of a wider US itinerary, Amtrak's USA Rail Pass may be a ticket to savings. Several types are available. Call, check the website or consult a travel agent to determine which one best suits your needs.

# GETTING AROUND

## AIR

Although it is possible to fly, say, from LA to San Diego or Palm Springs, the time and cost involved don't make air travel a sensible way to get around Southern California.

## BICYCLE

Cyclists must follow the same rules of the road as vehicles, but don't expect drivers to always respect your right of way. Helmets may give you a bad hair day but using one is not only the smart thing to do but mandatory for anyone under 18. Bicycling is allowed on all roads and highways – even along freeways if there's no suitable alternative like a smaller parallel road; all mandatory exits are marked.

Emergency roadside assistance is available from the **Better World Club** ( ☎ 866-238-1137; www.betterworldclub.com). Membership costs $40 per year, plus $10 enrolment fee, and entitles you to two free pickups and transportation to the nearest repair shop, or home, within a 30-mile radius.

Most airlines carry a bike in place of a checked bag without charge on international flights, although it may have to be in a box. On domestic flights there's usually a fee of about $80. Check before you buy the ticket.

Greyhound will carry bicycles as luggage for about $15 to $25, provided the bicycle is disassembled and placed in a box (available at terminals for $10).

Most of Amtrak's *Pacific Surfliner* trains (p369) feature special racks where you can secure your bike unboxed, but be sure to reserve a spot when making your ticket reservation. There's a fee of $5 to $10, depending on the destination. On trains without racks, bikes must be put in a box and checked as luggage ($5 fee, box $10).

## BUS

Within Southern California, buses operated by **Greyhound** ( ☎ 800-231-2222; www.greyhound.com) provide an economical and environmentally friendly way to travel between major cities and to points along the coast, but they won't get you off the beaten path or into parks and forests. Frequency of service varies from 'rarely' to 'constantly,' but main routes have service every hour or so, including a few nonstop express buses. Stopovers are allowed on full-fare tickets only.

Tickets are available at the terminal, over the telephone ( ☎ 800-229-9424, 214-849-8100 from outside the US or Canada) or online (US or Canadian residents only). If you order them at least 10 days in advance, they'll be mailed to you (US and Canadian addresses only) or you can pick them up at the terminal with proper identification.

Greyhound is most popular with the less-affluent strata of American society, but by international standards the service is really quite good. There's only one class and the buses are generally clean, comfortable and reliable. Amenities may include onboard lavatories, air-conditioning (bring a sweater) and reclining seats. Smoking onboard is prohibited.

Bus stations, on the other hand, are often dreary places located in sketchy areas. This is especially true of LA (see p192).

Greyhound can accommodate disabled travelers, but you should make your needs known either at the time of booking or by calling ☎ 800-752-4841 at least 48 hours in advance of travel.

### Costs

Greyhound is the cheapest method of getting around and there are ways to trim costs even further. Round-trips are generally cheaper than two one-way tickets. Children under 12 save 40% when accompanied by a passenger paying the full adult fare. Seniors get 5% off, while students in possession of a Student Advantage Card (see p354) save 15% off the full fare. Other promotions, including advance purchase or companion fares, become available all the time, although they may come with restrictions or blackout periods. Simply ask or check the website for the latest deals. For specific route and fare information, see the Getting There & Away section of the destination chapters. See the boxed text below for some sample fares.

### Reservations

Greyhound does not take reservations and even buying tickets in advance does not guarantee you a seat on any particular bus. Show up 45 minutes to one hour prior to the scheduled departure and chances are pretty good you'll get on. Allow more time on Friday and Sunday afternoons and around holidays.

## CAR & MOTORCYCLE
### Automobile Associations

For long road trips, an auto club membership is an excellent thing to have. The **American Automobile Association** (AAA; ☎ 800-874-7532; www .aaa.com), with offices throughout the country, is the main auto club in the US. Many AAA

**SAMPLE BUS FARES**

| Route | Adult Fare | Duration | Frequency |
|-------|-----------|----------|-----------|
| LA-San Diego | $16 | 2¼-3¾hr | up to 23 per day |
| San Diego-Anaheim (Disneyland) | $16 | 2¼-2½ | up to 7 per day |
| San Diego-Palm Springs | $27.50 | 4-5½hr | up to 3 per day |
| Santa Barbara-LA | $12 | 2½-3hr | up to 9 per day |

## ROAD DISTANCES (MILES)

| | Anaheim | Los Angeles | Palm Springs | San Diego |
|---|---|---|---|---|
| Los Angeles | 26 | | | |
| Palm Springs | 91 | 110 | | |
| San Diego | 96 | 120 | 140 | |
| Santa Barbara | 123 | 95 | 200 | 220 |

services, including 24-hour **emergency road-side assistance** ( ☎ 800-222-4357), are also available to members of its international affiliates such as CAA in Canada, AA in the UK and ADAC in Germany. The club also offers free trip-planning advice and maps, plus a range of discounts on hotels, car rentals, Amtrak tickets, admissions etc.

### Driver's License

Visitors can legally drive in California for up to 12 months with their home driver's license. If you're from overseas, an International Driving Permit (IDP) may give you greater credibility with traffic police and may be required for renting a vehicle, especially if your home license is not in English or doesn't have a photograph. IDPs are easy to obtain. Just grab a passport photo and your home license and stop by your local automobile association, which will make you one for a small fee. Always carry your home license along with the IDP.

### Fuel & Spare Parts

Gas stations in the US, nearly all of which are self-service, are ubiquitous except in sparsely populated desert areas (you should carry a filled gas canister as a backup, if possible). Gas is sold in gallons (1 gallon equals 3.78L). At the time of going to press the California average for mid-grade fuel was around $2.20.

Finding spare parts should not be a problem, especially in the cities, although actual availability depends on the age and model of your car. Always bring some tools and a spare tire and be sure to have an emergency roadside assistance number (see left) in case your car breaks down.

### Hire

#### CARS

As anywhere, rates for car rentals vary considerably by model and pick-up location, but you should be able to get an economy-size vehicle from about $20 per day, plus insurance and taxes. Expect surcharges for rentals originating at airports and train stations, as well as for additional drivers and one-way rentals. Child or infant safety seats are compulsory (reserve at the time of booking) and cost about $8 per day or $40 per week.

In order to rent your own wheels you generally need to be at least 25 years old and hold a valid driver's license and a major credit card. Some companies may rent to drivers between the ages of 21 and 24 for an additional charge (about $15 to $25 per day). Those under age 21 or not in possession of a credit card are usually out of luck.

Here is a list of the major international car-rental companies with dozens of branches throughout Southern California.

**Alamo** ( ☎ 800-462-5266; www.alamo.com)
**Avis** ( ☎ 800-437-0358; www.avis.com)
**Budget** ( ☎ 800-268-8900; www.budget.com)
**Dollar** ( ☎ 800-800-4000; www.dollar.com)
**Enterprise** ( ☎ 800-736-8222; www.enterprise.com)
**Hertz** ( ☎ 800-263-0600; www.hertz.com)
**National** ( ☎ 800-227-7368; www.nationalcar.com)
**Thrifty** ( ☎ 800-847-4389; www.thrifty.com)

Independent local agencies may offer lower rates, so it's worth checking into that as well. They're also more likely to rent to drivers under 25 and some may even accept cash or travelers checks as a deposit. About 300 independent agencies are represented by **Car Rental Express** ( ☎ 604-714-5911, 888-557-8188; www.carrentalexpress.com), which may yield savings as high as 25% over rates charged by the big chains.

Overseas travelers should look into prepaid deals or fly-drive packages arranged in your home country, which often work out cheaper than on-the-spot rentals. Search the rental and airline companies' websites as well as online travel agencies for deals.

**TRANSPORTATION**

## MOTORCYCLES

Motorcycle rentals and insurance are not cheap, especially if you've got 'Harley hunger.' Small bikes, such as Harley's Sportster 883, go for about $75 per day; three-day or one-week rentals cost around $210 or $455. Larger models, such as the Fat Boy, go for about $130, $345 or $750, respectively. Security deposits range from $1000 to $3000 (credit card required). Rates usually include helmets, unlimited miles and minimum liability insurance; collision insurance (CDW; right) costs extra. One-way rentals are available for a surcharge as well.

**Eagle Rider** ( ☎ 310-536-6777, 800-501-8687; www .eaglerider.com) The dominant company with outlets nationwide, including in Los Angeles, Palm Springs and San Diego.
**Moturis** ( ☎ 800-890-2909; www.moturis.com) Also rents recreational vehicles (RVs).

## RECREATIONAL VEHICLES

Traveling by RV is a popular way of exploring Southern California and great for those keen on getting away from the major population centers and into the forest or desert. For the widest choice, book as early as possible. Costs vary by size and model, but you can generally expect to pay from $100 per day for a small campervan sleeping two or three adults to as much as $300 for a mansion on wheels for up to seven people. Diesel-fueled RVs have considerably lower running costs. Your travel agency back home may have the best deals, or contact these companies directly:

**Cruise America** ( ☎ 800-327-7799; www.cruiseamerica .com) Also rents motorcycles.
**El Monte RV** ( ☎ 888-337-2214; www.elmonterv.com)
**Happy Travel Campers** ( ☎ 310-675-1335, 800-370-1262; www.camperusa.com)
**RV Central** ( ☎ 909-520-9940; www.rvcentral.com)

## Insurance

California law requires liability insurance for all vehicles. The minimum for bodily injury liability is $15,000 for one person or $30,000 for all injuries in one accident. You also have to carry at least $5000 of property damage liability. Car-rental contracts do not automatically include liability insurance, which inflates daily rental costs by about $12. You don't need to takeout this insurance if your home auto-insurance policy or travel insurance already provide adequate coverage.

Insurance against damage to the car itself, called Collision Damage Waiver (CDW) or Loss Damage Waiver (LDW), reduces or eliminates the amount you'll have to reimburse the rental company. Although it is optional, driving without a waiver is not recommended, despite costing a rather steep $15 per day. Some credit cards, especially the gold and platinum versions, cover CDW/LDW for a certain rental period if you use the card to pay for the entire rental and decline the policy offered by the rental company. Always check with your card issuer to see what coverage they provide in California.

Personal Accident Insurance (PAI) covers you and any passenger(s) for medical costs incurred as a result of an accident. If your travel insurance or your health-insurance policy at home does this as well (and most do, but check), then this is one expense (about $5 per day) you can do without.

## Road Rules

Californians drive on the right-hand side of the road. The use of seat belts and infant and child safety seats is required at all times, while motorcyclists must wear helmets.

Distances and speed limits are shown in miles. Unless otherwise posted, the speed limit is 65mph on freeways, 55mph on two-lane undivided highways, 35mph on major city streets and 25mph in business and residential districts and near schools. It's forbidden to pass a school bus when its rear red lights are flashing.

Except where indicated, turning right at red lights after coming to a full stop is permitted so long as you don't impede intersecting traffic, which has the right of way. Talking on a cell phone while driving is still legal in California. At four-way stop signs, cars proceed in the order in which they arrived. If two cars arrive simultaneously, the one on the right has the right of way. When emergency vehicles (ie police, fire or ambulance) approach from either direction, pull over to get out of their way.

On freeways, slower cars may be passed on either the left or right lane. If two cars are trying to get into the same central lane, the one on the right has priority. Lanes marked with a diamond symbol are reserved for cars with multiple occupants. California has strict anti-littering laws, and throwing trash from a vehicle can incur a fine up to $1000.

For full details, consult the *California Driver Handbook* or the *California Motorcycle*

*Handbook,* which may be picked up for free at any Department of Motor Vehicles office or downloaded from www.dmv.ca.gov/pubs /pubs.htm. For details about penalties for drinking and driving, see p359.

## LOCAL TRANSPORTATION

Buses are the most ubiquitous form of public transportation and practically all towns have their own system. Most are commuter-oriented and offer only limited or no service at all in the evenings and on weekends. Los Angeles also has a combination subway–light-rail network and San Diego operates a trolley to the Mexican border. Check the Getting Around sections of the destination chapters for local transportation options.

## TRAIN
### Amtrak

The *Pacific Surfliner* operated by **Amtrak** ( ☎ 800-872-7245; www.amtrak.com) is the main rail service within Southern California. The sleek, double-decker cars have comfortable seats with outlets for plugging in laptops or other electrical devices, and there's a café car as well. Smoking is prohibited on the train.

Up to 11 trains daily ply the LA–San Diego route, making stops in Solana Beach, Oceanside (for Legoland), San Juan Capistrano and Anaheim (for Disneyland), among others. As many as five trains continue north to Santa Barbara via Oxnard and Ventura. The trip itself, which hugs the coastline for much of the route, is a visual treat thanks to the stunning scenery. At some stations, trains are met by buses (called Amtrak Thruways) for onward connections to smaller destinations. Of Amtrak's long-distance trains (p365), the *Coast Starlight* stops in Santa Barbara and LA, while the *Sunset Limited* travels to LA and northern Palm Springs.

### COSTS

Tickets are available in person, by phone and online. Fares vary depending on whether you book a seat in coach or business class. The latter offers slightly more legroom as well as seats with nifty little video screens. See the boxed text below for sample standard adult fares. Fares are slightly higher between late May and early September. Round-trip tickets cost the same as two one-way tickets.

Seniors over 62 and students with a Student Advantage Card (see p354) receive a 15% discount, while up to two children aged two to 15 and accompanied by an adult get 50% off. Children under two travel for free. Special promotions can become available at any time, so be sure to ask or check the website. Reservations can be made any time from 11 months in advance to the day of departure. Some trains fill up quickly, so reserve as far in advance as possible.

### TRAIN PASSES

Amtrak's California Rail Pass costs $159 ($77.50 for children aged two to 15) and is valid on all trains and Amtrak Thruway buses for seven days of travel within a 21-day period. Unless your itinerary includes points outside of Southern California, however, this pass probably won't pay for itself.

### Metrolink

Southern California's major population centers are linked to LA by a commuter train network called **Metrolink** ( ☎ 800-371-5465; www .metrolinktrains.com). It connects Downtown LA's Union Station with the surrounding counties – Orange, Riverside, San Bernardino and Ventura – as well as northern San Diego County. Most trains depart between 6am and 9am and 3pm and 6pm Monday to Friday, with only one or two operating during the day. The most useful line for visitors is the Orange County Line that stops in Anaheim, Santa Ana, San Juan Capistrano and Oceanside. The Ventura County Line stops at Bob Hope Airport in Burbank. Tickets are available from vending machine at the stations and fares are zone based.

| SAMPLE TRAIN FARES | | | |
| --- | --- | --- | --- |
| **Route** | **Coach** | **Business Class** | **Duration** |
| LA-Santa Barbara | $17 | $28 | 2½hr |
| San Diego-LA | $26 | $38 | 2¾hr |
| San Diego-Santa Barbara | $26 | $41 | 5½hr |

# Health Dr David Goldberg

# BEFORE YOU GO

## INSURANCE

The USA, and Los Angeles in particular, offers possibly the finest health care in the world. The problem is that, unless you have good insurance, it can be prohibitively expensive. It's essential to purchase travel health insurance if your regular policy doesn't cover you when you're abroad.

Bring any medications you may need in their original containers, clearly labeled. A signed, dated letter from your physician that describes all medical conditions and medications, including generic names, is also a good idea.

If your health insurance does not cover you for medical expenses abroad, consider supplemental insurance. Check the Subway section of the **Lonely Planet website** (www.lonely planet.com/subwwway) for more information. Find out in advance if your insurance plan will make payments directly to providers or reimburse you later for overseas health expenditures.

## RECOMMENDED VACCINATIONS

No special vaccines are required or recommended for travel to the USA. All travelers should be up to date on routine immunizations: tetanus-diphtheria, measles, chicken pox and influenza.

## INTERNET RESOURCES

There is a wealth of travel health advice on the Internet. The World Health Organiza-tion publishes a superb book, called *International Travel and Health,* which is revised annually and is available online at no cost at www.who.int/ith. Another website of general interest is MD Travel Health at www .mdtravelhealth.com, which provides complete travel health recommendations for every country, updated daily, also at no cost.

It's usually a good idea to consult your government's travel health website before departure, if one is available:

**Australia** (www.dfat.gov.au/travel/)
**Canada** (www.hc-sc.gc.ca/english/index.html)
**UK** (www.doh.gov.uk/traveladvice/index.htm)
**United States** (www.cdc.gov/travel/)

# IN SOUTHERN CALIFORNIA

## AVAILABILITY & COST OF HEALTH CARE

In general, if you have a medical emergency, the best bet is to find the nearest hospital and go to its emergency room. If the problem isn't urgent, you can call a nearby hospital and ask for a referral to a local physician, which is usually cheaper than a trip to the emergency room. You should avoid stand-alone, for-profit urgent care centers, which tend to perform large numbers of expensive tests, even for minor illnesses.

Pharmacies are abundantly supplied, but you may find that some medications that are available over the counter in your home country require a prescription in the USA, and, as always, if you don't have insurance to cover the cost of prescriptions, they can be shockingly expensive.

## INFECTIOUS DISEASES

In addition to more common ailments, there are several infectious diseases that may be acquired by mosquito or tick bites.

### Giardiasis

This parasitic infection of the small intestine occurs throughout North America and the world. Symptoms may include nausea, bloating, cramps, and diarrhea, and may last for weeks. To protect yourself from *Giardia*, avoid drinking directly from lakes, ponds, streams and rivers, which may be contaminated by animal or human feces. The infection can also be transmitted from person to person if proper hand washing is not performed. Giardiasis is easily diagnosed by a stool test and treated with antibiotics.

## HIV/AIDS

As with most parts of the world, HIV infection occurs throughout the USA. Never assume, on the basis of someone's background or appearance, that they're free of this or any other sexually transmitted disease. Be sure to use a condom for all sexual encounters.

## West Nile Virus

This virus was unknown in the USA until a few years ago, but have now been reported in almost all 50 states. The virus is transmitted by culex mosquitoes, which are active in late summer and early fall and generally bite after dusk. Most infections are mild or asymptomatic, but the virus may infect the central nervous system, leading to fever, headache, confusion, lethargy, coma and sometimes death. There is no treatment for West Nile virus. For the latest update on the areas affected by West Nile, go to the **US Geological Survey website** (http://westnilemaps.usgs.gov).

## ENVIRONMENTAL HAZARDS
### Bites & Stings

The most effective ways to avoid bites and stings are common sense approaches: wear boots when hiking to protect from snakes, wear long sleeves and pants to protect from ticks and mosquitoes. If you're bitten, don't overreact. Stay calm and follow the recommended treatment.

### ANIMAL BITES

Do not attempt to pet, handle or feed any animal, with the exception of domestic animals known to be free of any infectious disease. Most animal injuries are directly related to a person's attempt to touch or feed the animal. Any bite or scratch by a mammal, including bats, should be promptly and thoroughly cleansed with large amounts of soap and water, followed by application of an antiseptic such as iodine or alcohol. The local health authorities should be contacted immediately for possible postexposure rabies treatment, whether or not you've been immunized against rabies. It may also be advisable to start an antibiotic, since wounds caused by animal bites and scratches frequently become infected.

### MOSQUITO BITES

When traveling in areas where West Nile or other mosquito-borne illnesses have been reported, keep yourself covered (wear long sleeves, long pants, a hat, and shoes rather than sandals) and apply a good insect repellent, preferably one containing DEET, to exposed skin and clothing. In general, adults and children over 12 should use preparations containing 25% to 35% DEET, which will usually last about six hours. Children between two and 12 years of age should use preparations containing no more than 10% DEET, applied sparingly, which will usually last about three hours. Neurological toxicity has been reported as a result of using DEET, especially in children, but appears to be extremely uncommon and generally related to overuse. DEET-containing compounds should not be used on children under age two.

Insect repellents containing certain botanical products, including oil of eucalyptus and soybean oil, are effective but last only 1½ to two hours. Products based on citronella are not effective.

Visit the **Center for Disease Control's website** (CDC; www.cdc.gov/ncidod/dvbid/westnile/prevention_info .htm) for further prevention information.

### SNAKE BITES

There are several varieties of venomous snakes in the USA, but unlike those in other countries they do not cause instantaneous death, and antivenins are available. The rattlesnake is the most common; most have triangular-shaped heads, diamond patterns along their backs and vary in length from 2ft to 6ft.

If you're bitten, place a light constricting bandage over the bite, keep the wounded part below the level of the heart and move it as little as possible. Stay calm and get to a medical facility as soon as possible. Bring the dead snake for identification if you can, but don't risk being bitten again. Do not use the mythical 'cut an X and suck out the venom' trick; this causes more damage to snakebite victims than the bites themselves.

**SPIDER & SCORPION BITES**

Although there are many species of spiders in the USA, the only ones that cause significant human illness are the black widow and brown recluse spiders. The black widow is black or brown in color, measuring about 15mm in body length, with a shiny top, fat body, and distinctive red or orange hourglass figure on its underside. It's found throughout the USA, usually in barns, woodpiles, sheds, harvested crops and bowls of outdoor toilets. The brown recluse spider is brown in color, usually 10mm in body length, with a dark violin-shaped mark on the top of the upper section of the body. It's usually found in the south and southern Midwest, but has spread to other parts of the country in recent years. The brown recluse is active mostly at night, lives in dark sheltered areas such as under porches and in woodpiles, and typically bites when trapped.

If bitten by a black widow, you should apply ice or cold packs and go immediately to the nearest emergency room. Complications of a black widow bite may include muscle spasms, breathing difficulties and high blood pressure. The bite of a brown recluse or hobo spider typically causes a large, inflamed wound, sometimes associated with fever and chills. If bitten, apply ice and see a physician.

The large (up to 6in in diameter), hairy tarantula looks much worse than it is; it rarely bites and then usually only when it is roughly handled. The bite is not very serious, although it is temporarily quite painful.

The only dangerous species of scorpion in the USA is the bark scorpion, which is found in the southwestern part of the country, chiefly Arizona. If stung, you should immediately apply ice or cold packs, immobilize the affected body part, and go to the nearest emergency room. To prevent scorpion stings, be sure to inspect and shake out clothing, shoes, and sleeping bags before use, and wear gloves and protective clothing when working around piles of wood or leaves.

## Sun

To protect yourself from excessive sun exposure, you should stay out of the midday

**TRADITIONAL MEDICINE**

American health-food stores and many regular groceries abound with so-called 'natural' remedies. These are a few of the more successful ones, in our opinion. They're not guaranteed, of course, but they may work great. You never know…

| Problem | Treatment |
| --- | --- |
| jet lag | melatonin |
| mosquito bite | oil of eucalyptus |
| motion sickness | ginger |

sun, wear sunglasses and a wide-brimmed hat, and apply sunscreen with SPF 15 or higher, providing both UVA and UVB protection. Sunscreen should be generously applied to all exposed parts of the body approximately 30 minutes before sun exposure and be reapplied after swimming or vigorous activity. Drink plenty of fluids and avoid strenuous exercise when the temperature is high.

## Heatstroke

Heatstroke may occur in those who are exposed to excessively high temperatures for a number of days. The elderly are at greatest risk, especially those with chronic medical problems. Heatstroke often occurs during physical exertion but, particularly in the elderly, may also occur at rest. The first sign may be an abrupt collapse, but there may be early, subtle warnings, including dizziness, weakness, nausea, headache, confusion, drowsiness, rapid pulse and unreasonable behavior. If early symptoms of heat illness are observed, remove the victim from direct sunlight, loosen clothing, give cold fluids and make sure the victim rests for at least 24 hours. In the event of heatstroke, the victim should be brought immediately to the nearest medical facility. To prevent heatstroke, drink plenty of fluids, eat salty foods, protect yourself from sun exposure and avoid alcohol and strenuous exercise when the temperature is high.

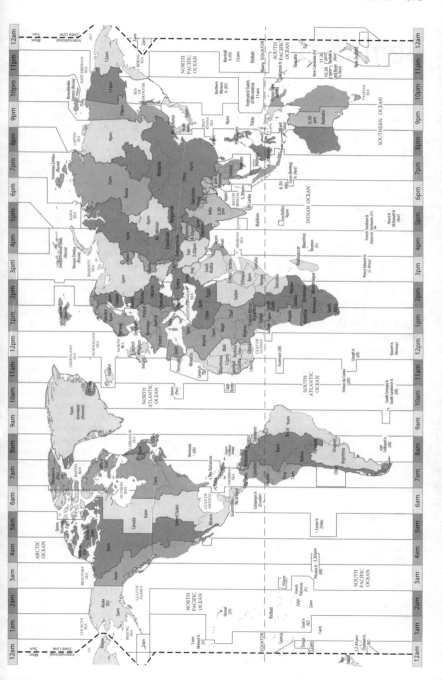

# Behind the Scenes

## THIS BOOK

This 1st edition of *Los Angeles & Southern California* was researched and written by Andrea Schulte-Peevers and John A Vlahides. Andrea coordinated the book and wrote Destination Los Angeles & Southern California, Getting Started, Itineraries, Snapshot, Directory, Transportation and the Los Angeles chapter. John wrote History, The Culture, Environment, Southern California Outdoors, Food & Drink and the Orange County, Palm Springs & the Deserts, San Diego and Santa Barbara chapters.

Dr David Goldberg wrote the Health chapter. John Payne wrote the Music section of the Culture chapter. Rose Dosti wrote the boxed text 'The LA Food Scene', Marisa Gierlich wrote the boxed text 'San Diego in 48 Hours' and Alisha Snider wrote the boxed text 'Living the Hollywood Cliché'.

## THANKS from the Authors

**Andrea Schulte-Peevers** Heartfelt thanks to my husband, David, who kept me sane during this book's intense write-up phase with his keen wit, delicious meals and bottomless empathy. Suki Gear: it was a treat to be reunited for another Lonely Planet book. I'm so glad you're back on board. Thanks for your good advice, patience and pep talks. Big thanks also to my coauthor, John Vlahides – you were truly a joy to work with and I hope we get to team up again. Andy Bender deserves a huge thank you for generously sharing his knowledge about gay LA, as does Andrea Mia for her insight into LA's film festivals. See you all at dinner soon.

**John A Vlahides** There would be no book without the kindness and support of my oh-so-fab commissioning editor Suki Gear and my kick-ass coauthor Andrea Schulte-Peevers.

Thanks to all my friends who put up with my disappearance while I toiled over this text, especially Jim Aloise, Karl Soehnlein, Jake Torrens, Sondra Hall, Tristy Taylor and Stanley Fuller. You, too, Brian Busta. (Are we friends again? I hope so.) I owe a debt of gratitude to sparkling and joyful Christine Murray for the stellar primer on her old stomping ground. Kate Brady, Liz Costello and David Booth: nobody beats your wise literary guidance. My life would have been miserable during the research of this guidebook were it not for the invaluable help of Shannon Brooks, Lauren Yacker, Joe Timko, Robert Arends, Elizabeth Ranta, Genevieve Anton, Jeff Hocker, Kathleen Spalione and giggly Gail Ossipoff. Special thanks, too, to Kevin McGuire and Brian Dobbins – ready the guestroom; I'm coming back.

## CREDITS

*Los Angeles & Southern California* 1 was commissioned and developed in Lonely Planet's Oakland office by Suki Gear. Cartography for this guide was developed by Alison Lyall and Laurie Mikkelsen. Production was coordinated by Gabbi Wilson (editorial) and Laurie Mikkelsen (cartography). Overseeing production was Eoin Dunlevy (project manager).

Editorial assistance was provided by Imogen Bannister, Monique Choy, Margedd Heliosz, Kristin Odijk, Charlotte Orr and Nina Rousseau. Cartographic assistance was provided by Anneka

### THE LONELY PLANET STORY

The story begins with a classic travel adventure: Tony and Maureen Wheeler's 1972 journey across Europe and Asia to Australia. There was no useful information about the overland trail then, so Tony and Maureen published the first Lonely Planet guidebook to meet a growing need.

From a kitchen table, Lonely Planet has grown to become the largest independent travel publisher in the world, with offices in Melbourne (Australia), Oakland (USA) and London (UK). Today Lonely Planet guidebooks cover the globe. There is an ever-growing list of books and information in a variety of media. Some things haven't changed. The main aim is still to make it possible for adventurous travelers to get out there – to explore and better understand the world.

At Lonely Planet we believe travelers can make a positive contribution to the countries they visit – if they respect their host communities and spend their money wisely. Every year 5% of company profit is donated to charities around the world.

Imkamp and the climate charts were produced by Owen Eszeki. Wayne Murphy produced the back cover map. The book was laid out by Jacqui Saunders and Pablo Gastar. The cover was designed by Gerilyn Attebery and cover artwork was by Jane Hart. Layout assistance was provided by Laura Jane, David Kemp and Mik Ruff. The book was indexed by Gabbi Wilson. And last but not least, *muchas gracias* to our brilliant authors.

## THANKS from Lonely Planet
**Thanks to the travelers who wrote to us with helpful hints, useful advice and interesting anecdotes:**
**A** Morten Andersen-Gott, Trygve Anderson, Jessica Andrews, Josée Arsenault **B** J Baker, George Baxter Smith, Ray Beebe, Bruce K Belknap, Maria & Tony Benfield, Bruce Berger, Emma H Black, Joseph Blum, Rick Blyth, Samantha Blyth, Sheila Bryans, Matthias Bode, Darryl Brock, Liza Brown, Wiliam & Helen Bull, Brad Burkman, Heidi & Richard Buxton **C** Michael Chang, Jennifer Charpentier, Beng Wan Chua, Rob Ciampa, Kate Claisse, Liz Clark, John Cojeen, Sharon Cooper, Caroline Coppin, Rupert Cousens, Scott Crawford, Paul Crowe **D** Siobhain Danaher, B Dark, Rosalie de Boer, Justin Delemus, Christina Demetriou, Kimberly Dempsey, Richard Desomme, AB DiLucente, Dennis DiLucente, Elizabeth Doherty, Alexa Donnelly, Guy Dowman **E** Patrick Easterling, Cammy Elquist, Nivine Emeran **F** Colin Falls, Sean Fargo, Jean Feilmoser, Anne-Katrin Feldkamp, Elsa Flores, Andy Foltz, Eleanor Friedman, Barbara Friedrich, Jean Fruend **G** Nicolas Gaere, Simon Gale, Joe Ganesh, Len Gierach, Emma Giesen, Ronalie Green, Joost Groot, Iris Gumm **H** Stuart Hale, Ellenise Hall, Ian Harris, Stephen Harris, Kay Harry, Marese Hickey, Bruce Hicks, Ian Hicks, BJ Hill, Garrit Huysman **I** Susan Irwin, Eleanor, Christopher & Susannah Inglis **J** Bailey T James, Jane James, Fabricio Jimenez, Darryl Jones, Gretchen Joseph, Christiane Jung, Holger Jung **K** Beth A Kaplan, Udo Keil, Bas Kempen, Christy Khattab, Don Kilburg, Rebecca Kirby, Michaela Klink, Catherine Koch, Hartmut Kuhne **L** Judy Lake, John Lam, SW Lam, Nancy Lee, Celine Lescaut, Derek Lycke **M** Youval Marks, Elona Masson, Kate Mathhams, Jade Mawbey, Sally Maynard, Daniel McChesney-Young, Iain McCormick, Pete McCusker, Christian Mena, Rich Mick, John Mitchell, Fiona Mocatta, Heather Monell, TRW Moore, Peter Mynors **N** Joe Nekrasz, Lucy Newman, Magnus Norstrom, David Nutt **O** Leah Oehlert, April Orcutt, Martin Oswell-Penton **P** Markku Paalanen, Marco Pace, Michelle Pauling, Katerina Pavlou, Eliza Penrose, Grace PerLee, Matthieu Permentier, Duke Peters, Denny Pierce **R** Donna Reddin, Donna Regan, Gerry Renshaw, Joe Repetski, Maxine Ressler, Nick Reynolds, Brett Rhodes, Vittorio Riguzzi, Sarah Robinson, Jan Roehlk, Ben Roman, Claudia Royston, Roland Rücker, Rob Ruschak, S Russell **S** Elaine Said, Jane Salty, Hannah Salvidge, Darren Sault, Lee Savage, Sean Savage, Randy Schisler, Petra Schneider, Link Schrader, Christina Schulte, Brian Shaw, Mary Sheesley, Kristina Shih, Don Shirley, Sandy Sillman, Claire Snel, John Sparks, Tina Sparks, Caroline Stout **T** Ken Tanji, Mark Terry, Anna Theodorou, Brian Tiernan, Sarah Tilley, Dawn Toles, Jane Toon, Hugo Torres **V** Huub van der Linden, Stijn van Rest, Craig & Linda Vandermeer, Rok Veber **W** Kate Waters, Darien Werfhorst, Nicola Westermann, Lesley & Paul Willetts, Wolfgang Wilfling, Duncan Williamson, Rachael Woodcock **Y** Andrew Young, Mary Young **Z** Adriana Zambojova, Suki Zoe

## ACKNOWLEDGMENTS
Many thanks to the following for the use of their content: Globe on back cover © Mountain High Maps 1993 Digital Wisdom, Inc.

### SEND US YOUR FEEDBACK
We love to hear from travelers – your comments keep us on our toes and help make our books better. Our well-traveled team reads every word on what you loved or loathed about this book. Although we cannot reply individually to postal submissions, we always guarantee that your feedback goes straight to the appropriate authors, in time for the next edition. Each person who sends us information is thanked in the next edition – and the most useful submissions are rewarded with a free book.

To send us your updates – and find out about Lonely Planet events, newsletters and travel news – visit our award-winning website: **www.lonelyplanet.com/feedback**.

Note: We may edit, reproduce and incorporate your comments in Lonely Planet products such as guidebooks, websites and digital products, so let us know if you don't want your comments reproduced or your name acknowledged. For a copy of our privacy policy visit www.lonelyplanet.com/privacy.

# Index

INDEX

**000** Map pages
**000** Location of color photographs

**000** Map pages
000 Location of color photographs

**000** Map pages
**000** Location of color photographs

## MAP LEGEND

### ROUTES

| | |
|---|---|
| Tollway | Walking Path |
| Freeway | Unsealed Road |
| Primary Road | Pedestrian Street |
| Secondary Road | Stepped Street |
| Tertiary Road | Tunnel |
| Lane | One Way Street |
| Walking Tour | Walking Trail |

### TRANSPORT

| | |
|---|---|
| Ferry | Rail |
| Metro | Rail (Underground) |
| Monorail | Tram |

### HYDROGRAPHY

| | |
|---|---|
| River, Creek | Mangrove |
| Intermittent River | Mudflats |
| Canal | Reef |
| Lake (Dry) | Swamp |
| Lake (Salt) | Water |

### BOUNDARIES

| | |
|---|---|
| International | Ancient Wall |
| State, Provincial | Cliff |
| Regional, Suburb | Marine Park |

### POPULATION

| | |
|---|---|
| ○ CAPITAL (NATIONAL) | ◉ CAPITAL (STATE) |
| ● Large City | ○ Medium City |
| ● Small City | ○ Town, Village |

### AREA FEATURES

| | |
|---|---|
| Airport | Forest |
| Area of Interest | Land |
| Beach, Desert | Mall |
| Building | Park |
| Campus | Reservation |
| Cemetery, Christian | Sports |

### SYMBOLS

**SIGHTS/ACTIVITIES**

| | |
|---|---|
| 🏖 | Beach |
| ☸ | Buddhist |
| 🏰 | Castle, Fortress |
| ✝ | Christian |
| ☯ | Confucian |
| 🤿 | Diving, Snorkeling |
| 🍷 | Drinking |
| 🕉 | Hindu |
| ☪ | Islamic |
| | Jain |
| ✡ | Jewish |
| 🗿 | Monument |
| 🏛 | Museum, Gallery |
| 🧺 | Picnic Area |
| • | Point of Interest |
| | Ruin |
| | Shinto |
| | Sikh |
| | Taoist |
| | Winery, Vineyard |
| | Zoo, Bird Sanctuary |

**INFORMATION**

| | |
|---|---|
| ❸ | Bank, ATM |
| ✉ | Embassy/Consulate |
| ✚ | Hospital, Medical |
| ❶ | Information |
| @ | Internet Facilities |
| Ⓟ | Parking Area |
| ⛽ | Petrol Station |
| 👮 | Police Station |
| ✉ | Post Office, GPO |
| ☎ | Telephone |
| 🚻 | Toilets |

**SLEEPING**

| | |
|---|---|
| 🛏 | Sleeping |
| ⛺ | Camping |

**EATING**

| | |
|---|---|
| 🍴 | Eating |

**DRINKING**

| | |
|---|---|
| 🍺 | Drinking |
| ☕ | Café |

**ENTERTAINMENT**

| | |
|---|---|
| 🎭 | Entertainment |

**SHOPPING**

| | |
|---|---|
| 🛍 | Shopping |

**TRANSPORT**

| | |
|---|---|
| ✈ | Airport, Airfield |
| 🚏 | Border Crossing |
| 🚌 | Bus Station |
| 🚲 | Cycling, Bicycle Path |
| 🚐 | General Transport |
| 🚕 | Taxi Rank |
| 🥾 | Trail Head |

**GEOGRAPHIC**

| | |
|---|---|
| ⚠ | Hazard |
| 🗼 | Lighthouse |
| 🔭 | Lookout |
| ▲ | Mountain, Volcano |
| 🏞 | National Park |
| 🌴 | Oasis |
| )( | Pass, Canyon |
| → | River Flow |
| 🏠 | Shelter, Hut |
| + | Spot Height |
| ⛲ | Waterfall |

*NOTE: Not all symbols displayed above appear in this guide.*

## LONELY PLANET OFFICES

### Australia
Head Office
Locked Bag 1, Footscray, Victoria 3011
☎ 03 8379 8000, fax 03 8379 8111
talk2us@lonelyplanet.com.au

### USA
150 Linden St, Oakland, CA 94607
☎ 510 893 8555, toll free 800 275 8555
fax 510 893 8572, info@lonelyplanet.com

### UK
72–82 Rosebery Ave,
Clerkenwell, London EC1R 4RW
☎ 020 7841 9000, fax 020 7841 9001
go@lonelyplanet.co.uk

### Published by Lonely Planet Publications Pty Ltd
ABN 36 005 607 983